# UNDERSTANDING
# FORTRAN 77

### with structured problem solving

# UNDERSTANDING FORTRAN 77

## with structured problem solving

### michel Boillot

Pensacola Junior College

## WEST PUBLISHING COMPANY

St. Paul • New York • Los Angeles • San Francisco

**COPY EDITOR**
Pamela S. McMurry

**COMPOSITION**
Carlisle Graphics

**COVER AND CHAPTER OPENING PHOTOGRAPHS**
Laser Photography by Floyd Rollefstad,
Laser Fantasy Production

**Library of Congress Cataloging in Publication Data**

Boillot, Michel H.
　　Understanding Fortran 77 with structured problem solving.

　　Includes index.
　　1.　FORTRAN (Computer program language)　2.　Structured
programming.　I.　Title.
QA76.73.F25B646　1984　　　001.64'24　　　83-26030
ISBN 0-314-77845-4

# contents

*v*

# THREE

# read, flowcharts, pseudo code and the if then else statement  *81*

FOUR

# program structure:
## the counting process, and loop control with the while do   *155*

## FIVE

# the accumulation process and the do loop   225

**SIX**

# data representation:
## substrings, the l, e, and, d format codes, and complex-numbers  *287*

**SEVEN**

# one dimensional arrays and the dimension statement  *331*

# EIGHT

# two- and three-dimensional arrays  *413*

# nine

# functions  *469*

TEN

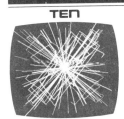

# subroutines   *519*

ELEVEN

# file processing   *563*

# preface

This text presents a unique approach to teaching and learning FORTRAN. Each chapter begins with a completely defined problem and a programmed solution to the problem. This program introduces the new language features and syntax that will be discussed in the chapter. Displaying a complete program before discussing the material in the chapter is intended to stimulate the student's curiosity by confronting him or her with a conceptual whole. The student can capture the essence of the program without much difficulty, and he or she is warned not to spend too much time on the introductory programming example. Subsequent sections will clarify the details of the program; at this point, they are unimportant.

The remaining sections of each chapter also have a specific purpose. The second and third sections explain new features, syntax, and programming techniques. Numerous short, illustrative examples are included to show both correct and incorrect coding and applications of programming techniques.

Another section of each chapter contains two or three worked-out problems that apply the language features and programming techniques covered in the preceding sections. All programs contain a data dictionary of variables, and the input and output (results) files are displayed along with the FORTRAN code.

Many chapters have an optional section containing material that is included for the sake of complete presentation of the FORTRAN language, but that is not necessarily essential to all students. Each instructor can decide whether to include or omit these sections.

A section entitled "You Might Want to Know" is in question-and-answer format. It attempts to anticipate commonly asked questions and provides informally phrased answers. Many of the questions point out predictable pitfalls for novice programmers.

Interspersed in the chapter are many "Do It Now" exercises and coding problems, which let students test their understanding of the material just covered. Answers to these exercises, including partial program code, are provided for immediate feedback.

All chapters conclude with exercises. The first section, "Test Yourself" lets the reader test his or her understanding of the material covered in the chapter and practice writing short FORTRAN coding segments covering important programming techniques. Answers to "Test Yourself" are provided at the end of each chapter. The following section contains programming exercises, an extensive collection of problems ranging over a wide variety of subject areas and levels of difficulty. Problems are generally presented in graduated order of difficulty. The instructors or students should be able to find problems that relate to their own areas of interest. There are some "fun" problems dealing with the simulation of processes or environments (a random number generator function is supplied in chapter 9 for use in these problems), "total" problems requiring the student to design a complete system, and, of course, more traditional problems. Some instructors may wish to present one of these problems as the first programming example of the chapter. In any event, the abundance of problems will allow the instructor to assign different problems semester after semester.

The organization of the text as a whole should also be noted. The initial discussions of input and output are placed in separate chapters. This enables the student to concentrate on each topic separately instead of having to master them simultaneously. Format-free as well as format-controlled input/output is presented in chapters 2 and 3. Formatted input/output lets the student produce good-looking results or reports starting with the very first program. On the other hand, format-free input/output is very convenient during the program development, testing, and debugging stages. Both options should be made available to the student from the very beginning.

Chapters 3 and 4 deal with program structure. Flowcharts and pseudo code are presented as tools for developing program logic. Since many FORTRAN 77 versions do not support the WHILE DO construct, the WHILE *condition* DO is simulated in most programming examples through such statements as:

```
10      IF NOT condition GO TO 20
            procedure
            GO TO 10
20 continue with program
```

Discussion of mathematical functions is deferred until chapter 9. Some instructors may wish to discuss the FORTRAN-supplied functions (in the first part of chapter 9) with chapters 2 and 3.

I would like to thank Mona, Zette, Raymond, Anne Marie, Marie Therese, Pierre, Octavie, Félix and Mms. Georges Claude for helping me through this writing adventure. Few successful textbooks are ever produced without the assistance and better judgments of reviewers. A special note of thanks goes to Janet and Edward Suppiger, Wayne Horn, Wayne Madison, Juris Prusis, Sally Goodwin, Richard Yankosky and Maurice Superville for their comments and suggestions. I am also greatly indebted to David Whitney for his superb and truly outstanding reviews—David's candid criticisms and humorous annotations throughout the manuscript and galleys made the entire writing process so much more lively. I found myself eagerly awaiting David's next set of trenchant remarks. In the end, to a point (got it David?) our differences are truly minimal—rien qu'un bon verre ne guérirait pas. Incidentally David wrote the instructor's manual—a very interesting manual indeed. I would also like to express my sincere thanks to Pamela McMurry who has painstakingly gone through the manuscript to free it of errors. Her contribution to style and prose has made this text easier to read and to understand. Penultimately I would like to thank the extraordinary people of Carlisle Graphics who have made a miracle out of a manuscript.

Not to be forgotten is our good WEST editor and friend, Gary Woodruff, and his efficient and cheerful developmental assistant Phyllis Calhoun who made this project a reality. Finally I would like to thank Keith Hobbie, Tim Danielson, Renee Grievous, Beth Hinzman and the remaining silent personnel at WEST.

Michel Boillot

# computers
# and
# computing

## CHAPTER ONE

# computers and computing

## 1-1  The Electronic Brain

*News Item*:   When the *Apollo 13* flight was jeopardized by unforeseen events, new flight plans were produced by computers in just 84 minutes. One person working on the problem could have performed the task in 1,040,256 years. With a desk calculator, the time could have been cut to 60,480 years.

*News Item*:   Mathematical Application Group, Inc., has announced a commercially available animation technique called Synthavision, which uses the computer to construct visuals that resemble conventionally produced cartoons when photographed.

*News Item*:   ARTRA, Inc. has announced the availability of HOUSEMASTER, a computer-based system that will control household lighting, heating, air-conditioning, appliances, and security alarm systems, as well as provide time services and assorted entertainment programs. The system is voice-controlled; it responds to verbal commands and includes a voice synthesizer to produce spoken responses.

*New Item*:   The U.S. Postal Service has announced the availability of an electronic mail system. Users' computers transmit mail (typically bills or advertising) to regional postal service computer centers via telephone. The computer at the regional center produces a printed version of the mail for next day home delivery.

The computers mentioned in these news items are the high-speed, internally programmed, electronic computers that have become the unseen "brain" behind most of the business transactions of everyday life. Computers have also had an incalculable influence on government, science, and the arts in the years since the first fledgling computer was invented in the mid-1940s.

## 1-2  Computers—What Are They?

Computers are automatic electronic machines that can:

1. Accept (read) data.

2. Store the accepted data in memory.

3. Manipulate the stored data according to directions given by the user.

4. Produce intelligible reports (results) from the manipulated data.

## 1-2-1 Data, Instructions and Information

The objective of computer data processing is to convert raw data into information that can be used for decision making. *Data* refers to raw facts that have been collected from various sources. Consider, for example, the number 2909. Is that number someone's street address or is it the balance in his/her checking account? The number 2909 is data, but once it has meaning it becomes information. *Information* is data that has been processed to give it meaning.

Data is generally fed to a computer to produce information; i.e., data is input to the computer and information is output from the computer (see Figure 1-1). Data is manipulated and organized by the computer by means of *instructions* that humans have written. A set of instructions written to solve a particular problem is called a *program*.

**FIGURE 1-1** DATA VERSUS INFORMATION

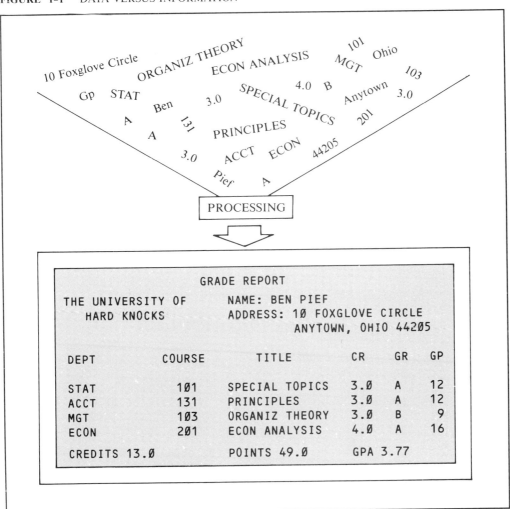

The computer can accept:

**1.** The set of instructions (program) that tells it what to do, i.e., how to solve a particular problem.

**2.** The data needed by the program to produce the desired report.

Thus the program and the data are clearly independent entities. Figure 1–2 illustrates the difference between program and data—the program is the set of instructions to sort an accepted list of names into ascending alphabetical order, and the data is the list of names. Note that a program can process different sets of data; e.g., the program in Figure 1–2 can process different lists of names.

**FIGURE 1–2**    INPUT, PROCESSING AND OUTPUT OF DATA

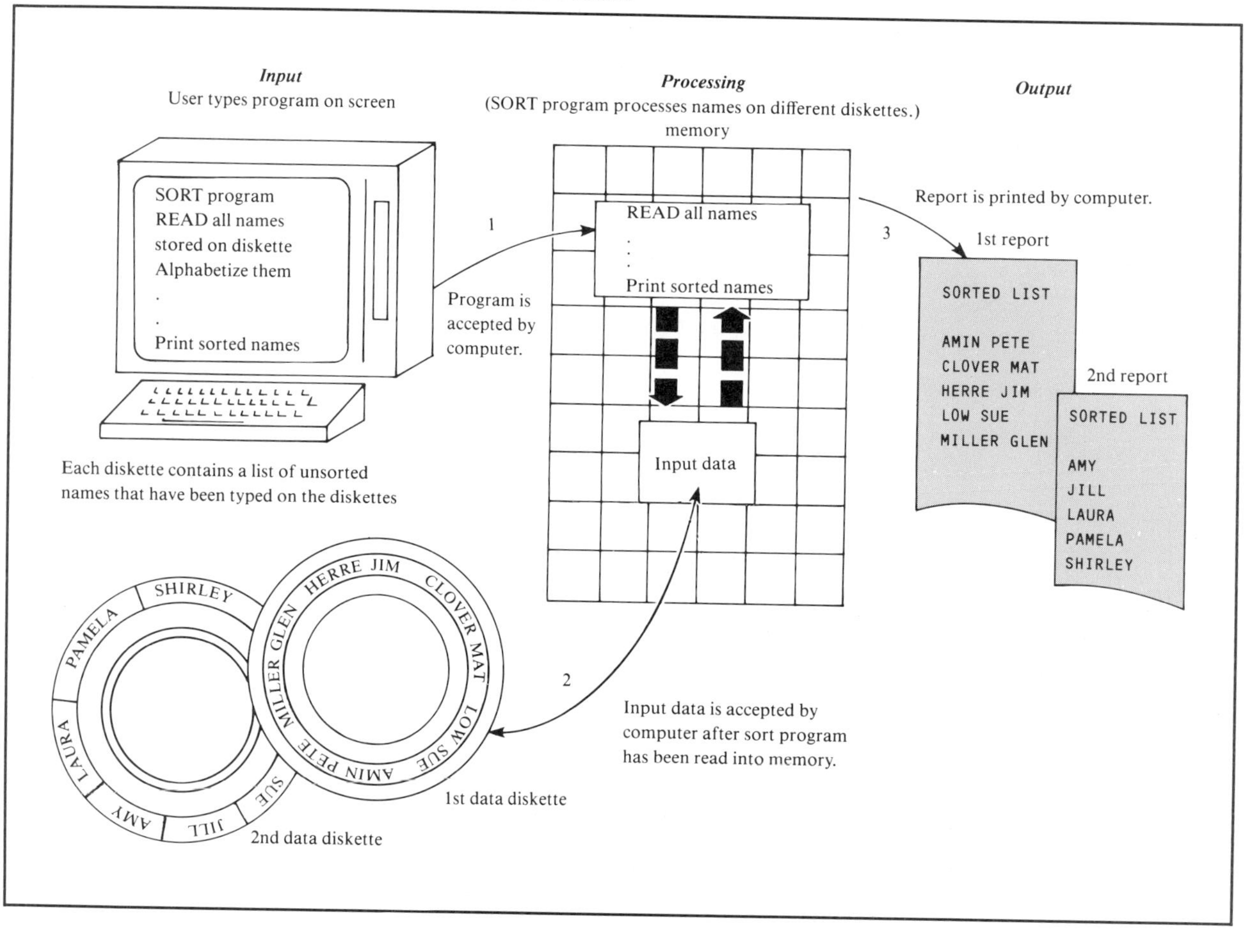

*Input*
User types program on screen

SORT program
READ all names
stored on diskette
Alphabetize them
.
.
Print sorted names

Each diskette contains a list of unsorted names that have been typed on the diskettes

*Processing*
(SORT program processes names on different diskettes.)
memory

1    Program is accepted by computer.

READ all names
:
:
Print sorted names

Input data

2    Input data is accepted by computer after sort program has been read into memory.

1st data diskette
2nd data diskette

PAMELA SHIRLEY LAURA AMY JILL SUE AMIN PETE LOW SUE CLOVER MAT HERRE JIM MILLER GLEN

*Output*

Report is printed by computer.

3    1st report

SORTED LIST

AMIN PETE
CLOVER MAT
HERRE JIM
LOW SUE
MILLER GLEN

2nd report

SORTED LIST

AMY
JILL
LAURA
PAMELA
SHIRLEY

## 1-2-2  What Do Computers Consist Of?

Computers accept (read) information from a variety of input devices. Punched cards used to be a common way to feed data to a computer. The punched card has now given way to other forms of data entry. Interactive terminals allow the user to enter instructions directly on the computer either on a visual screen (cathode ray tube, CRT) or on a hard copy terminal (paper display typewriters). Such communication is interactive in the sense that a continuous dialogue is established between user and computer. Flexible magnetic disks, called diskettes or floppy disks, have also replaced punched cards as a medium for data entry. The user typically inserts a diskette into a slot (disk drive) on the terminal, and by means of certain commands uses the keyboard to write the input data or programs onto the diskette. These programs and data can then be read and processed by the computer at a time convenient to the user.

Compared to punched cards, these devices are faster, more economical, and much more convenient in terms of operation and data editing (corrections, insertions, deletions, and so forth). Figure 1–3 displays these modes of data entry.

FIGURE 1–3    A CRT (LEFT), PAPER DISPLAY (CENTER), FLOPPY DISK (RIGHT)

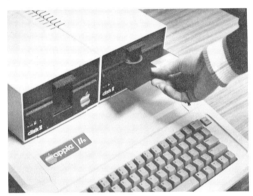

The data to be processed by a computer is stored in the computer's memory, which consists of numerous cells (locations) into which numbers, program instructions, and results can be stored. This memory is often referred to as *primary* storage (see Figure 1–2).

Once the program is stored in memory, the central processing unit (CPU) of the computer carries out (executes) the instructions one by one. Executing an instruction may mean adding or multiplying numbers or comparing two numbers to determine the larger of the two. It can also involve input/output operations such as reading data into storage and printing results onto a terminal, a printer, or some other type of storage device such as a magnetic disk. Storage devices such as magnetic disks, which are not part of memory, are referred to as *secondary* storage devices (see Figure 1–4).

FIGURE 1–4    A LINE PRINTER (LEFT) AND TWO TYPES OF MAGNETIC DISKS (RIGHT)

From this discussion, we can see that a typical computer system generally consists of input and output devices and a processing unit (see Figure 1–5), which is generally composed of the following units:

1. Memory — Programs and data are stored in memory cells.

2. Arithmetic/Logic — This unit can add, subtract, multiply, divide, and raise to a power. It can also compare numbers algebraically and compare words (one character at a time).

3. Control — The control unit fetches program instructions or data in memory and executes each instruction in conjunction with the arithmetic/logic unit.

The term *hardware* refers to the physical components of the computer, such as the input/output devices and CPU, whereas the term *software* refers to programs or systems of programs written by people to accomplish specific tasks. The software is then what makes the hardware come to life.

**FIGURE 1–5** FUNCTIONAL UNITS OF A COMPUTER

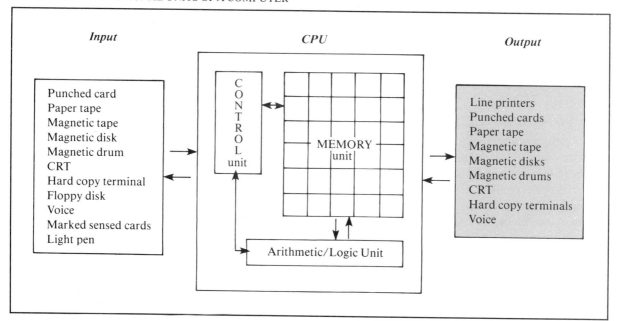

## 1-2-3 Computer Programs

An electronic computer may be called an electronic brain, but its function and problem-solving ability depend on the intelligence of the human beings who direct and control the machine. These people (*programmers* and *operators*) give the computer a set of instructions consisting of the necessary steps required to solve a given problem and see that those instructions are carried out by the computer. The set of instructions that controls the computer is called a *program*.

A program can be executed (processed) by the computer only when it is stored in the computer's memory and is in machine language code. Machine language is the only language the computer can understand. It is a language in which all operations are represented by machine-recognizable numeric codes and in which memory locations containing data and program instructions are represented by numeric addresses. Machine language programs are very detailed and difficult to write. Machine languages vary from one computer manufacturer to another; they are machine dependent, reflecting the design of each computer. Other types of languages (called *high-level languages*) have been developed to allow the user to formulate problems in a much more convenient and efficient manner. Such languages are problem-oriented rather than machine-oriented. High-level languages are essentially machine independent, which means that programs written in such languages can be processed on any type of computer. Programs written in a high-level language must ultimately be translated into machine language before they can be executed by the computer (see Figure 1–6). Special programs called *language translators* or *compilers* have been developed to provide this translation service. FORTRAN is an example of a high-level language. Its name is an acronym for FORmula TRANslation.

The following discussion will help you understand how and why a language like FORTRAN, instead of the computer's machine language, is used by the programmer: Each memory location has an *address*. Suppose we wanted to add the data contained in memory locations 065 and 932 and store the result in location 752. The machine instruction for this might be 43065932752 (In memory, the machine language instruction would actually be represented in binary 1's and 0's). The first two digits are called the *operation code*. This code is used by the control unit to determine what action (add, multiply, and so on) is to be performed on the data in the specified memory locations. After an operation is specified, the *operands* are given. Operands are the addresses of the data to be used. In our example, the data to be added are in memory locations 065 and 932, and the result will be stored in location 752. The machine language instruction is broken down as follows:

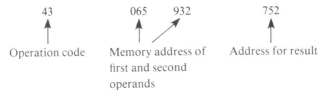

FIGURE 1–6   COMPILATION AND EXECUTION

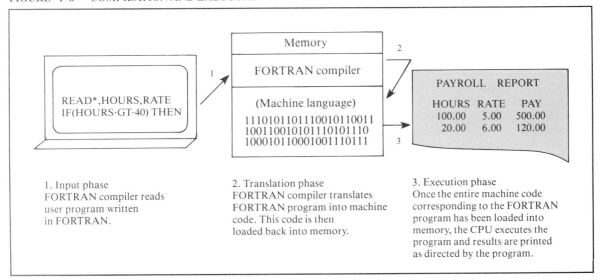

1. Input phase
FORTRAN compiler reads user program written in FORTRAN.

2. Translation phase
FORTRAN compiler translates FORTRAN program into machine code. This code is then loaded back into memory.

3. Execution phase
Once the entire machine code corresponding to the FORTRAN program has been loaded into memory, the CPU executes the program and results are printed as directed by the program.

In FORTRAN programs, arithmetic operations are indicated by the symbols + (addition), − (subtraction), * (multiplication), / (division), and ** (exponentiation). Each memory location is assigned a symbolic name. Let us call location 065 by the symbolic name P, location 932 by X, and location 752 by A. Then the FORTRAN instruction equivalent to the machine language instruction 43065932752 would be:

$$A = P + X$$

In practice, the high-level language programmer never needs to worry about machine addresses or operation codes. The FORTRAN compiler takes care of all these details, allowing the programmer to focus attention on the logic of the problem.

## 1-2-4 Types of Computing Systems

The very first computers required the user to prepare a program in some suitable form (usually punched cards) and submit it to the computer for processing. The computer executed each program one at a time. The user received his/her results, generally in printed form, at some later time. This mode of operation (known as *batch processing*) has several limitations, particularly in today's fast-paced environment. The user must wait some period of time between submitting his/her program and receiving the results. This is particularly annoying when a student is learning a new computer language and is apt to make mistakes. It may require many submissions of a program to receive an error-free output.

An alternative to batch processing is *interactive processing*, in which the user communicates directly with the computing system via a communication terminal (hard copy or CRT). A program called an *editor* enables the user to build a program by entering statements one at a time. The editor has provision for correcting errors, inserting and replacing statements, obtaining listings of the program, and so on. When a complete program has been entered, the system can then execute (*run*) the program, providing the results almost immediately.

There are two types of systems providing interactive computing capabilities: the *microcomputing* system and the *time-sharing* system. Microcomputing systems such as the widely used Apple, IBM, and Radio Shack systems are generally self-contained systems completely under the control of the computer user. Time-sharing systems, on the other hand, consist of a network of terminals communicating with a central computer system. The communication link between the terminal and the computer takes many forms. Telephone links are quite commonly used. To initiate communications via the telephone, the user must dial the number of the computer and place the telephone receiver in a special device (called a *modem*) that is attached to the communications terminal.

When using a microcomputing system, the user generally must enter some initial data such as the date and time. In a time-sharing system, the user must establish his/her identity to the computer by means of an account number and a password before using the computing facility. This is done to enable the system to account for the time used, to bill users accordingly, and to establish what resources are available to individual users. If the user's account number and password match a list kept by the computing system, the user is allowed to proceed; if not, the user may not have access to the computing facility. These steps, called a *sign-on* procedure, are quite specific to a particular computing system. An equally important operation is the *sign-off* procedure, which is followed when the user is finished. Almost all systems have a command such as "GOOD BYE" or "BYE" that terminates the user's communications with the system and releases the terminal for another user. It is important that the sign-off procedure be followed after each session at a terminal. If a user does not sign off, the next person can continue without signing-on, and the time used by both persons will be charged to the first user's account; stored information may also be lost.

### 1-2-5  Do It Now

1. What is the name of the computer you will be using?

2. Is the system batch or interactive?

3. If a batch system is to be used, how will programs be submitted?

4. If the system is interactive, is it a microcomputing or a time-sharing system?

5. If it is a microcomputing system, what procedure is needed to begin programming in FORTRAN?

6. If it is a time-sharing system, what is the sign-on/sign-off procedure? What commands are needed to begin entering a FORTRAN program?

7. If a batch system is to be used, what system control statements or job control language (JCL) will be required to enter a FORTRAN program?

### 1-2-6  Software

The term *software* is generally used to describe the set of programs written by the programmer that causes the computer hardware to function. There are three basic software categories:

1. Translation programs

2. Operating system programs

3. Applications programs

*Translation programs* (compilers) are programs used by the computer system to translate high-level languages or problem-oriented languages into machine language. These translation programs may be supplied by the hardware manufacturer or purchased from other sources. In traditional computing systems, the translated program (called the *object* program) is stored on the mass storage device (usually disk). In a subsequent step, the operating system loads the object program into memory for execution. Some computers use a modified version of this system called an *in-memory compiler* or a *compile-and-go system*. In a system of this type, the FORTRAN program is translated into an object program as before, but the object program is retained in main memory instead of being placed in mass storage. When the program is completely translated, the compiler causes the immediate execution of the program. The advantage of a compile-and-go system is that time and secondary storage space are saved by not producing an external copy of the object program. On the other hand, if the program is needed later, it must be translated again. Hence the compile-and-go system is practical for use only when programs are being developed and tested but are not being executed on a routine basis. This situation characterizes most of the work done on academic computers, therefore compile-and-go systems are widely used by schools and colleges.

*Operating system* programs are usually supplied by the computer manufacturer to assist in the overall operation of the computer system. They are used to regulate and supervise the sequence of activities going on in the system at any time. These programs minimize operator intervention in the actual operation of the computer and ensure a smooth, fast, and efficient transition among the varied tasks performed by the system. Other operating system programs aid the programmer in his/her own work; examples of such programs are utility and library programs. The following functions are performed by some of the more important operating system programs:

1. Load programs into memory from secondary storage.

2. Print messages for the operator and the programmer regarding the status of the program.

3. Perform job accounting by keeping track of who uses the computer and for how long.

4. Handle requests for input/output from executing programs.

5. Handle the collection of data from telecommunications lines (in a time-sharing system).

6. Schedule the slice of time to be allocated to each user's program (in a time-sharing system or multiprogramming system).

7. Perform some routine processing of data such as sorting and copying the contents of one data set onto a specified device.

8. Maintain the store of programs on the mass storage device—adding programs to the store, deleting those no longer needed, and so forth.

9. Attempt to recover from and/or correct errors that may occur in any segment of the computing system.

10. Interpret the job set up and job control instructions specified by the programmer.

At the heart of most operating systems is a program variously called the *supervisor*, the *executive*, or the *monitor*. This program is usually resident in memory at all times and performs many essential tasks, such as program loading and error checking. This resident portion of the operating system loads other, less often used routines as they are required.

*Applications programs* are written by individual users to solve particular problems. They may be written in a generalized fashion and modified as needed to fit the peculiar requirements of a particular system, or they may be constructed exactly to satisfy specific needs. For example, a company may construct its own payroll system, or it may purchase (or rent) a general set of payroll programs and modify them if necessary. Companies guard all of their processing programs as a very important company asset. Extensive security measures are taken to avoid the loss or theft of programs. A considerable store of programs is usually available to a computer user; in fact, the usefulness of a computer may well depend more on the variety and efficiency of the available software than on the characteristics of the hardware.

### 1-2-7 **Do It Now**

1. List the hardware components of the computing system you will be using.

2. How much memory does the CPU of your system have? One K (1K) of memory refers to 1024 memory locations, each capable of storing one character. Thus a 16K memory implies space for 16384 characters (1024 × 16).

3. Is FORTRAN implemented as a traditional system or compile-and-go system on your computer.

4. What is the name of the operating system you will be using?

5. Make a list of the more commonly used features of your operating system and the procedure required to use each feature.

## 1-2-8 **my system is different**

*Features, Commands, and Examples*

This section is left blank for you to list pertinent information about your system.

## 1-3  A Brief Preview of Program Flowcharts and Structured Code

A flowchart is a pictorial representation of the method (logic) used to solve a particular problem. It diagrams the sequence of steps that must be taken (from beginning to end) to arrive at the solution of the problem, and it turns out to be a very valuable tool. For example, the flowchart in Figure 1–7 identifies some of the activities that a person might perform upon waking in the morning. Figure 1–7 is so important to the understanding of structured programming concepts that the reader is asked to visually walk through the complete flow-chart very carefully, as many times as needed to try to understand the process involved. Note the two distinct types of activities:

1. Physical or processing activities, such as GET OUT OF BED, LIE DOWN, and so forth.

2. Mental or sensory activities involving decisions, the outcome of which is always expressed in terms of YES and NO; these decisions result in nonsequential transfer to a particular instruction, depending on a certain condition, for example IS IT 10TH PUSH-UP? or ENOUGH SUGAR?

Note, by the way, the two different types of geometric symbols (blocks) in the flowchart corresponding to these two distinct types of activities.

Eventually, program flowcharts must be translated into particular high-level languages. Figure 1–7 illustrates different language approaches differing not in their grammar but in their structure and organization. The language displayed is obviously not a programming language that can be processed by a computer. It is an example of *pseudo code*, which is an informal design language somewhat similar to FORTRAN. Pseudo code does not have to be extremely precise, and grammatical considerations are of secondary importance. One example of this pseudo code, the traditional version in Figure 1–7, is essentially an exact copy of the flowchart (line-to-line similarity) in which the flowchart decision block is expressed through English sentences of the form:

If the condition is true, transfer to a specific statement number.
Otherwise (if the condition is false), take the instruction
immediately following the IF statement.

For example, the GO TO statement at statement 15 skips four lines of code. This traditional approach illustrates the characteristics of nonstructured code, while the structured version in Figure 1–7 reflects current practices of program development. In the traditional version, the reader has to skip visually "all over the code" to follow the sequence of instructions; in contrast, the structured version is much smoother in terms of readability and comprehension. There are no offensive GO TO statements to break the reader's concentration, no numeric labels such as 10, 15, 30 … are needed. The reader simply starts at the top of the code and effortlessly moves on down as if he/she were reading a page of a novel! The statement IF-THEN-ELSE seems to be the logical way to express the outcome of a condition, while the WHILE DO statement is quite self-explanatory: a task is repeated until a particular condition is met, then the task is stopped. Note that with this type of design there are no statement numbers—none are needed!

Studies have shown that structured code is easier to develop, easier to read, easier to understand, and easier to modify than nonstructured code. In addition, fewer errors are likely to occur. It should be noted that not all versions of FORTRAN allow the IF-THEN-ELSE and the WHILE-DO statements. The older FORTRANs do not support the IF-THEN-ELSE instruction; hence GO TO statements are necessary. Most current FORTRANs reflect standards adopted in 1977, which do permit the IF-THEN-ELSE but which do not necessarily permit the WHILE DO instruction. This text assumes that your FORTRAN does not support the WHILE DO. In chapter 4 we will discuss a method to simulate the WHILE DO, which will allow us to design programs that are well structured.

**FIGURE 1-7** STRUCTURED VERSUS NONSTRUCTURED CODE

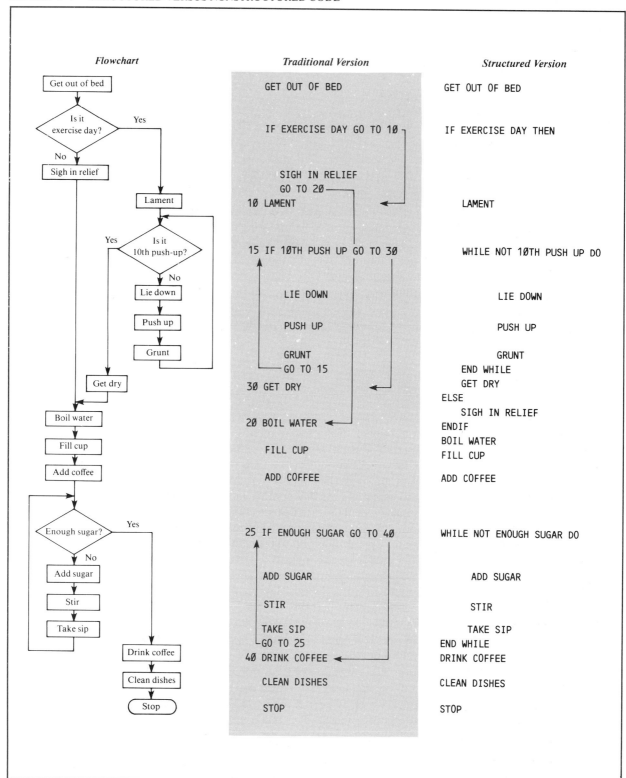

## 1-4  You Might Want to Know

**1.** How long has FORTRAN been around?

*Answer*: Development of the first FORTRAN compiler began in 1954 under the direction of John Backus of IBM; the project was completed in 1957.

**2.** Does FORTRAN vary from one computer to the other?

*Answer*: In 1966 the American National Standards Institute (ANSI) adopted a standard FORTRAN language. This initial standard of 1966 was revised in 1977. Not all computer manufactuers and software companies have adhered strictly to those standards. Many have added their own features to the language, while others have provided extensions to certain statements; as a result, a particular program run at your installation may not "work" at another installation without minor modifications. A technical reference manual developed by the computer manufacturer for the FORTRAN used at your computer installation is a worthwhile investment and may save hours of frustration and inconvenience. The serious student should consult a FORTRAN user's guide while studying this text.

**3.** What is the history of structured programming?

*Answer*: In 1966 the *communications of the ACM* (a publication of the Association for Computing Machinery) published a paper by Messrs. Boehm and Jacopini, presented two years earlier during an international colloquium of algebraic linguistics. In essence, the paper demonstrated that a program with one entry and one exit could be written using only three control patterns: the sequence, the section (IF-THEN-ELSE) and the DO WHILE patterns.

In 1968 Mr. E. Dijkstra of the Netherlands proposed that program code could be written without using the GO TO statement. Mr. Dijkstra considered the GO TO statement harmful and stated, "I discovered why the use of the GO TO statement has such disastrous effects, and I became convinced that the GO TO statement should be abolished from all higher level programming languages. . . ."

Subsequently, Dr. Mills of the IBM Corporation wrote an article on the mathematical foundation of structured programming. With Mr. Baker of IBM, the "New York Times" project was developed using structured program concepts.

From 1971 on, structured programming has been a replacement to the traditional program development methods that are progressively disappearing from the programming scene.

**4.** What other high-level languages are there besides FORTRAN?

*Answer*: One survey reported 600 computer languages in more or less widespread use. Among these are COBOL (Common Oriented Business Language), RPG (Report Program Generator—for small shops), Algol (scientific and system language), BASIC (Beginners All-purpose Symbolic Instruction Code), PL/1 (combining both FORTRAN and COBOL capabilities, well suited for business and for scientific problems), and Pascal.

**5.** In terms of coding productivity, how does structured programming compare to traditional FORTRAN programming?

*Answer*: Studies in the mid-1960s revealed that professional programmers would code approximately 12 lines of tested code per day. Some studies show that this figure jumps to 100 lines of tested code per day when structured designs are used.

**6.** Hardware costs have come down precipitously in the last few years. Can the same be said about software costs?

*Answer*: Software development costs have soared to the point where now, in a typical computer operation, approximately 90% of the total computer system budget is earmarked for software costs, as opposed to only 10% in 1950.

**7.** Just how fast do computers operate?

*Answer*: The latest model computers operate at speeds measured in *nanoseconds* (1 nanosecond = 1 billionth of a second). For example, the Cray 2 computer is capable of executing 100 to 200 million instructions per second; that is, one instruction takes 5 to 10 nanoseconds to execute.

**8.** I cannot conceive of how fast a nanosecond is. Can you help me?

*Answer*: Perhaps. One nanosecond is to 1 second as 1 second is to 32 years. In other words, there are approximately 1 billion seconds in 32 years. One nanosecond is the approximate time required for light to travel 1 foot.

**9.** Is there any limit to the internal speeds of a computer?

*Answer*: Electrical signals are propagated at speeds approaching the speed of light (1 foot/nanosecond). Integrated circuits packing many thousands of transistors per square inch have been designed to minimize the length of interconnections through which electrical signals are propagated, thereby reducing the time it takes a signal to travel from one transistor to another in that circuit. Figures 1–8 and 1–9 illustrate the size and density of an integrated circuit "chip."

**FIGURE 1–8** MAGNIFIED VIEW OF THE INTEL 8748
SINGLE CHIP MICROCOMPUTER
(COURTESY INTEL CORPORATION)

**FIGURE 1–9** FUNCTIONAL MAP OF THE 8748
MICROCOMPUTER (ACTUAL SIZE: 5.6 × 6.6
MILLIMETERS)

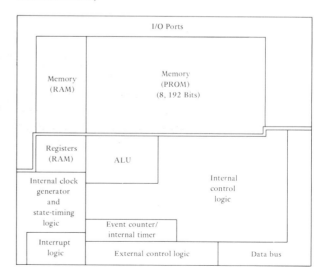

**10.** Computers may be very fast and powerful devices, but aren't there problems that even the fastest and largest of them cannot handle?

*Answer*: Yes. If a computer a billion times faster than the fastest computer available today were to analyze all possible outcomes of a chess game, it would require on the order of $10^{100}$ hours (many billions of years) to make the first move in the game.

# 1-5  Exercises

## 1-5-1  Test Yourself

**1.** List four parts of a computer and explain the function of each.

**2.** Define the following:

| | | |
|---|---|---|
| a. CPU | g. primary storage | m. compile-and-go |
| b. CRT | h. secondary storage | system |
| c. program | i. batch environment | n. microcomputer |
| d. data | j. interactive computing | o. source program |
| e. nanosecond | k. compiler | p. object program |
| f. machine language | l. software | |

**3.** Which of the following is used for input as well as output?

| | | |
|---|---|---|
| a. CRT terminal | c. magnetic tape | e. none of the above |
| b. printer | d. all of the above | |

**4.** A compiler is

    a. a program that translates machine code into a high-level language
    b. another name for FORTRAN
    c. a program that loads FORTRAN into memory
    d. a program that translates a high-level language program into machine code

**5.** The part of the machine-language instruction that tells the computer what to do is called

    a. an operand    b. a compiler    c. an operation code    d. a translator

**6.** Are the following statements true or false?

    a. Each memory location has a corresponding address.
    b. A machine language operand may indicate where the result of a particular operation is to be placed.
    c. Computer hardware consists of all the physical components of computer system.
    d. High-level languages are essentially machine-independent.
    e. The term *software* refers to such material as paper, magnetic tape, floppy disks, and so forth.
    f. In a batch-processing environment, the user receives an almost instantaneous response to his/her program.
    g. Time-sharing is made possible by the use of time slices.

## 1-5-2 Other Problems

1. a. If you will be working in an interactive computing environment, determine sign-on, sign-off, and other procedures necessary to compile and execute a FORTRAN program.
   b. If you will be working in a batch processing environment, determine the operating system instructions and the exact statements necessary to compile and execute a FORTRAN program.

2. Write a structured program for the following recipe:

> Bring to a boil in a saucepan 2 cups of milk, 2 tablespoons of butter, 1 teaspoon of sugar and 1 teaspoon of salt. Add 2 tablespoons of frozen orange juice and let mixture set until lukewarm. Meanwhile, dissolve 1/4 cup of yeast and 1 teaspoon of rum in 1/2 cup of hot water. When this rum mixture is cool, add it to the first preparation and stir in 3 cups of flour. Add in sufficient flour until dough is moist and does not stick to hands. Pour dough into cake pan and cover for two hours or until dough has risen 1 1/2 times its original size. Heat oven to 400 degrees. Place pan into oven and bake for 10 minutes. Then reduce heat to 300 degrees and leave pan until cake surface is golden.

## 1-5-3 Answers to Test Yourself

1. *Input*: device which reads information from some medium.
   *Output*: device which writes information onto some medium.
   *Memory*: stores program instructions and data.
   *Arithmetic/logical*: circuitry which performs arithmetic and decisions on the data.
   *Control*: executes program instructions.

2. a. *CPU*: central processing unit—memory, arithmetic/logical, and control units.
   b. *CRT*: cathode ray tube—input/output visual display device.
   c. *Program*: instructions to solve a problem.
   d. *Data*: information to be processed by a program (numbers, lists of names, etc.).
   e. *Nanosecond*: one billionth of a second.
   f. *Machine language*: numerical language inherent in the design of the particular computer.
   g. *Primary storage*: the memory of the computer residing in the CPU.
   h. *Secondary storage*: supplementary memory storage in the form of magnetic disks, and so forth.
   i. *Batch environment*: computing system in which programs and data are processed some period of time after submission of programs.
   j. *Interactive computing*: computing system in which user's instructions and data are analyzed and processed immediately.
   k. *Compiler*: a program that translates a high-level language such as FORTRAN into machine language for subsequent execution.
   l. *Software*: a set of programs that causes the computer to function.
   m. *Compile-and-go system*: programming system in which the object program is placed in memory and executed immediately after the compiler has finished the translation process.

    n. *Microcomputer*: small, stand-alone computing system based on a central process-
       ing unit contained on a microcircuit (chip).

    o. *Source program*: program written in high-level language such as FORTRAN.

    p. *Object program*: a machine language version of a source program produced by a
       compiler.

**3.**   a

**4.**   d

**5.**   a

**6.**   a. T       b. T       c. T       d. T
      e. F       f. F       g. T

# variables,
# replacement statement,
# write, print*, errors

## CHAPTER TWO

# variables, replacement statement, write, print*, errors

## 2-1   Programming Example

*Problem Specification:*   Mr. X. owns two rectangular lots. The width (W1) of lot 1 is 75.6 and its length (E1) is 121.5. The width (W2) of lot 2 is 98.5 and its length (E2) is 110.6. Calculate and print the area of each lot and the combined area of the two lots.

A FORTRAN program to solve this problem is shown in Figure 2–1, which contains the listing of the original program and the results printed by the FORTRAN program. Notice the five types of FORTRAN statements in this program:

1. The replacement (assignment) statement used for calculations; for example A1 = W1*E1

2. The WRITE statement, which tells which results are to be printed.

3. The FORMAT statement, used to position the numeric values (results) and the alphabetic messages on the output line.

**FIGURE  2–1**    CALCULATION OF THE AREA OF TWO LOTS

*FORTRAN Code*

| *Explanation* | Columns |
|---|---|

```
Set width of lot 1 to 75.6        W1  =  75.6
Set length of lot 1 to 121.5      E1  =  121.5
Compute area of lot 1             A1  =  W1*E1
Set width of lot 2 to 98.5        W2  =  98.5
Set length of lot 2 to 110.6      E2  =  110.6
Compute area of lot 2             A2  =  W2*E2
Compute sum of areas              SUM = A1+A2
WRITE area of lot 1               WRITE(6,10)A1
WRITE area of lot 2               WRITE(6,11)A2
WRITE sum of areas                WRITE(6,13)SUM
Terminate processing              STOP
                             10   FORMAT(3X,'AREA LOT1 IS',2X,F7.1)
                             11   FORMAT(3X,'AREA LOT2 IS',2X,F7.1)
                             13   FORMAT(3X,'TOTAL AREA IS',1X,F7.1)
                                  END
```

```
Output produced by program   {  AREA LOT1 IS   9185.4
                             {  AREA LOT2 IS  10894.1
                             {  TOTAL AREA IS 20079.5
```

**4.** The STOP statement to terminate execution of the program.

**5.** The END statement, which *must* be the last statement in any FORTRAN program.

### 2-1-1  Do It Now

**1.** Would the following code produce the same result as the program in Figure 2–1?

```
      W1=75.6
      W2=98.5
      E1=121.5
      E2=110.6
      A1=W1*E1
      A2=W2*E2
      WRITE(6,10)A1
      WRITE(6,11)A2
      ATOTAL=A1+A2
      WRITE(6,13)ATOTAL
      STOP
10    FORMAT (3X, 'AREA LOT1 IS' , 2X, F7.1)
11    FORMAT (3X, 'AREA LOT2 IS' , 2X, F7.1)
13    FORMAT (3X, 'TOTAL AREA IS' ,1X, F7.1)
      END
```

**2.** What do you think would happen if all the WRITE statements followed the STOP statement?

### *Answers*

**1.** Yes. The two names ATOTAL and SUM are different, but the same value is associated with each name.

**2.** No printout would ever be produced! The STOP statement terminates execution of the program, so the WRITE statements would not be executed.

## 2-2  Practical Considerations: Typing Your Program

### 2-2-1  Text Editors

A FORTRAN program consists of a sequence of FORTRAN instructions called FOR-TRAN statements. In the "old days" FORTRAN statements were punched on data cards, one statement per card. A typical card and a deck of cards containing a FORTRAN program are shown in Figure 2–2. The following fields were used in punching a FORTRAN statement:

■ card columns 1–5      statement number (optional except for formats)

■ card column  6        continuation (optional)

■ card columns 7–72     body of FORTRAN statement (always required)

■ card columns 73–80    identification (optional)

**FIGURE 2-2** FORTRAN PROGRAM ON PUNCHED CARDS

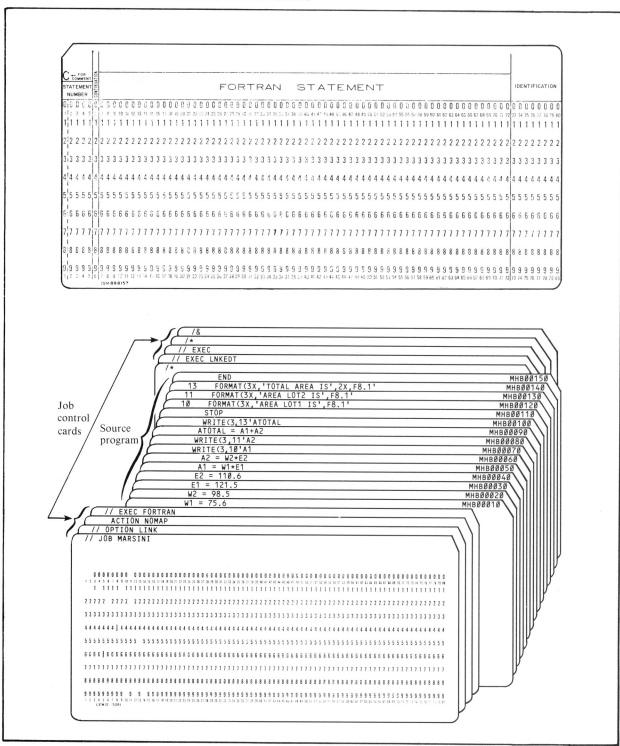

Advances in hardware technology have now made punched cards obsolete, and terminals (CRTs and hard copy printers) have replaced punched cards. Programs are now typed on screens or on printer keyboards and saved on magnetic disks (permanent, hard disks or flexible disks or magnetic tape). Conceptually, however, nothing has really changed in terms of the various fields that make up a FORTRAN statement. Whether you use a CRT or a printer keyboard, FORTRAN statement numbers are still typed in positions 1–5, the body of the FORTRAN statement uses positions 7–72, and so forth. The only difference is in the *editing* process. To correct a character when punched cards were used, you simply re-typed a new card and threw the old one away; when you wanted to insert a statement between two other statements, you physically inserted a card with the coded statement in its appropriate position in the deck of cards; and when you had finished with your program, you simply walked away with your deck of cards in hand! Working on a terminal is quite different!

Today's systems have text editors that make it possible to delete or insert a character or line within a program. Some of these editors are very user-friendly and make your life extremely easy in terms of changing information on the screen. They allow you to move a cursor in any direction on the screen and make any desired corrections (deletions or insertions). These editors are called full-screen editors. Other text editors (called line editors) only allow you to change one line at a time. They use special commands to delete, to insert lines, and so forth. Text editors vary greatly from one system to another. On some systems, the editing process requires that each line be numbered, i.e., each line of text must have a numeric label so that you can specify which line you want to edit (change). Even though these line numbers actually show up on the terminal, they are not used by FORTRAN, i.e., as far as FORTRAN is concerned, position 1 starts after the numeric label. These numeric line numbers (the number of digits may vary) are either provided automatically by the text editor every time the ENTER or RETURN key is pressed, or in some cases they are provided by the user. The program of Figure 2–1 might appear on a terminal as follows:

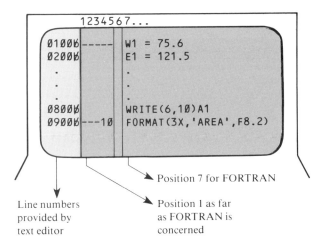

Once a program has been typed on a terminal, special text editor commands such as SAVE allow you to store the text that you have typed (edited) on magnetic disk or flexible diskette, under a user-chosen name. This same text (program) can then be loaded back into the memory of the computer by a text editor command such as LOAD or EDIT, for changes or corrections.

## 2-2-2 my system is different

*Features, Commands, and Examples.*

This section is left blank so that you can describe the way your text editor functions. Write down the various commands and a complete example of how to run a program at your installation.

## 2-2-3 The FORTRAN Coding Sheet

A statement number is an unsigned integer number (no decimal point) that identifies a particular FORTRAN statement. Statement numbers can be from one to five digits long and are entered in positions 1–5. The digits should be entered in consecutive positions. Many compilers require the number to be right-justified in positions 1–5 because blanks are interpreted as zeros. Statement numbers need not be sequential and are required only when a statement is to be referred to by another FORTRAN statement in the program. Many programmers number their statements in sequential fashion; this makes it easier to locate statements in the program.

The FORTRAN statement itself can be entered anywhere in positions 7–72. For program readability, the beginning programmer may wish to start all statements in position 7. If a statement is too long to fit one record in positions 7–72, it can be continued onto another record by using the continuation field (see chapter 3, section 3–8–3).

Positions 73–80 can be used to identify the author and/or for sequencing purposes, or they can be left blank. FORTRAN coding sheets (see Figure 2-3) are available commercially to help the novice identify the various fields. The coding sheet simplifies the transcription of the program into machine-readable form.

Positions 73–80 of the record are generally included in the program listing but are not translated by the compiler.

**FIGURE 2-3** A FORTRAN CODING FORM

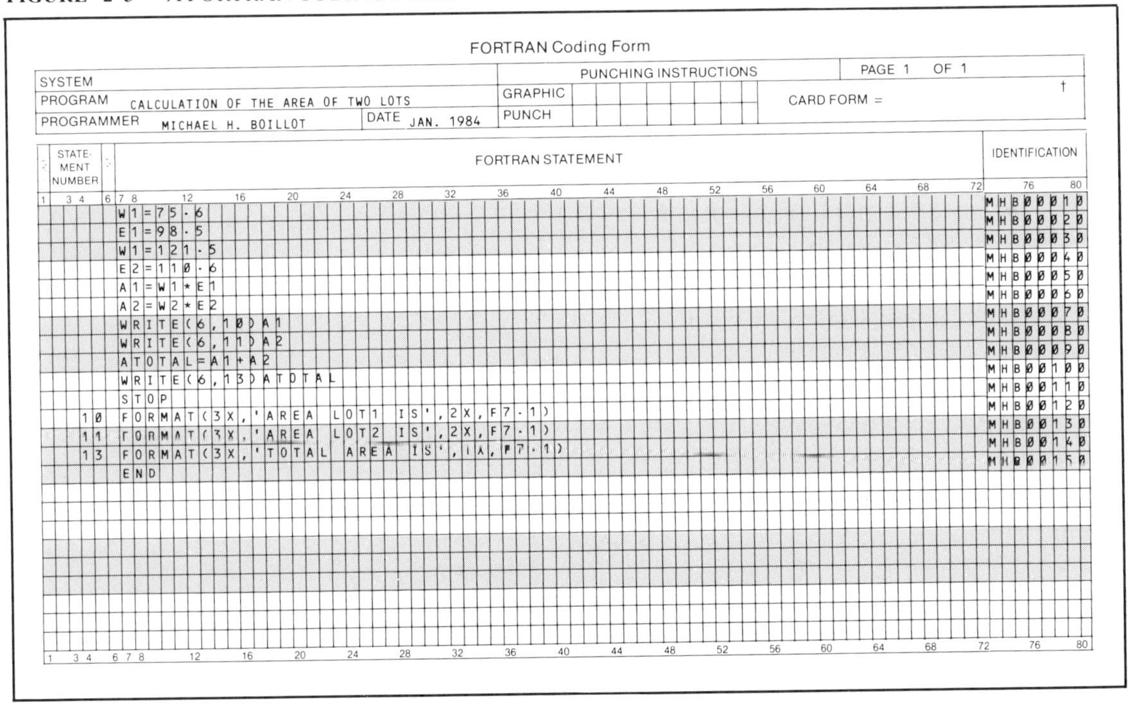
FORTRAN Coding Form

SYSTEM | PUNCHING INSTRUCTIONS | PAGE 1 OF 1
PROGRAM CALCULATION OF THE AREA OF TWO LOTS | GRAPHIC | CARD FORM =
PROGRAMMER MICHAEL H. BOILLOT | DATE JAN. 1984 | PUNCH

STATEMENT NUMBER | FORTRAN STATEMENT | IDENTIFICATION

```
      W1=75.6                                                           MHB00010
      E1=98.5                                                           MHB00020
      W1=121.5                                                          MHB00030
      E2=110.6                                                          MHB00040
      A1=W1*E1                                                          MHB00050
      A2=W2*E2                                                          MHB00060
      WRITE(6,10)A1                                                     MHB00070
      WRITE(6,11)A2                                                     MHB00080
      ATOTAL=A1+A2                                                      MHB00090
      WRITE(6,13)ATOTAL                                                 MHB00100
      STOP                                                              MHB00110
   10 FORMAT(3X,'AREA LOT1 IS',2X,F7.1)                                 MHB00120
   11 FORMAT(3X,'AREA LOT2 IS',2X,F7.1)                                 MHB00130
   13 FORMAT(3X,'TOTAL AREA IS',1X,F7.1)                                MHB00140
      END                                                               MHB00150
```

## 2-2-4 Program Documentation: The Comment Statement

In a real-life environment, a programmer seldom writes a program just for himself/ herself; it is usually for a friend, a customer, or the company for which he/she works. Thus, the program needs to be understood by others. Indeed, the program may need to be revised, updated, expanded, and so forth. It is, therefore, very important that the program be self-documenting and that it contain explanations and comments to help the reader understand its nature and purpose. For this reason, FORTRAN allows the programmer to intersperse comments throughout the FORTRAN code. Such a practice is very helpful when the programmer (or someone else) later decides to review or make revisions to some parts of the program. Comment statements can help the programmer recapture the essence of some of his/her original thoughts.

Comment lines can be inserted anywhere in a program by entering a C in position 1 of the FORTRAN statement. When the compiler reads the C in position 1, it realizes that the information in that statement is just for the programmer; it does not view the statement as a FORTRAN instruction and does not translate it into machine language. The C in position 1 causes the content of that statement to be listed on the output device with all other FORTRAN instructions.

As we will discuss in chapter 4, it is good practice to start a program with a comment identifying the purpose of a program. It is also an excellent idea to start a program with a dictionary of all the variables used in the program, where each variable is briefly described in terms of the role it plays in the program. For example, you could start our simple area calculation program as follows:

```
1234567-----------------------------------------------------...73
C      CALCULATION OF AREAS
C
C      W1: WIDTH OF LOT 1
C      E1: LENGTH OF LOT 1
C      A1: AREA OF LOT 1
          .
          .
          .
C      THE FOLLOWING INSTRUCTION COMPUTES THE AREA OF LOT 1
       A1 = W1 * E1
```

## 2-3  Getting Started

In general, FORTRAN statements consist of certain elements (key words, constants, variables, and special characters) strung together under strict grammatical rules. The following example illustrates the various grammatical components of a FORTRAN replacement statement.

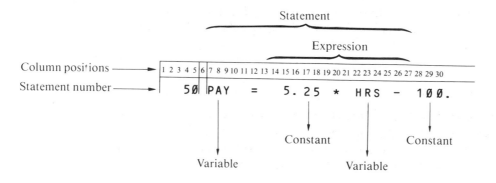

## 2-3-1  The Character Set

The characters used in FORTRAN are grouped into three classes:

■ alphabetic characters:    (blank), A, B, C, ..., Y, Z

■ numeric characters:      0 through 9

■ special characters:       + − * / = . ' ( ) ,

*Character data* refers to any of the symbols available on your keyboard.

## 2-3-2  Numeric Constants

A constant is a fixed numerical value that is explicitly stated; in other words, it is a number. A constant can be expressed in *integer* mode or *real* mode. An integer constant is always written without a decimal point; a real constant is always written with a decimal point. Either type may be preceded by a sign. If the number is negative, a minus sign must be used; if the number is positive, the plus sign is optional.

*Example 1*

| | | | | | |
|---|---|---|---|---|---|
| 300 | − 2 | 63247 | + 4 | 0 | are integer constants. |
| 6.32 | − 3.21 | .0005 | + 63.04 | 0. | are real constants. |

An imbedded blank (blanks between the first and last digit) in a constant has no effect on the value of the constant.

*Example 2*    The following constants have the same value:

```
6    32
632
6   3   2
```

*Example 3*    The following constants are invalid:

| | |
|---|---|
| 632,000 | No commas allowed. |
| 23.34. | Only one decimal point is permitted. |
| $30.50 | Special character $ is invalid. |
| 111-333-444 | Special character - is invalid. |

The allowable size (magnitude) of integer and real constants and their internal representation on a computer are discussed in detail in chapter 6. Integers and real numbers have different internal representations.

## 2-3-3  Character Constants

Character constants consist of any sequence of characters that your keyboard can produce; they are enclosed in apostrophes or single quotes (')—not double quotes ("). The apostrophes are not part of the string; they simply identify the start and the end of the string. Most FORTRAN versions allow character constants up to 127 characters.

*Examples*

| Constant | Number of Characters |
|---|---|
| `'DONKEY  '` | 8 (includes two trailing blanks) |
| `'3210 NORTH 10TH ST.'` | 19 |
| `'$23.45'` | 6 |
| `'111-21-8444'` | 11 |
| `'33'` | 2 |
| `'HE SAID "FORGET IT SAM"'` | 23 |

Note that character constants cannot participate in arithmetic operations. For example, '1' * '4' is an invalid operation; so is 2* '3'.

To use an apostrophe within a character constant, use two apostrophes instead of one, as in

`'MONA''S CAT'`   to mean MONA'S CAT
`''''`                  to mean '

## 2-3-4  Variables

Unlike a constant, a variable can assume different values. You can think of a variable as the name given to a memory location into which data is to be stored. Instead of referring to a value contained in a memory location by that location's numeric address, we use a symbolic name to refer to that location. Thus we can store a value such as 33.3 into SLOT or into POT or into DOG!

Judicious choice of variable names helps make the purpose of a particular FORTRAN statement understandable, as in

PAY = HRS*RATE

where PAY, HRS, and RATE are variable names.

Variable names can be from one to six characters in length. The first character of a variable name must be alphabetic; succeeding characters can be alphabetic or numeric. No special characters can be used in a variable name.

*Example 1*    The following are valid variable names:

X
Q1
COUNT
ABC
X12345

The following are invalid variable names:

| | |
|---|---|
| INVOICE | Too long. |
| A — B | Special character ( — ). |
| 1PAY | Numeric first character. |
| LIGHT. | Period is invalid. |

Any blanks between the characters of a variable name are ignored.

*Example 2*    The following are names for the same variable:

ABC

A   BC

A   B   C

Since variables are names for memory locations and since memory locations can contain integer, real, or character constants, you might expect that there would be three different types of variables to contain these three types of constants. Integers generally occupy less memory storage than real numbers, and arithmetic operations involving integer operands are faster than operations involving real numbers. Hence it is desirable to designate those variables that are to process integer values, those variables that are to process real numbers, and those variables that contain character data (names, addresses, and so forth). Internally these three types are coded differently, so FORTRAN needs to know which is which to ensure proper internal code. You can specify the types (modes) through the following FORTRAN **type** statements: INTEGER, REAL, CHARACTER. These statements should be placed at the "top" of the program (before any executable statements). Consider the following examples:

*Example 3*

If you want variables SUM, K, and FICA to represent integer variables, you can declare these variables as follows:

```
INTEGER SUM,K,FICA
or
INTEGER SUM
INTEGER K
INTEGER FICA
```

You can declare PAY, JET, and LENGTH to contain real constants with the statement:

```
REAL PAY,JET,LENGTH
```

If variables MESSG and ERROR are to contain character data, you *must* declare these variables and the maximum number of characters they will contain as follows:

```
CHARACTER MESSG*1Ø,ERROR*4,X
or
CHARACTER MESSG*1Ø     Variable MESSG can contain up to 10 characters.
CHARACTER ERROR*4      Variable ERROR can contain up to 4 characters.
CHARACTER X            Since the * is omitted, only 1 character is reserved for X.
```

Type declarations for variables containing character data can also have the following form:

```
CHARACTER*1Ø X,Y,Z     X, Y and Z can each contain up to 10 characters each. Note the po-
                       sition of the asterisk.
```

A typical program might start with the following **type** declarations:

```
REAL X,ISUM,JELL
INTEGER K,SEX
CHARACTER NAME*22
```

The types can appear in any order but they must appear before executable statements such as arithmetic, condition, or input/output statements.

A practice that is becoming more and more common in writing programs is identifying all the variables that will be used in the program at the start of a program. This can be done by **TYPING** each variable, i.e., by declaring each variable as INTEGER, REAL, or CHARACTER type. As we will discuss in chapter 4, this practice provides for better program documentation and for accountability of all variables used in a program. It also informs the reader of the way in which each variable is treated.

It should be noted that **typing** integer or real variables is *not* mandatory, although it is mandatory to **type** character variables. If the user does not **type** real or integer variables, then the type of the variable is implicitly defined by its name: If the first letter of the variable starts with I, J, K, L, M or N, the variable is integer; otherwise the variable is real. Thus, ISAM and KLM are integer variables, while HIM and SOCSEC are real variables.

An integer variable name represents a memory cell in which the number stored will have no decimal point, while a real variable represents a cell in which there is a decimal point. Consider the following real and integer variables with corresponding arbitrary memory contents; in this case, the numeric variables have not been **typed**, but the character variables have been **typed** with the statement: `CHARACTER X,N103*4`

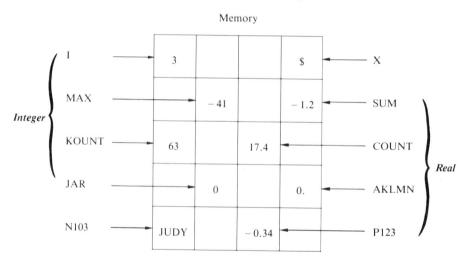

Variable names are automatically assigned to memory locations by the computer system.

In programs that make extensive use of integers and/or real variables, it becomes cumbersome to list all such variables in explicit mode declaration statements. For this reason the IMPLICIT specification statement allows the programmer to formulate his/her own conventions for type declaration. For example, the statement IMPLICIT REAL (I) would cause all variables with names beginning with the character I to be real. It is also possible to specify a range of letters in alphabetical order in the IMPLICIT statement; for example, the statement IMPLICIT INTEGER (A–D) would make any variable beginning with A, B, C, or D an integer variable. The general form of the implicit statement is:

IMPLICIT *type* (*a*[,*a*] . . . )[,*type*(*a*[,*a*] . . .)] . . .

where *type* can be INTEGER, REAL, or other mode type,
  *a* can be a single letter or a range of letters denoted by $I_1 - I_2$, where $I_1$ and $I_2$ are single letters of the alphabet.

The IMPLICIT statement must be the *first* of all the specification statements. Note that implicit typing does not necessarily negate the automatic implicit roles for integer or real variables, i.e., IMPLICIT INTEGER (C–F) does *not* mean that only variables starting with C through F will be integer variables—variables starting with I through N will *also* be integer variables.

*Examples*

1. IMPLICIT INTEGER(A,C–F),REAL(I–N)
2. IMPLICIT REAL (C), INTEGER (A,B)
3. IMPLICIT CHARACTER (G,I), CHARACTER * 15 (N)
4. IMPLICIT CHARACTER*3 (A–D)

In the first statement variables beginning with A, C, D, E, and F are implicitly integer; all other variables are real. In the second statement, variable names starting with the letter A or B become integer variables, (along with those starting with I–N). REAL (C) does not change the mode of C since it is implicitly real. In the third statement, any variable starting with the letter G or I will be a character variable of length 1, while all variables starting with the letter N will be character variables of length 15. In the fourth statement, all variables starting with A, B, C, or D will be character variables of length 3.

## 2-3-5 **Do It Now**

1. Classify each of the following as a valid or invalid constant. For valid constants, specify the mode (type). If invalid, explain why.

   a. $25
   b. 23,672
   c. −1.2

   d. 1432
   e. −.1270
   f. 4A

   g. 23.24.
   h. '111-22-111'
   i. '"'

2. Classify each of the following as a valid or invalid variable name. For valid variable names, specify the mode (type). If invalid, explain why.

   a. JJ2
   b. A4
   c. 4A

   d. BETAMAX
   e. KORN
   f. A*B

   g. A$
   h. 'MODULE'
   i. ABC.

### *Answers*

1. a. invalid because of $ sign
   b. invalid because of comma
   c. valid, real
   d. valid, integer
   e. valid, real

   f. invalid because of alphabetic character
   g. invalid because of 2 decimal points
   h. valid, character
   i. valid, character

**2.** a. valid, integer
   b. valid, real
   c. invalid because of numeric first character
   d. invalid because too long
   e. valid, integer

   f. invalid because of special character
   g. invalid because of $
   h. invalid because this is character constant
   i. invalid because of period

### 2-3-6 Integer and Real Arithmetic

The primary distinction between integer and real data is that real data can contain a fractional part while integer data cannot. When arithmetic is performed using two integer constants and/or variables, **no decimal part is retained** (everything to the right of the implied decimal point is truncated. For example, the integer 7 divided by the integer 4 yields the integer 1, and *not* 1.75!—the result is **truncated,** *not* **rounded off.**) With two real constants, the fractional part is retained.

*Examples*

| Expression | Value | |
|---|---|---|
| 3/4 | 0 | 3 and 4 are integers; no fractional part is retained. |
| 8/3 | 2 | 8 and 3 are integers; no fractional part is retained. |
| 3./4. | .75 | 3. and 4. are real; fractional result is computed. |
| 8./3. | 2.66667 | Note the round off of the fractional result for 8./3. |
| 1/2 + 1/2 | 0 | 1/2 = 0 since numerator and denominator are integers! |
| 1./2. + 1./2. | 1. | 1., 2., and the result are real. |

### 2-3-7 Expressions

An expression can be a constant or a variable or any combination of constants and/or variables linked by arithmetic operators. Parentheses can be included to denote the order of computations. No two arithmetic operators may be side by side. The arithmetic operators are:

| | |
|---|---|
| + | Addition |
| − | Subtraction |
| * | Multiplication |
| / | Division |
| ** | Exponentiation |

Both integer and real constants and variables can be used in an expression; thus 1 + 3.2, SUM*3 and A * I are valid mixed-mode expressions. In mixed-mode operations, the computer converts the integer values to real values before the arithmetic operations are carried out.

*Examples* The following are valid expressions:

| Algebraic Expressions | FORTRAN Expressions |
|---|---|
| $a$ | A |
| 14 | 14 |
| $\dfrac{a}{b} \cdot c$ | (A/B*C) |
| $a \cdot b - 30$ | A*B-30. |

| Algebraic Expressions | FORTRAN Expressions |
|---|---|
| $-c$ | $-C$ |
| $(ab)^2$ | $(A*B)**2$ |
| $(-c + b)d$ | $(-C+B)*D$ |
| $a^b$ | $A**B$ |
| $-3.7$ | $-3.7$ |
| $\sqrt{a}$ | $A**.5$ |
| $\sqrt[4]{(a - b)^3}$ | $((A-B)**3)**.25$ |
| $\text{PMT} \dfrac{(1 + i \cdot c)^n}{i \cdot c} \qquad 1$ | $PMT*(1+I*C)**N/(I*C)-1.$ |
| $a\left(x + \dfrac{b}{2a}\right)^2 + \dfrac{4ac - b^2}{4a^2}$ | $A*(X+B/(2*A))**2+(4*A*C-B*B)/(4*A**2)$ |
| $\dfrac{-2v(x^2 + y^2)}{(u^2 + v^2)^2}$ | $-2.*V*(X*X+Y*Y)/(U*U+V*V)**2$ |
| $\sqrt{\dfrac{2\mu(E + V_o)}{h^2}}$ | $(2*MU*(E+VO)/(H*H))**.5$ |
| $F\left(\dfrac{\lambda - 1}{\rho} - \dfrac{l(l + 1)}{\rho^2}\right)$ | $F*((LAM-1)/RO-L*(L+1)/(RO*RO))$ |

The following are examples of invalid expressions:

| | |
|---|---|
| $3(A+JB)$ | Operator missing after the 3. |
| $A-(B+C*(K)$ | Unpaired parentheses; should be $A - (B + C*(K))$. |
| $X*-3$ | Two operators side by side; should be $X*(-3)$. |

When there are parentheses in an expression, the operation within the parentheses is performed first.

*Example 1*

| Expression | Evaluation |
|---|---|
| $3*(4 + 5)$ | $3*(4 + 5) = 3*9 = 27$ |

If parentheses are nested in an expression, then the operation in the innermost set of parentheses is performed first.

*Example 2*

| Expression | Evaluation |
|---|---|
| $3*(4 + (8/2))$ | $3*(4 + (8/2)) = 3*(4 + 4) = 3*8 = 24$ |

Operations within an expression are performed according to the following rules of precedence:

| Operation | Symbol | Precedence |
|---|---|---|
| grouping | ( ) | high precedence |
| exponentiation | ** | |
| multiplication/division | * / | |
| addition/subtraction | + − | low precedence |

Operations with higher precedence are performed before operations with lower precedence, thus

$$4*3**2 = 4*9 = 36$$

Additions/subtractions, multiplications/divisions are performed in order from left to right according to the rules of precedence. Thus

$$2 + 3/4*2 = 2 + 0*2 = 2 \text{ (integer division)}$$

Exponentiations are performed in order from right to left. The following example illustrates the sequence of operations:

| | |
|---|---|
| 3**2 + (2 * 2** 3 / 4 + 1) − 2 / 3 | Grouping then exponentiation |
| 3**2 + (2 * 8/ 4 + 1) − 2 / 3 | Multiplication (left to right) |
| 3**2 + ( 16 / 4 + 1) − 2 / 3 | Division |
| 3**2 + (4 + 1) − 2 / 3 | Add (because of parentheses) |
| 3**2 + 5 − 2 / 3 | Exponentiation |
| 9 + 5 − 2 / 3 | Division |
| 9 + 5 − 0 | Addition |
| 14 − 0 | Subtraction |

*Example 3   Evaluation of real expressions*

**1.** A−B+C

   3.−2.+5.

B is subtracted from A and the result is added to C.

(3. − 2.) + 5. = 1. + 5. = 6.

**2.** A+B*C

   3.+2.*3.

Since multiplication has priority, B*C is computed and the result is then added to A, giving A + (B*C).

3. + (2.*3.) = 3. + 6. = 9.

**3.** A/B*C

   9./4.*2

Since multiplication and division have the same priority, B is first divided into A (A/B), and the result of the division is multiplied by C. (This is different from A/(B*C).)

(9./4.)*2 = 2.25*2. = 4.50

**4.** A/B/C

   8./4./2.

First A/B is performed, and the result is then divided by C. You will get the same answer if you calculate A/(B*C).

(8./4.)/2. = 2./2. = 1.

**5.** (A+B)/C*D

   (3.+6.)/3.*6.

The parentheses indicate that the addition A + B is to be performed first. The sum is then divided by C and the result is multiplied by D, giving

$$\frac{A + B}{C} * D \text{ not } \frac{A + B}{C*D}$$

$$\frac{9.}{3.} *6. = 3.*6. = 18.$$

**6.** A+B*C**2

   3.+3.*2.**2.

Since exponentiation has highest priority, $C^2$ is computed. This result is then multiplied by B, since multiplication has the next highest priority. Finally, this result is added to A, giving A + (B*(C**2)).

3. + 3.*(2.**2) = 3. (3.*4.) = 3. + 12. = 15.

7. `A**B**C`                    Exponentiations are evaluated from right to left; therefore, B is raised to the power C. This result is used as the power of A, giving A**(B**C) not (A**B)**C

   `3.**2.**3.`                 3.**(2.**3.) = 3.**8. = 6561., not

                               (3**2.)**3. = 9.**3. = 729.

*Evaluations of mixed mode expressions*

| *Expression* | *Value* | |
|---|---|---|
| `3/2.` | 1.5 | The integer 3 is converted to real 3. |
| `3./2` | 1.5 | The integer 2 is converted to real 2. |
| `4.+3/2` | 5. | The operation 3/2, involving integers, is performed first, resulting in 1. Then 4. + 1 is a mixed-mode expression evaluating to 5. |
| `4+3/2.` | 5.5 | 3/2. is mixed mode and evaluates to 1.5, which is added to 4, giving 5.5. |
| `I+7.2` | 6.2 | If I = −1, the expression evaluates to 6.2. |
| `4.*3/2` | 6. | The operation 4.*3 is performed first, yielding 12., which is then divided by 2 to give 6. |
| `4.*(3/2)` | 4. | (3/2) is performed first, giving 1, which is then multiplied by 4., yielding 4. |

Note that 4.*3/2 is algebraically equal to 4.*(3/2), yet these two expressions evaluate to different results because of integer division and rules of precedence!

## 2-3-8  Do It Now

Write FORTRAN expressions for each of the following:

1. $\dfrac{N(1+N)}{-2}$

2. $-Y{\cdot}X$

3. $V{\cdot}T - \dfrac{G{\cdot}T^2}{2}$

4. $x^3 - .73x + c$

5. $\dfrac{9}{T} - \dfrac{1}{(T-1)}$

6. $\dfrac{(X+Y)(A-B)}{(C+T)^2}$

7. $\sqrt{\dfrac{N(\text{SUM}) - \text{SUM}^2}{N(N-1)}}$

8. $\sqrt[6]{(-T)^5}$

## *Answers*

1. (N*(1 + N))/(−2)

2. −Y*X

3. V*T − (G*T**2)/2.

4. X**3 − .73*X + C

5. 9./T − 1./(T − 1.)

6. (X + Y)*(A − B)/(C + T)**2.

7. ((N*SUM − SUM**2)/(N*(N − 1)))**.5

8. (−T**5)**(1./6.) or (−T)**(5./6.)
   Note that (−T)**(5/6) would not be correct, since 5/6 = 0 with integer arithmetic.

### 2-3-9  The Replacement Statement

A replacement statement specifies the expression to be evaluated and the location (variable) into which the computed value is to be placed. The general form of the replacement statement is:

$$variable = expression$$

The value of the *expression* is first computed, then the result is placed (stored) in the *variable* on the left-hand side of the statement. The equals sign in a replacement statement must be understood as a replacement sign rather than a mathematical equality. Accordingly, the statement $X = X + 1.$ is completely legal: it means add 1. to whatever value is in memory cell X and store the result in X. The following examples are valid replacement statements.

*Examples*

| | |
|---|---|
| `X=3.123` | Define X to be 3.123 (place 3.123 in location X). Whatever value was in X before is now destroyed. |
| `C1=(A+B)/C` | Compute A + B, divide by C, and call result C1. |
| `Z=3.**2.` | Let Z be equal to 9. |
| `SK=(Z+4.)**.5` | SK is computed as the square root of the quantity Z + 4. (Recall that raising a number to the one-half power is the same as taking its square root.) |
| `CHARACTER MESSG*8,LONG*10,SMALL*4` | |
| `MESSG = 'WE AM US'` | Store 8 characters in MESSG. |
| `SMALL = MESSG` | Store 1st 4 characters in SMALL. SMALL contains W, E, blank and A |
| `LONG = MESSG` | The characters WE AM US followed by two trailing blanks are stored in LONG. |
| `MESSG = 'CAT'` | MESSG contains the characters C, A, T and 5 trailing blanks. |
| `MESSG = 'NIGHTINGALE'` | MESSG contains the 8 characters N, I, G, H, T, I, N, G. |
| `MESS = 'ERROR'` | MESS was *not* declared as a character variable, so an error would occur. |

The following are examples of invalid replacement statements:

| | |
|---|---|
| `3.16=X` | A variable (memory location), not a constant, must be on the left-hand side of the equals sign; how can one store the value of X into 3.16? |
| `X+Y=1.` | An expression cannot be on the left-hand side of the equals sign; how could one store a 1 in the sum of two memory locations? |
| `HRS*RATE+BONUS` | There is no variable specified into which the result is to be stored. |

Recall that blanks can be interspersed anywhere in positions 7–72 within a FORTRAN statement; thus imbedded blanks are permissible in variables, constants, or FORTRAN key words, i.e., blanks outside quotes have no effect. For example the statement 50 PAY = 5.25*HRS − 100. could theoretically be typed as follows:

| 1 2 3 4 5 6 7 8 9 10 11 12 13 14 15 16 17 18 19 20 21 22 23 24 25 26 27 28 29 30 31 32 33 34 35 36 37 38 39 40 41 |
|---|

```
50      P  A Y =    5   . 2    5    *  H R S    -   1 0  0 .
```

## 2-3-10 Do It Now

**1.** State whether the following are constants, variables, expressions, or statements.

| a. '1' | d. X = X + X | g. 1 − 1 |
|---|---|---|
| b. '2 + 3' | e. Y = Y | h. − .3 |
| c. X + 1 | f. 1 + 2 + 3.4 | i. P = − H + R |

**2.** State whether the following are constants, variables, expressions, or statements; if any are invalid, state the reason.

| a. 3 = 2 + 1 | e. X + Y = X + Y | i. A = (X + Y) / K. |
|---|---|---|
| b. PAY = HOURS + RATE | f. 0 = 0 * 4 | j. 'A' = 'C' |
| c. 'A = X + 1' | g. B + 3 / 2 / − 4 | k. A = '1' * '2' |
| d. '3 = 4' | h. A = 'HELLO' | |

## *Answers*

**1.**

| a. constant | d. statement | g. expression |
|---|---|---|
| b. constant | e. statement | h. constant |
| c. expression | f. expression | i. statement |

**2.**
   a. *Invalid statement*: a variable should be on the left-hand side of the equal sign.
   b. *Valid statement*.
   c. *Valid character* constant.
   d. *Valid character* constant.
   e. *Invalid statement*: X + Y is an expression on the left-hand side of the equal sign.
   f. *Invalid statement*: zero (0) is not a variable name.
   g. *Invalid expression*: two operators side by side (/ − ).
   h. *Valid statement* if A is declared as character type.
   i. *Invalid statement*: K. is an invalid variable name.
   j. *Invalid statement*: there is a constant on the left-hand side of the equal sign
   k. *Invalid expression*: one cannot multiply character constants.

## 2-3-11 Mixed-Mode Replacement Statements

A mixed-mode replacement statement is a replacement statement in which the type of the variable on the left is different from the type of the evaluated expression on the right. In this case the type of the value of the expression is converted to the type of the variable on the left-hand side of the equals sign before the resulting value is stored in the variable. The type of the variable on the left-hand side of the equals sign determines the type of the final value of the expression; the expression on the right is evaluated first, using the rules of precedence, and the final answer is stored in the type of the variable on the left.

*Examples*

| | |
|---|---|
| IX = 3.2 | The value stored in IX will be the integer 3. When a real value is converted to integer, any fractional part is truncated. |
| X = 3+2 | The value of X will be 5., not 5, since X is real. |
| J = 3./2 | The value of the expression is 1.5, but the value stored in J will be 1, since J is an integer variable. |
| KX = 4/3+6.8 | 4/3 is 1, since both numbers are integers. 1 + 6.8 = 7.8 since one of the operands is real. The value stored, however, is 7, since KX is integer. |

### 2-3-12 Do It Now

For each of the following, assume that A = 2., B = 3. and L = −2; what value will be stored in the variable on the left of the equal sign after execution of each of the following replacement statements?

**1.** X = A/B

**2.** IX = A/B

**3.** QQ = L/3

**4.** JJ = L/3.

**5.** Y = A**L

**6.** IY = A** 1/2 + 1/2

### *Answers*

**1.** A/B = 2./3. = .6666... ; value of X is .6666...7

**2.** A/B = .6666... ; value of IX is integer part of .6666..., which is 0 (without a decimal point).

**3.** L/3 = −2/3 = 0 (integer arithmetic); value of QQ is 0. (it must have decimal point).

**4.** L/3. = −2/3. = −2./3. = −.6666... ; value of JJ is integer part of −.6666... which is 0 (without a decimal point)

**5.** A**L = 2.**(−2) = 1./4. = .25 ; value of Y is .25.

**6.** IY = 1 (A** 1/2 = (A ** 1)/2 = 2./2 = 1.)

### 2-3-13 The Complete FORTRAN Job

As we noted in chapter 1, section 1–2–3, FORTRAN is a high-level language. FORTRAN allows a user to communicate with a computer in a semi-English scientific language which should not be too difficult to learn—after all, there are certain easily recognizable words, such as READ, WRITE, FORMAT, STOP, and END. The FORTRAN programmer can express problems through mathematical relationships and formulas. The computer, however, does not understand FORTRAN directly; its native language is machine language. To the computer, FORTRAN is a foreign language (see Figure 2–4), which must be translated

**FIGURE  2-4**   LANGUAGE BARRIER

**FIGURE  2-5**   LANGUAGE BARRIER RESOLVED

into machine language before it can be processed (executed). In the early days of computers, machine language specialists would translate high-level languages into machine language. Today, special language translator programs (*compilers*) perform this translation at extremely high speeds, without human intervention. The compiler reads a FORTRAN program (*source code*) and produces a resulting set of machine instructions (*object code*) that can then be executed by the CPU (see Figure 2–5.)

Processing a program on a computer requires more than submitting a source code written in a high-level language. The computer system must be told, among other things, what high-level language to expect so that it can direct the appropriate compiler for the translation process; it must also be told the name of the user, the user's password (if any), and so on. All in all, the programmer must give the computer certain administrative information by means of "job control" or "workflow" instructions. A typical FORTRAN job generally consists of FORTRAN instructions, data to be processed, and control statements telling the computer what to do. The control statements vary from one system to the other, and you are advised to check your installation for the particular control statements needed.

# 2-4 Output: FORMAT-Controlled and List-directed Output

There are two FORTRAN statements that can be used to generate output:

> 1. the PRINT statement, which specifies a list of output items to be printed, or
> 2. the WRITE statement used in conjunction with the FORMAT statement.

The PRINT statement is a list-directed output instruction. The system, *not* the user, decides where the output items are to be placed on the output line(s). (To those familiar with BASIC, the FORTRAN PRINT instruction is similar to the BASIC PRINT instruction.)

The WRITE statement is a format-controlled output instruction. The user is responsible for specifying where on the output line each output item is to be printed. This is done through the FORMAT statement. The WRITE statement gives the list of output items. (To those familiar with BASIC, the WRITE statement is conceptually similar to the PRINT USING.)

The PRINT statement is easier and more convenient to use than the WRITE instruction. However it is important to understand and become familiar with format-controlled output, since formatted output reflects industry procedures. Format-controlled output allows you to produce clean, professional-looking results or reports.

The PRINT statement will be discussed in section 2–4–10.

## 2-4-1 The WRITE Statement

The general form of the WRITE statement is:

> WRITE (*device number, format statement number*) [*variable list*]

where *device number* is a code (integer constant) representing the output device to be used (printer, tape, disk, and so forth);

*format statement number* is the number of a FORMAT statement that describes the output operation (layout design);

*variable list* is a list of variable names separated by commas; when the WRITE statement is executed, the contents of the variables specified in the variable list are written onto the specified output device according to the specified format.

(In the general form of the FORTRAN statements discussed in this text the capitalized words are FORTRAN key words, lower case words are user supplied and the brackets mean optional.)

*Example 1*

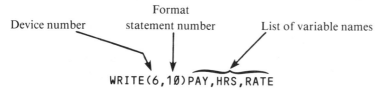

Device number     Format statement number     List of variable names

WRITE(6,10)PAY,HRS,RATE

This WRITE statement can be interpreted as follows: Write the contents of memory location PAY, HRS, and RATE onto device number 6, according to the layout description given by the FORMAT labeled 10.

The device number associated with specific devices depends on the computer system being used. (You should check with your computer center to determine which codes are used at your installation). A typical assignment might be:

| *Device-number* | *Physical Device* |
| --- | --- |
| 5 | Keyboard, card reader |
| 6 | Printer |
| 7 | Card Punch |
| 1 to 4, 8 or greater | Other devices (magnetic tapes, disks, etc.) |

A typical size for the output line of a printer is 132 characters or print positions.

*Example 2*   The following are valid WRITE statements:

| | |
| --- | --- |
| 65 WRITE(6,11)A,IJT | The values contained in A and IJT will be written onto device 6. FORMAT statement 11 will be used to describe the output line. |
| WRITE(7,15)Q | The value of Q will be written on device number 7 according to FORMAT statement 15. |

The following are examples of invalid WRITE statements:

| | |
| --- | --- |
| WRITE(6,14)4 | The variable list must consist of variables, not constants. |
| WRITE(6,16)X+Y | X + Y is an expression, not a variable. |
| WRITE(6,11)'THE SUM IS',X | Character data cannot be specified in the variable list. |
| WRITE(6,15.)X,Y | 15. is an incorrect statement number; the period is not allowed. |

## 2-4-2  The FORMAT Statement

It is apparent that the WRITE statement by itself does not give the computer sufficient information about how the write operation is to be carried out; for example, the following questions are unanswered:

1.  Where should each result be printed on the output line (which print positions?)

2.  How many digits to the right of the decimal point does the programmer need for the results? (For example, in the case of dollars and cents, only two digits should suffice.)

3.  How many print positions should be allocated for each result on the line?

A FORMAT statement is needed in conjunction with the WRITE statement to inform the computer precisely how the WRITE operation is to be carried out. Each WRITE statement must specify a format statement number, and each FORMAT statement must have a statement number by which it can be referred to. The WRITE instruction is processed according to the specifications described in the FORMAT. The FORMAT statement is processed only when the WRITE statement is processed, so the FORMAT statement can be placed anywhere in a program (before the END statement). Some programmers prefer to place all their formats at the end or beginning of their programs, while others like to have them immediately follow their associated WRITE statements. Recall that the link between the WRITE and the FORMAT statement is the format statement number specified within the parentheses of the WRITE statement.

The image of the line to be printed is formed in memory before it is actually printed. When all the output values have been placed in their proper positions in the image, that image is then printed as one output record (output line) on the printer. However, the first character of the image in memory is *never* printed, it is actually a special code to indicate whether the printer is to advance one line before printing, advance two lines before printing, skip to the top of the next page, and so forth. For example, if the first character in the image line is a blank, the printer advances to the next line before printing. These various characters are called *carriage control codes*; they are discussed in more detail in section 2–4–12.

*Example*

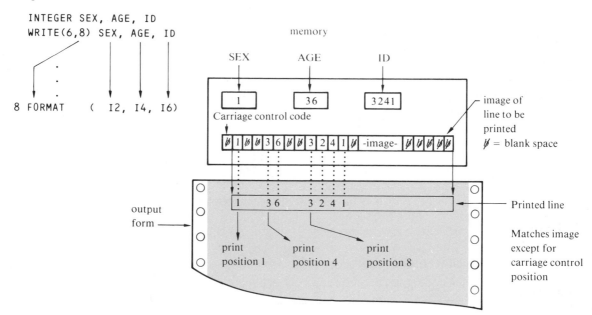

This output operation can be interpreted as follows: write three numbers (three variables are named) on output device 6 according to the data layout described by the FORMAT statement labeled 8. The actions of the FORMAT can be interpreted as: The first variable (SEX) is to be placed as an integer value (specified by the I format code) in the first two image positions (I2), the next variable is placed in the next four positions (I4), and the last variable (ID) is placed in the next six positions (I6). Note that these values are *right-justified* in the output field (the right-most digit is placed in the right-most position of the field), and that leading blanks are provided to complete the field width. Note that the carriage control code is the 1st character of the image, i.e., the leading blank space of the SEX field; this blank space tells the printer to advance one line before printing the image on the output line. The first print position on the output form (paper/screen) will display the number 1, *not* the carriage control code, which *never* gets printed.

The general form of the FORMAT statement is

> *statement number* FORMAT ($fd_1, fd_2, ..., fd_n$)

where *statement number* is the format label referred to in a WRITE statement, and $fd_1$, $fd_2, ..., fd_n$ are format codes that can be either:

**1.** Data format codes used to identify the mode of the data items to be printed: I for integer, F for real numbers, and A for character data; or

**2.** Edit codes used to control the placement and editing of the data items in the output record: X for spacing, single quote (') for literal data, and T for specifying the beginning print position for an output field.

Note that all format codes should be separated by commas.

## 2-4-3 The X Format Code

The X format code is an edit code used to specify spaces on an output line. It is generally used to provide margins or to separate output fields by a certain number of blank spaces. The general form of the X format code is:

> $n$X

where $n$ is an integer specifying the number of spaces (blanks) desired.

*Example*

The code shown below can be interpreted as follows: Write the number K on a line with the help of format number 11. Before printing K, allow three blank spaces (the first one of which is the carriage control code), then print an integer (I2) using two print positions. Note that the X format code does not have a corresponding item in the variable list of the WRITE statement.

```
   K=14
   WRITE(6,11)K
11 FORMAT(3X,I2)
```

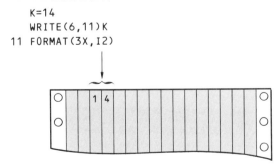

Two spaces precede the digits 14 on the output line.

### 2-4-4 The I Format Code

The I format code describes *integer data* for an output operation. The general form of the I format code is:

$$I w$$

where I specifies that an integer is to be written out, and *w* specifies the width of output field, i.e. the number of spaces to be reserved for the integer on the output line.

The I format code can be used only to describe integer type variables. Since a negative sign occupies one space (print position), an extra space for the sign should be included in the total number of spaces allocated for the output field (*w*).

*Example 1*

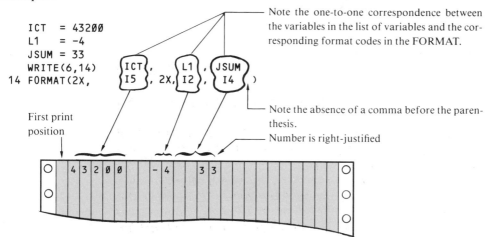

The first variable, ICT, in the variable list is associated with the first numeric format code, I5; the second variable, L1, is associated with the second numeric format code, I2, and so on. All numbers are *right-justified* (the right-most digit is placed on the right-most print position of the output field) with blanks inserted to the left in place of leading zeroes.

*Example 2*

```
    K = 35
    J = -5
    WRITE(6,12)K
12  FORMAT(2X,I3)
    L = -K*J
    WRITE(6,11)L,J
11  FORMAT(6X,I3,1X,I3)
```

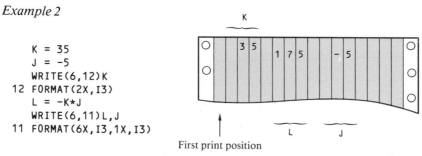

Note that a separate output line is printed for each WRITE statement. The first WRITE statement prints one number on one line, whereas the second WRITE statement prints two entries on a new line.

Care must be exercised to provide enough space in an I format code for all the digits of the number (including the negative sign, if required). If not enough spaces are allocated, an error message will be printed. The exact form of the message will differ among systems. In the following example a set of asterisks indicates insufficient field width.

*Example 3*

```
      K = 1234
      J = -14
      WRITE(6,15)K,    J,     J



15 FORMAT(3X,I3,1X,I2,2X,I4)
```

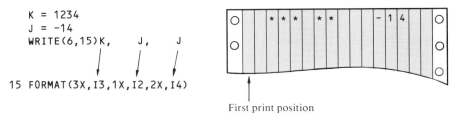

First print position

## 2-4-5  The F Format Code

Real data is described by the F format code, which has the general form:

$$\mathrm{F}w.d$$

where F specifies that a real number is to be printed out

  *w* specifies the number of spaces (print positions) to be reserved for the number on the output record (line)

  *d* specifies the number of digits that are to be printed to the right of the decimal point.

The decimal point is *always* printed. It occupies one print position in the output field and hence must be included in the total number of spaces (*w*) allocated for the real value. One print position must also be allowed for the negative sign.

The F format code can be used *only* for real variables. You might wonder why it is necessary to worry about the number of digits to the right of the decimal point on the output. Internally, the computer carries out computations to many decimal places; for example, the result of 10.12 * 5.24 is stored internally as 53.0288, and the programmer may only be interested in the first two decimal positions (e.g., for dollars and cents). Hence it is always the programmer's responsibility to specify the number of digits wanted for the fractional part of the result. The F format rounds the printed values, i.e., if the internal value 14.636 is to be printed with 2 digits to the right of the decimal point, then 14.64 will be printed. If that same value is to be printed with no digits to the right of the decimal point, 15. will be printed since 14.6 rounds off to 15.

*Example 1*

```
      A = 63.426
      B = -4.2
      WRITE(6,15) A ,        A ,        A ,     B ,    B


15 FORMAT(1X, F6.3,     F9.5 , 1X,    F6.1,    F6.1,    F4.0)

```

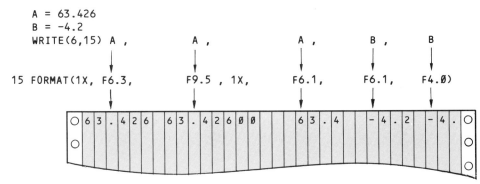

Note that if the number of digits to be printed is less than the width of the field reserved for it, the number is right-justified in the field, with blanks inserted to the left instead of leading zeroes.

Depending on the number of digits (*d*) specified in the format code F*w.d*, the data will be rounded as necessary, as shown in the following example.

*Example 2*

```
A = 12.6534
B = 13.7
WRITE(6,16)    A,          A ,        A ,        B

16 FORMAT(2X,  F9.3,       F6.1,      F5.0,      F7.3)
```

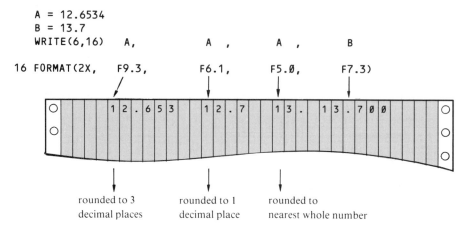

rounded to 3 decimal places    rounded to 1 decimal place    rounded to nearest whole number

Note that the value 13.700 is printed for the variable B, since the format specifies three fractional positions.

With F format codes, care must be exercised to provide enough print columns for all digits to the left of the decimal point of the real number. If not enough print columns are allocated, an error message will be printed. The exact form of the message differs among systems.

It is important to understand the way in which digits are printed on output, given the format F*w.d*. The computer first tries to print the *d* digits, then the decimal point, and then the remaining digits. If at any given time there is insufficient space, an execution time format error occurs.

For example, suppose we wanted to print 56.78 and we specified F4.2. The computer would first try to print the 8, then the 7, then the decimal point, then the 6; at this point the field width (4) is filled, and a format error occurs. Consider another example:

*Example 3*

```
A = -123.456
B =  2509.01
C = 12.
WRITE(6,12) A ,        A ,        B,        C

12 FORMAT(1X,  F7.3, 1X,F5.1, 1X,F6.2, 1X,F5.4)
```

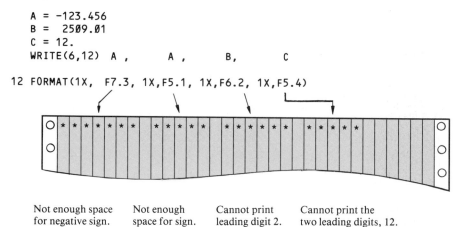

Not enough space for negative sign.    Not enough space for sign.    Cannot print leading digit 2.    Cannot print the two leading digits, 12.

To provide a field (*w*) sufficiently large to represent a real number, the following rule can be used.

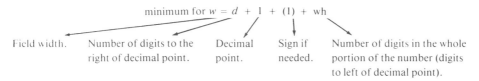

minimum for $w = d + 1 + (1) + wh$

Field width.    Number of digits to the      Decimal    Sign if      Number of digits in the whole
                right of decimal point.      point.     needed.      portion of the number (digits
                                                                     to left of decimal point).

The beginning programmer is warned again that any real variables that are to be printed *must* be described by F format codes in the FORMAT. For example, the next code segment is invalid:

```
    WRITE(6,11)A,B,C
11  FORMAT(I2,I4,I3)        Should be   FORMAT(1X,F2.0,F4.0,F3.0).
    WRITE(6,12)J,J,K
12  FORMAT(F2.0,F2.0,F3.0)  Should be   FORMAT(1X,I1,I2,I3)
```

## 2-4-6 The A Format Code

The A format code is used to print character data. A stands for *alphanumeric* (letters of the alphabet and other characters). The general formats of the A format code are

A
A*w*

where *w* specifies the width of the output field.

If *w* is not specified, then the size of the output field is determined by the size of the variable declared in the CHARACTER statement.

*Example*

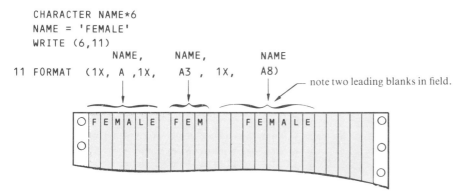

```
    CHARACTER NAME*6
    NAME = 'FEMALE'
    WRITE (6,11)
              NAME,      NAME,          NAME
11  FORMAT  (1X, A ,1X,  A3 ,  1X,      A8)
```
— note two leading blanks in field.

| O | F | E | M | A | L | E | | F | E | M | | | F | E | M | A | L | E | | | | | O |

Note that if the output field *w* is less than the size *s* of the variable declared in the CHARACTER statement (i.e., if the text is larger than the output field size), then only the leftmost characters of the character variable are printed. If the output field *w* is longer than the number of characters *s* of the character variable (i.e., the text is less than output field size), then $w - s$ leading blanks precede the entire contents of the character variable, i.e., the text is right-justified.

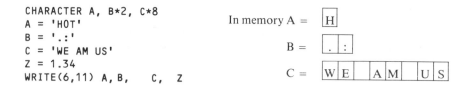

```
CHARACTER A, B*2, C*8
A = 'HOT'
B = '.:'
C = 'WE AM US'
Z = 1.34
WRITE(6,11) A, B,    C,  Z
```

In memory A =  H

B =  . :

C =  W E   A M   U S

```
11 FORMAT (1X,A3,A1,1X,A2,F3.1)
```

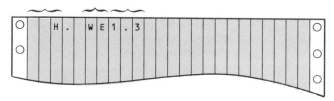

### 2-4-7  The T Format Code

The T format code is a printer control code used to specify the beginning position of a data field on the output line. The general form of the T format code is:

$$Tn$$

where *n* specifies the beginning column number of the next field to be positioned in the image of the output line.

The T format code can be used to provide margins and act as a tab feature of sorts; it is also extremely convenient when numerous variables must be printed in predesignated print positions where the data output layout is already specified (business forms, checks, tables, reports, and so forth).

Because of the carriage control code in the image, T3 implies that the output field will start in position 2 on the output line. If the output field is to start at position 20 then T21 should be used.

*Example*

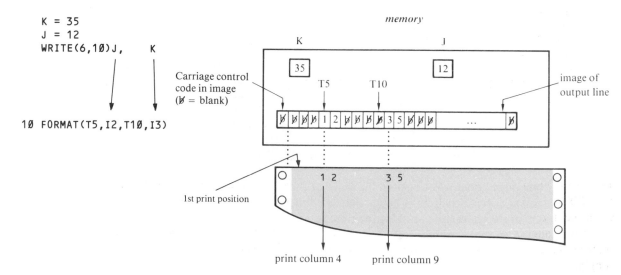

The format code T5 specifies that the output field for J is to start in print position 4, and T10 specifies that the output field for K is to start in print position 9. The T format code arbitrarily allows the programmer to skip to any desired position on the line. Note that using 4X instead of T5 in the FORMAT would have started J at the same print position.

## 2-4-8 The Format Code for Literal Data

Using apostrophes (') around a string of characters in a FORMAT specifies that the string (all characters within the two single quotes) is to be placed on the output line wherever the printer happens to be at that time. Literal strings are generally used to create headings, identify numerical results, or provide messages or explanation.

*Example 1*

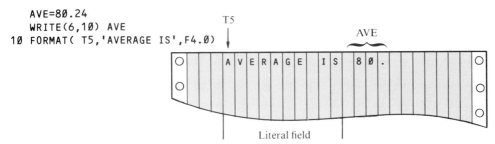

The character string AVERAGE IS, consisting of ten characters (including the blank), is printed starting in print position 4. Immediately following the literal string is the numerical field for AVE. Blanks within the single quotes are part of the literal and hence are printed on the output form.

A format can describe more than one literal string as in:

*Example 2*

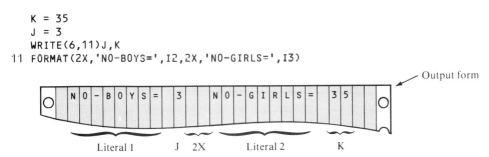

Before the variable J is printed, the printer is asked to start in print position 2 and write NO-BOYS = ; then J is printed. Before K is printed, the printer is asked to space two print positions and write NO-GIRLS = . Then the value for K is printed.

The reader is warned that literals may not appear in the list of variables of a WRITE instruction. Literals must be specified in the FORMAT itself, as shown in the following example.

*Example 3*

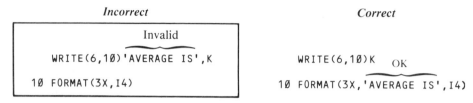

Literals can be very useful for providing headings.

*Example 4*

```
    M  = 5
    ID = 25
    IY = 84
    WRITE(6,5)M,ID,IY
  5 FORMAT(T61 ,'XYZ COMPANY PAYROLL REPORT DATE',1X,I2,'/',I2,'/',I2)
```

Output line ────▶ ┼ ──── ──── |XYZ COMPANY PAYROLL REPORT DATE  5/25/84

Print position 1 . . .    60                                      90

Finally, it is possible to have a WRITE statement without any variable list.

*Example 5*

```
    WRITE(6,11)◀── note, no variable list
 11 FORMAT(2X,'XYZ CORPORATION')
```

These statements will produce the output line

X Y Z   C O R P O R A T I O N

Such WRITE statements are generally used to produce headings or page titles.

## 2-4-9  Do It Now

Show the output produced by the following sets of statements, assuming that

A = −123.45
B = 67.2
L = 123
C = −.06

1.    ```
      WRITE(6,11)A,L,C
   11 FORMAT(2X,F6.1,2X,I4,1X,F6.3)
      ```

2.    ```
      WRITE(6,12)B,A,C
   12 FORMAT(1X,F3.1,1X,F4.0,1X,F3.1)
      ```

3.    ```
      WRITE(6,13)L,B,C
   13 FORMAT(1X,I2,3X,F6.0,1X,F3.0)
      ```
      ```

4.  ```
       WRITE(6,14)A
    14 FORMAT(T3,'A IS',F8.3)
    ```

5.  ```
       CHARACTER GREET*3, PRNN*4
       GREET = 'HELLO'
       PRNN  = 'HE'
       WRITE(6,10)GREET,PRNN,GREET,GREET,PRNN
    10 FORMAT(1X,A5,'F4.1',A1, 1X,A,1X,A2,A3)
    ```

## Answers

1. ` ` `-` `1` `2` `3` `.` `5` ` ` ` ` `1` `2` `3` ` ` `-` `0` `.` `0` `6` `0`
   └─Note Round Off

2. `*` `*` `*` ` ` `*` `*` `*` `*` ` ` `-` `.` `1`
   First Two Fields Are Too Small

3. `*` `*` ` ` ` ` ` ` ` ` `6` `7` `.` ` ` `-` `0` `.`
   Field Too Small

4. ` ` `A` ` ` `I` `S` `-` `1` `2` `3` `.` `4` `5` `0`

5. ` ` ` ` `H` `E` `L` `F` `4` `.` `1` `H` ` ` `H` `E` `L` ` ` `H` `E` `H` `E`

      A5        A1   A   A2  A3

   GREET    PRNN GREET GREET PRNN

### 2-4-10  List-Directed Output

So far we have discussed format-controlled output, which uses the WRITE statement. This form of output enables the programmer to decide exactly where the various output items are to be printed on the output line by means of various format edit codes. A format-free output is available to the user who is not concerned about the layout of the output. With format-free (or list-directed) output, the system determines where it will place the results on the output; it simply *lists* the results one after the other on the output line(s). List-directed output does *not* require any format.

The general form of the list-directed output statement is:

PRINT*, *list*

where *list* can contain variable names, character strings (including the space set off in single quotes), and arithmetic expressions; these items should be separated by commas.

The resulting list values are written on the output line separated by spaces or by commas, depending on the system. If all the values do not fit on one line, as many lines as needed will be used to print the entire list. The number of items per line, as well as the width of each output item, varies from one system to the next. Decimal points will be printed if the value to be printed is real.

*Example*    Assume X = 1., Y = 2., Z = 143.2, K = 1

*Output*

1. `PRINT*,'PAY=',Z`

2. `PRINT*,'X=',X,'Y=',Y,'Z=',Z`

3. `PRINT*,X+Y`

4. `PRINT*,K,K,K,K,Y,Y,Y,Y,Z,K`

5. `PRINT*,'$',Z`
   `PRINT*,Y/X+1`

6. `PRINT*, 'HELLO','MIKE', 3.1`

```
PAY= 143.2

X=  1.  Y=  2.  Z= 143.2

3.

1   1   1   1   2.   2.   2.   2.
143.2   1

$ 143.2
3.

HELLOMIKE 3.1
```

Examples of incorrect PRINT statements;

```
PRINT A,B          The initial asterisk and comma are missing.
PRINT*,SUM IS',S   Missing first apostrophe around SUM IS.
PRINT*,Z=X+4       Z = X + 4 is a statement, not an expression.
```

### 2-4-11  Do It Now

Specify the output obtained from the following:

1. 
```
CHARACTER NAME*7
NAME = 'CHARLES'
PRINT*, 'GOT IT ',NAME,'?'
NAME = 'SUE'
PRINT*, 'WELL, ',NAME'HOW ABOUT THAT!'
```

2. 
```
CHARACTER*3 NAME
K = 3
NAME = 'SUE ELLEN'
PRINT*, NAME,'''','S DOG WAS ',NAME,'D',K,'TIMES!'
NAME = 'E'
PRINT*, NAME,'.'
```

### *Answers*

1. 
```
GOT IT CHARLES?
WELL, SUE    HOW ABOUT THAT!
```

2. 
```
SUE'S DOG WAS SUED  3   TIMES!
E  .
```

### 2-4-12  Carriage Control Characters for FORMAT-Controlled Output

The first character of every line (image line) sent to the printer is used as a code to determine the vertical spacing on the paper. This code is *never* printed. It is just a signal to the printer to tell it to single-space, double-space, skip to the top of a new page, and so forth. The list in figure 2–6 summarizes permissible codes and the meaning associated with each.

**FIGURE 2–6    CARRIAGE CONTROL CHARACTERS**

| Code (character) | Meaning |
|---|---|
| 1 | Skip to the top of a new page |
| 0 | Double-space. |
| + | Do not space; i.e., stay on the same line. |
| blank | Single-space. |
| other characters | May have special installation printer control effects. |

The vertical movement of the output form (page) is effected at the very beginning of the WRITE instruction when the printer interprets the carriage control code specified by the FORMAT in the image line; before the printer writes anything, it checks the carriage control code to decide whether to space a line, double-space, skip to the top of a new page, and so forth. Then it writes the output line. The vertical spacing of the form is *not* performed at the end of the WRITE operation.

The X format code or the T format code can be used to provide a blank as the first character in the image line; this causes the printer to advance to the next line (single space).

*Example 1*

```
   AV = 62.0
   WRITE(6,10)AV
10 FORMAT(1X,F4.1,'(AVERAGE)')
```

This code segment will result in the following output:

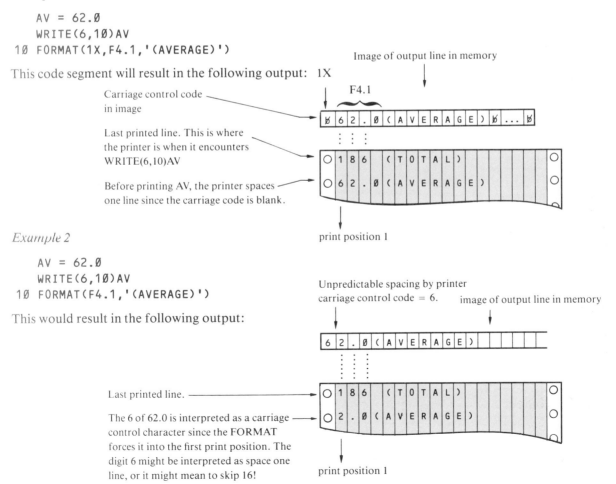

*Example 2*

```
   AV = 62.0
   WRITE(6,10)AV
10 FORMAT(F4.1,'(AVERAGE)')
```

This would result in the following output:

Printer control can be achieved by placing the desired carriage control code as a literal in the first position of the output line.

*Example 1*

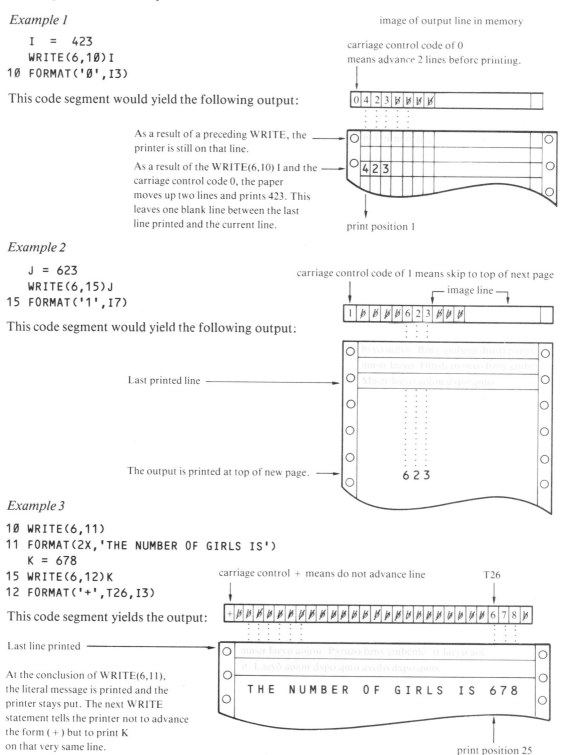

```
    I  =  423
    WRITE(6,10)I
10 FORMAT('0',I3)
```

This code segment would yield the following output:

image of output line in memory

carriage control code of 0
means advance 2 lines before printing.

As a result of a preceding WRITE, the printer is still on that line.

As a result of the WRITE(6,10) I and the carriage control code 0, the paper moves up two lines and prints 423. This leaves one blank line between the last line printed and the current line.

print position 1

*Example 2*

```
    J = 623
    WRITE(6,15)J
15 FORMAT('1',I7)
```

This code segment would yield the following output:

carriage control code of 1 means skip to top of next page

image line

Last printed line

The output is printed at top of new page.

6 2 3

*Example 3*

```
10 WRITE(6,11)
11 FORMAT(2X,'THE NUMBER OF GIRLS IS')
    K = 678
15 WRITE(6,12)K
12 FORMAT('+',T26,I3)
```

carriage control + means do not advance line

T26

This code segment yields the output:

Last line printed

At the conclusion of WRITE(6,11), the literal message is printed and the printer stays put. The next WRITE statement tells the printer not to advance the form ( + ) but to print K on that very same line.

THE NUMBER OF GIRLS IS 678

print position 25

It is important that a carriage control character be included explicitly in a FORMAT statement used for printed output. The system will use *whatever* character appears in the first print position of the image line as a carriage control character; it does not matter to the system whether this character originated as a literal or a data item from an F or I field.

*Example 4*

```
      K = 123
      L = -24
      WRITE(6,16)K,L
16 FORMAT ( I3 ,2X,I3)
```

This code will produce the following output:

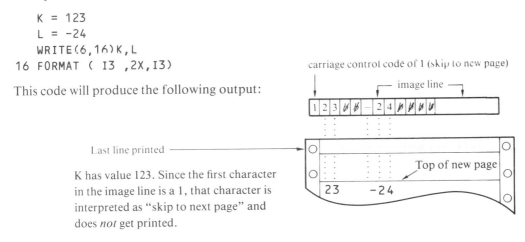

carriage control code of 1 (skip to new page)

image line

Last line printed

K has value 123. Since the first character in the image line is a 1, that character is interpreted as "skip to next page" and does *not* get printed.

Top of new page

## 2-4-13 The STOP Statement

The general form of the STOP statement is:

STOP

The STOP statement is used to terminate execution of a program. *At least one* STOP statement should occur in every FORTRAN program; more than one can be used if desired.

## 2-4-14 The END Statement

The general form of the END statement is:

END

The last statement in every FORTRAN program must be the END statement. Only one END statement can be used in a program. END is a message to the compiler and is therefore nonexecutable; it should not be assigned a FORTRAN statement number. (See section 2–6, question 8).

## 2-4-15 Do It Now

Write the code to produce the following display, beginning at the top of a new page and replacing the dashes with the appropriate numbers. The tax should be 4% of the subtotal.

```
            INVENTORY ANALYSIS
      ITEM    QUANTITY      COST      TOTAL


      NUTS       58         .07        -
      BOLTS      64         .11        -


      SUBTOTAL                         -
      TAX                              -
      GRAND TOTAL                      -
```

*Answer*

```
      INTEGER QN,QB
      QN = 58
      QB = 64
      CN = .07
      CB = .11
      TN = QN * CN
      TB = QB * CB
      SUBTOT = TN + TB
      TAX = .04 * SUBTOT
      GTOT = SUBTOT + TAX
      WRITE(6,11)
   11 FORMAT('1',T12,'INVENTORY ANALYSIS')
      WRITE(6,12)
   12 FORMAT(1X,'ITEM',T9,'QUANTITY',T21,'COST',T29,'TOTAL')
      WRITE(6,13)QN,CN,TN
   13 FORMAT('0NUTS,T11,I1,T21,F3.2,T29,F6.2)
      WRITE(6,14)QB,CB,TB
   14 FORMAT(1X,'BOLTS',T11,I2,T21,F3.2,T25,F6.2)
      WRITE(6,15)SUBTOT
   15 FORMAT('0SUBTOTAL',T29,F6.2)
      WRITE(6,16)TAX
   16 FORMAT(1X,'TAX',T29,F6.2)
      WRITE(6,17)GTOT
   17 FORMAT(1X,'GRAND TOTAL',T29,F6.2)
      STOP
      END
```

## 2-5 Errors and the Editing Process: Bugs

The reader will quickly realize how easily one can make errors on a computer. Errors, commonly called *bugs*, come in four varieties: typographical, syntactical, logical, and system errors.

### 2-5-1 Typographical Errors

Everyone, at some time or another, mistypes characters. These errors are usually interpreted by the computer as syntax errors. Such errors are self-evident and can be minimized by concentration. A common error is to type the letter $O$ instead of the digit zero 0, or the lowercase letter $l$ for 1.

## 2-5-2 Syntax Errors

Syntax errors reflect the programmer's inability to observe the "grammatical" rules of the FORTRAN language. Syntax errors include misspelled key words, forgotten statement numbers, faulty punctuation, mismatched parentheses, incorrect word order, and so forth. The computer will identify the line number(s) where the error(s) occurred during the compilation process.

*Examples*

```
P+1.                      Typographical error; typed + instead of =
X = A(B+C)                Missing operator; could be A * (B + C)
PRINT*,'HELLO' S1 S2      Comma missing before and after S1
Z = (3+X*(4+T)            Missing right parenthesis…(4 + T))
WRITE(6,11)Z              Statement 11 (FORMAT) is missing.
FORMAT(1X,F4.1)           Missing statement number.
```

Depending on the gravity of the syntactical errors, most systems will abort the job at the conclusion of the compilation (why execute a set of unsound instructions?).

## 2-5-3 Logical Errors

Logical errors are the traditional enemies of beginning and professional programmers alike. Logical errors are present in a program whenever the program does not solve the intended problem, i.e., the results produced by the computer are incorrect. Such incorrect results may occur because of one silly but critical typographical error or because of incorrect reasoning or an incorrect sequence of instructions. In between these two extremes lie hundreds of other possible sources of errors.

Logical errors are the hardest ones to find in a program because the computer generally prints no error message during the execution of the program, i.e. as far as FORTRAN is concerned, the instructions are all syntactically sound and therefore the results must be correct.

Logical errors are often very well camouflaged and can look perfectly innocent to the programmer as well as to the computer. However, the program does not solve the intended problem if logical errors are present. For example, the instruction $Y = K/N$ is a perfectly valid instruction, syntactically speaking, yet it could be a time bomb during the execution of the program if the value of N is 0. If indeed $N = 0$, the computer will give out an error message, since it (like any human being) cannot divide a number by 0. Somehow N should not be 0 and the programmer must play detective in order to find out why the value of N is 0 when that instruction is executed.

Logical errors can also be the result of careless mistakes. For example, you might want to print the result stored in memory location R, but instead you write the instruction PRINT*,S; this yields an incorrect answer, yet as far as FORTRAN is concerned, this is perfectly valid, since PRINT*,S is grammatically correct. The instruction $P = H + R$ to compute a pay, given a number of hours H and a rate R, is perfectly valid to the computer, but it is a logical error as far as you are concerned, since the formula is incorrect!

Always remember that the compiler merely translates FORTRAN statements into machine instructions; it does not execute the machine instructions and hence cannot determine whether the instructions (commands) are feasible or not. In the cartoon of Figure 2–5, the American tourist might ask, "How about getting me a dinosaur steak?" the translator would dutifully translate the sentence into French, but the French chef would be unable to fulfill his request.

**Thus, it is important that the programmer not put blind faith in whatever the computer prints out. The fact that the computer prints out numbers does not necessarily mean that those numbers are correct! The programmer should always check and analyze computer-produced results most carefully.**

A logical error can also be picked up by the operating system. Consider the following infinite loop:

```
5 GO TO 5
```

An error message dealing with "time exceeded" would probably be printed. Certain execution errors can cause immediate cancellation of the job. A list of execution-time errors with their codes and meanings is provided by the system on the printout form. It is recommended that the reader consult the manufacturer's FORTRAN technical reference manual for a complete description and explanation of each of the different types of execution-time errors.

### 2-5-4 System Errors

System errors are caused by the components of the computer system itself, such as the telephone lines, the printers, the tapes, or the diskettes. For example, a printer may not be turned on when the CPU needs it, thus generating a special error message. A diskette may be "bad" (especially in microcomputer systems): a user diskette may not have been formatted, or an input/output failure may have occurred when saving or loading a program from tape or disk. The user should contact the lab manager or computer center personnel when system errors occur.

### 2-5-5 Do It Now

Mrs. X has purchased $12,500 worth of A&L stock which yields a 13.5% interest return. Mrs. X is in the 27% tax bracket, which means that she pays 27 % of her income to the government. The program below attempts to compute and print the following:

1. the yearly interest on the stock
2. the total accumulated principal after one year
3. the federal tax to be paid on the earned interest
4. Mrs. X's net holdings (after federal income tax)

Identify syntax and logical errors in the following program:

```
1.    STOCK = 12,500
2.    INT = STOCK * 13.5          Compute interest.
3.    WRITE(6,10)INT
4. 10 FORMAT(1X,YEARLY INTEREST,I4)
```

```
5.      INT + STOCK = TOTAL                Compute total principal.
6.      WRITE(6,11)TOTAL
7.      FEDTAX = TOTAL * .27               Compute federal tax on interest.
8.      HOLD = 1.135 * 12500 - .135 * .27 * 12500  Compute net holding.
9.      END
```

## Answers

*Syntax errors:*

| | |
|---|---|
| Line 1 | Invalid comma; should be 12500 |
| Line 4 | YEARLY INTEREST should be within apostrophes |
| Line 5 | Invalid statement; should be TOTAL = INT + STOCK |
| Line 6 | FORMAT 11 is missing |

*Logical errors*:

| | |
|---|---|
| Line 2 | INT is truncated. |
| Line 2 | The percentage should be expressed as .135 |
| Line 7 | Federal tax on interest should be INT * .27 and not TOTAL * .27 |
| | Mrs. X's holdings are not printed. |
| | There is no STOP instruction. |

# 2-6    You Might Want to Know

1. What happens if I insert extra unnecessary sets of parentheses in an expression?

   *Answer*: Extra sets of parentheses have no effect on the evaluation of an expression.

   *Example*

   $$(X + (Y*(Z+W)))$$ is equivalent to $X + Y*(Z+W)$

   The important point is that parentheses must occur in matched pairs. For each left parenthesis, there must be a right parenthesis. Too many parentheses may slow down the compilation process, however.

2. How long can a printed line be? How can I print a blank line?

   *Answer*: This depends on the particular system. Typical lengths vary from 80 to 144 characters. To print a blank line, use PRINT*,'   ' or
   $$\text{WRITE(6,3)}$$
   $$\text{3 FORMAT(1X)}$$

3. What if my printer can accommodate up to 80 characters, but my FORMAT specifies more than 80 characters? What will happen to the extra characters?

   *Answer*: Some systems might truncate the line to 80 characters, others will stop execution of the program with an execution-time format error and some will wrap around to the next line.

4. How does the computer represent repeating decimal numbers (rational numbers)? For example, how can the computer represent exactly 1./3. in decimal form?

   *Answer*: It can't; only the first few digits are retained. For instance, on an IBM 370 computer 1./3. = .3333333 and 8./9. = .8888888

**5.** How many WRITE statements can reference a FORMAT statement?

*Answer*: As many as desired. One FORMAT can be shared by many WRITE statements.

**6.** What happens if I try to divide by zero?

*Answer*: An execution-time diagnostic will be printed, and your program will usually be terminated. Division by zero is not a permissible operation.

**7.** What happens when I multiply (or divide, add, or subtract) two numbers and the result is too large to be represented as a number on my computer system? Also, what happens if the number is too small to be represented on the system (less than $10^{-76}$ for IBM 370)?

*Answer*: In the first case an overflow condition will occur; an execution-time error may appear to that effect. The program will generally not terminate, and execution of the program will continue. The user should check the logic or scale numbers if necessary.

In the second case an underflow occurs with a corresponding error message. The variable is generally set to 0, and the program will proceed. Check the logic to understand why such a condition would arise.

**8.** I am confused about the difference between STOP and END. Can you help?

*Answer:* The END statement is processed at compilation time to inform the compiler that there are no more FORTRAN statements to be translated (no FORTRAN code follows; the physical end of the FORTRAN program has been reached—not the physical end of the complete job, control statements and all, but just the FORTRAN source statements). The END statement is not translated into a machine-language instruction. If the END statement is not the last of the FORTRAN statements, the remaining FORTRAN statements will not be read (processed) by the compiler. In the context of the cartoon in Figure 2–5, the American could use an END statement to tell the translator that the message preceding the END statement is all he wants translated. The world's shortest FORTRAN program is just an END statement all by itself!

The STOP statement on the other hand, is translated into a machine-language instruction and is therefore executed by the CPU during execution time to inform the system that all machine instructions (corresponding to the program) have been carried out, all results (if any) have been printed out, and that as far as this job is concerned there is nothing else to do; i.e., the STOP causes execution to terminate and represents the logical end of the program as opposed to the physical end designated by the END statement. The STOP statement causes control to be returned to the operating system, which will process other programs (if any). As we will see in chapter 3, the STOP statement can be placed anywhere in the program (before the END).

**9.** I am performing some arithmetic computations on some data, and I do not know how many digits I should reserve for my output field (I,F) in the FORMAT.

*Answer:* Most of the time you can estimate an upper limit and use that length for your width, *w*. Otherwise, make your field as large as possible—I20 or F20.1, for example. The result will be right-justified anyway, with blanks on the left. If you are working with very large magnitudes, use the E format discussed in chapter 6.

**10.** You know, it's really funny, yesterday I visited the computing center and I overheard someone say, "There's a bug somewhere in my program." I was tempted to say, "call the exterminator." What do you think this person meant?

*Answer:* A "bug" in the computer science jargon simply refers to an error or a mistake of some kind. To "debug" a program means to get rid of the bugs or errors in it.

**11.** Can I use a negative number as a base in exponentiation? For example, is $(-3)**2$ or $(-3.)**2.$ valid?

*Answer:* To a certain extent this depends upon the compiler being used. In many systems, exponentiation involving small integer exponents is implemented by repeated multiplication. For example, $(-3)**2$ is implemented as $(-3)*(-3)$, which would cause no problems. However, for larger integer exponents and for all real exponents, most compilers use logarithms to evaluate the expression. In these cases the use of a negative number as a base in exponentiation will result in an error, since the logarithm of a negative number is undefined. For example $(-3.)**2.$ would result in an execution-time error.

**12.** Can an exponent be negative?

*Answer:* Yes. For example, $3.**(-2)$ is evaluated as $\dfrac{1.}{3.^2} = \dfrac{1}{9.}$

**13.** In everyday life we don't differentiate between integer and real (floating point) numbers when performing arithmetic operations. Why do we in FORTRAN?

*Answer:* Actually, we do allow for a difference in everyday-life computations as well as in FORTRAN. Sometimes we have to figure the position of the decimal point when multiplying or dividing two real numbers. Obviously, operations involving decimal points are more time-consuming than those without a decimal point. When some computers rent for $82 per minute or more and only integer arithmetic is desired, it would be uneconomical and a waste of time to worry about the position of an unneeded decimal point during computations. On a typical computer, real number operations may be 10 times slower than integer number operations.

In a scientific environment, too, it may be necessary to work with very large numbers requiring the use of exponents and decimal points. It would be impractical to write $10^{70}$ as an integer; hence, an alternative arithmetic is required (real arithmetic). The exponent notation for real numbers is discussed in chapter 6.

**14.** Is it possible to use nested parentheses to reduce the number of operations required to evaluate an expression?

*Answer:* Yes. Consider, for example, the evaluation of $2x^3 + 3x^2 - 6x + 1$. A straightforward way to code this expression is:

```
2.*X**3.+3.*X**2.-6.*X+1.
```

Evaluation of this expression will require 2 exponentiations
3 multiplications
2 additions
1 subtraction.

This expression can, however, be simplified by factoring as follows:

$$2x^3 + 3x^2 - 6x + 1 = (2x^2 + 3x - 6)x + 1$$
$$= ((2x + 3)x - 6)x + 1$$

This can then be coded as

```
((2.*X+3.)*X-6.)*X+1.
```

Evaluation of this expression will require 3 multiplications
2 additions
1 subtraction.

**15.** How do I print an apostrophe as a part of a literal string?

*Answer:* The difficulty with an apostrophe is that it is used to enclose literal strings; a format code such as 'DON'T' is ambiguous to a compiler. Many compilers use the following rule to avoid ambiguity: In order to print an apostrophe as a part of a literal string, use two apostrophes in succession. The compiler will insert one apostrophe on the output line in place of the two present in the format code.

*Example*

```
WRITE(6,16)
16 FORMAT(3X,'SUSAN''S GRANDMOTHER')
```

would produce the following line:

```
| | |S|U|S|A|N|'|S| |G|R|A|N|D|M|O|T|H|E|R| | | |
```

# 2-7  Problem Example

## 2-7-1  An Investment Decision

Mrs. Gabroudy would like to deposit $1,500 at a savings institution. She considers a local bank and a credit union. The credit union requires a nonrefundable membership fee of $15 (up front); deposits earn 12.75%, and interest is compounded once a year. Deposits at the bank earn 11.75%, and interest is compounded quarterly (4 times/ year). Mrs. Gabroudy will need the money in 2½ years. Which institution should Mrs. Gabroudy select? The formula to compute the value of the investment $T$ is:

$$T = P(1 + I/J)^{N*J}$$

where $T$ is the principal and accumulated interest
  $P$ is the principal
  $I$ is the interest rate expressed in fractional form
  $J$ is the number of times the interest is compounded
  $N$ is the duration of the investment in years

Write a program to print the total value of the investments as well as the accumulated interest for each case.

A program to solve this problem is shown in Figure 2–7. It has several features that should be noted: the interest rate (12.75%) is typed as .1275. N*J1 is enclosed in parentheses for exponentiation. Finally, the accumulated interest is the difference between the final value of the investment and the original principal.

## 2-7-2  How Good Is Your Computer With Numbers?: Finite and Infinite Sums

Consider the following three sums, S6, S7 and S8:

$S6 = 9/10 + 9/10^2 + 9/10^3 + 9/10^4 + 9/10^5 + 9/10^6$
$S7 = 9/10 + 9/10^2 + 9/10^3 + 9/10^4 + 9/10^5 + 9/10^6 + 9/10^7$
$S8 = 9/10 + 9/10^2 + 9/10^3 + 9/10^4 + 9/10^5 + 9/10^6 + 9/10^7 + 9/10^8$

**FIGURE 2-7** AN INVESTMENT DECISION

```
C INVESTMENT DECISION PROBLEM
C    P:  PRINCIPAL
C    I1: CREDIT UNION INTEREST    J1: COMPOUND ONCE A YEAR
C    A1: ACCUMULATED  INTEREST    T1: TOTAL CREDIT UNION VALUE
C    I2: BANK INTEREST RATE       J2: COMPOUND 4 TIMES YEAR
C    A2: ACCUMULATED INTEREST     T2: TOTAL BANK VALUE
C    N:  NUMBER OF YEARS
C
       REAL P,I1,A1,T1,I2,A2,T2,N,J1,J2
       P  = 1500.00          Principal
       I1 = .1275            Credit union interest
       J1 = 1                Number of times interest is compounded
       I2 = .1175            Bank interest
       J2 = 4                Number of times interest is compounded
       N  = 2.5              Duration of investment
C
C COMPUTE FINAL INVESTMENTS
       T1 = (P-15.0)*(1. + I1/J1)**(N*J1)  Credit union final investment
       T2 = P*(1. + I2/J2)**(N*J2)         Bank final investment
       A1 = T1 - P
       A2 = T2 - P
C
       WRITE(6,10)T1,A1        Print total credit union value and interest
       WRITE(6,11)T2,A2        Print total bank value and interest
       STOP
10     FORMAT(1X,'CREDIT AMOUNT',1X,F7.2,20X,'CREDIT INTEREST',1X,F6.2)
11     FORMAT(1X,'BANK AMOUNT',3X,F7.2,10X,'BANK INTEREST',3X,F6.2)


CREDIT AMOUNT 2004.55          CREDIT INTEREST 504.55
BANK AMOUNT   2003.67          BANK INTEREST   503.67
```

As more terms are added to these sequences, do the successive sums get closer and closer to a particular value, or do the sums grow larger than any arbitrary value by simply adding more and more terms? Does the infinite sum S, shown below, get closer and closer to a particular value (converge) or does the value of the infinite sum itself become infinite (diverge)?

$$S = 9/10 + 9/10^2 + 9/10^3 + \ldots + 9/10^{100} + \ldots$$

In mathematics a sequence of numbers like this one is called a geometric progression, i.e. each new term of the sequence is equal to the preceding term multiplied by the number $1/10$ (the ratio between two successive terms is constant and equal to $1/10$).

The formula to compute the sum of $n$ terms of a geometric progression is:

$$\text{Sum of } n \text{ terms} = \frac{\text{first term of sequence} * (1 - \text{ratio}^n)}{1 - \text{ratio}}$$

The formula to compute the sum of the infinite progression is:

$$\text{Sum of infinite terms} = \frac{\text{first term}}{1 - \text{ratio}}$$

Let us write a program to compute the three finite sums S6, S7, and S8, the infinite sum S, and the difference between the infinite sum and each of the finite sums. We will assume that our computer gives 6 significant digits on output. The program is shown in Figure 2–8.

Note that the infinite sum S is equal to 1. The reader should expect this result, since the infinite sum S is actually

$$S = .9 + .09 + .009 + .0009 + .00009 + \ldots = .99999 \ldots = 1 \text{ at infinity!}$$

Note also that the value computed for S7 and S8 is 1. In fact, as far as the computer is concerned, all finite sums after the first seven terms are included are equal to 1. This is due to the computer's inability to work with more than six significant digits.

**FIGURE 2–8** FINITE AND INFINITE SUMS

```
C ERRORS INDUCED BY ARITHMETIC OPERATIONS ON SMALL NUMBERS
C   S: INFINITE SUM
C   S6, S7, S8: 6TH, 7TH AND 8TH FINITE SUMS
C   D6, D7, D8: DIFFERENCES BETWEEN FINITE AND INFINITE SUMS
        REAL S6,S7,S8,D6,D7,D8,S
C
        S6 = .9 * (1. - .1**6) / .9
        S7 = .9 * (1. - .1**7) / .9
        S8 = .9 * (1. - .1**8) / .9
C
C COMPUTE INFINITE SUM
        S = .9 / (1. - .1)
C
C COMPUTE DIFFERENCES BETWEEN FINITE AND INFINITE SUMS
        D6 = S - S6
        D7 = S - S7
        D8 = S - S8
C
        WRITE(6,10)S
        WRITE(6,11)S6,S7,S8
        WRITE(6,12)D6,D7,D8
        STOP
10      FORMAT(1X,'INFINITE SUM = ',F4.2)
11      FORMAT('    S6 =',F9.6,'       S7 =',F9.6,'    S8 =',F9.6)
12      FORMAT(' S - S6 =',F9.6,'   S - S7 =',F9.6,'   S - S8 =',F9.6)
        END
INFINITE SUM = 1.00
     S6 =  .999999        S7 = 1.000000        S8 = 1.000000
 S - S6 =  .000001    S - S7 =  .000000    S - S8 =  .000000
```

### 2-7-3 Do It Now

Run the program in Figure 2–8 on your system and see if you obtain the same results. If D8 is not 0, compute S9 and D9 = S − S9. How many more terms do you need to add to the sum so that DN = S − SN = 0?

## 2-8 Exercises

### 2-8-1 Test Yourself

1. What is the difference between an expression and a statement? Between a constant and a variable? Between integer and real data?

2. Define the terms: *source statement, job control instructions, execution time,* and *compile time.*

3. Characterize each of the following as either an integer, a real or a character constant, or an integer, a real, or a character variable. If some are invalid, explain why.

   a. F  b. I123  c. FORTRAN  d. X1.3
   e. − 1234  f. 3ABC  g. 'XRAY'S'  h. .000000006
   i. + 72  j. 4(Y)  k. A1B2C.  l. 234-567-999
   m. − 1,314.6  n. IRAY  o. 'COUNT'  p. KOUNT
   q. 3 + 4  r. I2 + 1  s. $300.50  t. '3 < 4'

4. Translate the following algebraic expressions into FORTRAN:

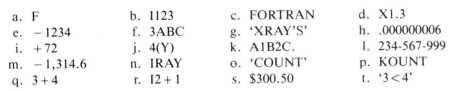

   a. $x(y + z)$   b. $\dfrac{a}{b} \cdot c$   c. $\dfrac{a}{b^5}$

   d. $ax^2 + bx + c$   e. $\dfrac{a}{bs}$   f. $y^{1/3}$

   g. $\pi r^2$   h. $\dfrac{a}{x+y} - \dfrac{.5}{xz}$   i. $2(xy^{-1})$

   j. $-x^2$   k. $a^{x+y} + 3.5$   l. $y + a^x$

   m. $\dfrac{y - y_0}{y_1 - y_0} \cdot \dfrac{x - x_0}{x_1 - x_0}$   n. $z - 1 + \dfrac{1}{2 + \dfrac{3}{1 - x}}$   o. $\dfrac{-b + \sqrt{b^2 - 4ac}}{2a}$

   p. $u^{2n}$   q. $\sqrt{\dfrac{4(x_1^2 + x_2^2 + x_3^2) - (x_1 + x_2 + x_3)^2}{3(3 - 1)}}$

5. Fill in the blanks with the appropriate words:
   a. The _____ instruction denotes the logical end of a FORTRAN program.
   b. Variables not starting with the letters _____ are real variables.
   c. _____ statements are used to describe the layout of the data in an I/O operation.
   d. Print position 1 of the output form is used as a _____.
   e. _____ can be used to refer to or identify a particular FORTRAN instruction.
   f. The _____ instruction denotes the physical end of the FORTRAN program.
   g. Integers and real numbers are examples of _____.
   h. Letters of the alphabet and the digits 0 through 9 are referred to as _____ characters.
   i. _____ are used to refer symbolically to memory locations.

    j. 3*X + 1 is an example of an _____.

    k. In a FORTRAN statement, positions 73–80 are used for _____.

    l. *Variable = expression* is the general form of a FORTRAN _____.

    m. _____ instructions are generally used in addition to the FORTRAN program to make up a complete job.

    n. The output code generated by the FORTRAN compiler is called _____, while the input to the compiler is called _____.

    o. To identify real and integer numbers in a FORMAT, the codes _____ and _____ are used.

    p. The _____ or _____ format code can be used to space data on the output form.

    q. Two FORTRAN statements with identical statement numbers would result in a _____ time error, while computing the square root of a negative number would result in an _____ time error.

    r. Dividing one integer by another integer will result in _____.

    s. _____ are used to enclose character strings.

**6.** Identify the order of the operations by placing an appropriate number above each arithmetic operator in the expression, for example:

$$\overset{\text{⑤}}{A} + 1 \overset{\text{③}}{/} 3 \overset{\text{⑥}}{+} B \overset{\text{⑦}}{-} (3 \overset{\text{①}}{+} 4) \overset{\text{④}}{/} Z \overset{\text{②}}{**} 2$$

    a. `3 * 4 - (B - C)`

    b. `1 / 8 + 5 ** 2 / 4`

    c. `(-3 + X) * (B + C) + 3 / X + (C - 1)`

    d. `X / A * 1 - B + (3 - Y)`

**7.** Which of the following are identical to A*(B + C)/D?

    a. (B + C)* A/D   b. (A*(B + C))/D   c. (B + C)/D*A   d. (A/D)*(B + C)

**8.** What values will be stored in X and Y as a result of the following?

| a. | b. | c. | d. |
|---|---|---|---|
| `X = 9.` | `X = 9.` | `X = 9.` | `X = 3.` |
| `Y = 4.` | `Y = 3.` | `Y = 10.` | `Y = 8.` |
| `Y = Y-X` | `X = Y` | `T = X` | `Y = .3` |
| | `Y = X` | `X = Y` | |
| | | `Y = T` | |

**9.** Write the statements to perform the following:

    a. Double what is in C and print out result with the prefix $.

    b. Replace X by half of its square root.

    c. Add $X^3$ to whatever was in X.

    d. Store the characters SAM in a memory location.

**10.** Write the FORTRAN code to convert $-139.65°$ Fahrenheit into Centigrade. The formula is:

$$C = \frac{5}{9} (F - 32)$$

**11.** Write the FORTRAN code to compute and print the length of the hypotenuse of a right triangle, given its two legs .0056 and 135.77.

12. Write the FORTRAN code to interchange the values contained in memory locations S and T.

13. Run a program to compute the following, and explain the results.

    a. 1./3.

    b. 2./3.
    c. 2./3. + 1./3.

    d. 10000000 + 999999

    e. $\dfrac{1}{10^7} + \dfrac{1}{10^8}$

14. Mr. X is a widower with three children aged 12, 16, and 19. His monthly salary is $1,023.36. His monthly contribution to a retirement plan is 4.5% of his first nine month's salary. For each child under 18, he receives $119.25 in child support from social security. His monthly social security deduction is 6.13% of his monthly income, and his federal income tax is 13.6% of his yearly gross (deducted on a monthly basis). Monthly payments for life insurance equal 9.6% of his monthly salary after social security and federal tax deductions. Write a program to compute Mr. X's monthly spendable income after taxes, deductions, and supplemental support income.

15. Which of the following output instructions are invalid (assume 6 represents the output device)? Explain why.

```
a.      WRITE(6,10),A,B,C          b.      WRITE(6,5)I,J
   10 FORMAT(1X,F1.0,F2.0,F3.0)       5 FORMAT(I1,I4)
c.      WRITE(6,11)4,5.23          d.      WRITE(6,16)A,I,J
   11 FORMAT(T5,I2,F4.2)             16 FORMAT(T3,F4.5,I2,I1)
e.      WRITE(6,7)A,K,C            f.      WRITE(6,9)'RESULT IS',J
    7 FORMAT(F5.2,I3,F4.)            9 FORMAT(3X,I3)
g.      WRITE(6,12.)X,Y            h.      WRITE(6,15)I,X,K
   12 FORMAT(2X,F3.1,F3.1)          15 FORMAT(1X,I2,I3,I1)
i.      WRITE(6,11)X - Y           j.      WRITE(5,9)KL,M1
   11 FORMAT(F3.2,F4.0)              9 FORMAT(3X,I3,I3)
k.      PRINT * A,B                l.      PRINT*, A+B/2.1,-2
```

16. Are the following statements true or false?
    a. Statement numbers must be sequentially numbered.
    b. Integer variables that have not been typed must start with one of the letters I, J, K, L, M, or N.
    c. The statement END denotes the logical end of the program.
    d. Statement numbers cannot exceed 99999.
    e. Syntax errors are detected at execution time.
    f. FORMATs can be located anywhere in the program before the END record.
    g. The STOP is used by the compiler to terminate the translation process.
    h. SAM. is a valid, real variable name.
    i. Statement numbers must start in column 1.
    j. A FORMAT can be referred to by any number of WRITE statements.
    k. X = X + 1. is a valid FORTRAN expression.
    l. WRITE(6,11) is an invalid output statement.
    m. 4./4/5 evaluates to the same as 4./(4/5).
    n. 2*J = 3 is a valid replacement statement.
    o. The maximum number of characters for a FORTRAN variable name depends on the particular system.

p. Depending on the integer values I and J and the real variable C, I*J*C ≠ I*C*J.
q. K = − (K) is a valid statement.
r. In describing the output format Fw.d for a real number, the value d should always be less than or equal to w.
s. The output field F3.1 refers to a field allowing for 1 fractional digit and 3 digits to the left of the decimal point.
t. All character variables must be declared in a CHARACTER statement.
u. CHARACTER A, CHARACTER*1 A, CHARACTER A*1 are identical

17. For A = 3., B = − 2., I = 6, and J = 0, evaluate each of the following expressions.

a. A**2 + B       b. I + 2/3       c. A**B
d. A*3. + B*4.     e. A/B        f. A/B* 3. + A
g. A/B/2.        h. A/B + 2.     i. J/I
j. I/J          k. A**I        l. (A + I)/B
m. A**2**3      n. B**B       o. J**B

18. What value will be stored in X or IX by each of the following statements, if A = 3.2, B = − 2., I = 6, and J = 0?

a. X = I         b. IX = A       c. X = (I + 3)/2
d. IX = − A + B    e. X = I**B     f. X = J*I/.1
g. X = J        h. X = B**J     i. IX = J*A

19. As a result of the following program code, indicate what value will be placed in memory locations S, J, and JK.

```
I = 4.
A = 1
B = 2
S = (3/I)*3
J = (3./9)*3
JK = (A + 2./B)/2
```

20. Show that if I and J are integer variables and C is real, it is possible to have the following situation:

a. $\dfrac{I}{J} \cdot C \neq \dfrac{I\,C}{J}$            b. $C \cdot I/J \neq C \cdot (I/J)$

21. Show the printed output field (print positions) for A, given the following format specifications:

a. A = 743.25    1X,F10.3        d. A = 328.74    1X,F5.2
b. A = − 643.281   1X,F7.2        e. A = .37        1X,F5.2
c. A = − 4768.6   1X,F6.0

22. What output will be produced by each of the following program segments?

a.
```
    X=3.2
    Y=X*.16
    WRITE(6,10)X,Y
 10 FORMAT(3X,F4.0,T10,F9.2,'ALL')
```
b.
```
    I=+1632
    J=-4
    K=I/J
    WRITE(6,11)I,J,K
 11 FORMAT(T8,I4,3X,I1,'+',I5)
```

c.
```
     XXX=4.3257
     YYY=-.0007
     ZZZ=XXX+YYY
     WRITE(6,12)XXX,YYY,ZZZ
  12 FORMAT(T3,F7.3,F7.3,F7.3)
```

d.
```
     ABC=19.2
     IJ3=4
     WRITE(6,13)ABC,IJ3
  13 FORMAT(2X,I4,3X,F6.0)
```

e.
```
     I=.8
     J=.6
     Z=1+J
     WRITE(6,11)Z
  11 FORMAT(1X,F2.0,'I2,F4.1')
```

f.
```
     I=11
     WRITE(6,12)I
  12 FORMAT(I2)
     WRITE(6,13)
  13 FORMAT('1','1','ALL')
```

**23.** What will be printed by the following code

```
CHARACTER A*4,B*6
A = ' HELLO '
B = 'MIKE'
PRINT*, A, B,'!'
B = A
PRINT*,B,' ','MIKE'
```

## 2-8-2 Exercises

**1.** Write the code to produce the remainder (expressed as an integer) of A/B. For example, the remainder of 13/2 is 1, while the remainder of 29/6 is 5.

**2.** Write a program to compute the simple interest $i = prt$ for $r = .08$ $t = 3$ $p = 100$. Write the results with appropriate headings.

**3.** With an interest rate $I$ of 6% and a principal $P$ of \$1,956.45 deposited for an 11-year period in a savings account, write a program to compute a total principal $T$, given the formula:

$$T = P(1 + I)^N$$

where $N$ is the number of years.

**4.** Suppose the interest of exercise 3 is compounded daily for 11 years. Write a program to compute

a. The total principal given by the formula:

$$T = P \left(1 + \frac{I}{J}\right)^{J*N}$$

where $J$ is the number of times the interest is compounded per year.

b. Compute and print the difference between total amounts when the principal is compounded once and 365 times a year. Also print the corresponding interests.

c. What would the principal be after 11 years and 7 months? (Hint: Express $N$ as total months divided by 12.)

5. A wholesaler accepts a $5,000 promissory note at 7% in lieu of cash payment for delivered goods. Write a program to compute the maturity value of the note for a 30-, 60-, and 90-day short-term loan. The formula to compute the maturity value $S$ is:

$$S = P(1 + I * N)$$

where $P$ is the principal, $I$ is the interest rate, and $N$ is the number of years (express $N$ as number of days divided by 360).

6. Write a program to evaluate each of the formulas for the indicated values (use $\pi = 3.1416$) and print the answers with appropriate literal headings.

a. Simple interest        $i = Prt$          for $r = 4\%$    $t = 3$    $p = 100$
b. Volume of a cube     $v = c^3$          for $c = 3.167219$
c. Area of a circle       $A = \pi r^2$        for $r = 6.2$
d. Volume of a cone     $v = \frac{1}{3} \pi r^2 b$     for $r = 9.1$    $b = 4.932747$

[Expected answers: $i = 120$    $v = 31.77$    $A = 120.76$    $v = 427.76$]

7. Write a program to compute and print the area and the length (perimeter) of a. and b. and the volume of the sphere in c.

a. 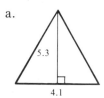    b.     c.

8. The lowest temperature ever recorded in the Antarctic is $-126.9°$ Fahrenheit. Write a program to convert this temperature in degrees Centigrade and print the result with appropriate captions. The formula is $C = \frac{5}{9}(F - 32)$.

9. Write a program to compute and print the length of the hypotenuse of a right triangle, given its two legs A1 = .0056 and A2 = 135.77.

10. Write a program to compute and print (7./3.)*3. and (3.*7.)/3. Do you expect the result to be 7.? Think about formats.

11. Write a program to approximate the Julian date (introduced by Julius Caesar in 46 B.C.) equivalent to the calendar date given in the form month, day. The Julian date is the day of the year. January 1 has Julian date 1, February 2 has Julian date 33, December 31, has Julian date 365, etc. A formula to approximate the Julian date is (month − 1) * 30 + day. Determine the Julian dates for November 7, May 25, and March 21.

12. Write a program to print out your initials by magnifying them. For example,

```
MMM            MM         BBBBBB
MMMM         MMMM         BBB    B
MMMMM     MMMMM           BBBBBB
MMM  MMMM  MMM            BBB    B
MMM     MM     MMM        BBBBBB
```

13. Mr. X is a bricklayer. Last year his gross pay was $23,564.99. After deducting 6.85% for social security and 23.5% for federal income tax from his gross pay, was his net income greater than Mrs. Y's net income? Mrs. Y is a teacher who grossed $19,874 but had $850.45 deducted for her income retirement plan and 16.03% of her gross income deducted for income tax purposes. Print the salaries of Mr. X and Mrs. Y.

14. The truth in lending law requires that money-lending institutions disclose the annual interest rate charged on loans. The approximate rate is given by the formula:

$$R = \frac{(2 + N) * F}{P(n + 1)}$$

where $N$ is the number of payments per year, $F$ = the finance charge in dollars, $P$ is the principal, and $n$ = the number of scheduled installment payments. Write a program to determine the annual percentage rate for a loan of $5,000 for 36 months at 162.50 dollars per month. (Finance charge = 36 * 162.5 − 5000 = 850).

15. a. Miss T. drove 1050 miles in 17½ hours and spent $86.75 for gas. Her car averages 14.5 miles per gallon. Write a program to compute her average speed, number of gallons used and the average cost per gallon. The output should be as follows:

```
MILES =                1050
HOURS DRIVEN =         17.5
GAS COST =             86.75
AVERAGE SPEED =        _____
NO. GALLONS =          _____
COST/GALLON =          _____
```

b. Miss T. estimates that she spent 12% of the traveling time on miscellaneous stops. How does this change her average speed?

16. Write a program to produce the following report on the cost $c$ of operating electrical devices:

**Cost Analysis**

| Watts | Hours | Cost/KW | Cost |
|-------|-------|---------|------|
| 65    | 6     | .087    | --   |
| 100   | 6     | .087    | --   |

The formula is: $C = \dfrac{W \cdot T \cdot K}{1000}$  where $W$ = number of watts
$T$ = time in hours
$K$ = cost in cents per kilowatt hours

17. The date for any Easter Sunday can be computed as follows. Let N be the year for which Easter Sunday is to be computed.

Let NA be the remainder of the division of N by 19.
Let NB be the remainder of the division of N by 4.
Let NC be the remainder of the division of N by 7.
Let ND be the remainder of the division of (19·NA + 24) by 30.
Let NE be the remainder of the division of (2·NB + 4·NC + 6· ND + 5) by 7.

The date for Easter Sunday is then March $(22 + ND + NE)$. Note that this can give a date in April. In order to compute the remainder, NR, of the division of NUM1 by NUM2, the following statement can be used:

$$NR = NUM1 - NUM1/NUM2*NUM2$$

i.e., the remainder of the division of 17 by 3 is $17 - 17/3*3 = 17 - 5*3 = 2$

Write a program to read a year N and compute the date for Easter Sunday for that year using the formula $22 + ND + NE$. The resulting day can be in either March or April.

18. Fifteen seconds after dropping a stone into a well, the stone hits the surface of the water. Determine the height of the well, given the formula $d = \frac{1}{2}gt^2$ where $d$ is the distance, $g$ is the force of gravity (9.81 meter/s), and $t$ is the time in seconds.

19. For four resistors $R_1$, $R_2$, $R_3$, and $R_4$ in parallel, the overall resistance $R$ is given by:

$$\frac{1}{R} = \frac{1}{R_1} + \frac{1}{R_2} + \frac{1}{R_3} + \frac{1}{R_4}$$

where $R_1$, $R_2$, $R_3$, and $R_4$ are respectively 1.5, 3, 4.5, and 6 ohms. Write a program to compute $R$ and print the results as follows:

```
R1 = 1.5   R2 = 3.   R3 = 4.5   R4 = 6.
THE OVERALL RESISTANCE R = XX.X
```

20. Write a program to determine whether $x = 1.3$ is a root of the polynomial

$$\frac{17}{3}x^{17} + 4x^8 - .76x^2 - 686$$

21. Write a program to compute the infinite sum of each of the following geometric progressions (whenever possible). See section 2–7–2 for formulas.

a. $1 + 2 + 4 + 8 + 16 + \ldots$
b. $3 - 9 + 27 - 81 + \ldots$
c. $4 + 2 + 1 + 1/2 + 1/4 + \ldots$
d. $9/10 + 9/100 + 9/1000 + \ldots$

22. Mr. Grand wants to purchase a $32,356 Jaguar. He can manage a down payment of $7,800. The trade-in allowance for his old Volvo is $2,945. Current dealer interest rates are an annual 15.6% for 2½ years. What will be Mr. Grand's monthly payment for the next 2½ years? The formula to compute the monthly payment is:

$$R = iP \left[ \frac{(1 + i)^m}{(1 + i)^m - 1} \right]$$

where $i$ = interest rate per month, $P$ = principal (purchase price – down payment – trade-in-allowance), and $m$ = the number of monthly payments.

23. Write a program to generate unit-price shelf labels for a grocery store. For example, process the data:

| Price | .59 | Standard unit size | 16 |
| Size | 11.5 | Description of unit | oz. |
| Item description | green beans | | |

The output should display all of the above data. The unit price is computed as:

$$\text{unit price} = \frac{\text{price}}{\text{size}} \times \text{standard unit size}$$

For our example, the output should be similar to:

```
.59       GREEN BEANS      11.5 OZ.
UNIT PRICE      .82      FOR 16 OZ.
```

24. Write a program to produce a magic square. In a magic square, the sum of each row, column, and diagonal is equal. For example, the following is a magic square in which the sum is 3:

| | | |
|---|---|---|
| −2 | 2 | 3 |
| 6 | 1 | −4 |
| −1 | 0 | 4 |

The secret of the magic square is this: for any values of $x$, $y$, and $z$, a magic square can be formed from:

| | | |
|---|---|---|
| $x-z$ | $x+z-y$ | $x+y$ |
| $x+y+z$ | $x$ | $x-y-z$ |
| $x-y$ | $x+y-z$ | $x+z$ |

In the above example, $x=1$, $y=2$, $z=3$.

25. A balance sheet showing the financial position of a business has the following format. Assets are generally listed in the order specified. This balance sheet will be referred to repeatedly in later chapters.

**XYZ Corporation**
**Balance Sheet**
**April 30, 1984**

| *Assets* | | *Liabilities and Stockholders' Equity* | |
|---|---|---|---|
| Cash | 3500 | Liabilities: | |
| Accounts Receivable | 500 | Accounts Payable | 3000 |
| Supplies | 100 | | |
| Land | 2000 | | |
| Buildings | 10000 | Stockholder's Equity: | |
| Machines and Equipment | 3000 | Capital Stock | 18100 |
| Patents | 2000 | | |
| | | Total Liabilities and | |
| Total Assets | 21100 | Stockholders' Equity | 21100 |

a. Write a program to duplicate this balance sheet. Define each asset and liability with a variable name as in CASH = 3500. Variables for the various entries should appear in the WRITE statements.

b. Write a program to generate a similar balance sheet for the Triple Star Corporation for the month of September 1984, given the following data:

Cash = $3,200            Accounts receivable = $1,300
Capital stock = $5,000   Repair supplies = $700
Accounts payable = $2,500   Land = ?

Use variable names to define these entries and let the computer determine the value of the land in such a way that Total Assets = Liabilities + Stockholders' Equity.

26. The Sullivans would like to take a summer trip abroad in a year and a half. They estimate that their expenses will be just over $3,500. They save regularly at a credit union where 6.5% interest is paid on deposits. What should the Sullivans' minimum monthly deposit be to afford the vacation abroad? What would their deposits have to be if they made four equal deposits per year? The formula to calculate the regular deposit $R$ is:

$$R = P \left( \frac{i/n}{(1+i/n)^{n \cdot y} - 1} \right)$$

where $P$ = amount to be saved (future value)
$i$ = interest rate
$n$ = deposits/year
$y$ = number of years

27. Mary and John Soule would very much like to buy the Pitts' house. The Pitts are asking $76,000 conventional with $7,000 down or $84,000 for VA with nothing down. In either case, a 30-year mortgage is sought. Financing charges are 13.5% for VA and 14% for conventional. (Equal monthly payments will be made.) The Soules have another option: Mary's father is willing to give them $9,000 for a down payment, on the condition that they assume with him a 14.5% interest mortgage for the next 22 years and 8 months on the remainder of the conventional price, with equal payments four times a year. In terms of today's dollar value, what is the Soule's best financial arrangement? Identify in each case the total costs involved as well as the interest paid. The formula to compute the regular payments $R$ (monthly, quarterly, etc.) is:

$$R = \frac{iP/n}{1 - \left( \dfrac{i}{n} + 1 \right)^{ny}}$$

where $P$ = principal, $i$ = interest rate, $n$ = number of payments/year, and $y$ = number of years. (If the number of years is given in years and months, convert it to months and divide by 12.)

## 2-8-3 Answers to Test Yourself

1. An expression is a part of a statement; an expression should always be on the right-hand side of the = sign. The value of a constant does not change; the value of a variable can change. Integer data cannot have decimal points; real data always have decimal points.

2. A source statement is a statement written in a high-level language such as FORTRAN. Job control instructions are required for communication with the computer's operating system to compile and execute a program. Execution time is the time during which the computer is executing the translated program. Compile time is the time during which the computer is translating a program into machine language.

**3.** a. real variable
   b. integer variable
   c. invalid variable, too many characters
   d. invalid variable, contains special character
   e. integer constant
   f. invalid variable, numeric first character
   g. invalid character constant, missing apostrophe
   h. real constant
   i. integer constant
   j. invalid variable, numeric first character and special characters
   k. invalid variable, decimal point
   l. invalid constant, imbedded −
   m. invalid constant, comma
   n. integer variable
   o. character constant
   p. integer variable
   q. invalid constant, imbedded +
   r. invalid variable, special character
   s. invalid constant, $ must not be used
   t. valid character constant

**4.** a. `X*(Y + Z)`
   b. `A/B*C`
   c. `A/B**5`
   d. `A*X**2 + B*X + C`
   e. `A/(B*S)`
   f. `Y**(1./3.)`
   g. `3.14*R**2`
   h. `A/(X + Y) - .5/(X*Z)`
   i. `2.*(X*Y**(-1))`
   j. `-X**2`
   k. `A**(X + Y) + 3.5`
   l. `Y + A**X`
   m. `(Y - YØ)/(Y1 - YØ)*(X - XØ)/(X1 - XØ)`
   n. `Z - 1. + (1./(2. + 3. /(1. - X)))`
   o. `(-B + (B*B - 4.*A*C)**.5)/(2.*A)`
   p. `U**(2.*N)`
   q. `((4.*(X1*X1 + X2*X2 + X3*X3) - (X1 + X2 + X3)**2)/(3.*(3.-1.)))**.5`

**5.** a. STOP      b. I through N     c. FORMAT        d. carriage control code
   e. Statement number        f. END         g. numeric constants
   h. alphanumeric            i. Variables      j. expression
   k. sequencing/identification   l. statement    m. Job control
   n. object code, source code      o. F, I        p. X or T
   q. compilation, execution        r. truncation of fractional part
   s. apostrophes

**6.**
   a.  ② ③ ①
       3  *  4  − (B − C)
   b.  ② ④ ① ③
       1  / 8 + 5 ** 2 / 4
   c.  ① ④ ② ⑥ ⑤ ⑦ ③
       (−3 + X) * (B + C) + 3 / X + (C − 1)
   d.  ② ③ ④ ⑤ ①
       X  / A * 1 − B + (3 − Y)

**7.** All are identical

**8.** a. X = 9., Y = −5.
   b. X = 3., Y = 3.
   c. X = 10., Y = 9.
   d. X = 3., Y = .3

**9.** a. `PRINT*,'$',2.*C`
   b. `X = X**.5/2.`
   c. `X = X + X**3.`
   d. `CHARACTER A*3`
      `A = 'SAM'`

**10.** 
```
F = -139.65
C = 5./9.*(F-32.)
PRINT*,C
```

**11.** 
```
A = .0056
B = 135.77
H = (A**2 + B**2)**.5
PRINT*,H
```

**12.** 
```
X = S
S = T
T = X
```

**13.** The results depend on the system used. On a system with six significant digits on output, we would have:
   a. 0.333333
   b. 0.666667
   c. 1.
   d. depends on system
   e. .000000

**14.**
```
      CHILD=119.25
      SALMON=1023.36
      RETIRE=(9.*SALMON*.045)/12.
      SSTAX=.0613*SALMON
      TAXINC=.136*SALMON
      PAYNET=SALMON-(RETIRE+SSTAX+TAXINC)
      PAYLIF=.096*(SALMON-TAXINC-SSTAX)
      PAY=PAYNET-PAYLIF
      PAY=PAY+2.*CHILD
      WRITE(6,14)PAY
   14 FORMAT(2X,'SPENDABLE INCOME',F7.2)
      STOP
      END
```
`SPENDABLE INCOME 946.55`

**15.** a. There should be no comma after (6,10); also, the field for A is too small, it should be at least two positions long.
   b. Value of variable I will be used as a carriage control character.
   c. The WRITE statement can contain only variables, not constants.
   d. F4.5 is an invalid FORMAT code since 5 > 4.
   e. F4. is invalid; there must be a digit after the decimal point.
   f. The WRITE statement list must not contain literal strings.
   g. No . is used after the format statement number.
   h. The variable X must be described with a real format code.
   i. The WRITE statement list must not contain expressions.
   j. Unit 6, not unit 5, represents the output device.
   k. Missing comma after asterisk
   l. Valid

**16.** a. F   b. T   c. F   d. T   e. F   f. T   g. F   h. F
   i. F   j. T   k. F   l. F   m. F   n. F   o. F   p. F
   q. T   r. F; *d* should be less than *w*.   s. F   t. T   u. T

**17.** a. 7.   b. 6   c. .111111   d. 1.   e. −1.5   f. −1.5
g. −.75   h. .5   i. 0      j. error.   k. 729.   l. −4.5
m. 6561.   n. Error, base is negative.      o. undefined.

**18.** a. 6.   b. 3   c. 4.   d. −5   e. .0277778   f. 0.
g. 0.   h. 1.   i. 0

**19.** S = 0.    J = 0 or 1 on some systems    JK = 1

**20.** a. 3/4*4. = 0. but (3*4.)/4 = 3.    b. 2.*3/4 = 1.5 but 2.*(3/4) = 0.

**21.** a. `      7 4 3 . 2 5 0`   b. `  − 6 4 3 . 2 8`

c. `  − 4 7 6 9 .`   d. `  * * * * *`   e. `        . 3 7`

**22.** a. `      3 .             . 5 1 A L L`

b. `          1 6 3 2     * +   − 4 0 8`

c. `      4 . 3 2 6   − 0 . 0 0 1   4 . 3 2 5`

d. ABC and IJ3 should be defined respectively by F and I format codes.

e. `  0 . I 2 , F 4 . 1`

Some systems will not write text after list is satisfied.

f. `  1`      Top of new page.

`  1 A L L`      Top of new page.

**23.**    ␢HELMIKE␢␢!
␢HEL␢␢␢MIKE

# read, flowcharts, pseudo code, and the if then else statement

CHAPTER THREE

# read, flowcharts, pseudo code and the if then else statement

## 3-1  Programming Example

*Problem/Specification:*　Mr. Loh is paid at a regular rate of $6.50 per hour for the first 40 hours of work per week. The overtime rate for hours in excess of 40 is 1.5 times the regular rate. Write a FORTRAN program to read the number of hours worked and compute and print out Mr. Loh's gross pay.

　　A FORTRAN program to solve this problem is shown in Figure 3–1 along with the corresponding pseudo code. New FORTRAN statements in this program include:

**1.** The READ statement, which is used to read data from an input file.

**2.** The IF THEN ELSE and ENDIF statements, which are used to carry out certain program statements depending on the outcome of a particular condition.

**FIGURE 3-1**　　CALCULATION OF A GROSS PAY

|  |  |
|---|---|
| | *FORTRAN Program* |
| ***Pseudo Code*** | `1234567` |
| * Calculation of gross pay | `C CALCULATION OF GROSS PAY` |
| | `C    PAY:   GROSS PAY` |
| | `C    PAY1:  PAY FOR 40 HOURS` |
| | `C    PAY2:  OVERTIME PAY` |
| | `C    HOURS: NUMBER OF HOURS WORKED` |
| | `C    OVTM:  OVERTIME HOURS` |
| | `C    RATE:  HOURLY RATE` |
| | `C` |
| | `     INTEGER HOURS,OVTM` |
| | `     REAL PAY,RATE,PAY1,PAY2` |
| Set hourly rate to 6.50 | `     RATE = 6.50` |
| READ number of hours worked | `   5 READ(5,10) HOURS` |
| IF hours worked is ≤ 40 THEN | `     IF(HOURS .LE. 40) THEN` |
| 　　compute pay for hours worked | `        PAY  = HOURS * RATE` |
| ELSE | `     ELSE` |
| 　　compute 40 hours at regular rate | `        PAY1 = 40.* RATE` |
| 　　compute overtime hours | `        OVTM = HOURS - 40` |
| 　　compute overtime pay | `        PAY2 = OVTM * RATE * 1.5` |
| 　　compute total pay | `        PAY  = PAY1 + PAY2` |
| ENDIF | `     ENDIF` |
| WRITE out the pay | `     WRITE(6,20) PAY` |
| END | `  20 FORMAT(4X,'GROSS PAY IS',F7.2)` |
| | `  10 FORMAT(I2)` |
| | `     STOP` |
| Input file | `     END` |
| `64` | `GROSS PAY IS 494.00` |
| | ↓ |
| | output |

## 3-2 Input Considerations

So far, we have defined variables (given them a value) by means of the replacement statement; for example, in the problem of section 3-1 we defined the rate with RATE = 6.50. The problem with defining variables this way is that the program is too specific; in our example, pay can be computed only for a fixed rate of $6.50. If we want to use the same program for different values of RATE, we have to reset RATE each time, and every time we do, the entire program has to be completely recompiled because one statement was changed. This is time-consuming, inefficient, and inconvenient.

Another way to assign value to a variable is to use the READ statement. The READ statement allows the program to accept data during the execution of the program, i.e., after the program has been successfully compiled.

### 3-2-1 Data Records and Placement of Data Records in the Complete FORTRAN Job

Because of the many types of operating systems and the wide variety of computers, ranging from the micros to the large main-frame computing systems, the way in which FORTRAN programs are submitted varies considerably from one computing installation to another. This is particularly true when the FORTRAN program needs to read data records. There are essentially three different types of job configurations for the complete FORTRAN job.

### Case 1

In many systems, the data records that are to be read by the source program are actually entered along with the FORTRAN program, in one package and at the same time. Job control instructions, which are *not* part of the FORTRAN language, separate the FORTRAN source program from the data records. Figure 3-2 illustrates a typical FORTRAN job with this configuration. Note the three types of components that make up the complete job:

1. the job control instructions, which tell the operating system what to do

2. the FORTRAN source program to solve the user's problem

3. the data records that are to be processed by the FORTRAN program

Usually the entire job is entered through a text editor on a terminal. Each line of the job, whether a job control instruction, a source program instruction, or a data line, would be numbered on the terminal. Note, once again, that with this arrangement the data records are part of the complete job, i.e., if you need to edit the data records, you must bring back onto the terminal the complete job, i.e., the job control instructions, the FORTRAN program itself, and the data records.

### Case 2

On many other systems, the job is broken down into two separate entities: the source program with the job control instructions and the separate data file. In this situation, the two files are typed independently. Using a text editor, the user creates the data file (data records) consisting of all the input records that are to be read by the FORTRAN program. He/She then stores that data file on magnetic disk under a given name (the data file is thus catalogued). If the user wishes to edit that file, he/she can do so through the same text editor. A

**FIGURE 3-2**   SAMPLE JOB WITH DATA RECORDS

```
Job control       ⎧   // JOB BOILLOT
instructions      ⎨   // OPTION LINK
                  ⎩   // EXEC FORTRAN
                  ⎧          READ(5,1) N1
                  │          READ(5,1) N2
                  │          READ(5,1) N3
FORTRAN           │          WRITE(6,2)N1,N2,N3
program           ⎨          STOP
                  │   1      FORMAT(I6)
                  │   2      FORMAT(1X,3I7)
                  ⎩          END
Job control       ⎧   /*
instructions      ⎨   // EXEC LNKEDT
                  ⎩   // EXEC
                  ⎧   999999 ◄── This record will be used to get value for N1
Data records      ⎨   123456 ◄── This record will be used to get value for N2
                  ⎩   543210 ◄── This record will be used to get value for N3
Job control       ⎧   /*
instructions      ⎨   /&
```

job control instruction is used to specify the name of the data file catalogued on disk to tell FORTRAN where to "find" the input file at execution time when it is time to read the data records.

## Case 3

This version is very similar to the version discussed in case 2; it also applies to all microcomputer FORTRAN systems. Through a text editor, the user creates two separate files, the FORTRAN source program and the data file, which are catalogued under different names, for example, PAYROLL for the source program and DATAPAY for the data file. To link the source program to the data file, the user typically uses the FORTRAN OPEN instruction in his/her source program: OPEN (5,FILE = 'DATAPAY'). This tells FORTRAN that whenever a READ(5,...) instruction is encountered in the program, the READ operation is to be carried out on the data records found in file DATAPAY. The OPEN statement directs the READ operation to the appropriate input file, in much the same way that the job control instruction specified the data file in case 2. The numeric label 5 in the OPEN statement is associated with the data file DATAPAY so that a READ (5...) operation will be directed to the input file DATAPAY.

### 3-2-2  Compilation and Execution

Just like output, input can be carried out with the list-directed READ*, instruction (section 3-4) or with the format-controlled READ instruction (section 3-3). Before any READ instructions are carried out, the FORTRAN program must first be compiled, i.e., each FORTRAN instruction must be translated into machine language (the result of this translation is called the *object* code.) Syntax errors are detected by the compiler during this translation phase. If no errors occur, the machine language code (object code) is loaded into the memory of the computer. Up to this point, each READ instruction has been translated into machine code, but no data records have been read. When the object code has been loaded into the computer's memory and control has been passed to the object code (the translated version of the FORTRAN program), the data records are read by the various READ statements as they (or actually their machine language equivalents) are encountered in the program (see figure 3–3).

**FIGURE 3–3** EXECUTION OF A SAMPLE JOB

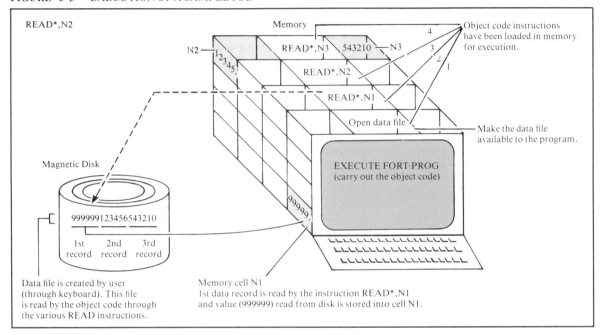

## 3–2–3 my system is different

*Preparing a Simple Program with Input Functions*

Use this space to identify the sequence of steps necessary to create and run a program that will read an input record and print the input record read.

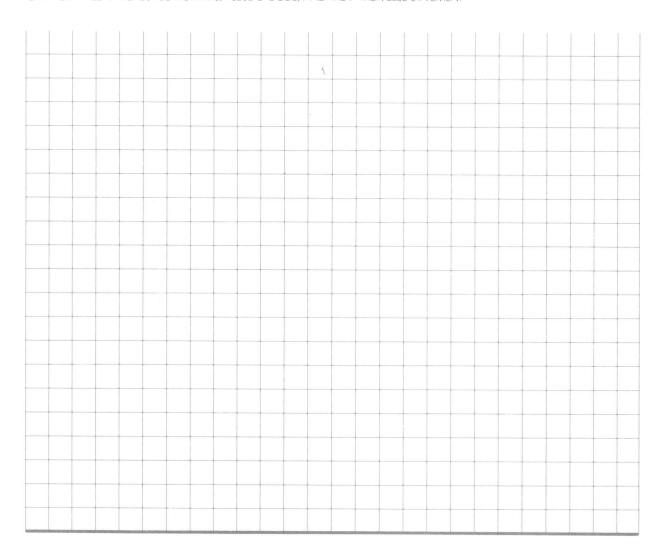

## 3-3  **Format Controlled Input**

One form of the READ statement is:

> READ *(device number, format statement number) variable list*

where *device number* is an integer specifying the input device (address of device),
for example, card reader, magnetic tape, disk, and so forth. These numbers will vary
from installation to installation. Throughout this text the number 5 will be used to
refer to the input device. In some installations the number 1 is used for this purpose.

*format statement number* is a user-selected statement number describing the layout
of the data on the input record, and

*variable list* specifies the names of values to be read from the input medium; each
data item on the input record will be stored in the corresponding named memory location specified in the variable list.

*Example*

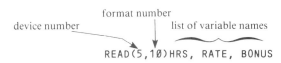

```
                     format number
    device number         |      list of variable names
                                 _____
            READ(5,10)HRS, RATE, BONUS
```

This READ statement can be interpreted as follows: Read three numbers from one or more records (device number 5 may be any input device, depending on the system) and store these three numbers in memory location HRS, RATE, and BONUS, respectively.

## 3-3-1  The FORMAT Statement

It is apparent that the READ statement by itself does not provide the computer sufficient information to know the following:

**1.** How many items there are per record.

**2.** In what position each data item starts.

**3.** How many positions are used for each data item (length of data item).

**4.** The type of the data field—integer, real or character.

This information is provided by a FORMAT statement, which is used in conjunction with the READ statement; the FORMAT statement tells the computer precisely how the READ operation is to be performed, that is, how to process the various data items on the input record.

Each READ statement must specify a FORMAT statement number; each FORMAT statement must have a statement number by which it can be referred to. The READ is an executable statement while the FORMAT is nonexecutable. The READ instruction is carried out according to the specifications described in the FORMAT. For this reason the FORMAT statement can be placed anywhere in the program (before the END statement).

Some programmers prefer to place all their FORMATs at the beginning or end of their programs, while others place them immediately following the associated READ statements.

*Example*

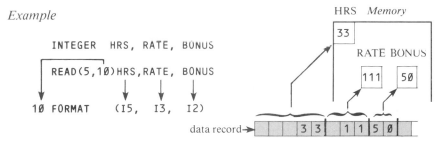

```
    INTEGER  HRS, RATE, BONUS
     _____
    READ(5,10)HRS,RATE, BONUS

10 FORMAT    (I5,  I3,  I2)
```

This input operation can be interpreted as follows:

Read three numbers (three variables are named) from a record (device number 5) according to the data layout described by the FORMAT labeled 10. FORMAT 10 can be interpreted as follows: The first number (HRS) will be an integer number (specified by the I format code) found in the first five positions (1–5). The next number (RATE) will be an integer number found in the next three positions (6–8), and the last number (BONUS) will be an integer found in the next two positions (9–10).

The general form of the FORMAT statement is:

> *statement number* FORMAT ($fd_1, fd_2, ..., fd_n$)

where *statement number* is the format label referred to in a **READ** statement; and $fd_1, fd_2, ..., fd_n$ are format codes, which can be either:

1. Data format codes to identify data on the record as either integer, real number, or character data, or

2. Edit codes to control editing of the input record.

Data format codes can be any of the following codes:

- F indicates a real number; that is, real data is to be read from the input record.

- I indicates an integer number.

- A indicates character data.

Edit codes allow the programmer to provide spaces between input fields (the X code, section 3–3–7), to control positioning of each input field (the T code, section 3–3–6), and to skip records (the slash '/' code, section 4–5–3).

### 3-3-2  The I Format Code

The general form of the I format code is:

$I w$

where I specifies that an integer is to be read and
      *w* specifies the width of the integer field (number of positions).

One position must be reserved for the minus sign if the integer is negative. Any blanks within the integer data field, whether leading, intermediate, or trailing, are interpreted as zeros; hence the integer number must be right-justified within the field. Integer data can consist only of the digits 0 through 9 and the + and − sign; any other character entered in an I field will result in an execution time READ error. The corresponding variable in the READ list must be an integer variable.

*Example*

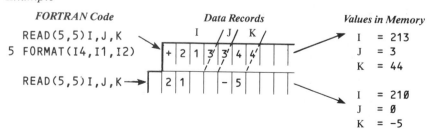

In this example the READ list specifies three numbers to be read. Since the FORMAT has three data format codes, this means that three numbers are to be read from one record.

Note that the leading and trailing blanks are read as zeros. Also note that the plus sign for I in the first data record is not really needed to identify a positive number. Reading starts at the first position of the record unless otherwise specified by T or X edit format codes. Each new field immediately follows the preceding field on the data record, as long as there are no other intervening control format codes.

### 3-3-3  The F Format Code

The general form of the F code is:

$$Fw.d$$

where F specifies that a real number is to read,

    *w* specifies the field width (number of positions), and

      *d* tells the system where to assume the decimal point in the number read into memory, in case no decimal point is entered in the number field.

If no decimal point is entered in the number field on the data record, *w* columns (positions) are read, and the number is stored in memory with the decimal point assumed to be *d* positions to the left of the rightmost digit specified in the field.

If a decimal point is entered in the number field, the number is read as is, into memory, and the implied position of the decimal point specified by *d* is disregarded. The presence of a decimal point on the data record overrides the implied position *d* which can be any number between 0 and *w*. For grammatical considerations, *d* must always be specified in the format even though it might not be used (as is the case when the decimal point is typed in the input field).

In all cases *d* must be such that $d \leq w$. Blanks within the field are treated as zeros. One position must be reserved in the input field for the minus sign if the real number is negative, and another position must be reserved for the decimal point if it is to be entered in the number field. Remember that *w* represents the number of positions to be read. If a decimal point is entered in the field, this position is counted as part of the field length *w*.

Variables in the READ list that are described by an F code in the format *must* be real type variables.

*Example 1*

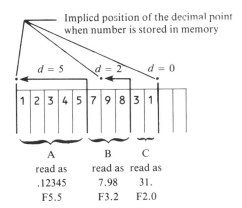

In this example three real numbers are to be read. The first one is located in the first five positions. Since no decimal point is entered in these five positions, the decimal point is assumed to be five positions to the left of the rightmost digit ($d = 5$); hence A = .12345; that is, A has five digits to the right of the decimal point. For B the decimal point is implied to be two positions to the left of the rightmost digit, 8, and hence B = 7.98. For C, the implied position of the decimal point is at the rightmost position of the field ($d = 0$).

*Example 2*

```
 READ(5,1)X,  Y,  Z
1 FORMAT(F5.5,F3.2,F2.0)
```

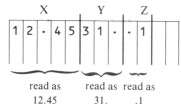

In this example decimal points have been entered in each field, hence the values for X, Y, and Z are those entered in the three fields. The explicit position of the decimal point overrides the implicit position as defined by $d$.

*Example 3*

```
 READ(5,5)X,  Y,  Z,   W
5 FORMAT(F1.1,F2.0,F3.2, F4.3)
```

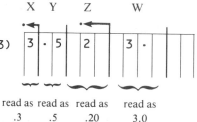

This example illustrates two ways to identify the position of the decimal point in data fields: explicitly (Y,W) and implicitly (X,Z).

*Example 4*

```
 READ(5,8)X,  Y,  Z
8 FORMAT(F4.2,F5.1,F2.0)
```

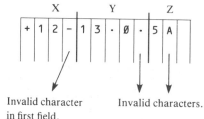

In this example a READ error would occur at execution time as a result of the invalid character ($-$) in the fourth position, the second decimal point in the Y field, and an illegal character (A) in the Z field. The program would generally stop at the first error spotted and an error message would be printed. Similar READ errors would also occur while reading integer data with invalid characters in the data fields.

## 3-3-4 Mixed-Mode Input

It is permissible to combine both real and integer variables in a READ list. The programmer must then make sure that each variable name in the READ list is properly described by a format code of the corresponding type. If a real variable name is read, its corresponding format code should be F; if an integer variable name is read, its corresponding format code should be I. If the names and corresponding format codes are not consistent, number conversion will take place, changing the value of the input data and thereby causing logical errors in the program. In some systems a READ error will occur terminating the program.

*Example*

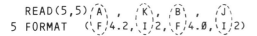

```
     READ(5,5) A ,  K ,  B ,  J
   5 FORMAT   (F4.2, I2, F4.0, I2)
```

Note the type correspondence between the variable names and their format codes.

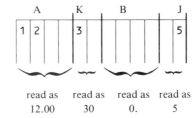

```
        A       K       B       J
     1  2     | 3     |       | 5
```

read as   read as   read as   read as
12.00      30        0.        5

### 3-3-5  The A Format Code

The A format code is used to read character type data. The general form of the A format code is:

$$
\begin{array}{c}
A \\
Aw
\end{array}
$$

where A specifies that character data is to be read and

w specifies the width of the input field on the input record. If w is omitted, the size of the input field is equal to the length of the variable specified in the CHARACTER statement.

*Example 1*

```
   CHARACTER*6 A,B,C
   READ(5,6)        A,        B,        C
 6 FORMAT (         A,        A3,       A8 )
```

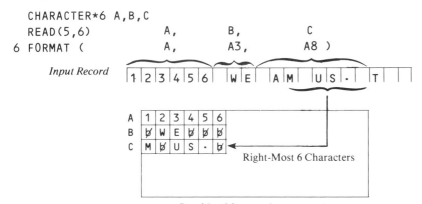

*Resulting Memory Arrangement*

Note that if the input field w is less than the size s of the character variable (as declared in the CHARACTER statement), the w characters are read from the input field and stored left-justified in memory with blanks to the right, to complete the memory width of the variable. If the input field w is larger than the size s of the character variable, the right-most s characters of the input field are read and stored in memory.

*Example 2*

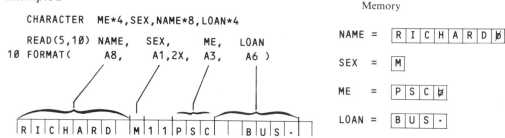

```
CHARACTER   ME*4,SEX,NAME*8,LOAN*4
READ(5,10) NAME,    SEX,     ME,    LOAN
10 FORMAT(   A8,     A1,2X,   A3,    A6 )
```

Memory

NAME = | R | I | C | H | A | R | D | ∅ |

SEX  = | M |

ME   = | P | S | C | ∅ |

LOAN = | B | U | S | . |

*Example 3*

Given the following record, the code to read the name, address, account number, and social security number would be:

| 01 02 03 | 04 05 06 07 08 09 10 11 | 12 | 13 14 15 16 17 18 19 20 21 22 23 24 25 | 26 | 27 28 29 30 31 32 33 | 34 | 35 36 37 38 39 40 41 42 43 |
|---|---|---|---|---|---|---|---|
| | Name | | Address | | Acct.Number | | Social Security # |

```
CHARACTER NAME*8, ADRESS*13, ACCT*7, SSNO*9
READ(5,7) NAME,ADRESS,ACCT,SSNO
7 FORMAT(T4,A,T13,A,T27,A,T35,A)
```

(The T format code is described in the following section.)

### 3-3-6  The T Format Code

The general form of the T format code is:

$$Tj$$

where $j$ is an integer specifying the starting position of the next input field to be read. The T code causes a data field to be read starting in column $j$.

*Example*

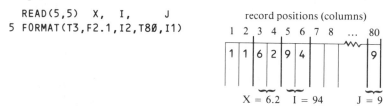

```
READ(5,5)  X,  I,     J
5 FORMAT(T3,F2.1,I2,T80,I1)
```

record positions (columns)

```
1 2 3 4 5 6 7 8 ... 80
1 1 6 2 9 4         9
```

X = 6.2   I = 94   J = 9

The T feature is generally not used to control the spacing between fields; it only identifies the first position of the field. This example can be interpreted as follows: Starting in position 3 (skip 1st two columns) find a real number two digits in length (positions 3 and 4); read it and store it in memory location X, then find an integer in the next two positions (5 and 6) and store it into I. Then go to position 80 and read one digit into J.

The T feature is extremely useful with prearranged data layouts where each field is known to start at a specific record position.

### 3-3-7 The X Format Code

The general form of the X format code is:

where $n$ is an integer specifying the number of positions to be skipped. The effect of the X code is to skip $n$ positions between fields.

*Example 1*

```
    READ(5,5)  X,       I,    J
  5 FORMAT(4X,F2.1,2X,I3,1X,I1)
```

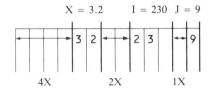

This example can be interpreted as follows: First skip four positions, and starting in position 5 find a two-digit real number, then skip two positions and find a two-digit integer, then skip one position and find a one-digit integer number.

A combination of both T and X can be used in the same format statement as in:

*Example 2*

```
    READ(5,7)  X,       I,    J,    Z
  7 FORMAT(T10,F3.2,2X,I1,3X,I2,T30,F4.1)
```

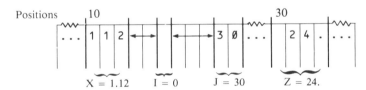

### 3-3-8 Do It Now

The data record below is to be read by each of the following READ statements. What value will be stored in each variable? (Assume CHARACTER V*4).

**Data Record**

```
| - | 2 | 3 | . | 4 | 5 | 0 | 0 | 6 |   |   | 3 | L | 0 | 0 | P | S |   |   |
```

1. 
```
    READ(5,7)I,A,B
  7 FORMAT(1X,I2,F3.0,F3.1)
```

2. 
```
    READ(5,8)X,Y,Z,V
  8 FORMAT(F4.2,F2.2,3X,F3.0,A5)
```

3. 
```
    READ(5,9)J1,J2,J3,V
  9 FORMAT(4X,I2,I3,I2,T16,A)
```

4. 
```
    READ(5,10)QR,ST,V
 10 FORMAT(T2,F3.0,T5,F2.2,5X,A2)
```

5. 
```
    READ(5,6)V,K
  6 FORMAT(A5,3X,I5)
```

## *Answers*

**1.** I = 23, A = .45, B = .6

**2.** X = −23., Y = .45, Z = 3., V = 'OOPS'

**3.** J1 = 45, J2 = 6, J3 = 0, V = 'PS*bb*'

**4.** QR = 23., ST = .45, V = '3L'

**5.** V = '23.4'; Read error, invalid character L.

### 3-3-9 The Duplication Factor

Many times a sequence of variables is read or printed, and each variable has the same format code description.

*Example 1*

```
    READ(5,101),X,Y,Z
101 FORMAT(F4.0, F4.0,F4.0)
```

In such instances the list of the format codes can be recorded using a duplication factor to specify the repetition of the format code. The following FORMAT statement is equivalent to statement 101 above:

$$\text{101 FORMAT(3F4.0)}$$

Any data format code can be duplicated in this way. A more general form for the data format codes is:

$$\boxed{n\text{F}w.d} \qquad \boxed{n\text{I}w} \qquad \boxed{n\text{A}w}$$

where *n* is the optional duplication factor; *n* must be an unsigned integer.

*Example 2*

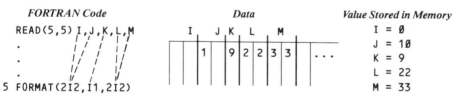

| FORTRAN Code | Data | Value Stored in Memory |
|---|---|---|
| READ(5,5) I,J,K,L,M | I  J K  L  M | I = 0 |
| . | 1 9 2 2 3 3 ... | J = 10 |
| . | | K = 9 |
| . | | L = 22 |
| 5 FORMAT(2I2,I1,2I2) | | M = 33 |

Five numbers are to be read. Instead of writing I2,I2,I1,I2,I2, the format list is made more compact by use of duplication factors: 2I2,I1,2I2.

*Example 3*

```
  WRITE(6,5)A,J,B,K,L,M,N
5 FORMAT(3X,2(F3.1,I2),3(2X,I1))
```

This format is equivalent to (3X,F3.1,I2,F3.1,I2,2X,I1,2X,I1,2X,I1)

with the first underbrace labeled 2 and the second underbrace labeled 3.

*Example 4*

```
  CHARACTER*8, NAME1, NAME2, NAME3
  READ(5,6)NAME1, NAME2, NAME3
6 FORMAT(3(A7,1X))
```

**Data Record**

| S | U | S | A | N | | | A | S | T | E | R | I | X | E | | S | O | N | I | A | | |
|---|---|---|---|---|---|---|---|---|---|---|---|---|---|---|---|---|---|---|---|---|---|---|

**Value Stored in Memory**

| NAME1 | S | U | S | A | N | | | |
|---|---|---|---|---|---|---|---|---|
| NAME2 | A | S | T | E | R | I | X | |
| NAME3 | | S | O | N | I | A | | |

*Example 5*

A literal string within a FORMAT can be repeated by enclosing the string within parentheses and specifying the duplication factor

```
   WRITE(6,7)
 7 FORMAT(1X,80('*'))
```

This will produce a string of 80 asterisks on the output line.

## 3-4 List-Directed Input

So far we have discussed FORMAT-controlled input through the READ statement. This form of input enables the programmer to decide exactly where the various input items are to be found or placed on the input record. In many commercial installations, input data is already preformatted, i.e., specific fields are reserved for the various input items. In such situations, only format-controlled input can be used since the user is given a data file whose record layout *cannot* be changed.

A format-free input is available to the user who is not really concerned about the layout of input records. The user simply lists (types) his/her input items one after the other on data records (data lines), separating each item in the input list by a comma or one or more spaces.

The general form of the list-directed input statement is:

READ*,*list*
where *list* is a list of variable names separated from one another by commas or spaces.

- Input items, which can be integer, real, or character constants, are read from data record(s) and placed into the memory locations corresponding to the variables in the READ list.
- Character constants *must* be enclosed within apostrophes.
- There must be agreement in type between each variable and the corresponding input item.
- As many data records (data lines) will be read as are needed to satisfy the READ list.
- An error message will result if there is insufficient data, i.e., if a variable is read but there is no corresponding input item.
- Each READ statement processes a new data record (data line).

*Example 1*    Assume the following type declarations:

```
CHARACTER NAME*8
INTEGER   COUNT
REAL      SUM
```

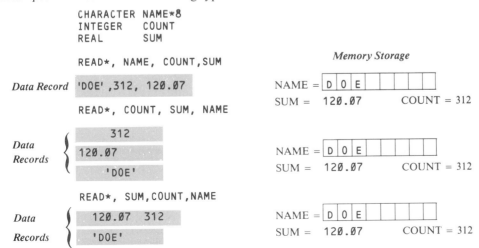

*Example 2*

```
CHARACTER*5 FIRM1,FIRM2
REAL A
INTEGER K
```

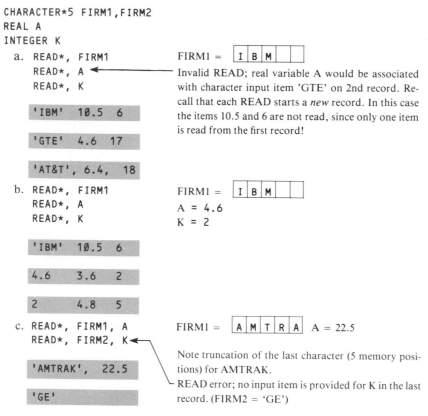

a. 
```
   READ*, FIRM1
   READ*, A  ◄─
   READ*, K
```
FIRM1 = | I | B | M |   |   |

Invalid READ; real variable A would be associated with character input item 'GTE' on 2nd record. Recall that each READ starts a *new* record. In this case the items 10.5 and 6 are not read, since only one item is read from the first record!

```
'IBM'  10.5  6

'GTE'  4.6  17

'AT&T', 6.4,  18
```

b. 
```
   READ*, FIRM1
   READ*, A
   READ*, K
```
FIRM1 = | I | B | M |   |   |

A = 4.6

K = 2

```
'IBM'  10.5  6

4.6    3.6   2

2      4.8   5
```

c. 
```
   READ*, FIRM1, A
   READ*, FIRM2, K ◄─
```
FIRM1 = | A | M | T | R | A |    A = 22.5

Note truncation of the last character (5 memory positions) for AMTRAK.

READ error; no input item is provided for K in the last record. (FIRM2 = 'GE')

```
'AMTRAK',  22.5

'GE'
```

The repetition factor * can be used as follows:

```
INTEGER A,B,C
REAL X,Y,Z,T
READ*, A,B,C,X,Y,Z,T
```

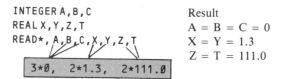

Result
A = B = C = 0
X = Y = 1.3
Z = T = 111.0

The asterisk * does not mean multiply, it indicates repetition of the input field.

### 3-4-1 **Do It Now**

Given the following coding segment, identify the value of each of the variables read.

```
CHARACTER NAME*4,LE*2
REAL A,B,C
INTEGER I,J,K
READ*, A,B,C,I
READ*, J
READ*, K,NAME,LE
```

```
2.3  4.1  2.0
2  3
5  'ELLA'
6
'UNITED',''''
```

*Answers*

A = 2.3
B = 4.1
C = 2.0
I = 2
J = 5
K = 6
NAME = | U | N | I | T |
LE = |   ' |   |

## 3-5 Flowcharts and Pseudo Code

The computer can function as a problem solver only if it is given instructions on how to proceed. A set of instructions for solving a problem is called an *algorithm*. People use algorithms of one type or another every day to solve such routine problems as baking a cake, operating an electrical appliance, or solving a quadratic equation. Algorithms can be expressed in verbal or symbolic form. To be useful, an algorithm must be expressed in a way that can be understood and executed by the person (or machine) for which it is intended. A computer *program* is a specific example of an algorithm intended for a machine. It is expressed in a symbolic language that the computer can readily understand and execute.

### 3-5-1 Flowcharts

The *flowchart* was one of the earliest techniques adopted by programmers for describing computer algorithms. A flowchart is a graphical representation of an algorithm. It illustrates the sequence of steps that are to be carried out in order to solve a particular problem. As an example, consider the flowchart in Figure 3–4, which a rather narrow-minded stu-

**FIGURE 3–4**   ALGORITHM FOR SELECTING COURSE SECTION

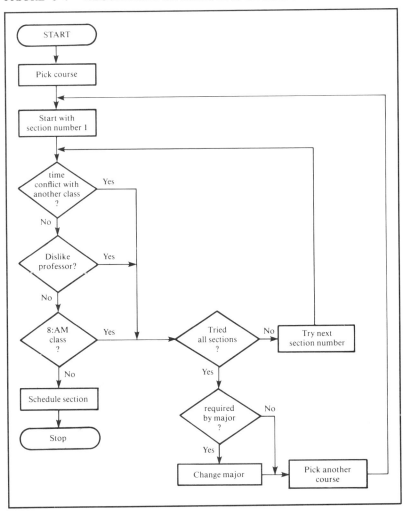

dent might use for selecting classes. The various block shapes represent the standard types of operations that are used in an algorithm, such as process (arithmetic calculations, data movement, and so forth), comparison, and input/output operations. English descriptions or algebraic expressions are placed inside the boxes to describe what actions are to be performed in each step of the algorithm. The lines connecting the boxes are called *flow lines*; they show the order in which steps are to be performed.

## Blocks

The oval, rectangle, diamond, and parallelogram are the four basic blocks used in flowcharting:

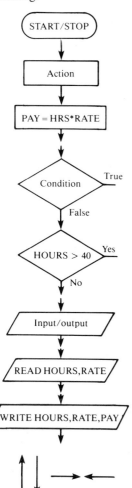

**Oval**—*terminal block*. This either marks the start or end of the algorithm.

**Rectangle**—*process block*. An explicit action such as the evaluation of an arithmetic expression is to be carried out.

**Diamond**—*decision block*. A question is posed, and the answer determines the next step to be performed. A decision box always has at least two flow lines coming out of it. Each is labeled to indicate which line to follow, based on whether the condition is currently true or false.

**Parallelogram**—*input/output block*. Data is either to be brought into the algorithm (READ) or results are to be written out by the algorithm (WRITE).

**Flowlines.** The sequence of instructions to be executed in a flowcharted algorithm is denoted by straight lines. The direction of flow is always in the direction indicated by the arrowhead.

## Connector Blocks

Connectors are often used when it is inconvenient to draw flowlines to connect one area of the flowchart to another. Connectors serve two purposes:

1. to label a block for reference purposes, and

2. to indicate transfer to another labeled block.

The symbol used for a connector is a small circle ◯ . A numeric or alphabetic label is placed in the connector block. When the flowline points away from the connector ◯→ , the connector denotes an entry point, that is, a block to which transfer will be made from some other point in the flowchart. When the flowline points toward the connector ◯← , the connector is being used to indicate a transfer, that is, execution will resume at an entry point with the same symbol as used in the connector at the transfer point. For example, consider the following flowchart segment:

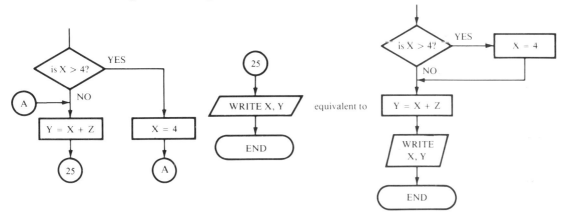

If the value of X is less than or equal to 4, the block containing Y = X + Z is executed and transfer is made to the entry point marked 25, which is the WRITE instruction. If the value of X is greater than 4, the block containing X = 4 is executed and transfer is made to the entry point labeled A. Note that in a flowchart it is possible to have many transfer connectors with the same label, such as Ⓐ→ , but there can be only one entry connector →Ⓐ in a flowchart.

## Flowchart Statements

In this section we consider the particular actions, conditions, and input/output lists specified in the flowchart rectangles, diamonds, and parallelograms.

A difficult decision in writing algorithms in the form of flowcharts is how to write the statements in the flowchart blocks. Should the statements be written using an algebraic notation or in English? How detailed should the statements be? Should the statements essentially mirror FORTRAN instructions? The answer to the last question is a definite no. The whole purpose of developing a flowchart is to avoid becoming entangled in the details of a particular programming language. As we will see in chapter 4, top-down design encourages the use of very general statements in our first attempt at a solution. Later, after the structure of the entire algorithm has been developed, the details can be added as needed.

The choice between English and an algebraic notation is partly a matter of personal style. In many cases, however, a verbal description of the step can provide more information about what is to be done than the equivalent algebraic statement would provide. For example, the statement "compute overtime pay" may have more meaning than:

$$\text{overtime} = (\text{hours} - 40) \times \text{rate} \times 1.5$$

when we are trying to understand and construct the overall logic of a payroll program. The ultimate choice of how to write a particular statement or condition is a personal choice, but you should never lose sight of the purpose of a flowchart, which is to provide a clear and easily understood description of an algorithm.

## Variable Names

A second concern is the choice of variable names in an algorithm. In chapter 2 we learned that FORTRAN restricts our choice of names. In designing an algorithm, however, there is no real need to be limited by FORTRAN restrictions. If a 10-character or two-word name does a good job of describing the function of a variable, then why not use it? The purpose of a variable named "hourly__pay" is obvious; the abbreviation HRPAY may not be as obvious. After the algorithm is developed, the names used in the algorithm can easily be translated into valid FORTRAN names. In this text we will use the underline symbol (__) to connect a multi-word name as a way to emphasize that this is a name for a single variable.

A flowchart of the payroll problem in section 3–1 is shown in Figure 3–5. Study this flowchart and notice how the flow lines lead us from step to step in the algorithm and how the decision boxes cause alternative actions to be performed based on the input data.

## Limitations of Flowcharts

A flowchart is an excellent tool for presenting the structure and logic of an algorithm. As you might imagine, however, the flowchart can be a cumbersome tool to use during the developmental stage when an algorithm is being changed frequently. A correction or change in the logic can require redrawing the entire flowchart. It is also difficult to convert a flowchart into actual code in a straightforward manner; the horizontal and vertical dispersion of the various blocks must somehow be translated into a vertical sequence of FORTRAN instructions. Because of these disadvantages, a newer design tool, called *pseudo code*, has gained widespread acceptance as a developmental tool for describing algorithms.

**FIGURE 3–5**   FLOWCHART FOR PAYROLL PROBLEM

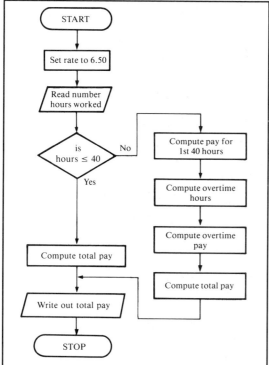

## 3-5-2  **Do It Now**

**1.** Is a recipe in a cookbook an example of a flowchart? an algorithm? a program?

**2.** Determine the output produced by the following flowcharts, given the following data records:

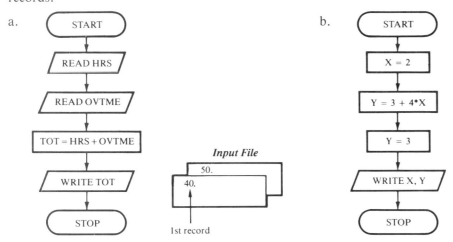

a.

b.

### *Answers*

**1.** A recipe, if carefully written, is an example of an algorithm.

**2.** a.  90    b.  2,3

## 3-5-3  **Pseudo Code**

*Pseudo code* provides an Englishlike mechanism for describing algorithms. As we saw in the pseudo code solution to the payroll problem in Section 3–1, algorithms expressed in pseudo code are compact and easy to read. Modifications to pseudo code algorithms are relatively straightforward, since they involve little more than deleting or moving existing instructions or inserting new instructions.

Even though pseudo code is a more flexible development tool than flowcharts, algorithms expressed in pseudo code must still conform to basic standards and be in a form that is easily understood and that can be easily translated into a computer language. In this section we will establish the pseudo code notation that will be used throughout this text. In chapter 4 we will find that converting a well-written pseudo code algorithm into FORTRAN is a relatively direct and natural process.

### *Statements*

The guidelines for writing statements for flowcharts also apply to pseudo code algorithms. The purpose of a statement is to clearly state what action is to be carried out at this point in the algorithm. We shall follow the convention of writing pseudo code in lowercase characters, reserving uppercase characters for key words such as IF THEN ELSE, WHILE DO, IF, and STOP. These key words have special meanings that will be described later.

## Variables

Variables also serve the same function as they did in flowcharts. Because of the Englishlike nature of pseudo code, careful choice of descriptive variable names can make an algorithm particularly easy to read and understand.

## Input/Output

The pseudo code instructions READ and WRITE serve the same function as the parallelogram block in a flowchart. The command READ indicates that data should be brought into the algorithm; WRITE indicates that results should be listed.

## STOP

The STOP pseudo code statement simply marks the end of the algorithm.

## Comments

Lines that begin with an asterisk (*) are comments that provide additional information on what the algorithm is doing. They serve the same purpose as comment statements in a FORTRAN program. Although pseudo code is already very descriptive, there is still a need to summarize the function of groups of statements and describe how they relate to the logic of the overall algorithm. Pseudo code comments can be incorporated into the FORTRAN program when it is coded. Your algorithm should always begin with comments that describe the problem being solved by the algorithm. A descriptive comment should also precede each major step in the algorithm.

# 3-6  The GO TO and IF Statements

### 3-6-1  The Unconditional Transfer Statement GO TO

The general form of an unconditional transfer statement GO TO is:

```
GO TO transfer statement number
```

FORTRAN processes the statements in a FORTRAN program one after another in sequential order. When a FORTRAN program encounters a GO TO statement during execution, it will transfer control to the statement specified; that is, processing will continue at the transfer statement number. This allows the programmer to bypass certain instructions in the program. It also allows the program to branch back to repeat (reprocess) certain instructions or certain procedures; this is called *looping*. (If we added the statement GO TO 5 immediately after the WRITE statement in the program of Figure 3–1, the computer could execute the entire program again and again, with a new value for HOURS each time.)

*Example*

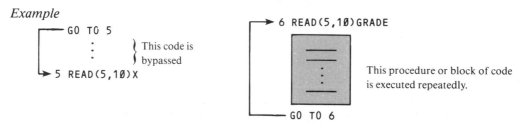

Once again the reader is reminded that FORTRAN statement numbers need not be in ascending or descending order; statement numbers, however, must be entered in positions 1 through 5.

## 3-6-2 Types of Comparisons

The logical unit of the central processing unit can compare two numeric operands or two character operands, but it *cannot* compare a numeric operand with a character operand. Numbers (numeric operands) are compared algebraically, based on their signs and magnitudes, for example:

$$1 < 23456$$
$$-345 < -12$$

Character data are compared character by character from left to right according to the collating sequence shown below. If the two character operands to be compared are of unequal length, the shorter operand is filled with blanks to the right until it is as long as the other operand. In FORTRAN the following collating sequence is always used:

$$\text{blank} < A < B < C < ... < Y < Z$$
$$\text{and}$$
$$0 < 1 < 2 < ... < 8 < 9$$

Depending on the code used to represent characters internally (EBCDIC/ASCII), the digits may all be "less" than the letters of the alphabet (ASCII code) or "larger" than the letters of the alphabet (EBCDIC code).

*Examples*

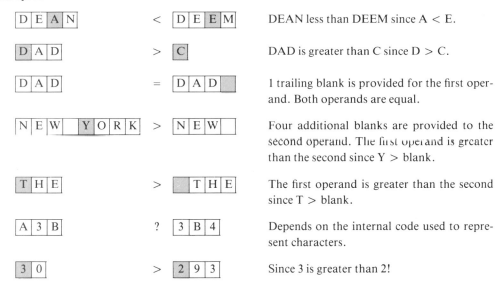

| | | |
|---|---|---|
| DEAN | < DEEM | DEAN less than DEEM since A < E. |
| DAD | > C | DAD is greater than C since D > C. |
| DAD | = DAD_ | 1 trailing blank is provided for the first operand. Both operands are equal. |
| NEW YORK | > NEW | Four additional blanks are provided to the second operand. The first operand is greater than the second since Y > blank. |
| THE | > _THE | The first operand is greater than the second since T > blank. |
| A3B | ? 3B4 | Depends on the internal code used to represent characters. |
| 30 | > 293 | Since 3 is greater than 2! |

## 3-6-3 The Logical IF Statement, Version 1

Recall that the central processing unit (CPU) has a unit to carry out logical operations. This hardware feature enables the computer to compare numbers or character strings and make decisions based on those comparisons. The computer's ability to make decisions is probably one of its most powerful and desirable characteristics. A computer stripped of its logical capability would be no more than an extremely fast calculator that could only process sequential arithmetic and input/output instructions.

The IF statement allows the computer to transfer to a nonsequential instruction in a program, depending on whether certain conditions are met. In this way a program can contain several alternate paths that are data dependent. Certain blocks of FORTRAN statements can be bypassed in the program by transferring to a nonsequential instruction.

A very useful form of the logical IF statement is:

IF *(logical expression)* GO TO *statement number*

where *logical expression* consists of two arithmetic expressions or two character operands linked together by one of the relational operators shown in Figure 3–6. The reader can think of a logical expression as a proposition, i.e., a statement that is either true or false. For example, the statements "I am 36" and "NAME = 'SUSAN'" are either true or false.

*Statement number* is the statement transferred to if the logical expression is true, that is, if the condition specified in the decision statement is met. If the condition is not met (logical expression is false), control is passed to the statement immediately following the IF statement.

The logical IF can be flowcharted as follows:

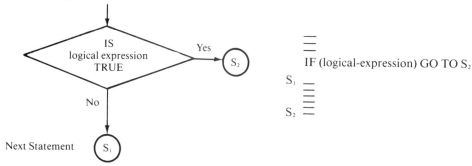

Note that $S_1$ immediately follows the IF statement, whereas $S_2$ can precede the IF statement or be anywhere after $S_1$.

**FIGURE 3–6**   FORTRAN RELATIONAL OPERATORS

| *FORTRAN Relational Operators* | *Mathematical Symbols* | *Meaning* |
|---|---|---|
| .EQ. | = | Equal to |
| .LT. | < | Less than |
| .GT. | > | Greater than |
| .NE. | ≠ | Not equal to |
| .LE. | ≤ | Less than or equal to |
| .GE. | ≥ | Greater than or equal to |

*Example*

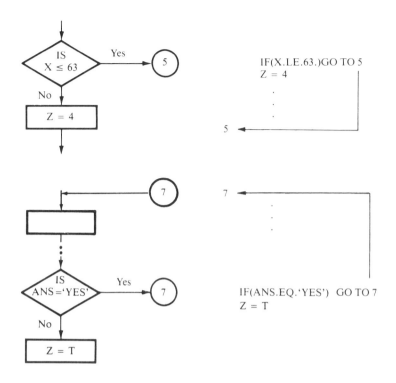

Figure 3-7 displays numerous examples of logical IFs and their meanings.

**FIGURE 3-7** EXAMPLES OF LOGICAL IF STATEMENTS

| *Logical IF Statements* | *Meaning* |
|---|---|
| 1 IF(X .EQ. 0.)GO TO 5<br>  A=4. | If X = 0., transfer to statement 5; otherwise (if X is less than or greater than 0), process the next statement. |
|   IF (CITY .EQ. 'PARIS')GO TO 9<br>    CITY='ROME' | CITY must be declared as CHARACTER data. IF CITY = 'PARIS' transfer to 9, otherwise store 'ROME' in location CITY. |
| 4 IF((X-Y)**2 .LT. Z)GO TO 40<br>8 IF(Z.GT.2.)GO TO 60 | If $(X - Y)^2 < Z$, process statement 40; otherwise (if $(X - Y)^2 \geq Z$), fall through and execute statement 8. |
| 5 IF(SQRT(X) .GE. 2.)GO TO 50<br>  WRITE(6,11)X | If $\sqrt{X} \geq 2$, go to 50. If $\sqrt{X} < 2$, process the next sequential statement. |
| 2 IF(X+Y .NE. (J-K))GO TO 70<br>  READ(5,5)A | If X + Y = J − K, process the next statement; otherwise go to statement 70. |

To better understand the logical IF statement and its interaction with other FOR-TRAN statements in a program, consider the following examples:

*Example 1*

Read an integer number I from a record and determine whether I is even or odd. Since integer division results in the truncation of all digits to the right of the decimal point, the following statements are true:

If I is even, then 2*(I/2) = I     For example, if I = 4, then 2*(4/2) = 2*2 = 4
IF I is odd, then 2*(I/2) ≠ I     For example, if I = 5, then 2*(5/2) = 2*2 = 4 ≠ 5

This example is flowcharted and coded in Figure 3–8.

The reader should analyze the FORTRAN program of Figure 3–8 to understand why the STOP statement is needed. If this statement were omitted, both messages I IS ODD and I IS EVEN would be printed every time I was odd. The STOP statement is required to by-pass statement number 15. Actually the statement GO TO 5 could have been used instead of the STOP statement.

FORTRAN logical IF statements allow for only a two-way transfer; that is, either the condition tested for is met or it is not met. If a decision involves a three-way outcome, two logical IF statements are required.

**FIGURE 3–8**   THE LOGICAL IF STATEMENT

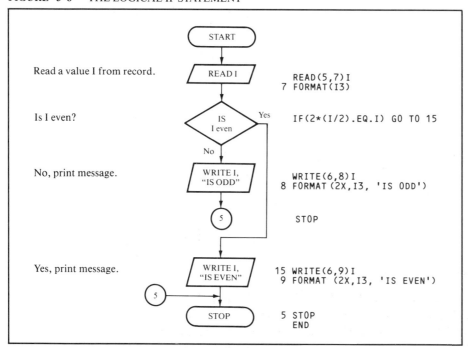

*Example 2*   Read a number N and write a program to do the following:

If N > 0, write the code POS on the output medium.
If N = 0, write the code ZERO on the output medium.
If N < 0, write the code NEG on the output medium.

**FIGURE 3-9** A THREE-WAY DECISION

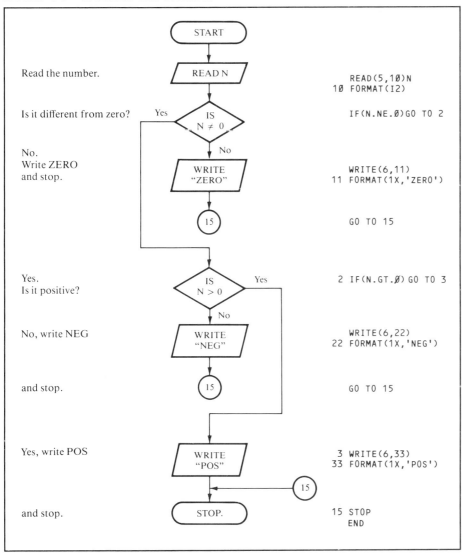

The flowchart and program are shown in Figure 3-9.

As displayed in Figure 3-9, the sequence of FORTRAN instructions parallels the physical sequence of the flowchart blocks. Note the importance and necessity of the two GO TO 15 statements after the WRITE(6,11) and WRITE(6,22) instructions. If N were zero and the two GO TO 15s were omitted, the message ZERO would be written as a result of the WRITE(6,11), then the computer would execute the instruction WRITE(6,22), which would write NEG, and finally the WRITE(6,33) would be processed, printing the message POS. Altogether, three messages would be printed instead of the single correct one. Note, however, that there is no need for a GO TO 15 after statement 3 since the STOP statement is the next executable statement following statement 3.

### 3-6-4 Do It Now

Write the FORTRAN code for each of the following flowcharts:

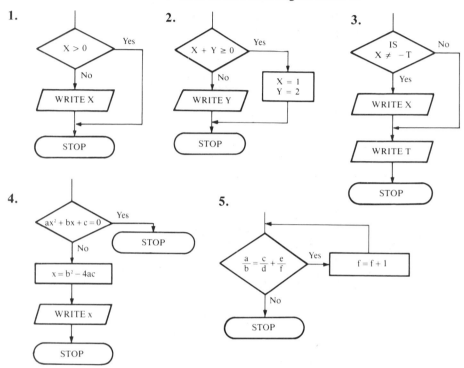

*Answers*   (the FORMAT statements have been omitted):

```
1.      IF(X .GT. Ø.) GO TO 1Ø
        WRITE(6,11)X
    1Ø STOP
```

```
2.      IF((X+Y) .GE. Ø.) GO TO 2Ø
        WRITE(6,12)Y
        STOP
    2Ø X=1.
        Y=2.
        STOP
```

```
3.      IF(X .EQ. −T) GO TO 4Ø
        WRITE(6,13)X
    4Ø WRITE(6,13)T
        STOP
```

```
4.      IF(A*X**2 + B*X + C .EQ. Ø.) GO TO 3Ø
        X = B**2 − 4.*A*C
        WRITE(6,14)X
    3Ø STOP
```

```
5.      3Ø IF(A/B .EQ. C/D + E/F) GO TO 4Ø
        STOP
    4Ø F = F+1.
        GO TO 3Ø
```

### 3-6-5 The Logical IF Statement, Version 2

The logical IF is somewhat more powerful than has been previously shown. The general form of the IF statement is:

IF *(logical expression) statement*

where *logical expression* consists of two arithmetic expressions or two character operands linked by one of the logical operators .LE., .GT., .EQ. and so forth, and *statement* is any executable statement *except* another IF statement or DO statement (see chapter 5). Note that only *one* statement is permitted on the same line as the IF.

If the condition described by the logical expression is met (the value of the logical expression is true), the statement on the same line as the IF statement is executed after which control is passed to the statement following the IF statement. If the condition is not met (the value of the logical expression is false) control is passed to the statement following the IF.

*Examples*

```
5 IF(A.LT.B)K=K+1
10 IF(A.EQ.4.) GO TO 1
```
If A < B, the statement K = K + 1 will be executed. Then statement 10 will be processed. If A ≥ B, statement 10 is processed next.

```
8 IF (CODE.NE.0.)WRITE(6,1)A
6 STOP
```
If CODE ≠ 0., A will be printed before terminating. If CODE = 0., the program is terminated.

```
7 IF(A.GT.3.)IF(A.LT.1.)K=K+1
8 Y = 0.
```
This is an invalid logical IF. The statement may not be another IF.

Since only one statement is grammatically permissible on the same line as the logical IF statement, an unusual code is required for the following flowchart:

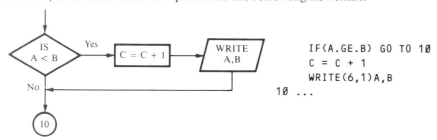

```
IF(A.GE.B) GO TO 10
   C = C + 1
   WRITE(6,1)A,B
10 ...
```

Another situation where a particular flowchart requires a cumbersome code is as follows:

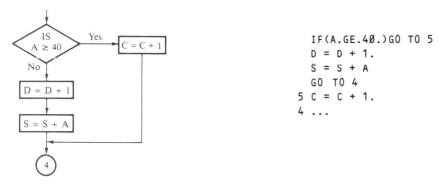

```
   IF(A.GE.40.)GO TO 5
   D = D + 1.
   S = S + A
   GO TO 4
 5 C = C + 1.
 4 ...
```

If the above flowchart were coded as follows:

```
   IF(A.GE.40.)C = C + 1.
   D = D + 1.
   S = S + A
 4 ...
```

Every time statement C = C + 1. is carried out the statements D = D + 1. and S = S + A will also be carried out. This is contrary to the flowchart.

then when $A \geq 40$, statements $D = D + 1$ and $S = S + A$ would be executed in addition to $C = C + 1$. This is clearly wrong.

The reader also should not be tempted to code the flowchart as:

```
IF(A.GE.40)C = C + 1, GO TO 4
```

Only one statement is permitted on the same line as the IF statement.

### 3-6-6  Do It Now

**1.** Write the code to solve the following:

    If code = 1 set BONUS equal to 100
    If code = 2 set BONUS equal to 300
    If code = 3 set BONUS equal to 500
    Otherwise        set BONUS to 1000

**2.** Write the FORTRAN code corresponding to the following flowchart:

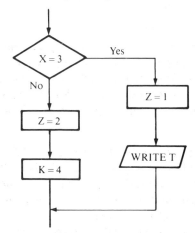

### *Answers*

**1.**
```
INTEGER CODE, BONUS
BONUS = 1000
IF(CODE .EQ. 1) BONUS = 100
IF(CODE .EQ. 2) BONUS = 300
IF(CODE .EQ. 3) BONUS = 500
```

**2.**
```
    INTEGER X,Z,K
    IF(X .EQ. 3) GO TO 10
    Z = 2
    K = 4
    GO TO 60
10  Z = 1
    WRITE(6,8)T
60
```

### 3-6-7  The Selection Structure: IF THEN ELSE

ANSI 1977 FORTRAN provides another way to express logical IF statements. This feature, the IF THEN ELSE statement, enhances the clarity and readability of FORTRAN code by reducing the use of the GO TO statements.

The following diagram illustrates the general form of the IF THEN ELSE structure:

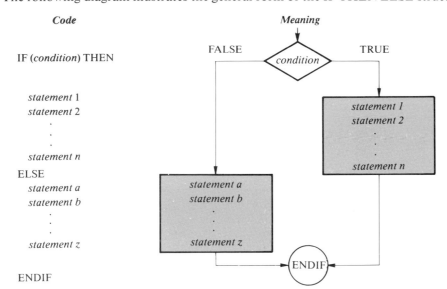

| Code | Meaning |
|------|---------|

IF (*condition*) THEN

    *statement* 1
    *statement* 2
    .
    .
    *statement n*
ELSE
    *statement a*
    *statement b*
    .
    .
    *statement z*

ENDIF

where *statement 1*,... can be any FORTRAN statements. If *condition* is true, *statement 1, statement 2,..., statement n* (i.e., all statements up to the ELSE word) are executed, after which control is passed to the statement following the ENDIF statement. If *condition* is false, *statement a, statement b,..., statement z* (i.e., all statements between ELSE and ENDIF) are executed, after which control is passed to the statement following the ENDIF statement.

Note the indentation of the statements within the IF/ELSE and ELSE/ENDIF intervals to improve readability and comprehension. The ENDIF key word must be included if the IF/THEN option is used. The three key words IF, ELSE, and ENDIF should be aligned; a common practice is to set off the inner statements of the IF/THEN structure at least four positions to the right of the IF, ELSE, and ENDIF key words.

The ELSE and ENDIF statements should not have numeric labels, meaning that one should not transfer to (GO TO) either the ELSE or ENDIF statements.

The pseudo code representing the IF THEN ELSE statements takes on the same structure as the IF THEN ELSE FORTRAN instruction, as shown in the following example.

*Example 1*
Read a number of hours worked and a rate of pay to compute an employee's paycheck.

| Pseudo Code | FORTRAN Code |
|-------------|--------------|
| READ hours and rate | `READ(5,6)HRS,RATE` |
| IF hours < = 40 THEN | `IF  (HRS.LE.40.) THEN` |
|     compute gross__pay | `    TOTPAY=HRS*RATE` |
| ELSE | `ELSE` |
|     compute overtime__pay | `    OVTPAY=(HRS-40.)*RATE*1.5` |
|     compute gross__pay | `    TOTPAY=OVTPAY + 40.*RATE` |
| ENDIF | `ENDIF` |
| WRITE gross__pay | `WRITE(6,8)TOTPAY` |
|  | `6 FORMAT(F5.1,F6.2)` |
|  | `8 FORMAT(1X,'TOTAL PAY=',F9.2)` |

The code could be shortened by the use of the logical IF as follows:

```
TOTPAY = HRS * RATE
IF (HRS .GT. 40.) TOTPAY = TOTPAY + .5*(HRS - 40.)*RATE
WRITE(6,8) TOTPAY
```

Sometimes an alternate action is not required if *condition* is false. In that case, the ELSE key word can be omitted, which leads to the simpler structure:

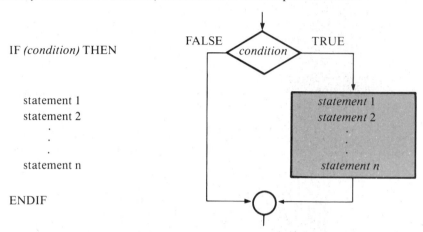

IF *(condition)* THEN

    statement 1
    statement 2
    .
    .
    .
    statement n

ENDIF

If *condition* is true, the block of statements, *statement 1,..., statement n*, is executed and control is passed to the statement following the ENDIF. If *condition* is false, control is passed to the statement following the ENDIF.

*Example 2*

Read SALES, HOURS and RATE. Compute the pay (HOURS*RATE). If SALES exceeds $10,000, add a bonus equal to 10% of SALES to the pay and print the bonus. Otherwise there is no bonus. Print out the total pay.

| *IF THEN Structure* | *Logical IF Structure* |
|---|---|
| `READ(5,8)SALES,HRS,RATE` | `READ(5,8)SALES,HRS,RATE` |
| `BONUS=0.` | `BONUS=0.` |
| `IF (SALES.GT.10000.) THEN` | `IF (SALES.GT.10000.) GO TO 8` |
| `   BONUS=.1*SALES` | `GO TO 7` |
| `   WRITE(6,5)BONUS` | `8 BONUS=.1*SALES` |
| `ENDIF` | `   WRITE(6,5)BONUS` |
| `PAY=HRS*RATE+BONUS` | `7 PAY=HRS*RATE+BONUS` |
| `WRITE(6,6)PAY` | `   WRITE(6,6)PAY` |

The unstructured (logical IF) code could have been simplified somewhat by using the statement IF (SALES.LE.10000); however, this does not translate directly the phrase "If the amount of sales exceeds $10,000..." stated in the problem.

## Nested IF/THEN Structures

We often need to include an IF THEN ELSE structure within another IF THEN ELSE structure. This usually occurs when more than two alternative actions are associated with the value of a single variable. Consider the following problem. A salesperson is assigned a commission on the following basis:

| *Sales* | *Commission (percentage of sales)* |
|---|---|
| Under $500 | 2% |
| $500 and under $5000 | 5% |
| $5000 and over | 8% |

Two different approaches to this problem and two different nested structures are:

## Approach 1

```
IF (SALES.LT.500.) THEN

    COM=.02*SALES
ELSE
    IF(SALES.LT.5000.)THEN

        COM=.05*SALES
    ELSE
        COM=.08*SALES

    ENDIF
ENDIF

WRITE(6,5)COM
```

## Approach 2

```
IF (SALES.GE.500.)THEN

    IF(SALES.GE.5000.)THEN

        COM=.08*SALES
    ELSE
        COM=.05*SALES
    ENDIF
ELSE
        COM=.02*SALES
ENDIF

WRITE(6,5)COM
```

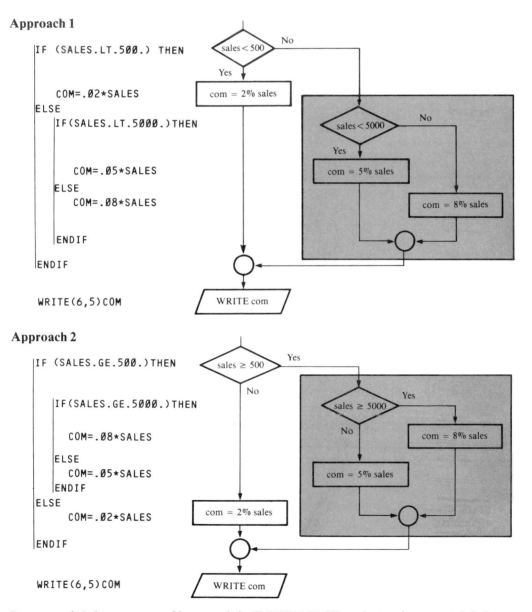

In approach 1 the sequence of key words is IF THEN ELSE...whereas in approach 2 the sequence is IF THEN IF... The first approach may be easier to read in this case.

IF THEN [ELSE] structures may be nested within one another as long as they are wholly contained within an IF ELSE, or an ELSE ENDIF or an IF ENDIF (no ELSE) coding segments. Each IF THEN statement requires a separate ENDIF statement as shown in the following examples:

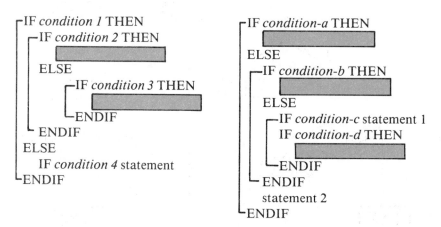

Note that the logical IF statement can be included in such nested structures as in the above examples with condition 4 and condition-c.

### 3-6-8 Do It Now

Test your IFFY judgment

**1.** Which of the following are equivalent?

```
IF (X.EQ.1)THEN          IF(X.EQ.1)A=1
    A=1                  IF(X.EQ.2)B=1
ELSE                     IF(X.EQ.3)THEN
    IF(X.EQ.2)THEN           C=1
        B=1              ELSE
    ELSE                     D=1
        IF(X.EQ.3)THEN   ENDIF
            C=1
        ELSE
            D=1
        ENDIF
    ENDIF
ENDIF
```

**2.** Compare these codes under the following conditions:

(1) K is neither 1 nor 2, and
(2) for all values of K.

```
IF(K.NE.2)THEN           IF(K.NE.1)THEN
    B=1                      A=1
    IF(K.NE.1)THEN           IF(K.NE.2)THEN
        A=1                      B=1
    ENDIF                    ENDIF
ENDIF                    ENDIF
```

### Answers

**1.** not equivalent; see what happens if X = 1 for example.
**2.** case 1, equivalent; case 2, not equivalent

### 3-6-9 The ELSE IF THEN Statement

The ELSE IF THEN structure is a more compact notation for a series of IF THEN ELSE structures. In the following diagram the numbered blocks 1, 2, 3 and 4 represent possible other IF THEN ELSE ENDIF, IF THEN ENDIF, logical IF's and ELSE IF THEN structures; these must have their controlled statements within their own block.

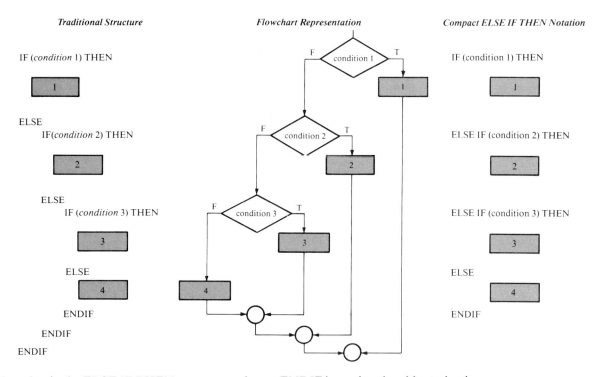

| Traditional Structure | Flowchart Representation | Compact ELSE IF THEN Notation |

Note that in the ELSE IF THEN structure only *one* ENDIF is used and no identation is necessary. Also note that if block 1 is executed, control is then passed to the ENDIF statement, as it is after execution of blocks 2, 3, and 4.

*Example*

Write the code to read a numerical marital status code (1 = married, 2 = divorced, 3 = single, 4 = widowed) and print the corresponding English word. If the code is neither 1, 2, 3, or 4, print an error message

```
READ*, MS                   read marital status code
IF(MS.EQ.1) THEN
    PRINT*,'MARRIED'
ELSE IF(MS.EQ.2) THEN
    PRINT*,'DIVORCED'
ELSE IF(MS.EQ.3) THEN
    PRINT*,'SINGLE'
ELSE IF(MS.EQ.4) THEN
    PRINT*,'WIDOWED'
ELSE                        If no error message were to be printed the
    PRINT*'ERROR'           last ELSE statement would have been omitted.
ENDIF
```

## 3-6-10 Do It Now

**1.** A special code K is used for student classifications as follows:

| Value of K | Verbal Description |
| --- | --- |
| 1 | Freshman |
| 2 | Sophomore |
| 3 | Junior |

Write the FORTRAN code to read a numeric value for K and print the verbal description (word) corresponding to the value of K. If K is neither 1, 2, or 3, print an error message.

**2.** Write the FORTRAN code for the following flowcharts using the IF THEN ELSE:

a.                                b.

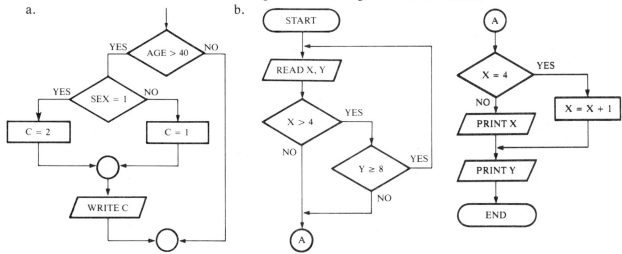

**3.** Which of the following are equivalent coding segments?

a.
```
   IF(X .EQ. '1') THEN            IF(X .EQ. '1') THEN
      PRINT*,A                       PRINT*,A
   ENDIF                         ELSE
   IF(X .EQ. '2') THEN              IF(X .EQ. '2') THEN
      PRINT*,B                         PRINT*,B
   ENDIF                            ENDIF
                                 ENDIF
```

b.
```
   IF(X .GT. 1) THEN             IF(X .GT. 1) THEN
      A = A+1                       A = A+1
   ELSE                          ENDIF
      IF(X .GT. 2) THEN          IF(X .GT. 2) THEN
         C = C+1                    C = C+1
      ENDIF                      ENDIF
   ENDIF
```

c.
```
   IF(KODE .EQ. 1) THEN          IF(KODE .EQ. 1) THEN
      PRINT*,B                      PRINT*,B
      IF(KODE .EQ. 2) THEN       ELSE
         PRINT*,D                   IF(KODE .EQ. 2) THEN
      ENDIF                           PRINT*,D
   ENDIF                            ENDIF
                                 ENDIF
```

In parts d through f, assume K takes on values 1, 2, or 3.

d.
```
   IF(K .NE. 1) THEN             IF(K .EQ. 2) THEN
      PRINT*,A                      IF(K .EQ. 3) THEN
   ENDIF                              PRINT*,A
                                   ENDIF
                                 ENDIF
```

```
e. IF(K .NE. 1) THEN        IF(K .EQ. 1) THEN     IF(K.EQ.2 .OR. K.EQ.3)THEN
       PRINT*,A                PRINT*,B              PRINT*,A
    IF(K .NE. 2) THEN       ELSE                  ELSE
       PRINT*,B                PRINT*,A              PRINT*,B
    ENDIF                   ENDIF                 ENDIF
    ENDIF
```

```
f. IF(K .GT. 1) THEN        IF(K .LE. 1) THEN
       A = A+1                 IF(K .LE. 2) THEN
    ELSE                          C = C+1
       IF(K .GT. 2) THEN       ELSE
          B = B+1                 B = B+1
       ELSE                   ENDIF
          C = C+1           ELSE
       ENDIF                   A = A+1
    ENDIF                   ENDIF
```

4. Assume that K takes on integer values between 1 and 6 in the following two coding segments. Which variables (A, B, C, D, E, or F) will be printed for each value of K?

```
a. IF(K .NE. 1) THEN       b. IF(K .GE. 3) THEN
    IF(K .NE. 4) THEN          IF(K .LT. 5) THEN
    IF(K .GT. 3) THEN             PRINT*,A
       PRINT*,F                ENDIF
    ELSE                      ENDIF
       PRINT*,E               IF(K .GT. 3) THEN
    ELSE                      IF(K .EQ. 6) THEN
       PRINT*,D                  PRINT*,B
    ELSE                      ELSE
       IF(K .NE. 2) THEN         IF(K .LE. 6) THEN
       IF(K .GT. 3) THEN            PRINT*,D
          PRINT*,C               ENDIF
       ELSE                   ENDIF
          PRINT*,B           ELSE
       ELSE                     PRINT*,C
          PRINT*,A           ENDIF
       ENDIF
       ENDIF
    ENDIF
    ENDIF
    ENDIF
```

## Answers

```
1.   READ(5,6)K              READ(5,6)K
     IF(K .EQ. 1) THEN       IF(K .EQ. 1) THEN
        PRINT*,'FRESHMAN'       PRINT*,'FRESHMAN'
     ELSE                    ELSE IF (K .EQ. 2) THEN
        IF(K .EQ. 2) THEN  or   PRINT*,'SOPHOMORE'
           PRINT*,'SOPHOMORE'  ELSE IF (K .EQ. 3) THEN
        ELSE                   PRINT*,'JUNIOR'
           IF(K .EQ. 3) THEN  ELSE
              PRINT*,'JUNIOR'    PRINT*,'ERROR'
           ELSE              ENDIF
              PRINT*,'ERROR'
           ENDIF
        ENDIF
     ENDIF
```

2. a.
```
IF(AGE .GT. 40) THEN
    IF(SEX .EQ. 1) THEN
        C = 2
    ELSE
        C = 1
    ENDIF
    PRINT*,C
ENDIF
```

b.
```
10 READ*,X,Y
   IF(X .GT. 4) THEN
       IF(Y .GE. 8) GO TO 10
   ENDIF
   IF(K .EQ. 4) THEN
       X = X+1
   ELSE
       PRINT*,X
   ENDIF
   PRINT*,Y
   STOP
```

3. a. Identical.
   b. Not identical. For example, suppose X = 3. In case 1, 1 will be added only to A, whereas in case 2, 1 will be added to A and C.
   c. Not identical. D will never be printed in case 1.
   d. Not identical. If K = 3, then A will be printed in case 1, whereas A will never be printed in case 2.
   e. The last 2 cases are identical.
   f. Identical.

4. a.

| K | |
|---|---|
| 1 | B |
| 2,3 | E |
| 4 | D |
| 5,6 | F |

b.

| K | |
|---|---|
| 1,2 | C |
| 3 | A,C |
| 4 | A,D |
| 5 | D |
| 6 | B |

## 3-7  Programming Examples

### 3-7-1  Compound Interest Problem

*Problem/Specification*:   Write a program to read an interest rate (*R*), a principal (*P*), and a number of years (*N*). If the principal and earned interest are left in the account, compute the total value of the investment after *N* years. The formula to calculate the total value is $V = P(1 + R)^N$. The input and output can be visualized as follows:

*Output*

*Input*

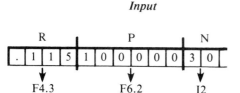

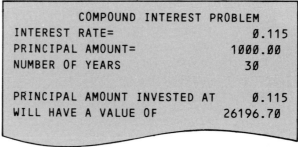

A program to solve this problem is shown in Figure 3–10

**FIGURE 3-10** COMPOUND INTEREST PROBLEM

```
C   COMPOUND INTEREST PROBLEM
C   R: INTEREST RATE
C   P: PRINCIPAL
C   N: NUMBER OF YEARS
C   V: TOTAL VALUE
        REAL R,P,V
        INTEGER N
        READ(5,10),R,P,N
        WRITE(6,11)
        WRITE (6,12)R
        WRITE(6,13)P
        WRITE(6,14)N
        V=P*(1.+R)**N
        WRITE(6,15)R
        WRITE(6,16)V
        STOP
     10 FORMAT(F4.3,F6.2,I2)
     11 FORMAT('1',T50,'COMPOUND INTEREST PROBLEM')  Skip to top of new page.
     12 FORMAT('0',T40,'INTEREST RATE=',T69,F9.3)      Double space before writing.
     13 FORMAT(1X,T40,'PRINCIPAL AMOUNT= ',T69,F8.2)
     14 FORMAT(1X,T40,'NUMBER OF YEARS',T69,I5)
     15 FORMAT('0',T40,'PRINCIPAL AMOUNT INVESTED AT',T69,F9.3)
     16 FORMAT(T40,'WILL HAVE A VALUE OF',T69,F8.2)
        END
```

## 3-7-2 Largest of Three Values

*Problem/Specification:* Write the pseudo code and the program to read three values from one data record and print the largest value. If all values are equal, print any of the three values. Use only two decision statements.

The pseudo code and the program to solve this problem are shown in Figure 3-11.

**FIGURE 3-11** FINDING THE LARGEST OF THREE NUMBERS

```
* Find largest of three values          C FINDING LARGEST OF 3 VALUES
                                                INTEGER N1,N2,N3,LARGE
READ the 3 values N1, N2 and N3                 READ(5,10)N1,N2, N3
IF N1 > N2 THEN                                 IF(N1 .GT. N2) THEN
      Largest__so__far = N1                         LARGE = N1
ELSE                                            ELSE
      Largest__so__far = N2                         LARGE = N2
ENDIF                                           ENDIF
IF Largest__so__far < N3 THEN                   IF(LARGE .LT. N3) THEN
      Largest__so__far = N3                         LARGE = N3
ENDIF                                           ENDIF
WRITE Largest__so__far                          WRITE(6,11)LARGE
END                                             STOP
                                             11 FORMAT(1X,I3)
                                             10 FORMAT(3I3)
                                                END
```

Testing the code requires four different sets of input values, for example

```
10 20 30
30 20 10
10 30 20
10 10 10
```

Note that in the FORTRAN code the last IF/THEN statement could have been coded using just one line as: IF(LARGE .LT. N3)LARGE = N3. This saves two lines of code.

### 3-7-3  Real Roots of a Polynomial

*Problem/Specification*:  Develop an algorithm to find the roots of the polynomial $ax^2 + bx + c$ ($a \neq 0$), where $a$, $b$, and $c$ are provided as input. Recall that the roots of a polynomial can be computed by applying the formulas:

$$r_1 = \frac{-b + \sqrt{b^2 - 4ac}}{2a} \qquad r_2 = \frac{-b - \sqrt{b^2 - 4ac}}{2a}$$

The expression $b^2 - 4ac$ is referred to as the discriminant.

■ If the discriminant is negative, the message NO REAL ROOTS should be printed.

■ If the discriminant is zero, print SINGLE ROOT = _ _ _ _ _

■ If the discriminant is positive, print ROOT1 = _ _ _ _ _ _ ROOT2 = _ _ _ _ _ _

*Problem/Solution*:  The pseudo code and the FORTRAN code are shown in Figure 3–12.

*Problem/Testing*:  To test the correctness of the algorithm, we need three different sets of values of $a$, $b$, and $c$, such as:

$a = 1, b = 0, c = 1$     (no real roots)
$a = 1, b = 0, c = -1$    (two roots: $r_1 = -1, r_2 = 1$)
$a = 1, b = 1, c = 1$     (one root: $r = -1$)

### 3-7-4  Year-end Bonus

*Problem/Specification*:  Employees at Sarah's Style Shop are to receive a year-end bonus. The amount of the bonus depends on the employee's weekly pay, position code, and number of years with the store. Each employee is assigned a bonus based on the following rules:

| Position Code | Bonus |
|---|---|
| 1 | One week's pay |
| 2 | Two weeks' pay; maximum of $700 |
| 3 | One and a half week's pay |

Employees with more than 10 years' experience are to receive an additional $100, and employees with fewer than 2 years' experience are to receive half the usual bonus.

**FIGURE 3–12** ROOTS OF A POLYNOMIAL

```
* Find roots of polynomial ax² + bx + c
* Read in the coefficients
READ a, b and c
* Compute the discriminant
Discriminant = b² − 4ac
IF discriminant < 0 THEN
        WRITE "no real roots"
ELSE
        root1 = (−b + √discriminant) / 2a
        IF discriminant = 0 THEN
                WRITE single root root1
        ELSE
                root2 = (−b − √discriminant) / 2a
                WRITE root1 and root2
        ENDIF
ENDIF
STOP
```

$$root1 = \frac{-b + \sqrt{discriminant}}{2a}$$

$$root2 = \frac{-b - \sqrt{discriminant}}{2a}$$

Input file

```
A   B   C
1.00.01.0
1.00.0-1.
1.02.01.0
```

If program is executed 3 times

output

NO REAL ROOTS
ROOT1 = 1.00 ROOT2 = − 1.00
SINGLE ROOT = − 1.00

```
C FINDING ROOTS OF POLYNOMIALS
C   A, B, C:          COEFFICIENTS
C   DISC:             DISCRIMINANT
C   ROOT1, ROOT2:   ROOTS OF POLYNOMIAL
C
      REAL A,B,C,DISC,ROOT1, ROOT2
      READ(5,4)A,B,C
C COMPUTE DISCRIMINANT
      DISC = (B*B - 4.*A*C)
      IF(DISC .LT. 0.) THEN
         WRITE(6,1)
      ELSE
         ROOT1 = (-B + DISC**.5)/(2.*A)
         IF (DISC .EQ. 0.) THEN
            WRITE(6,2) ROOT1
         ELSE
            ROOT2 = (-B - DISC**.5)/(2.*A)
            WRITE(6,3) ROOT1,ROOT2
         ENDIF
      ENDIF
      STOP
    1 FORMAT(1X,'NO REAL ROOTS')
    2 FORMAT(1X,'SINGLE ROOT=',F6.2)
    3 FORMAT(1X,'ROOT1=',F6.2,2X,'ROOT2=',F6.2)
    4 FORMAT(F3.1, F3.1, F3.1)
      END
```

```
NO REAL ROOTS
ROOT1=  1.00  ROOT2= -1.00
SINGLE ROOT= -1.00
```

Results for first input record
Results for 2nd input record
Results for 3rd input record

Read an employee number, a weekly pay, a position code, and a number of years; then compute and print the employee's bonus.

*Problem/Solution:* The best way to solve such a problem is to first work out a few examples manually. Make up artificial entries (pay, code, years) and figure out the answers to warm up for the flowchart/pseudo code phase. For example, assume that the weekly pay is $200, the position code is 3, and the employee has 15 years of experience. The position code tells you that the bonus corresponds to 1½ weeks' pay ($200 + $100 = $300). Since the employee has been with the company more than 10 years, add $100 to the bonus ($300 + $100 = $400). Now we have figured out the bonus for one particular employee.

Let's look at another case where the weekly pay is $500, the position code is 2, and the employee has 1 year of experience. In this case, the bonus is 2 weeks' pay ($1,000); however since the problem states that the maximum bonus is $700, the bonus is set to $700. (Had the weekly pay been $300, the bonus would have been 2 x $300 = $600, and the limitation would not apply.) Since the employee has less than 2 years of experience, the final bonus is cut in half ($350).

Now that we have some ideas about how to solve the problem, we start writing them down, using either a flowchart or pseudo code. These are shown in Figure 3–13, and the FORTRAN code is shown in Figure 3–14.

**FIGURE 3–13**    PSEUDO CODE AND FLOWCHART FOR YEAR-END BONUS

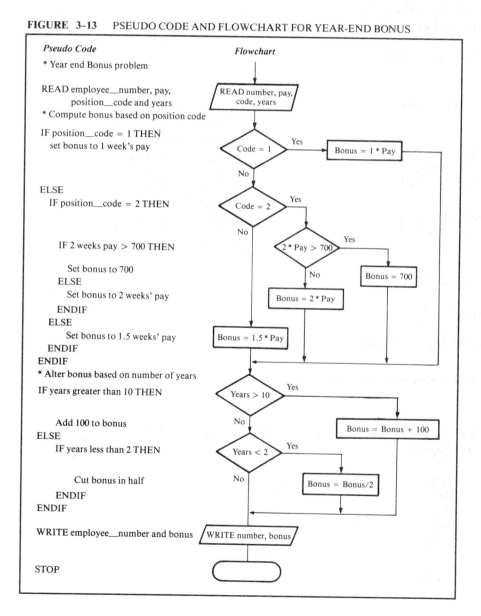

**FIGURE 3-14** FORTRAN PROGRAM FOR YEAR END BONUS

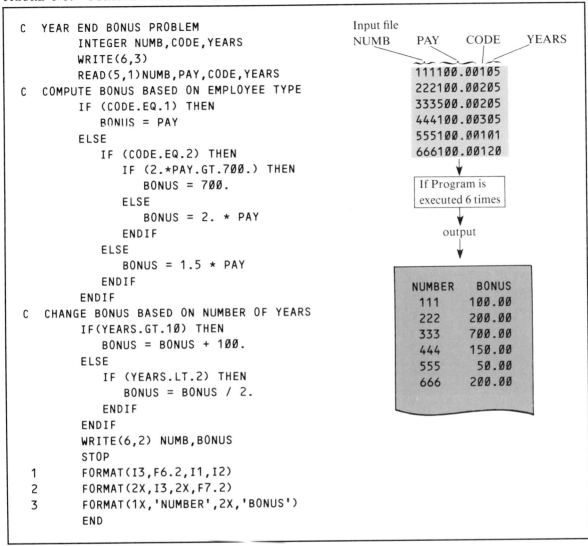

```
C   YEAR END BONUS PROBLEM
        INTEGER NUMB,CODE,YEARS
        WRITE(6,3)
        READ(5,1)NUMB,PAY,CODE,YEARS
C   COMPUTE BONUS BASED ON EMPLOYEE TYPE
        IF (CODE.EQ.1) THEN
            BONUS = PAY
        ELSE
            IF (CODE.EQ.2) THEN
                IF (2.*PAY.GT.700.) THEN
                    BONUS = 700.
                ELSE
                    BONUS = 2. * PAY
                ENDIF
            ELSE
                BONUS = 1.5 * PAY
            ENDIF
        ENDIF
C   CHANGE BONUS BASED ON NUMBER OF YEARS
        IF(YEARS.GT.10) THEN
            BONUS = BONUS + 100.
        ELSE
            IF (YEARS.LT.2) THEN
                BONUS = BONUS / 2.
            ENDIF
        ENDIF
        WRITE(6,2) NUMB,BONUS
        STOP
1       FORMAT(I3,F6.2,I1,I2)
2       FORMAT(2X,I3,2X,F7.2)
3       FORMAT(1X,'NUMBER',2X,'BONUS')
        END
```

Input file

| NUMB | PAY | CODE | YEARS |
|------|-----|------|-------|

```
111100.00105
222100.00205
333500.00205
444100.00305
555100.00101
666100.00120
```

If Program is executed 6 times

output

```
NUMBER    BONUS
  111     100.00
  222     200.00
  333     700.00
  444     150.00
  555      50.00
  666     200.00
```

*Problem/Testing:* To test the correctness of the algorithm, we need to process at least six sets of input records such as the following:

| Number | Pay | Code | Years |
|--------|-----|------|-------|
| 111 | 100 | 1 | 5 |
| 222 | 100 | 2 | 5 |
| 333 | 500 | 2 | 5 |
| 444 | 100 | 3 | 5 |
| 555 | 100 | 1 | 1 |
| 666 | 100 | 1 | 20 |

## 3-8  Probing Deeper

### 3-8-1  The Logical Operators: .NOT., .AND., and .OR.

Logical expressions can be compounded, as shown in the following examples:

```
INTEGER AGE,SEX,X,S
IF(AGE .LT. 40 .AND. SEX .EQ. 1) THEN ...
IF(.NOT. AGE .GT. 40) J = J + 1   meaning AGE ≤ 40
IF((SEX .EQ. 2.) .OR. (.NOT. ((X .EQ. 1).AND. (S .LT. 2)))) GO TO 10
```

A *compound* condition is formed when one or more conditions are connected by the logical operators .NOT., .AND. or .OR.. The meaning of those operators is illustrated by the following examples:

IF(*condition 1* .AND. *condition 2*) THEN  ...  Transfer to the THEN statements if both conditions are true; otherwise transfer to the ELSE statements, if any.

IF(*condition 1* .OR. *condition 2*) THEN  ...  If one condition or both conditions are true, transfer to the THEN statements; otherwise transfer to the ELSE statements, if any.

IF(.NOT. *condition*) THEN  ...  Transfer to the THEN statements if the condition is NOT true; otherwise transfer to the ELSE statements, if any.

The logical operators have the lowest priority in the rules of precedence governing operations:

| Operations | Precedence |
|---|---|
| Grouping via parentheses | Highest |
| (Arithmetic operations) | . |
| ** | . |
| *, / | . |
| +, − | . |
| (Conditions) | . |
| LT.,.GT.,.EQ.,.NE.,.LE.,.GE. | . |
| (Logical operators) | . |
| .NOT. | . |
| .AND. | . |
| .OR. | Lowest |

*Example 1*

To determine whether an age is between 18 and 30 (inclusive), the following statement could be used:

```
IF (AGE.GE. 18 .AND. AGE.LE. 30) PRINT*,'YES'
```

*Example 2*   Assume X = 30., Y = 40., and A = 10.

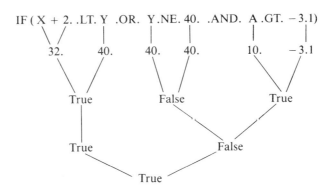

Arithmetic expressions
are evaluated first.

Relations are
evaluated next.

Logical operations are
evaluated last according to
the precedence rule.

Parentheses can be used to denote the order in which the compound conditions are to be evaluated. Consider, for example, the two following conditions, which have entirely different meanings:

```
IF(WEIGHT .LT. 140 .OR. AGE .LT. 30 .AND. EARNIN .GT. 100000.) THEN ...
IF((WEIGHT .LT. 140 .OR. AGE .LT. 30) .AND. EARNIN .GT. 100000.) THEN ...
```

In the first case, the condition is true if WEIGHT < 140, regardless of age and earnings, whereas in the second case the condition EARNIN > 10000 would have to be satisfied before the condition is true.

### *Caution:*

Just as in the case of relational operators, the logical operators .AND. and .OR. cannot be side by side in a compound expression. For example,

```
IF((AGE .GT. 7) .AND. .OR. .LT. 14)
```

is invalid. However, the .NOT. operator can be conjuncted to the .AND. or to the .OR., as in

```
IF((A .GT. B) .AND. (.NOT. (B .LT. C))) THEN ...
```

Relational operators may *not* be typed side by side with logical operators. For example

```
IF(AGE .GE. 25 .AND. .LT. 30) IHEN ...
```

is invalid. Instead, this condition should be expressed as:

```
IF(AGE .GE. 25 .AND. AGE .LT. 30) THEN ...
```

### 3-8-2  **Do It Now**

1. A marriage proposal letter will be written when the following condition is true. Under how many conditions will the letter be written? Specify the various conditions.

   ```
   IF(HAIR .EQ. 'BLACK' .AND. HEIGHT .GT. 5.8 .OR. EARNIN .GT. 100000.) ...
   ```

2. Assume X = 30.;  Y = 40.;  A = 1.;  B = 4.

   Is the following condition true or false?
   ```
   .NOT.(X + Y .LT. 100. .OR. A .EQ. 1.).AND. B .GT. 3.
   ```

3. Which of the following are valid? If invalid, explain why.

    a. `IF((X+Y)**2 .LT. -1. .AND. Y .GT. Z) THEN`
    b. `IF(X-Y .EQ. 0 .OR. Z .AND. X .EQ. 0.) THEN`
    c. `IF(-3. .LT. Z .OR. 1. .EQ. X) THEN`
    d. `IF(X .NOT. .GT. .4.) THEN`
    e. `IF(.NOT. (Y .NE. -1.)) THEN`

## Answers

1. A marriage proposal letter will be written under either of the following conditions:
    a. If earning > $100,000
    b. If hair is black and person is over 5.8 ft. tall.
    c. If both conditions a and b are satisfied.

2. False

3.   a. Valid
    b. Invalid: Z .AND. X (neither Z nor X are conditions).
    c. Valid
    d. Invalid: X .NOT. .GT. (juxtaposition .NOT. .GT. is meaningless).
    e. Valid

## 3-8-3 FORTRAN Statement Continuation

A FORTRAN statement is often too long to fit in columns 7–72. When this happens, the statement can be continued onto one or more succeeding lines. If any character other than a blank or zero is entered into column 6, the statement on that line is treated as a continuation of the preceding line. For example, statement 101 in the following example is continued by placing an asterisk "*" in column 6 of the "next" line. Note that statement 101 itself has no continuation character in column 6.

*Example 1*    The following two statements are equivalent:

```
        column 6
  101| FORMAT(3X,'AREA LOT1 IS',2X,F8.1,3X,'AREA LOT2 IS',2X,F8.1)

  101| FORMAT(3X,'AREA LOT1 IS',2X,F8.1,
      |*3X,'AREA LOT2 IS',2X,F8.1)         equivalent to line above
```

A statement can be continued onto several successive lines.

*Example 2*    Statements 100 and 101 are equivalent:

```
        column 6
  100| X = Y +
      |1Z +
      |2   Q
  101| X = Y + Z + Q
```

Caution must be exercised when continuing a literal string within quotes in a FORMAT.

*Example 3*

```
    WRITE(6,11)                                         column 72
 11 FORMAT(. . . ,'I DREAM OF THINGS THAT-----
    1NEVER WERE')
```

These statements will produce:

```
                              5 blanks
    I DREAM OF THINGS THAT-----NEVER WERE
```

If the following statement had been used,

```
                                            column 72
 11 FORMAT(. . . ,'I DREAM OF THINGS THAT NE
    *VER WERE')
```

the following output would be produced:

```
    I DREAM OF THINGS THAT NEVER WERE
```

## 3-8-4  The Computed GO TO Statement

A useful and convenient statement that transfers to different points in a program with just one FORTRAN statement is the computed GO TO. The general form of the computed GO TO is:

GO TO (*statement number-1, statement number-2,..., statement number-n*), *variable*

where *variable* must be an *integer* variable name and *statement number-1,2,...,* n are FORTRAN statement numbers defined in the program.

If the value of the integer variable is 1, control is transferred to statement number-1. If the value of the integer variable is 2, control is transferred to statement number-2. In general, if the value of the variable is *i*, control is passed to the *i*th statement in the list of statements.

*Example*

|                        | *Meaning*           |
|------------------------|---------------------|
| GO TO (3,57,100,4),N   | If N = 1, go to 3   |
|                        | N = 2, go to 57     |
| Note the comma!        | N = 3, go to 100    |
|                        | N = 4, go to 4      |

If N is less than 1 or exceeds the number of statement numbers within the parentheses, control is passed to the statement immediately following the computed GO TO.

The reader is cautioned that an integer variable must be used in the computed GO TO; no expressions are allowed, i.e., GO TO(2,3,4),2*I is invalid, since 2*I is not a variable.

Consider, for example, the following problem. We want to write out the meaning associated with a class code read from a data record. The possible codes and meanings are shown below:

| Class Code | Meaning |
|:---:|:---|
| 1 | Freshman |
| 2 | Sophomore |
| 3 | Junior |
| 4 | Senior |
| 5 | Graduate |

The program shown in Figure 3–15 could be used to solve this problem. The flowchart version of this program is shown in Figure 3–16.

**FIGURE 3–15**    COMPUTED GO TO EXAMPLE

```
       CHARACTER CLASS*12                 If KODE is not equal to
       READ(5,6)KODE                      1,2,3,4, or 5, then go to the
       GO TO(15,20,25,30,35),KODE         next statement and print an er-
       PRINT*, 'INVALID CODE'             ror message.
       STOP
    15 CLASS = 'FRESHMAN'
       GO TO 40
    20 CLASS = 'SOPHOMORE'
       GO TO 40
    25 CLASS = 'JUNIOR'
       GO TO 40
    30 CLASS = 'SENIOR'
       GO TO 40
    35 CLASS = 'GRADUATE'
    40 PRINT*, CLASS
       STOP
       END
```

**FIGURE 3–16**    FLOWCHART OF A COMPUTED GO TO EXAMPLE

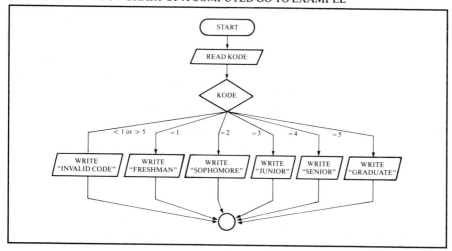

### 3-8-5  Do It Now

1. Consider the following computed GO TO statement:

```
GO TO(16,16,19,20,20), L
```

    a.  If L = 3, the next statement executed would be _____.
    b.  If L = 1 or L = 2, the next statement executed would be _____.
    c.  If L = 7, the next statement executed would be _____.

2. Rewrite the program of Figure 3–15 using IF statements

### Answers

1.    a.  19
    b.  16
    c.  next statement

2.
```
CHARACTER CLASS*12
READ*, KODE
CLASS = 'INVALID CODE'
IF(KODE .EQ. 1) CLASS = 'FRESHMAN'
IF(KODE .EQ. 2) CLASS = 'SOPHOMORE'
IF(KODE .EQ. 3) CLASS = 'JUNIOR'
IF(KODE .EQ. 4) CLASS = 'SENIOR'
IF(KODE .EQ. 5) CLASS = 'GRADUATE'
PRINT*, CLASS
STOP
END
```

### 3-8-6  The Arithmetic IF Statement

The arithmetic IF allows a three-way transfer out of a decision block, as opposed to the two-way transfer of a logical IF. For example, when comparing two numbers, A and B, the decision block can have three exits: one if A is less than B, a second one if A equals B, and third one if A is greater than B. The flowchart symbol for an arithmetic IF is:

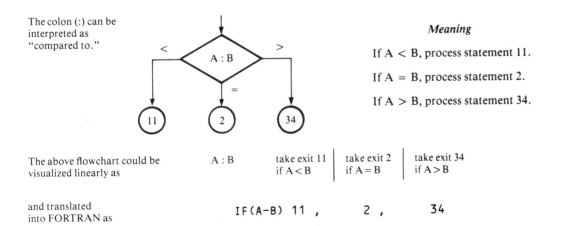

The colon (:) can be interpreted as "compared to."

**Meaning**

If A < B, process statement 11.

If A = B, process statement 2.

If A > B, process statement 34.

The above flowchart could be visualized linearly as

| A : B | take exit 11 if A < B | take exit 2 if A = B | take exit 34 if A > B |

and translated into FORTRAN as

```
IF(A-B) 11 ,    2 ,     34
```

The general form of the arithmetic decision statement is:

> IF *(expression) statement number* 1,*statement number* 2,*statement number* 3

where *expression* is any FORTRAN expression

*statement number* 1, 2, and 3 are FORTRAN statement numbers defined in the program.

The IF statement can be interpreted as follows:

**1.** Evaluate the expression.

**2.** If the result is negative, transfer to *statement number 1*.
If the result is equal to zero, transfer to *statement number 2*.
If the result is positive, transfer to *statement number 3*.

It should be noted that the three statement numbers in the IF statement always correspond to the sequence: less than 0, equal to 0, and greater than 0, in that order. The reader can visualize this sequence as follows:

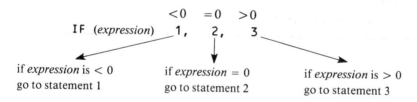

Two numbers, A and B, can be compared in an IF statement using the expression $A - B$ as follows:

$$IF(A-B)11,2,34 \quad \text{means} \quad \begin{array}{l} \text{if } A-B<0 \text{ or if } A<B, \text{ then go to } 11 \\ \text{if } A-B=0 \text{ or if } A=B, \text{ then go to } 2 \\ \text{if } A-B>0 \text{ or if } A>B, \text{ then go to } 34 \end{array}$$

In some cases a decision may require only a two-way transfer, in which case appropriate IF statement numbers can be combined as follows:

IF(A-B)1,5,1     means    if $A = B$, go to 5; otherwise go to 1 (unequal).

IF(A-B)11,11,4    means    if $A \leq B$, go to 11; otherwise go to 4 (greater).

Some valid IF statements and their meanings are:

| IF Statements | Meaning |
|---|---|
| IF(X)1,3,5 | If $X < 0$, go to 1; if $X = 0$, go to 3; if $X > 0$, go to 5. |
| IF(X - (-4))1,1,2 } | These two statements are logically the same |
| IF(X + 4)1,1,2 | and could be interpreted as comparing X with $-4$. |
| IF(X + Y*Z)3,4,3 | If $X + Y*Z = 0$, go to 4; otherwise go to 3. |
| IF(2*X + (Z-4)*X**2)1,2,3 | Evaluate the expression and transfer 1, 2, or 3 |

Some invalid IF statements are shown below:

| IF Statements | Reason |
|---|---|
| IF(A*B)1,2 | Missing a statement number. |
| IF(X:1Ø)1,2,3 | Invalid expression. Colon (:) is illegal. |
| IF A -B 2,3,5 | Missing both parentheses. |
| IF (2*(X+3)1,2,3 | Missing right parenthesis. |
| IF(X = 1Ø) GO TO 7 | Special character = invalid—so is GO TO 7 |

To better understand the arithmetic IF statement and its interaction with other FOR-TRAN statements in a program, consider the following example:

*Example*

Write a program read a number N and do the following:

    IF N > 0, write the message POS on the output form.
    IF N = 0, write the message ZERO on the output form.
    IF N < 0, write the message NEG on the output form.

The flowchart and programs are shown in Figure 3–17.

**FIGURE 3-17**    FLOWCHART AND FORTRAN PROGRAMS

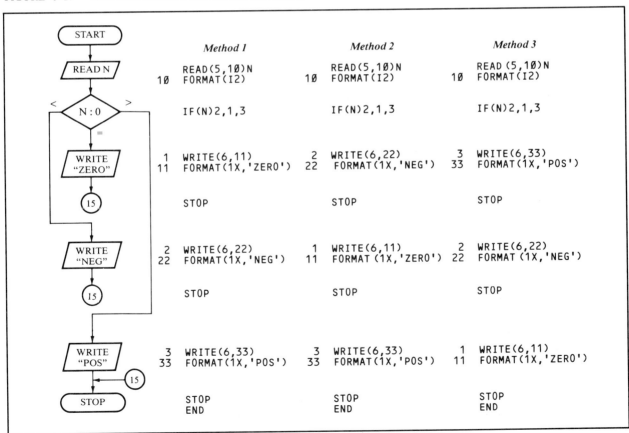

In method 1, the sequence of FORTRAN instructions parallels exactly the physical sequence of the flowchart blocks. This method is probably the easiest for the beginner to follow. Note the importance and necessity of the two STOP statements following statements 1 and 2. If N were zero and these two statements were omitted, the message ZERO would first be written as a result of statement number 1, then the computer would execute the next instruction at 2, which would write NEG, and then statement 3 would be processed, causing the message POS to be printed. Altogether, three messages would be printed when in fact only one should be printed.

Methods 2 and 3 also illustrate alternative FORTRAN programs, although their FORTRAN statements do not physically match the flowchart blocks. Nevertheless, they are correct. The important point to keep in mind is that the logical flowpath in the flowchart be preserved in the FORTRAN program. Whether statement 1, 2, or 3 immediately follows the IF statement is immaterial as long as the IF statement connects these statements logically (if not physically) as shown in the flowchart.

Once again, END denotes the physical end of the FORTRAN program (after the END statement there are no more FORTRAN statements); END is used by the compiler to stop translating the program into machine language, while the STOP statement is used at execution time to tell the CPU that processing (execution of the machine instructions corresponding to the FORTRAN program) is completed and that it is the (logical) end of the program.

### 3-8-7 Do It Now

Use arithmetic IF statements to code each of the following flowcharts:

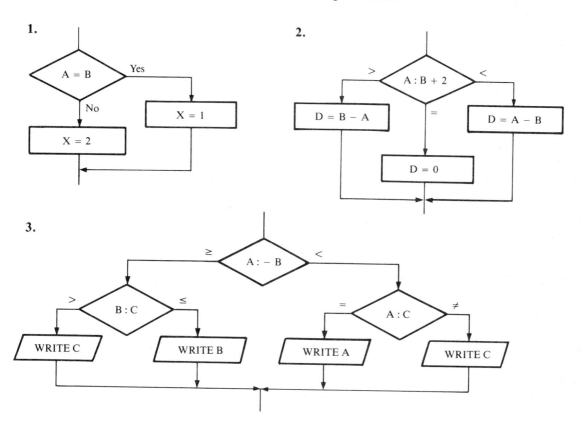

## Answers

**1.**
```
    IF(A-B) 6,7,6
  7 X = 1.
    GO TO 8
  6 X = 2.
  8
```

**2.**
```
    IF(A-(B+2.)) 1,2,3
  1 D = A-B
    GO TO 5
  2 D = 0.
    GO TO 5
  3 D = B-A
  5
```

**3.**
```
    IF(A+B) 1,2,2
  1 IF(A-C) 3,4,3
  4 PRINT*, A
    GO TO 9
  2 IF(B-C) 5,5,3
  5 PRINT*, B
    GO TO 9
  3 PRINT*, C
  9 ...
```

# 3-9  You Might Want to Know

**1.** When a data record is read, does the computer read only those fields specified by the data format codes in the FORMAT, or does it actually read all positions of the record?

*Answer:* Actually, the computer reads all characters from the record into memory but only selects and processes those fields described by the data format codes (I, F, and A). By processing, we mean converting each number or character into its proper internal machine representation and storing it into the corresponding memory location described in the READ list.

**2.** Do I need to initialize a variable to some value before I can use that variable in a READ list? For instance:

```
GR=0.
READ(5,10)GR
```

*Answer:* No. The fact that GR is in the READ list implies that a memory location will be reserved for it.

**3.** What happens during execution if my program needs to read data records but I forgot to include all or some of them in my job?

*Answer:* The computer will read the end-of-file record and report an execution error. End-of-file checks are discussed in chapter 4. The program is terminated.

**4.** Suppose that at execution time my program reads numbers from data records that have been entered incorrectly. For example, suppose that I enter an alphabetic character in a numeric field; what will happen?

*Answer:* A READ error will occur, causing termination of your program.

**5.** What happens if I try to read an integer or a real number from a data record and the field is blank?

*Answer:* Blanks are interpreted as zeroes.

**6.** What happens if I want to read a large number, as follows?

```
    READ(5,10)X
 10 FORMAT (F15.0)
```
| 1 | 2 | 3 | 4 | 5 | 6 | 7 | 8 | 9 | 0 | 1 | 2 | 3 | 4 | 5 | |

*Answer:* The number of significant digits that can be retained for real numbers varies depending upon the computer in use. Some computers store seven significant digits, hence the number X might be stored as 123456700000000 thereby resulting in an error of 89,012,345. (X should be declared as DOUBLE PRECISION—see chapter 6 for double precision and internal representation of numbers.)

**7.** How can I read imaginary or complex numbers?

*Answer:* See chapter 6 for a complete discussion.

**8.** Can I use the same format for more than one READ statement?

*Answer:* Yes, for example:

```
     READ(5,5)I,J
     READ(5,5)IPROD,KPROD
   5 FORMAT(I3,I3)
```

**9.** What happens if I write the following code?

```
     READ(5,6)I,J,K
   6 FORMAT(I3,T2,I3,T1,I1)
```

*Answer:* The T feature permits restarting a READ operation at different positions in a record. In this case, I = 139, J = 398, K = 1

**10.** Can you have more than one STOP statement in a program?

*Answer:* Yes, for example:

```
      IF(X.GT.0.)GO TO 15
      WRITE(6,12)
      STOP
   15 WRITE (6,11)
      STOP
   12 FORMAT(3X,'X IS NEGATIVE')
   11 FORMAT(3X,'X IS POSITIVE')
      END
```

Remember, though, you can have only *one* END statement, and it must be the last statement in your program.

**11.** When you read data, is it a good idea to print that data on the output form immediately?

*Answer:* Yes. In fact, it is strongly recommended that you print out all the original data that your program is reading. The user can then verify the accuracy of the input data, and the printed data can then be used for documentation for anyone reading the output who does not have access to the original data.

**12.** Was I surprised the other day! I knew I made a mistake, but the compiler didn't catch it. I entered GOTO51 instead of GO TO 51 and my program still ran. How about that?

*Answer:* The compiler is smarter than you think. Spaces within FORTRAN statements are ignored by the compiler.

13. Since certain *fractional* numbers are not always represented exactly in memory, because of binary representation of numbers, would K be set to 3 in the following example?

```
Y = .5
X = .1 + .1 + .1 + .1 + .1
IF (X .EQ. Y) K = 3
```

*Answer:* On many systems .1 is approximated by .09999999; hence X = .4999995. On the other hand, Y can be represented exactly as .5; hence, on some systems X may not equal Y, even though this is the case arithmetically. In such cases the user may want to ask whether X − Y is close enough to 0, (i.e., is X sufficiently close to Y?) This can be expressed as:

```
IF (ABS(X - Y) .LT. EPS) K = 3
```

where EPS = .01, .001, .0000001, etc., depending on the degree of accuracy needed, and ABS is the FORTRAN symbol for the absolute value function.

14. Suppose I want to print a line full of asterisks: ****...***. What is an easy way to do that?

*Answer:*

```
      WRITE(6,5)
    5 FORMAT (1X,132('*'))
```

Note that the format code 132 '*' would be invalid. A duplication factor can be applied to any sequence of format codes contained in parentheses.

15. Can I use a logical IF statement within an IF THEN ELSE structure?

*Answer:* Yes

## 3-10  Exercises

### 3-10-1 Test Yourself

1. Which of the following coding segments are valid? If invalid, state reasons.

```
a.     READ (5,10),A,B,C           b.     READ(5,5) I,J
    10 FORMAT(F1.0,F2.0,F3.0)           5 FORMAT(I1,I4)


c.     READ(5,6)A,I,J              d.     READ(5,7)A,B,C
     6 FORMAT(F4.5,I2,I1)              7 FORMAT(F5.2,I3,F4)


e.     READ(5,8)X,J,Y              f.     READ(5,5)X,I
     8 FORMAT(F3.1,F2.1,I4)            5 FORMAT(T5,F5.1,T2,I2)
```

2. Given the following READ statement with associated data records, what values would be read for I,J,K for the following formats?

```
      READ (5,5)I,J,K
```

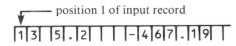

```
(a)  5 FORMAT(T1,I1,I1,I1)
(b)  5 FORMAT(T2,1X,I1,1X,I2,I5)
(c)  5 FORMAT(I3,I1,T6,I1)
```

position 1 of input record

`| 1 | 3 | | 5 | . | 2 | | | | - | 4 | 6 | 7 | . | 1 | 9 | | |`

(d)  5 FORMAT(I4,I3,I5)
(e)  5 FORMAT(T8,I1,I4,I1)
(f)  5 FORMAT(I2,T1,I1,T2,I4)
(g)  5 FORMAT(2(1X,I1),T10,I3)

3. You are to prepare an input data file with three fields per record

FLD1    FLD2    FLD3

a. Without entering decimal points on the data records, specify the READ instruction and accompanying format to read the following numbers (four records in all). The FORMAT should be the same for all four records. Display your arrangement of the input records.

| FLD1 | FLD2 | FLD3 |
| --- | --- | --- |
| − .5 | 2000.00 | .0 |
| 100.0 | 100000.00 | .8 |
| 47.8 | 99000.88 | .09 |
| 3.6 | 1001.02 | .06 |

b. Repeat part a, but this time enter the decimal points on the data records. What will the FORMAT look like in this case?

4. What values would be read for A, I, S as a result of the following READ operations?

```
READ(5,5)A,I,S
```

Position 1 of data record

`| 1 | . | 3 | | 2 | 5 | . | 1 | . | 5 | | |`

(a)  5 FORMAT(F4.0,I2,3X,F1.1)
(b)  5 FORMAT(T3,F4.3,1X,I1,F3.1)
(c)  5 FORMAT(2X,F2.1,I3,F3.0)
(d)  5 FORMAT(T2,F6.1,I1,F2.2)
(e)  5 FORMAT(T2,F1.1,I2,F2.0)

5. Simulate the output produced by the following program segments, indicating all print positions and blanks.

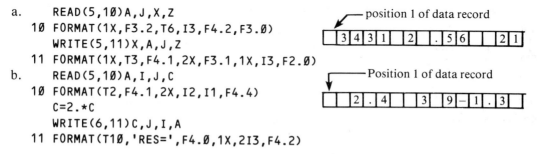

```
a.      READ(5,10)A,J,X,Z
     10 FORMAT(1X,F3.2,T6,I3,F4.2,F3.0)
        WRITE(5,11)X,A,J,Z
     11 FORMAT(1X,T3,F4.1,2X,F3.1,1X,I3,F2.0)
b.      READ(5,10)A,I,J,C
     10 FORMAT(T2,F4.1,2X,I2,I1,F4.4)
        C=2.*C
        WRITE(6,11)C,J,I,A
     11 FORMAT(T10,'RES=',F4.0,1X,2I3,F4.2)
```

6. Are the following statements true or false?

a. Only one STOP statement is allowed per program.
b. Position 1 of an input data record is reserved for record control.
c. A C in position 6 of a FORTRAN statement indicates a continuation from the preceding program line.

d. Data cannot be entered in position 73–80 of an input record (for a READ operation).
e. Input data records are read at compilation time.
f. FORMATs must immediately follow the READ instruction.
g. FORMATs are not required to have statement numbers.
h. The same FORMAT can be used for a READ and WRITE instruction.
i. A C in position 1 of a FORTRAN statement will cause a compilation error.
j. FORMATs are nonexecutable statements.
k. Running out of input data records will cause a compilation error.
l. The statement 5 GOTO5 is grammatically incorrect.
m. The statement READ(5,10)J,J,J is invalid.
n. The statement GO TO KODE3 is valid.
o. In a READ operation, either FORMAT(T2,...), or FORMAT(2X,...) will cause reading to start at the same record position.
p. Input data records can immediately follow the READ statement within the FORTRAN program.

**7.** What are some execution time errors that might occur when a READ instruction is executed? A WRITE instruction?

**8.** Write both arithmetic and logical IF statements for the following flowchart blocks.

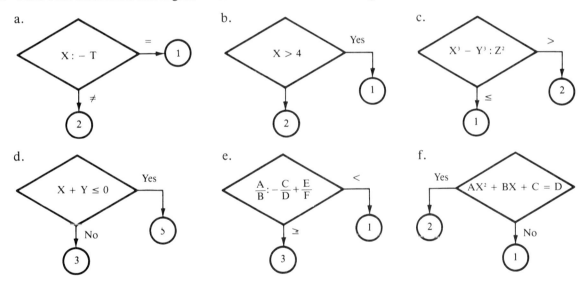

**9.** Write the FORTRAN logical and IF THEN ELSE statements for each of the following three-way decision blocks:

a.

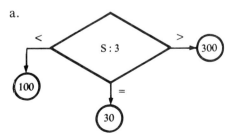

b.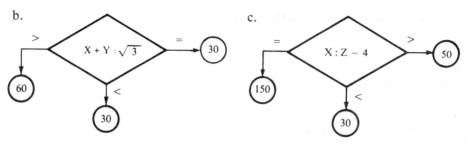
c.

**10.** Indicate the action taken by each of the following IF statements, given the following two cases:

Case 1     A = 3.      B = −2.     C = 2.
Case 2     A = −4.     B = −5.     C = 1.

a.     `IF(B**2.LE.4.*A*C)GO TO 4`
       `R=1.`
       :
       :
       `4 R=2.`

b.  `IF(A.GT.B) WRITE(3,1)A`
    `GO TO 3`

c.  `IF(A.LE.0.)A=-A`
    `WRITE(6,1)A`

d.  `IF(B.GE.C-4.)STOP`
    `C=0.`
    `WRITE(6,1)C`

e.  `IF(A.NE.C*3.)WRITE(3,1)C`
    `WRITE(6,2)A`

**11.** Find syntax errors in the following:

a. `IF(I=N) GO TO 15`
c. `IF G.GE.3. GO TO 41`
e. `IF(A.LE.(A+B)P=Q`
g. `IF(A.GE.7.),WRITE(3,1)A`
i. `IF(7.3+A.GT.2.+B)END`
k. `IF(A.LT.B)WRITE(3,1)A,GO TO 3`

b. `IF(X+Y.GT.3.4)X.EQ.2.`
d. `IF(X+Y)P=G**(.5)`
f. `7 IF(17..LE.B)GO TO 7`
h. `IF 3.*A.EQ.B,A=A+1.`
j. `IF(A.LT.B)IF(T.EQ.S)STOP`

**12.** Write the FORTRAN code for the following flowcharts:

a.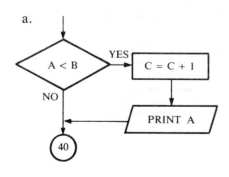

b.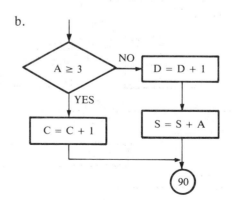

**13.** Convert the following pseudo code into flowchart and FORTRAN code.

> READ amount due
> READ amount received
> IF amount due < amount received THEN
> > compute credit owed
> > PRINT credit owed
>
> ELSE IF amount due = amount received THEN
> > > PRINT "nothing owed"
> >
> > ELSE compute a 2% service charge of the unpaid balance
> > > PRINT new amount due
> >
> > END-IF
>
> END-IF
> END

**14.** Write the FORTRAN code for the following flowcharts. Eliminate redundancy, if any.

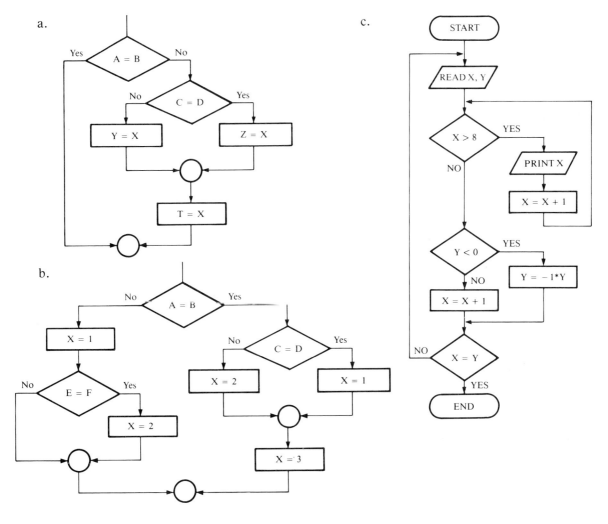

15. Write one or more FORTRAN statements to accomplish each of the following:
    a. Read in three sides of a triangle—the largest side is read last. Write the statements to print the sides of the triangle if the triangle is a right triangle then go to statement 4; otherwise, just go to statement 4.
    b. If B is larger than or equal to 60, increase C by 1, and then go to statement 4; otherwise, go to statement 4.
    c. If X is larger than MAX, assign this value to MAX; otherwise continue.
    d. If $B^2 - 4AC$ is negative, set $R = 1$; otherwise set $R = 2$.
    e. If HRS is greater than 40, compute and print the wage (wage = 1.2*rate*hrs).
       If HRS is equal to 40, compute and print the wage (wage = 1.05*rate*hrs).
       If HRS is less than 40, print the wage (wage = rate*hrs).

16. Assume code is a numeric code representing a student classification (1 = Freshman, 2 = Sophomore, 3 = Junior, Other = Error). Will the following pseudo code print the English word corresponding to the numeric code?

    a. IF code = 1 THEN
                WRITE word Freshman
       END-IF
       IF code = 2 THEN
                WRITE word Sophomore
       END-IF
       IF code = 3 THEN
                WRITE word Junior
       ELSE WRITE bad code
       END-IF

    b. IF code = 1 THEN
                WRITE word Freshman
       IF code = 2 THEN
                WRITE word Sophomore
       IF code = 3 THEN
                WRITE word Junior
       ELSE WRITE bad code
       ENDIF
       ENDIF
       ENDIF

17. Which of the following coding segments are equivalent? (Assume K takes on values 1, 2 or 3)

    a.
```
IF(K .NE. 1) THEN
    PRINT*, A
ENDIF
IF(K .NE. 2) THEN
    PRINT*, B
ENDIF
```
```
IF(K .NE. 2) THEN
    PRINT*, B
ENDIF
IF(K .NE. 1) THEN
    PRINT*, A
ENDIF
```

    b.
```
IF(K .EQ. 1) THEN
    A = A+1.
ELSE
    IF(K .EQ. 2) THEN
        B = B+1.
    ELSE
        C = C+1.
    ENDIF
ENDIF
```
```
IF(K .NE. 1) THEN
    IF(K .NE. 2) THEN
        C = C+1.
    ELSE
        B = B+1.
    ENDIF
ELSE
    A = A+1.
ENDIF
```

18. Without using compound conditions, translate each of the following into a sequence of IF THEN ELSE statements. Include statements to print 'TRUE' if true or 'FALSE' if false. TRUE or FALSE should be printed once.
```
    INTEGER HOURS,SEX,STAT
a.  IF(HOURS .EQ. 40 .OR. SEX .EQ. 2 .OR. STAT .EQ. 3) THEN
b.  IF(HOURS .EQ. 40 .AND. SEX .EQ. 2 .AND. STAT .EQ. 3) THEN
```

```
c. IF(NAME .EQ. 'FONDA' .OR. SEX .EQ. 1 .AND. STAT .EQ. 3) THEN
d. IF(.NOT. (HOURS .LT. 40) .AND. .NOT. (SEX .EQ. 1) .OR. STAT .EQ. 3) THEN
e. IF(.NOT. (HOURS .EQ. 40 .OR. SEX .EQ. 2 .OR. STAT .NE. 3)) THEN
```

19. Write the necessary compound IF statements to perform the following:

    a. If X is greater than 0 but less than 3*A, go to 7.
    b. If both A and B lie between 1 and 8 inclusively, go to 8; otherwise go to 4.
    c. If X exceeds 4 while Y is less than 5, or if X is less than 5 while Y is greater than 4, go to 10; otherwise stop.

20. Will a branch to 15 be taken as a result of the following code? What value is printed for X?

    ```
        X = 1./3. + 1./3. +1./3.
        WRITE(6,5)X
        IF(X .EQ. 1.) GO TO 15
      5 FORMAT(F4.2)
    ```

21. Omega Triple Pooh sorority girls are very selective about their blind dates. The house-mother keeps a record file of male characteristics of the local fraternities. Each record contains a code describing the following attributes:

    | Complexion | Build | Trait |
    |---|---|---|
    | fair (1) | tall (1) | meticulous (1) |
    | dark (2) | medium (2) | timid (2) |
    | olive (3) | small (3) | aggressive (3) |

    All dates must satisfy the following conditions:

    1. Tall but not dark, and between the ages of 20 and 30 or
    2. medium or small build, but neither meticulous nor with olive complexion and either under 18 or over 28
    3. but under no circumstances small and aggressive and over 75, or timid and tall under 19

    Write the code to perform the "blind date" selection for the Pooh girls by counting the number of such dates.

22. If a year is divisible by 4 it is a leap year with the following exception: years that are divisible by 100 but not by 400 are not leap years. Thus 1981 is not a leap year, 1984 is a leap year, 2000 is a leap year but 1900 is not a leap year (not divisible by 400). Write the pseudo code to read a year and determine whether it is a leap year.

### 3-10-2 Exercises

1. Final grades in a course are determined by adding scores obtained on three tests T1, T2, and T3. Students get a PASS grade if the sum of the three scores is above 185 and a FAIL otherwise. Write a program to enter three scores and determine the grade. Print the input scores, the average, and the final grade.

2. The FMT Corporation provides home mortgages up to $70,000. The down payment schedule is as follows:

3% of the first $30,000
10% of the next $22,000
20% of the remainder

Enter a mortgage amount and print the down payment required. Reject any application for an amount over $70,000.

3. A student in DP101 has her account number in record positions 1–4 and three test scores record positions 11–19. The student's average is based on her two best scores. Starting on a new page, print the student's account number and her average on one line and the three test scores on another line (double-space) as follows:

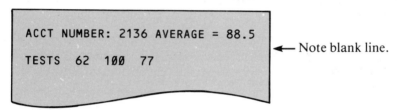

ACCT NUMBER: 2136 AVERAGE = 88.5     ◄— Note blank line.

TESTS  62  100  77

4. Change the program of Figure 3–11 (finding the largest of three numbers) to print a message if any two (but not three) numbers are equal.

5. An income tax agent is checking a file of wage earners in the income bracket $20,000 to $30,000. Each record contains the federal tax paid and gross earnings. If taxes paid are below 27.5% of gross earnings, compute the amount due and print a stern message to the wage earner specifying the amount due. (Assume that taxes are 27.5% of gross earnings in this tax bracket.) If the amount due is over $5,000, add a penalty charge of 1.5% of the amount due. Reject entries with incomes outside the range $20,000–$30,000. Produce a self-explanatory report.

6. A salesperson receives a commission of 10% on all sales if he/she has sold at least $10,000 worth of merchandise in a pay period, but only 8.5% if his/her sales are below $10,000. Write a program to input an amount of sales, compute the commission, and print the commission earned.

7. A salesperson is assigned a commission on the following basis:

| *Sale* | *Commission* |
|---|---|
| less than $500 | 1% |
| $500–$5000 | 5% |
| over $5000 | 8% |

Write a program to enter an amount of sales and calculate the commission.

8. Read an amount in cents between 0 and 100. Write a program to break down the amount read into the least number of half dollars, quarters, dimes, nickels, and pennies possible. For example, 76 cents = 1 half dollar, 1 quarter and 1 penny. [Hint: Divide by 50, then by 25 etc.]

9. The metric system is upon us! Some simple approximation rules for metric conversions are:

*Fahrenheit to centigrade*: Take half and subtract 15.
(86°F.: 86/2 = 43 − 15 = 28° C.)

| | |
|---|---|
| *Inches to centimeters*: | Double, then add half. |
| | (40 inches: 40 * 2 + 20 = 100 cms.) |
| *Miles to kilometers*: | Add 60 percent |
| | (100 miles: 100 + 60% of 100 = 160 kms.) |
| *Pounds to kilograms*: | Take half and then subtract 10% |
| | (60 lbs.: 60/2 = 30 − 10% of 30 = 27 kgs.) |

a. Write a program to read a Fahrenheit temperature, a number of inches, a number of miles, and a number of pounds, and convert these to corresponding metric measures. Identify all results with appropriate headers.

b. Write a similar program to convert metric measurements to Fahrenheit, inches, etc.

10. The Gull Power Electric Company charges supermarkets and small businesses for electricity according to the following scale:

| *Kilowatt Consumption* | *Cost* |
|---|---|
| 0–300 | $5 |
| 301–1000 | $5 + 6.113 cents for each kwh over 3000 (June thru Oct.) |
| | $5 + 5.545 cents for each kwh over 300 (other months) |
| over 1000 | Previous rate up to 1000 kwh and 98% of either 5.545 or 6.113 cents for each kwh over 1000, depending on season |

Write a program to accept a date (month, day, and year), an account number, a meter number, a current meter reading, and a previous meter reading and produce invoices similar to the following: (Don't forget the two dotted lines.)

```
-------------------------------------------------
   ACCOUNT NUMBER      METER NUMBER     DATE
      12300               SAE558       04/25/83


   METER READING        KW HOURS       AMOUNT
   PRESENT PREVIOUS        USED       WINTER RATE
      2335   1998           337          $7.05
-------------------------------------------------
```

11. Write a program to read a grade *N* between 0 and 99 and use the computed GO TO statement to print out the appropriate letter grade according to the following table:

| *Grades* | *Letter Grade* |
|---|---|
| 0–49 | F |
| 50–59 | D |
| 60–79 | C |
| 80–89 | B |
| 90–99 | A |

[*Hint:* Use N/10]

12. In baseball, a batting average is computed by dividing the total number of hits by the total number of times at bat. The slugging average is computed by dividing the total number of bases by the total number of times at bat. For this computation, a single is counted as one base, a double as two bases, etc. Write a program that will accept as input the number of singles, doubles, triples, and home runs, and the total number of

times at bat for a player. Compute and print the batting average and the slugging average. Use the following test data:

| Player | Singles | Doubles | Triples | Home Runs | At Bat |
|--------|---------|---------|---------|-----------|--------|
| 1 | 5 | 3 | 1 | 2 | 70 |
| 2 | 3 | 0 | 2 | 1 | 15 |
| 3 | 10 | 5 | 3 | 0 | 30 |

The expected output is:

| Player | Batting Average | Slugging Average |
|--------|-----------------|------------------|
| 1 | .157 | .314 |
| 2 | .400 | .867 |
| 3 | .600 | .967 |

13. The present value of an investment $P$ invested at interest rate $R$ for $T$ years with interest compounded $N$ times a year is given by the formula:

$$A = P\left(1 + \frac{R}{N}\right)^{T*N}$$

a. Read $P, R$, and $T$ and determine the difference between compounding once a year and 365 times a year.

b. Read a principal and an interest rate and, by trial and error, determine the number of years it will take before the original principal is doubled when compounded annually.

14. Salaries at the XYZ Corporation are based on job classification, years of service, education, and merit rating. The base pay for all employees is the same; a percentage of the base pay is added according to the following schedule:

| Job Classification | Percentage of Base Pay | Education | Percentage of Base Pay |
|--------------------|------------------------|-----------|------------------------|
| 1 | 0 | 1 (high school) | 0 |
| 2 | 5 | 2 (junior college) | 10 |
| 3 | 15 | 3 (college) | 25 |
| 4 | 25 | 4 (graduate degree) | 50 |
| 5 | 50 | 5 (special training) | 15 |

| Merit Rating | Percentage of Base Pay | Years of Service | Percentage of Base Pay |
|--------------|------------------------|------------------|------------------------|
| 0 (poor) | 0 | 0–10 years | 5 |
| 1 (good) | 10 | each additional year | 4 |
| 2 (excellent) | 25 | | |

Write a program to accept numerical codes for each of the four variables and calculate the employee's salary as a percentage of a base pay.

**15.** Write a program to make daily weather reports. Read nine integer values giving the following information: current month, day, and year; high temperature for the day, low temperature for the day; year in which the record high for this day was set, record high temperature; year of record low for this day, record low temperature. After entering an input record, print a message of one of the following three types, depending on the data:

| 10/23/84 | HIGH TODAY | 52 |
| | LOW TODAY | 23 |
| 10/24/84 | HIGH TODAY | 71* |
| | LOW TODAY | 38 |

* (BEATS RECORD OF 70 SET IN 1906)

| 10/25/84 | HIGH TODAY | 73* |
| | LOW TODAY | − 10** |

* (BEATS RECORD OF 68 SET IN 1938)
** (BEATS RECORD OF − 8 SET IN 1918)

Read at least three records so that the three output reports are produced.

**16.** Write a program to perform an analysis of expenses for an automobile trip. Input into the program will be:

number of days
estimated mileage for each day
estimated miles per gallon
estimated cost of gas per gallon
estimated cost of room(s) per day
number of persons
estimated cost of breakfast/lunch/dinner per person

Assume that no more than four persons can occupy a room; if there are more than four persons, additional rooms will be required. Assume that breakfast on the first day and dinner on the last day are not included in trip expenses. Allow 15% of room plus meals per day per person for incidental expenses. (For example, if two persons are sharing a $40 per night room and total meals per day per person is $15, the estimate for incidental expenses per person per day would be $.15 \times (40/2 + 15) = 5.25$.) Allow 15% of total estimated cost of gas for incidental auto expenses.

Write a report showing all input data and a trip expense budget including:

total automotive costs (gas + incidental)
total cost of meals
total cost of rooms
total cost of incidental expenses
total trip estimated expenses.

**17.** The following flowchart calculates the exact date for Easter given any year after 1583. Write a program to compute the Easter date for any given year.

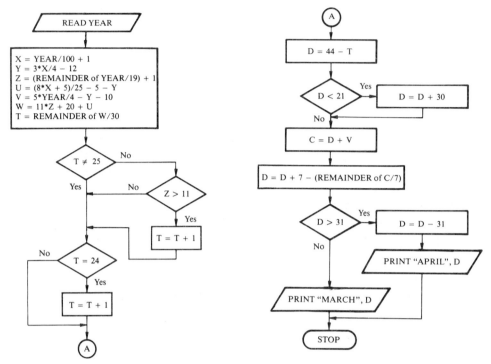

[Remainder of 17/3 is 2; remainder of 16/5 is 1, etc.]

### 3-10-3 Programming Problems: Scientific/Mathematical

**1.** Consider the polynomial $P(x) = x^2 - 1.596x + .266$, which has a root between 1.3 and 1.4. Use trial and error to find an approximation $r$ to that root such that $|P(r)| < 0.001$. (Recall that a root $s$ of P(x) is such that $P(s) = 0$.)

**2.** Write a program to read a value for x and compute and print the absolute value of $x$. Recall that $|x| = x$ if $x > = 0$ and $|x| = -x$ if $x < 0$.

**3.** Read three values and determine if they represent the three sides of a right triangle.

**4.** Write a program to compute the area of a triangle given three sides $a$, $b$, and $c$ using the formula:

$$\text{area} = \sqrt{s(s-a)(s-b)(s-c)} \qquad \text{where } s = \frac{a + b + c}{2}$$

(*Caution:* Not all possible values of $a$, $b$, and $c$ represent a triangle. How could your program detect such values?)

[*Hint:* The sum of any two sides must always be greater than the third.]

**5.** Read a three-digit number, $N$, between 100 and 999 and print out each digit as a separate number, i.e., the 100s, and 10s, and the unit's digits.

[*Hint*: divide first by 100, then by 10, using real and integer operations.]

6. The square root of a number $A$ can be computed by successive approximations using the iterative formula $x_{n+1} = \frac{1}{2}(x_n + A/x_n)$ which becomes $X = .5*(X + A/X)$ in FOR-TRAN. Starting with $x = 1$ as an initial approximation for the square root of A, a new approximation $x$ is computed using the above formula. This new approximation, in turn, can be substituted in the formula to compute a newer approximation $x$. This process can be continued until the square of the new approximation $x$ is close to $A$ within a prescribed degree of accuracy $\epsilon$ (where $\epsilon = 0.1, 0.01, 0.001$, etc. depending on the accuracy needed); that is,

$$|x - A| < \epsilon.$$

Write a program to read $A$ and E ($\epsilon$) to compute $\sqrt{A}$. Write an error message if $A \leq 0$. For example, to compute the square root of 24 we start as follows:

$$x_1 = \frac{1}{2}\left(x_0 + \frac{24}{x_0}\right) = \frac{1}{2}\left(1 + \frac{24}{1}\right) = 12.5$$
$$x_2 = \frac{1}{2}\left(x_1 + \frac{26}{x_1}\right) = \frac{1}{2}\left(12.5 + \frac{26}{12.5}\right) = 7.29$$
$$x_3 = \frac{1}{2}\left(x_2 + \frac{24}{x_2}\right) = \ldots$$

7. A certain metal is graded according to the results of three tests. These tests determine whether the metal satisfies the following specifications:

   a. Carbon content is below 0.67.
   b. Rockwell hardness is no less than 50.
   c. Tensile strength is greater than 70,000 psi.

   The metal is graded 1 if it passes all three tests, 9 if it passes tests 1 and 2, 8 if it passes test 1, and 7 if it passes none of the tests. Write a program to read a carbon content, a Rockwell constant, and a tensile strength and determine the grade of the metal.

8. Systems of equations can be solved by iterative techniques. For example, the system

$$\begin{cases} 2x + y = 3 \\ x - 3y = 2 \end{cases}$$

can be solved by solving for $x$ in terms of $y$ in the first equation, and for $y$ in terms of $x$ in the second equation, to obtain:

$$\begin{cases} x = (3 - y)/2 \\ y = (x - 2)/3 \end{cases}$$

Starting with an initial approximate solution $x = y = 0$, we refine this approximation by computing a new $x$ and $y$ as follows:

$$\begin{cases} x = (3 - y)/2 = (3 - 0)/2 = 1.5 \\ y = (x - 2)/3 = (1.5 - 2)/3 = -.1666 \end{cases}$$

This procedure is repeated by computing new values for $x$ and $y$ in terms of the values $x$ and $y$ just computed. The process can be terminated by substituting $x$ and $y$ in the original equation and verifying that:

$$\begin{cases} 2x + y \doteq 3 & \text{or} \quad 2x + y - 3 \doteq 0 \quad \text{or} \quad |2x + y - 3| < \epsilon \\ x - 3y \doteq 2 & \text{or} \quad x - 3y - 2 \doteq 0 \quad \text{or} \quad |x - 3y - 2| < \epsilon \end{cases}$$

where $\epsilon$ is a prescribed degree of accuracy ($\epsilon = 0.01, 0.0001$, etc.)

Write a program to solve the following system of equations using this iterative technique with $\epsilon = 0.01$

$$\begin{cases} 2.56x - .034y = -.56 \\ 3.14x + 1.32y = 50.76 \end{cases}$$

9. Write a program to solve the following system of three equations in three unknowns using the approach in exercise 9. Initially set $x = y = z = 0$ and use $\epsilon = 0.1$.

$$\begin{cases} 3.1x - y + 2z = -.4 \\ x - 10y - 1.3z = 10 \\ -2.1x - 3y + 10z = -103.2 \end{cases}$$

10. Determining the roots of a polynomial, $y = P(x)$, implies finding values, $x_i$, so that $y = P(x_i) = 0$. A systematic method to determine $x$ is presented as follows:

*Step 1.* Determine by visual inspection two values for $x$, i.e., *xpos* and *xneg* so that P(*xpos*) > 0 and P(*xneg*) < 0. This means that a root of P(*x*) exists in the interval *xpos*, *xneg*, since polynomials are continuous functions and the graph of $y = P(x)$ must intersect the $x$ axis somewhere between *xpos* and *xneg*.

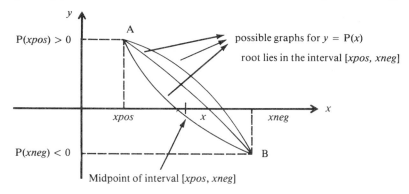

*Step 2.* For the next approximation $x$ to the root, take the midpoint of the interval *xpos*, *xneg*;

$$x = \frac{xpos + xneg}{2}$$

*Step 3.* Determine whether P($x$) > 0 or P($x$) < 0. If P($x$) > 0, then the root must lie between $x$ and *xneg*. If P($x$) < 0, then the root must lie between $x$ and *xpos*.

Then go back to step 2 and recompute a new (refined) approximation, $x$, making sure to replace *xpos* or *xneg* by $x$ depending on the sign of $y = P(x)$.

The above algorithm can be terminated when $y = P(x)$ is "sufficiently close" to zero; mathematically speaking, this means $|P(x)| < \epsilon$ where $\epsilon$ is a prescribed degree of accuracy.

Using the method described, compute a root of $y = x^3 - 2x^2 + x - 16$ in the interval [3,4]. Start with *xpos* = 4 and *xneg* = 3 and stop when $\epsilon$ = .1; i.e., $|P(x)| < .1$.

## 3-10-4 Answers to Test Yourself

1.  a.  Invalid; comma.
    b.  Valid.
    c.  Invalid; F4.5.
    d.  Invalid; integer format for real variable, B.   F4 is also invalid.
    e.  Invalid; real format for integer variable and vice versa for variable Y.
    f.  Valid.

2.  a.  1, 3, 0
    b.  0, invalid data in field, $-4$
    c.  130, 5, 2
    d.  1305, invalid data, $-46$
    e.  0, $-46$, 7
    f.  13, 1, invalid data
    g.  3, 5, $-46$

3.  a.

| | | $-$ | 5 | 0 | 0 | 2 | 0 | 0 | 0 | 0 | 0 | 0 | 0 |
|---|---|---|---|---|---|---|---|---|---|---|---|---|---|
| 1 | 0 | 0 | 0 | 1 | 0 | 0 | 0 | 0 | 0 | 0 | 0 | 8 | 0 |
| 0 | 4 | 7 | 8 | 0 | 9 | 9 | 0 | 0 | 0 | 8 | 8 | 0 | 9 |
| 0 | 0 | 3 | 6 | 0 | 0 | 1 | 0 | 0 | 1 | 0 | 2 | 0 | 6 |

```
READ(5,6)FLD1,FLD2,FLD3
6 FORMAT(F4.1, F8.2, F2.2)
```

b.

| | $-$ | . | 5 | 0 | 0 | 0 | 2 | 0 | 0 | 0 | . | 0 | 0 | . | 0 | 0 |
|---|---|---|---|---|---|---|---|---|---|---|---|---|---|---|---|---|
| 1 | 0 | 0 | . | 0 | 1 | 0 | 0 | 0 | 0 | 0 | . | 0 | 0 | . | 8 | 0 |
| 4 | 7 | . | 8 | 0 | 9 | 9 | 0 | 0 | 0 | . | 8 | 8 | 0 | . | 0 | 9 |
| 3 | . | 6 | 0 | 0 | 1 | 0 | 0 | 1 | . | 0 | 2 | 0 | 0 | . | 0 | 6 |

```
READ(5,6)FLD1,FLD2,FLD3
6 FORMAT(F5.0, F9.0, F3.0)
```

4.  a.  1.3, 25, .5        b.  3.025, 1, .5      c.  3.0, Invalid data, 1.5
    d.  Invalid data, 1, .5      e.  0., 30, 25.

5.  a.  A = 3.43,   J = 20,   X = .56,   Z = 21.

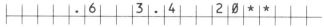

b.  A = 2.4,   I = 30,   J = 9,   C = $-1.3$

6.  a.  F.     b.  F.     c.  T.     d.  F.     e.  F.     f.  F.     g.  F.
    h.  T.     i.  F.     j.  T.     k.  F.     l.  F.     m.  F.     n.  F.
    o.  F.     p.  F.

7. READ instruction: invalid data in an input field, no more data records.
   WRITE instruction: format code is wrong mode for variable, data too large for field.

8. a.     `IF(X + T)2,1,2`              `IF(X.NE.(-T))GO TO 2`
                                                  `GO TO 1`

   b.     `IF(X - 4.)2,2,1`              `IF(X.GT.4.)GO TO 1`
                                                  `GO TO 2`

   c.     `IF(X**3 - Y**3 - Z**2)1,1,2`   `IF(X**3-Y**3 .GT. Z**2)GO TO 2`
                                                  `GO TO 1`

   d.     `IF(X + Y)5,5,3`               `IF(X+Y .LE. 0.)GO TO 5`
                                                `GO TO 3`

   e.     `IF(A/B - (-C/D + E/F))1,3,3`   `IF(A/B .LT. (-C/D+E/F))GO TO 1`
                                                  `GO TO 3`

   f.     `IF(A*X**2 + B*X + C - D)1,2,1`  `IF(A*X**2+B*X+C .EQ. D)GO TO 2`
                                                `GO TO 1`

9. a.
```
        IF(S .LT. 3.) GO TO 100    or  IF(S .LT. 3.) THEN
        IF(S .GT. 3.) GO TO 300            statement 100
    30                                 ELSE
                                           IF(S .GT. 3.) THEN
                                               statement 300
                                           ELSE
                                               statement 30
                                           ENDIF
                                       ENDIF
```

   b.
```
        IF(X .EQ. Z-4.) GO TO 150   or  IF(X .EQ. Z-4.) THEN
        IF(X .GT. Z-4.) GO TO 50            statement 150
    30                                 ELSE
                                           IF(X .GT. Z-4.) THEN
                                               statement 50
                                           ELSE
                                               statement 30
                                           ENDIF
                                       ENDIF
```

   c.
```
        IF(X+Y .GT. 3.**.5)GOTO 60  or  IF(X+Y .GT. 3.**.5) THEN
    30                                     statement 60
                                       ELSE
                                           statement 30
                                       ENDIF
```

10. a. Case 1: R = 2.            d. Case 1:  STOP.
        Case 2: R = 1.                Case 2:  0 is written.
   b. Case 1:  3 is written.        e. Case 1: 2 and 3 are written.
        Case 2:  −4 is written.           Case 2: 1 and −4 are written.
   c. Case 1: 3 is written.
        Case 2: 4 is written.

11. a. The = symbol is illegal; should be .EQ.    d. Missing relational operator.
   b. X.EQ.2 is not a statement.              e. Missing right parenthesis.
   c. Missing parentheses.                    f. Infinite loop if $17 \leq B$.

g. Comma illegal.
h. Missing parentheses; comma illegal.
i. END is not an executable statement.

j. IF in YES branch is illegal.
k. Only one statement allowed in YES branch.

12. a.
```
   IF(A .GE. B) GO TO 40        or        IF(A .LT. B) THEN
      C = C+1.                                 C = C+1.
      PRINT*, A                                PRINT*, A
40                                           ENDIF
```

b.
```
   IF(A .GE. 3) GO TO 40        or        IF(A .GE. 3.) THEN
      D = D+1                                  C = C+1.
      S = S+A                               ELSE
      GO TO 90                                 D = D+1.
40    C = C+1                                  S = S+A
90                                           ENDIF
                                       90
```

13.
```
   READ*, DUE
   READ*, RECEIV
   IF(DUE .LT. RECEIV) THEN
      CREDIT = RECEIV-DUE
      PRINT*, CREDIT
   ELSE
      IF(DUE .EQ. RECEIV) THEN
         PRINT*, 'NOTHING OWED'
      ELSE
         DUE = 1.02*(DUE-RECEIV)
         PRINT*, DUE
      ENDIF
   ENDIF
```

14. a.
```
   IF(A .NE. B) THEN
      T = X
      IF(C .EQ. D) THEN
         Z = X
      ELSE
         Y = X
      ENDIF
   ENDIF
```

b.
```
   IF(A .EQ. B) THEN
      X = 3.
   ELSE
      IF(E .EQ. F) THEN
         X = 2.
      ELSE
         X = 1.
      ENDIF
   ENDIF
```

c.
```
      READ*, X,Y
   10 IF(X .GT. 8.) THEN
         PRINT*, X
         X = X+1.
         GO TO 10
      ELSE
         IF(Y .LT. 0.) THEN
            Y = -1.*Y
         ELSE
            X = X+1.
         ENDIF
      ENDIF
      IF(X .NE. Y) GO TO 10
      STOP
```

15. a.
```
4 READ(5,6)A,B,C
  IF(C**2.EQ.A*A+B*B)WRITE(6,7)A,B,C
  GO TO 4
```

b.
```
IF(B.GE.60.)C=C+1.
  GO TO 4
```

c.
```
IF(X.GT.MAX)MAX=X
```

d.
```
  IF(B*B-4.*A*C.LT.0.)GOTO6
  R=2.
  GO TO 5
6 R=1.
5
```

e.
```
  IF(HRS-40.)1,2,3
3 W=1.2*R*HRS
  GO TO 6
2 W=1.05*R*HRS
  GO TO 6
1 W=R*HRS
6 WRITE(6,5)W
```

16. a. No, because every time code ≠ 3 an error message will be printed.
    b. No, because you never get to test codes 2 and 3.

17. a. Equivalent    b. Equivalent

18. a.
```
IF(HOURS .EQ. 40) THEN
    PRINT*, 'TRUE'
ELSE
   IF(SEX .EQ. 2) THEN
      PRINT*,'TRUE'
   ELSE
      IF(STAT .EQ. 3) THEN
         PRINT*, 'TRUE'
      ELSE
         PRINT*, 'FALSE'
      ENDIF
   ENDIF
ENDIF
```

b.
```
IF(HOURS .EQ. 40) THEN
   IF(SEX .EQ. 2) THEN
      IF(STAT .EQ. 3) THEN
         PRINT*, 'TRUE'
      ELSE
         PRINT*, 'FALSE'
      ENDIF
   ELSE
      PRINT*, 'FALSE'
   ENDIF
ELSE
   PRINT*, 'FALSE'
ENDIF
```

c.
```
IF(NAME .EQ. 'FONDA') THEN
    PRINT*, 'TRUE'
ELSE
   IF(SEX .EQ. 1) THEN
      IF(STAT .EQ. 3) THEN
         PRINT*, 'TRUE'
      ELSE
         PRINT*, 'FALSE'
      ENDIF
   ELSE
      PRINT*, 'FALSE'
   ENDIF
ENDIF
```

d.
```
IF(STAT .EQ. 3) THEN
    PRINT*, 'TRUE'
ELSE
   IF(HOURS .GE. 40) THEN
      IF(SEX .NE. 1)
         PRINT*, 'TRUE'
      ELSE
         PRINT*, 'FALSE'
      ENDIF
   ELSE
      PRINT*, 'FALSE'
   ENDIF
ENDIF
```

e.
```
IF(HOURS .NE. 40) THEN
   IF(SEX .NE. 2) THEN
      IF(STAT .EQ. 3) THEN
         PRINT*, 'TRUE'
      ELSE
         PRINT*, 'FALSE'
      ENDIF
   ELSE
      PRINT*, 'FALSE'
   ENDIF
ELSE
   PRINT*, 'FALSE'
ENDIF
```

**19.** a.
```
      IF(X .GT. Ø. .AND. X .LT. 3.*A) GO TO 7
```
b.
```
      IF(A .GE. 1. .AND. A .LE. 8. .AND. B .GE. 1. .AND. B .LE. 8.) GO TO 8
    4 ...
```
c.
```
      IF((X .GT. 4. .AND. Y .LT. 5.) .OR. (X .LT. 5. .AND. Y .GT. 4.)) GO TO 10
      STOP
```

**20.** On many systems, X will be stored internally as 1. On any system, the value 1.00 will be printed because the FORMAT rounds X to two decimal places.

**21.** The third test for the "under no condition" should be tested first since the characteristics specified in conditions 1 and 2 could conceivably satisfy condition 3. (Assume all variables are integers.)
```
      IF(.NOT.(HGHT .EQ. 3 .AND. TRAIT .EQ. 3 .AND. AGE .GT. 75
    1      .OR.(TRAIT .EQ. 2 .AND. HGHT .EQ. 1 .AND. AGE .LT. 19))) THEN
        IF(HGHT.EQ.1 .AND. COMP.NE.2 .AND. AGE.GE.2Ø .AND. AGE .LE.3Ø
    1                            .OR.
    2      HGHT.NE.1 .AND. COMP.NE.3 .AND. TRAIT.NE.1
    3                            .AND.
    4              (AGE.LT.18 .OR. AGE.GT.28)) THEN
            KOUNT=KOUNT+1
```

**22.** READ year
Divide year by 4 and keep remainder r
IF r = 0 THEN
    divide year by 100 and keep remainder r
    IF r = 0 THEN
        divide year by 400 and keep remainder r
        IF r = 0 THEN
            WRITE leap-year
        ELSE
            WRITE not leap-year
        ENDIF
    ELSE
        WRITE leap-year
    ENDIF
ELSE
    WRITE not leap year
ENDIF

# program structure:
## the counting process, and loop control with the while do

CHAPTER FOUR

# program structure:
## the counting process, and
## loop control with the while do

## 4-1  Programming Example

*Problem/Specification:*    Lurnalot University in Florida has four student classifications for billing purposes: in-state full-time, out-of-state full-time, in-state part-time, and out-of-state part-time. A student who enrolls for less than 12 hours of courses is considered to be a part-time student. The schedule of charges for each classification is summarized in the following table:

*Schedule of Charges*

|  | full-time | | part-time | |
|---|---|---|---|---|
|  | in-state | out-of-state | in-state | out-of-state |
| Tuition & Fees | $545 | $1,184 | $44/hour | $94/hour |
| Fixed Fee (All students) | $60 | | | |
| Board | $425 | | | |

The university needs a computer program to compute student bills. The input to the program is a file of student records where each record contains a student's:

■ name

■ residence status: the state abbreviation. Florida or 'FL' implies in-state status.

■ scheduled hours

■ request for board: 'yes' if requested, 'no' otherwise.

The output should list each student's name and total bill. The input and output can be visualized as follows:

*Input File*

| Name | State | Hours | Board |
|---|---|---|---|
| EDMUND | SC | 10 | YES |
| LITTLE | SC | 20 | YES |
| ZONE | SC | 10 | NO |
| HUGHES | SC | 20 | NO |
| DANGER | FL | 09 | YES |
| RANT | FL | 09 | NO |
| DOE | FL | 15 | YES |
| MIGHT | FL | 15 | NO |

*Output*

| NAME | STATE | HOURS | BOARD | BILL |
|---|---|---|---|---|
| EDMUND | SC | 10 | YES | 1425.00 |
| LITTLE | SC | 20 | YES | 1669.00 |
| ZONE | SC | 10 | NO | 1000.00 |
| HUGHES | SC | 20 | NO | 1244.00 |
| DANGER | FL | 9 | YES | 881.00 |
| RANT | FL | 9 | NO | 456.00 |
| DOE | FL | 15 | YES | 1030.00 |
| MIGHT | FL | 15 | NO | 605.00 |

The pseudo code and flowchart to solve this problem are shown in Figure 4–1, while the FORTRAN code is shown in Figure 4–2.

**FIGURE 4-1**   PSEUDO CODE AND FLOWCHART FOR STUDENT BILLING PROBLEM

### Pseudo Code

\* Student billing problem—compute student
\* bills based on in-state/out-of-state residency,
\* hours scheduled, and request for board
\*
\* Process individual student bills
\*

WHILE end-of-input-file-not-encountered DO

   \*Read student record

   READ name, state, hours, and board

   \* Initialize bill to fixed fees

   Bill = 60

   \* Determine tuition and fee charges
   IF hours ≥ 12 THEN
      \* Full__time student

      IF state = Florida THEN
         charge = 545
      ELSE
         charge = 1184
      ENDIF
   ELSE
      \* Part__time student

      IF state = Florida THEN
         charge = hours \* 44
      ELSE
         charge = hours \* 94
      ENDIF

   ENDIF
   add charge to bill
   \* Determine whether to charge for board

   IF board = 'yes' THEN
      add 425 to bill
   ENDIF
   PRINT bill
END WHILE
STOP

### Flowchart

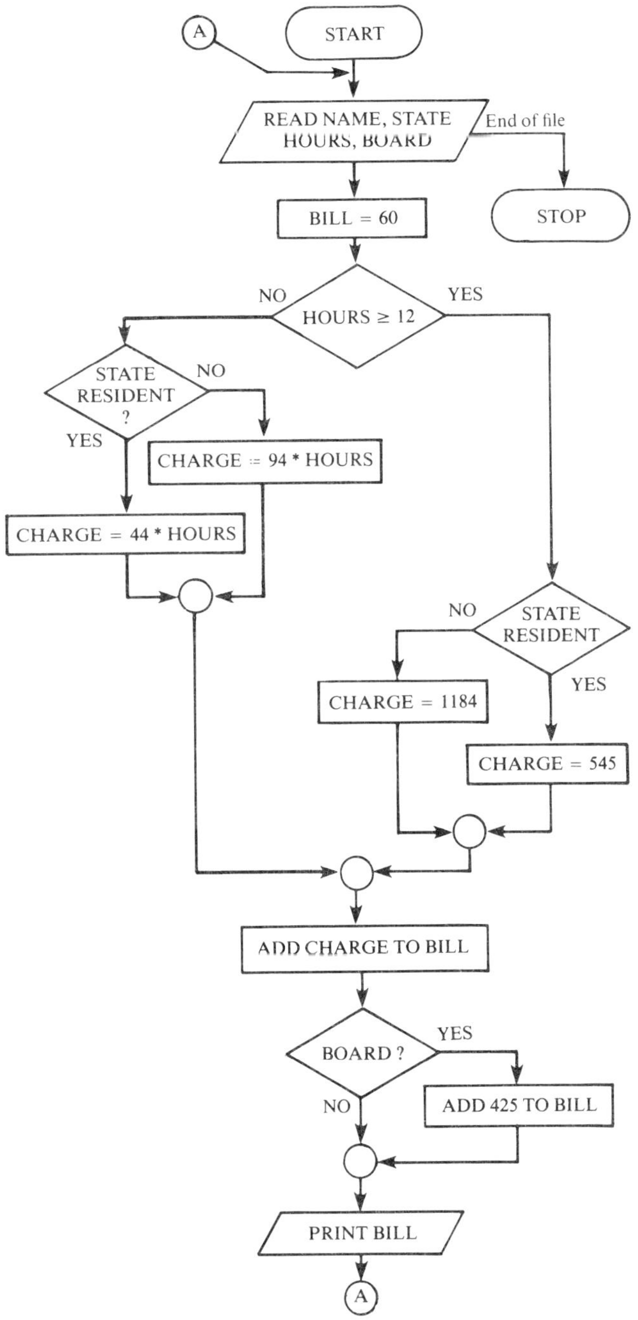

**FIGURE 4–2**   A STUDENT BILLING PROGRAM

```
C STUDENT BILLING PROGRAM
C   NAME:    STUDENT NAME
C   STATE:   RESIDENCY (FL IS IN-STATE)
C   BOARD:   ROOM & FOOD (EITHER 'YES' OR 'NO')
C   HOURS:   NUMBER OF CREDIT HOURS
C   CHARGE:  TUITION
C   BILL:    TOTAL COST TO STUDENT
C
      CHARACTER NAME*8, STATE*2, BOARD*3
      REAL BILL, CHARGE
      INTEGER HOURS
      WRITE(6,9)
      WRITE(6,5)
   10 READ(5,6,END=88)NAME,STATE,HOURS,BOARD
C INITIALIZE BILL TO FIXED FEE
      BILL = 60.00
C DETERMINE TUITION AND FEE CHARGES
      IF(HOURS .GE. 12) THEN
C FULL-TIME STUDENT
         IF(STATE .EQ. 'FL') THEN
            CHARGE = 545.00
         ELSE
            CHARGE = 1184.00
         ENDIF
      ELSE
C PART-TIME STUDENT
         IF(STATE .EQ. 'FL') THEN
            CHARGE = HOURS * 44.
         ELSE
            CHARGE = HOURS * 94.
         ENDIF
      ENDIF
      BILL = BILL + CHARGE
C DETERMINE WHETHER TO CHARGE FOR BOARD
      IF(BOARD .EQ. 'YES') THEN
         BILL = BILL + 425.00
      ENDIF
      WRITE(6,8) NAME,STATE,HOURS,BOARD,BILL
      GO TO 10
   88 STOP
    5 FORMAT(1X)
    6 FORMAT(A,A,I2,A)
    8 FORMAT(1X, A, 3X, A, 5X, I2, 5X, A, 3X, F7.2)
    9 FORMAT(1X,'NAME',6X,'STATE',2X,'HOURS',2X,
     1'BOARD',3X,'BILL')
      END
```

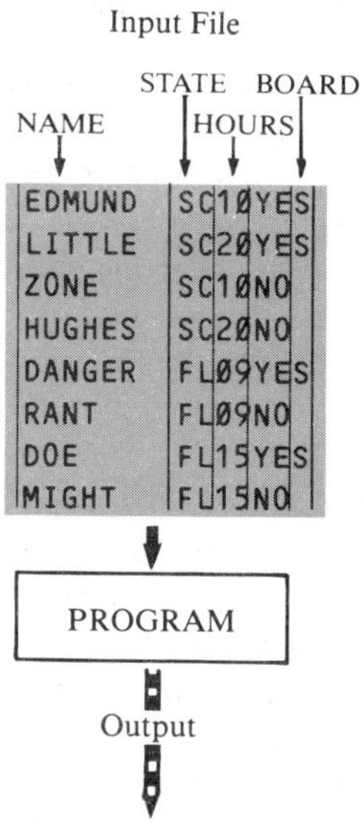

Input File

STATE  BOARD

| NAME | | HOURS | |
|------|------|------|------|
| EDMUND | SC | 10 | YES |
| LITTLE | SC | 20 | YES |
| ZONE | SC | 10 | NO |
| HUGHES | SC | 20 | NO |
| DANGER | FL | 09 | YES |
| RANT | FL | 09 | NO |
| DOE | FL | 15 | YES |
| MIGHT | FL | 15 | NO |

PROGRAM

Output

| NAME | STATE | HOURS | BOARD | BILL |
|------|-------|-------|-------|------|
| EDMUND | SC | 10 | YES | 1425.00 |
| LITTLE | SC | 20 | YES | 1669.00 |
| ZONE | SC | 10 | NO | 1000.00 |
| HUGHES | SC | 20 | NO | 1244.00 |
| DANGER | FL | 9 | YES | 881.00 |
| RANT | FL | 9 | NO | 456.00 |
| DOE | FL | 15 | YES | 1030.00 |
| MIGHT | FL | 15 | NO | 605.00 |

## 4-2 The Program Development Process

### 4-2-1 Major Programming Activities

Computer programming is a complex, creative task that demands a disciplined, organized approach to problem solving. Students often assume that proficiency in one or more computer languages (such as FORTRAN or COBOL) is all that is required to be a good computer programmer. This is equivalent to assuming that proficiency in English ensures the success of a novelist or proficiency in draftsmanship insures the success of an architect.

The computer programmer must first be able to convert a problem to an *algorithm*, a sequence of well-defined steps that can be carried out by a computer. In some cases, such as computing the area of a rectangular lot, this process is relatively straightforward, since the details of the solution are well understood. In other cases, such as computing the orbit of a spacecraft or predicting weather patterns, the programming process can become quite complex and time-consuming. Even after an algorithm has been developed and converted into a computer language, the programmer must still make sure that the program is correct and will function as desired in all situations. The actual process of writing statements in FORTRAN or some other language often represents only a small portion of the time spent on a programming project.

The program development process involves the following five major activities:

- Problem Specification
- Algorithm Design
- Coding
- Testing
- Documentation

In the following sections we will describe the purpose of each of these activities and techniques of program design.

### 4-2-2 An Analogy

Before considering the details of the programming process, let us first consider an analogous situation in which an architect is asked to develop plans for a building, as illustrated in Figure 4–3. In the first step, the client must clearly specify the purpose, function, and requirements for the building. If these specifications are not clearly described or if they are incomplete, the architect might design a structure that would not meet the client's needs. This would be a waste of time and money, and the process would have to start again with a more complete set of specifications. The analogous stage in the programming process requires the programmer and problem originator (often the same person) to carefully define the problem to be solved on the computer.

After the client and architect agree on the building specifications, the architect begins a design phase. The architect will probably first develop a general idea of what the structure should look like. Various tools such as sketches and models will be used to help the architect and the client visualize the structure. After many modifications and refinements to the general design, the architect is ready to develop a detailed set of blueprints that describe exactly how the building should be constructed. The programmer also begins by developing a general approach to the problem's solution. The end result of the design stage is an algorithm that describes the solution as a sequence of well-defined steps. Various program design tools such as flowcharts and pseudo code are used to describe and develop algorithms.

**FIGURE 4–3** PROGRAM DEVELOPMENT ACTIVITIES

| | | |
|---|---|---|
| | Specification | Given a number of hours worked . . .<br>. . . write a program to produce an employee payroll . . .<br><br>| NAME | HOURS | OVERTIME PAY | PAY |<br>\|---\|---\|---\|---\|<br>\| SMITH \| 40 \| 0.00 \| 200.00 \|<br>\| LADD \| 60 \| 200.00 \| 600.00 \| |
| | Design | Flowchart      Pseudo code<br><br>START<br><br>WHILE ... DO<br>  READ...<br><br>  IF hours ≤ 40 THEN<br>    Pay = ...<br>  ELSE<br><br>    Pay = ...<br>END    END WHILE |
|  | Coding | ```10 READ(5,6,END=88)NAME,HOURS,RATE```<br>```   IF (HOURS.LE.40) THEN```<br>```      PAY=HOURS*RATE```<br>```   ELSE```<br>```   .```<br>```   .```<br>```   ENDIF```<br>```   WRITE(6,8)NAME,HOURS,PAY```<br>```   .```<br>```   .```<br>```   END``` |
|  | Testing | input file      output<br><br>SMITH 40 5<br>LADD 60 -<br><br>\| NAME \| HOURS \| PAY \|<br>\| SMITH \| 40 \| 200.00 \|<br>\| MAZUR \| 20 \| 38400.00 \| |
| | Documentation | ```C    XYZ COMPANY PAYROLL PROGRAM```<br>```C    READ THE NAME,HOURS AND RATE```<br>```10 READ(5,6,END=88)NAME,HOURS,RATE```<br>```   .```<br>```C    IF EMPLOYEE HAS WORKED OVERTIME```<br>```   .```<br>```C    COMPUTE FINAL PAY```<br>```   PAY=PAY1 + PAY2```<br>```   .``` |

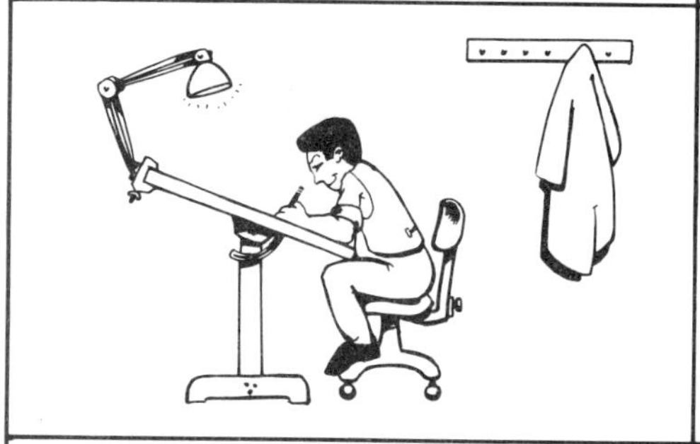

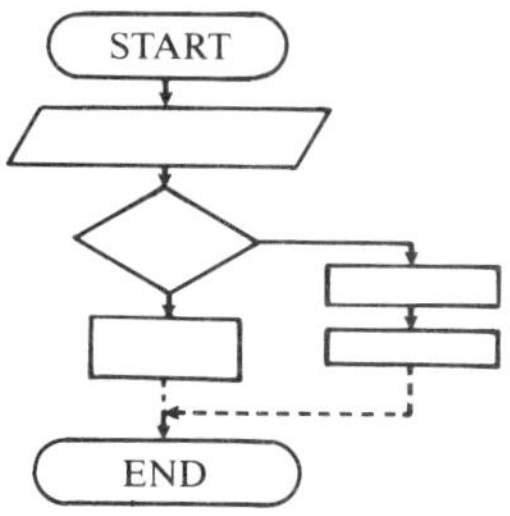

After the blueprints are completed and carefully checked for errors, the actual construction begins. This stage will probably require the innovative use of building techniques and materials, but for the most part the construction stage is simply a translation of the design into a physical structure. The equivalent stage in programming is called *coding* and involves the translation of the program design into a computer language.

When construction is completed, the architect and client can inspect the building for flaws. Minor construction and design errors can be corrected at some inconvenience and added expense. Major flaws that have progressed beyond the design stage are usually unacceptable and can seriously damage the architect's reputation (e.g., failure to provide access to the fourth floor of a building would impress future clients!). Similarly, the programmer tests a program after it has been translated into a programming language. Like the architect, the good programmer will probably discover and correct a few errors during the design stage. Invariably, however, some errors will exist in the initial program version. Some errors will be obvious minor ones that are easily corrected. Even the best programmers, however, find that it is not uncommon for major flaws to exist in the initial program run! The programmer does not have the advantage of being able to visualize a physical, static structure. The *testing* stage, during which the programmer tries to develop a reasonable level of confidence in the correctness of a program, often consumes a substantial proportion of the time spent on a program.

A separate, parallel activity that both the architect and programmer must perform is to provide *documentation* on the project. The architect will provide the client with blueprints, maintenance procedures, constructions details, and so forth. The programmer also must provide documentation on what the program does, how to use it, and how to keep it up-to-date.

Figure 4–4 illustrates the sequence of programming activities, the time involved in each one, and the typical overlap between the various activities. Many programming projects have failed because one or more of these activities were not given sufficient attention. Students often make the mistake of allowing only enough time to carry out the coding process without regard to the other more time-consuming activities of design and testing. Students who make this mistake usually end up wasting time since they must engage in a long and very frustrating testing phase during which they are continually convinced that their program is *almost* working.

In the following section we will review these activities and establish techniques for developing algorithms and programs.

## 4-3 Design Techniques

### 4-3-1 Problem Specification

A programmer must obviously understand what the problem is before he/she can hope to solve it. Many programmers, however, have experienced the frustration of writing a program that works perfectly well only to find out that the program does not satisfy the requirements of the problem. For example, suppose that the specifications for the area of two lots problem in section 2–1 had simply said: *Write a program that will find the area of two rectangular lots.* The programmer would be left with many uncertainties and would have to resolve the questions:

■ What type of data will be used by the program?　■ What output should this program produce?

■ How will the data be provided?　■ Should the total area of the two lots be computed?

**FIGURE 4-4    PROGRAMMING ACTIVITIES—TIME REQUIREMENTS AND TYPICAL OVERLAP**

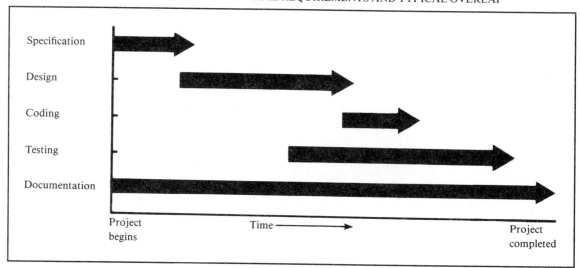

The programmer's interpretation of these sketchy specifications might result in a program that is quite different from the one presented in chapter 2. Suppose, for example, that the programmer decides against computing and printing the total area of the two lots. If the person who originated the problem really did want to know the total area, the programmer would have to modify the program to add this feature. In this simple example the modification is very straightforward; in a more complex example, however, the modification might easily take as much time as the original solution!

The problem specification stage, therefore, requires that the problem originator clearly state the *function* of the program, what *results* it should produce, and any *special considerations* or methods that should be used in arriving at the results. It is then the programmer's responsibility to study the specifications carefully and to seek clarification on any points that are ambiguous or omitted. Even when the problem originator and the programmer are the same person, the success of the programming project depends on a clear understanding of what is to be achieved.

## 4-3-2  Structured Programming and Algorithm Design

Once the programmer understands what is to be accomplished, he/she can proceed with the development of an algorithm. This stage requires two skills: a technique for developing a solution and a mechanism for expressing the solution. Both of these areas have received considerable attention in recent years. Until the early seventies there were few formal techniques or guidelines for developing algorithms. Then, in response to the chaotic situation caused by a multitude of individual styles and methods, a new programming discipline called *structured programming* emerged. An exact definition of structured programming is difficult to state since it is usually defined in terms of the alternatives, i.e., the undisciplined approaches of the past. In the most general sense, however, structured programming provides an organized and disciplined approach to design, coding, and testing through the use of the three control structures: sequence, selection, and loop iteration.

## Control Structures

In a flowchart, the order in which instructions are to be carried out is specified by the flow-lines that connect the boxes. In pseudo code the order is specified by the use of three well-defined *control structures*: sequence, selection (IF THEN ELSE), and loop (WHILE DO). The *exclusive* use of these three control structures in writing algorithms is a key principle of structured programming.

One of the more difficult tasks in programming is developing the logic that controls the order in which instructions are performed. A haphazard approach can result in a situation in which following the order of the instructions is like trying to visually pick out the individual strands in a bowl of spaghetti—the logic of the algorithm is so intertwined that the structure is obscured and difficult to comprehend. Structured programming avoids this problem by restricting the ways in which the control logic can be specified. The result is an algorithm that is easier to develop, understand, and modify.

In section 4–4 we will find that these three control structures are easily implemented in FORTRAN, even on systems that do not support the WHILE DO structure.

## The Sequence Structure

The programs in chapter 2 only used the simplest and most basic control structure, the *sequence* structure. As the name implies, the instructions in a sequence are to be performed one after another. In pseudo code we specify a sequence by simply listing the instructions in the order in which we want them to be performed. A pseudo code sequence and its flowchart equivalent are shown as follows:

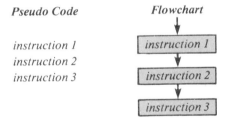

## The Selection Structure

The *selection* structure, which we used in chapter 3, allows alternative actions to be carried out based on the current value of variables in the algorithm. The general form of the selection control structure in pseudo code and in flowchart form is:

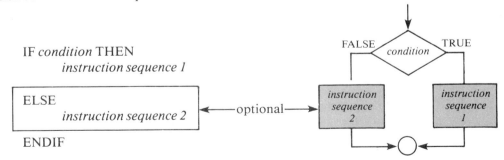

Note that indentation in the pseudo code enhances readability by providing important visual cues to associate actions with conditions.

### The Loop Structure: *WHILE DO*

The loop control structure allows a set of sequential instructions to be repeated zero or more times. The general form of the WHILE DO in pseudo code and in flowchart form is:

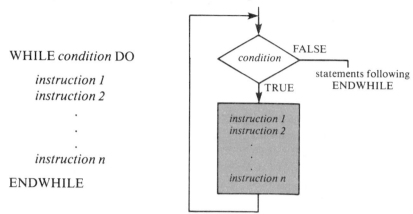

WHILE *condition* DO

    *instruction 1*
    *instruction 2*
    .
    .
    .
    *instruction n*

ENDWHILE

As in the IF THEN ELSE statement, the condition in the WHILE DO statement is a question with a true or false answer. If the condition is true, the instruction sequence *instruction 1, instruction 2,..., instruction n* is processed. The ENDWHILE causes the condition to be tested again. If the condition is still true, the instruction sequence is repeated. This continues until at some point the condition tested is false, at which time control passes to the statement following the ENDWHILE.

If the loop is ever to end, the instructions within the loop must perform an action that will eventually cause the condition to be false. Otherwise the instruction sequence will be repeated forever!

It is very important to understand the following points:

1. The condition tested by the WHILE DO statement is tested first, before the instruction sequence is carried out. If the condition is already false when the WHILE DO statement is first encountered, the instruction sequence is *not* carried out and control passes to the statement following the ENDWHILE, i.e., the instruction sequence is skipped.

2. Even though the condition specified by the WHILE DO may be met near the beginning of the instruction sequence, this does *not* mean that control is immediately passed to the statement following the WHILE DO. Only when *all* the instructions specified in the WHILE DO have been carried out will the condition be tested again and the loop end (if the condition is false). Consider the following example:

| | |
|---|---|
| X = 1 | |
| WHILE X ≠ 0 DO | Since X ≠ 0 the instruction sequence is carried out. |
|   READ name, sex, earning | At this point, X = 0 and the condition |
|   X = 0 | specified in the WHILE statement is false. |
|   add earning to total | Nevertheless the last three instructions are |
|   WRITE name, sex, earning | carried out before the loop terminates, since the test |
|   add 1 to count | for X ≠ 0 is made at the ENDWHILE. |
| ENDWHILE | |

The WHILE DO FORTRAN instruction may not be available on your system. If this is the case, the WHILE DO can be expressed very simply (simulated) in standard FORTRAN, as we will show in section 4–4 and Figure 4–8.

In summary, note that any algorithm can be expressed in pseudo code by using combinations of the loop, selection, and sequence control structures. The selection and the loop control structures incorporate the sequence control structure, but selection and loop structures themselves can also be combined to form larger sequence structures, as shown in Figure 4–5. Thus we can view an algorithm initially as a sequence of general actions; the algorithm is then refined to incorporate the loop and selection structures necessary to carry out the general actions.

## 4-3-3  Top-Down Design

The problem of "not being able to see the forest for the trees" can easily occur in the process of developing algorithms. The computer's limited intuitive abilities (compared to those of a human) require that a great deal of detail be incorporated in any problem solution. A programmer can easily become lost in a maze of details if he/she attempts to fully solve each component of a problem before moving on to the next.

A more productive approach is to first formulate the solution in terms of generalized statements. This first version of the algorithm is typically limited to expressing the general logic of the solution, not the details of any particular computation or any specific action. Once the general algorithm has been developed, it can be refined by adding the details that are necessary to perform the general actions. For a complicated problem, this refinement process may be repeated several times with each version containing more detail than the last. The process stops when the translation of the algorithm to a programming language is obvious. This approach, referred to as *stepwise refinement*, is part of a design philosophy called *top-down design*. By using top-down design, we can delay becoming involved in details until the problem has been broken into more manageable segments.

**FIGURE  4–5**    ALGORITHM STRUCTURE

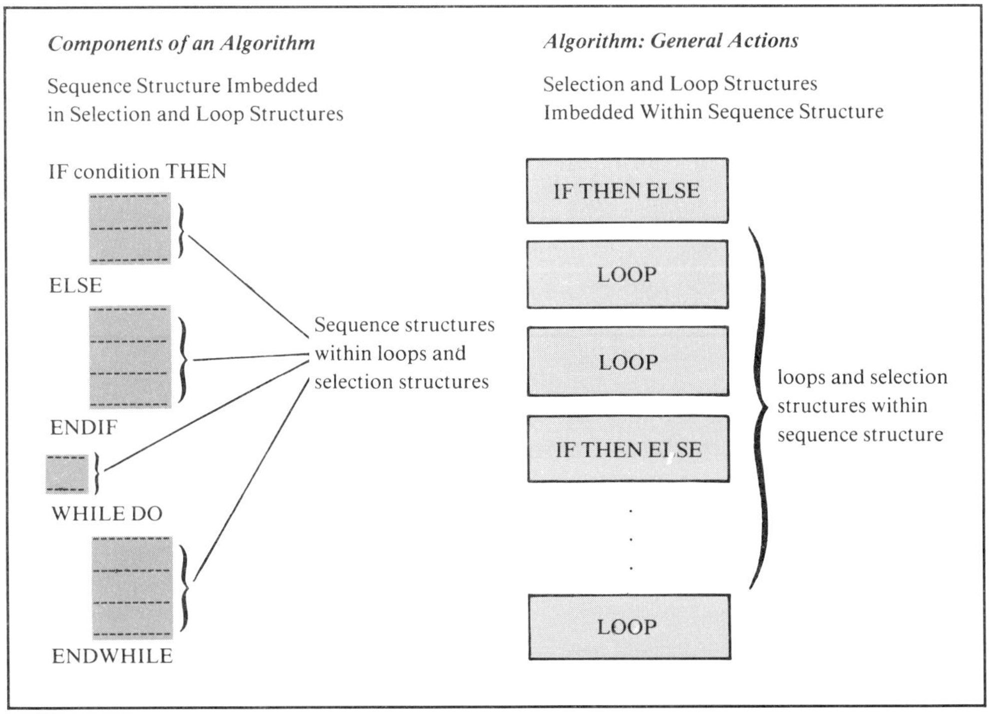

As an example of the top-down design process, consider the following pseudo code versions of the student billing problem of section 4–1. We begin by considering the actions that are needed to process one student's bill:

■ READ the student's record,　　■ Compute the bill,　　■ WRITE the bill.

These very general actions for a single student must obviously be repeated for each student, so we make our first attempt at an algorithm, by including these actions in a loop:

```
* student billing problem.
* version 1—general algorithm
WHILE the end of the input file is not encountered DO
        READ student record
        compute bill
        WRITE student bill
ENDWHILE
STOP
```

The statement to "compute bill" is obviously very general, but at this point in the development process we are simply trying to identify the major components of the problem. The next version includes somewhat greater detail on how to compute the bill:

```
* student billing problem
* version 2—add some details on bill computation.
* process individual student bills.
WHILE the end of the input file is not encountered DO
        READ student record
        initialize bill to fixed fee
        add tuition and fees charge to bill
        if requested, add board charge to bill
        WRITE student bill
ENDWHILE
STOP
```

These statements are still very general. We still have not considered the details of how to compute the tuition and fees, for example. A further refinement of the algorithm might expand this by distinguishing between full-time and part-time students:

```
* student billing problem
* version 3—additional details on bill computation
* process individual student bills
WHILE the end of the input file is not encountered DO
        READ student record
        initialize bill to fixed fee
* determine tuition and fee charge
        IF full-time student THEN
                determine full-time tuition and fees charge
        ELSE
                determine part-time tuition and fees charge
        END IF
        add tuition and fees charge to bill
        if requested, add board charge to bill
        WRITE student bill
ENDWHILE
STOP
```

In this version we continue to delay consideration of the difference between in-state and out-of-state student charges. Incorporating too many details in one refinement step will only obscure the general logic of the algorithm that we are trying to develop.

The final refinement of this algorithm was given in Figure 4–1. Note the addition of the details on how to compute in-state versus out-of-state tuition and fees. This stepwise refinement process is illustrated in Figure 4–6.

## 4-3-4  Testing the Design

This is probably the most crucial phase in the program development process, since the fate of the real-life programmer is determined by the correctness of his/her computer-generated results. In an environment where managers and corporate executives increasingly make decisions based on computer-produced reports, a programmer whose program results are faulty has a dismal job outlook. Yet many beginning (and some not-so-beginning) programmers put blind trust in whatever output is produced by their programs, arguing that since no errors showed up during execution, and since captions and numeric values were printed, the results must be correct. Nothing, of course, could be further from the truth. Computer-generated results are often incorrect—the numbers simply do not add up!

The remedy to this problem is to check your results to make sure that they are correct. This, of course, may require a great deal of time. The best way to proceed is to manufacture hypothetical data that will force the program to test each and every path that can be taken during execution of the program. (In a parallel context, if you built a lawn-watering system with numerous cutoff valves, you would want to check that no particular line or pipe was obstructed, i.e., that water would flow through each and every line. Checking just one particular circuit or one component of the pipeline and observing that it worked would not imply that the other lines also worked!) In a programming environment, different types of input values may need to be "invented" so that the action of the program on these dummy values can be observed and checked out. This process is known as *tracing* through a pro-

FIGURE  4–6    THE STEPWISE REFINEMENT PROCESS

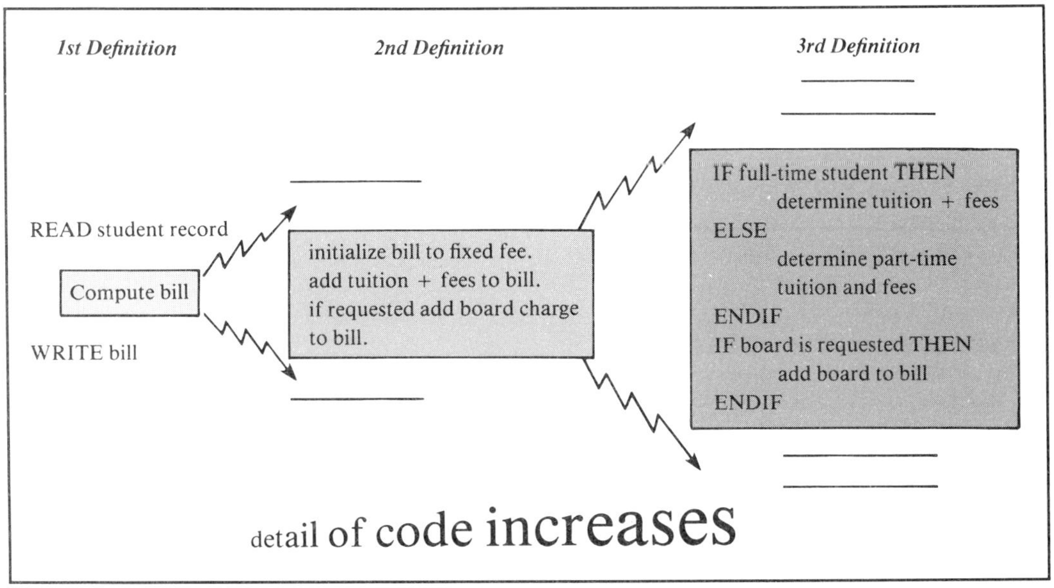

gram, flowchart, or pseudo code. You must follow and record what happens to each experimental input item as it travels through the network of instructions until the end of the program is reached. (See Figure 4–7.) You should manufacture as many experimental items as there are paths in the pseudo code or flowchart and you should follow each item through the entire network.

Input data validation is another part of design testing. Even though a program may be perfect in the sense that it contains no syntax or logical errors, it may not perform perfectly in the hands of others. For example, what would a program do at execution time if it expected to read a value of 1 or 2 for a particular variable X, but the value submitted by the user was 3? Ideally, the program should inform the user that the value read is incorrect and ask the user to change it to a 1 or 2! The program therefore cannot assume that the value for X will always be a 1 or 2; in fact, when dealing with humans, the value read could be a 1, a 2, or any other character on the keyboard! Hence, to avoid input mistakes the program should test X for the value 1, and then, if X is not 1, test for the value 2. If X is not 2, then the human goofed, and an appropriate action should be taken by the computer.

Testing every input item for every imaginable (or unimaginable) value can soon become a programmer's nightmare, and adding the extra code to take care of the input validation process can swell a "skinny" program into the obese league in no time at all! Yet, theoretically, a program should be written in such a way that it is "human-goof-proof".

**FIGURE  4–7**    VALID VERSUS INVALID TESTING

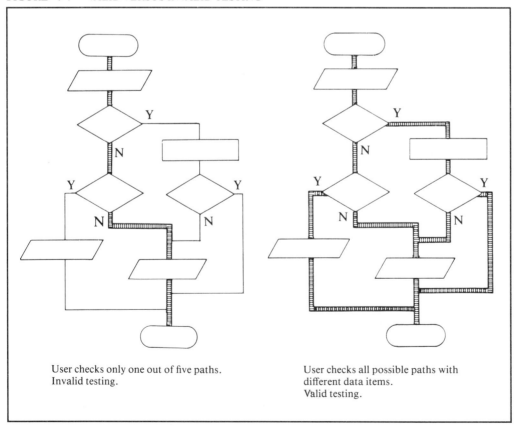

User checks only one out of five paths.
Invalid testing.

User checks all possible paths with different data items.
Valid testing.

For these reasons, the input validation process is a very important part of the problem-solving process. Its importance becomes even more critical during application of the program or system.

### 4-3-5 **Do It Now**

In the student billing program of Figure 4–1, what should the program do if the state abbreviation is incorrectly recorded, for example, FA instead of FL? Should that student be charged out-of-state tuition—a whopping additional $600.00 or so for the difference between an A and an L? What if the HOURS were recorded as 100 instead of 10 for a part time out-of-state student? Would he or she be charged $1,184? As this program is now coded, that is what would happen! What would you do to prevent these two types of errors from happening?

# 4-4 **The Counting Process**

Counting is an essential technique in programming. Counting can be used to read a specified number of data records from a file, to repeat a procedure a certain number of times *(loop control)*, to count the occurrences of specific events, or to generate sequences of numbers for computational uses. In any event, the computer cannot count by itself, and therefore the programmer must resort to certain counting techniques.

### 4-4-1 **Enumeration: Counting by 1's to Infinity**

Let us write the code to count by 1's and print the resulting numbers 1, 2, 3, 4, .... First, we choose a variable—for example, I—to serve as a counter, and we initially set I to 1. We print I, then we add 1 to I (increment I by 1) so that the new value of the counter I becomes 2 (we do this through the statement $I = I + 1$). Then we go back to the PRINT I statement, as shown here:

```
    I = 1            I is the counter, initially set to 1.
10 PRINT*, I         Print the value of the counter.
    I = I + 1        Add 1 to the counter
    GO TO 10         and go back to print the new value of the counter.
```

The statement $I = I + 1$ is of such paramount importance that we reemphasize its meaning:

$I = I + 1$ means
add 1 to I and call this new value I (the new value for I is equal to the old value plus 1).

Internally, this statement causes the computer to fetch the contents of memory location I, add 1 to it, and store the result back into location I. This, of course, causes destruction of the value that was previously stored in I.

### 4-4-2 **Do It Now**

1. If you are using a monitor (screen), and the output is displayed on the screen, run the code given in the preceding section. What do you think would be the highest value of I?

**2.** Write the codes to print the following sequences (part e should be in decimal, not fractional, form).

a. 2, 4, 6, 8, ...
b. 0, − 1, − 2, − 3, ...
c. 1, 3, 5, 7, ...

d. 2, 4, 8, 16, 32, ...
e. 1. 1./2. 1./3. 1./4., ... (1., .5, .3333..., .25)
f. − 1, 1, − 1, 1, − 1, ...

## Answers

**1.** The answer depends on the computer. A maximum value would be reached, at which point other unpredictable values would be printed.

**2.**

a.
```
  I = 2
5 PRINT*, I
  I = I + 2
  GO TO 5
```

b.
```
  I = Ø
5 PRINT*, I
  I = I-1
  GO TO 5
```

c.
```
  I = 1
5 PRINT*, I
  I = I+2
  GO TO 5
```

d.
```
  I = 2
5 PRINT*, I
  I = 2*I
  GO TO 5
```

e.
```
  X = 1.
5 Y = 1./X
  PRINT*, Y
  X = X+1.
  GO TO 5
```

f.
```
  I = 1
5 PRINT*, I
  I = (-1)*I      (or I = -I)
  GO TO 5
```

### 4-4-3  Loop Control: the WHILE DO

In most cases, we do not want to go on counting forever—we want to stop at some point—so we need to control the number of times we repeat a set of instructions. This process is known as loop control.

As we learned in section 4–3–2, the WHILE DO control structure allows us to repeat a set of instructions as long as a particular condition is met (true). The pseudo code and the flowchart form of the WHILE DO are:

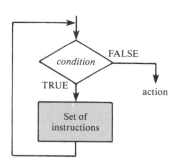

WHILE *condition* DO

> set of instructions
> to be carried out
> as long as
> condition is true

ENDWHILE
Action

An important application of the WHILE DO control structure is *loop control*. Loop control allows the programmer to repeat a procedure (task) a predetermined number of times by using a counter to keep track of the number of times the procedure is being carried out (*loop*). Exit from the loop is achieved when the counter reaches the designated value. Consider the following problem:

> An input file consists of three records, each containing a score. Write the code to read and print each of the three scores.

The WHILE DO structure suggests that we take the following approach:

1. Initialize a counter to 1.

2. As long as the counter is less than or equal to 3, repeat steps 3, 4, and 5. When the counter is greater than 3, end the loop and stop.

3. Read a score.

4. Print the score. } loop

5. Add 1 to the counter.

Let us write these instructions in pseudo code, using the WHILE DO.

| | |
|---|---|
| Set the counter to 1 | Initially, the counter is 1. |
| WHILE counter ≤ 3 DO | Since 1 ≤ 3, the 1st score is processed and the counter becomes 2. |
|     READ a score | Since 2 ≤ 3, the 2nd score is processed and the counter becomes 3. |
|     WRITE the score | Since 3 ≤ 3, the 3rd score is processed and the counter becomes 4. |
|     add 1 to the counter | Since 4 is not ≤ 3, control is passed to the instruction following |
| ENDWHILE | the ENDWHILE. |
| STOP | |

    To better visualize the mechanism of the loop process, we can trace through the loop and, for each cycle through the loop, record the values assumed by the different variables, thus constructing a table of values. This process is called *tabulation*. The flowchart and table corresponding to this program are:

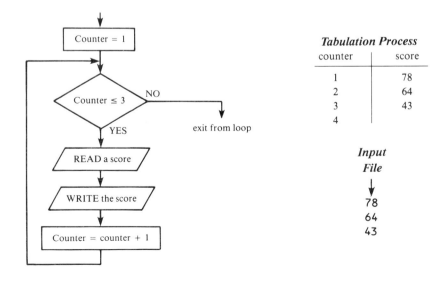

***Tabulation Process***

| counter | score |
|---|---|
| 1 | 78 |
| 2 | 64 |
| 3 | 43 |
| 4 | |

***Input File***

↓

78
64
43

If your FORTRAN system supports the WHILE DO, then you can translate the pseudo code into FORTRAN as follows:

```
INTEGER SCORE
I = 1
WHILE (I .LE. 3) DO        Note that the condition must be enclosed in parentheses.
    READ*, SCORE
    PRINT*, SCORE
    I = I+1
ENDWHILE
STOP
```

If your FORTRAN system does *not* support the WHILE DO instruction, the same structure can easily be simulated in standard FORTRAN. The problem of reading and printing three scores would become:

1. Initialize a counter to 1.

2. When the counter is greater than 3, transfer out of the loop and stop. Otherwise execute steps 3, 4, 5, and 6.

3. Read a score.

4. Print the score.

5. Add 1 to the counter.

6. Go back to step number 2.

Let us, then, write the corresponding FORTRAN code and interpret its action:

```
    INTEGER SCORE
       I = 1
10  IF(I.GT.3)GO TO 20
    READ*,SCORE
    PRINT*,SCORE
    I = I+1
    GO TO 10
20  STOP
```

I is 1. Since 1 is not greater than 3, the first score is processed and I becomes 2.
Since 2 is not greater than 3, the second score is processed and I becomes 3.
Since 3 is not greater than 3, the third score is processed and I becomes 4.
Since 4 is greater than 3, control is passed to 20, terminating the looping process.

The generalized implementation of the WHILE DO control structure for standard FORTRAN (FORTRAN 77 or FORTRANs that do not support the FORTRAN statement WHILE DO) is shown in figure 4–8.

## Structured Code

Writing structured code implies the following:

1. The WHILE DO pseudo code will be used to express loop structures in the design of our programs, regardless of whether the FORTRAN in use supports the WHILE DO instruction. (An alternative to the WHILE DO is the DO loop discussed in chapter 5.)

**FIGURE 4-8**  IMPLEMENTATION OF THE WHILE DO IN STANDARD FORTRAN

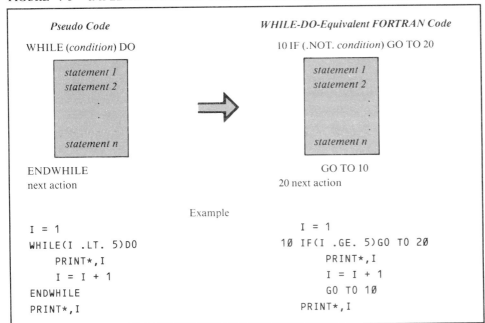

2. If the FORTRAN in use does not support the WHILE DO instruction, we will express the WHILE DO in the equivalent FORTRAN code shown in Figure 4-8.

While this systematic approach (using only the WHILE DO to express loop structures) may seem inflexible, its consistent usage will ultimately benefit the novice programmer. Other languages, such as COBOL and PASCAL, use similar structures. If you wish to write structured code, then you *must* use the three control structures described in section 4-3: the sequence, the selection, and the WHILE DO structures.

This does not mean, of course, that there are no alternatives to the WHILE DO to express the loop process. There are indeed many ways to code loops—pretests, posttests, middle tests, and so forth. This variety of methods is the affliction of unstructured code. In an unstructured environment, programmers naturally develop individual programming styles reflecting their own ways of thinking, their particular strategies, their understanding or misunderstanding of the language, and so forth. Poor program design and tortured code often emerge as a result.

Many highly complex programming systems are now the result of team efforts, so it is extremely desirable that a commonality of structure and coding practices exist in all of the system's components. Indeed, such systems (which could well be the programs you write for your instructor) require "universal" understanding so that they can be comprehended, used, maintained, and modified by a variety of users other than their originators. In that perspective, structured programming is a tool for standardized communication. Structured programming not only encourages well thought-out logic, it also provides the means to standardize and simplify the development of the program design; this is one of our reasons for using the WHILE DO and its FORTRAN implementation to represent loop processes.

*Example 1*

Write the pseudo code and the corresponding FORTRAN code to print the numbers 1, 3, 5, ..., 227 and stop.

```
Set counter to 1                    I = 1
WHILE counter ≤ 227 DO          10 IF(I .GT. 227)GO TO 20
    PRINT the counter                  PRINT*,I
    add 2 to the counter               I = I + 2
ENDWHILE                               GO TO 10
STOP                            20 STOP
```

Note that when I becomes 229 in the FORTRAN code, control is passed to statement 20 and the value 229 is *not* printed.

You may wonder why this WHILE DO pseudo code is translated into a logical IF with a GO TO statement, instead of an IF THEN ENDIF structure, as follows:

```
Set counter to 1                    I = 1
WHILE counter ≤ 227 DO          10 IF(I .LE. 227)THEN
    PRINT the counter                  PRINT*,I
    Add 2 to the counter               I = I + 2          undesirable practice
ENDWHILE                               GO TO 10
STOP                               ENDIF
```

Such FORTRAN code *is* valid; however the version in Figure 4–8 is preferable. The GO TO statement imbedded in the IF THEN structure gives an aborted appearance to the IF THEN, since the ENDIF statement is not actually used if the condition is true.

In general, the IF THEN ELSE selection structures should be self-contained entities. If possible, they should not be linked to outside structures through internal GO TO statements. For that reason, we will use the logical IF model of Figure 4–8 to represent the WHILE DO.

*Example 2*

Write the pseudo code and FORTRAN code to print the 7's multiplication table, as follows:

```
7X  1 =  7
7X  2 = 14
     .
     .
7X 12 = 84
```

In this example, we need to generate a counter that takes on the values 1 through 12. The solution can be written as follows:

```
Set counter to 1                    N = 7
                                    L = 1
WHILE counter ≤ 12 DO           20 IF(L .GT. 12) GO TO 50
    Multiply 7 by the counter          K = 7 * L
    WRITE the results                  WRITE(6,5)N,L,K
    Add 1 to counter                   L = L + 1
ENDWHILE                               GO TO 20
STOP                            50 STOP
                                 5 FORMAT(1X,I1,'X',I2,' = ',I2)
```

*Example 3*  Nested WHILE Control Structures

Suppose we were to write the code to print out the multiplication tables from 2 to 12 with blank lines separating each table, as follows:

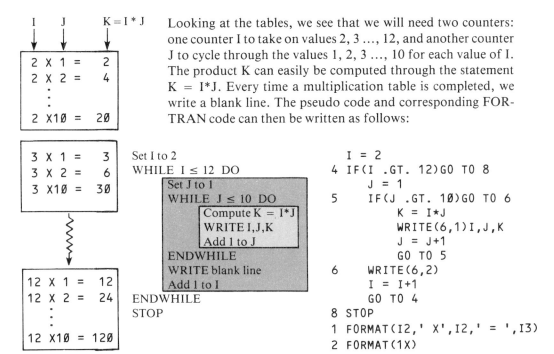

Looking at the tables, we see that we will need two counters: one counter I to take on values 2, 3 ..., 12, and another counter J to cycle through the values 1, 2, 3 ..., 10 for each value of I. The product K can easily be computed through the statement K = I*J. Every time a multiplication table is completed, we write a blank line. The pseudo code and corresponding FORTRAN code can then be written as follows:

```
Set I to 2                              I = 2
WHILE I ≤ 12  DO                    4 IF(I .GT. 12)GO TO 8
    Set J to 1                             J = 1
    WHILE J ≤ 10  DO               5     IF(J .GT. 10)GO TO 6
        Compute K = I*J                     K = I*J
        WRITE I,J,K                         WRITE(6,1)I,J,K
        Add 1 to J                          J = J+1
    ENDWHILE                                GO TO 5
    WRITE blank line              6     WRITE(6,2)
    Add 1 to I                            I = I+1
ENDWHILE                                  GO TO 4
STOP                               8 STOP
                                   1 FORMAT(I2,' X',I2,' = ',I3)
                                   2 FORMAT(1X)
```

The process of incrementing the two counters can be visualized as follows:

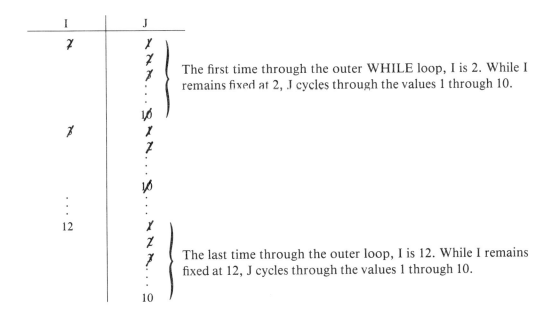

## *Common Pitfalls with Nested Structures*

As we have seen in chapter 3 and in this chapter, it is possible to nest IF THEN ELSE structures within other IF THEN ELSE structures, and to nest WHILE DOs within other WHILE DOs. Clearly IF THEN ELSE structures can be nested in WHILE DOs and vice versa. In so doing one has to ensure that each structure is wholly contained within another structure, not straddling across other structures. Each structure must have a beginning and an end, i.e., header statements (WHILE DO and IF statements) and terminal statements (END WHILE and ENDIF). If these rules are observed, a variety of structures can be built as follows:

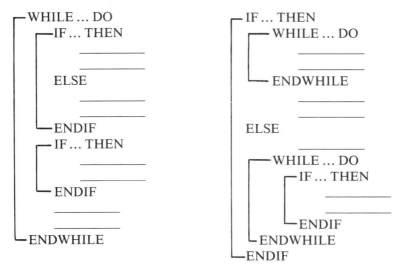

Make sure that the nested structures do not overlap, as in:

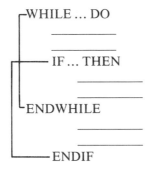

To avoid this type of problem, use a line to connect each WHILE to its corresponding ENDWHILE and each IF to its corresponding ENDIF. If the lines intersect, the structure is incorrect.

Even if the FORTRAN WHILE DO instruction is not available on your system, the corresponding FORTRAN implementation of Figure 4–8 can be used to create these structures.

### 4-4-4 Counting for Occurrences of Events

A poll was conducted in a political science class to determine students' feelings about isolationism. The code used to record students' opinions was as follows:

| Code | Meaning |
|------|---------|
| 0 | Against isolationism. |
| 1 | Neutral. |
| 2 | For isolationism. |

All responses were gathered and recorded, one per record, with the special code 9 as the last data item to indicate the physical end of the results. Write a program to read the data records and determine the number of students who are against isolationism, the number who are neutral, and the number who are for isolationism.

This problem requires the use of three counters: one counter for the anti-isolationists, another counter for the neutrals, and another for the pro-isolationists. Initially, before we start reading the records, these counters should be set to 0.

One remaining problem is that we do not know the number of records in the input file. We only know that the last record is a 9, not a 0, 1, or 2. One possible method for processing this input file would be: as long as the code read is *not* 9, process the code and find out if it is a 0, 1, or 2. This approach lends itself very well to the WHILE DO structure:

```
Set the 3 counters to 0
WHILE code not equal to 9 DO
        Read code
        Process the code
ENDWHILE
WRITE the results
```

One problem with this approach is that the value for code in the WHILE DO statement is undefined the first time through the loop,—it has not yet been read! One way to solve this problem is to read the first record all by itself, so that code is initially defined, and then read all the other records with a separate READ statement at the foot of the WHILE DO structure. This method is called the *prime READ method* and is used in the following pseudo code and FORTRAN code:

```
* Initialize the 3 counters to 0
Set counter for anti to 0
Set counter for neutral to 0
Set counter for pro to 0
* Read the first record all by itself
READ code
WHILE code ≠ 9 DO
    IF code = 0
        Add 1 to Anti__count
    ELSE
        IF code = 1
            Add 1 to Neutral__count
        ELSE
            Add 1 to Pro__count
        ENDIF
    ENDIF
READ code
ENDWHILE
* When all records have been processed
WRITE the three counts
STOP
```

```fortran
      INTEGER ANTI,PRO,NEUTRL,CODE
      ANTI   = 0
      NEUTRL = 0
      PRO    = 0
      READ*, CODE
    5 IF(CODE .EQ. 9)GO TO 8
          IF(CODE .EQ. 0)THEN
             ANTI = ANTI + 1
          ELSE
             IF(CODE .EQ. 1)THEN
                NEUTRL = NEUTRL + 1
             ELSE
                PRO = PRO + 1
             ENDIF
          ENDIF
      READ*, CODE
      GO TO 5

    8 PRINT*, ANTI,PRO,NEUTRL
      STOP
      END
```

Note that with this method the first value for code is read by the independent READ statement outside the loop. Also note that the loop terminates if the code read within the loop is 9, since the very next instruction after the READ is the test for the code. If the code read is not 9, then the WHILE DO is carried out, processing the code just read.

In this problem we use a special last record code to tell us that there are no more records in the input file, i.e., this special terminal code (sometimes called a *trip* or a *trigger*, or a *sentinel* code) warns us that we have reached the end of the file. In essence, it simulates an end-of-file condition. In section 4–4–6, we will discuss a simpler method of reading an input file with an unknown number of records, without having to manufacture an artificial (dummy) last record.

### 4-4-5 Do It Now

1. Write the pseudo code to perform an input data validation for the poll problem in the preceding section.

2. Each record of an input file contains a score (1–100). A negative value that is *not* a score identifies the last record of the input file. The following pseudo code is supposed to print all scores below 50. Why is the logic in the code incorrect?

   ```
   Set score to 0
   WHILE score ≥ 0 DO
         READ score
         IF score < 50 THEN
               WRITE score
         ENDIF
   ENDWHILE
   ```

3. Complete the condition so that 6 data records will be read.

   a. SET I TO 7
      WHILE I _____ DO
            READ RECORD
            SUBTRACT 1 FROM I
      ENDWHILE

   b. SET I TO 0
      WHILE I _____ DO
            ADD 1 TO I
            READ RECORD
      ENDWHILE

4. How many records will be read by the following?

   a. SET I TO 9
      WHILE I ≥ 1 DO
            READ RECORD
            SUBTRACT 1 FROM I
      ENDWHILE

   b. SET I TO 1
      WHILE I ≠ 3 DO
            ADD 1 TO I
            READ RECORD
      ENDWHILE

5. Write the pseudo code and the FORTRAN code to print the following sequences of numbers:

   a. 100, 95, 90, ..., 10, 5
   b. 1, 10, 100, ..., 100000

6. An input file consists of six records, where each record contains a score between 1 and 100. Write the pseudo code to compute and print the percentage of passing scores and print each passing score. A passing score is a score above 70.

**7.** Assume the input file in problem 6 above consists of an unknown number of records, where the last record contains any number over 100. Write the pseudo code to compute and print the percentage of passing scores.

## Answers

**1.** Add following code after the second ELSE statement:
> IF code = 2
>> Add 1 to Pro__count
> ELSE
>> write error message
> ENDIF

**2.** The WHILE DO will process the value on the last record as a valid score, i.e., the negative score will be printed in addition to all the other scores below 50. This clearly should not happen: the trip value on the last record should not be processed like all other input values. This is one reason why we use the prime READ to process an input file.

**3.**  a.  I ≠ 1
   b.  I ≠ 6

**4.**  a.  9
   b.  2

**5.**  a.  Set counter to 100
   WHILE counter ≥ 5 DO
     WRITE the counter
     Subtract 5 from counter
   ENDWHILE

```
  I = 100
5 IF(I .LT. 5) GO TO 1
    PRINT*, I
    I = I-5
    GO TO 5
1 STOP
```

   b.  Set counter to 1
   WHILE counter ≤ 100000
     WRITE counter
     Multiply counter by 10
   ENDWHILE

```
  K = 1
5 IF(K .GT. 100000) GO TO 1
    PRINT*, K
    K = 10*K
    GO TO 5
1 STOP
```

**6.** * Set counter to count from 1 to 6
   Counter = 1
   * Set counter to count passing scores to 0
   Passing__count = 0
   * Process the 6 records
   WHILE counter ≤ 6 DO
     READ*, score
     IF score > 70 THEN
       Add 1 to passing__count
       PRINT*, score
     ENDIF
     Add 1 to counter
   ENDWHILE
   * Compute percentage of passing scores
   Percentage__passing__scores = passing__count/6*100
   WRITE percentage__passing__scores
   STOP

7. Since we need the total number of scores to find the percentage passing, we need two counters: one to count all scores and the other to count the passing scores. Also since we do not know how many records to read, we use the prime READ method to read the input file.

```
* Initialize counter to count all scores read, call it total
total = 0
* Initialize counter to count passing scores, call it pass
pass = 0
* Read the 1st record independently of the others
READ score
* Process the record just read as well as all remaining records
WHILE score ≤ 100 DO
IF score > 70 THEN
    add 1 to pass
ENDIF
add 1 to total
* Read next record
READ score
* and go back and process record just read
ENDWHILE
* Compute percentage of passing scores
Percent__passing = pass/total * 100
WRITE percent__passing
STOP
```

### 4-4-6  End-of-File Processing

As we noted in chapter 1, computers can read from a variety of devices or mediums: magnetic disks, data cards, magnetic tape, terminals, and so forth. Data on such mediums is organized into *fields;* for example, if data cards are used, a field is defined as a group of related card columns. A field identifies a particular fact about an entity; a *record* is a group of related fields and hence describes many characteristics of an entity. An employee record might consist of a social security number field, a name and address field, and so forth, all entered on one record. A *file* is a collection of related records.

When reading a file it is important not to attempt to read more records than are present in the file; this causes a read error and the system terminates the program. When the computer is programmed to read an unknown number of records, it is necessary to determine when the file ends. There are several ways to do this. Two of these end-of-file techniques are the automatic end of file and the last record code technique (section 4-4-4).

### *Automatic End of File*

On most systems the programmer can use a feature of the READ statement to instruct the computer to keep reading records until they run out; when that happens the computer transfers control to a particular statement designated by the user. The computer automatically senses the end of file (no more data records to read) and is told where to go and what to do when this condition arises (see Figure 4–9). With this method the programmer is relieved of the task of simulating an end of file using the last record code method (section 4-4-4).

**FIGURE  4-9**    AUTOMATIC END-OF-FILE PROCESSING

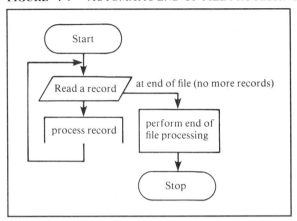

## *Processing Input Files with the Automatic End-of-File Option*

The general format for the extended READ is:

---

*Format-directed input*

READ (*device number*, *format statement number*, END = *statement number*) *list*
*Example:*  `READ(5,6,END=88)X,Y,Z`
          Read 3 values on logical device 5 according to FORMAT 6
          If the end-of-file is read, transfer to statement 88.

*List-directed input*

READ(*device number*,*,END = *statement number*) *list*
*Example:*  `READ(*,*,END=88)X,Y,Z`
          Read 3 values from the system input device (terminal = '*')
          If the end-of-file is detected, transfer to statement 88.

---

The automatic end-of-file record is a record that identifies the physical end of a particular file. If the user creates an input file similar to the one discussed in section 3-2-1, Figure 3-2, then he/she must add the end-of-file record to the data file. This end-of-file record differs from one system to another, depending on the operating system. Some systems use /* as an end-of-file record. If the user creates a data file on diskettes or magnetic disk, the system will automatically insert an end-of-file record at the end of the data file. In any event, this end-of-file marker can be sensed by the READ statement with the END= option.

Figure 4–10 shows the pseudo code and the equivalent FORTRAN code for reading an input file with an unknown number of records using the automatic end-of-file option.

**FIGURE 4–10**    PROCESSING AN INPUT FILE WITH AN UNKNOWN NUMBER OF RECORDS

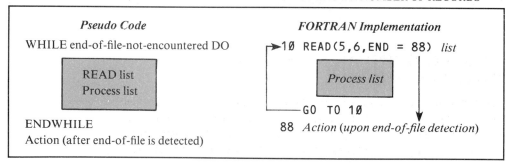

To read an input file using the automatic end-of-file, use the FORTRAN code in Figure 4–10. To represent the automatic end of file process in pseudo code, use the statement WHILE end-of-file-not-encountered DO.

Note that when the end-of-file is detected, **no input data** is read into the variable(s) specified in the input list of the READ statement.

*Example 1*

| Input Records | Code | Memory |
|---|---|---|

```
12.1   3      10 READ(5,6,END=88)X,I      X  |  I
                       .                 12.1 | 3  1st record
14.2   5               .                 14.2 | 5  2nd record
                       .
■ end of file     GO TO 10
               88 STOP
                6 FORMAT(F4.1,2X,I2)
```

The last values read into X and I are 14.2 and 5, respectively.

*Example 2*

An input file consists of records, each containing a student's name and test score. Write the code to read and print the students' names, scores, and test results (PASS if score > 90, FAIL otherwise) and the total number of scores.

Using the structure outlined in Figure 4–10, we proceed as follows:

```
* Set up a counter to count all scores
count = 0                            CHARACTER NAME*8, GRADE*4
WHILE end-of-file-not-encountered DO INTEGER SCORE, COUNT
READ name, score                     COUNT = Ø
    add 1 to count                 5 READ(5,6,END = 88) NAME,SCORE
    IF score > 90 THEN                 COUNT = COUNT+1
        grade = 'PASS'                 IF(SCORE .GT. 90) GRADE = 'PASS'
    ELSE                               IF(SCORE .LE. 90) GRADE = 'FAIL'
        grade = 'FAIL'                 WRITE(6,1) NAME,SCORE,GRADE
    ENDIF                              GO TO 5
    WRITE name, score, grade       88 WRITE(6,3) COUNT
ENDWHILE                              STOP
* Print count at end of file         1 FORMAT(1X,A,1X,I3,1X,A)
WRITE count                          3 FORMAT(1X,'COUNT SCORES=',I3)
STOP                                 6 FORMAT(A8,I3)
```

Note that the counter that counts all scores is printed only after the end of file has been encountered, not before.

### Processing an Input File with the WHILE DO Instruction and with the Last Record Code Technique

The automatic end-of-file method illustrated in Figure 4–10 does not make use of the WHILE DO FORTRAN instruction. If your system supports this instruction and if you do not wish to use the automatic end-of-file method, you must simulate an end-of-file condition by adding to your data file a last record containing "unusual" values for the variables that are to be read, i.e., values that are intentionally different from the preceding ones. For example, if you are reading an age field and a sex field (1 = male, 2 = female), either sex or age can be used as a "trip" or "sentinel" variable to detect the end of file: The trip value could be 3 for the sex code or 1000 for the age field in the *very last* input record. The corresponding WHILE DO condition could then be:

WHILE age < 1000 process the input file
or
WHILE sex < 3 process the input file

When the last record is read, the condition in the WHILE DO will be false and an exit from the loop will be taken.

A first attempt at writing the corresponding pseudo code might be:

WHILE age < 1000 DO
    READ sex, age
    [ process record read ]    For example, "process record read" might mean
    ENDWHILE    "count the number of people over 90."

There are, however, two problems with the above code: the value of age is undefined the first time the WHILE statement is executed, and, more important, the WHILE DO will process the simulated end of file record as a valid record before realizing that it is the "artificial" last record. Obviously the last record should not participate in the count process; otherwise the count of people over 90 would incorrectly include a person 1000 years old!

We can avoid this problem by reading the first record by itself before the WHILE DO is carried out:

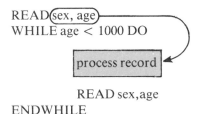

READ the first record.
This first record will be processed within the WHILE DO the first time through the loop. Then the second record is read by the READ statement in the loop. If the record read is the trip record, exit is taken; otherwise that record is processed in the *process record* block.

Recall from section 4–4–4 that this method of reading the first record independently is called the prime READ method. Its structure is shown in Figure 4–11.

**FIGURE  4-11**    THE PRIME READ METHOD USING THE WHILE DO INSTRUCTION

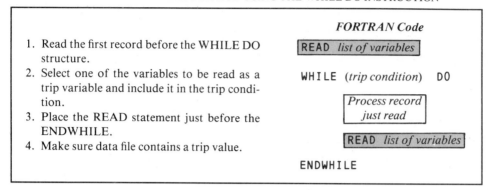

*FORTRAN Code*

1. Read the first record before the WHILE DO structure.

```
READ  list of variables
```

2. Select one of the variables to be read as a trip variable and include it in the trip condition.

```
WHILE (trip condition)   DO
```

3. Place the READ statement just before the ENDWHILE.

```
        Process record
          just read

        READ  list of variables
```

4. Make sure data file contains a trip value.

```
ENDWHILE
```

*Example*

Each record of an input file contains a name and a sex code (1 = male, 2 = female). Write the code to compute the percentage of females.

Let us use the sex field as a trip, with value 3. (We could just as well have chosen the name as a trip, with value 'XXXX'.) We now write the code as follows:

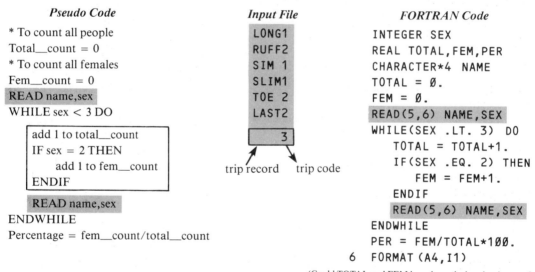

*Pseudo Code*

```
* To count all people
Total__count = 0
* To count all females
Fem__count = 0
READ name,sex
WHILE sex < 3 DO

    add 1 to total__count
    IF sex = 2 THEN
        add 1 to fem__count
    ENDIF

    READ name,sex
ENDWHILE
Percentage = fem__count/total__count
```

*Input File*

```
LONG1
RUFF2
SIM 1
SLIM1
TOE 2
LAST2

    3
```

trip record    trip code

*FORTRAN Code*

```
INTEGER SEX
REAL TOTAL,FEM,PER
CHARACTER*4 NAME
TOTAL = 0.
FEM = 0.
READ(5,6) NAME,SEX
WHILE(SEX .LT. 3) DO
    TOTAL = TOTAL+1.
    IF(SEX .EQ. 2) THEN
        FEM = FEM+1.
    ENDIF
    READ(5,6) NAME,SEX
ENDWHILE
PER = FEM/TOTAL*100.
6   FORMAT (A4,I1)
```

(Could TOTAL and FEM have been declared as integers?

[*Hint*: What would be the value of PER?])

### 4-4-7  Do It Now

1. Can you use the method shown in Figure 4–10 to read an input file if you know exactly how many records you are going to read?

2. Suppose your system does not allow you to use the list-directed READ with the END option. How would you write the code for example 2 in the previous section, where students' names and scores were read and then printed along with their test results and the total number of scores?

## Answers

1. Yes. In fact, to simplify your life, you can always use the END option.

2. If you cannot use the END option, add to the data records a last record containing a name and a *negative* score. Then use the score to allow you to detect this simulated end-of-file condition as follows:

```
READ name, score
WHILE score not negative DO
    Process score
        READ name, score
ENDWHILE
```

Note that if the input file contains no data records other than the last artificial record, the WHILE DO statements are bypassed since the first score would be negative.

# 4-5 Specification Statements and the Slash (/) Format Code

There are a number of FORTRAN statements that are classed as *specification statements* because they specify certain attributes of variables to the FORTRAN compiler. For example, the specification statements INTEGER, REAL, CHARACTER, and IMPLICIT can be used to specify the mode (type) of a variable. In this section we will learn how the DATA statement (another specification statement) is used, and other specification statements will be introduced later.

All specification statements are nonexecutable (see section 4–8, question 7) and should precede the first executable statement (replacement, condition, READ, WRITE, and so forth) in the FORTRAN program.

## 4-5-1 The DATA Statement

The DATA statement can be used to specify an initial value for a variable. The general form of the DATA statement is:

> DATA *variable list/constant list/*[,variable list/contant list/...]

where *variable list* is a list of variables separated by commas, and
*constant list* is a list of constants separated by commas.

The first variable in the variable list is associated with the first element in the constant list, the second variable with the second constant, and so forth. The number of constants in the constant list must match the number of variables in the variable list, and the type of a variable must match the type of its associated constant.

The DATA statement should follow such statements as the CHARACTER, INTEGER, REAL and IMPLICIT statements. It is recommended (not necessary) to place DATA statements before the first executable statement in the program.

*Example 1*

```
DATA  A,J/3.2, 4/
```

The value of A is 3.2 and the value of J is 4.

Note the agreement in number and type between the variables and constants. J is integer 4 while A is real 3.2.

*Example 2*

The following DATA statements are invalid:

```
DATA A,J,K/3.2,4/          Only two constants for 3 variables!
DATA CODE,LL/0,3.2/        Invalid: type mismatch
```

*Example 3*

```
CHARACTER*2,KODE,J,NAME*8
DATA KODE,A,NAME/'MO',3.14,'HILARY'/
```

*Memory*

KODE: MO
A:     3.14
NAME: HILARYbb

More than one *variable list/constant list/* can be included in a DATA statement. Repetitions must be separated by a comma.

*Example 4*

```
DATA A,B/3.,0./, I,J/1,0/     Note comma required.
```

A is 3., B is 0., I is 1 and J is 0

Remember that DATA statements *must* be placed after other specification statements.

*Example 5*

```
CHARACTER*5 L,C,B
INTEGER    A           Note position of DATA statements
REAL       I
DATA       A,I/1,-3.2/,B,C/'HE','IS'/
READ(5,6)X,Y
```

Finally, the DATA statement can include repetition factors. Suppose we wanted I, J, and K to be initialized to 0, and A, B, C, and D to be initialized to $-4.1$ and X and Y to 'NAME'. The following statement could be used:

*repetition factors*

```
DATA I,J,K/3*0/,A,B,C,D/4*-4.1/,X,Y/2*'NAME'/
```

The asterisks in this context mean repetition, not multiplication.

It is important to remember that the DATA statement is a *nonexecutable* statement, that is, the values specified by the DATA statement are initialized during the compilation process. The DATA statement cannot be used during execution to set or reset variables to particular values. The DATA statement can have *no* statement number. Consider the following code:

```
┌─►5 C=Ø.
│    DATA R,F/3.,2./
│    :
│    :
│    R=X+1.
│    :
│    :
└───IF(C.LT.3.)GO TO 5
```

Before the program is executed, the values of R and F are 3. and 2., respectively. The DATA statement is not carried out at execution time and hence cannot be used to reset variables R and F to 3. and 2., if R and F have been changed somewhere in the program. Only a replacement or a READ statement can reset R and F to 3. and 2.

### 4-5-2  Do It Now

1. Consider the following specification statements:

```
IMPLICIT INTEGER (X), REAL (K-L)
INTEGER AA, B2, C
REAL I, J3
DATA X3, L2/4, 2.2/
DATA AA, B, B2/4, -6.2, Ø/, I, J3/ 2*Ø.1/
```

What will be the type and initial value of each of the following variables?

a. AA      e. J3
b. B2      f. X3
c. C       g. L2
d. I

2. Given the specification statements

```
REAL A,B,C,D
INTEGER X,Y,Z
CHARACTER NAME, FIRST
```

identify errors in each of the following DATA statements:

a. DATA/X,Y,Z/1.,2.,3./
b. DATA A,B,C,D/4*Ø./NAME/'HELLO'/
c. DATA NAME,AB,X,Y/'SEE',2*1., 1,2/
d. DATA X,A,B/3,2.3,CLOSE/
e. DATA A,B,D,Y,Z/1.1,2.2,3.,4/

### *Answers*

1.
a. AA   INTEGER   4
b. B2   INTEGER   0
c. C    INTEGER   unknown initial value
d. I    REAL      0.1

e. J3   REAL      0.1
f. X3   INTEGER   4
g. L2   REAL      2.2

**2.**  a.  First slash is illegal, also X,Y,Z are integer and the constant list contains real numbers.

b.  Missing comma after second slash. NAME is just one character (HELLO will be truncated to H).

c.  There are 4 variables but 5 constants. The character S will be stored in NAME. X is an integer but is assigned the real value 1.

d.  B is not a character constant, CLOSE should be enclosed in single quotes.

e.  Insufficient number of constants for the 5 variables.

### 4-5-3  The Slash (/) Format Code

So far our FORMAT statements have described one physical input or output record, i.e., one input record or one line of print. We can describe more than one input or output record with one FORMAT statement by using the control format code /. The / format code can be interpreted to mean "end of physical record"; it is used to separate lists of format codes describing different physical records. A comma is optional between the / and other format codes.

For a READ operation the / implies reading a new record; for a WRITE operation format control looks at the carriage control code specified implicitly or explicitly by the "next" record to determine what action to take in terms of vertical paper movement.

*Example 1*

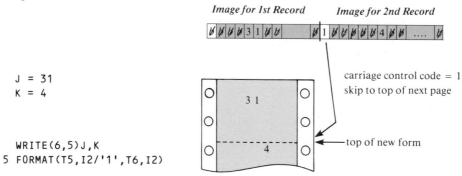

```
J = 31
K = 4


WRITE(6,5)J,K
5 FORMAT(T5,I2/'1',T6,I2)
```

Implied in T5 is a blank character for the carriage control code (the 1st character of the image line is a blank) which tells the printer to advance to the next line before printing J. Format control then encounters the slash in the FORMAT which tells it that a new record is to be processed. Format control checks the carriage control code for this new record and finds out it is a 1; the printer then skips to the top of the next page before printing the value for K.

If the format had been FORMAT(T5,I2/1X,I2), then J would be printed on one line and since the carriage control code starting the second record is blank (1X), the printer would advance to the next line and print K.

If the format had been FORMAT(T5,I2/T10,I2), J would be printed on one line; and since T10 implies a blank for the carriage control code of the next record, the printer advances one line and prints K.

*Example 2*

The ' + ' carriage control code can be very useful for underlining. To underline a particular heading use the following code (if the underline character is available on your keyboard/printer):

```
   WRITE(6,5)
5  FORMAT(T50,'JULY REPORT'/'+',T50,4('_'),1X,6('_'))
```

underline graphic symbol

This will produce the following output:

JULY REPORT

If the underline character is not available, use a row of hyphens on the next print line.

*Example 3*

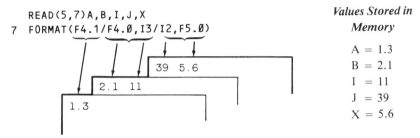

```
   READ(5,7)A,B,I,J,X
7  FORMAT(F4.1/F4.0,I3/I2,F5.0)
```

**Values Stored in**
**Memory**

A = 1.3
B = 2.1
I = 11
J = 39
X = 5.6

The READ list specifies that five variables are to be read from three records. The value for A is taken from the first data record. The / means "end of this record; select a new record and continue processing at the beginning of the new record." Hence the values for B and I come from the second record, while those for J and X are taken from the third data record.

*Example 4*

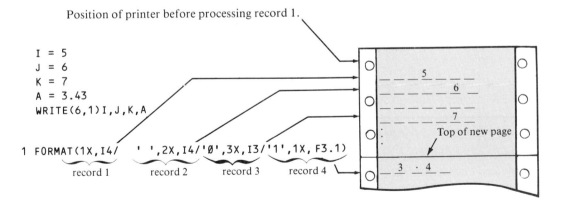

Position of printer before processing record 1.

```
   I = 5
   J = 6
   K = 7
   A = 3.43
   WRITE(6,1)I,J,K,A

1  FORMAT(1X,I4/  ' ',2X,I4/'0',3X,I3/'1',1X, F3.1)
     record 1      record 2    record 3    record 4
```

Four variables are to be written as four distinct records. The carriage control for the first record is blank as a result of 1X, so the printer spaces one line and writes the value for I. The second output record is then processed and a "blank" carriage control character causes the printer to space one line and print the value for J. Record 3 is then processed, and the printer double spaces and prints the value for K. Finally, the fourth record is processed, and the value of A is written at the top of a new page.

*Example 5*

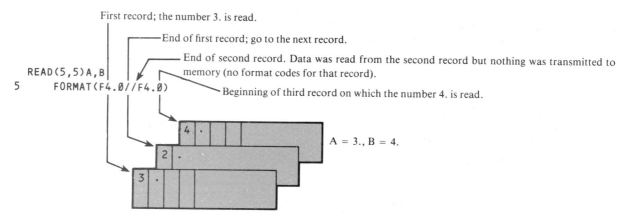

Three records are read in this example. Any data contained on record 2 is read, but no data on it will be transmitted to memory, since the record has no accompanying data format code. The slash means "end of the record; go to the next record."

*Example 6*

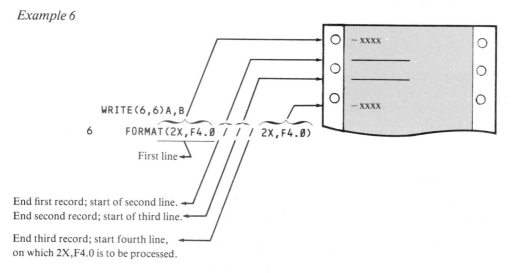

In this example, line 1 contains the value of A, and the fourth record (line 4) contains B.

*Example 7*

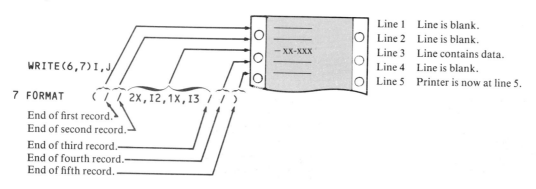

If the next WRITE statement used a + carriage control character, data would be printed on the fifth line. If, on the other hand, the next WRITE statement used a (blank) carriage control, line 5 would be blank and printing would start of the following line.

Finally, the slash can be extremely useful to create headings or distribute data items over more than one record with just one WRITE statement.

*Example 8*

```
      WRITE(6,5)REV ,EXP ,ANC
    5 FORMAT('1'/T50,'PACIFIC COMPANY'/T50,'INCOME STATEMENT'/T53,
    *'JUNE1984'//T45,'REVENUES',164,F7.2/
    *T45,'EXPENSES',T64,F7.2/T45,'NET INCOME',T64,F7.2)
```

This will produce the following output:

```
              PACIFIC COMPANY
              INCOME STATEMENT
                JUNE 1984

       REVENUES          8800.00
       EXPENSES          7800.00
       NET INCOME        1000.00
```

### 4-5-4 **Do It Now**

**1.** Consider the following input file:

```
     -324      1st record
     0064        .
     +123        :
     0000      4th record
```

What will be the value of each variable after the following statements?

a.     READ(5,11) A, I2, B
    11 FORMAT(F4.0/I4//F4.0)

b.     READ(5,12) X, Y, Z
    12 FORMAT(/2F2.0//F2.0)

**2.** Suppose I = 4 and A = − 3.2. What output will be produced by each of the following?

a.     WRITE(6,13) I, A
    13 FORMAT(3X,I3//2X,F4.1)

b.     WRITE(6,14) A, I
    14 FORMAT(//'0',F4.1,I3)

*Answers*

**1.**   a.  A = − 324.
       I2 = 64
       B = 0.

    b.  X = 0.
       Y = 64.
       Z = 0.

**2.**   a.                    b.

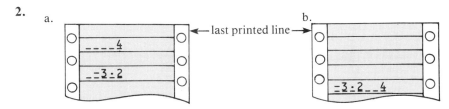

## 4-6 Programming Examples

### 4-6-1 Computing a Percentage of Passing Grades

*Problem/Specification:* An input file consists of several sets of records, each containing grades obtained by different class sections of an introduction to management course (see illustration below). Each set is identified by a header record specifying the number of scores for a particular section and the section number. Write a program to determine the number and percentage of passing scores for each section. Passing scores are those scores above 70. The program should list each section's scores and the output should be similar to the one shown below:

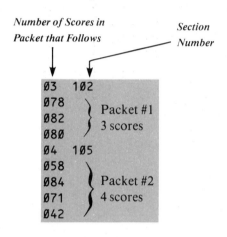

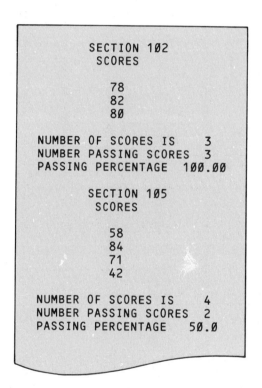

*Problem/Solution:* To understand the problem, we manufacture some "dummy" input data as shown above, and we then try to solve the problem manually. The header record tells us how many scores we need to process, and what the class section number is. The section number is important because we need to print it out. The number of scores tells us how many more data items we need to read before we encounter the next packet of information. For the first packet in the example, we need to read 3 scores: 78, 82 and 80. Since they all exceed 70, the percentage of passing grades is 100 percent and the count of passing scores is 3. Since we have read the 3 scores, we know that the next record will be a header record and, in the above case, we will need to process the 4 scores of section 105. The logic of the problem is captured in pseudo code in Figure 4–12 while the FORTRAN code is shown in Figure 4–13.

**FIGURE  4-12**    COMPUTING A PERCENTAGE OF PASSING SCORES—PSEUDO CODE

```
* Computing a percentage of passing scores
WHILE end-of-file-not-encountered DO
    * Read the header record of packet
    READ number__scores and section__number
    WRITE section__number
    * Set up a counter pass to count passing scores
    * and another counter n to process however many scores there are in the packet
    pass − 0
    n = 1
    WHILE n ≤ number__scores DO
        READ a score and print it
        IF score > 70 THEN
            add 1 to the counter of passing scores pass
        ENDIF
        add 1 to n
    ENDWHILE
    * After all scores of a packet have been read, compute percentage of passing scores
    Compute percentage = pass/n*100
    WRITE the results
ENDWHILE
STOP
```

**FIGURE  4-13**    COMPUTING A PERCENTAGE OF PASSING SCORES—FORTRAN CODE

```
C COMPUTING PERCENTAGE OF PASSING SCORES
C   SCORE: INDIVIDUAL SCORES
C   PASS:  COUNT OF PASSING SCORES
C   SECT:  SECTION NUMBER
C   PER:   PERCENTAGE PASSING SCORES
C   N:     NUMBER SCORES PER PACKET
C
      INTEGER N, SECT, SCORE, PASS
      REAL PER
  20 READ(5,6,END=88) N,SECT
         WRITE(6,1) SECT
         PASS = 0
         I = 1
  10     IF(I .GT. N) GO TO 15
            READ (5,2) SCORE
            WRITE(6,9) SCORE
            IF(SCORE .GT. 70) PASS = PASS + 1
            I = I + 1
            GO TO 10
  15     PER = PASS * 100./N
         WRITE(6,3) N, PASS, PER
         GO TO 20
  88 STOP
   1 FORMAT('0',7X,'SECTION',1X,I3/ 9X,'SCORES')
   2 FORMAT(I3)
   3 FORMAT('0','NUMBER OF SCORES IS',3X,I2/ 1X,'NUMBER PASSING SCORES'
     B,1X,I2/1X,'PASSING PERCENTAGE',2X,F5.1)
   6 FORMAT(I2,2X,I3)
   9 FORMAT(10X,I3)
      END
```

### 4-6-2  A Car Rental Problem

*Problem/Specification:*   Acme Rental charges customers for use of its rental cars based on type of car, insurance purchased, mileage, and number of days. The company rents three types of cars:

| Type | Daily Rental | Mileage Charge |
|------|--------------|----------------|
| 1 | $40.00 | .06 |
| 2 | $45.00 | .08 |
| 3 | $50.00 | .12 |

The company offers two insurance plans:

| Plan | Cost |
|------|------|
| 1 | 5% of the combined daily and mileage charges, $10 minimum |
| 2 | $6 per day of use |

Write a program to read records that contain the type of car, the insurance plan selected (1 or 2), the mileage, and the number of days, and print a report showing this information and the total charge. Print an error message if the code for the car type is unrecognized. The input and output will have the following form:

*Input File*

INSURANCE PLAN
MILES
TYPE ┐ │ ┌ DAYS

```
11050001
12050004
21010002
22010002
31010002
32010002
52010001
11001001
12050001
31060005
```

*Output*

| TYPE CAR | INS PLAN | MILEAGE | DAYS | INVOICE |
|----------|----------|---------|------|---------|
| 1 | 1 | 500 | 1 | 80.00 |
| 1 | 2 | 500 | 4 | 214.00 |
| 2 | 1 | 100 | 2 | 108.00 |
| 2 | 2 | 100 | 2 | 110.00 |
| 3 | 1 | 100 | 2 | 122.00 |
| 3 | 2 | 100 | 2 | 124.00 |
| INVALID CODE TYPE 5 | | | | |
| 1 | 1 | 10 | 1 | 50.60 |
| 1 | 2 | 500 | 1 | 76.00 |
| 3 | 1 | 600 | 5 | 222.60 |

Many approaches can be taken to solve this problem. One approach is as follows:

1. The daily rental charge and mileage charge figures do not need to be stored in variables since these figures can be used directly in the formulas for computing the daily rental costs and the mileage cost.
   The total daily charges to drive a type 1 car M miles for D days are:
   $$C = 40 * D + .06 * M$$
   Similarly, the total daily charges for a type 2 car are
   $$C = 45 * D + .08 * M$$
   and the charges for a type 3 car are
   $$C = 50 * D + .12 * M$$

In the program, these formulas have been broken down into two parts, in case we want to print the mileage cost and the daily rental charges separately. Since there are three types of cars, three tests are needed to check the type to specify the correct formula. If the car type is neither a 1, a 2, or a 3, the type read is invalid and an error message is printed out.

2. After the total daily charges have been computed, we are ready to deal with the insurance plan. If the insurance plan code is 1, the insurance cost is 5% of the total daily charges, *but* if that figure is less than $10, the insurance cost is the $10 minimum (the insurance cost is the larger of two figures: 5% of the total daily charges or 10 dollars). If the insurance plan code is 2, the insurance cost is simply 6 * D.

3. The final total charge is the sum of the insurance cost and the total daily charges.

These steps are captured in flowchart form in Figure 4–14, which also displays the FORTRAN program.

*Problem/Discussion:* Suppose the company changed its daily mileage rates and its insurance rates frequently. How would you change the program of Figure 4–14 to reflect these changes?

Answer: With the code as shown, you would have to locate and change every constant in the program and hope that you found them all! In this particular program five different line alterations would be required (in a more complex program, hundreds of lines might be involved). A much better way to handle this situation is to collect and name *all* the constants in one DATA statement and then use these variable names throughout the program. Then all the constants can be easily updated with just one alteration if the need arises.

## 4-6-3  Impact of Interest Rates on Monthly Payments. Nested Loops

*Problem/Specification:*   A good friend of yours has been looking at 60, 70, and 80 thousand dollar homes. She knows you have a computer and has asked you to figure out the monthly payments that she would have to make on such homes given 30-year mortgage rates of 11.5, 12.5 and 13.5%. She states the problem rather vaguely, "can you print out the monthly payments for all the different rates and costs? I'd also like to know the total mortgage payments over 30 years for the four prices of homes."

*Problem/Solution:*   First, to understand and to solve the problem, you need the formula to compute the monthly payment, based on the mortgage amount A, the duration time D in years, and the interest rate I (expressed as a fractional value). That formula is

$$\text{monthy payment} = \frac{A \cdot \dfrac{I}{12}}{1 - \left(\dfrac{1}{1 + \dfrac{I}{12}}\right)^{D \cdot 12}}$$

To get a feel for the problem, work out an example with A = $60,000, an interest rate of 11.5% and a duration D of 30 years (write the interest rate in decimal form):

$$\text{monthly payment} = \frac{60000 \times (0.115/12)}{1 - (1 / (1 + 0.115/12))^{30 * 12}}$$

**FIGURE 4–14   A CAR RENTAL PROBLEM**

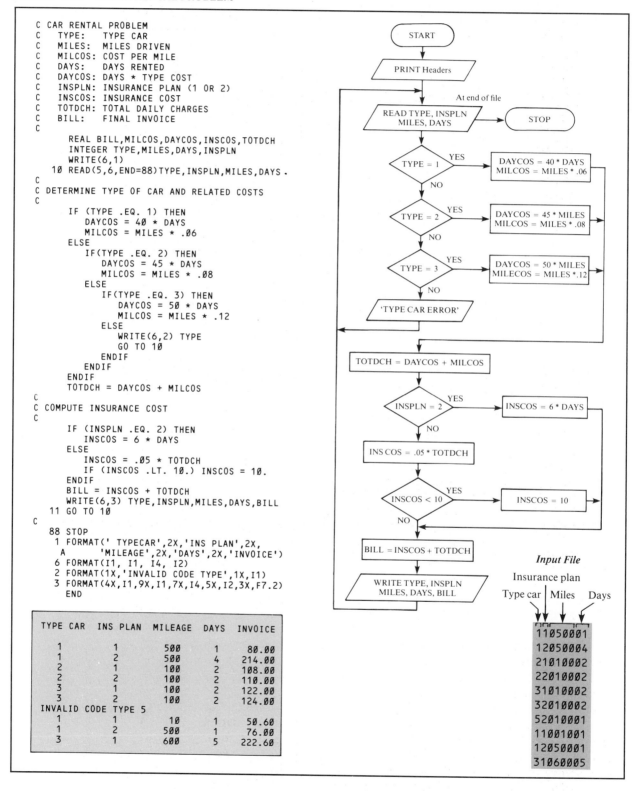

```
C CAR RENTAL PROBLEM
C   TYPE:    TYPE CAR
C   MILES:   MILES DRIVEN
C   MILCOS:  COST PER MILE
C   DAYS:    DAYS RENTED
C   DAYCOS: DAYS * TYPE COST
C   INSPLN: INSURANCE PLAN (1 OR 2)
C   INSCOS: INSURANCE COST
C   TOTDCH: TOTAL DAILY CHARGES
C   BILL:   FINAL INVOICE
C
      REAL BILL,MILCOS,DAYCOS,INSCOS,TOTDCH
      INTEGER TYPE,MILES,DAYS,INSPLN
      WRITE(6,1)
   10 READ(5,6,END=88)TYPE,INSPLN,MILES,DAYS .
C
C DETERMINE TYPE OF CAR AND RELATED COSTS
C
      IF (TYPE .EQ. 1) THEN
         DAYCOS = 40 * DAYS
         MILCOS = MILES * .06
      ELSE
         IF(TYPE .EQ. 2) THEN
            DAYCOS = 45 * DAYS
            MILCOS = MILES * .08
         ELSE
            IF(TYPE .EQ. 3) THEN
               DAYCOS = 50 * DAYS
               MILCOS = MILES * .12
            ELSE
               WRITE(6,2) TYPE
               GO TO 10
            ENDIF
         ENDIF
      ENDIF
      TOTDCH = DAYCOS + MILCOS
C
C COMPUTE INSURANCE COST
C
      IF (INSPLN .EQ. 2) THEN
         INSCOS = 6 * DAYS
      ELSE
         INSCOS = .05 * TOTDCH
         IF (INSCOS .LT. 10.) INSCOS = 10.
      ENDIF
      BILL = INSCOS + TOTDCH
      WRITE(6,3) TYPE,INSPLN,MILES,DAYS,BILL
   11 GO TO 10
C
   88 STOP
    1 FORMAT(' TYPECAR',2X,'INS PLAN',2X,
    A       'MILEAGE',2X,'DAYS',2X,'INVOICE')
    6 FORMAT(I1, I1, I4, I2)
    2 FORMAT(1X,'INVALID CODE TYPE',1X,I1)
    3 FORMAT(4X,I1,9X,I1,7X,I4,5X,I2,3X,F7.2)
      END
```

| TYPE CAR | INS PLAN | MILEAGE | DAYS | INVOICE |
|---|---|---|---|---|
| 1 | 1 | 500 | 1 | 80.00 |
| 1 | 2 | 500 | 4 | 214.00 |
| 2 | 1 | 100 | 2 | 108.00 |
| 2 | 2 | 100 | 2 | 110.00 |
| 3 | 1 | 100 | 2 | 122.00 |
| 3 | 2 | 100 | 2 | 124.00 |
| INVALID CODE TYPE 5 | | | | |
| 1 | 1 | 10 | 1 | 50.60 |
| 1 | 2 | 500 | 1 | 76.00 |
| 3 | 1 | 600 | 5 | 222.60 |

Flowchart:

START

PRINT Headers

READ TYPE, INSPLN MILES, DAYS → (At end of file) → STOP

TYPE = 1 —YES→ DAYCOS = 40 * DAYS  MILCOS = MILES * .06
  NO

TYPE = 2 —YES→ DAYCOS = 45 * MILES  MILCOS = MILES * .08
  NO

TYPE = 3 —YES→ DAYCOS = 50 * MILES  MILECOS = MILES *.12
  NO

'TYPE CAR ERROR'

TOTDCH = DAYCOS + MILCOS

INSPLN = 2 —YES→ INSCOS = 6 * DAYS
  NO

INS COS = .05 * TOTDCH

INSCOS < 10 —YES→ INSCOS = 10
  NO

BILL = INSCOS + TOTDCH

WRITE TYPE, INSPLN MILES, DAYS, BILL

**Input File**

Insurance plan

Type car | Miles | Days

```
11050001
12050004
21010002
22010002
31010002
32010002
52010001
11001001
12050001
31060005
```

To get the total payment over 30 years, you need to multiply the monthly payment by the number of months in 30 years (30 * 12). You also need to compute monthly payments for the 70, and 80 thousand dollar homes at the three interest rates, as well as do the calculations for the 60 thousand dollar home at the other interest rates. You can see that you will have to print a lot of results, so you must design an output that your friend will be able to understand. The output design is very important in this case because it will also help you organize the steps you will need to take in your program.

| MORTGAGE AMOUNT | YEARS | INTEREST RATE | MONTHLY PAYMENT | TOTAL PAYMENT |
|---|---|---|---|---|
| 60000. | 30 | 11.50 | 594.17 | 213901.20 |
| 60000. | 30 | 12.50 | 640.35 | 230526.00 |
| 60000. | 30 | 13.50 | 687.25 | 247410.00 |
| 70000. | 30 | 11.50 | 693.20 | 249552.00 |
| 70000. | 30 | 12.50 | 747.08 | 268948.80 |
| 70000. | 30 | 13.50 | 801.79 | 288644.40 |
| 80000. | 30 | 11.50 | 792.23 | 285202.80 |
| 80000. | 30 | 12.50 | 853.81 | 307371.60 |
| 80000. | 30 | 13.50 | 916.33 | 329878.80 |

Looking at the output, you can see that you will need two loops. In fact, one loop will be part of another loop (a nested loop). When A is 60000, we will need to run the interest rate from 11.5 to 13.5% in increments of 1%. Then A will become 70000 and the interest rate will run through its cycle again. Hence an outer loop will control A, which will increase in increments of 10000, and an inner loop will control I, which will increase in increments of 1%. The FORTRAN program to solve this problem is shown in Figure 4–15.

## 4-7  Programming Techniques

### 4-7-1  Search for a Maximum/Minimum

It is often necessary to go through a list of values to identify the largest or smallest value in that list. To illustrate such a search technique, consider the following problem:

An input file consists of an unknown number of scores.
Write the code to determine the highest score.

To determine the highest score we must compare each new score with the highest score found so far (use the variable name MAX for highest score). If MAX is less than the score read, we replace MAX with the score just read; otherwise, we keep on reading scores until we find one that is larger than MAX (if there is one). When the end-of-file is encountered, MAX is the highest score.

To start the comparison between MAX and the other scores, we read the first score in a separate READ statement and call that value MAX. (After all, if there were only one score, then MAX would be that score.) All other scores are then read by another READ statement. This method is shown in flowchart form in Figure 4–16.

**FIGURE 4-15** AN EXAMPLE OF NESTED LOOPS

```
C MONTHLY MORTGAGE PROBLEMS
C   YEARS:   MORTGAGE DURATION IN YEARS
C   I:       INTEREST RATE IN FRACTIONAL FORM
C   INT:     INTEREST RATE (100 * I)
C   A:       MORTGAGE AMOUNT
C   MONTH:   MONTHLY PAYMENT
C   TOTAL:   TOTAL PAYMENT OVER THE YEARS
C
      REAL MONTH, I, INT, A, TOTAL
      INTEGER YEARS
      DATA A,YEARS/60000.,30/
      WRITE(6,1)
      WRITE(6,2)
C
C OUTER WHILE DO LOOP
C
    4 IF(A .GT. 80000.) GO TO 7
        I = .115
C
C INNER WHILE DO LOOP
C
    5    IF(I .GT. .135) GO TO 6
           MONTH = (A*I/12.) / (1. - (1./ (1.+ I/12.)) ** (YEARS*12) )
           TOTAL = 12.* YEARS * MONTH
           INT   = 100 * I
           WRITE(6,3) A, YEARS, INT, MONTH, TOTAL
           I = I + .01
           GO TO 5
    6    WRITE(6,2)
         A = A + 10000.
         GO TO 4
C
    7 STOP
    2 FORMAT (1X)
    1 FORMAT(' MORTGAGE',2X,'YEARS',2X,'INTEREST',2X,'MONTHLY',4X,
     A 'TOTAL' / '  AMOUNT',11X,'RATE', 5X,'PAYMENT',3X,'PAYMENT')
    3 FORMAT(2X,F6.0,4X,I2,5X,F5.2,4X, F6.2,3X,F9.2)
      END
```

| MORTGAGE AMOUNT | YEARS | INTEREST RATE | MONTHLY PAYMENT | TOTAL PAYMENT |
|---|---|---|---|---|
| 60000. | 30 | 11.50 | 594.17 | 213901.20 |
| 60000. | 30 | 12.50 | 640.35 | 230526.00 |
| 60000. | 30 | 13.50 | 687.25 | 247410.00 |
| 70000. | 30 | 11.50 | 693.20 | 249552.00 |
| 70000. | 30 | 12.50 | 747.08 | 268948.80 |
| 70000. | 30 | 13.50 | 801.79 | 288644.40 |
| 80000. | 30 | 11.50 | 792.23 | 285202.80 |
| 80000. | 30 | 12.50 | 853.81 | 307371.60 |
| 80000. | 30 | 13.50 | 916.33 | 329878.80 |

**FIGURE 4-16** SEARCH FOR HIGHEST SCORE

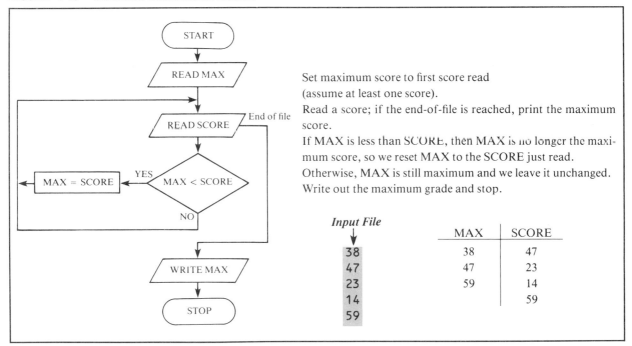

Set maximum score to first score read (assume at least one score).
Read a score; if the end-of-file is reached, print the maximum score.
If MAX is less than SCORE, then MAX is no longer the maximum score, so we reset MAX to the SCORE just read.
Otherwise, MAX is still maximum and we leave it unchanged.
Write out the maximum grade and stop.

*Input File*

| | MAX | SCORE |
|---|---|---|
| 38 | 38 | 47 |
| 47 | 47 | 23 |
| 23 | 59 | 14 |
| 14 | | 59 |
| 59 | | |

## 4-7-2 Sequence Check

In many instances, a programmer will need to process lists of names or item numbers that are supposed to be arranged in a particular order (ascending or descending). It is conceivable, though, that some of these items might be out of order. Thus, when processing the list, it may be necessary to perform a *sequence check* and flag (identify) those elements that are out of sequence. Consider the following problem:

> An input file contains a list of scores supposedly arranged in ascending order. Write the code to verify that the list is indeed in ascending order. Print all scores and place an asterisk by those that are out of sequence.

To get a preliminary feel for this problem, let us look at a few lists of numbers:

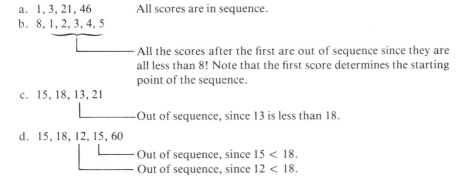

a.  1, 3, 21, 46          All scores are in sequence.
b.  8, 1, 2, 3, 4, 5
                          All the scores after the first are out of sequence since they are all less than 8! Note that the first score determines the starting point of the sequence.
c.  15, 18, 13, 21
                          Out of sequence, since 13 is less than 18.
d.  15, 18, 12, 15, 60
                          Out of sequence, since 15 < 18.
                          Out of sequence, since 12 < 18.

Note that, in example d, the score 15 is out of sequence even though it *is* in sequence compared to 12. The point is that 12 is out of sequence and hence should *not* be used in determining whether or not the next score is in sequence.

To determine whether the scores are in ascending order, we check whether the score just read (let's call it NEW) is larger than the previous score (called OLD). Clearly, this process needs to be repeated for every new score read. If NEW is greater than OLD, then the two scores are in sequence; otherwise NEW is out of sequence. To understand what happens next, consider a specific example:

$$\text{OLD} \quad \text{NEW}$$
$$\downarrow \quad \downarrow$$
$$...15, 18, 20,...$$

In this case, NEW is greater than OLD, so 15 and 18 are in sequence. What we want to do now is read the next score 20 (which becomes the new NEW!) and ask whether that NEW score is greater than the one we were calling NEW for the previous comparison, i.e., 18. However, by reading the next score (20) into NEW, we have destroyed the value 18! Hence, before we read NEW (20), we need to save the current NEW, i.e., save 18 into OLD! Then, on the next go-round, we will be comparing NEW with OLD or 20 with 18, which is just what we want to do:

$$\text{OLD} \quad \text{NEW}$$
$$\downarrow \quad \downarrow$$
$$...15, 18, 20,...$$

If we did *not* set OLD to NEW before reading the next score, the value of OLD would *never* change, and thus we would always compare a new score with the same OLD score (in this case 15)!

What happens now if NEW is less than OLD? For example,

$$\text{OLD} \quad \text{NEW}$$
$$\downarrow \quad \downarrow$$
$$...15, 12, 14,...$$

In this case, NEW is less than OLD, so 12 is out of sequence! Before we read the next NEW score (14), we do *not* save 12 into OLD. (If we did, then on the next go-round, NEW (14) would be greater than OLD (12), which would imply that 14 is in sequence. This is clearly not the case, since any new score read must be greater than the last score in sequence (15).) When a score is out of order, we leave OLD unchanged.

To begin the comparison between NEW and OLD, we read the first score independently of all others and assign that value to OLD. We then use a different READ statement to read all remaining NEW scores. The entire process is shown in flowchart form and in pseudo code in Figure 4–17.

### 4-7-3 **Do It Now**

1. In the search for a maximum in section 4–7–1, is it possible to write the algorithm with just one READ statement instead of two? Assume the scores range in the interval 0 to 100.

**FIGURE 4-17** A SEQUENCE CHECK

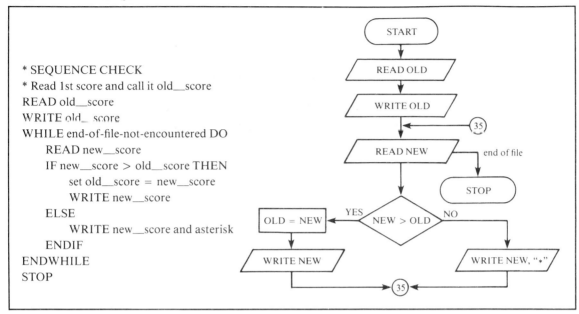

```
* SEQUENCE CHECK
* Read 1st score and call it old_score
READ old_score
WRITE old_ score
WHILE end-of-file-not-encountered DO
    READ new_score
    IF new_score > old_score THEN
        set old_score = new_score
        WRITE new_score
    ELSE
        WRITE new_score and asterisk
    ENDIF
ENDWHILE
STOP
```

2. Each record of an input file consists of an age field and a sex code (1 = male, 2 = female). Write the FORTRAN code to print the age and sex (write the caption "male" or "female") of the youngest person.

## *Answer*

1. Yes, it is possible. Replace the first statement in the flowchart with MAX = 0. When the first score is read, that score will be compared to 0. Since that score is greater than 0, MAX will be set to the first score.

2.
```
   C INITIALIZE THE VARIABLE CONTAINING THE MINIMUM AGE TO 1000!
         CHARACTER DESCR*6
         INTEGER AGE, MINAGE, SEXCOD, SEX
         MINAGE = 1000
      10 READ(5,6,END = 88) AGE,SEXCOD
         IF(MINAGE .LT. AGE) GO TO 10
   C STORE THE PERSON'S SEX CODE IN SEX; IF SEXCOD = 1 THEN SEX = 1 ETC.
            SEX = SEXCOD
            MINAGE = AGE
            GO TO 10
   C WHEN THE END OF FILE IS ENCOUNTERED SEX WILL REFLECT SEX OF YOUNGEST PERSON
      88 IF(SEX .EQ. 1) THEN
            DESCR = 'MALE'
         ELSE
            DESCR = 'FEMALE'
         ENDIF
         WRITE(6,2)MINAGE, DESCR
         STOP
       6 FORMAT(I3,I1)
       2 FORMAT(1X,'MINIMUM AGE=',I3, 1X, A6)
         END
```

## 4-8   You Might Want to Know

1. I don't like writing long variable names. Can't I just use names like X, Y, and Z?

   *Answer:* An algorithm is difficult enough to develop, but hiding the function of a variable behind a meaningless name only complicates the process. Today you may be able to remember what X represents, but will you tomorrow? and what about a reader? You will find that the time invested in writing descriptive names is well spent.

2. There seem to be few rules for writing statements in flowcharts and pseudo code. How do I know if I am doing it correctly?

   *Answer:* A statement in a flowchart or pseudo code algorithm is your way of describing the action that should be carried out at this point in the algorithm. You should always ask yourself the following question: If I handed this algorithm to someone else, could he/she understand it and carry out the intended action? If the answer is no, you must describe the desired actions more clearly.

3. When I see someone else develop a general solution to a problem and refine it, the process seems quite simple and natural. When I try it, however, I have trouble making an initial decomposition and then deciding on how to proceed. What am I doing wrong?

   *Answer:* Probably nothing that a little practice won't cure. As with anything, you have to develop some skills and a set of tricks. One of the most important skills is the ability to recognize an attempted solution whose basic structure is wrong; you must be willing to discard such a solution and start over again. This process is far less painful during the design stage than after the algorithm is coded in FORTRAN.

4. Some "experienced" programmers that I have talked with say that design is a waste of time. They claim that they can get programs working by simply sitting down and writing FORTRAN statements. Will I ever get to that stage?

   *Answer:* Let's not hope. Let's use the example of the builder again. If you ask him to build a sandbox, he may well build a beautiful sandbox without any plans. But if you ask him to do the same thing for a three-story house, the results are likely to be far less satisfactory. Programmers who refuse to invest time in the design stage quickly run into their own limitations. These are the same programmers who complain bitterly (or brag) about the long hours they spend at the computer center and the amount of time it takes them to find and correct errors. The programmer should start by carefully constructing a design; this will minimize waste of time and ensure program reliability.

5. For a given problem, is there just one correct algorithm?

   *Answer:* No. Every programmer will have his/her own approach to arriving at a solution. The final algorithms for a given problem, therefore, may be quite different, but the results generated by the algorithms must be the same.

6. If a DATA statement can be replaced by a replacement statement, why use the DATA statement?

   *Answer:* The primary reason is programmer convenience. One DATA statement can initialize a great many variables that otherwise would require many replacement statements. The DATA statement also saves time during the execution of a program. The DATA statement is interpreted by the compiler once to accomplish the initialization; replacement statements must be repeated each time the program is executed. Thus the

DATA statement saves time if the program is to be run a number of times without being recompiled each time.

7. I don't understand the difference between a nonexecutable statement and an executable statement. Can you help?

*Answer:* I'll try! The nonexecutable statements that have been encountered so far are END, FORMAT, INTEGER, REAL, DATA, IMPLICIT, CHARACTER while the executable statements have been READ, WRITE, IF THEN ELSE, computed GO TO, GO TO, STOP, and the replacement statement. Nonexecutable instructions are processed by the compiler and not by the CPU at execution time. Executable instructions are those instructions translated by the compiler into machine language and then executed by the CPU. Essentially, nonexecutable instructions are instructions to the compiler that do not get translated into machine language. The END statement, for instance, is not translated into a machine instruction; it merely informs the compiler that there are no more FORTRAN statements to be translated (the physical end of the FORTRAN statements has been reached). The INTEGER specification statement is not translated into machine language but tells the compiler that whenever an INTEGER-specified variable is encountered in the program it is to be processed as an integer. The FORMAT informs the compiler how to complete the translation of the READ/WRITE instructions. The statement X = 2. is an executable instruction. It is translated into a set of machine instructions that causes the CPU to store the number 2. in memory location X at execution time.

8. Is it possible to use the DATA statement to reset variables to specified values during execution of a program?

*Answer:* No. The values of variables specified in a DATA statement are already set at the beginning of execution of a program. The DATA statement is not an executable statement and hence cannot be executed by the program to reset the values of variables. To reset the variable, use a replacement statement.

# 4-9 Exercises

## 4-9-1 Test Yourself

1. Which of the following will read 10 records?

   a. Set I to 1
      WHILE I ≤ 10 DO
         READ record
         add 1 to I
      ENDWHILE

   b. Set I to 10
      WHILE I ≥ 0 DO
         READ record
         Subtract 1 from I
      ENDWHILE

   c. Set I to 0
      WHILE (I ≤ 10 AND I ≠ 10) DO
         Add 1 to I
         READ record
      ENDWHILE

   d. Set K to 7
      WHILE K < 17 DO
         add 1 to K
         READ record
      ENDWHILE

**2.** Complete the condition so that 6 data records will be read.

a.  Set I to − 1
    WHILE I _____ DO
        READ record
        add − 1 to I
    ENDWHILE

b.  Set I to 1
    WHILE I _____ DO
        READ record
        add .5 to I
    ENDWHILE

**3.** Write the WHILE DO pseudo code and the WHILE DO equivalent FORTRAN code to generate the following sequences of numbers:

a.  0, 5, 10, 15, ..., 100
b.  2, 4, 8, 16, ..., 4096
c.  1, − 2, 3, − 4, ..., − 100
d.  N, N − 1, ... 3, 2, 1 where N is read from an input record

**4.** Each record of an input file contains the following data:

    Employee number
    Employee's yearly base pay
    Employment duration in years (1.5 means one year and a half)
    Employee classification: 1 = hourly, 2 = salaried
    Rating: 1 = satisfactory, 2 = unsatisfactory

The policy for determining employee Christmas bonuses at Santa-Claus Inc. is as follows:

Employees must have been employed with the company at least six months. Employees with a satisfactory rating are paid one week's pay if they are hourly employees or 20% of monthly pay if they are salaried employees. If the rating is unsatisfactory, one day's pay (1/240 of base pay) will be paid to hourly employees and 5% of monthly pay to salaried employees.

Employees with more than 10 years of service and a satisfactory rating receive an additional bonus of $400.

Write the pseudo code to compute the bonus.

**5.** Each record of an input file contains the name of a city and its record high temperature for the year. Cities have been sorted by ascending temperature order. Write the pseudo code to print the name of the first city with a temperature of 100 degrees or above. Flush out all remaining input records, if any; i.e., read remaining records, but do not process them.

**6.** Each record of an input file contains a dollar amount. Write the pseudo code to print the message 'YES' if *all* the dollar amounts in the file are greater than 10000; otherwise print 'NO.'

**7.** Personpower Inc. needs to find in a hurry the telephone number of the first individual in their personnel file satisfying the following characteristics:

Male, between 20 and 40 with either 2 years of college or a certificate degree.

Write the pseudo code to print either the telephone number of the individual or a message specifying that no one meets the description. A sample record is shown below:

Sex:   1 = male, 2 = female
College:   1, 2, 3 or 4
Certificate:   'YES' or 'NO'

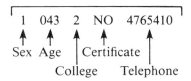

**8.** Each record of an input file, contains the following fields:

Student name
Age
Sex       1 = male, 2 = female
Class     1 = freshman, 2 = sophomore

Write a program to list the names of students over 21 years of age and compute the number of male freshmen, the number of female freshmen, the number of male sophomores, and the number of female sophomores.

**9.** An input file contains an unknown number of records, each record containing a number between − 99 and 99. Write the FORTRAN code to print the numbers read up to and including the first number that changes sign. For example:

| | | |
|---|---|---|
| Given 3,4,8,4, − 3, − 2, − 1, | the program would print | 3,4,8,4,−3 |
| Given − 2,1, − 3, | the program would print | −2,1 |
| Given 1,2,3,4,5, | the program would print | 1,2,3,4,5 |
| Given 1,0, − 1,2 | the program would print | 1,0,−1 |

**10.** Determine the number of records processed (read) or the number of lines generated by the following statements, given the various formats:

```
        READ(5,5)I,J                    WRITE(6,6)I,K
a.  5 FORMAT(I4/I3)              f.  6 FORMAT(/1X,I2///1X,I3)
b.  5 FORMAT(/I4,I3)            g.  6 FORMAT('0',I2/1X,I3/1X)
c.  5 FORMAT(/I4,I3/1X)        h.  6 FORMAT(//T2,I2/1X,I3)
d.  5 FORMAT(//I4,I3/1X)       i.  6 FORMAT(//1X,I2/1X/I4///1X)
e.  5 FORMAT(//I4//I3//1X)     j.  6 FORMAT(/'0',I2/'0',I3)
```

**11.** Which of the following statements are true?

a. Specification statement errors are detected at execution time.
b. DATA statements can be inserted anywhere before the END statement.
c. Specification statements are nonexecutable statements.
d. The statement INTEGER ISAM,SAM,KKK is valid.
e. Automatic end-of-file can be used in certain cases when printing an unknown number of values.
f. IMPLICIT INTEGER A-Z is an invalid specification statement.
g. Three consecutive slashes at the beginning of an output format (///) mean three blank lines.
h. The statements      `READ(5,6)X,I,Y`                will read three records.
                       `6 FORMAT(F5.1/I3/F5.1)`
i. The statements      `READ(5,7)I,X,K`
                       `7 FORMAT(I1,F1.1,I2,F2.2,F3.3)`   will read five records
j. The statements      `READ(5,6)I,J`
                       `6 FORMAT(I2/'+',I3)`          will read the same record twice.

k. The prime READ method can be used when it is known exactly how many records are to be read.

## 4-9-2 Programming Exercises: General/Business

1. Write a program to print out the following board (exactly).

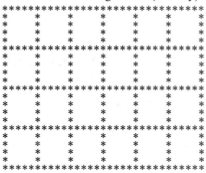

2. The formula to compute the simple interest *I* on a loan of *P* dollars at an interest rate *R* for *T* days is:

$$I = P * R * T/360$$

Write a program to read a dollar amount and an interest rate and produce a table showing the interest to be paid as T varies from 30 days to 5 years in steps of 1 month (30 days). Provide captions and skip to the top of the next page for each year.

3. An input file contains an unknown number of positive and negative numbers varying from −1,000 to +1,000. Write a program to determine how many positive numbers, how many negative numbers, and how zeros there are in the input file.

4. a. A file contains ten pairs of grades (one pair per record). Write a program to print out each pair and its corresponding sum.
   b. Suppose that the first record in an input file contains the number of records that follow, for example:

   3 ◄——————— 3 data records follow
   45    60  ⎫
   80    100 ⎬ Three data records
   36    49  ⎭

   Modify the program written for part (a) above to process this type of data file.

5. Each record of an input file contains a name and a corresponding earning. Write the code to print the names of the persons with highest/lowest earnings. Assume no two earnings amount are the same.

6. An input file contains 30 grades, one per record. Write a program to compute and print out the number of grades greater than 49 and less than or equal to 63.

7. A data file contains positive or negative numbers (two numbers per record). Write a program to stop reading the file whenever two successive numbers have opposite signs. These two successive numbers may or may not be on the same record.

8. An input file consists of an unknown number of records. Each record contains two integers. Count the occurrence of positive numbers, negative numbers, and zeros. Print all numbers read and their corresponding counts using the following format:

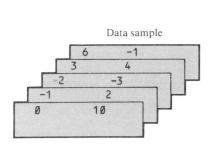

Data sample

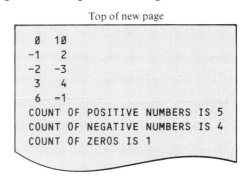

Top of new page

```
 0   10
-1    2
-2   -3
 3    4
 6   -1
COUNT OF POSITIVE NUMBERS IS 5
COUNT OF NEGATIVE NUMBERS IS 4
COUNT OF ZEROS IS 1
```

9. Each data record in a file contains two items: an age and a code for marital status (1 = single, 2 = married, 3 = divorced, and 4 = widowed). Write a program to compute and print:

a. The percentage of people over 30 years of age.
b. The number of people who are either widowed or divorced.
c. The number of people who are over 50 or less than 30 and who are not married.
Don't forget to print all the input data.

10. An IRS agent is checking taxpayers' returns in the $20,000 to $30,000 income bracket (gross earnings). Each record of the returns file contains a social security number, gross earnings, and an amount of tax paid. If taxes paid are below 18.5% of gross earnings, compute tax due. Assume all taxes in that bracket are 18.5% of gross. If the amount due is above $1,400, add a penalty charge of 1.5% of the amount due. Take care of refunds if necessary. Records of gross earnings outside the interval $20,000 to $30,000 are not checked. Print appropriate messages with the results.

11. Drs. Smith and Jones both teach principles of management. Information about students enrolled in the course is recorded as follows:

| Record Positions | Meaning | Section | Teacher | Time |
|---|---|---|---|---|
| 1–6 | Student ID | 1 | Smith | Day |
| 10 | Course Section (1–4) | 2 | Smith | Night |
| 15–17 | Grade point average 0.0–4.0 | 3 | Jones | Day |
| 20 | Type code 1 = part-time, | 4 | Jones | Night |
| | 2 = full-time | | | |

Write a program to compute and print:
a. The percentage of students who are part-time.
b. The total number of students in Dr. Smith's sections.
c. A list of the ID numbers of students enrolled in night classes.
d. The number of day students having a GPA of 2.0 or higher.
e. The name of the teacher in whose class the highest GPA is to be found.

12. An input file contains 100 numbers (one number per record). Write a program to read these numbers, and stop whenever the number 4 (by itself) has been read three times. Print the total number of items read. (It is possible that the number 4 may not occur three times.)

**13.** In a physical education class, students get either a pass or a fail for the course. If the average of the student's three test scores is below 70, the student fails the course. The student's three test scores are recorded as follows:

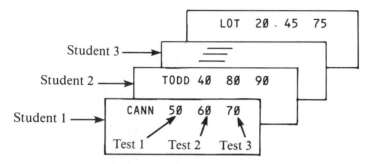

Write a program to produce the following output:

```
STUDENT    TEST1    TEST2    TEST3    AVERAGE    FINAL GRADE
  CANN       50       60       70       60.0        FAIL
  TODD       40       80       90       70.0        PASS
   .          .        .        .         .           .
   .          .        .        .         .           .
   .          .        .        .         .
  LOT        20       45       75       46.6        FAIL
THE PERCENTAGE OF STUDENTS WHO FAILED IS XXX.X
```

**14.** Data for a store shows daily sales for corresponding days of succeeding years. The first value on the record is the amount of sales for a given day in the first year; the second value is the amount of sales for the corresponding day in the second year. Find the number of days in which the second year's daily sales exceeded the first year's daily sales by more than 10% of the first year's sales. The output should be similar to the following:

*Sample Data*

```
500 550
400 441
300 500
600 448
```
1st year   2nd year

*Sample Output*

```
FIRST YEAR      SECOND YEAR
   500             550
   400             441 **
   300             500 **
   600             448
NUMBER OF SUPERIOR SALES DAYS 2
```

(Note that ** identifies those records for which the second year's daily sales exceeds the first year's daily sales by more than 10%.)

**15.** Each record of an input file contains a last name and a final test score. The names are supposed to be in descending alphabetical order (Z–A). Write a program to identify records that are not in sequence by name. If all names are in order, print the message "NAMES ARE IN ORDER".

**16.** An input file contains numbers supposedly arranged in numerical ascending order. Write a program to print the message IN ORDER if they are *all* in order and the message OUT OF ORDER if they are not. Read *all* records whether in order or not.

**17.** The FHA insures home mortgages up to $60,000. The down payment schedule is as follows:

  a.  Three percent of the amount up to $25,000.
  b.  Ten percent of the next $10,000.
  c.  Twenty percent of the remainder.

  Each record in the input file contains a social security number and a mortgage amount. The output should contain the applicant's social security number and the down payment required. Reject any application over $60,000 and indicate this on the output.

**18.** Salaries at the XYZ Corporation are based on job classification, years of service, education, and merit rating. The base pay for all employees is the same; a percentage of the base pay is added to salaries according to the following schedule:

| Job Classification | Percentage of Base Pay | Education | Percentage of Base Pay |
|---|---|---|---|
| 1 | 0 | 1(high school) | 0 |
| 2 | 5 | 2(junior college) | 10 |
| 3 | 15 | 3(college) | 25 |
| 4 | 25 | 4(graduate degree) | 50 |
| 5 | 50 | 5(special training) | 15 |

| Merit Rating | Percentage of Base Pay | Years of Service | Percentage of Base Pay Per Year |
|---|---|---|---|
| 0(poor) | 0 | 0–10 years | 5 |
| 1(good) | 10 | each additional year | 4 |
| 2(excellent) | 25 | | |

  Write a program to accept numerical codes for each of the four variables and calculate the employee's salary as a percentage of base pay.

**19.** Each employee working at Slimpower, Inc. is paid at a regular hourly rate of $5.00 for the first 40 hours. The overtime rate is 1.5 times the regular rate. The number of hours worked by each employee is typed into record positions 1–4.

  a.  Write a program to compute each employee's pay and produce an output similar to the following:

```
HOURS   RATE   OVERTIME HOURS      PAY
10.00   5.00        0            50.00
50.00   5.00        10          275.00
  .       .         .              .
  .       .         .              .
  .       .         .              .
```

  b.  Repeat part a, but now the number of hours and the rate of pay are read from data records in positions 1–4 and 7–11. Also, 6.1% of each employee's pay for the first 30 hours is subtracted from the gross pay for a pension plan. The output should be similar to:

```
HOURS    RATE    PENSION PLAN      PAY
50.00   10.00        18.30      531.70
  :       :            :           :
  :       :            :           :
  :       :            :           :
```

c. Repeat part b, but now a bonus amount for each employee is recorded in positions 15–18 as a three-digit number. If the employee's pay exceeds $500, the bonus is added to the employee's pay; if not, the bonus field is left blank on the output and is not computed into the pay, for example,

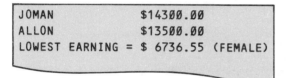

```
HOURS    RATE    PENSION PLAN    BONUS     PAY
50.00   10.00        18.30        100    631.70
10.00    5.00         3.05       ____      46.95
  :       :            :                    :
  :       :            :                    :
  :       :            :           ↑        :
```

[Note blank field]

20. Each record of a data file contains the following information: a name, a sex code (1 = M, 2 = F), and an amount of earnings. Write a program to print the earnings and the names of females earning between ten and twenty thousand dollars; also print the lowest earnings and indicate whether it was earned by a male or a female. Specify MALE or FEMALE on the output. For example, either of the following outputs could be produced:

```
JOMAN                 $14300.00
ALLON                 $13500.00
LOWEST EARNING = $ 6736.55 (FEMALE)
```

```
GANDY                 $11000.50
LOWEST EARNING = $ 5244.00 (MALE)
```

21. Computerized checkbook: The first record of an input file contains the balance from the previous month. Each succeeding record contains two entries: a check number and a dollar amount. This dollar amount can be a positive number (deposit) or a negative number (withdrawal). Write a program to produce a checkbook report similar to the following:

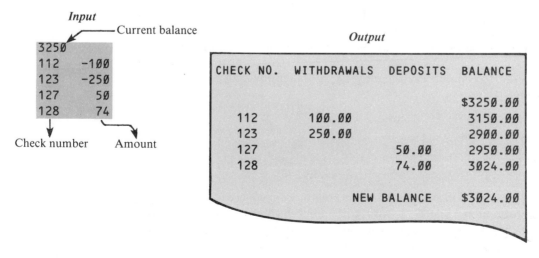

*Input*

Current balance

```
3250
112   -100
123   -250
127    50
128    74
```

Check number    Amount

*Output*

| CHECK NO. | WITHDRAWALS | DEPOSITS | BALANCE |
|---|---|---|---|
|  |  |  | $3250.00 |
| 112 | 100.00 |  | 3150.00 |
| 123 | 250.00 |  | 2900.00 |
| 127 |  | 50.00 | 2950.00 |
| 128 |  | 74.00 | 3024.00 |
|  |  | NEW BALANCE | $3024.00 |

**22.** Write a program to produce the following comparative mortgage tables for principals varying from 50,000 to 100,000 dollars in steps of 10,000, interest rates varying from 9.50% to 12.50% in increments of 0.25% and durations of 20, 25, and 30 years.

```
                    MORTGAGE PAYMENT PLAN
                          JOHN DOE

    PRINCIPAL    INTEREST RATE    DURATION    MONTHLY-PAYMENT
      50000          9.50            20           XXXX.XX
                                     25           XXXX.XX
                                     30           XXXX.XX

                     9.75            20           XXXX.XX
                                     25           XXXX.XX
                                     30           XXXX.XX
                      :
                    12.50            20           XXXX.XX
                                     25           XXXX.XX
                                     30           XXXX.XX

      60000          9.50            20           XXXX.XX
                                     25           XXXX.XX
                                     30           XXXX.XX
                      :
                    12.50            20           XXXX.XX
                                     25           XXXX.XX
                                     30           XXXX.XX
       :
     100000          9.50            20           XXXX.XX
                                     25           XXXX.XX
                                     30           XXXX.XX
                      :               :            :
```

Note blank lines after every third monthly payment.

The formula to compute the monthly payment is:

$$M = \frac{P \cdot I/12}{1 - \left(\dfrac{1}{1 + I/12}\right)^{T \cdot 12}}$$

where
$P$ is the principal
$I$ is the interest rate
$T$ is the mortgage duration in years

**23.** To be eligible for promotion, teachers at Franzia College must have taught there for at least 5 years or somewhere else in the state for at least 7 years. Teachers are not eligible for promotion after 25 years of teaching. To be eligible for promotion to the following ranks, teachers must meet the requirements shown:

| *Rank* | *Requirements* |
|---|---|
| assistant professor | master's degree in teaching |
| associate professor | master's degree plus 30 hours in teaching field |
| full professor | doctorate |

In addition, no teacher is eligible for promotion if he/she has not served three full years in his/her rank. The rank below assistant professor is instructor; only four ranks exist at Franzia College. Design a record layout form for personnel to record all faculty data, and write a program to identify the faculty eligible for promotion.

**24.** The first record of a store's inventory file contains the current date expressed as YYXXX where YY and XXX represent the year and Julian date. For example, 84245 represents the 245th day of 1984. Each succeeding record contains (among other items) the date of the last time an item was sold, the number of items on hand, the cost per item, and the regular selling price. A store plans a sale to try to sell slow-moving items. The purpose of the program is to produce a report showing recommended sale prices as follows:

> If an item has not been sold in the last 30 days, discount is 10%.
> If an item has not been sold in the last 60 days, discount is 20%.
> If an item has not been sold in the last 90 days, discount is 40%.

However, any item that has sold in the last 30 days is not to be placed on sale. If there is only one of an item left in stock, it is not to be placed on sale no matter when the last day of sale occurred. The amount of discount allowed is also subject to the following rule: sale prices cannot be lower than cost.

Write a program to read the input file and produce a report similar to the following one.

```
CURRENT DATE 84:220
ITEM    LAST SALE    DAYS      NO. IN    COST    REG.    SALE
NO.       DATE       ELAPSED   STOCK             PRICE   PRICE

302        200         20        20     10.00   15.00   15.00
400        189         31         5      6.50   10.00    9.00
101        159         61        15      3.00    5.00    4.00
100        101        119        50      2.00    3.00    2.00
901        100        120         1     12.00   25.00   25.00
999        180         40         2      6.50    7.15    6.50
222        360        225        60     10.00   12.00   10.00
174        100        485         1     30.50   35.50   35.50
```

How would you change your program to handle the case where there is an overlap in years, for example, '84 to '85?

**25.** Amortization schedule: Suppose you take out a loan of $1,000 at a yearly interest rate of 12% and you intend to repay that loan at $200 (including the interest payment) per month until the loan has been fully repaid. You would like to have an amortization schedule showing the following entries: the interest charge, the payment towards the loan, the remaining balance, and the accumulated interest to date. One way to solve this problem is shown here (the monthly interest rate is 1% since the yearly rate is 12%):

| | | | |
|---|---|---|---|
| The interest for month 1 is | $1000 * | .01 | = $ 10 |
| The payment to capital is | $200 − | 10 | = $190 |
| The remaining balance is | $1000 −190 | | = $810 |
| The interest for month 2 is | $810 * | .01 | = $ 8.10 |
| The payment to capital is | $200 − | 8.10 | = $191.90 |
| The remaining balance is | $810 −191.90 | | = $618.10 |

The final schedule can then be drawn as follows:

```
                    AMORTIZATION TABLE
           PRINCIPAL  $1000.00  INTEREST 12.00
                 REGULAR PAYMENT  $200.00

   NO.   INTEREST    AMORTIZED   BALANCE   INTEREST TO DATE
    1     10.00       190.00     810.00        10.00
    2      8.10       191.90     618.10        18.10
    3      6.18       193.82     424.28        24.28
    4      4.24       195.76     228.52        28.52
    5      2.29       197.71      30.81        30.81
    6      0.31        30.81       0.00        31.12
   LAST PAYMENT  = $31.12
```

Write a program to read a loan amount, a monthly repayment amount, and an interest rate in percentage form (such as 12.75%) and produce a repayment schedule similar to the one above.

26. This is the same as exercise 25, except that the person taking the loan decides to repay the loan for a fixed number of months at a fixed monthly amount. Note that in such a case the last payment may not be the same as the regular monthly payment. Consider the following two examples:

```
                    AMORTIZATION TABLE
   PRINCIPAL  $1000.00  INTEREST 12.00  DURATION 3 MONTHS
                 REGULAR PAYMENT  $300.00

   NO.   INTEREST    AMORTIZED   BALANCE   INTEREST TO DATE
    1     10.00       290.00     710.00        10.00
    2      7.10       292.90     417.10        17.10
    3      4.17       417.10       0.00        21.27
   LAST PAYMENT = $421.27
```

```
                    AMORTIZATION TABLE
   PRINCIPAL   750.00  INTEREST 12.00  DURATION 3 MONTHS
                 REGULAR PAYMENT  $300.00

   NO.   INTEREST    AMORTIZED   BALANCE   INTEREST TO DATE
    1      7.50       292.50     457.50         7.50
    2      4.57       295.43     162.07        12.07
    3      1.62       162.07       0.00        13.69
   LAST PAYMENT = $163.69
```

Write a program to read a loan amount, a monthly payment, an interest rate, and the term of the loan (such as 5 months, or 1 year and 3 months) and produce a repayment schedule similar to the one above.

27. A wholesaler accepts a $5,000 promissory note from a retailer at 10% in lieu of cash payment for delivered goods. Write a program to compute the maturity value of the

note for a 30-, 60-, and 90-day short-term loan. (The formula for the maturity value is $S = P(1 + I \cdot N)$. $S$ is maturity value, $P$ is principal, $I$ is interest rate, and $N$ is the number of years, or, if less than 1 year, the number of days/360.)

**28.** The simple discount is the amount deducted from the maturity value $S$ (see problem 27) of an obligation sold before its date of maturity. The formula is $SD = S \cdot D \cdot N$, where $SD$ = simple discount, $S$ = maturity value, $D$ = discount rate, and $N$ = term of loan, that is, time remaining before maturity.

A wholesaler receives a \$10,500 promissory note for goods sold to a retailer. The note matures in $N$ months and bears an $I\%$ interest rate. One month later the wholesaler sells the note to a bank at a 9% discount rate. Write a program to compute:

a. The maturity value of the note for $N$ = 30, 60, and 90 days with interest rate of $I$ = 4%, 5% and 6%. (That is, $N$ = 30 for $I$ = 4%, 5%, and 6%; $N$ = 60 for $I$ = 4%, 5% and 6%, and so forth.)

b. The proceeds received by the wholesaler as a result of selling the note to the bank for $N$ = 30, 60, and 90 days with interest rate of 4%, 5%, and 6%, respectively.

**29.** Ms. Small is thinking of borrowing \$5,000 for $N$ months at a 12% simple discount rate to purchase a new automobile. Write a program to compute the proceeds of this loan for the following values of $N$: 6 months, 1 year, 2 years, and 3 years. The proceeds ($P$) is the sum remaining after the discount is deducted; it is given by the formula: $P = S(1 - SD \cdot N)$ (see problem 28).

**30.** The Kiddie Up Company manufactures toys for adults. The company expects fixed costs for the next year to be around \$180,000. With the demand for adult toys increasing, the company is looking for sales of \$900,000 in the year to come. The variable costs are expected to run at about 74% of sales.

a. Write a program to determine the breakeven point (BEP) (the dollar amount of sales that must be made to incur neither a profit nor a loss), and compute the expected profit. The formula to compute the BEP is

$$BEP = \frac{\text{total fixed costs}}{1 - \dfrac{\text{variable costs}}{\text{sales}}}$$

b. The Kiddie Up Company management is arguing that with the current rate of inflation, variable costs will run higher for the next year—probably anywhere from 75 to 83% of sales. With sales still projected at \$900,000, the management directs its data processing staff to generate the following report to determine the breakeven point and the profits and losses for varying variable costs. Sales and fixed costs remain constant.

```
                      KIDDIE UP COMPANY
                  1984 OPERATIONS FORECAST

    PROJECTED SALES: 900,000
    FIXED COSTS:     180,000
    VARIABLE      VARIABLE COST    BREAK EVEN     PROFIT    DEFICIT
     COSTS        PERCENTAGE         POINT
    675000            75            720000        180000      ***
      .                .              .             .          .
      .                .              .             .          .
      .                .              .             .          .
    747000            83           1058823         ***       205882
```

Write a program to complete the above report. Place three stars (***) in the profit column if there is no profit. Do the same for deficit.

c. The company employees have just won a new contract. As a result, variable costs are expected to reach 81 or 82% of next year's projected $900,000 sales. A recent internal study carried out by the company on the various aspects of the manufacturing operations disclosed production inefficiencies. Corrective measures could significantly lower fixed costs. Project a range of fixed costs to show a company profit of anywhere from 50 to 100,000 dollars, given that variable costs are expected to reach 81 or 82% of sales next year.

**31.** XSTAR is a small company supplying major auto parts companies with a single item. The total fixed costs to run the company amount to $40,000 per year. The company has had a steady dollar breakeven point value (BEP) for the last three years, and the president of the company would like to keep the BEP at about the same level ($117,647) for the coming year. The president believes that the selling price per item could range anywhere from $1.10 to $1.30, but that the variable cost per item should not fall below $.75 nor exceed $.83. To help the president consider the options, write a program displaying different combinations of selling prices ($1.10 to $1.30 in increments of one cent) and corresponding variable costs, all yielding a constant BEP of $117,647; that is, generate a table with headings as follows:

| SELLING COSTS | VARIABLE COST/UNIT | BREAKEVEN POINT | DECISION |
|---------|---------|---------|---------|
| $1.10 | 73 | 117647 | TOO LOW |
| 1.11 | | 117647 | . |
| . | . | . | . |
| . | . | . | . |
| . | | . | . |
| 1.30 | 86 | 117647 | TOO HIGH |

If the variable cost per unit falls outside the interval of $.75–$.83, state in the decision column that the variable cost is either too low or too high. The formula to compute the BEP is given by:

$$BEP = \frac{\text{total fixed costs}}{1 - \dfrac{\text{variable cost/unit}}{\text{selling price/unit}}}$$

**32.** One method for calculating depreciation is to subtract a fixed percentage of the original value of the item each year. Thus a $100 item depreciated at 10% would be valued at $90 at the end of the first year, $80 at the end of the second, and so forth. Another method for calculating depreciation is to subtract a fixed percentage of the present value of the item. A $100 item depreciated by 10% would be valued at $90 at the end of the first year, $90 − .1 × 90 = $81, at the end of the second year, and so forth. Write a program to accept as input the original value ($V$), the depreciation rate ($R$), and a number of years ($N$), and produce a table showing the value of the items for the first, second, third,... $N$th year using both depreciation methods.

**33.** You have been hired by E. Naddor, Inc., a world-famous firm specializing in inventory control problems, to write a computer program for one of Naddor's largest customers, the Shopping Basket. This firm would like to computerize part of its reordering system to cut down on the cost of replenishing inventories.

Each Friday at the close of business, the ending inventory of each product is compared to the fixed reorder point for that product. If the ending inventory is equal to or below the reorder point for that product, the Shopping Basket orders enough of the item to bring the amount on hand up to a predetermined order level. Any order placed on Friday is delivered over the weekend so that the company can begin a new week of business with well-stocked shelves. It is possible for the ending inventory to be negative, indicating that demand exceeded supply during the week and some orders were not filled. Shopping Basket policy is to order enough to cover this backordered demand.

To aid you in your task, you have been given some old records that illustrate how the reorder system works:

| Item Number | 15202 | 67180 | 51435 | 49415 | 24361 |
| Description | Tuna Fish | Charcoal Lighter Fluid | Mouthwash | Pizza Mix | Asparagus |
| --- | --- | --- | --- | --- | --- |
| Unit price (per case) | 4.27 | 8.48 | 12.29 | 9.27 | 15.32 |
| Order level (cases) | 30 | 25 | 55 | 75 | 15 |
| Reorder point (cases) | 5 | 8 | 10 | 25 | 2 |
| Ending inventory (cases) | 9 | 5 | 7 | −10 | 6 |

Your task is to write a program to read five data records (using the sample data in the above inventory summary) to determine which items must be ordered and the respective quantities to be ordered for each item. The program should also calculate the cost of such orders and the total cost for all items ordered. The sample input layout is shown below:

**Input Layout**

| Positions | Field Description |
| --- | --- |
| 1–5 | Item number |
| 31–34 | Unit price (dollars and cents) |
| 35–37 | Order level (cases) |
| 38–40 | Reorder point (cases) |
| 41–44 | Ending inventory |

For example, the data record corresponding to the tuna fish would be:

```
15202    427    30    5    9
Item     Unit   Order Reorder Ending
number   price  level point  inventory
```

Some helpful rules are:

a. Order an item only if ending inventory is less than or equal to the reorder point for the item.

b. Amount to order = order-level − ending inventory.
c. Cost of ordering an item = amount ordered * unit price.

A sample output for the records given above would be:

```
                    THE SHOPPING BASKET
                      ORDER REPORT
    ITEM    UNIT    ORDER   REORDER    ENDING
   NUMBER   PRICE   LEVEL    POINT    INVENTORY   ORDER    COST

   15202    4.27     30        5          9         0      0.00
   67180    8.48     25        8          5        20    169.60
   51435   12.29     55       10          7        48    589.92
   49415    9.27     75       25        -10        85    787.95
   24361   15.32     15        2          6         0      0.00
                                          —
                                    TOTAL COST $1547.47
```

**34.** A rent-a-car company has the following system for computing a customer's rental car bill:

| Car Type | Rent/day 150 Miles | Rent/week 1050 Miles | Extra Mileage | Extra Hours |
|----------|--------------------|-----------------------|---------------|-------------|
| 1 | $24.95 | $140.00 | .18 | $3.60 |
| 2 | $32.95 | $184.80 | .24 | $4.80 |
| 3 | $44.95 | $256.95 | .26 | $7.00 |

The daily rate includes 150 mileage allowance, and the weekly rate includes 1050 mileage allowance.

The extra mileage column indicates the additional cost for each mile above the mileage allowance for the different car types.

The extra hours column specifies the additional hourly charge for each hour that the vehicle is used in excess of one day or in excess of one week.

Passenger collision insurance is optional and costs $3.75 per day.

Destination extra charges: There is no extra charge if the vehicle is returned to the renting station; however, if the receiving station is not the renting station, there is an additional charge of 14 cents per mile for the total number of miles driven (including the mileage allowance).

If a car is rented for fewer than 24 hours, the lesser of the following rates is applied: (1.) the number of hours of use times the hourly charge (the extra hours charge in the table) or (2.) the daily rental charge.

The final invoice should also include a 4% sales tax.

Write a program to compute a customer's bill, based on the charges described above. The input parameters are shown in the following example:

| *Input Parameters* | *Example* |
|---|---|
| Rent code: day = 1, week = 2 | 1 |
| Number of miles driven | 1080 |
| Car type | 1 |
| Possession of car | |
|   Days | 5 |
|   Hours | 0 |
| Insurance code 1-yes 2-no | 1 |
| Destination extra charge | 1 |

The output should be similar to:

```
      CAR TYPE          HOURS USED              RENT CODE
         1                120.                      1

   MILES DRIVEN         1080.
   LESS MILES ALLOWED    750.
   CHARGEABLE MILES      330. @         .18       $ 59.40
   NUMBER DAYS             5. @       24.95       $124.75

                        SUBTOTAL                  $184.15
   DESTINATION CHARGES                            $151.20
   COLLISION INSURANCE                            $ 18.75

                        TAXABLE CHARGE            $354.10
                        STATE TAX                 $ 14.16
                        NET AMOUNT                $368.26
```

## 4-9-3  Programming Exercises: Scientific/Mathematical

1. Make your family a temperature conversion chart that displays the temperatures in Fahrenheit and centigrade from $-35°F$ to $125°F$.  $(F = 9/5*C + 32)$.

2. The radii of circles vary from 2, 7, 12, 17,..., 47, inclusively. Print out the radius, circumference, and area of each circle.

3. Write a program to perform octal counting up to $27_8$, that is, print the numbers 1, 2,..., 7, 10, 11,..., 17, 20, 21,..., 27. Can you generalize your program for counting in octal up to a number N read from a data record?

4. Write a program to read a value for J $(J > 0)$ and:
   a. Print the positive even integers that are less than or equal to J,
   b. Print the first J odd integers starting with 1.

5. Read 30 grades already sorted into ascending order and compute the mode. The mode is defined as the score that occurs most frequently. For example, given the grades 10, 15, 15, 17, 17, 17, 20, 21, the mode is 17.

**6.** Read N grades (one per record) already sorted into ascending order (N is to be read from the first record) and compute the median. The median is the grade that divides a distribution of scores into two equal parts, for example:

10, 11, 12, 13, 14, 15, 16     The median is  13.

10, 11, 12, 13     The median is  $\dfrac{11 + 12}{2} = 11.5$.

**7.** Write the code to determine whether a particular number K is a prime number. A prime number is a number that is divisible only by itself and 1. One unsophisticated approach is to divide K by all the numbers starting with 1 up to one less than K. If K is not divisible evenly by any of these numbers, it is prime. Another method, a little more efficient than the one above, is to divide K by all numbers from 2 up to the square root of K.

**8.** The greatest common factor for two integers is the largest integer that will divide both numbers evenly. For example, the greatest common factor (*gcf*) of 9 and 12 is 3 since 3 is the largest number to divide evenly into both 9 and 12. The *gcf* of 8 and 9 is 1; the *gcf* of 27 and 18 is 9. An interesting algorithm (attributed to the mathematician Euclid) for computing the greatest common factor is shown here in flowchart form. [The remainder of $12 \div 9$ is 3, while the remainder of $17 \div 3$ is 2 i.e., $17 \div 3 = 5 + 2/17$] Write a program to implement the Euclidean algorithm. Can you explain why it works?

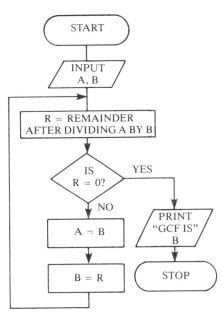

**9.** The number *e* can be defined as the limit of $(1 + 1/n)^n$ as *n* (integer) gets larger and larger. Write a program to approximate a value for *e*. Stop when the difference between two successive approximations is less than 0.001. Print out the values for *e* and *n*. For example,

$$e_1 = \left(1 + \frac{1}{1}\right)^1 = 2$$

$$e_2 = \left(1 + \frac{1}{1}\right)^2 = 2.25$$

$$e_3 = \left(1 + \frac{1}{3}\right)^3 = 2.37$$

The difference between $e_3$ and $e_2$ is still greater than 0.001; hence new values for *e* have to be computed until $e_{n+1} - e_n < 0.001$.

10. Management of any group of people is made more complex by the many types of relationships between the manager and the subordinates and among groups of subordinates. There are three types of relationships.

   a. Direct single: the manager relates directly to each subordinate. The number of these relationships is equal to $n$, the number of subordinates.
   b. Direct group: the manager relates to each distinct group of subordinates. The number of these relationships is $2^n - 1$.
   c. Cross: each subordinate relates to other subordinates. The number of these relationships is $n(n - 1)$.

   The total number of relationships in the group is $2^n + n^2 - 1$. Write a program to calculate the number of direct single, direct group, cross, and total number of relationships for 1 to 50 subordinates. Have your program print these in tabular form for each number of subordinates in the range specified. The mode used for the variables in this program will have a significant effect on the results produced. Try using all integer variables, then all real variables. Which results are the most useful?

11. The Fibonacci sequence is formed by assigning the value 1 to the first two terms and then computing each successive term as the sum of the two preceding terms. Thus $a_1 = 1, a_2 = 1, a_3 = a_1 + a_2 = 1 + 1 = 2, a_4 = a_2 + a_3 = 1 + 2 = 3$, and so on. The first ten terms of the Fibonacci sequence are: 1,1,2,3,5,8,13,21,34,55,...

   a. Write a program to generate the first 20 terms of the Fibonacci sequence.
   b. A number is said to be a Fibonacci number if it occurs as a term of the Fibonacci sequence. Write a program to read a number and determine if it is a Fibonacci number.

12. The golden mean was used by ancient roman architects in the design of structures. A building in which the ratio of the length to the width equalled the golden mean (which is approximately equal to 1.618) was believed to be most pleasing aesthetically. It can be shown that the limit of the ratio of successive terms of the Fibonacci sequence (see exercise 11) is equal to the golden mean. Write a program to compute terms of the Fibonacci sequence and the ratio of each term to its predecessor. How many terms are required before the difference between successive ratios is less than 0.01? 0.0001? How many terms are required before successive ratios are equal? (The answers to these questions depend on the data representation of the computer is use; the ratios should become equal in fewer than 100 terms.)

13. The following formula provides an approximation for the $n$th term in the Fibonacci sequence:

$$0.447264 \times (1.61803)^{n-1}$$

   Write a program to generate the actual terms of the Fibonacci sequence, the approximation, the absolute difference between the actual term and the approximation, and the relative error (difference divided by actual value). What happens to the values of relative error for successively larger values of $n$? How "good" is the approximation? Can you improve on the approximation formula?

14. Write a program to make daily weather reports. Each data record should contain nine integer values giving the following information: current month, day, and year; high

temperature for the day, low temperature for the day; year in which the record high for this day was set, record high temperature; year of record low for this day; record low temperature. After reading a data record, print a message of one of the following four types, depending on the data:

a. `10/23/84   HIGH TODAY   52`
   `            LOW TODAY    23`

b. `10/24/84   HIGH TODAY   71*`
   `            LOW TODAY    38`
   `*(BEATS RECORD OF 70 SET IN 1906)`

c. `10/25/84   HIGH TODAY   73*`
   `            LOW TODAY   -10**`
   `*(BEATS RECORD OF 68 SET IN 1938)`
   `**(BEATS RECORD OF -8 SET IN 1918)`

d. `10/26/84   HIGH TODAY   22`
   `            LOW TODAY   -18*`
   `*(BEATS RECORD OF -5 SET IN 1900)`

15. Write a program to compute the weight of a person on the following planets, based on the data:

| Planet | Percentage of Earth Weight |
|--------|---------------------------|
| Moon | 16 |
| Jupiter | 264 |
| Venus | 85 |
| Mars | 38 |

Create a table with weights ranging from 50 to 250 pounds in steps of 50 pounds. The same program should generate both of the following outputs, with output *a* displayed above output *b*.

a.
```
 EARTH   MOON   JUPITER   VENUS   MARS

   50     XXX     XXX      XXX    XXX
  100      .       .        .      .
    .
    .
  250     XXX     XXX      XXX    XXX
```

In part b, planet 1 is the moon, planet 2 is Jupiter etc.
On the output, part *b* of the problem should be displayed below the results for part a.

b.
```
 PLANET   EARTH   WEIGHT

    1       50     XXX
           100     XXX
            .       .
            .       .
            .
           250     XXX

    2       50     XXX
           100     XXX
            .       .
            .       .
           250     XXX
    .
    .
    4       50     XXX
           100     XXX
            .       .
            .       .
           250     XXX
```

## 4-9-4 Answers to Test Yourself

**1.** a. 10 records
   b. 11 records
   c. 10 records
   d. 10 records

**2.** a. I ≠ −7      b. I ≠ 4      There are alternative answers to problem 2.

**3.** a. Set I to 0
    WHILE I ≤ 100 DO
        PRINT I
        add 5 to I
    ENDWHILE

```
    I = 0
  5 IF(I .GT. 100) GO TO 10
        PRINT*, I
        I = I+5
        GO TO 5
```

  b. Set I to 2
    WHILE I ≤ 4096 DO
        PRINT I
        multiply I by 2
    ENDWHILE

```
    I = 2
  5 IF(I .GT. 4096) GO TO 10
        PRINT*, I
        I = 2*I
    GO TO 5
```

  c. Set K = 1
    Set I = 1
    WHILE I ≤ 100 DO
        PRINT K*I
        multiply K by − 1
        add 1 to I
    ENDWHILE

```
    DATA K,I/2*1/
  5 IF(I .GT. 100) GO TO 10
        L = K*I
        PRINT*, L
        K = -K
        I = I+1
        GO TO 5
```

  d. READ N
    Set I to N
    WHILE I ≥ 1 DO
        PRINT I
        add − 1 to I
    ENDWHILE

```
     READ*, N
     I = N
  5 IF(I .LT. 1) GO TO 10
        PRINT*, I
        I = I - 1
     GO TO 5
```

**4.** WHILE end-of-file-not-encountered DO
    READ emp_no, base_pay, emp_time, class, rating
    IF emp_time < .5 THEN
        WRITE 'no bonus'
    ELSE
        IF rating = 1 THEN
            IF class = 1 THEN
                bonus = Base_pay/52
            ELSE
                bonus = .2*Base_pay/12
            ENDIF
            IF emp_time > 10 THEN
                add 400 to bonus
            ENDIF
        ELSE
            IF class = 1 THEN
                bonus = base_pay/240
            ELSE
                bonus = .5*base_pay/12
            ENDIF
        ENDIF
    ENDIF
ENDWHILE

5. * Flag is a variable name used to record whether or not
   * an action has taken place during execution of some code
   Set flag to 0
   WHILE end-of-file-not encountered DO
       READ city__name, temperature
       IF flag = 0 THEN
           IF temperature ≥ 100 THEN
               WRITE city__name
               set flag to 1
           ENDIF
       ENDIF
   ENDWHILE

6. Alternative 1
   * Set counter to count number of amounts exceeding 10000
   * Set counter to count the number of records in the file
   over__10000 = 0
   total = 0
   WHILE end-of-file-not-encountered DO
       READ dollar__amount
       IF dollar__amount > 10000 THEN or
           add 1 to over__10000
       ENDIF
       add 1 to total
   ENDWHILE
   IF over__10000 = total THEN
       WRITE 'yes'
   ELSE
       WRITE 'no'
   ENDIF
   STOP

   Alternative 2
   WHILE end-of-file-not-encountered DO
       READ dollar__amount
       IF dollar__amount ≤ 10000 THEN
         WRITE 'no'
         STOP
       ENDIF
   ENDWHILE
   WRITE 'yes'
   STOP

7. WHILE end-of-file-not-encountered DO
       READ sex, age, college, certificate, telephone__number
       IF (sex = 1) and (age between 20 and 41) and (college or certificate)
           WRITE telephone number__number
           STOP
       ENDIF
   ENDWHILE
   WRITE 'no candidate found'

**8.**
```
      CHARACTER*8 SN
      INTEGER FM,FF ,SM,SF ,AGE,CLASS, SEX
      DATA FM,FF,SM,SF/4*Ø/
   10 READ(5,1,END=5)SN,AGE,SEX, CLASS
      IF(AGE.GT.21)WRITE(6,2)SN
      IF(CLASS.EQ.1.AND.SEX.EQ.1) FM=FM+1
      IF(CLASS.EQ.1.AND.SEX.EQ.2)FF=FF+1
      IF(CLASS.EQ.2.AND.SEX.EQ.1)SM=SM+1
      IF(CLASS.EQ.2.AND.SEX.EQ.2)SF=SF+1
      GO TO 10
    5 WRITE(6,3)FM,FF,SM,SF
    8 STOP
    2 FORMAT(1X,A8)
    1 FORMAT(A8,I2,2I1)
    3 FORMAT('Ø',4I8)
      END
```

**9.**
```
      READ(5,6,END = 8)I
      WRITE(6,6)I
    3 READ(5,6,END = 8)K
          WRITE(6,6)K
          IF(K .EQ. Ø)GO TO 3
          IF(I*K .LT. Ø)GO TO 8
          I = K
          GO TO 3
    8 STOP
    6 FORMAT(1X,I3)
      END
```

**10.** a. 2.   b. 2.   c. 3.   d. 4.   e. 7.   f. 5   g. 4.   h. 4.   i. 8.   j. 5.

**11.** a. F.   b. T.   c. T.   d. T.   e. F.   f. T.   g. T.   h. T.
i. F(1 record).   j. F(carriage control applies to output.)      k. T.

# the accumulation process and the do loop

CHAPTER FIVE

# the accumulation process and the do loop

## 5-1 Programming Example

*Problem/Specification*:    Write a FORTRAN program to compute the sum of the first N positive integers, where N is an integer read from an input record.

A program to solve this problem is shown in figure 5–1. Note the new FORTRAN instruction DO 5 I = 1,N which generates the integers 1 through N in steps of 1 and causes statement 5 to be carried out N times automatically.

Also note the way in which numbers are accumulated at line 5. This process is called the accumulation process; it is an extension of the counting process discussed in chapter 4.

**FIGURE 5–1**    SUM OF N INTEGERS

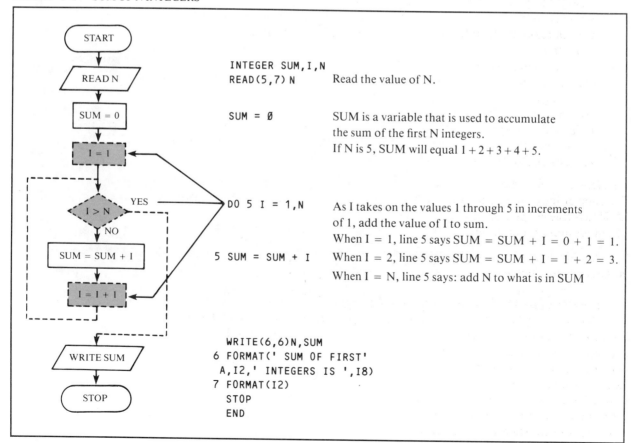

# 5-2  FORTRAN Statements

### 5-2-1  The DO Statement

The DO statement represents no new programming concepts; in fact, any FORTRAN program can be written without the DO statement. The purpose of the DO statement is strictly convenience to the programmer. It is used primarily for loop control. The usual procedure for loop control is to initialize a counter to a certain value, then increment that counter by a constant, and finally compare the counter to a terminal value for loop exiting. With one DO statement, the user can specify the initial value, the increment, and the terminal value of the counter (index) and the range of the DO, within which all statements are to be processed a specific number of times.

The general form of the DO statement is:

DO *statement number  index = initial, test* [, *increment*]

where *statement number* is the number of the last statement in the body of the loop, sometimes called the *foot* of the loop.

*index* is an integer variable name (sometimes called the DO variable); it essentially counts the number of times the body of the loop will be executed. In many FORTRAN compilers the index can be a real variable.

*initial* is an integer constant or integer variable specifying the initial value of the index. In many FORTRAN compilers *initial* can be an arithmetic expression (integer or real).

*test* is an integer constant or variable against which the index is tested to determine whether an exit from the loop should be taken. In many FORTRAN compilers *test* can be an arithmetic expression (integer or real).

*increment* is an optional integer constant or integer variable specifying the increment to be added to the index after each pass through the body of the loop. If the increment is omitted, its value is assumed to be 1. In many FORTRAN compilers, *increment* can be an arithmetic expression (integer or real).

*Restrictions*:   The increment must not evaluate to 0.

The foot of loop cannot be a GO TO, IF THEN ELSE, STOP, END, an arithmetic IF, RETURN (see chapter 9), or another DO statement.

The index must not be altered by any statement in the body of the loop.

You should check with your FORTRAN technical reference manual to determine whether *initial*, *test*, and *increment* can be arithmetic expressions.

The effect of a DO statement can be visualized in flowchart form, as shown in Figure 5–2. (A more complete discussion of the way in which FORTRAN formally treats the index is found in question 4, section 5–6.) In essence, if the increment is positive, you are counting "up"; if the increment is negative, you are counting "down." When counting "up," the body of the loop is processed once for each value taken on by the index; the index takes on values ranging from the initial value up to the last value not greater than *test*, going up in steps of *increment*. The body of the loop consists of all the statements after the DO statement, up to and including the foot of the loop (see Figure 5–2). In the following example, statements 15 and 90 will be carried out 303 times:

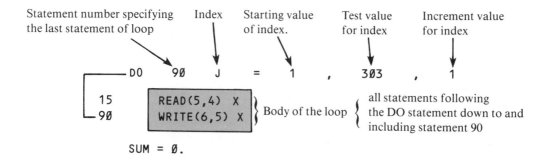

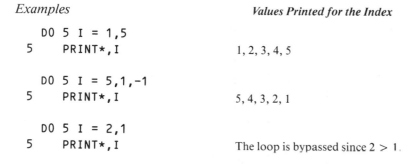

To improve readability, the body of the loop is indented at least four positions to the right of all other FORTRAN statements.

The following examples illustrate the counting mechanism of the DO loop. Refer to the flowcharts in Figure 5–2 to understand the counting process.

| *Examples* | *Values Printed for the Index* |
|---|---|
| `DO 5 I = 1,5`<br>`5    PRINT*,I` | 1, 2, 3, 4, 5 |
| `DO 5 I = 5,1,-1`<br>`5    PRINT*,I` | 5, 4, 3, 2, 1 |
| `DO 5 I = 2,1`<br>`5    PRINT*,I` | The loop is bypassed since 2 > 1. |

**FIGURE 5–2**    THE MEANING OF A DO LOOP

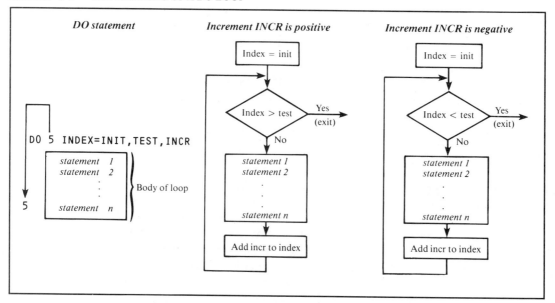

| *Examples* | *Values Printed for the Index* |
|---|---|

```
    DO 5 I = 1,1
  5    PRINT*,I
```
1

```
    DO 5 I = -1,-1
  5    PRINT*,I
```
−1

```
    DO 5 I = -2,-1
  5    PRINT*,I
```
−2, −1

```
    DO 5 I = -1,-1,-1
  5    PRINT*,I
```
−1

```
    DO 5 I = -2,-1,-1
  5    PRINT*,I
```
No value is printed
(−2 is less than −1).

```
    DO 5 X = .5,1.3,.3
  5    PRINT*,X
```
.5, .8, and 1.1

Sometimes it is convenient to use the index not just as a counting mechanism for loop control but also as a variable (number generator) within the body of the DO loop, as follows:

```
┌─ DO 15 I=3,100,2
│     ISQR=I*I
│     SQROOT=I**.5
└─15   WRITE(6,1)I,ISQR,SQROOT
   1 FORMAT(2X,I3,I7,F6.2)
```

This code will generate a table of the square root and the square of the numbers 3, 5, 7,..., 99.

It is often convenient to express the terminal value of a DO loop as a variable:

```
      READ(5,1)N
┌─  DO 15 K = 1,N
└─15  ▓▓▓▓▓▓▓▓▓▓
```

The increment in the DO statement is omitted, so the increment value is assumed to be 1. The body of the loop will be repeated N times.

The initial, terminal, and increment values can all be expressed with variables as follows:

```
      READ(5,1)N,M,INC
┌─ DO 16 L=N,M,INC
└─16  ▓▓▓▓▓▓▓▓▓
```

Section 5–6 shows how to determine the number of times the body of the loop will be executed.

*Caution:*

It is very important not to change the value of the index while in the DO loop, i.e., avoid the following type of error:

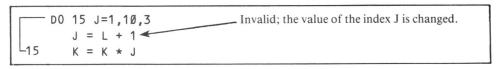

```
┌─ DO 15 J=1,10,3          ── Invalid; the value of the index J is changed.
│     J = L + 1  ◄
└─15  K = K * J
```

If a loop goes through its complete cycle (i.e., there is no transfer out of the loop through an IF or a GO TO statement), the value of the index is undefined outside the body of the loop. This means that you cannot expect the index to retain its last value after the loop has completed its full cycle and exit has been taken. Consider the following example:

```
┌─DO 5 I = 1, 10          The last value of I in the loop is 10.
└5    WRITE(6,8)I          The values 1, 2, 3,..,10 will be written.
     WRITE(6,8)I          I is undefined, because I is outside the loop and
                          the loop has gone through its complete cycle.
```

Contrast this situation with the following:

```
     DO 5 I = 1, 10
 ┌───── IF(I .EQ. 10) GO TO 9    The loop does not go through its complete cycle,
 │   5 WRITE(6,11)I              since there was a transfer out of the loop
 │        :                     through the IF statement.
 │        :                     Even though I is outside the loop, it is defined (10)
 └→  9 WRITE(6,11)I              because the loop stopped short of its full cycle.
```

### 5-2-2 Do It Now

**1.** Write the WHILE DO pseudo code and its equivalent FORTRAN code to represent the following DO loops:

```
a.    DO 5 I = 1,3
      5    PRINT*,I

b.    DO 5 K = 10,5,-2
      5    PRINT*,K
```

**2.** Identify the values taken on by the index in the following examples:

```
a. DO 5 X = -2., 2.3, .5
b. DO 5 I = -3, -4
c. DO 5 I = 0, 2
d. DO 5 I = 3/2, 8/3, 3
```

**3.** Identify any errors in the following coding segments:

```
a. DO 16 K = -2,N          b.    DO 5 L = 2,3,9
        PRINT*,K                      READ*,J,K,L
   X = 1                      5 PRINT*,J,K,L
```

**4.** What output is produced by the following DO loops?

```
a.    DO 5 L = 1,4          b.    DO 5 L = 2,21,3
      5    PRINT*,L,L**2,L**.5     5 PRINT*,L

c.    DO 5 T = 3.,1.        d.    DO 5 T = 1.,-1.,-.5
          X = T + 1                   X = 10. - T
      5    PRINT*,X          5 PRINT*,X
```

**5.** Using a DO loop, write the code to generate the following sequences of numbers (write the sequence for part d in decimal form):

a. 1, 3, 5, 7, ..., 51

b. −10, −9, −8, ..., −1

c. $5^2, 6^2, 7^2, ..., 21^2$

d. 1., 1./2., 1./3., ..., 1./99.

## *Answers*

**1.** a. Set I to 1
   WHILE I ≤ 3 DO
      PRINT*,I
      add 1 to I
   ENDWHILE

```
      I = 1
    6 IF(I .GT. 3) GO TO 10
         PRINT*,I
         I = I + 1
         GO TO 6
   10 -------
```

b. Set K to 10
   WHILE K ≥ 5 DO
      PRINT*,K
      add −2 to K
   ENDWHILE

```
      K = 10
    6 IF(K .LT. 5) GO TO 8
         PRINT*,K
         K = K - 2
         GO TO 6
    8 -------
```

**2.** a. −2., −1.5, −1., −.5, 0, .5, 1., 1.5, 2.

b. The loop will not be executed since −3 > −4

c. 0, 1, 2

d. 1

**3.** a. The foot of the loop is missing, i.e., statement 16 is undefined.

b. The value of the index L is changed by the READ statement.

**4.** a.
```
1   1    1
2   4    1.414
3   9    1.732
4   16   2
```
   b. 2, 5, 8, 11, 14, 17, 20

c. Nothing is printed since the starting value of the index is greater than the terminal value.

d. 9., 9.5, 10., 10.5, 11.

**5.** a.
```
   DO 5 I = 1, 51, 2
 5 PRINT*,I
```
   c.
```
   DO 5 I = 5, 21
      K = I**2
 5 PRINT*,K
```

b.
```
   DO 5 I = -10, -1
 5 PRINT*,I
```
   d.
```
   DO 5 T = 1, 99
      X = 1./T
 5 PRINT*,X
```

## 5-2-3 The CONTINUE Statement

Many non-DO controlled loops terminate with an IF or GO TO statement. Coding these loops with a DO statement may be difficult, since the last statement of a DO loop cannot be a transfer or an IF THEN ELSE statement. The dummy statement CONTINUE provides the programmer with a grammatical way out. Consider the problem of reading 100 grades and counting those greater than 90:

<table>
<tr><td align="center">*Incorrect Code*</td><td align="center">*Correct Code*</td></tr>
</table>

```
      K = Ø
┌──── DO 1Ø I = 1,1ØØ
│  5    READ(5,1)GRADE
│       IF(GRADE.GT.9Ø.)K=K+1
└─1Ø GO TO 5
       X = 1.
```

```
      K = Ø
┌──── DO 1Ø I = 1,1ØØ
│       READ(5,1)GRADE
│       IF(GRADE.GT.9Ø.)K=K+1
└─1Ø CONTINUE
   16 X = 1.
```

Incorrect code (even though it seems to make sense). A GO TO is not allowed at the foot of the loop.

The CONTINUE statement causes loop processing to continue if I does not exceed 100 (i.e., go back to first statement of the body of the loop). If I exceeds 100, the CONTINUE causes the next sequential statement to be processed (statement 16).

The general form of a CONTINUE statement is:

| *statement number*  CONTINUE |
|---|

A CONTINUE statement at the foot of the DO loop acts as a visual bracket to denote the end of a DO range. It helps delineate the range of the loop while not causing any operation to take place. Many programmers always use a CONTINUE statement as the terminal statement of the body of a DO loop, for example

```
┌──── DO 1Ø I = 1,1Ø
│       READ(5,1)X
│       WRITE(6,1)X
└─1Ø CONTINUE
```

The following examples are invalid but show common mistakes made by most beginning students. Study them carefully to understand why they will not work. The program is supposed to read 100 grades and count those grades above 90; the correct code was shown above.

<table>
<tr><td align="center">*Incorrect Codes*</td></tr>
</table>

```
      K = Ø
┌──── DO 1Ø I = 1,1ØØ
│  5    READ(5,1)GRADE
│       IF(GRADE.LE.9Ø.)GO TO 5
└─1Ø K = K + 1
```

In order to increment the index I of the DO loop, the foot of the loop must be processed. In the incorrect code, the foot of the loop is bypassed every time a grade 90 is encountered; this means that the index is not incremented. If one or more grades is less than or equal to 90, an end-of-file condition will occur at statement 5.

```
      K = Ø
┌─1 DO 1Ø I = 1,1ØØ
│       READ(5,2)GRADE
│       IF(GRADE.LE.9Ø)GO TO 1
└─1Ø    K = K + 1
```

Every time the grade is ≤ 90, transfer is made to statement 1, which means that the index I is reset to 1. An end-of-file condition will occur if one or more grades are less than or equal to 90.

### 5-2-4 **Transfer Into and Out of Loops**

The rules for transferring into and out of loops are best illustrated by considering the following situations.

## *Case 1*

It is not permissible to transfer from a statement outside a loop to a statement within the body of a loop.

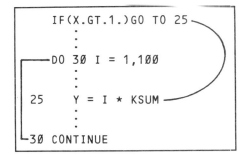

*Not* permissible.

This would not make sense, since the value of I would be unknown. A loop must be entered at the DO statement.

## *Case 2*

Transfer can be made to a loop if the transfer target is the DO statement.

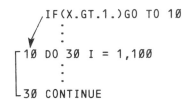

Permissible.

In this case I is properly initialized.

## *Case 3*

Transfer can be made from one statement to another within the same loop.

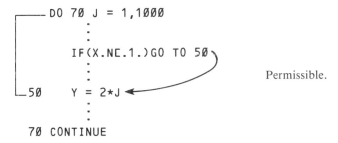

Permissible.

## *Case 4*

Transfer can be made from a statement in the loop to the foot of the loop.

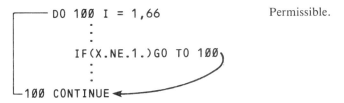

Permissible.

## Case 5

Transfer from a statement within a loop to a statement outside the loop is permissible.

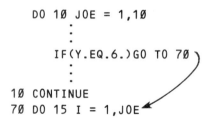

Permissible.

The value of JOE at line 70 will be the value of the index at the time the exit was taken from the loop. If the loop went through its complete cycle, i.e., exit from the loop was made through the CONTINUE statement, then the value for JOE would be undefined.

The statement JOE = 10 could be inserted between statements 10 and 70 to handle this situation.

## Case 6

The following example illustrates a typical beginner's attempt to transfer out of a loop to perform a particular task (as a result of a certain condition) and then come back into the loop after completing that task. This practice is to be avoided—the task to be performed should be coded within the loop.

*Bad Practice: Task Outside Loop*

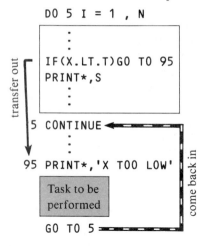

*Good Practice: Task Within Loop*

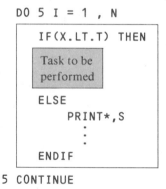

Suppose, for example, we are to read an input file consisting of 100 grades and print and count the number of grades over 90:

<table>
<tr><td>Incorrect Code</td><td>Correct Code</td></tr>
</table>

```
        K = 0
        DO 10 I = 1,100
            READ(5,1)GRADE
            IF(GRADE.GT.90.)GO TO 5
   10 CONTINUE
    5 K = K + 1
        WRITE(6,6)GRADE
        GO TO 10
```

```
    K = 0
    DO 10 I = 1,100
        READ(5,1)GRADE
        IF(GRADE.LE.90.)GO TO 10
        K = K + 1
        WRITE(6,6)GRADE
10 CONTINUE
```

There is no need to transfer out of the DO loop to complete some task and then to come back into the DO loop. The simplest way to avoid this problem is to use the IF THEN ELSE statement:

```
      K = 0
----DO 10 I = 1,100
        READ(5,1)GRADE
      ┌IF(GRADE .GT. 90.)THEN
      │   K = K + 1
      │   WRITE(6,6)GRADE
      └ENDIF
└---10 CONTINUE
```

Recall that no GO TO statements and therefore no FORTRAN statement numbers are needed when you use the IF THEN ELSE. The code becomes more readable.

Finally, remember that the value of the index of a DO loop is no longer defined once the loop has gone through its complete cycle, i.e., if exit from a loop is made through the foot of a loop, the value of the index at that point is undetermined. For example:

```
      DO 10 I = 1,2
         PRINT*,I
   10 CONTINUE
         PRINT*,I
```

Values printed for I will be 1 and 2. Do not expect I to be 3; it is undefined since exit from the loop was made through the CONTINUE.

This does *not* mean that the value of the index is undetermined if an exit is made out of the loop *before* the loop has completed its full cycle. In this situation the index will have whatever value it had at the time of the exit. Consider the following example: Assume an input file contains at most 100 records. Will the value of I at line 5 reflect the number of records read?

```
   ┌---DO 10 I = 1,100
   │     READ(5,6,END=5)GRADE
   └--10 CONTINUE
        .
        .
        .
    5 WRITE(6,11)I
```

If fewer than 100 grades are read, transfer is made to statement 5 where I reflects the number of grades read + 1 (end of file record). If 100 grades are read the value of I at statement 5 is meaningless since exit from the loop is made through the foot of the loop.

To avoid this situation, use DO 10 I = 1,101 to force a premature exit from the loop. In this way, exit will *never* be made through the foot of the loop and the value of the index is preserved.

### 5-2-5 Do It Now

1. Which of the following coding segments are invalid? Explain why.

```
a.      IF(X .LT. 4.) GO TO 68          b.      IF(X .LT. 4.) GO TO 6
           .                                        .
           .                                        .
    68 DO 5 I = 1,N                             DO 6 K = 1,N
           .                                        .
           .                                        .
           PRINT*,I                          8 S = S + T
           IF(L.GT.6)GOTO98                     CONTINUE
           .                               6 DO 5 I = 1,10
           .                               4     IF(X .LT. 2.)GOTO6
     5 CONTINUE                                  PRINT*,I
           .                               5 CONTINUE
           .
           GO TO 68
    98 -----
```

2. Write the code to print the integer value of X in the range 1 to 10 that satisfies the condition

$$X^2 - X - 6 = 0$$

If there are no such values, print an appropriate message.

## *Answers*

1. a. Valid
   b. Invalid foot of loop at line 6; possible infinite loop between lines 6 and 4.

2.
```
     DO 10 IX = 1,10
         IF(IX**2 - IX - 6 .EQ. 0) GO TO 20
  10 CONTINUE
     WRITE(6,11)
  11 FORMAT(1X,'NO VALUE SATISFIES CONDITION')
     STOP
  20 WRITE(6,12)IX
  12 FORMAT(1X,I3,' SATISFIES CONDITION')
     STOP
     END
```

### 5-2-6  Nested Loops

It is often necessary to repeat an entire loop a certain number of times. This is done by placing a loop within a loop or, more exactly, making a complete loop part of the body of another loop. In such cases each pass though the outer loop causes the inner loop to run through its complete cycle. The following code illustrates the mechanism of *nested* loops:

Outer loop.

Since I varies from 1 to 3 the inner loop will be processed three times.

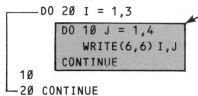
```
 ┌──DO 20 I = 1,3
 │    ┌─DO 10 J = 1,4
 │    │     WRITE(6,6) I,J
 │    └─CONTINUE
 │  10
 └──20 CONTINUE
```

Inner loop.

The inner loop causes the WRITE statement to be processed four times. Since the outer loop is processed three times, the WRITE statement will be processed altogether 12 times.

This code will produce

| I | J | |
|---|---|---|
| 1 | 1 | |
| 1 | 2 | First time through the inner loop |
| 1 | 3 | (outer loop index I = 1). |
| 1 | 4 | |
| 2 | 1 | |
| 2 | 2 | Second time through the inner loop |
| 2 | 3 | (outer loop index I = 2). |
| 2 | 4 | |
| 3 | 1 | |
| 3 | 2 | Third time through the inner loop |
| 3 | 3 | (outer loop index I = 3). |
| 3 | 4 | |

In nested loops, the inner loop always cycles more rapidly than the outer loop.

Any number of DO statements can share the same foot or the same CONTINUE statement. The above program segment could be coded as follows:

```
 ┌──DO 20 I = 1,3
 │ ┌──DO 20 J = 1,4
 │ │     WRITE(6,10)I,J
 └─┴20 CONTINUE
```

The inner loop is repeated four times for each of the three repetitions of the outer loop. For readability, it is a good idea to provide a separate CONTINUE statement for each loop.

As an example, let us write the code to generate the 6's, 7's, 8's, 9's, and 10's multiplication tables.

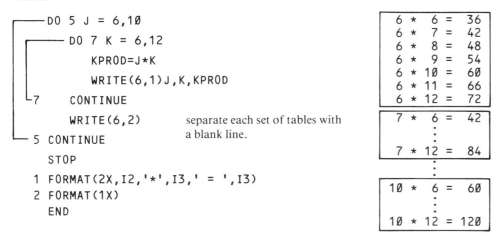

```
      DO 5 J = 6,10
         DO 7 K = 6,12
            KPROD=J*K
            WRITE(6,1)J,K,KPROD
7        CONTINUE
         WRITE(6,2)          separate each set of tables with
                             a blank line.
5     CONTINUE
      STOP
1     FORMAT(2X,I2,'*',I3,' = ',I3)
2     FORMAT(1X)
      END
```

```
6  *  6  =   36
6  *  7  =   42
6  *  8  =   48
6  *  9  =   54
6  * 10  =   60
6  * 11  =   66
6  * 12  =   72

7  *  6  =   42
          .
          .
7  * 12  =   84
          .
          .
10  *  6  =   60
          .
          .
10  * 12  =  120
```

It is important to keep in mind that each nested loop must lie totally within the body of an outer loop. Consider, for example, the following graphical illustrations of valid and invalid loops:

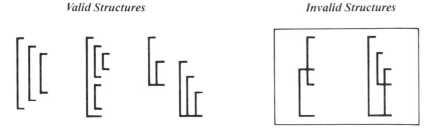

*Valid Structures*          *Invalid Structures*

DO loops can also be nested within WHILE DO and IF THEN structures, and vice versa. Once again, each nested structure should have a header and a terminal statement that lie wholly within the other structure. To avoid errors and confusion, it is strongly recommended that the terminal statement of a DO loop always be a CONTINUE statement. The following are examples of valid structures:

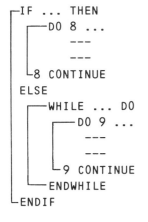

```
IF ... THEN
   DO 8 ...
      ---
      ---
8  CONTINUE
ELSE
   WHILE ... DO
      DO 9 ...
         ---
         ---
9     CONTINUE
   ENDWHILE
ENDIF
```

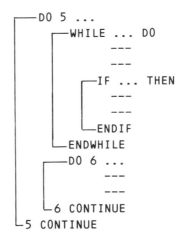

```
DO 5 ...
   WHILE ... DO
      ---
      ---
      IF ... THEN
         ---
         ---
      ENDIF
   ENDWHILE
   DO 6 ...
      ---
      ---
6  CONTINUE
5  CONTINUE
```

Obviously, such nested structures can be difficult to understand. Whenever possible, use simple structures!

*Example*   Nested DO's and IF's within WHILE DO Loops

An input file consists of an unknown number of packets of records, where each packet contains a header record identifying the number of records that follow in the packet. Each record, except the header record, contains a name field and a sex code (1 = male, 2 = female). Write the code to print the names of all females and the percentage of males in each given packet. A negative or zero entry on a header record identifies the end of the file. The input and output have the following forms:

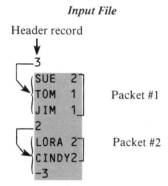

*Input File*

Header record

```
 3
SUE   2
TOM   1     Packet #1
JIM   1
 2
LORA  2     Packet #2
CINDY2
-3
```

*Output*

```
GROUP 1
SUE
PERCENTAGE MALES = 66.6

GROUP 2
LORA
CINDY
PERCENTAGE MALES = 0.0
```

The pseudo code and FORTRAN code for this problem are as follows:

```
* Count each packet to identify group
Set group__count to 1
* Read number of records in packet
READ header__count
WHILE header__count > 0 DO
    PRINT group__count
    Set male__count to 0
    DO as I goes from 1 to header__count
        READ name, sex__code
        IF sex__code = 2 THEN
            PRINT name
        ELSE
            add 1 to male__count
        ENDIF
    CONTINUE
*    Print percentage of males for packet
        PRINT male__count/header__count
        add 1 to group__count
        READ header__count
ENDWHIILE
STOP
```

```fortran
      INTEGER HDCNT,MALE,GROUP,SEX
      CHARACTER NAME*8
      REAL PER
      GROUP = 1
      READ*,HDCNT
6     IF(HDCNT .LE. 0)GO TO 8
          PRINT*,'GROUP',GROUP
          MALE = 0
          DO 5 I = 1,HDCNT
              READ*,NAME,SEX
              IF(SEX .EQ. 2)THEN
                  PRINT*,NAME
              ELSE
                  MALE = MALE + 1
              ENDIF
5         CONTINUE
          PER = MALE*100./HDCNT
          PRINT*,PER
          GROUP = GROUP + 1
          READ*,HDCNT
          GO TO 6
8     STOP
```

### 5-2-7  Do It Now

**1.** How many times will the PRINT statement be executed?

a.
```
   DO 3 I = 2,3
      DO 2 J = 1,4
         DO 1 K = 0,2
            PRINT*,K
   1 CONTINUE
   2 CONTINUE
   3 CONTINUE
```

b.
```
   DO 2 J = 40,60
      DO 1 K = 1,3
         PRINT*,K
   1  CONTINUE
   2 CONTINUE
```

c.
```
   DO 3 I = 2,8,2
      DO 2 J = 1,4
         DO 1 K = 1,4,2
            PRINT*,K
   1     CONTINUE
   2  CONTINUE
   3 CONTINUE
```

d.
```
   DO 5 I = 1,4
      DO 6 J = 2,I
         PRINT*,J
   6  CONTINUE
   5 CONTINUE
```

**2.** What output would be produced by each of the following? List all the values taken by I and J during execution of the code.

a.
```
    DO 110 I = 2,10,2
       DO 100 J = 1,10
          WRITE(6,11)I,J
100    CONTINUE
110 CONTINUE
```

b.
```
    N = 4
    DO 210 I = 1,N
       DO 200 J = 1,I
          WRITE(6,11)I,J
200    CONTINUE
210 CONTINUE
```

### *Answers*

**1.**  a.  24; (2 x 4 x 3)
    b.  63; (21 x 3)
    c.  32; (4 x 4 x 2)
    d.  6; (0, 1, 2, 3)

**2.**  a.

| I | J |
|---|---|
| 2 | 1 |
| 2 | 2 |
| . | . |
| . | . |
| 2 | 10 |
| 4 | 1 |
| 4 | 2 |
| . | . |
| . | . |
| 4 | 10 |
| . | . |
| . | . |
| 10 | 1 |
| 10 | 2 |
| . | . |
| . | . |
| 10 | 10 |

b.

| N | I | J |
|---|---|---|
| 4 | 1 | 1 |
|   | 2 | 1 |
|   | 2 | 2 |
|   | 3 | 1 |
|   | 3 | 2 |
|   | 3 | 3 |
|   | 4 | 1 |
|   | 4 | 2 |
|   | 4 | 3 |
|   | 4 | 4 |

## 5-3 The Accumulation Process

We have already seen how to count through repeated execution of such statements as I = I + 1, where I is initially set to a beginning value. Each time I = I + 1 is executed, the value 1 is added to the counter I, which will take on successive values 1, 2, 3, 4, and so on, if I is set initially to zero. Counting can be thought of as "accumulating a count." The main difference between counting and accumulating is that in accumulating, instead of repetitively adding a constant (1, for example) to a counter, a variable is added repetitively to an accumulator, which is a special variable used to keep track of running sums or partial sums (see Figure 5-3). An accumulator can also be used to accumulate a partial product; this is done by repetitively multiplying the accumulator by a variable.

**FIGURE 5-3** COUNTING VERSUS ACCUMULATING

| Counting | Accumulating |
|---|---|
| C = 0 | 60 70 80 20 } input file |
| | S = 0 |
| | READ G |
| C = C + 1 ... 1 / 4 3 2 1 | S = S + G ... 1 / 230 210 130 60 |
| Each time the constant 1 is added to the previous count (C). | Each time a new grade G is added to the current sum S. |

The following examples illustrate the accumulation process.

*Example 1* Computing an average

An input file consists of exactly five scores. Write the code to print the five scores and compute the average score. The output should be similar to the following:

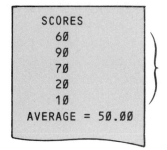

```
    SCORES
      60
      90
      70
      20
      10
AVERAGE = 50.00
```

This caption is printed once, outside the loop.
As each score is read, the score is printed.
Every time a score is read, it is added to the previous score to form a sum of scores. When five scores have thus been summed, the sum is divided by 5 to give the average.

The program to solve this problem is shown in Figure 5-4. Analyze the accumulation process carefully to see how the sum of all scores is obtained.

**FIGURE 5-4**    COMPUTING AN AVERAGE OF SCORES

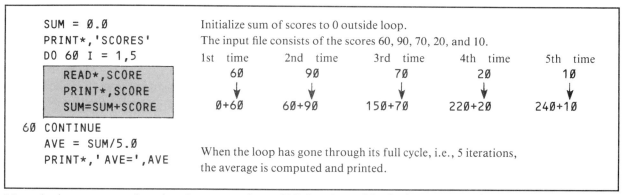

Note the importance of setting the accumulator SUM to 0 outside the loop. Every time a new score is read, it is immediately added to the current sum of scores at line 10; this is shown in Figure 5–4.

*Example 2*    Computing the product of the first 15 integers

Let us write the code to compute PROD $= 1 * 2 * 3 * 4 * ... * 15$. To do this, we need:

1. an accumulator PROD, which will be initially 1, then $1 * 2$, then $1 * 2 * 3$, and so forth, and

2. a counter I to generate the numbers 1, 2, 3, ..., 15, which will be used to develop the partial products in PROD.

   Every time we generate a new value for I, we will immediately multiply PROD by I to obtain a product. The DO loop can be used to generate the numbers 1, 2, 3, ... as follows:

```
      INTEGER PROD
      PROD = 1
      DO 5 I = 1,15          PROD will take on the values
         PROD = PROD*I       1*1,  1*1*2,  1*1*2*3,... ,  1*1*2*3*...*15
    5 CONTINUE
      PRINT*,PROD
```

## 5-3-1 Do It Now

1. Write the code to compute the following:

   a. $5 + 10 + 15 ... + 675$
   b. $-1 - 2 - 3 ... - 17$
   c. $1. + 1./2. + 1./3. ... + 1./100.$
   d. $1 + (1+2) + (1+2+3) + ... + (1+2+3+4...+99+100)$

2. What will be the output for each of the following?

   a.
```
      M = 0
      DO 5 K = 1,10
         M = M - (-1)**K * K
    5 CONTINUE
      PRINT*,M
```

```
b.     A = 0.
       DO 100 I = 1,4              Data File
           READ*,X                 ───────
           A = A - X                 20.
   100 CONTINUE                      40.
       PRINT*,A                      70.
       STOP                          90.
```

## *Answers*

1.  a.
```
       SUM = 0.
       DO 5 I = 5,675,5
     5 SUM = SUM + I
       PRINT*,SUM
```

c.
```
       SUM = 0.
       DO 5 I = 1,100
     5 SUM = SUM + 1./I
       PRINT*,SUM
```

  b.
```
       SUM = 0.
       DO 5 I = -1,-17,-1
     5 SUM = SUM + I
       PRINT*,SUM
```

d.
```
       SUM = 0.
       BIGSUM = 0.
       DO 5 I = 1,100
       SUM = SUM + I
     5 BIGSUM = BIGSUM + SUM
       PRINT*,BIGSUM
```

2.  a.  M = 1 − 2 + 3 − 4 + ... + 9 − 10 = −5

  b.

| A | I | X |
|------|---|-----|
| 0. | 1 | 20. |
| -20. | 2 | 40. |
| -60. | 3 | 70. |
| -130. | 4 | 90. |
| -220. | | |

Expected output:   −220

# 5-4   Programming Examples

### 5-4-1   An Amortization Schedule

*Problem/Specification*:   Suppose you take out a loan of $1,000 at a yearly interest rate of 12% and you intend to repay that loan at $200 (including the interest payment) per month until the loan is fully repaid. You would like to have an amortization schedule like the following one:

```
                    AMORTIZATION TABLE
           PRINCIPAL  $1,000.00   INTEREST  12.00%
                 REGULAR PAYMENT $ 200.00

   NO.   INTEREST   AMORTIZED   BALANCE   INTEREST TO DATE
    1      10.00     190.00     810.00        10.00
    2       8.10     191.90     618.10        18.10
    3       6.18     193.82     424.28        24.28
    4       4.24     195.76     228.52        28.52
    5       2.29     197.71      30.81        30.81
    6       0.31      30.81       0.00        31.12

   LAST PAYMENT = $ 31.12
```

Write a program to read a loan principal, an interest rate, and a monthly repayment amount and generate an amortization table like the one above.

*Problem/Solution*:    If no interest were charged, it would take 5 months to repay a $1,000 loan at $200 per month. When interest is charged, the $200 monthly payment must repay the capital (i.e., pay back the $1,000 loan) and pay the interest on the outstanding balance of the loan. The part of the monthly payment that goes to repay the capital is called the *amortized* amount. The interest taken from the monthly payment is the interest on the unpaid balance; this amount represents the cost of borrowing money.

In this problem, a 12% yearly interest rate means a 1% monthly interest rate, i.e.,

| | | | |
|---|---|---|---|
| the interest for month 1 is | $1,000 * | 0.01 | = $ 10 |
| the payment to capital is | $ 200 – | 10 | = $190 |
| the remaining balance is | $1,000 – 190 | | = $810 |
| | | | |
| the interest for month 2 is | $ 810 * | 0.01 | = $ 8.10 |
| the payment to capital is | $ 200 – | 8.10 | = $191.90 |
| the remaining balance is | $1,000 – 191.90 | | = $808.10 |

This process continues until the remaining balance is less than or equal to $200 (in this example, $30.81). Since that amount will be paid at the end of the last month, an interest of 1% is computed on that amount (31 cents), so that the last payment is $30.81 + .31 = $31.12. At that point the remaining balance is set to 0. The accumulated interest is $31.12; if the borrower had made just one interest payment at the end of 6 months, the interest would have been 1000 * 6% = 60 dollars.

The program to solve this problem is shown in Figure 5-5. This problem illustrates the counting and accumulation mechanisms. The variable K counts the number of payments, and the monthly balance BAL is equal to the old balance minus the payment to capital; the payment to capital is equal to the monthly payment minus the interest on the remaining balance.

## 5-4-2  Charlie's Eatery

*Problem/Specification*:    Whenever a meal is sold at Charlie's Eatery, the cost of the order and a corresponding meal code (B = breakfast, L = lunch, D = dinner) are recorded on a terminal. At the end of the day, Charlie would like to obtain the following information:

■ the day's total sales      ■ the average breakfast cost      ■ the lowest dinner cost

Write a program to read an input file where each record consists of a meal cost and a meal code and produce a report like the following one:

```
MEAL COST       MEAL CODE
    7.36            B
    6.78            L
    9.87            D
    4.00            B
    2.78            D

TOTAL SALES = 30.79
AVERAGE BREAKFAST COST = 5.68
MINIMUM DINNER COST = 2.78
```

**FIGURE 5–5** AN AMORTIZATION SCHEDULE

```
C AMORTIZATION PROBLEM
C  BAL:    BALANCE
C  RATE:   INTEREST RATE
C  MONPAY: MONTHLY FIXED PAYMENT
C  K:      COUNTS THE PAYMENTS
C  ACCINT: ACCUMULATED INTEREST
C  AMORT:  MONTHLY AMORTIZED AMOUNT
C  INTBAL: INTEREST ON CURRENT BALANCE
C  LASPAY: LAST PAYMENT
C
       REAL BAL,RATE,MONPAY,ACCINT,AMORT,INTBAL,LASPAY
       INTEGER K
       READ(5,7) BAL, RATE, MONPAY
       WRITE(6,1)BAL, RATE, MONPAY
       RATE = RATE/100./12.          Convert to monthly decimal interest.
       K = 0                         Counts the number of payments.
       ACCINT = 0.                   Accumulates the monthly interest payments.
    10 IF(BAL .LE. MONPAY)GO TO 20   Exit from the loop when balance < monthly payment.
          K = K + 1
          INTBAL = RATE * BAL        Computes interest on current balance.
          ACCINT = ACCINT + INTBAL   Accumulate the monthly interests
          AMORT  = MONPAY - INTBAL   Amortized amount = monthly payment - interest
          BAL    = BAL - AMORT       New balance = old balance - amortized amount
          WRITE(6,5)K,INTBAL,AMORT,BAL,ACCINT
          GO TO 10
    20 K = K + 1                     Count the last payment.
       INTBAL = BAL * RATE           Compute interest on last payment.
       ACCINT = ACCINT + INTBAL      Add last interest to accumulated interest.
       AMORT  = BAL                  Amortized amount equals last balance.
       BAL    = 0.                   Set balance to 0; loan has been repaid.
       WRITE(6,5)K,INTBAL,AMORT,BAL,ACCINT
       LASPAY = AMORT + INTBAL       Add the last month's interest to amortized amount.
       WRITE(6,6) LASPAY             Print the last payment.
       STOP
C
    1  FORMAT('                        AMORTIZATION TABLE'/
    A  '              PRINCIPAL  $',F7.2,4X,'INTEREST    ',F5.2,'%'/
    B  '                  REGULAR PAYMENT $',F6.2/1X/
    C  ' NO.   INTEREST   AMORTIZED   BALANCE   INTEREST TO DATE')
    5  FORMAT(2X,I1,6X,F5.2,6X,F6.2,6X,F6.2,8X, F5.2)
    6  FORMAT(' LAST PAYMENT= $',F6.2)
    7  FORMAT(F7.2, F2.0,F6.2)
       END
```

```
                    AMORTIZATION TABLE
           PRINCIPAL  $1000.00    INTEREST    12.00%
                  REGULAR PAYMENT $200.00

NO.   INTEREST   AMORTIZED   BALANCE   INTEREST TO DATE
 1      10.00      190.00     810.00        10.00
 2       8.10      191.90     618.10        18.10
 3       6.18      193.82     424.28        24.28
 4       4.24      195.76     228.52        28.52
 5       2.29      197.71      30.81        30.81
 6        .31       30.81        .00        31.12

LAST PAYMENT= $ 31.12
```

Input File

1000.0012200.0

BALANCE  MONTHLY PAYMENT

INTEREST RATE

*Problem/Solution*:  To compute the daily total sales, the program simply accumulates the various meal costs as they are read. To compute the average breakfast cost, the number of breakfasts must be counted and the breakfast costs accumulated. To find the minimum dinner cost, we can arbitrarily initialize the minimum cost to an unrealistic figure, say $1000, so that when that "minimum" is compared to the first dinner cost, that dinner cost will obviously be less than $1000 and will become the new minimum.

This program requires three techniques: (1) counting (breakfasts), (2) accumulating (total sales and breakfast sales), and (3) finding a minimum value (minimum dinner cost). The entire logic of the problem can be captured in flowchart form as shown below and in FORTRAN code as shown in Figure 5–6.

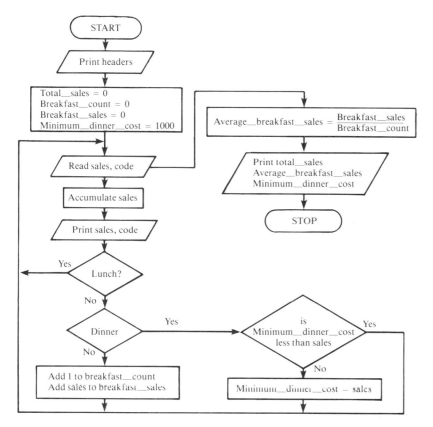

A minimum of five input records is needed to test this program: two dinner records (for the minimum cost), two breakfast records (for the breakfast average), and one lunch record.

*Problem/Discussion:*

1. What would happen to the minimum dinner cost if no dinner records were present in the input file? Change the program to respond appropriately.

2. What would happen if no breakfasts were served? Change the program accordingly.

**FIGURE 5-6**    CHARLIE'S EATERY: DATA ANALYSIS

```
C CHARLIE'S EATERY PROBLEM
C  TOTCOS:   ACCUMULATES ALL MEAL COSTS
C  TOTBKC:   ACCUMULATES ALL BREAKFASTS COSTS
C  BKCNT:    COUNTS ALL BREAKFASTS
C  MINDIN:   MINIMUM DINNER COST
C  MEALC :   USED TO READ MEAL COST
C  MEALKD:   USED TO READ MEAL CODE
C  AVGBKF:   AVERAGE BREAKFAST COST
C
      CHARACTER MEALKD*1
      INTEGER BKCNT
      REAL TOTCOS, TOTBKC, MINDIN, MEALC, AVGBKF
      DATA TOTCOS,TOTBKC,BKCNT,MINDIN /0.,0.,0,1000./
      WRITE(6,1)
C
   10 READ(5,4,END=88)MEALC, MEALKD
          TOTCOS = TOTCOS + MEALC
          WRITE(6,2)MEALC, MEALKD
          IF(MEALKD .EQ. 'D') THEN
              IF(MEALC .LT. MINDIN) MINDIN = MEALC
          ENDIF
          IF(MEALKD .EQ. 'B') THEN
              BKCNT = BKCNT + 1
              TOTBKC = TOTBKC + MEALC
          ENDIF
          GO TO 10
C
   88 AVGBKF = TOTBKC/BKCNT
      WRITE(6,3)TOTCOS, AVGBKF, MINDIN
      STOP
C
    1 FORMAT(' MEAL COST',4X,'MEAL CODE'/)
    2 FORMAT(3X, F5.2, 10X, A1)
    3 FORMAT('0TOTAL SALES = ',F6.2/
   A        ' AVERAGE BREAKFAST COST =',F5.2/
   B        ' MINIMUM DINNER COST =',F5.2)
    4 FORMAT(F7.2, A1)
      END
```

| MEAL COST | MEAL CODE |
|-----------|-----------|
| 7.36 | B |
| 6.78 | L |
| 9.87 | D |
| 4.00 | B |
| 2.78 | D |

TOTAL SALES = 30.79
AVERAGE BREAKFAST COST = 5.68
MINIMUM DINNER COST = 2.78

Input file

Meal cost        Meal code

```
0007.36B
0006.78L
0009.87D
0004.00B
0002.78D
```

3. Change the program to print error messages if the meal code is invalid or if any meal cost exceeds $1,000.

4. Change the program to print BREAKFAST, LUNCH and DINNER in the report instead of codes B, L, and D.

### 5-4-3  Do It Now

1. Run the amortization program of Figure 5–5 for BAL = 5000, I = 12%, and monthly payment = $200. In the report, skip a line when 12 payments have been made (1 year) and start the next year with numbers 1, 2, 3, ... rather than 13, 14, 15.

2. Change the program of Figure 5–5 so that payments will be made quarterly; for example, in problem 1 $600 would be paid every 3 months instead of $200 every month.

3. Determine how much faster the loan in problem 1 would be repaid if, at the end of each month, the borrower paid the interest for the next month in advance.

4. Determine what happens to the program in Figure 5–6 if there are no dinner records in the input file. How could you correct this situation?

### 5-4-4  Standard Deviation

*Problem/Specification*:  The general formula to compute the standard deviation for $n$ grades $x_1, x_2, x_3, ..., x_n$ is

$$SD = \sqrt{\frac{n(x_1^2 + x_2^2 + x_3^2 + ... + x_n^2) - (x_1 + x_2 + x_3 + ... + x_n)^2}{n(n-1)}}$$

Write a program to read $n$ grades and compute the average and the standard deviation.

*Problem/Solution*:  If you are unsure of the meaning of the standard deviation, consider the following illustration. The following tables show the final scores obtained in two introduction to computers classes taught by two different instructors.

| Class A | Class B |
|---------|---------|
| 40 | 90 |
| 55 | 20 |
| 60 | 80 |
| 45 | 10 |

At the end of the semester, the two instructors discuss how their classes did that semester. Both recall that their class average was 50, whereupon both express surprise at this coincidence. Little do they realize how different their ranges of scores are. The average does not reflect this. In Class A, all the scores are close together, while in Class B the scores spread out considerably; yet the averages are identical. If the average does not capture the spread of the scores, what mathematical measure does? Answer: the standard deviation.

The standard deviation gives us a feel for the distribution of scores. In Class A the spread between the outermost scores and the average is 10, while in Class B that spread is 40 (90–50 or 10–50). In general, the standard deviation gives an indication of how much, on the average, the scores deviate from the average. A small deviation implies that most of the scores are clustered, while a large deviation implies a large spread among the scores. A deviation of 0 means that all the scores are the same. If the standard deviation is 15 and the score average is 70, this means that the great majority of scores fall in the interval 70 + 15 to 70 − 15 (between 85 and 55).

To understand the mechanics involved, let us compute the standard deviation for class A, where $x_1$, $x_2$, $x_3$, and $x_4$ are 40, 55, 60, and 45, and $n = 4$.

**Sum of the square of each score**

**Sum of the scores squared**

$$\textit{Standard Deviation} = \sqrt{\frac{4(40^2 + 55^2 + 60^2 + 45^2) - (40 + 55 + 60 + 45)^2}{4(3)}} = 9.13$$

Note that the numerator is simply $n*$(sum of all scores$^2$) − (sum of scores)$^2$

The program to solve this problem must accumulate two types of sums: a sum of scores and the sum of the square of each score. Every time a score is read, it is added to the sum of scores ($x_1 + x_2 + x_3 + \ldots$) and it is multiplied by itself and added to the sum of squares ($x_1^2 + x_2^2 + \ldots$).

This process continues until the end-of-file is reached, then the standard deviation is calculated. The logic of the problem is expressed in the following pseudo code and in the FORTRAN code in Figure 5–7.

**FIGURE 5–7** A STANDARD DEVIATION

```
C STANDARD DEVIATION PROBLEM
C    SUM:    SUM OF SCORES              X₁ + X₂ + X₃ + . . . + Xₙ
C    N:      COUNT OF SCORES
C    SUMSQ:  SUM OF EACH SCORE SQUARED  X₁² + Xₓ² + X₃² + . . . + Xₙ²
C    SCORE:  VARIOUS SCORES READ
C    NUM:    NUMERATOR OF FORMULA       N * SUMSQ - SUM * SUM
C    DENOM:  DENOMINATOR OF FORMULA     N * (N - 1)
C    AVE:    AVERAGE OF SCORES
C    STD:    STANDARD DEVIATION         (NUM / DENOM) ** .5
C
      INTEGER N
      REAL  NUM,DENOM,STD,AVE,SUM,SUMSQ,SCORE
      N     = 0
      SUM   = 0.
      SUMSQ = 0.
    5 READ(5,1,END=88) SCORE
         SUM   = SUM + SCORE
         SUMSQ = SUMSQ + SCORE**2
         N     = N + 1
         GO TO 5
   88 NUM   = N * SUMSQ - SUM**2
      DENOM = N * (N - 1)
      AVE   = SUM / N
      STD   = (NUM / DENOM)**.5
      WRITE(6,2) AVE, STD
      STOP
    1 FORMAT (F5.1)
    2 FORMAT(1X,'AVERAGE = ',F6.2/
   A         1X,'DEVIATION =', F6.2)
      END
```

*Input File*

SCORE

```
034.0
078.0
098.0
087.0
060.0
067.0
```

Program

```
AVERAGE = 70.67
DEVIATION = 22.54
```

```
AVERAGE = 70.67
DEVIATION = 22.54
```

```
* To compute a standard deviation
set sum of scores to 0 (sum)
set count of scores to 0 (n)
set sum of each score squared to 0 (sumsq)
WHILE end-of-file-not-encountered DO
      READ score
      add score to sum
      add score² to sumsq
      add 1 to n
ENDWHILE
Numerator = n * sumsq − sum²
Denominator = n * (n − 1)
Standard__deviation = square root of (numerator/denominator)
WRITE standard__deviation
STOP
```

*Problem/Discussion:*

1. What happens in the program of Figure 5–7 if N is either 0 or 1. Change the program appropriately.

2. Can the formula to compute the standard deviation in the program of Figure 5–7 be written using only one statement?
   [STD = ((N * SUMSQ − SUM**2)/(N * (N−1)))**.5]

## 5-4-5  An Approximation to the Sine Function

*Problem/Specification:*   The general formula to compute an approximation for the sine of $x$, where $x$ is any angle measured in radians, is:

$$\sin x = \frac{x^1}{1!} - \frac{x^3}{3!} + \frac{x^5}{5!} - \dots - \frac{x^{11}}{11!} + \dots$$

Write a program to read a value for $x$ and compute and print the sine of $x$ using the first six terms of the formula. Recall that 5! (read as 5 factorial) is equal to 1*2*3*4*5.

*Problem/Solution:*   The reader may recall that the sine of 90° ($\pi/2$) is 1, or that the sine of 30° ($\pi/6$) is 1/2, while the sine of 0 is 0. The above formula can be used to compute an approximation of the sine of an angle. This approximation becomes more accurate as more terms of the formula are computed. Let us, for example, compute the sine of $\pi/2$ (which is exactly equal to 1) using the first three terms of the formula. Note that $\pi/2 \approx 1.57080$

$$\text{sine } (1.57080) = 1.57080 - \frac{(1.57080)^3}{3!} + \frac{(1.57080)^5}{5!}$$

$$= 1.57080 - 0.64597 + 0.07969 = 1.00452$$

This result is fairly accurate, since the real answer is supposed to be 1.

A program to compute the sine of $x$ must do the following:

a. Read $x$

b. Keep accumulating a product of integers (PRODUCT) in such a way that
PRODUCT is first 1
then 1*2*3
then 1*2*3*4*5
PRODUCT serves as the denominator in the terms of the formula.

c. Accumulate the terms $\frac{x}{\text{PRODUCT}}, \frac{x^3}{\text{PRODUCT}}, \frac{x^5}{\text{PRODUCT}}, \ldots$ as each new PRODUCT is computed.

d. Capture $x^1$, $x^3$, $x^5$, ... through the use of $x^i$ where $i$ is initially set to 1 and incremented by 2's to obtain successive odd powers of $x$.

e. Generate the oscillating sequence of terms: $x$, $-x^3$, $x^5$, $-x^7$, ...
To do that, we note that $(x)^1, (-x)^3, (x)^5, (-x)^7$ gives rise to $x$, $-x^3$, $x^5$ and $-x^7$.
Hence we replace $x$ by $-x$ when generating successive terms of the sequence.

The logic of the program can be translated into FORTRAN code as follows:

| Code | Explanation |
|---|---|
| `READ*,X` | |
| `PROD = 1.` | Used to compute 1, then 1*2*3, then 1*2*3*4*5, etc. |
| `SUM = 0.` | Used to accumulate X, $\frac{-X^3}{3!}, \frac{X^5}{5!}, \ldots$ |
| `DO 5 I = 1 ,11, 2` | I is used for the exponent and for PROD. |
| `   SUM = SUM + (X**I)/PROD` | $\frac{X^1}{1}, X^1 - \frac{X^3}{1\cdot2\cdot3}, X^1 - \frac{X^3}{1\cdot2\cdot3} + \frac{X^5}{1\cdot2\cdot3\cdot4\cdot5}, \ldots$ |
| `   PROD = PROD*(I+1)*(I+2)` | Generates 1*2*3, then 1*2*3*4*5, . . . |
| `   X = -X` | Generate the oscillating sequence −, +, −, +, . . . |
| `5 CONTINUE` | |

## 5-4-6 Do It Now

1. When computing the sine of 1.57, how many terms of the formula would you need to accumulate before the difference between any two successive approximations is less than 0.0001 in absolute value? Would computing the sine of 3.14 require as many terms to get the same difference between two successive approximations (0.0001)?

2. Determine whether the following coding segments also compute the sine of $x$.

a.
```
   READ(5,3)X
   XSQ = X*X
   S = 0.
   IFACT = 1
   DO 10 I = 1,5
      S = S + X/IFACT
      X = X*XSQ
10 IFACT = -IFACT*(2*I)*(2*I+1)
   WRITE(6,6)S
 6 FORMAT(4X,F8.4)
 3 FORMAT(F3.0)
   STOP
```

b.
```
   DATA K,SUM,N/1,0.,1/
   READ(5,5)X
   X = -X
20 SUM = SUM + (-X)**N/K
   N = N + 2
   K = K*(N-1)*N
   IF(N.LE.11)GO TO 20
   WRITE(6,6)SUM
 5 FORMAT(F3.0)
 6 FORMAT(F8.4)
   STOP
```

## Answers

**1.** 6 terms for 1.57 and 8 terms for 3.14     **2.** Both codes compute the sine of x.

### 5-4-7  Reports and Control Breaks

The observation that computer-produced reports should be easy to read, easy to understand, and attractively designed appears so evident that one might feel this subject warrants no further comment. Yet the physical appearance of a report is of dramatic importance. Decisions are made daily by people of all walks of life that are based on computer-produced reports—detailed reports, summarized reports, etc.

A "good" report is self-explanatory, accurate (obviously), self-contained, and organized in a way that allows the reader to capture the essence of the report as well as the detail. These characteristics should be reflected in a design that is neat, clear, and pleasant to the eye. It is impossible to list all the ingredients that comprise an ideal report; a partial list, however, follows:

1. Major or documentary headings: Identification of the purpose of the report. Date of the report or transaction. Identification of the company, agency, or other producer or subject of the report.

2. Subheadings: Titles or labels should be provided for each column of information listed. (In some cases underlining might improve the appearance of the report).

3. Summary or intermediate results should be printed whenever necessary to provide subtotals for a group of entries that are similar in nature; for instance, sales subtotals for a given salesperson in a sales report, or item subtotals in an inventory.

4. Overall or grand totals reflecting sum of subtotals. A descriptive explanation should precede numerical results.

*Problem/Specification*:   Suppose we have a file in which each record contains a salesperson number and an amount of sales, and all records for a given salesperson occur in a group. Note that in the sample file shown below, the number of records for a given salesperson is variable; for example, salesperson 100 has made two sales, while salesperson 200 has made one sale. Let us write a program to produce a report that will summarize both the total sales for all salespeople and the total sales for each individual salesperson. A sample input and output are shown as follows:

**Input File**

*Salesperson     Sales*
*Number*

```
100  150.50
100  150.60
300  034.70
200  456.70
400  654.20
400  567.80
```

```
NUMBER   SALES    SUBTOTALS
 100    150.50
 100    150.60
                   301.10
 300     34.70
                    34.70
 200    456.70
                   456.70
 400    654.20
 400    567.80
                  1222.00

TOTAL SALES        2014.50
```

For this type of report we keep accumulating a salesperson's total sales (minor total) until a change occurs in the salesperson number. If a record pertains to the same salesperson as the preceding record, the sales amount is added to the current minor total. If the record read is for a new salesperson, a *control break* has been found. At this point the minor total for the previous salesperson is printed and the accumulator for the new minor total is set to 0 (see Figure 5–8). Since the salesperson number read belongs to a new salesperson, we store that number in OLD; then when we read the NEW salesperson number, we compare NEW with OLD, the most recent salesperson number. If we did not change OLD, we would always be comparing NEW with the first salesperson number.

To start the comparison between OLD and NEW, we read the first record separately from the remainder of the records and call the first salesperson number read, OLD.

Figure 5–8 shows the flowchart for this problem, and Figure 5–9 illustrates the FORTRAN code.

**FIGURE 5–8**    A CONTROL BREAK PROBLEM

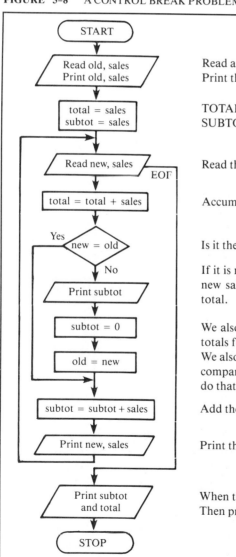

Read a salesperson number and call it OLD.
Print the first number and the first sales.

TOTAL accumulates the sum of all sales.
SUBTOT accumulates the totals for each salesperson.

Read the next salesperson number and sales.

Accumulate the sales just read into TOTAL.

Is it the same salesperson?

If it is not the same salesperson number, then we have encountered a new salesperson and we must print the previous salesperson's subtotal.

We also need to reset SUBTOT to 0 to start accumulating new subtotals for the salesperson whose number has just been read.
We also reset the OLD number to the NEW number, since we need to compare that number with the next number to be read. If we did not do that, OLD would never change!

Add the sales just read to the current subtotal.

Print the salesperson number and sales.

When the end of file is reached, print the last salesperson's subtotals. Then print the total sales.

**FIGURE 5-9    A CONTROL BREAK PROBLEM**

```
C CONTROL BREAK PROBLEM
C   OLDNO:  OLD SALESMAN NUMBER
C   NEWNO:  NEW SALESMAN NUMBER
C   TOTAL:  TOTAL SALES FOR ALL SALESPEOPLE
C   SUBTOT: TOTAL SALES FOR EACH SALESPERSON
C
      INTEGER OLDNO, NEWNO
      REAL TOTAL, SALES, SUBTOT
      WRITE(6,1)
      READ(5,2,END=88) OLDNO,SALES        Read first record.
      WRITE(6,3) OLDNO, SALES
      TOTAL  = SALES                      Set total sales to sales just read.
      SUBTOT = SALES                      Set subtotal to sales just read.
C
    7 READ(5,2,END=88) NEWNO, SALES
        TOTAL = TOTAL + SALES             Accumulate all sales.
        IF(NEWNO.NE.OLDNO) THEN           Check for CONTROL BREAK.
           WRITE(6,4) SUBTOT              If different salesperson, print subtotal of previous salesperson.
           SUBTOT = 0.                    Reset subtotal to 0 for new salesperson.
           OLDNO  = NEWNO                 Set old salesperson number to salesperson number just read.
        ENDIF
        SUBTOT = SUBTOT + SALES           Accumulate subtotal.
        WRITE(6,3) OLDNO, SALES
        GO TO 7                           Process next record.
C
   88 WRITE(6,4) SUBTOT                   At end of file print last subtotal and total sales.
      WRITE(6,5) TOTAL
      STOP
    1 FORMAT(1X,'NUMBER',3X,'SALES',2X,'SUBTOTALS')
    2 FORMAT(I3,1X,F5.2)
    3 FORMAT(2X,I3,3X,F7.2)
    4 FORMAT(18X,F7.2)
    5 FORMAT('0','TOTAL SALES',6X,F7.2)
      END
```

| NUMBER | SALES | SUBTOTALS |
|--------|-------|-----------|
| 100 | 150.50 | |
| 100 | 150.60 | |
| | | 301.10 |
| 200 | 34.70 | |
| | | 34.70 |
| 300 | 456.70 | |
| | | 456.70 |
| 400 | 654.20 | |
| 400 | 567.80 | |
| | | 1222.00 |
| TOTAL SALES | | 2014.50 |

**Input File**

*Salesman Number* ⌐ ↓ ⌐ *Sales*

```
100 150.50
100 150.60
200 034.70
300 456.70
400 654.20
400 567.80
```

### 5-4-8  Do It Now

Study flowcharts 1 and 2 carefully and determine whether they will solve the control break problem of section 5-4-7.

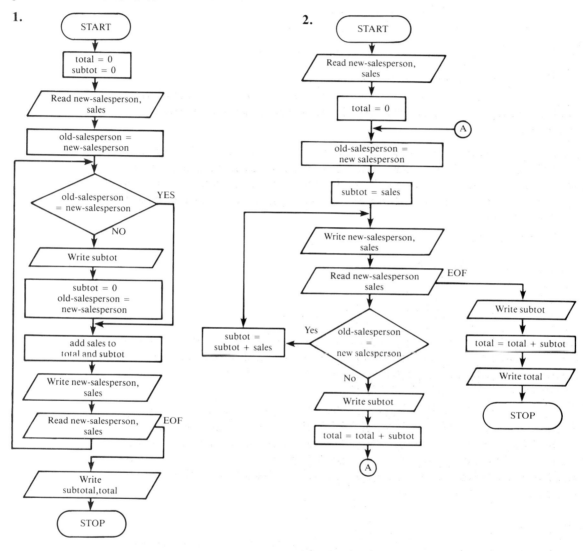

### Answers

1. Yes          2. Yes

## 5-5  Probing Deeper

### 5-5-1  Relationship between the List of Variables and List of Format Codes

If there are more data format codes in a FORMAT statement than there are variables in the corresponding list of variables in the READ/WRITE statement, the unused data format codes are ignored.

*Example 1*

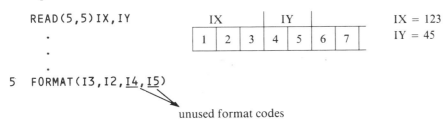

```
READ(5,5)IX,IY
    .
    .
    .
5   FORMAT(I3,I2,I4,I5)
```

unused format codes

Only two numbers are to be read, and they are described by the first two data format codes, I3 and I2. The remaining format codes (I4 and I5) are not processed, since only two numbers are to be read.

On the other hand, if there are more variables in the list of variables than there are data format codes, the sequence of format codes is reused (starting at the beginning of the FORMAT) until all variables have been satisfied. Each FORMAT statement describes one record; hence reusing the sequence of format codes causes a new input record to be selected or output record to be produced.

*Example 2*

| | Input File | Memory |
|---|---|---|
| READ(5,5)I,J,K | 39 | I = 39 |
| 5   FORMAT(I2) | 33 | J = 33 |
| | 44 | K = 44 |

This READ list specifies that three numbers are to be read. Since the FORMAT has only one data format code, only one number will be read per record. Hence three records will be read to satisfy the READ list. The three integers will be read from the first two positions of each of the three data records.

The list of variables in the READ statement tells the computer how many variables it *must* read; the number of data format codes (I, F, A) in the FORMAT specifies how many items are to be read per record. For example, if there are three data format codes in the FORMAT and the READ list specifies eight variables, three records will be read with only two items read on the third record (assuming the control code / is not used). Consider the following examples:

*Example 3*

| READ Statement | FORMAT Statement | Number of Records Read | Number of Items Read from Last Record |
|---|---|---|---|
| READ(5,6)A,B,C,D,E,F | FORMAT(7F5.1) | 1 | 6 |
| READ(5,6)A,B,C,D,E,F | FORMAT(6F5.1) | 1 | 6 |
| READ(5,6)A,B,C,D,E,F | FORMAT(5F5.1) | 2 | 1 |
| READ(5,6)A,B,C,D,E,F | FORMAT(4F5.1) | 2 | 2 |
| READ(5,6)A,B,C,D,E,F | FORMAT(3F5.1) | 2 | 3 |
| READ(5,6)A,B,C,D,E,F | FORMAT(2F5.1) | 3 | 2 |
| READ(5,6)A,B,C,D,E,F | FORMAT(F5.1) | 6 | 1 |

Thus FORMAT codes are reused when a WRITE list contains more variables than the number of FORMAT codes.

*Example 4*

```
    A = 3.2
    B = -6.0
    C = 4.9
    D = 0.
    WRITE(6,10)A,B,C,D
10  FORMAT(3X,2F6.1)
```

This WRITE list contains four variables; however FORMAT statement 10 places only two items on one line of output. The sequence of format codes is reused to complete the output of the four variables. Each reuse of the format codes results in a separate output line.

### 5-5-2  Do It Now

Identify the number of records (input records or output lines) processed by each of the following pairs of statements. If the statements are invalid, explain why.

1.  ```
    READ(5,6)A,K,C
    6 FORMAT (F5.1)
    ```

2.  ```
    WRITE(6,6)I,J,I,I,J
    6 FORMAT(2I3)
    ```

3.  ```
    WRITE(6,6)I,A,J,B,K,C
    6 FORMAT(1X,I4,F4.1)
    ```

4.  ```
    WRITE(6,6)I,J
    6 FORMAT(1X,I3,I4,'RESULT',I2)
    ```

5.  ```
    WRITE(6,6)I,A,J,B,K,C
    6 FORMAT(1X,I3,F4.1,I2)
    ```

### *Answers*

1.  Invalid: K should be read under an I format code.

2.  3

3.  3

4.  1 (Note that the literal "RESULT" may or may not be printed.)

5.  Invalid: variable B needs an F format not an I format (I3 is reused).

### 5-5-3  Random Numbers

Random numbers are introduced here because some of the exercises in this chapter and the following ones will require the use of random numbers to simulate certain real-life events. Such exercises can be interesting and fun, since in many instances the outcome cannot be predicted (unless you have a knowledge of statistics). Random numbers are often used in
    ```

programs that simulate probabilistic events. For example, consider the throwing of a die. The outcome of this event can be 1, 2, 3, 4, 5, or 6; each outcome is equally likely to occur. A program can use random numbers in the range 1 to 6 to simulate the outcome of a single throw of a die.

There is no standard method for generating random numbers from a FORTRAN program. However, most computer installations have random number routines stored in their libraries and these routines can be accessed by the user. Typically there is a built-in function (which might be called RANDOM, RANF, or RAND) that returns a random number in some range. For example, Y = RAND(1) will cause the computer to store in Y a random number between 0. and 1. Every time this statement is executed, a new random value will be stored in Y.

*Example:*

|  |  | *Output* |
|--|--|--|
| Y1 = RAND(1) | | .263884 |
| Y2 = RAND(1) | | .708429 |
| Y3 = RAND(1) | | .002562 |
| WRITE(6,3)Y1,Y2,Y3 | | |
| 3   FORMAT(1X,F10.6) | | |

You must determine the specifics of random number generation for your installations before attempting any programming exercises using random number generation. If you have no random number generator routine, you can append to your FORTRAN program the random number program shown in Figure 5–11.

The random number function can be very useful in the simulation of random events or in games where the computer is one of the players. Many times, though, the fractional numbers (between 0 and 1) generated by RAND are not too convenient in that particular form. Suppose, for example, that we wished to pick integer random numbers between 1 and 6 to simulate the throw of a die. How could we go from a fractional number in the interval (0,1) to an integer in the interval (1,6)? The following sequence of transformations illustrates how this can be accomplished.

|  | *Value of RAND* | *Value of RAND* | *Value of RAND* |
|--|--|--|--|
|  | Case 1 | Case 2 | Case 3 |
| T1 = RAND(1) | .263884 | .708429 | .002562 |
| T2 = RAND(1)*6. | 1.583304 | 4.250574 | .015372 |
| T3 = RAND(1)*6.+1. | 2.583304 | 5.250574 | 1.015372 |
| I  = RAND(1)*6.+1. | 2 | 5 | 1 |

Hence the formula I = RAND(1)*6. + 1. can be used to transform the set of random fractional numbers between 0 and 1 into the set of integers 1, 2, 3, 4, 5 and 6!

In general, to generate real or integer random numbers between LOW (low) and HIGH (high), the following formulas can be used:

| Real values between LOW and HIGH | X = RAND(1)*(HIGH – LOW) + L |
|--|--|
| Integer values between LOW and HIGH | I = RAND(1)*(HIGH – LOW + 1) + LOW |

## A Programming Example: Simulation of Moles and Mazes

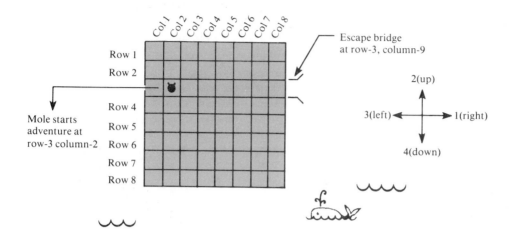

The above diagram represents an island surrounded by water. The island can be thought of as a square grid divided into 8 rows and 8 columns. One bridge leads off the island at row 3 and column 9. Let us place an imaginary mole at the black square (row = 3, column = 2). The mole moves one square at a time in one of 4 directions: right, up, left, or down. A random number between 1 and 4 tells the mole what direction to take for each move, i.e., we arbitrarily associate a move to the right with the number 1, move up with the number 2, and so forth. The mole keeps moving from one square to the next until it either hits the water and drowns or gets to the bridge and escapes.

Write a program to determine the mole's chances of escape. Express its chances in percentage form, for example, 1.8%.

In this problem, the sequence of moves ending in either an escape or a drowning is called a mole "adventure." Adventures can last anywhere from two moves (shortest distance to water) to hundreds of moves.

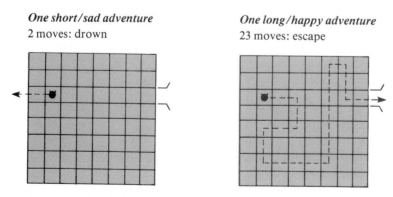

*One short/sad adventure*
2 moves: drown

*One long/happy adventure*
23 moves: escape

Obviously, 10 or even 50 such adventures may not be enough to determine the mole's chances of escape. The mole may never escape in its first 50 adventures. For the results to be meaningful, let us give the mole the opportunity to have 500 distinct adventures, i.e., let us restart the mole at the starting block 500 times and count the number of times it escapes or drowns.

The key questions in this problem are: How do we move the mole around? and how do we know when the mole drowns or escapes?

Initially we position the mole at row 3 and column 2 by writing R = 3 and C = 2. (We will use the variables R and C to keep track of the row and column positions of the mole.) We then generate a random number K between 1 and 4 (K = RAND(1)*4 + 1., for example) to tell us the direction of the next move (1 = right, 2 = up, 3 = left, 4 = down).

If K has value 2, we move the mole up one square, i.e., we go from row 3 to row 2. Hence we need to subtract 1 from the current value of R (in FORTRAN code, R = R − 1).

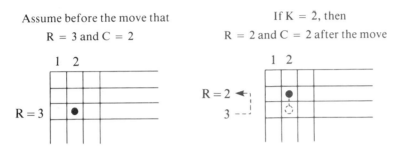

Note that when moving in an upward direction, the column C does *not* change.

In general, if the mole is at position (R,C) and the random number is 2 (move up), we set R = R − 1.

If K has value 3, and we are initially at R = 3 and C = 2, we need to move the mole from column 2 to column 1 (C = C − 1).

If K has value 4, we need to add 1 to R (R = R + 1).

If K has value 1, we need to add 1 to C (C = C + 1).

After we move the mole to its new position, we must check to see where the mole has landed, i.e., has the mole hit the water (R = 0, R = 9, C = 0, C = 9), or has it escaped (R = 3, C = 9)? It is fairly evident that when the mole is moving upward, it can drown only at row 0! (When moving up, the mole cannot drown to the left or to the right or backwards!) Hence, if the row is not 0, the mole is still on the island and we need to pick another random number for the next move. If, on the other hand, the mole moves left (K = 3), we need to check whether column C is 0; obviously we do not need to check for R = 0, C = 9, or R = 9, when moving in a leftward direction.

When moving down, we should check if R = 9 (drown) and when moving to the right we should check if C = 9. If C = 9, the mole can escape if the row R is 3. Hence, when moving right, we should check for C = 9 *and* R = 3. If both these conditions are satisfied, we increment the escape counter by 1. If C = 9 but R ≠ 3, the mole has drowned. If C does not equal 9, then the mole is still on the island, and we go to the random number generator for the next move.

An adventure ends when the mole either drowns or escapes. Before we start a new adventure by repositioning the mole at its starting block (R = 3 and C = 2), we must determine whether we have gone through 500 adventures. If we have completed 500 adventures, we compute the percentage of escapes by computing E * 100/500 or E/5 (E is the number of escapes). Note that the number of escapes plus the number of accidents should equal 500. A flowchart that parallels the above discussion is shown in Figure 5–10. The program is shown in Figure 5–11. Note how the code has been made somewhat easier to read and understand by means of the logical operators .AND. and .OR. This code may not be as efficient as the code corresponding to the flowchart; however, it is much more readable.

**FIGURE 5-10** OF MOLES AND MAZES

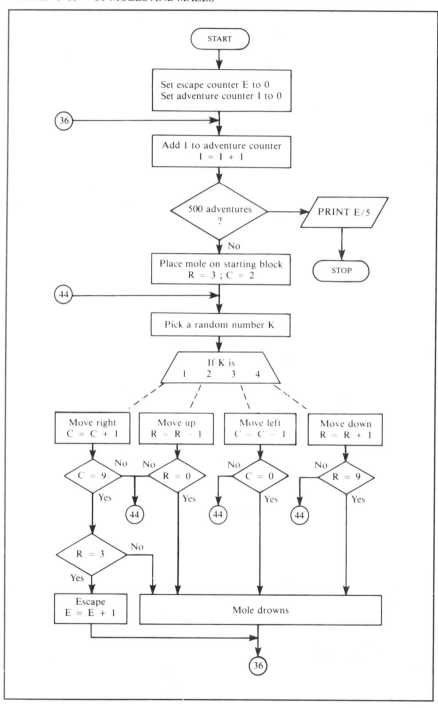

**FIGURE 5-11** OF MOLES AND MAZES

```
C      MOLE PROJECT
C
C      DATA DICTIONARY
C      R: KEEPS TRACK OF ROW POSITION
C      C: KEEPS TRACK OF COLUMN POSITION
C      E: COUNTS THE NUMBER OF ESCAPES
C      P: PERCENTAGE OF ESCAPES (E/5)
C      I: COUNTS NUMBER OF ADVENTURES
C      K: RANDOM DIRECTION FOR MOLE
C         1=RIGHT; 2=UP; 3=LEFT; 4=DOWN
       INTEGER R,C,I,K
       REAL P,E
       E = 0
C      START 500 ADVENTURES
       DO 500 I = 1, 500
C          POSITION MOLE AT ROW 3 AND COLUMN 2
C          AFTER EACH ACCIDENT OR ESCAPE
           R = 3
           C = 2
C          MOVE MOLE RANDOMLY
  205      K = RAND(1) * 4. + 1.
           IF (K .EQ. 1) C = C + 1          Mole moves right.
           IF (K .EQ. 2) R = R - 1          Mole moves up.
           IF (K .EQ. 3) C = C - 1          Mole moves left.
           IF (K .EQ. 4) R = R + 1          Mole moves down.
C          IF THE NEXT CONDITION IS TRUE, THE MOLE
           HAS DROWNED UP, DOWN, OR TO THE LEFT
           IF (R.EQ.0 .OR. C.EQ.0 .OR. R.EQ.9) GO TO 500
           IF (C.EQ.9 .AND. R.EQ.3) GO TO 450  Mole has escaped.
           IF (C.NE.9) GO TO 205               Move mole randomly.
           GO TO 500                           Mole has drowned if column = 9.
  450      E = E + 1
  500  CONTINUE
C      COMPUTE PERCENTAGE OF ESCAPES
  500  P = E / 5.
       PRINT*, 'PERCENTAGE ESCAPES IS', P
       STOP
       END
```

```
C      TYPE THE FOLLOWING CODE IF YOU NEED A RANDOM NUMBER GENERATOR
       FUNCTION RAND(K)
       INTEGER IM, IB, IA
       DATA IM,IB,IA/ 25211,32767,19727/          } optional
       IA = MOD(IM*IA, IB)
       RAND = FLOAT(IA) / FLOAT(IB)
       RETURN
       END
```

```
PERCENTAGE ESCAPES IS    1.2
```

## 5-6   **You Might Want to Know**

**1.** To what depth or level can loops be nested?

*Answer:* It depends on the compiler. It is safe to assume up to 16 nested loops.

**2.** Given the initial value (INIT), the increment (INC) and the test value (ITEST) for a DO statement, how many times will the following loop be executed?

```
DO 10 I = INIT,ITEST,INC
```

*Answer:* The number of times the loop is executed is given by the formula:

$$NT = \frac{ITEST - INIT}{INC} + 1$$

where only the integer result of the division is kept.

*Example 1*

```
DO 10 K = 3,10,2
```
The number of times through the loop is:

$$NT = \frac{10 - 3}{2} + 1 = \frac{7}{2} + 1 = 3 + 1 = 4$$

The values assumed by K will be 3, 5, 7, and 9.

The DO loop is bypassed whenever $NT \leq 0$, i.e., control is passed to the statement following the foot of the loop; in older compilers the loop is carried out once.

*Example 2*

```
6  Y = 1.
   DO 5 I = 10,1
      ⋮
5  CONTINUE
7  X = 1.
```
Since INIT > ITEST, the loop is bypassed and control is passed from statement 6 to statement 7.

In this case $NT = \dfrac{1 - 10 + 1}{1} = -8 \leq 0$.

```
   DO 5 I = 1,10,-1
      ⋮
      ⋮
5  CONTINUE
```
The loop will be bypassed since $NT = \dfrac{10 - 1}{-1} + 1 = -8 \leq 0$.

**3.** Can the CONTINUE statement appear anywhere other than at the foot of a DO loop?

*Answer:* Yes, if it is not used at the foot of a DO loop, the CONTINUE statement passes control to the next statement in the program.

*Example 3*

```
   IF (X.EQ.3.)GOTO6
      ⋮
   IF (Y.LT.4.2)GOTO6
      ⋮
      ⋮
6  CONTINUE
17 DO 5 I = 1, 7
```
GO TO 6 is identical to GO TO 17.

The CONTINUE statement provides an alternative reference to statement 17.

**4.** Given the DO loop DO  5  I = BEG,TEST,STEP how does FORTRAN control the number of times the loop is carried out?

*Answer:* It uses an iteration count, as follows:

   a.  The iteration count is initially set to the larger of the two values:

$$0 \text{ or } \frac{TEST - BEG}{STEP} + 1 \quad \text{where the fractional digits are discarded.}$$

       The iteration count is thus 0 if BEG > TEST  and  STEP > 0
                                or if BEG < TEST  and  STEP < 0 .

   b.  The iteration count is tested. If it exceeds 0, the body of the loop is carried out otherwise the loop is bypassed (exit).

   c.  Upon encountering the foot of the loop, the value of the index is incremented by the initial value of STEP.

   d.  The iteration count is decremented by 1.

   e.  Control is passed to step (b).

**5.** What flowchart symbols are used to represent DO loops?

*Answer:* The hexagon or rectangle can be used:

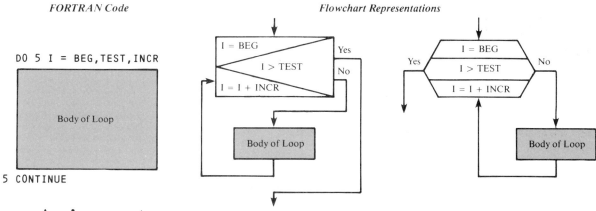

## 5-7   **Assignments**

### 5-7-1   **Test Yourself**

**1.** Using DO loops, write the code to print the following sequences of numbers:

   a.  1,3,5,7, ..., 99
   b.  $-1, 1, -1, 1, \ldots$   (25 terms)
   c.  1./1.,  1./1./2.,  1./1./2./3.,  ... 1./2./3./4./ ... /X   (X is read)
   d.  N, N − 2, N − 4, ..., 0   where N is an even positive number
   e.  1./9., 1./99., 1./999., ... 1./9999999.
   f.  .25, .50, .75, ..., 2.00

**2.** Trace through the following flowchart and record all values taken on by the variables K, A, and B in the table below. The first set of values is already recorded in the table.

The values to be read are shown in the input file. Also show the output that will be printed.

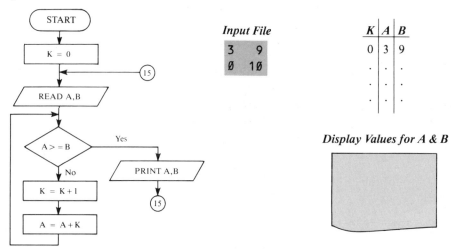

*Input File*

| 3 | 9 |
|---|----|
| 0 | 10 |

| K | A | B |
|---|---|---|
| 0 | 3 | 9 |
| . | . | . |
| . | . | . |
| . | . | . |

*Display Values for A & B*

3. Write the code to accumulate the following values (use DO loops):

   a. $1^2 + 2^2 + 3^2 + ... + 10^2$
   b. $2 + 4 + 8 + 16 + ... + 1024$
   c. $1 - 2 + 3 - 4 + ... - 1000$
   d. $1 + (1*2) + (1*2*3) + (1*2*3*4) + ... + (1*2*3* ... *50)$
   e. $1. + 1./3. + 1./5. + ... + 1./77.$

4. Which of the following are valid DO loops? If a loop is invalid, explain why.

   a.
   ```
       DO 10 I = 1,5
         .
         .
         .
   10 CONTINUE
   ```
   b.
   ```
       DO 20 IJ = 2,6.5
         .
         .
         .
   20 CONTINUE
   ```

   c.
   ```
       DO 30 K = 1,10
          DO 40 K = 1,40
            .
            .
            .
   40     CONTINUE
   30 CONTINUE
   ```
   d.
   ```
       DO 15 I = I,6
         .
         .
         .
   15 CONTINUE
   ```

   e.
   ```
       DO 50 I - 1 = 2,6
         .
         .
         .
   50 CONTINUE
   ```
   f.
   ```
       DO 60 I = 1,5
          DO 70 J = 1,10,-1
            .
            .
            .
   70     CONTINUE
   60 CONTINUE
   ```

   g.
   ```
       DO 60 I = 1,5
          DO 70 J = 1,10
            .
            .
            .
   60     CONTINUE
            .
            .
            .
   70 X = 1.
   ```
   h.
   ```
       DO 80 A = I,N
         .
         .
         .
   80 CONTINUE
   ```

```
i.     DO 90 L = 1,5                    j.     DO 21 M = 10,6,1
       DO 91 K = 2,8                           .
       S = S + G                               .
   90 CONTINUE                               CONTINUE
                                         21 CONTINUE
```

```
k.     DO 5 K = 1,5                     l.     DO 20 L = 8,1
       .                                        DO 30 K = 1,3
       .                                        L = L + 1
       .                                30     CONTINUE
    5 IF(L - 80)3,3,2                   20 CONTINUE
```

```
m.     DO 5 I = 1,3                     n.     DO 6 I = 1,10
       .                                        J = I*I + 1
       .                                  6 CONTINUE
       .
       IF(Q.EQ.6.) GO TO 5
       DO 5 K = 1,10
       SUM = SUM + J
    5 CONTINUE
```

```
o.     DO 8 K = 1,6                     p.     DO 10 I = 1,17
       READ(5,5)K1,K                    15     X = X + SUM
       SUM1 = SUM1 + K1                         IF(X.GT.10.) GO TO 17
    8     SUM2 = SUM2 + K               10 CONTINUE
                                         17 IF(SUM.NE.T) GO TO 15
```

```
q.     DO 8 K = 1,110,5                 r.     DO 9 J = 40,60
       .                                        DO 9 K = 1,3
       .                                        .
    8 SUM = SUM + X                             .
       DO 9 K = 1,15                      9 IF(M.GT.K+J) GO TO 8
       .                                        .
       .                                        .
    9 CONTINUE                            8
```

```
s.     DO 85 I = 1,4                    t.     DO 9 J = 5,8
       .                                        X = 1.
       .                                        DO 6 K = 1,5
       CONTINUE                                 IF(J.GT.5) GO TO 9
   85 DO 90 J = 3,6,1                           PRINT*,J
       .                                  6 CONTINUE
       .                                        PRINT*,K
   90 X = 10.3                            9 CONTINUE
```

**5.** What output will be produced by each of the following coding segments?

```
a.     DO 5 I = 1,10,2                  b.     DO 7 J = 6,18,3
    5 WRITE(6,1)I                        2 FORMAT(2X,I3)
    1 FORMAT(2X,I3)                      7 WRITE(6,2)J
```

```
c.     DO 8 K = 4,1                     d.     DO 6 I = 1,3
    8 WRITE(6,3)K                               K = 10**I
    3 FORMAT(2X,I3)                      6 WRITE(6,5)K
                                         5 FORMAT(I4/'+',I5/'+',I6)
```

**6.** Assuming all loops go through their complete cycle, how many times will statement 3 be processed?

a.
```
      DO 20 I = 1,3
      DO 20 J = 1,4
      DO 20 K = 1,10
   3    X = 1.
  20 CONTINUE
```

b.
```
      DO 33 I = 2,20
        DO 33 J = 3,17,5
          :
          :
   3    X = 1.
  33 CONTINUE
```

c.
```
      DO 10 I0 = 2,8,2
      DO 10 IM = I0,2,1
      DO 10 II = 1,4,2
   3    X = 1
  10 CONTINUE
```

d.
```
      DO 10 K = 1,6,2
      DO 5 I = 1,K
   3 SUM = SUM + I
   5 CONTINUE
  10 CONTINUE
```

**7.** Determine whether the following code will result in a compilation execution-time or logical error.

a.
```
  15 DO 10 I = 1,5
        WRITE(6,1)I
        IF(I.GT.5)GO TO 15
  10 CONTINUE
```

b.
```
      DO 6 I = 1, 10
        SUM = SUM + I
   6 CONTINUE
      AVG = SUM / I
```

**8.** Will the following codes compute the average of ten grades?

a.
```
      SUM = 0.
      DO 10 I = 1,10
        READ(5,1)GRADE
  10 SUM = SUM + GRADE
      AVERAG = SUM/I
   1 FORMAT(F5.1)
```

b.
```
      SUM = 0.
      DO 15 I = 1,10
        READ(5,1)GRADE
        SUM = SUM + GRADE
  15 AVE = SUM/I
      WRITE(6,6)AVE
```

**9.** What will the final value of J be?
```
      J = 0
      DO 4 I = 1,10
   4 J = J + .1
```

**10.** How many records will be processed by the following READ instructions using the various accompanying FORMATs?

a.
```
      READ(5,5)A,B,C
                with FORMATS
```
$\begin{cases} 5 \text{ FORMAT(F5.1,F5.1,F5.1)} \\ 5 \text{ FORMAT(F5.1,F5.1)} \\ 5 \text{ FORMAT(4F5.1)} \end{cases}$

b.
```
      READ(5,6)I,J,K,L,M,N
                with FORMATS
```
$\begin{cases} 6 \text{ FORMAT(I1,I2,I2)} \\ 6 \text{ FORMAT(I1,I2,I3,I4)} \end{cases}$

c.
```
      READ(5,7)A,I,D
                with FORMATS
```
$\begin{cases} 7 \text{ FORMAT(F5.1,I3,F4.1)} \\ 7 \text{ FORMAT(F5.1/I2)} \\ 7 \text{ FORMAT(F5.1)} \end{cases}$

11. Which of the following statements are true? If false, explain why.

   a. DO 10 IX2 = N, N + 1 is a valid statement.
   b. The index of a DO loop can be a real variable.
   c. If the initial value of the index of a DO loop is not specified, it is assumed to be 1.
   d. The CONTINUE statement can only be used as the last statement in the range of a DO loop.
   e. The body of a loop will always be processed at least once.
   f. A nonexecutable statement in the body of a DO loop can be processed more than once at execution time.
   g. When a DO loop has completed its full cycle, the value of its index becomes undefined.
   h. A DO loop should always be entered at the DO statement.
   i. Accumulating and counting are synonymous terms.
   j. A comment statement in the range of a DO loop will be listed at least once and probably more than once, depending on the number of times the body of the loop is executed.

12. Identify at least six errors in the following program; identify compilation errors.

```
      INTEGER A,B,STAT,STAT10,STAT100,X
      DATA X,Y,A,I/4*0./
      DATA PI,E/3.14159,2.71828/
      READ(5,10) K,L,N
   10 FORMAT(3I5.0)
      IF (K.EQ.L) THEN L = L + 1
      GO TO (10,20,30,30) L
   20 STOP
   30 WRITE(6,25) L
   25 FORMAT(I6)
      DO 100 I = 1,10
      DO 300 J = 1,3
   77 M = I*J
      WRITE(6,200)M
  100 CONTINUE
  300 CONTINUE
      IF(I*J*L)GO TO 77
      STOP
      END
```

13. To determine how "good" your random number generator is, generate 1000 random numbers between 1 and 4 and count their occurrence. Use a DO loop.

14. Draw a flowchart for a program to read an amount of money (in cents) less than or equal to a dollar and express it in the least number of quarters, dimes, nickels and pennies (use repeated subtractions).
   For example: 93 cents = 3Q + 1D + 1N + 3P
   [*Hint*: Keep subtracting 25 from the amount then 10 …]

15. Write a program for the following problem: The principal $P$ left in a savings account for $T$ years at interest rate $R$, compounded yearly, yields a total amount $A$ given by the

formula $A = P(1 + R)^T$. Compute and write the total amount, $A$, given a principal of $1,000 at different interest rates varying from 5 to 8% in steps of 1% for a time period of one to three years. The output should be similar to the following:

```
AMOUNT    YEARS    INTEREST
1050.00     1        .05
1060.00     1        .06
1070.00     1        .07
1080.00     1        .08

1102.50     2        .05
1123.60     2        .06
1144.90     2        .07
1166.40     2        .08

1157.62     3        .05
1191.01     3        .06
1225.04     3        .07
1259.71     3        .08
```

## 5-7-2 Programming Problems: Business/General

1. Write a program to compute $3 + 5 + 7 + 9 + \ldots + 225 + 227$.

2. Write a program to compute $1! - 2! + 3! - 4! + 5! \ldots - 20!$

3. A data file contains positive and negative numbers varying from $-100$ to $100$. Write a program to compute the sum of the positive numbers and the sum of negative numbers. Print both sums.

4. Grades are recorded on records with two grades per record. The first negative number indicates the end of the data file. Write a program to determine the largest and smallest grades and the average of the grades; use a DO loop.

5. Mrs. X has just invested $9,000 at 13.5% yearly interest rate (compounded once a year). She has decided to withdraw the accumulated interest as soon as that interest exceeds $11,000.00. Write a program to determine how many years Mrs. X will have to wait before she can withdraw at least $11,000 of accumulated interest. Could you be more specific and identify the number of years and months?

6. Mr. Sly convinced his employers to pay him for 30 days as follows: The first day he gets paid 1 cent, the second day 2 cents, the third day 4 cents, the fourth day 8 cents, and so forth. Each day's pay is twice the previous day's pay. Print a table showing Mr. Sly's earnings during the last 10 days. (Make sure the earnings are displayed in dollar figures.)

7. The post office charges 20 cents for the first ounce or part thereof for a first class letter and 17 cents for each additional ounce or part thereof. Write a program to accept letter weights in ounces and print the required postage.

8. You own a bookstore that sells both paperback and hardback books. For every book you sell, you have a record with two numbers: the price of the book and either a 0 or a 1

(0 if the book is a paperback, 1 if the book is hardback). Write a program to obtain the following information:

    a. total sales
    b. total number of books sold
    c. average price per book
    d. minimum price of a hardback book
    e. average price of a paperback book

9. A data file consists of records, each containing the following information concerning items produced at the XYZ manufacturing plant: a department number, an item number, a quantity, and a cost per item. Assume the file has been sorted into order by ascending department number. Write a program to produce a summary report as follows:

| DEPARTMENT | ITEM | QUANTITY | COST/ITEM | VALUE | TOTALS |
|---|---|---|---|---|---|
| 15 | 1389 | 4 | 3.20 | 12.80 | |
| 15 | 3821 | 2 | 7.00 | 14.00 | |
| | | | | | 26.80 |
| 16 | 0122 | 8 | 2.50 | 20.00 | |
| | | | | | 20.00 |
| 19 | 1244 | 100 | .03 | 3.00 | |
| 19 | 1245 | 20 | 4.00 | 80.00 | |
| 19 | 2469 | 4 | 16.00 | 64.00 | |
| | | | | | 147.00 |
| | | | | GRAND TOTAL | 193.80 |

Could you alter the program to write each subtotal on the same line as the last entry for each department? Make your own data file.

10. Write a program to simulate a bank's handling of a savings account. Each record input into the program will contain a transaction amount, a transaction date (day of the month), and a transaction code with the records in ascending date order for a particular month. The meaning of the codes are as follows:

| Code | Meaning |
|---|---|
| 1 | Balance forward |
| 2 | Deposit |
| 3 | Withdrawal |
| 4 | End of transactions (the transaction amount will be ignored while the transaction date will be used for final balance) |

Print a report showing all transactions and the account balance after each transaction. The final balance should be clearly labeled. Your report should be similar to the following:

| DAY | AMOUNT | TRANSACTION TYPE | BALANCE |
|---|---|---|---|
| 1 | 300.00 | BALANCE FORWARD | 300.00 |
| 4 | 49.00 | DEPOSIT | 349.00 |
| 6 | 50.00 | WITHDRAWAL | 299.00 |
| 19 | 99.00 | WITHDRAWAL | 200.00 |
| 31 | | FINAL BALANCE | 200.00 |

**11.** Modify the program written for problem 10 to compute and credit interest to the account. Assume that interest is based on the average daily balance for the number of days from the beginning of the statement (the date on the balance forward transaction) up to and including the end of the statement (the date of the end of transactions). The interest should be credited to the account on the date of the end of transactions. The average daily balance is computed by adding the daily balances and dividing by the number of days. In the example above, the average daily balance would be

$$\frac{3 \times 300 + 2 \times 349 + 13 \times 299 + 12 \times 200 + 200}{31} = 260.81$$

since the account had a balance of $300 for 3 days, $349 for 2 days, $299 for 13 days, $200 for 12 days, and a balance of $200 on the date ending the period.

**12.** Mrs. Spander is spending her money faster than she earns it. She has now decided to keep track of all her expenses. For every purchase or expense, she enters on her home computer the expense description, the amount, and an expense category code (1 = household, 2 = medical, 3 = recreation, 4 = utilities). Then every Sunday night she runs her budget program to obtain an analysis like the following one:

```
                          BUDGET ANALYSIS

                  HOUSEHOLD    MEDICAL    RECREATION    UTILITY
                  EXPENSES     EXPENSES    EXPENSES      BILLS

   PLANTS           12.33
   MOVIES                                    6.50
   MORTGAGE        389.75
   DENTIST                      154.25
   GAS                                                   99.66
   VACATION                                 1156.56

   SUBTOTALS       402.08       154.25     1163.06       99.66

      TOTAL EXPENSES        $1819.05
```

Write a program to read the expenses and provide a weekly summary for Mrs. Spander.

**13.** The Meals on Wheels Company operates a fleet of vans that deliver cold foods at various local plants and construction sites. The management is thinking of purchasing a specially built $18,000 van equipped to deliver hot foods. This new addition to the fleet is expected to generate after-tax earnings $E_1$, $E_2$, ..., $E_6$ (as displayed in the following table) over the next six years, at which time the van's resale value will be zero. Projected repair and maintenance costs $C_0$, $C_1$, $C_2$, ..., $C_6$ over the six years are also shown in the table.

| *Projected Earnings* | | *Projected Costs* | |
|---|---|---|---|
| | | $C_0$ | $18,000 (purchase cost of the van) |
| $E_1$ | $2,500 | $C_1$ | 610 |
| $E_2$ | 2,500 | $C_2$ | 745 |
| $E_3$ | 3,000 | $C_3$ | 820 |
| $E_4$ | 4,500 | $C_4$ | 900 |
| $E_5$ | 6,000 | $C_5$ | 950 |
| $E_6$ | 6,000 | $C_6$ | 1,000 |

a.  Write a program to determine whether or not the company should acquire the van. The decision depends on the benefit/cost ratio *(BCR)* (grossly speaking, earnings/expenditures) given by the formula:

$$BCR = \frac{E_1(1 + i)^6 + E_2(1 + i)^5 + \ldots + E_6(1 + i)^1}{C_0 + C_1(1 + i)^6 + C_2(1 + i)^5 + \ldots + C_6(1 + i)^1}$$

where $i$ is the rate of investment of earnings by the company (11% in this problem). If the $BCR < 1$, then the company should not acquire the van. Use the accumulation process to compute the $BCR$. The first data record contains $E_1$ and $C_1$, the second data record contains $E_2$ and $C_2$, and so forth.

b.  When shown the projected maintenance costs for the next six years, the repair and maintenance shop foreman argues that these cost figures are unrealistic and proposes instead the following costs for the first through sixth years: 1,000, 1,500, 2,000, 2,000, 2,100, 2,400. Using these figures, determine whether the company should purchase the van.

c.  Having found out that the $BCR$ is less than 1 with the projected maintenance costs shown in part b, the management decides to recompute the $BCR$ with the same figures as in part b but setting the resale value of the van at $1,000.00 (the sale of the van represents earnings). Use your program to recompute the $BCR$.

14.  A large clothing store keeps track of its inventory by department (1 = men's wear, 2 = ladies' wear, 3 = girls' wear, and 4 = boys' wear). The store's inventory file consists of four packets of data, each packet representing a particular department. A typical input file is shown below, where each record consists of: a department number, an item description, an item quantity, a cost figure, and a market figure (cost to the customer).

| Dept. No. | Item | Quantity | Cost to Store | Cost to Customer |
|---|---|---|---|---|
| 1, | SUITS, | 300, | 100, | 92 |
| 1, | COATS, | 200, | 60, | 65 |
| 1, | SHIRTS | 1000, | 12, | 13 |
| 2, | DRESSES, | 400, | 60, | 65 |
| 2, | COATS, | 185, | 184, | 200 |
| 2, | SHOES, | 600, | 40, | 30 |
| 3, | JEANS, | 200, | 40, | 35 |
| 3, | SHOES, | 200, | 30, | 34 |
| 4, | JEANS, | 300, | 4?, | 43 |

a. Write a program to process the input file to compute the store's inventory at lower cost (the lesser of cost or market value for each whole department). The output should be similar to the following:

```
                    PAN AMERICAN APPAREL COMPANY
                        INVENTORY EVALUATION
                            05/06/84


                        UNIT COST              EXTENDED

            QUANTITY   COST   MARKET      COST          MARKET    LOWER COST
MENS DEPT
  SUITS       300      100     92        30000         27600
  COATS       200       60     65        12000         13000
  SHIRTS     1000       12     13        12000         13000
  TOTAL                                $ 54000       $ 53600     $ 53600
LADIES DEPT
  DRESSES     400       60     65        24000         26000
  COATS       185      184    200        34040         37000
  SHOES       600       40     30        24000         18000
  TOTAL                                $ 82040       $ 81000     $ 81000
GIRLS DEPT
  JEANS       200       40     35         8000          7000
  SHOES       200       30     34         6000          6800
  TOTAL                                $ 14000       $ 13800     $ 13800
BOYS DEPT
  JEANS       300       42     43        12600         12900
  TOTAL                                $ 12600       $ 12900     $ 12600

        INVENTORY AT LOWER COST                                $161000
```

Note the various subtotals for each of the four departments, as well as the grand total.

b. Compute the lower cost inventory line by line instead of for the whole department. For example, for the men's department the cost inventory is: 27,600 + 12,000 + 12,000 = 51,600

**15.** A large supermarket is organized into departments such as meats, perishables, and dairy products. The supermarket's management would like to follow the monthly sales trends in the various departments. They have instructed their data processing staff to produce monthly reports that will identify departments showing unusually sluggish or unusually active sales: If the current month's sales are more than 15% greater than the average of the previously recorded monthly sales for that department, an appropriate message such as HIGH should be printed. If the current month's sales are less than 90% of the average of the previously recorded monthly sales, then a different message such as LOW should be printed.

All departments have sales records for at least the last three months, and some have records going back beyond three months. The input file consists of records that are arranged in sequence by department number. Within each department the monthly sales are arranged in ascending date order. Write a program to produce a report similar to the following one (the averages do not reflect the most recent month):

**Output**

```
NO.   DATE   SALES       AVERAGES    ALERT
11    02/01  15,000.40
      03/01  14,000.55
      04/01  14,500.20
      05/01  13,800.48   14,500.38

22    01/01  23,400.64
      02/01  30,500.88
      03/01  32,600.46
      04/01  29,400.00
      05/01  25,000.00   28,975.56   LOW

33    02/01  40,000.80
      03/01  45,876.20
      04/01  44,784.88
      05/01  51,080.40   43,553.96   HIGH
```

**Input**

| Dept. No. | Date | Amount | |
|---|---|---|---|
| 11 | 0201 | 1500040 | Last 3 months' sales records for dept. 11. |
| 11 | 0301 | 1400055 | |
| 11 | 0401 | 1450020 | |
| 11 | 0501 | 1380048 | Current monthly sales for dept. 11. |
| 22 | 0101 | 2340064 | |
| 22 | 0201 | 3050088 | |
| 22 | 0301 | 3260046 | |
| 22 | 0401 | 2940000 | |
| 22 | 0501 | 2500000 | |
| 33 | 0201 | 4000080 | |
| 33 | 0301 | 4587620 | |
| 33 | 0401 | 4478488 | |
| 33 | 0501 | 5108040 | Current monthly sales for dept. 33 |

**16.** All academic departments at Franzia College are charged for the use of the college's computer system. The amount charged is based on the utilization of 6 specific resources:

| Resources | Input Code | Cost in Cents |
|---|---|---|
| Cards read | 10 | .0012/card |
| Cards punched | 11 | .0012/card |
| Lines printed | 20 | .0003/line |
| CPU time (seconds) | 30 | .0600/second |
| Memory (words) | 40 | .0012/word |
| I/O operations | 50 | .0013/operation |

Utilization of any of the above resources is recorded on data records like those shown in the sample input file below:

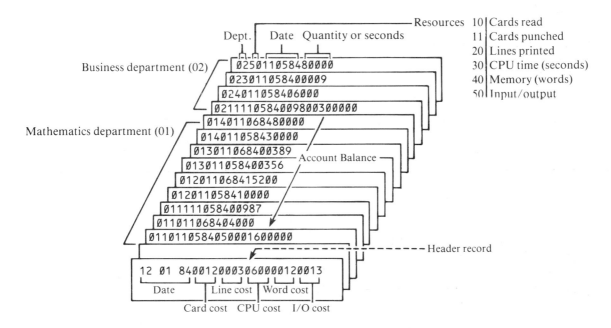

***Item Positions***

| 1–2 | | 3–4 | 5–10 | 11–15 |
|---|---|---|---|---|
| Department code | { 01 Math<br>02 Business<br>03 Chemistry | Resources code (described above) | Date of computer transaction | Amount used (no. of cards, seconds, etc.) |

The first record of the input file is a header record that identifies the date of the report and the five costs associated with the six resources. All remaining transaction records are grouped by department; within each department, transaction records are grouped by resources.

In addition to the department code, resource code, date of computer transaction, and amount of resource used, the very first transaction record for each department also contains an account balance for the department, i.e., how much money is left to spend (position 16–22).

Write a program to produce a report similar to the output shown below. Note that the numeric codes for the various departments have been converted to words (MATHEMATICS, BUSINESS, and so forth). Codes for resources have also been expressed in words. New account balances should be computed for each department.

```
            COMPUTER RESOURCES BILLING STATEMENT
12 01 84 DEPT: MATHEMATICS
PREVIOUS BALANCE                                      $16000.00
     110584 CARDS READ         05000 a .0012   6.00
     110684 CARDS READ         04000 a .0012   4.80
                                                     10.80
     110584 CARDS PUNCHED      00987 a .0012   1.18
                                                      1.18
     110584 LINES PRINTED      10000 a .0003   3.00
     110684 LINES PRINTED      15200 a .0003   4.56
                                                      7.56
     110584 CPU TIME (SECS)    00356 a .0600  21.36
     110684 CPU TIME (SECS)    00389 a .0600  23.34
                                                     44.70
     110584 MEMORY (WORDS)     30000 a .0012  36.00
     110684 MEMORY (WORDS)     80000 a .0012  96.00
                                                    132.00
     TOTAL COMPUTER CHARGE                          196.24
NEW ACCOUNT BALANCE                                  $15803.76
12 01 84 DEPT: BUSINESS
PREVIOUS BALANCE                                      $3000.00
     110584 CARDS PUNCHED      00980 a .0012   1.17
                                                      1.17
     110584 MEMORY (WORDS)     00600 a .0012   7.20
                                                      7.20
     110584 CPU TIME (SECS)    00009 a .0600    .54
                                                       .54
     110584 INPUT/OUTPUT (SECS) 80000 a .0013 104.00
                                                    104.00
     TOTAL COMPUTER CHARGE                          112.91
NEW ACCOUNT BALANCE                                  $2887.09
```

## 5-7-3  Programming Problems: Scientific/Mathematical

1. Write programs to accumulate and print the following:

   a. $1 + 3 + 5 + 7 \ldots + 225$   Is accumulation necessary in this problem?
   b. $1^1 + 2^2 + 3^3 + 4^4 + \ldots N^N$   where N is read from a data record.
   c. $2*4*6*8* \ldots *N$   where N is read from a data record.
   d. the values for *x, y,* and *z*, where $z = x^2 + y^2$, *y* takes on values 1, 2, and 3, and *x* takes on values 2, 4, 6, and 8 (use all possible combinations of *x* and *y*).

2. Write a program to read a value for N and compute the sum of the squares of the first N even integers. For example, if N = 4, the sum is $2^2 + 4^2 + 6^2 + 8^2$.

3. Write a program to compute $1 + (1+2) + (1+2+3) + (1+2+3+4) + \ldots + (1+2+3+4\ldots+11)$.

4. Write a program to read a value for N and compute $1*N + 2*N + 3*N + \ldots + 40*N$. For example, if N = 3, compute $1\cdot3 + 2\cdot3 + 3\cdot3 + \ldots 40\cdot3$.

5. Using a DO loop, write a program to determine whether a number N read from a record is prime. A prime number is any number that can be divided only by itself and by 1.

6. Write a program to compute the following sequences of sums:

$$S_1 = 1$$
$$S_2 = 1 + \frac{1}{2}$$
$$S_3 = 1 + \frac{1}{2} + \frac{1}{3}$$
$$S_4 = 1 + \frac{1}{2} + \frac{1}{3} + \frac{1}{4}$$
$$\vdots$$

   How many different sums would you have to compute before a sum exceeds 3.5?

7. Write a program to approximate the value of $\pi/4$ using the formula:

$$\frac{\pi}{4} = 1 - \frac{1}{3} + \frac{1}{5} - \frac{1}{7} + \frac{1}{9} - \ldots$$

   First approximation is $\pi/4 = 1$
   Second approximation is $\pi/4 = 1 - 1/3$
   Third approximation is $\pi/4 = 1 - 1/3 + 1/5$
   $\vdots$

   Stop when the difference between two successive approximations is less than 0.01.

8. Write the code to print the following sequence of numbers and stop when the sum of the terms exceeds 1000.

$$1, 1, 2, 3, 5, 8, 13, \ldots$$

   [*Hint*: Each term is equal to the sum of the two preceding terms.]

9. The number *e* can be approximated by the formula

$$e_4 = 1 + \frac{1}{1}\left(1 + \frac{1}{2}\left(1 + \frac{1}{3}\left(1 + \frac{1}{4}\right)\right)\right)$$

However, a better approximation would be

$$e_{100} = 1 + \frac{1}{1}\left(1 + \frac{1}{2}\left(1 + \frac{1}{3}\left(1 + \frac{1}{4}\left(1 + \frac{1}{5}\left(1 + \frac{1}{6}\left(\cdots + \frac{1}{99}\left(\cdots 1 + \frac{1}{100}\right)\right)\cdots\right)\right.\right.\right.\right.$$

Write a program to compute $e_{100}$.

10. It can be shown that the irrational number $e = 2.71828\ldots$ can be approximated by taking as many terms as desired in the relation

$$e = 1 + 1/1! + 1/2! + 1/3! + 1/4! + \ldots$$

Draw a flowchart to approximate the value of $e$ using this method. Stop when two successive approximations differ by less than 0.001.

For example:  1st approximation is 1
2nd approximation is $1 + 1/1! = 2$
3rd approximation is $1 + 1/1! + 1/2! = 2.5$
4th approximation is $1 + 1/1! + 1/2! + 1.3! = 2.666$, etc.

11. Write a program to convert binary numbers to decimal. One method that can be used is shown in the following example:

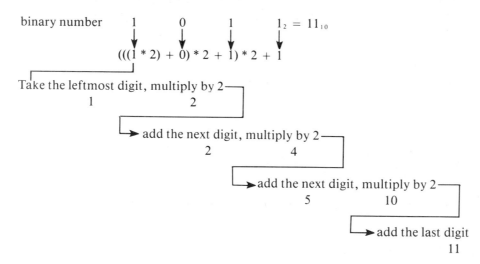

This method assumes that we can decompose a binary number into separate digits. One method of decomposition is shown as follows for decimal numbers: To decompose 143 into 3 digits (1, 4, and 3) consider the following (assume FIRST, REM, SECOND, THIRD are integer variables)

FIRST   = 143/100            = ①
REM     = 143 − (100 * FIRST) = 43      } 143!
SECOND  = REM/10             = ④
THIRD   = REM − (10 * SECOND) = ③

The same technique can be used to decompose $1011_2$ into successive digits.

12. Assume each of the variables I, J, K, and L contains one digit. Write the code to fuse these 4 digits into the variable M, for example, if I = 2, J = 8, K = 3, and L = 6, then M = (I)(J)(K)(L) = 2836; M is now a numeric variable equal to 2836!

[*Hint*: This uses the same method as the first part of Problem 11, except that you will multiply by 10, not by 2.]

13. Given a six-digit number such as 134578, decompose it into six variables in such a way that I = 1, J = 3, K = 4, L = 5, M = 7, N = 8.

[*Hint*: See the second part of Problem 11.]

14. *Straight line fitting*: Imagine that you are running an experiment for a physics or a biology project, and you obtain six points with coordinates $x$ and $y$ that you graph carefully as shown. The points seem to fit a straight line, and you would like to find the equation of the line that best fits these points. The equation could then be used to find corresponding $y$ values for points on the $x$-axis—these points could be between $x_1$ and $x_6$ or they could be outside the experimental range.

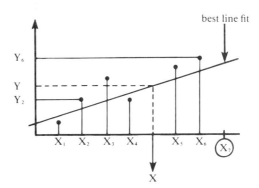

The least squares method can be used to find the equation of the straight line that best fits the experimental points. In this example, we will fit six experimental points $(x_1, y_1)$, $(x_2, y_2), \ldots, (x_6, y_6)$ to the straight line:

$$y = m * x + b$$

where $m$ (the slope) and $b$ (the $y$ intersect) are given by the following formulas:

$$m = \frac{N * SUM_{xy} - SUM_x * SUM_y}{N * SUM_{x^2} - (SUM_x)^2}$$

$$b = \frac{SUM_{x^2} * SUM_y - SUM_x * SUM_{xy}}{N * SUM_{x^2} - (SUM_x)^2}$$

Notice that the two denominators are the same. The meanings associated with the above variables are

| | |
|---|---|
| N | is the total number of points, six in this case. |
| $SUM_{xy}$ | is the sum of the $x*y$ product for each point: $x_1*y_1 + x_2*y_2 + \ldots + x_6*y_6$ |
| $SUM_y$ | is the sum of the $y$'s, i.e., $y_1 + y_2 + \ldots + y_6$ |
| $SUM_x$ | is the sum of the $x$'s, i.e., $x_1 + x_2 + \ldots + x_6$ |
| $SUM_{x^2}$ | is the sum of all the $x$'s squared, i.e., $x_1^2 + x_2^2 + \ldots + x_6^2$ |

Write a program to compute $m$ and $b$ for the following two sets of experimental data:.

| Experiment 1 | $x$ | 5 | 29.7 | 48.4 | 73 | 98 | 8.2 |
|---|---|---|---|---|---|---|---|
| 6 points | $y$ | 6.883 | − 51.13 | − 94.02 | − 150 | − 208.6 | 0.03 |

| Experiment 2 | $x$ | 0.43 | 0.28 | 0.39 | 0.62 | 0.36 | 0.7 | 0.67 | 0.62 | 0.23 | 0.59 |
|---|---|---|---|---|---|---|---|---|---|---|---|
| 10 points | $y$ | 0.0047 | 0.0027 | 0.0036 | 0.0065 | 0.0035 | 0.007 | 0.0064 | 0.0056 | 0.0021 | 0.0064 |

Then, using the RESTORE statement, compute the difference between each experimental $y$ value and the corresponding $y$ value obtained from the least squares straight line.

Identify the experimental point that seems to be the least accurate in terms of its relationship with the least squares straight line and the other experimental points.

15. A study was conducted to determine whether using different computer communication modes could affect a student's attitude toward programming. In a computer-related course, 13 students used the batch-processing mode to solve problems on the computer, while 12 other students used the conversational (interactive) mode to solve the same problems. The following entries reflect the average score obtained by each student for the 20 questions of the Attitude Test Toward Programming (ATTP) given at the end of the semester:

**Mode of Communication**

| Batch-Processing | Conversational |
|---|---|
| 2.75 | 4.15 |
| 2.95 | 3.70 |
| 3.00 | 3.55 |
| 3.10 | 4.45 |
| 4.50 | 4.20 |
| 4.75 | 3.95 |
| 2.50 | 3.80 |
| 3.35 | 4.00 |
| 4.00 | 3.00 |
| 3.05 | 3.65 |
| 2.00 | 4.00 |
| 3.35 | 4.35 |
| 4.10 | |

Students using the conversational approach had a higher average score than students using the batch-processing approach. Write a program to determine if this difference is significant. The difference is significant if $t > 2.069$, where $t$ is given by the following formula:

$$t = \frac{\overline{X}_c - \overline{X}_b}{\sqrt{\frac{(N_c - 1) S_c^2 + (N_b - 1)S_b^2}{(N_c + N_b - 2)} \cdot \frac{N_c + N_b}{N_c \cdot N_b}}}$$

where $\overline{X}_c$ and $\overline{X}_b$ are the averages of the conversational and batch scores, respectively;
$S_c$ and $S_b$ are the standard deviations for conversational and batch modes respectively (see section 5-4-4 for the programming example of a standard deviation); and
$N_c$ and $N_b$ are the number of scores for conversational and batch processing, respectively. [Expected answer = 2.202]

**16.** Legendre Polynomials are defined by the following equations:

$$P_0 = 1$$
$$P_1 = x \text{ where } -1 \le x \le 1$$
$$P_i = \left(\frac{2i-1}{i}\right) x P_{i-1} - \left(\frac{i-1}{i}\right) P_{i-2} \text{ for } i = 2,3,\ldots$$

Write a program to produce a table of Legendre polynomials $P_0, P_1, \ldots, P_{10}$ for equally spaced values of $x$ such as $-1.0, -.95, -.90,\ldots,.95, 1.00$.

**17.** The natural logarithm (base $e$) of $x$ can be approximated using the series

$$\ln(x) = \left(\frac{x-1}{x}\right) + \frac{1}{2}\left(\frac{x-1}{x}\right)^2 + \frac{1}{3}\left(\frac{x-1}{x}\right)^3 + \ldots$$

Write a program to approximate the value of $\ln(x)$, with the approximation correct to 3 decimal places. Use the function LOG(X) to compare your results.

**18.** Write a program to find a five-digit number $d_1 d_2 d_3 d_4 d_5$ that when multiplied by a digit $k$ between 2 and 9 will give a result of $d_5 d_4 d_3 d_2 d_1$, i.e.,

$$\begin{array}{r} d_1 \ d_2 \ d_3 \ d_4 \ d_5 \\ \times \ k \\ \hline d_5 \ d_4 \ d_3 \ d_2 \ d_1 \end{array}$$

**19.** Write a program to compute the area under a curve, $y = f(x)$:

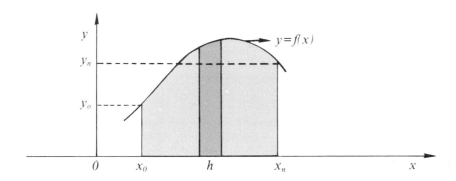

The darkened area under a curve, $y = f(x)$, can be approximated by breaking the interval $(x_0, x_n)$ into $n$ equal intervals of size,

$$h = \frac{x_n - x_0}{n}$$

and computing the sum of the areas of the $n$ trapezoids with base $h$. The smaller the interval $h$, the closer the approximation is to the exact area. The formula to compute the sum of the areas of the $n$ trapezoids is:

$$A = \frac{h}{2} (y_0 + 2y_1 + 2y_2 + \ldots + 2y_{n-1} + y_n)$$

where $y_0, y_1, y_2, \ldots, y_n$ are the values of the function at the points $x_0, x_1, x_2, \ldots, x_n$
Your program should approximate the area under the curve $y = e^{-x^2/2}$ for $x$ between 1 and 2 for three different values of $h$, .1, .01, .001. (This is equivalent to obtaining an approximation for the integral $\int_1^2 e^{-x^2/2}$.) The value computed should be approximately 0.34.

20. A *perfect* number is a number that is the sum of all its divisors except itself. Six is the first perfect number; the only numbers that divide 6 evenly are 1, 2, 3, 6, and $6 = 1 + 2 + 3$. An *abundant* number is one that is less than the sum of its divisors (e.g., $12 < 1 + 2 + 3 + 4 + 6$); a *deficient* number is greater than the sum of its divisors (e.g., $9 > 1 + 3$). Write a program to generate a table of the first N integers (N is read from a record) and classify each as perfect, abundant, or deficient.

## 5-7-4 Programming Problems: Random Numbers

1. Write a program to generate 100 random real numbers and 100 random integers in the range 0–10. Determine the average of the numbers. What would you expect the results to be?

2. Marc and Laura each toss a six sided die. What is the probability that they will toss the same number? Write a program to simulate the toss of a die.

3. Sue Ellen and Anabelle each toss a pair of six-sided dice. What is the chance that both will toss a 2 (i.e., each tosses two 1's)? a 3? a 4? a 12? Simulate the toss of a die.

4. Charlie tosses a pair of six-sided dice. What number (sum of the face values of both dice) is most likely to be thrown (a 2 is a combination of 1 and 1; a 7 is a combination of 4 and 3, 5 and 2, or 6 and 1, and so forth). Simulate the toss of a die.

5. On a multiple-choice test consisting of ten questions, each question has five answers to choose from—A, B, C, D, or E. Margie does not know the answers to questions 3 and 7. What is the probability of her guessing both answers correctly? One answer? Neither? Simulate the answers to both questions 3 and 7.

6. A dog is lost in a tunnel at node 0 (see diagram). It can move one node at one time in either direction right or left with equal probability (1 = right, 2 = left). When the dog hits node $L_2$, however, a force of nature always propels him directly to node $L_4$. The dog escapes from the tunnel when he either hits $L_5$ or $R_4$. Write a program to determine:
   a. Whether the dog has a better chance to exit from the right or the left: in fact, what are the odds that he will exit from $R_4$? From $L_5$?
   b. How long, on the average, the dog stays in the tunnel (each node takes one minute to cover).
   c. Do the same problem as in part a, but let node $L_2$ propel the dog to $L_4$ only when traveling in a left direction. If node $L_2$ is reached when traveling to the right, the node $L_2$ has no effect.
   Restart the dog at node 0 a thousand times and count the number of times he escapes through $R_4$ or $L_5$.

NODE 0

| EXIT ← | $L_5$ | $L_4$ | $L_3$ | $L_2$ | $L_1$ | | $R_1$ | $R_2$ | $R_3$ | $R_4$ → EXIT |

7. Write a program to determine the least number of random integer numbers between 1 and 100 that must be generated so that the average of these numbers lies in the interval 47 to 53.

8. John Jones has $200,000 to invest in speculative gold stock. The gold mines are of such a nature that they either go broke, leaving stock worthless, or strike gold and make the stockholders wealthy. Mr. Jones's goal is to retire with $2,000,000. He plans to invest in blocks of $100,000. He estimates that the probability of losing each $100,000 investment is 75%, while the probability of making $1,000,000 from the same investment is 25%. In the latter case, he will sell the stock and make further $100,000 investments of the same nature.

   a. What is the probability of Mr. Jones's retiring with $2,000,000? [*Hint*: Simulate the 75%/25% lose/win probability by generating random numbers in the range 1 to 4. Arbitrarily choose one number to represent a win. The probability of getting any value in this range is 1/4 = 25%.] Simulate 100 such investment sequences and count the wins (makes $2,000,000) and losses (goes broke); from these figures, determine the probability for a successful retirement.

   b. Determine whether, in the course of the 100 investment trials, Mr. Jones ever won $1,000,000 only to lose it, i.e. does he ever win $1,000,000 but fail to retire with $2,000,000?

   c. Instead of a return of $1,000,000 for a $100,000 investment, suppose that the return was only $500,000. How would this change Mr. Jones's chances of success? Experiment with returns varying from $300,000 to $3,000,000 in steps of $100,000 and see how the odds for successful retirement change.

9. You are now at the famous Monte Carlo casino and you have $1,000 to burn. You are not a sophisticated roulette player, so you decide to place bets on the even or odd. The roulette ball lands on any of 37 numbers (0–36). The number 0 is the house's lucky number, and the croupier rakes in everything on the board (i.e., you lose your bet). Correct bets on even or odd squares double your input bet. A correct bet on any of the numbers 1 through 36 gives you 20 times the original amount you bet. Write a program to continuously accept bets, and print your remaining balance. The game should go on till you have either run out of cash or doubled your initial investment. Play 10 such games and keep track of how many you win and how many you lose. What are your chances of doubling your initial investment?

10. A submarine has been trapped into an enemy bay with only one escape channel leading out of the bay. The bay is surrounded by mines as shown below. All navigating equipment is malfunctioning, and the blind submarine is now moving randomly in any of the four cardinal directions one square at a time. If the sub hits any of the mines, it is instantly destroyed. The sub escapes when it reaches row 2 column 5.

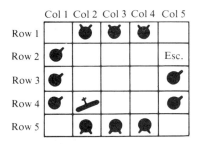

Directional Chart

a. Write a program to determine the sub's escape chances from its present position of row 4 and column 2.

b. Compute the submarine's chances of escape for each of the squares in the above grid.

c. Allow the submarine to restart at row 4, column 2, 10,000 times. In those 10,000 attempts, determine the least number of steps the submarine took to escape. Do you think the answer will be 5?

d. Assume there is another moving blind submarine in row 3, column 4. What are the chances of the submarines' colliding with each other? Take into account the fact that both submarines can escape!

e. Change the program to allow the submarine to travel also in any diagonal direction. Do you expect the sub's chances of escape are improved with the sub's increased versatility?

11. Refer to the mole problem of Figure 5–10.

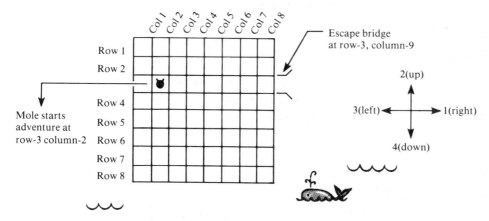

a. Compute the average number of moves the mole takes before it either drowns or escapes.

b. In the course of the 1000 adventures, record the maximum number of steps taken by the mole before it escapes.

c. The above island (maze) has now been transformed into a closed arena from which no mole can escape. One mole is placed in row 1, column 1 and another mole in row 6, column 6. Moles move about the arena as described in part a above. Upon hitting a wall, the mole bounces back to the position it occupied prior to hitting the wall. Both moles move at the same time. Write a computer program to determine, on the average, how many mole moves are made before a mole collision occurs. [*Hint*: After each collision, restart the moles back in $R = 1, C = 1$ and $R = 6, C = 6$ one thousand times.]

12. An approximation for $\pi$ can be found by selecting random points in a square into which a circle of radius $r$ has been inscribed. The area of the square times the quotient of the number of points lying inside the inscribed circle of radius $r$ divided by the number of points sampled is approximately $\pi$.

Write a program to select random points in the square in the following diagram, where the circle has radius 1; then use the method described to compute an approximation for $\pi$. Recall that the equation for the unit circle is $x^2 + y^2 = 1$. Therefore the values of $x$ and $y$ where $x^2 + y^2 \leq 1$ represent points that lie within the circle.

In this example

$$\pi \doteq 4 \cdot \frac{6}{8} = 3$$

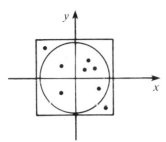

## 5-7-5  Answers to Test Yourself

1.  a.
```
       DO 5 I = 1,99,2
     5 PRINT*,I
```

d.
```
       DO 5 I = N,Ø,-2
     5 PRINT*,I
```

  b.
```
       DO 5 I = 1,25
     5 PRINT*,(-1)**I
```

e.
```
       DO 5 I = 1,7
     5 PRINT*,1./(10**I - 1.)
```

  c.
```
       P = 1.
       READ*,X
       DO 5 I = 1,X
       P = P/I
     5 PRINT*,P
```

f.
```
       DO 5 I = 25,200,25
       P = I/100.
     5 PRINT*,P
```

2.

| K | A | B |
|---|---|---|
| ~~Ø~~ | ~~3~~ | ~~Ø~~ |
| ~~1~~ | ~~4~~ | |
| ~~2~~ | ~~6~~ | |
| ~~3~~ | ~~9~~ | |
| ~~4~~ | ~~Ø~~ | 10 |
| ~~5~~ | ~~4~~ | |
| ~~6~~ | ~~9~~ | |
| | 15 | |

```
  9   9
 15  10
```

3.  a.
```
       S = Ø.
       DO 5 I = 1,10
     5     S = S + I*I
```

d.
```
       P = 1.
       S = Ø.
       DO 5 I = 1,50
           P = P*I
     5     S = S + P
```

  b.
```
       S = Ø.
       DO 5 I = 1,10
     5     S = S + 2.**I
```

  c.
```
       S = Ø.
       DO 5 I = 1,1000
     5     S = S - (-1)**I*I
```

e.
```
       S = Ø.
       DO 5 I = 1,77,2
     5     S = S + 1./I
```

**4.** a. valid    b. valid    c. invalid; index must not be changed    d. invalid; inconsistent use of I    e. invalid index    f. valid    g. invalid; body of interior loop overlaps body of outer loop    h. valid    i. invalid; foot of loop 91 is missing    j. valid    k. invalid foot    l. invalid; L is redefined in loop    m. valid    n. valid    o. invalid; index K cannot be modified within loop    p. invalid; cannot branch into body of loop after normal exit from loop    q. valid    r. valid    s. invalid; foot of loop cannot be a DO statement    t. value printed for K is meaningless

**5.** a. 1,3,5,7,9.    b. 6,9,12,15,18.    c. No output; the loop is bypassed.    d. 10,100,000 on 3 separate lines, with 000 at the top of the next page.

**6.** a. 120.    b. 57.    c. 2.    d. 9.

**7.** a. Neither. The value of I will never be greater than 5.    b. logical error: division by I.

**8.** a. No; the value of the index I is indeterminate after normal/complete exit from loop and should not be used.    b. Yes.

**9.** J = 0

**10.** a. 1,2,1.    b. 2,2.    c. 1,3, error (I is integer, but is described by F type).

**11.** a. T.    b. T.    c. F; initial value must always be specified.    d. F; the CONTINUE statement can be used anywhere in a program.    e. F; if the index is greater than starting value, the loop will be bypassed (if the increment is positive).    f. F; nonexecutable statements are processed at compilation time, not execution time.    g. T.    h. T.    i. F.    j. F; the comment will be listed once at compilation time.

**12.** STAT100 is seven characters long.
X, A, and I are integers and should not be initialized to 0. but to 0
3I5.0 is incorrect in statement 10; it should be 3I5
Comma needed in the computed GO TO(10, 20, 30, 30),L.
The computed GO TO should transfer to an executable statement not a FORMAT (statement 10).
Incorrect placement of the two CONTINUE statements.
In the last IF statement, I*J*L is neither true nor false!
GO TO 77 is invalid since it causes a transfer into the midst of a DO loop.
FORMAT 200 is missing.
Note that THEN L = L + 1 is not a compilation error since THEN L is a variable.

**13.**
```
    DATA K1,K2,K3,K4/4*0/
    DO 5 I = 1 ,1000
        L = RAND(1)*4. + 1.
        IF(L.EQ.1)K1 = K1 + 1
        IF(L.EQ.2)K2 = K2 + 1
        IF(L.EQ.3)K3 = K3 + 1
        IF(L.EQ.4)K4 = K4 + 1
  5 CONTINUE
    PRINT*,K1,K2,K3,K4
```

14.

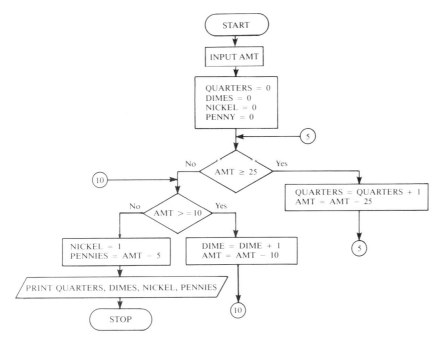

15. 
```
C     COMPOUND INTEREST PROBLEM
      INTEGER YEARS
      WRITE(6,1)
      P = 1000.
      DO 40 YEARS = 1,3
         DO 35 IR = 5,8
            R = IR/100.
            A = P*(1.+R)**YEARS
            WRITE(6,2)A,P,YEARS,R
  35     CONTINUE
      WRITE (6,3)
  40 CONTINUE
   2 FORMAT(1X,F7.2,T13,I1,T21,F3.2)
   1 FORMAT(T3,'AMOUNT',T11,'YEARS',T18,'INTEREST')
   3 FORMAT(1X)
      STOP
      END
```

# data representation:
## substrings, the l, e,
## and, d format codes,
## and complex-numbers

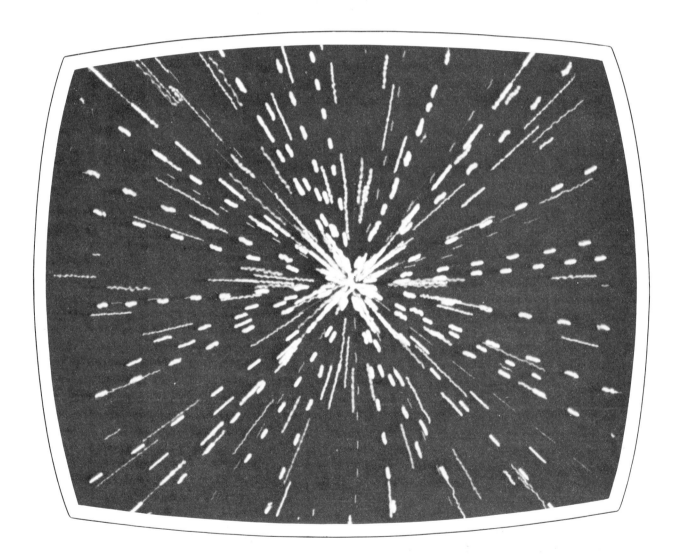

**CHAPTER SIX**

# data representation:
## substrings, the l, e, and, d format codes, and complex-numbers

## 6-1    Programming Example

Each record of an input file contains a student's name and the student's final score. Write a program to assign each student a letter grade, using the cutoffs shown below and produce an output similar to the following one.

| Score | Letter Grade |
|-------|--------------|
| score ≥ 90 | A |
| 80 ≤ score < 90 | B |
| 60 ≤ score < 80 | C |
| 50 ≤ score < 60 | D |
| score < 50 | F |

*Output*

```
NAME              SCORE      GRADE

ANTONIONI L         58         D
DELLA CROC M        91         A
LUCIANNO F          91         A
INVALID SCORE    MARANGANO T   680
PALOMINO P          68         C
TOMBALO R           34         F
GALANTE M           83         B

HIGHEST SCORE = 91
(OBTAINED BY 2 OR MORE STUDENTS)
```

This message is printed only if the highest score is obtained by at least two students; otherwise, it is not printed.

A program to solve this problem is shown in Figure 6–1. Notice the logical variable ONEMAX and the LOGICAL statement; these new FORTRAN features will be described in detail later in this chapter.

## 6-2    Substrings

### 6-2-1    Referencing Character Substrings

Character constants are examples of character strings. Through the CHARACTER specification statement we can reserve a specific number of character positions for a particular character variable (note that the CHARACTER statement does not generally initialize character variables to blanks). In many programming applications it is important to be able to process one or more characters (substrings) within a given string. FORTRAN allows us to operate on substrings through an index mechanism that identifies the position of a character within a string. The general form of a substring reference is:

*string variable* (*start position* : *last position*)

**FIGURE 6-1**   LOGICAL VARIABLES

```
C EXAMPLE OF PROGRAM WITH LOGICAL VARIABLES
C    NAME:    STUDENT NAME
C    SCORE:   STUDENT SCORE
C    MAX:     MAXIMUM SCORE
C    GRADE:   STUDENT GRADE
C    ONEMAX:  LOGICAL VARIABLE
C
      CHARACTER NAME*12, GRADE
      INTEGER SCORE,MAX
      LOGICAL ONEMAX                 ONEMAX is a logical variable that contains either the value
      WRITE(6,45)                    .TRUE. or .FALSE.
      MAX = 0
      ONEMAX = .TRUE.
C WE MAKE THE ASSUMPTION THAT THERE IS ONLY ONE MAXIMUM (ONEMAX) SCORE
C IN THE INPUT FILE. WE EXPRESS THIS BY SETTING ONEMAX TO .TRUE.
C AS SOON WE FIND OTHER SCORES EQUAL TO MAX WE RESET ONEMAX TO .FALSE.
C WHEN ALL SCORES HAVE BEEN READ THE VALUE OF ONEMAX WILL EITHER BE
C .TRUE. OR .FALSE. IF ONEMAX IS .FALSE. THEN THE MESSAGE "OBTAINED BY
C TWO OR MORE STUDENTS" WILL BE PRINTED, OTHERWISE NO MESSAGE IS PRINTED
C
   10 READ(5,50,END=40) NAME, SCORE
      IF (SCORE.LT.0 .OR. SCORE .GT.100) THEN       Screen scores for proper range.
         WRITE(6,55) NAME, SCORE
         GO TO 10
      ELSE IF (SCORE .GE. 90) THEN
                              GRADE = 'A'
      ELSE IF (SCORE .GE. 80) THEN
                              GRADE = 'B'
      ELSE IF (SCORE .GE. 60) THEN
                              GRADE = 'C'
      ELSE IF (SCORE .GE. 50) THEN
                              GRADE = 'D'
      ELSE
                              GRADE = 'F'
      ENDIF
      WRITE(6,60) NAME, SCORE, GRADE
      IF (MAX .GT. SCORE) GO TO 10         If MAX is still highest score we read the next score.
      IF (MAX .LT. SCORE) THEN             If score just read is greater then MAX, then
         MAX = SCORE                       we have found a new MAX and since it is the
         ONEMAX = .TRUE.                   first time that this MAX has occurred we set
      ELSE                                 ONEMAX to .TRUE.
         ONEMAX = .FALSE.                  If another score also happens to be equal to
      ENDIF                                MAX, then it is no longer true that there is only
      GO TO 10                             one MAX, so we reset ONEMAX to .FALSE.
   40 WRITE(6,65) MAX
      IF ( .NOT. ONEMAX) WRITE(6,70)       If there is not one maximum, print the message.
      STOP
   45 FORMAT(1X,'NAME',11X,'SCORE',2X,'GRADE')
   50 FORMAT(A12,I3)
   55 FORMAT(1X,'INVALID SCORE  ', A12, I4)
   60 FORMAT(1X,A12,4X,I3,5X,A1)
   65 FORMAT('0','HIGHEST SCORE =',I4)
   70 FORMAT(1X,'(OBTAINED BY 2 OR MORE STUDENTS)')
      END
```

| NAME | SCORE | GRADE |
|------|-------|-------|
| ANTONIONI L | 58 | D |
| DELLA CROC M | 91 | A |
| LUCIANNO F | 91 | A |
| INVALID SCORE | MARANGANO T | 680 |
| PALOMINO P | 68 | C |
| TOMBALO R | 34 | F |
| GALANTE M | 83 | B |

HIGHEST SCORE = 91
(OBTAINED BY 2 OR MORE STUDENTS)

*Input File*

```
ANTONIONI L 058
DELLA CROC M091
LUCIANNO F  091
MARANGANO T 680
PALOMINO P  068
TOMBALO R   034
GALANTE M   083
```

where *string variable* is the name of a CHARACTER variable

> *start position* identifies the position of the first character of the substring; if omitted, the default position is 1.

> *last position* identifies the position of the last character in the substring; if omitted, the default position is the position of the last character in the string.

Both start position and last position can be arithmetic expressions.

*Example*

```
CHARACTER LINE*20,A*5,B*7,C*4,D*4
```

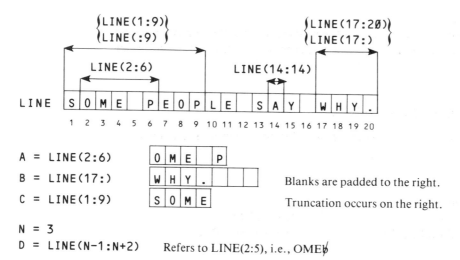

```
A = LINE(2:6)
```
```
O M E   P
```
```
B = LINE(17:)
```
```
W H Y .
```
Blanks are padded to the right.
```
C = LINE(1:9)
```
```
S O M E
```
Truncation occurs on the right.

```
N = 3
D = LINE(N-1:N+2)    Refers to LINE(2:5), i.e., OMEb
```

In general, LINE(I:J) where I ≤ J refers to the segment of the string starting at position I up to and including the Jth position. The values of I and J must be such that $1 \leq I \leq J \leq$ length of LINE as declared in the CHARACTER statement.

**LINE(2:6) is just like any other CHARACTER variable and can be used in the same way as other character variables in IF statements, input/output statements, and so forth.** It looks different, but it is just another character variable!

## 6-2-2 Substrings in Replacement Statements

For assignment purposes, substring variables can appear on the left of the equal sign in a replacement statement. The DATA statement can also be used to assign characters to substrings.

*Example*

```
CHARACTER DAY*9,M*3
DATA M /'NES'/
```

DAY

```
DAY = 'SUNDAY'
```
```
S U N D A Y
```
Trailing blanks provided.
```
DAY(1:3) = 'WED'
```
```
W E D D A Y
```
Replace first 3 characters.
```
DAY(7:) = 'DAY'
```
```
W E D D A Y D A Y
```
Replace last 3 characters.
```
DAY(4:6) = M(2:)
```
```
W E D E S   D A Y
```
Replace characters 4, 5, and 6.

No substring may be "equated" to a substring of the same parent string if there is a resulting overlap in position assignments, for example, the following assignment is invalid due to the overlap of characters in positions 3 and 4:

```
DAY(2:4) = DAY(3:5)    Overlapping characters not allowed.
DAY(2:5) = DAY(6:9)    Valid assignment, no overlap.
```

Such a restriction can be circumvented by using a temporary variable.

```
TEMP = DAY(3:5)    where TEMP is a character variable at least 3 positions long.
DAY(2:4) = TEMP
```

A character string assignment normally takes place in several steps unlike replacement of numbers and hence part of a string might be altered before the completion of the assignment.

## 6-2-3  Substrings in Input/Output Statements

Substrings can appear in list directed and format controlled input/output statements.

*Example 1*

```
CHARACTER FAMILY*16
FAMILY = 'MARC ANDREW GOOD'
WRITE(6,1) FAMILY(13:)              will print GOOD
PRINT*,FAMILY(:5),FAMILY(13:)      will print MARC GOOD
```

*Example 2*

```
CHARACTER FAMILY*16                          Input Record
DATA FAMILY/16*' '/
READ*,FAMILY(8:),FAMILY(1:6),AGE     'MANSOOR', 'TIM', 17.

PRINT*, FAMILY                       TIMϕϕϕϕMANSOORϕϕ
PRINT*,FAMILY(8:),FAMILY(1:6),AGE    MANSOORϕϕTIMϕϕϕ  17.
```

  9 characters will be printed    6 characters will be printed

## 6-2-4  Substrings in IF Statements

Substring variables can be used in IF statements in the same way that character variables are used.

*Example 1*    Count the occurrence of the letter E in a word.

```
CHARACTER WORD*8
WORD = 'SENTENCE'
K = Ø
DO 5 I = 1,8
    IF(WORD(I:I) .EQ. 'E')K = K+1
5 CONTINUE
PRINT*,K        The value 3 will be printed.
```

*Example 2*  Replace the words MIGUEL and LAURA in a line of text by the words MICHEL and LAURE.

```
CHARACTER TEXT*80
READ*,TEXT
DO 5 I = 1,73
    IF(TEXT(I:I+7) .EQ. ' MIGUEL ')THEN
        TEXT(I:I+7) = ' MICHEL '
    ELSE
        IF(TEXT(I:I+6) .EQ. ' LAURA ') THEN
            TEXT(I:I+6) = ' LAURE '
        ENDIF
    ENDIF
5 CONTINUE
```

In this case we are searching for strings of 7 and 8 characters (2 blanks plus the name) and replacing it with different strings of the same length.

## 6-2-5  Concatenation of Strings

To chain or fuse two or more strings into one string, we use the double slash operator // between the strings, i.e., *string 1//string 2* fuses *string 1* and *string 2* into one string. No additional spaces are inserted between the strings.

*Example*

```
CHARACTER A*3,TAG1*6,TAG2*7,TAG3*5,B*5,TAG4*8
A = 'XYZ'
B = 'HI'
TAG1 = 'ABC'//'DEF'        TAG1 = | A | B | C | D | E | F |
TAG2 = A//'DEF'            TAG2 = | X | Y | Z | D | E | F |
TAG3 = A//' '//A           TAG3 = | X | Y | Z |   | X |       Truncation occurs.
TAG4 = B//A(1:2)           TAG4 = | H | I |   |   | X | Y |   B has size 5.
PRINT*,A//' CORPORATION'   will print XYZCORPORATION
```

Note that the concatenation operator can be used in IF statements as in:

```
IF(COIN//TEMP .EQ. C(1:K+1))THEN ...
IF(A//B//C .EQ. WORD//CONT)THEN ...
```

The concatenation process can be very convenient when we want to remove one or more characters from a particular string. Suppose, for example, that we wanted to remove the first period encountered in the string TEXT = 'HE SAID TO T. CARSON' in order to obtain 'HE SAID TO T CARSON'. To do this, we need to tie the first 12 characters of TEXT to the character substring in positions 14 through 20. Hence we concatenate the first 12 characters with the last 7 characters, as follows:

TEXT(:12)   TEXT(14:)

```
CHARACTER*20 TEXT, TEMP
TEMP = TEXT(1:12)//TEXT(14:)        | HE SAID TO T | bCARSON |
TEXT = TEMP
```

TEXT was originally 20 characters long; even though we have removed one character, the length of TEXT does *not* shrink by 1—it is still 20 characters long, meaning that there will be a blank in position 20. The complete code to extract the first period found in a sentence is:

```
      CHARACTER*20 TEXT,TEMP        Assume TEXT contains a complete sentence.
      DO 5 I = 1,20
          IF(TEXT(I:I) .EQ. '.')GO TO 6    Locate the position of the period.
    5 CONTINUE
      PRINT*,'NO PERIODS FOUND'
      STOP
    6 IF(I .EQ. 20)THEN              If the period is in position 20,
          TEMP = TEXT(:19)          retain only the first 19 characters.
      ELSE
          TEMP = TEXT(:I-1)//TEXT(I+1:)    Excise the period. Trailing blanks
      ENDIF                         are provided for TEMP.
      TEXT = TEMP                   Place text back into TEXT.
      PRINT*,TEXT
```

Other character string functions (the INDEX, LEN, ICHAR, and CHAR functions) are discussed briefly in section 6–7, question 1.

## 6-2-6  Do It Now

**1.** Specify the output for the following:

```
      CHARACTER MESSG*6,PLUS*5,ONE*3
      MESSG = 'WEAMUS'
```
a. `PRINT*,MESSG(:4)`
b. `PRINT*,MESSG(6:6)`
c. `PRINT*,MESSG(3:)`
d. `PRINT*,MESSG(3:7)`
e. `ONE = '3+'`
   `PLUS = ONE//'4=8'`
   `PRINT*,PLUS`

**2.** Determine the output produced by the following code: (Assume LINE contains blanks.)

```
      CHARACTER LINE*10
```

a.
```
      DO 5 I = 1,10
    5     LINE(I:I)='.'
      PRINT*,LINE
```
b.
```
      DO 5 I = 1,7
          LINE(I:I)='.'
    5     PRINT*,LINE
```
c.
```
      DO 5 K = 1,10
          LINE(K:K)=' '
    5 PRINT*,LINE(:K)//'HELLO'
```

**3.** What does the following code accomplish? Assume TEXT consists of N characters.

```
      DO 10 I = 1,N/2
          TEMP = TEXT(I:I)
          TEXT(I:I) = TEXT(N-I+1:N-I+1)
          TEXT(N-I+1:N-I+1) = TEMP
   10 CONTINUE
```

**4.** Determine what is stored in Z as a result of the following code:

```
CHARACTER*4 X,Y,Z
X = '.'
Y = X//X
Z = X//Y
```

**5.** How could you type and store your English term paper, which contains 80 character lines, into a character string of 10000 positions, i.e., CHARACTER TEXT*10000?

## Answers

**1.**  a. WEAM  　　　　d. Invalid; too many characters
　　b. S  　　　　　　e. 3+ 4=
　　c. AMUS

**2.**  a. . . . . . . . . . .  (10 periods)  　　c.  HELLO
　　b. .  　　　　　　　　　　　　HELLO
　　　. . 　　　　　　　　　　　　HELLO　　 ⎫
　　　. . . 　 ⎫ 7 lines 　　　　　. 　　　　 ⎬ 10 lines
　　　. . . . 　⎬ 　　　　　　　　. 　　　　 ⎭
　　　. . . . . 　　　　　　　　. HELLO
　　　. . . . . . ⎭
　　　. . . . . . .

**3.** Reverses the sentence, for example, WE AM US would become SU MA EW

**4.** Z contains ⎡.⎢ ⎢ ⎢ ⎤  Remember, X, Y, and Z are each 4 characters long!

**5.** CHARACTER TEXT*10000,LINE*80

Read a line of your paper into LINE and concatenate it to TEXT.
Read a 2nd line of text and concatenate it to TEXT(81:), and so forth.

### 6-2-7  A Programming Example

An input file consists of an unknown number of records, where each record consists of a line of text, i.e., 80 characters of information. Write a program to compute the number of characters and words in the entire text file, and determine the average word length.

Assume that no word is hyphenated from one line to the next, and that punctuation characters are followed by one or more blank space to the right and preceded by a non-blank character to the left, i.e., the word DOG could be in any one of the following forms:

DOG.　　DOG　　DOG?　　DOG,　　DOG;　　DOG!

In the context of this problem, a word is a sequence of nonblank contiguous characters. If the word terminates with a punctuation symbol, the punctuation symbol is not counted as a character.

One way to proceed is to analyze each character, one at a time, and ask if that character is a nonblank character. If it is a nonblank character, we determine whether the character that follows it is a blank. If it is blank, then we have found the end of a word. The program to solve this problem is shown in Figure 6–2.

**FIGURE 6-2** A WORD COUNT PROBLEM

```
C COUNTING WORDS
C   LINE: A LINE OF TEXT
C   CHARS: NUMBER OF CHARACTERS
C   WORDS: NUMBER OF WORDS
C   AVE: AVERAGE NUMBER OF WORDS
C
      CHARACTER LINE*81,NEXT
      INTEGER I,WORDS,CHARS
      REAL AVE
      CHARS = 0
      WORDS = 0
      LINE(81:81) = ' '                     Because of the index I + 1 at line 12
  10 READ(5,6,END=88)LINE(:80)              Read 80 characters from input device.
         DO 5 I = 1,80
            IF(LINE(I:I) .EQ. ' ')THEN       Transfer to foot of loop if blank character
               CONTINUE                      i.e., don't count blanks
            ELSE
  12           NEXT = LINE(I+1:I+1)          Look ahead to next character
               IF(NEXT.EQ.'.'.OR.NEXT.EQ.','.OR.NEXT.EQ.'?'.OR.NEXT.EQ.';')THEN
                  CONTINUE                   Don't count punctuation characters.
               ELSE
                  CHARS = CHARS+1
                  IF(NEXT .EQ. ' ') WORDS = WORDS + 1
               ENDIF
            ENDIF
   5     CONTINUE
         GO TO 10
  88 AVE = 1.*CHARS/WORDS          use of 1. forces real division
      WRITE(6,11)CHARS,WORDS,AVE
      STOP
  11 FORMAT(1X,'NO. CHARACTERS=',I5,' NO. WORDS=',I4,'AVERAGE LENGTH=',F5.1)
   6 FORMAT(A)
      END
```

# 6-3   Number Representation

## 6-3-1  Internal Data Representation

### *Integer Data*

The internal form for integer data differs from that used for real or alphanumeric data. On most computers integer data is represented in binary form (also called *fixed point*, because the decimal point is assumed fixed to the right of the rightmost digit). Each integer in memory occupies a computer word consisting of a fixed number of *binary digits* (*bits*). Thus integer variable names are just names for computer words. Word lengths on different computers vary from 8 to 60 bits; some typical lengths for specific computers are shown in Figure 6–3. The range of values that can be represented in integer mode is directly proportional to the word length used. Integer value ranges for some computers are also shown in Figure 6–3.

## Real Data

Real data is represented internally in a form called *floating-point form* (the decimal point is allowed to move or float anywhere in the number). Floating-point notation permits representation of numbers with decimal points and exponents. A floating-point number can be expressed as follows:

$$fraction \times base^{\,exponent} \quad (fraction = \text{number expressed in fractional form})$$

For example, in base 10 the number 6325.3 might be expressed as

$$\overbrace{.63253}^{\text{Fractional part}} \times 10^{4} \quad \text{exponent}$$

base (most machines use base 2,8 or 16)

It should be noted that a real number occupies one computer word, which consists of a fixed number of bits (see Figure 6–4). In many systems the sign is reflected by the first bit. Internally, the computer word is broken into two parts—an exponent and a fractional part—and the number is normalized, meaning that the first digit to the right of the decimal point is nonzero, (the exponent is adjusted accordingly).

**FIGURE 6–3** WORD LENGTH AND MAXIMUM INTEGER VALUES

| Computer | Word Length (Bits) | Range of Integer Value | Number of Decimal Digits |
|---|---|---|---|
| TRS-80 II | 16 | $-2^{15}$ to $2^{15}-1$ | 5 |
| IBM 370/30xx/43xx | 32 | $-2^{31}$ to $2^{31}-1$ | 10 |
| Burroughs 6900 | 48 | $-2^{38}$ to $2^{38}-1$ | 15 |
| CDC Cyber 72 | 60 | $-2^{59}+1$ to $2^{59}-1$ | 18 |

**FIGURE 6–4** WORD LENGTH AND RANGE OF REAL NUMBERS

| Computer | Word Length (Bits) | Exponent Range | Digits in Fraction Part (Significant Digits) |
|---|---|---|---|
| TRS-80 II | 32 | $10^{38} - 10^{-38}$ | 7 |
| IBM 370/30xx/43xx | 32 | $10^{75} - 10^{-78}$ | 7 |
| Burroughs B6900 | 48 | $10^{67} - 10^{-47}$ | 11 |
| CDC Cyber 72 | 60 | $10^{308} - 10^{-308}$ | 15 |

*Example*

The number 6325.3 might be expressed as

$$.63253 \times 10^{\textcircled{4}}$$

and its internal representation might be

| 04 | 632530 | one word

exponent      implied position of decimal point      fractional part

The range of values that can be represented in floating-point form depends on the number of bits (digits 0 or 1) allowed for the exponent and on the number of bits allocated to the mantissa in each computer word. Some typical ranges are shown in figure 6–4.

## 6-3-2  Do It Now

Determine the word length and other details of integer and real data representation for the computer you are using.

## 6-3-3  Real Constants in Exponential Form and the E Format Code

A real constant in a FORTRAN program can be represented in two forms: a *basic* form and an *exponential* form. A real constant in basic form is a sequence of digits with a decimal point. The maximum number of significant digits is shown in Figure 6–4. For example:

X = −999.9901        is a valid real constant on the IBM/370.
Y = 1.00000000000099      is a valid real constant on the CDC CYBER.

If more than the allowed number of significant digits is used, the system will generally represent the constant in double precision mode, which we will discuss in section 6–3–5.

The exponential form for a real constant has the general form.

| *basic real constant* E *integer exponent* |

The value of a constant in this form is *basic real constant* $\times$ $10^{\text{integer exponent}}$

The number of digits allowed in the basic real constant and in the integer exponent varies depending on the system used.

*Example 1*

| *Exponential Form Constants* | *Value* |
|---|---|
| 6.2E + 4 | $6.2 \times 10^4$ = 62000. |
| − 4.32E14 | $-4.32 \times 10^{14}$ = − 432000000000000. |
| 0.034E − 2 | $0.034 \times 10^{-2}$ = .00034 |
| − 1.2E − 7 | $-1.2 \times 10^{-7}$ = − .00000012 |

Exponential form is typically used in place of the basic form for real constants with large or small magnitudes. The exponential form can be used in lieu of the basic form in any arithmetic expression.

*Example 2*

| Exponential Form | Basic Form |
|---|---|
| X = -.01E3*Y | X = -10.*Y |
| Y = 16.2E-4*Z + W | Y = .00162*Z + W |
| Z = 4.2E+20**2 - Z*.5E-21 | Only exponential form is practical. |

## The E Format Code

**Input of exponential numbers**. Numbers in exponential form can be read from data records using the E format code. Recall that an exponential number can be written as:

$$\text{basic real constant E integer exponent}$$

For example

$$\underbrace{-2134}_{\text{basic real constant}} \text{E} + \underbrace{30}_{\text{integer exponent}}$$

The general form of the E format code is:

$$Ew.d$$

where *w* represents the number of positions reserved for the data field, and *d* informs the system where to place the decimal point in the basic real constant in case no decimal point is entered in the input data field.

If there is no decimal point entered in the basic real constant, the basic real constant is adjusted (read) with *d* fractional digits (the decimal point is assumed *d* positions to the left of the character E in the field). This adjusted value is then raised to the specified integer exponent. If the decimal point is entered as part of the basic real constant, *d* is ignored and the basic real constant is raised to the specified integer power; *d* nevertheless must be included in the E format description.

*Example 1*

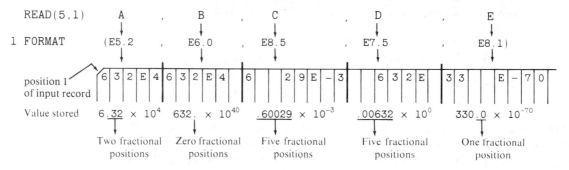

Note that blanks are treated as having value zero.

*Example 2*

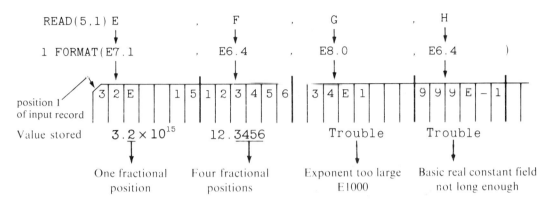

*Example 3*

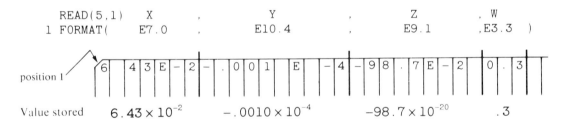

To avoid errors, the programmer should always try to right-justify numbers in their input fields. The exponent portion *must* be right-justified.

**Output of exponential numbers.** Any exponential number printed by E$w.d$ will generally have the following standardized output form:

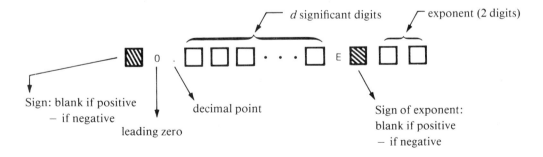

Hence the minimum print positions required to print a negative number with no significant digits is $-0. E-\square \square$, which means that $w$ must be greater than or equal to 7 to print the sign, the leading 0, the decimal point, the E, the sign of the exponent, and the two digits for the exponent. (If *w* is not large enough, some systems will not print the leading zero.) Consider the following examples:

| Value of Data Item in Memory | Output Format Code | Printed Value | Comments |
|---|---|---|---|
| 632000. | E10.3 | ƀ0.632Eƀ06 | Leading blank. |
| 632000. | E8.3 | .632Eƀ06 | No room for leading 0. |
| 632999. | E9.3 | 0.633Eƀ06 | Round off. |
| − .83247 | E12.5 | −0.83247Eƀ00 | Leading blanks and |
| − .83247 | E13.4 | ƀƀ−0.8325Eƀ00 | round off. |
| − .000004269 | E10.3 | −0.427E−05 | Round off. |
| − .000004269 | E10.1 | ƀƀ−0.4E−05 | Leading blanks. |
| − 98.5678 | E8.1 | −0.1Eƀ03 | Round off. |
| − 98.5678 | E8.0 | ƀ−0.Eƀ03 | No significant digits. |
| 123.4567 | E15.9 | ƀ.1234567ddEƀ03 | The digits dd are not significant if the system has 7 significant digits. |
| 3.256 | E8.4 | ******** | Missing at least one space. |

### 6-3-4 Do It Now

1. Write each of the following in exponential form.
   a. 13201.47      b. − 0.000327

2. Write each of the following as a basic real constant.
   a. 0.332E − 4      b. 0.034E4

3. If X = − 6324.705, what output would be produced by
   ```
       WRITE(6,11) X,X
    11 FORMAT(1X,E14.7,E14.3)
   ```

4. Suppose a data record containing the characters

   | − | | 3 | 2 | E | + | 4 | 1 | . | 3 | 2 | 4 |

   is read by the following statements:
   ```
       READ(5,12)Q,R
    12 FORMAT(E8.2,E5.2)
   ```
   What will be the values of Q and R?

5. Identify the output for the following fields and output fields:
   a. 3.162                E10.2
   b. − 0.12345678E04      E9.4
   c. − 0.12345678E4       E11.4
   d. 392.1E − 23          E10.2

### Answers

1.  a. .1320147E5
    b. − 3.27E − 4

2.  a.  0.0000332          b.  340.

3.  |–|Ø|.|6|3|2|4|7|Ø|5|E|  |Ø|4|  |  |  |  |  |–|Ø|.|6|3|2|E|  |Ø|4|

4.  Q = − 3200.
    R = 1.324

5.  a.  ⊘⊘Ø.32EⱮØ1                    c.  −Ø.1235EⱮØ4
    b.  Insufficient field width      d.  ⊘⊘Ø.39E−2Ø

## 6-3-5  Double Precision Numbers and the D Format Code

Some applications require a greater number of significant digits than can be maintained using real mode data. Many computers offer an extended version of floating-point data representation called *double precision*; it allows the retention of more significant digits. Figure 6–5 displays the number of significant digits available in double precision on certain computers.

Usually, the magnitude (exponent) of a real constant does not increase with double precision representation—only the number of digits in the fractional part is affected. (An exception is found in the Burroughs B6900/7900 systems, in which both the number of significant digits and the size of the exponent increase.) The only way to specify that a variable is in double precision mode is to declare the variable in a DOUBLE PRECISION statement. There is no implicit mode specification for double precision variables. The general form of the DOUBLE PRECISION statement is:

> DOUBLE PRECISION   *list of variables*

Each variable in the *list of variables* is assigned double precision mode. It should be noted that DOUBLE PRECISION affects *only real numbers, not integer numbers*. The double precision feature does not exist for integers. This does not mean that a variable name starting with I through M cannot be declared in a DOUBLE PRECISION list—such a variable would just represent a double precision real number.

*Example*

    DOUBLE PRECISION X,I
      X = 123456789012345.        Both X and I are double precision.
      I = .123456789012345D40     Exponential form using D instead of E.

FIGURE  6–5    DOUBLE PRECISION CHARACTERISTICS

| Computer | Word Length (Bits) | Exponent Range | Number of Significant Decimal Digits |
|---|---|---|---|
| TRS-80 II | 48 | $10^{38}$ to $10^{-38}$ | 10 |
| IBM 370/30xx/43xx | 64 | $10^{75}$ to $10^{-78}$ | 16 |
| Burroughs B6900 | 96 | $10^{29603}$ to $10^{-29581}$ | 24 |
| CDC Cyber 72 | 120 | $10^{308}$ to $10^{-308}$ | 33 |

DOUBLE PRECISION is a nonexecutable specification statement subject to the same restrictions as other specification statements.

Double precision constants can be represented in a basic form similar to the basic real constants, except that double precision constants will have more significant digits than can be stored in an ordinary floating-point word. For example, on IBM systems the constant 63217869.2, which contains more than seven significant digits, automatically becomes a double precision constant.

There is also an exponential form for double precision constants; it is analogous to the exponential form for real constants except that the character D is used in place of E.

*Example*

6.2D + 4 has value 62000.00...
− .0326798432156D − 4 has value − .00000326798432156

Double precision constants and variables can be mixed with real and integer constants and variables in any arithmetic expression. When any double precision operand and a non-double precision operand are involved in an arithmetic operation, the nondouble precision operand is converted to double precision. The operation is then carried out using double precision arithmetic, and the final result of the expression is a double precision number.

*Example*

```
DOUBLE PRECISION T,X
X = I*J/C**K + T
```

First C ∗∗K is performed in real mode.
Then I∗J is performed in integer mode.
Then (I∗J)/(C∗∗K) is performed in real mode.
Then (I∗J)/(C∗∗K) + T is performed in double precision.
Finally, the double precision result is stored in the double precision variable X.

If, in a replacement statement, a double precision value is to be placed into a real variable, significant digits may be lost. Consider the following example, which assumes that a real variable can hold at most seven significant digits:

| | *Results* |
|---|---|
| `DOUBLE PRECISION X,Y` | |
| `REAL A,B` | |
| `X = 1.23456789D3` | X will contain 1234.56789 |
| `A = X` | A will contain 1234.567 (no round off) |
| `Y = 999999999.D0` | Y will contain 999999999. |
| `B = Y` | B will contain 999999900. (no round off) |
| `I = 1.29456789D1` | I will contain 12 (no round off). |
| `J = Y` | J will contain 999999999 or fewer digits, depending on the number of significant digits. |

The D format code can be used for input/output of double precision data. The general form of the D format code is D*w.d*. The D format code is used in exactly the same as the E format code (section 6–3–3).

The F format code can also be used for double precision input and output, as in the following:

```
      DOUBLE PRECISION X,Y
      READ(5,1)X,Y
    1 FORMAT(F8.0,F10.4)
      WRITE(6,2)X,Y
    2 FORMAT(2X,F9.0,3X,D18.5)
```

Double precision data occupies more memory space than single precision real data. Operations performed on double precision operands take longer than the same operations with real arithmetic.

## 6-3-6 Do It Now

1. Determine the word length and other details of double precision data representation for the computer you are using.

2. Assuming an IBM system as described in the preceding pages, what output would be produced by each of the following:

   a.
   ```
         DOUBLE PRECISION X,Y
         X = 123.456789
         Y = 1.6D-4
         WRITE(6,14)X,Y
      14 FORMAT(1X,D14.7,D8.1)
   ```

   b.
   ```
         DOUBLE PRECISION QR,ST
         QR = 1.2DØ + (-.12E1)
         ST = .123456789D + 4
         UV = ST
         WRITE(6,15)QR,ST,UV
      15 FORMAT(1X,F4.Ø,D17.9,E16.9)
   ```

## Answers

2. (a) | | |Ø|.|1|2|3|4|5|6|8|D| |Ø|3| |Ø|.|2|D|-|Ø|3| | | | | | | | |

   (b) | | |Ø|.| | |Ø|.|1|2|3|4|5|6|7|8|9|D| |Ø|4|Ø|.|1|2|3|4|5|6|7|Ø|Ø|E| |Ø|4|

# 6-4  Logical Data

## 6-4-1  Logical Type Data and the L Format Code

We have already made extensive use of logical expressions, perhaps without your being aware of it. A logical expression can be thought of as a proposition (a statement that is either true or false). For example, the statement "I am 36 years old" is either true or false; similarly, the statement "X is greater than 63" is either true or false. We have already used expressions like these in IF statements. Syntactically, a FORTRAN logical expression can be defined as two arithmetic expressions or two character variables linked together by a relational operator (.GT., .GE., .LT., and so forth). Consider, for example the following elementary logical expressions whose values are either true or false:

|  | *Valid Logical Expression* | *Invalid Logical Expression* | |
|---|---|---|---|

```
      Valid Logical                    Invalid Logical Expression
       Expression
X .LT. 1.3              X + 23*Z            Is not true or false.
XAM .NE. Y              .LE. 100            Missing arithmetic expression.
(X+Y)**2 .EQ. 4.        (X .LT. Y) + Z      Logical values cannot be added.
2.*Y .GT. X-Y
NAME .LE. 'JONES'
```

Logical expressions, just like arithmetic expressions, can be processed in replacement statements and in IF statements. In either case, the logical expression is first evaluated and the result of this evaluation is one of the logical values .TRUE. or .FALSE. (these values are called *logical constants*), just as the evaluation of 3. + 5. results in the numerical value 8.0. These logical values, .TRUE. and .FALSE., can be stored in logical variables in the same way that arithmetic constants can be stored in variables. However, logical variables must be declared in a LOGICAL statement. The LOGICAL statement has the general form:

> LOGICAL    *variable list*

where *variable list* is a list of variable names.

*Example*

```
LOGICAL X,I,GUESS
```

X, I, and GUESS are now logical variables.

### Replacement Statements

Once a variable is declared LOGICAL, it can be assigned the values .TRUE. or .FALSE. through replacement statements, DATA statements or READ statements. It cannot, however, be assigned numeric or CHARACTER values. The general form for logical replacement statements is:

> *logical variable* = *logical expression*

The following code contains valid examples of logical replacement statements:

```
CHARACTER*5 LAST
LOGICAL A,B,C
DATA X,Y,B,LAST/4.,-2.,.TRUE.,'NEWS'/
A = .TRUE.              A is true. (.TRUE. is stored in A)
C = A                   C is true. (.TRUE. is stored in C)
B = X .LT. Y            B is false since    4 ≮ −2.
C = Y .NE. X**.5        C is true since   −2 ≠ 2.
B = (X + Y)**2 .EQ. 4.  B is true since    4 = 4.
C = 2.*Y .GT. X-Y       C is false since  −4 ≯ 6.
A = LAST .LE. 'NEW'     A is false since   S ≮ blank.
```

The following are examples of invalid logical replacement statements:

```
LOGICAL A,B,C
A = 2.1*X            Expression is arithmetic.
B = 2.*C             C is logical, 2. is numeric.
C = A + B            Cannot add two logical variables.
A = B .EQ. .TRUE.    Cannot compare two logical values.
C = A .LT. X         A is not numeric.
A = IF(X .LT. 4.)    Invalid logical expression, IF key word not allowed.
Z = .FALSE.          Z is not declared logical.
C = X.LT.Y + Z.GT.3. Cannot add logical values.
```

### Compound Logical Expressions

Sometimes it may be practical to create a more complex proposition by combining (*conjuncting*) elementary logical expressions. For example, it might be desirable to know whether "SEX is 1 and STATUS is 4" or "AGE is less than 18 or AGE is greater than 65." Such a combination of elementary logical expressions is called a *compound logical expression*. A compound logical expression can be defined as elementary logical expressions linked to one another by the logical operators .AND., .OR., and .NOT..

The effect of the logical operators on two logical expressions, $e_1$ and $e_2$, can be described as follows:

$e_1$ .AND. $e_2$    is .TRUE. if and only if $e_1$ and $e_2$ are both .TRUE..
$e_1$ .OR. $e_2$     is .TRUE. if either $e_1$ or $e_2$ (or both) are .TRUE..
.NOT. $e_2$          is .TRUE. if $e_2$ is .FALSE. (evaluate $e_2$ and negate it).

This can be illustrated in table form, as shown in Figure 6–6. Note that the .NOT. operator can only be connected to one logical expression.

**FIGURE 6–6**   TRUTH TABLES FOR LOGICAL OPERATORS

| $e_1$ | $e_2$ | $e_1$ .AND. $e_2$ | $e_1$ .OR. $e_2$ | .NOT. $e_1$ |
|---|---|---|---|---|
| .TRUE. | .TRUE. | .TRUE. | .TRUE. | .FALSE. |
| .TRUE. | .FALSE. | .FALSE. | .TRUE. | .FALSE. |
| .FALSE. | .TRUE. | .FALSE. | .TRUE. | .TRUE. |
| .FALSE. | .FALSE. | .FALSE. | .FALSE. | .TRUE. |

Some examples of compound logical expressions and their outcomes for X = 4, Y = 2, and Z = 2 are shown in the following table (assume X, Y and Z are integers).

| $e_1$ | Operator | $e_2$ | $e_1$ | $e_2$ | Outcome |
|---|---|---|---|---|---|
| X .GT. Y**.5 | .AND. | Y .EQ. Z | .TRUE. | .TRUE. | .TRUE. |
| X .LT. Z | .OR. | Y .NE. Z | .FALSE. | .FALSE. | .FALSE. |
| Y .LE. X | .OR. | Y+Z .LT. X | .TRUE. | .FALSE. | .TRUE. |
| X .GT. 5.1 | .AND. | X .EQ. 2*Z | .FALSE. | .TRUE. | .FALSE. |
|  | .NOT. | X .LT. Y+Z |  | .FALSE. | .TRUE. |

The values of compound logical expressions can be stored in logical variables. Consider the following examples:

```
LOGICAL A,B,C,D,E,F                           Logical Value Outcomes
CHARACTER T*1
DATA X,Y,T/3.,-2.3,'X'/
A = X.LT.Y .OR. T.GE.'Y'      A = .FALSE.   3 ≮ -2.3. and 'X' < 'Y'.
B = Y .LE. 20.                B = .TRUE.    -2.3 < 20.
C = A .AND. B                 C = .FALSE.   .FALSE. .AND. .TRUE. = .FALSE.
F = .NOT. X .LT. Y            F = .TRUE.    .NOT.X.LT.Y is same as X.GE.Y
D = A .OR. X .LT. 6           D = .TRUE.    since A is .FALSE. but X < 6 is .TRUE.
E = .NOT. C                   E = .TRUE.    since C is .FALSE..
F = A .AND. .NOT. B           F = .FALSE.   Both A and .NOT. B are .FALSE..
G = (.TRUE. .OR. .FALSE.) .AND. .TRUE.   G = .TRUE.   The expression is evaluated as .TRUE.
```

Some examples of invalid compound expressions are:

```
INTEGER X,Y,Z
LOGICAL A,B,C,CA
A = .NOT. X                   X is not logical
B = X + 1 .OR. Y + 6          X + 1 and Y + 6 are not logical expressions.
C = X .LT. Y + Z .GT. 3       Logical values cannot be added.
A = CA .OR. 'BUST'            BUST is not a logical value.
```

If more than one logical operator is used in a compound logical expression, parentheses may be used to specify which expression is to be evaluated first. Consider the logical expression $e_1$ .AND. $e_2$ .OR. $e_3$ with $e_1$ = .FALSE. and $e_2 = e_3$ = .TRUE.. Depending on the placement of parentheses, this logical expression could be interpreted two ways:

$$e_1 .\text{AND.} (e_2 .\text{OR.} e_3) = .\text{FALSE.}$$

or

$$(e_1 .\text{AND.} e_2) .\text{OR.} e_3 = .\text{TRUE.}$$

Since all of the arithmetic operations, arithmetic relation operations, and logical operations can appear in one expression, it becomes important to know the relative precedence (in the absence of parentheses) of the operations. This precedence or hierarchy of operations is summarized in the following table:

| Operation | Comment | Precedence |
|---|---|---|
| Grouping (parentheses) | Innermost parentheses first | Highest |
| Arithmetic operations. | According to usual rules of precedence. | |
| Arithmetic relations. | In order from left to right. | |
| (.LT.,.LE.,.GT.,.EQ.....) | | |
| .NOT. | Operates on expression to immediate right. | |
| .AND. | | |
| .OR. | | Lowest |

Parentheses can be used as necessary to change the implied precedence.

*Example 1*

Suppose X = 30 and Y = 40 are integers and A = .TRUE.

Arithmetic operations are performed first.

Arithmetic relations are evaluated next.

Logical operations last.

```
X + 2. .LT. Y .OR. Y .NE. 30. .AND. A
  32         40      40
        .TRUE.          .TRUE.      .TRUE.
                                .TRUE.
                .TRUE.
```

The above expression is evaluated as ((X + 2.).LT.Y) .OR. ((Y.NE.30).AND.A).

*Example 2*

Suppose X = 30, Y = 40, A = .TRUE. and B = .FALSE.

```
.NOT. (X + Y .LT. 100 .OR. A) .OR. B
         70
              .TRUE.
           .TRUE.
          .FALSE.
                              .FALSE.
```

## Logical Expressions and IF Statements

Any logical expression can be used in an IF statement, the general form of which is:

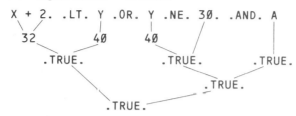

> IF (*logical expression*) *statement*
> IF (*logical expression*) THEN ...

If the value of *logical expression* is .TRUE., the statement or THEN statements is executed; if the value of *logical expression* is .FALSE., the statement following the IF or the ELSE statements are executed. Logical values cannot be compared to one another.

*Example*

```
Suppose X = 30, Y = 40
LOGICAL A,B,C
INTEGER X,Y
DATA B/.TRUE./
   .
   .
   .
IF(B) GO TO 30                  B is .TRUE., hence the branch to 30 is taken.
   .
   .
A = X .LT. Y                    A is .TRUE.; A .AND. B is TRUE.;
IF(A .AND. B)THEN               therefore C = .TRUE. is processed.
   C = .TRUE.
ELSE
   C = .FALSE
ENDIF                           X .GT. 100 is .FALSE.; .NOT. B is .FALSE.;
IF(X.GT.100. .OR. .NOT.B)GOTO7  therefore the next statement is executed.
```

## Input/Output of Logical Values: The L Format Code

Logical variables can participate in input/output statements. In order to assign a value to a logical variable via the READ or WRITE statements, the L format code must be used. The general form of the L code is:

where $w$ represents the field width.

When reading a logical variable, the system will scan the input field from left to right. If the first nonblank character is T, the value stored for the logical variable is .TRUE.; the value .FALSE. will be stored if no T is present. Any remaining characters in the field are ignored. On output, a T or an F is printed, depending on whether the variable is .TRUE. or .FALSE.. The character T or F is right-justified on the output field with $w - 1$ blanks to the left.

*Example*

```
        LOGICAL X,Y,Z
        READ(5,2)X,Y,Z
    2   FORMAT(L3,L1,L5)
        WRITE(6,2)X,Y,Z
        STOP
        END
```

The value of X and Z is .TRUE. and the value of Y is .FALSE..

### 6-4-2  Do It Now

1. Determine if the logical data type is supported by the compiler you are using.

2. What output would be produced by each of the following?

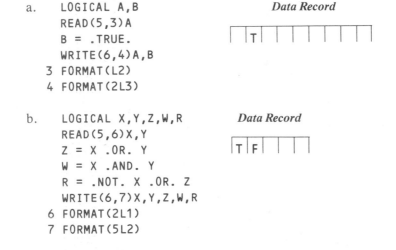

```
a.      LOGICAL A,B
        READ(5,3)A
        B = .TRUE.
        WRITE(6,4)A,B
    3   FORMAT(L2)
    4   FORMAT(2L3)
```

```
b.      LOGICAL X,Y,Z,W,R
        READ(5,6)X,Y
        Z = X .OR. Y
        W = X .AND. Y
        R = .NOT. X .OR. Z
        WRITE(6,7)X,Y,Z,W,R
    6   FORMAT(2L1)
    7   FORMAT(5L2)
```

3. A marriage proposal letter will be written when the following logical expression is .TRUE.. Under what conditions will the letter be written?

```
IF(HAIR.EQ.'BLOND' .AND. HEIGHT.GT.5.6 .OR. EARNIN.GT.100000.)THEN...
```

4. Assume X = 30., Y = 40., A = 1., and B = 4. Is the following statement true or false?

```
IF(.NOT. (X + Y .LT. 100 .OR. A .EQ. 1.) .AND. B .GT. 3.0) THEN...
```

5. Assume X = 3, Y = 2, Z = −1. Which of the following statements are valid?

```
a. IF((X + Y)**2 .LT. −1 .AND. Y .GT. Z) THEN...
b. IF(X − Y .EQ. 0.0 .OR. Z .AND. X .EQ. 0) THEN...
c. IF(−3.0 .LT. Z .OR. 1 .EQ. X) THEN...
d. IF( X + 1.0 .OR. Y + Z .GT. 3 ) THEN...
e. IF( X .NOT. .GT. 4. ) THEN...
f. IF( .NOT. (Y .NE. −1)) THEN...
```

## Answers

2.  a. 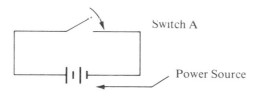   b.

3. A marriage proposal letter will be written under either of the following conditions:
    a. If earning exceeds $100,000
    b. If hair is blond and height is at least 5 foot 6

4. False

5.  a. Valid
    b. Invalid "Z.AND.X"   (Z or X are not logical values).
    c. Valid

    d. Invalid use of the .OR.
    e. Invalid .NOT. .GT.
    f. valid

## 6-4-3  A Programming Example: Switching Circuits

Consider an electrical circuit consisting of a power source and switches such as:

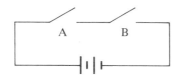

Switch A

Power Source

If the switch is up, no current travels through the circuit; if the switch is down, current flows through the circuit. Let us represent the switch A with a logical variable having value .TRUE. if the switch is down and .FALSE. if the switch is up.

Two switches can be arranged in series as:

A     B

In this case, current travels through the circuit only when both A and B are down. The expression A .AND. B represents the series circuit.

Two switches can also be arranged in parallel:

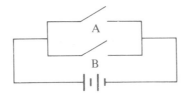

In this case, curre ⁺ travels through the circuit when either A or B (or both) are down. The expression A .OF   represents the parallel circuit.

It is possibl  ιo write logical expressions for any switching circuits:

*Examples*

| *Circuits* | *Logical Expressions* |
|---|---|

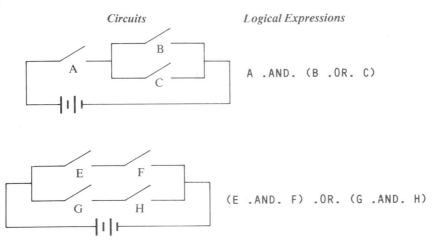

A .AND. (B .OR. C)

(E .AND. F) .OR. (G .AND. H)

The program shown in Figure 6–7 can be used to evaluate the above circuits for various values of the switches.

**FIGURE 6-7**    EVALUATION OF CIRCUIT EXPRESSIONS

```
    LOGICAL A,B,C,E,F,G,H,X,Y
  2 READ(5,1,END=10)A,B,C,E,F,G,H
    X = A .AND. (B. OR. C)
    Y = (E. AND. F) .OR. (G .AND. H)
    WRITE(6,3)A,B,C,X
    WRITE (6,4)E,F,G,H,Y
    GO TO 2
 10 STOP
  1 FORMAT(7L1)
  3 FORMAT(3X,'CIRCUIT1',3L2,'IS',L2)
  4 FORMAT(3X,'CIRCUIT2',4L2,'IS',L2)
    END
```

# 6-5 Complex Data

## 6-5-1 Definition and Form

A complex number is a number of the form:

$$a + bi \qquad \text{where } i = \sqrt{-1} \ (i^2 = -1) \text{ and } a, b \text{ are real numbers.}$$

real part   imaginary part

For example, the following are complex numbers:

$$4 + 3i$$
$$3.2 + (-4)i$$
$$-.6 + 70 \cdot i$$
$$3 \quad (3 + 0 \cdot i)$$

A FORTRAN complex constant is a number which is written as follows:

$$(a,b) \longleftarrow \text{parentheses required}$$

where $a$ and $b$ are real constants, with $a$ representing the real part of the constant and $b$ the imaginary part. Note the enclosing parentheses.

*Examples*

| *FORTRAN Constants* | *Value* |
|---|---|
| (4.,3.) | $4 + 3i$ |
| (3.2,-4.) | $3.2 + 4i$ |
| (24.3E-2,79.) | $.243 + 79i$ |
| (1.1E+10,.2E-3) | $11000000000 + .0002i$ |

The following examples are invalid complex constants:

| | |
|---|---|
| (Ø.,I) | I is not a constant. |
| 1.,1. | No parentheses. |
| (3115,3.4) | The real part is an integer. |
| (.ØØ4E+4,5.1D1Ø) | Difference in precision specification. |

Complex constants can be added, subtracted, multiplied, and divided as follows:

| | | |
|---|---|---|
| *Addition:* | $(a+bi) + (c+di)$ | $= (a+c) + (b+d)i$ |
| *Subtraction:* | $(a+bi) - (c+di)$ | $= (a-c) + (b-d)i$ |
| *Multiplication:* | $(a+bi) * (c+di)$ | $= (ac-bd) + (ad+bc)i$ |
| *Division:* | $(a+bi) / (c+di)$ | $= \dfrac{(ac+bd)}{c^2+d^2} + \dfrac{(bc-ad)}{c^2+d^2}i$ |

The absolute value of $(a+bi)$ is $\sqrt{a^2+b^2}$

Before a complex variable can be processed, it must be declared in the COMPLEX statement, which has the form:

| | |
|---|---|
| COMPLEX | *list of variable names* |

For example, COMPLEX A,B,X(10) specifies that A, B, and X of length 10 are complex variables.

Internally, each complex variable consists of two memory words, the first for the real part and the second for the imaginary part of the number. Complex expressions can be formed with complex constants in much the same way they are formed with real and integer constants. The result of evaluating an expression with a complex term is always a complex value.

*Examples*

```
REAL X
COMPLEX A,B,C
A = (2.,2.) + (0.,1.)
B = (5.,-1.)*2.
C = A + B - 5.
X = A - B
C = A*B
C = (3.,5.) - A
C = (A*B)/2.*(0.,1.)
C = A**2 - (2.,3.4)**3
C = (X,Z)
C = A + 2.
```

$A = 2 + 3i$
$B = 10 - 2i$
$C = 7 + i$
$X = -8.$ (X is real, the imaginary part is discarded.)
$C = 26 + 26i$
$C = 1 + 2i$
$C = -13 + 13i$
$C = 56.36 + 10.504i$
Invalid (X,Z not constants).
$C = 4 + 3i$

It should be noted that the exponent in a ** (exponentiation) operation cannot be complex; for example, 3.14**(1.,3.) is invalid. Additionally, complex numbers cannot be raised to a real power. Thus C = A**2. is invalid. However, complex numbers (expressions) can be raised to an integer power, i.e., C = A**2 is valid if A is complex.

Most FORTRAN libraries have complex functions available to the user to carry out COMPLEX operations. The following list shows the usually available COMPLEX functions:

| Functions | Arguments | Value | Meaning |
|---|---|---|---|
| REAL | 1 Complex | Real | Real $(a,b) = a$ $(a,b$ real constants) |
| AIMAG | 1 Complex | Real | Imaginary $(a,b) = b$ |
| CONJG | 1 Complex | Complex | Conjugate $(a,b) = (a, -b)$ |
| CABS | 1 Complex | Real | Absolute value $(a,b) = \sqrt{a^2 + b^2}$ |
| CSQRT | 1 Complex | Complex | Square root of $a + bi$ |
| CLOG | 1 Complex | Complex | Logarithm |
| CSIN | 1 Complex | Complex | Sine function |
| CCOS | 1 Complex | Complex | Cosine function |
| CEXP | 1 Complex | Complex | Exponential function |
| CMPLX | 2 Real | Complex | Cmplx $(a,b)$ refers to $a + bi$ |

A well-documented description of these functions is generally available in the FORTRAN technical reference manual for the particular computer system.

## Input/Output of Complex Variables

Input/output of complex variables requires two data descriptor format codes for each complex variable. The first format code describes the real part, and the second describes the imaginary part of the number.

*Example*

```
COMPLEX A,B,C
READ(5,1)  A ,       B
1 FORMAT(F4.0,F6.0,F3.2,F4.3)
```

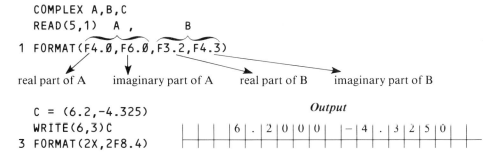

real part of A    imaginary part of A    real part of B    imaginary part of B

```
C = (6.2,-4.325)
WRITE(6,3)C
3 FORMAT(2X,2F8.4)
```

*Output*

| | | | | 6 | . | 2 | 0 | 0 | 0 | | − | 4 | . | 3 | 2 | 5 | 0 | | |

## 6-5-2  **Do It Now**

**1.** Determine if the complex data type is supported by the compiler you are using.

**2.** What output would be produced by each of the following?

a.
```
    COMPLEX A,B,C,D
    A = (-2.,3.)
    B = (1.,-2.)
    C = A + B
    D = (4.,2.)*A
    WRITE(6,11)A,B,C,D
11 FORMAT(1X,8F4.0)
```

b.
```
    COMPLEX A,B,C,D
    READ(5,12)A,B
12 FORMAT(4F2.0)
    C = CONJG(A)
    E = 4.0
    F = 6.0
    D = CMPLX(E,F)
    WRITE(6,13)A,B,C,D
13 FORMAT(1X,8F4.0)
```

*Data Record*

| − | 1 | | 3 | | 2 | − | 1 | | |

**3.** Compute the values for each of the following:

```
   REAL X
   COMPLEX C,Z
   A = 3.0
   B = -2.0
a. C = (-7.0, -4.0)/(2.0, 3.0)
b. Z = CMPLX(3.0,4.0) - CMPLX(A,B)
c. R = CABS((5.0, 12.0))
d. T = CMPLX(5.0 + 2.0, A+B)
e. X = (-.5, √ 3./2.)*(-.5, - √ 3./2.)
```

## *Answers*

**2.** a.  -2.  3.  1. -2. -1.  1.-14.  8.

b.  -1.  3.  2. -1. -1. -3.  4.  6.

**3.** a. $(-2.0, 1.0)$

b. $(0., 6.)$

c. 13.

d. $(7.0, 1.0)$

e. 1.

### 6-5-3 A Programming Example: Complex Roots of a Quadratic

The roots of $ax^2 + bx + c = 0$ are given by

$$x_1 = \frac{-b + \sqrt{b^2 - 4ac}}{2a} \qquad x_2 = \frac{-b - \sqrt{b^2 - 4ac}}{2a}$$

If $b^2 - 4ac \geq 0$, the values of $x_1$ and $x_2$ are real, otherwise, they are complex. The program shown in Figure 6–8 will determine the roots of the quadratic equation. If the solutions are real, the imaginary part of the roots will be zero (assume A1 $\neq$ 0).

FIGURE 6–8    COMPLEX ROOTS OF A QUADRATIC

```
      COMPLEX X1,X2,A1,B1,C1,D
    1 READ(5,2,END=10)A,B,C
      A1 = A
      B1 = B
      C1 = C
      D = CSQRT(B1**2 - 4.*A1*C1)        CSQRT requires complex arguments.
      X1 = (-B1 + D)/(2.*A1)
      X2 = (-B1 - D)/(2.*A1)
      WRITE(6,3)A,B,C,X1,X2
      GO TO 1
   10 STOP
    2 FORMAT(3F4.0)
    3 FORMAT(2X,'A=',F5.0,'B=',F5.0,'C=',F5.0,'X1=',2F7.3,'X2=',2F7.3)
      END
```

## 6-6    Probing Deeper

### 6-6-1 More on Floating-Point Numbers and Integers

Operations on floating-point data are performed using both the exponent and fractional part in much the same way that hand calculations are performed on numbers represented in scientific notation.

*Examples*

$$4.2 \times .003 = .42 \times 10^1 \times .3 \times 10^{-2} = (.42 \times .3) \times (10^1 \times 10^{-2}) = .126 \times 10^{-1}$$
$$4.2 + .003 = .42 \times 10^1 + .3 \times 10^{-2} = .42 \times 10^1 + .0003 \times 10^1 = .4203 \times 10^1$$

Much larger and much smaller numbers can be represented with floating-point than with fixed-point numbers. However, the number of significant digits is limited with floating-point representation. For example, on the IBM 370, 1000000999999999 is internally stored as 1000000000000000 since the computer can only retain seven significant digits. This really means that $10^{15} + 999,999,999 = 10^{15}$. Any operations performed on large magnitudes result in large *absolute errors*. For example, $10^{60} + 10^{52} = 10^{60}$, which means that $10^{52}$ is totally ignored. On the real number line there are gigantic gaps between the larger numbers. The number that immediately follows $10^{75}$ on the IBM 370 is $10^{75} + 10^{69}$, not $10^{75} + 1$ or even $10^{75} + 1,000,000,000,000$. The gap is $10^{69}$! In comparison, the numbers between 0 and 1 are extremely dense and well stocked.

The absolute error, such as the one above, is not as horrendous as one might suppose. After all, if the computer represents 1,000,000,400 as 1,000,000,000, the absolute error may be 400, but, relatively speaking, what is 400 compared to 1,000,000,400? Very little. For comparison, suppose the computer represented .6 as .5; then the absolute error would be .1, which is small, but, relatively speaking, an error of .1 in representing .6 is horrendous even though the absolute error is small. Hence we need another measure of error, the *relative error*, which may be more meaningful than the notion of absolute error.

The relative error of a computer-generated number is the absolute error divided by the computer approximation for that number. For example, if we have a true value of .00006 and a computer approximation of .00005, the absolute error is only $10^{-5}$ but the relative error is $.00001/.00005 = .2$ or 20%. If, on the other hand, we have a true value of 1,000,000,400 and an approximation of 1,000,000,000, the absolute error is 400 but the relative error is $400/1,000,000,000 = .4 \times 10^{-8}$ or nearly zero, percentagewise.

Fixed-point arithmetic is much faster than floating-point arithmetic, hence if execution time is critical it may be wise to use integer mode data and arithmetic whenever possible. There is some inherent error in the representation of data in floating-point schemes. During the number conversion process, some decimal numbers cannot be translated exactly into binary; for example, $0.1_{10}$ has no exact binary representation. The resulting binary value is an approximation of $0.1_{10}$ to within seven digits of accuracy (IBM). There are also other rational numbers that have no finite decimal or binary representation, such as $1./3. = 0.3333333$.

After any calculation, only a given number of digits are stored for the result. In a program with many calculations this error (called *round-off error*) may encroach on one or more of the digits of the calculated result, causing fewer than the anticipated number of digits to be correct. For example, on IBM systems

$1.0007*1.007 = 1.007705$      while by hand      $1.0007*1.007 = 1.0077049$.

There is a difference of only one digit in the sixth fractional position. However, if the result were to be multiplied by $10^{10}$, this would result in an absolute error of 1,000.

# 6-7 You Might Want to Know

1. Does FORTRAN support any other string functions not discussed in section 6–2?

   *Answer:* Many FORTRANs support the following functions (check with your reference manual).

   a. INDEX searches a string for a desired substring; it returns the starting position of the substring.

   ```
   K = INDEX('THE DOG','DO')      K = 5 i.e., DO starts at position 5 in the string.
   K = INDEX('THE CAT','DOG')     K = 0 i.e., DOG does not exist in the string.
   K = INDEX('YOU ARE ALL','A')   K = 5 picks up first occurrence of A.
   K = INDEX(LINE(3:12),' ')      searches characters 3 through 12 of LINE for a blank.
   ```

b. LEN returns the length of the string.

```
M = LEN('THE DOG')   M = 7
M = LEN(LINE)         M = length of string LINE
```

c. ICHAR (*character*)    Returns the integer value of the internal code representing *character*. See question 6 for internal character codes.

```
J = ICHAR('A')       J = 65   These values depend on the collating sequence.
K = ICHAR('D')       K = 68   If the ASCII code is used.
```

d. CHAR (*integer*)    Returns the character corresponding to the integer value in the collating sequence. See question **6** for collating sequence.

```
CHARACTER M
M = CHAR(65)          M will contain the character A, i.e., M = 'A'
```

Examples of uses of the ICHAR and CHAR functions are shown in section 9-4-9 chapter 9. Note that CHAR(ICHAR (*character*)) = *character* while ICHAR (CHAR (*integer*)) = *integer*.

2. What are "significant digits"?

*Answer:* Generally speaking, significant digits are those digits used to represent any number. Leading zeroes (before or after the decimal point) are not significant. For example:

1001.56   has six significant digits
0012.4    has three significant digits
.000315   has three significant digits ($.000315 = .315 \times 10^{-3}$)

Trailing zeroes may or may not be significant, depending on the context in which they are used. For example, in the set of measurements 10.5, 13.6, and 10.0, the number 10.0 has three significant digits. In a different set of measurements (11.356, 12.555, and 10.000) the number 10.000 has five significant digits; yet 10.0 = 10.000.

Computers represent numbers and carry out operations using a fixed number of significant digits, $n$, which depends on the computer's hardware. Any number or any result of an operation must then be expressed as accurately as possible with those $n$ digits.

Since computers cannot, in general, represent nonterminating decimal numbers exactly, those numbers are rounded off or truncated, depending on the computer. Rounding off a number to $n$ significant digits amounts to finding the closest approximation to that number with $n$ or fewer nonzero digits; this means discarding all digits to the right of the $n$th significant digit. If the first discarded digit is 5 or greater, 1 is added to the $n$th digit; otherwise, the $n$th digit is unchanged.

*Example*

The following numbers are rounded off to seven significant digits (as on IBM systems):

| | | |
|---|---|---|
| 41.239824 | rounded to 41.23982 | $= .4123982 \times 10^2$ |
| .0011145678 | rounded to .001114568 | $= .1114568 \times 10^{-2}$ |
| 315.00075 | rounded to 315.0008 | $= .3150008 \times 10^3$ |
| 1000001499999.98 | rounded to 1000001000000.00 | $= .1000001 \times 10^{13}$ |

In the last example, note the loss of precision in the final number representation (499,999!).

**3.** Does "significance" of digits imply accuracy of result? That is, if the computed result of an operation is carried out to seven significant digits, does this mean that the computer result represents the first seven digits of the true answer?

*Answer:* No. Significance and precision or accuracy of results are not synonymous. Consider the following example: Two carpenters must saw a board in seven equal parts. They use a computer for their calculations and it carries out operations to seven significant digits. Both carpenters feel very satisfied with the accuracy of their measurement of the board—40.01 and 39.89 inches respectively. A computer printout yields an answer of 5.715714 (40.01/7) and 5.698541 (39.89/7) for one-seventh of the board. The very presence of seven digits on the computer printout form might so overwhelm the carpenters that each might think that all seven of his/her digits must be correct. Yet the two results have only one digit in common! How many of these digits are then truly meaningful? One? Two? Precision depends on the accuracy of the measurements, not on the seven significant digits. Many programmers have blind faith in computer printouts; yet much of a computer's input data in real life deals with approximate measurements of weights, distances, temperatures, forces, and so forth. The number of significant digits will not affect the precision of results to any great extent. Hence results should always be interpreted with the greatest of care even if 15 digits are used to express a result and even if DOUBLE PRECISION is used.

If it is known that the input data are 100% accurate, then of course the number of significant digits used in carrying operations can affect the precision of the results. The reader might be interested in the subject of error analysis, which treats the effects of significant digits or roundoff on numerical operations.

**4.** It is true that most decimal numbers don't have an exact internal representation on the computer?

*Answer:* Yes. In fact 99.999...% of the numbers that we use in everyday life are not represented exactly on a computer; this is not surprising when we realize that the set of real numbers on a computer is finite. Numbers with small magnitudes have the best chance of being the most accurately represented on a computer. There are literally thousands and thousands more computer real numbers in the interval {0,1} than there are, say, in the interval between 100,000 and 100,001; and the interval or gap between any two successive computer real numbers widens dramatically as the numbers grow in magnitude. For example, on IBM systems the real number following 3,000,000,000 is 3,000,001,000, not 3,000,000,001 (using single precision).

It should be noted, however, that all *integers* are represented exactly in memory up to the number of significant digits allowed by the computer system (see Figure 6–3). Note also the difference in significant digits for real versus integer numbers (see Figures 6–3 and 6–4). Integers are represented exactly in memory because the integer conversion to binary is exact. In the case of floating-point number conversion, the fractional part generally does not convert exactly in binary; for example, $0.1_{10} = 0.00011001100..._2$, which must be truncated.

**5.** Does the DOUBLE PRECISION statement give me more significant digits for integer numbers?

*Answer:* No. The DOUBLE PRECISION statement affects only real numbers. There is no double precision for integers. If an integer variable is declared in a DOUBLE

PRECISION statement, that variable becomes automatically a real variable and should be described by an F, D, or E edit code in a READ/WRITE format.

6. What is the collation sequence for the alphanumeric characters that can be processed by CHARACTER related instructions?

*Answer:* There are two codes for internal representation of characters. The ASCII (pronounced Ask-ee) and EBCDIC (pronounced ebb-si-dic) code.

The EBCDIC code (Extended Binary Coded Decimal Interchange code) is a code where each character is represented internally using 8 bits; for example, the character A is C1 in hexadecimal or 11000001 in binary. The EBCDIC code is used by such computers as IBM, Digital PDP-11 series, and Amdahl.

The ASCII code (American Standard Code for Information Interchange) is a 7-bit code used by large computers and by most of the microcomputers.

The collating sequence for the two codes is shown as follows:

| ASCII Code | | | EBCDIC Code | | |
|---|---|---|---|---|---|
| *Character* | *Decimal* | *Hex* | *Character* | *Decimal* | *Hex* |
| space | 32 | 20 | space | 64 | 40 |
| ! | 33 | 21 | . | 75 | 4B |
| " | 34 | 22 | < | 76 | 4C |
| # | 35 | 23 | ( | 77 | 4D |
| $ | 36 | 24 | + | 78 | 4E |
| % | 37 | 25 | ! | 79 | 4F |
| & | 38 | 26 | & | 80 | 50 |
| single quote | 39 | 27 | $ | 91 | 5B |
| ( | 40 | 28 | * | 92 | 5C |
| ) | 41 | 29 | ) | 93 | 5D |
| * | 42 | 2A | ; | 94 | 5E |
| + | 43 | 2B | minus − | 96 | 60 |
| comma | 44 | 2C | / | 97 | 61 |
| − | 45 | 2D | comma | 107 | 6B |
| . | 46 | 2E | % | 108 | 6C |
| / | 47 | 2F | > | 110 | 6E |
| 0 | 48 | 30 | ? | 111 | 6F |
| ⋮ | ⋮ | ⋮ | : | 122 | 7A |
| 9 | 57 | 39 | # | 123 | 7B |
| : | 58 | 3A | @ | 124 | 7C |
| ; | 59 | 3B | single quote | 125 | 7D |
| < | 60 | 3C | = | 126 | 7E |
| = | 61 | 3D | " | 127 | 7F |
| > | 62 | 3E | a | 129 | 81 |
| ? | 63 | 3F | b | 130 | 82 |
| @ | 64 | 40 | ⋮ | ⋮ | ⋮ |
| A | 65 | 41 | z | 169 | A9 |
| ⋮ | ⋮ | ⋮ | A | 193 | C1 |
| Z | 90 | 5A | ⋮ | ⋮ | ⋮ |
| a | 97 | 61 | Z | 233 | E9 |
| ⋮ | ⋮ | ⋮ | 0 | 240 | F0 |
| Z | 122 | 7A | 9 | 249 | F9 |

Thus in EBCDIC the following is true:

special characters < letters of alphabet < digits 0-9

**7.** I need more significant digits than DOUBLE PRECISION can give me on the system that I use. What can I do?

*Answer:* You will have to write you own code. See exercises 9, 10 and 11, section 7-10-3, for some thoughts on this matter.

**8.** Was I surprised the other day when a result of $-0.$ was printed for my answer. I didn't know the computer used negative zeros!

*Answer:* Some do and some do not. But your result wasn't really $-0.$ Your FORMAT just didn't leave enough places to print additional fractional digits. For example:

```
    X = -.04
    WRITE (6,1)X          This statement would cause - 0.0 to be printed.
  1 FORMAT(2X,F4.1)
```

**9.** What is the advantage of using logical variables and logic processing?

*Answer:* Decisions can be expressed in a straightforward fashion, and use of logical variables saves both memory storage and processing time. Also, logical variables can be employed in Boolean algebra, which can be used as a mathematical tool or model in the study of sets, in the study of switching circuits, and in applications that make use of truth or decision tables.

**10.** Can I initialize logical variables in a DATA statement and can the IMPLICIT statement be used to declare DOUBLE PRECISION, LOGICAL and COMPLEX variables?

*Answer:* Yes on both counts!

*Example*

```
    IMPLICIT COMPLEX (W-Z), LOCICAL (D-H)
    IMPLICIT DOUBLE PRECISION (A,X-Z)
    LOGICAL X
    DATA X/.TRUE./
```

# 6-8 Exercises

### 6-8-1 Test Yourself

**1.** Specify the outcome of each condition (use collation tables in question 6, section 6-7):

    a. '1' .NE. '1'
    b. '100' .LT. '20'
    c. '<' .LT. '>'
    d. 'NEW YORK' .GT. 'NEWARK'
    e. '3' .GT. 'Z'
    f. 'THE'//'DOG' .LT. 'THE DOG'
    g. 'AXE' .LT. 'AX' .OR. '3' .EQ. '3'

**2.** Show the contents of each variable as a result of the following codes. Identify any errors.

```
    CHARACTER NAME*8,WORD*6, TEMP * 6
    CHARACTER*5 FIRST,LAST,MIDDLE
    WORD = 'SHE IS'
a.  NAME = 'SALLY MCGOON'
b.  FIRST = NAME(:6)
c.  LAST = NAME(6:)
d.  MIDDLE = NAME(1:2)//'L'//NAME(4:5)
e.  NAME(1:2) = NAME(7:)
f.  NAME(2:5) = 'NONO'//NAME(4:7)
g.  NAME = 'TALLYHO'
h.  TEMP = NAME(1:4)//NAME(3:)
i.  TEMP(3:) = WORD(1:2)//WORD(3:)
```

**3.** Show the contents of variable Z. Identify any errors.

```
    CHARACTER Z*5,A,B
a.  Z = 'A'//'B'//'ᵇᵇᵇC'
b.  A = '542'
    Z = A//'542'
```

**4.** Show the contents of each variable. Identify errors, if any.

```
    CHARACTER N*5
    N = 'MICHEL'
a.  N = N(5:5)//N(4:4)//N(3:3)//N(2:2)//N(1:1)
b.  N = '123456'
    N = N(1:)//N(2:)//N(3:)//N(4:)//N(5:)
```

**5.** Specify what the following coding segment does. Assume SEN is not all blanks.

```
    CHARACTER SEN*51,DUP*51
    SEN(51:51) = ' '
    DO 5 I = 50,1, -1
        IF(SEN(I:I) .NE. ' ') GO TO 6
  5 CONTINUE
  6 DUP = SEN(I + 1:)//SEN(:I)
```

**6.** What advantage is there in using double precision mode variables and constants? What is the price that you pay for double precision mode, however?

**7.** What restrictions are there on the placement of specification statements in FORTRAN programs?

**8.** Express each of the following exponential constants in basic form:

a.  3.2E–4

b.  .0034E10

c.  –132.4E6

d.  –132.4E–6

e.  432.4D2

f.  –163.94872D–10

g.  1632543.11D–8

h.  .0000324D15

9. What value will be stored for each of the following data items as a result of a READ operation? The result should be expressed as $0.ddddddd \times 10^{ee}$, where d and e are the significant digits and the decimal exponent, respectively.

| Input Data | READ FORMAT Code | Value Stored |
|---|---|---|
| a. 632E4 | E5.2 | |
| b. − .623E14 | E8.2 | |
| c. 1234E − 2 | E7.0 | |
| d. − 1234E − 5 | E8.2 | |
| e. 69.52D4 | D7.2 | |
| f. 000003241 | E9.3 | |
| g. − 00002561E4 | E11.4 | |
| h. 333.447E − 50 | E11.0 | |

10. What output will be produced for each of the following?

| Value in Memory | Output FORMAT Code | Output Results |
|---|---|---|
| a. .0032456 | E8.2 | |
| b. − 98.9437 | E15.1 | |
| c. .0032456 | E11.4 | |
| d. 31245.E − 31 | E15.2 | |
| e. − 12340000. | E13.4 | |
| f. − 12340000. | D16.7 | |
| g. − .0000006972 | E8.1 | |
| h. + 212.E + 26 | E7.1 | |
| i. 212.E26 | E6.1 | |
| j. 123.4567891 | E17.10 | |
| k. 123.4567891 | D16.8 | |

11. Are the following statements true or false?

   a. If X is real then X (:2) is a valid substring of X.
   b. DATA statements must be the first statements in a FORTRAN program.
   c. Specification statements are nonexecutable statements.
   d. The statement LOGICALISAM,SAM,KKK is valid.
   e. Double precision numbers provide twice as many significant digits as ordinary real constants.
   f. A real constant has the same internal representation as an exponential real constant.
   g. Double precision numbers also exist for integers.
   h. The statement DOUBLE PRECISION I,J,K is valid.
   i. The REAL statement may be used to define a double precision constant.
   j. The statement X = 12345678901134.56 causes X to become a double precision variable.
   k. Integers are always fixed in length in terms of memory representation. For instance, the constant 1 uses the same number of bits as 1234567
   l. Double precision always provides a greater number of significant digits and a greater range for the exponent.

m. The F, E, and D format codes can be used to read real numbers in nonexponential form.

n. The A format code can be used to read any data that can be read by an I,F,E or D format code.

o. The statement A(4:6) = A(2:4) is invalid while A(4:6) = A(1:3) is valid.

p. B = 'ALPHABET' followed by B(4:) = 'INE' gives B = 'ALPINEβ. β'.

q. Real numbers can be concatenated to yield double precision values.

r. Given CHARACTER P*4 it is valid to write P = P//P.

**12.** Which of the following statements are correct?

a. A + B could be a valid logical expression, depending on how A and B are specified.

b. X + Y.LT.5. is an elementary logical expression.

c. B.OR.10 is a compound logical expression.

d. A.NOT.B is an invalid, compound logical expression.

e. The value of A.AND.(.NOT.A) is .FALSE..

f. Y.AND.X could be a valid logical expression.

**13.** Evaluate each of the following logical expressions if A = 3.0, B = −4., and C = 0.

a. A .LT. B

b. .NOT. A .GT. 0.

c. B .LT. C .OR. A .LT. B

d. B .LE. C .AND. A .LT. B

e. C .GT. B .AND. (A .LE. 16.0 .OR. B .EQ. 4.)

f. .NOT.(A .GT. B .OR. C .EQ. 0.)

g. .NOT. A .GT. B .OR. C .EQ. 0.

h. A .EQ. B .AND. B .LT. C .OR. (.NOT. A .LT. B)

**14.** Determine the value of the following expressions, given A = .TRUE., B = .TRUE., C = .FALSE..

a. A.OR.B

b. .NOT.C

c. (A.OR.B).AND.C

d. .TRUE..OR.C

e. .TRUE..AND.C (read it quickly!)

f. .NOT.C.ÓR.B

**15.** Using compound statments write one IF-statement that will have the same effect as the statements below.

a.
```
    IF(J.GT.0)GO TO 20
      GO TO 30
 20 IF(J.LT.10)STOP
 30 ...
```

b.
```
    IF(X.GT.10.)GO TO 20
    IF(X.LT.0.)GO TO 20
      GO TO 30
 20 STOP
 30 ...
```

**16.** Write a LOGICAL expression involving two LOGICAL variables, A and B, which has the value .TRUE. if only A is .TRUE. or if only B is .TRUE. and which has the value .FALSE. if both A and B are .TRUE. or both are .FALSE.. (This expression is called the *exclusive or*.)

**17.** Represent each of the following circuits with a logical expression.

a.

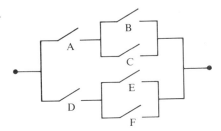

b.

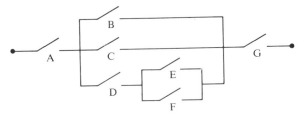

c.

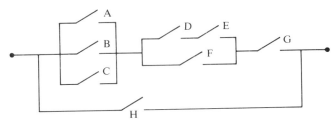

d.

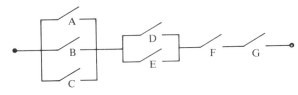

e.

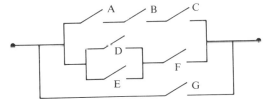

**18.** Which of the following are valid complex constants:

   a.  (0.0)           c.  (12.3, $-1.2E-3$)

   b.  (6,4)             d.  (X,Y)

**19.** Determine the values of the following expressions:

   a.  2.*(1.4, $-3.7$)       c.  C*(1.,0.) + D*(0., +1.) where C = 2., D = $-3$.

   b.  (0.,1.)**2          d.  A*(1., $-1$) where A = (2., $-3$.)

**20.** Write the code to print all characters recognized by FORTRAN (Hint: use CHAR).

## 6-8-2 Programming Problems

1. Write a program to list the content of a file containing records of length 80.

2. A file contains two fields per record: a name and marital status code (1 = single, 2 = married, 3 = divorced, 4 = widowed). Produce a listing (using *only* one PRINT* statement or only one FORMAT) of the names and their corresponding alphabetic marital status.

   *Example*

   | Output | | Input | |
   |--------|--------|--------|--------|
   | JONES | MARRIED | JONES | 2 |
   | SALEM | SINGLE | SALEM | 1 |

3. In a physical education class, students get either a pass or a fail for the course. If the average of the student's three test scores is below 70, the student fails the course. The student's three test scores are recorded on records, as follows:

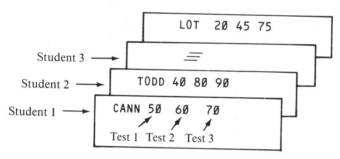

Student 3 → 

Student 2 → TODD 40 80 90

Student 1 → CANN 50  60  70

Test 1  Test 2  Test 3

Write a program to produce the following output:

| STUDENT | TEST1 | TEST2 | TEST3 | AVERAGE | FINAL GRADE |
|---------|-------|-------|-------|---------|-------------|
| CANN | 50 | 60 | 70 | 60 | FAIL |
| TODD | 40 | 80 | 90 | 70 | PASS |
| . | . | . | . | . | . |
| . | . | . | . | . | . |
| . | . | . | . | . | . |
| LOT | 20 | 45 | 75 | 46 | FAIL |

```
THE PERCENTAGE OF STUDENTS WHO FAILED IS XXX.X
HIGHEST AVERAGE WAS OBTAINED BY TODD
(HIGHEST AVERAGE WAS ALSO OBTAINED BY OTHER STUDENTS)
```

Message is printed if appropriate.

4. Omega Triple Pooh sorority girls are very selective about their blind dates. The house-mother keeps a record file of characteristics of the members of the local fraternities. Each record contains an age code describing the following attributes:

| Complexion | Build | Personality |
|------------|-------|-------------|
| fair (1) | tall (1) | meticulous (1) |
| dark (2) | medium (2) | timid (2) |
| olive (3) | small (3) | aggressive (3) |

All dates must satisfy the following conditions:

a. tall but not dark, and between the ages of 20 and 30 or

b. medium or small build, but neither meticulous nor with olive complexion, and either under 18 or over 28

c. but under no circumstances small and aggressive and over 75, or timid and tall and under 19.

Write the code to perform the "blind date" selection for the Pooh girls by counting the number of potential dates.

5. Each record of an input file consists of the following six items:

| Item | Description/code |
|------|------------------|
| 1. Marital status | (1 = single, 2 = married, 3 = divorced, 4 = widowed) |
| 2. Sex | (1 = female, 2 = male) |
| 3. Age | (1 = over 30, 2 = under 30) |
| 4. Contentment | (1 = happy, 2 = unhappy) |
| 5. Family name | |
| 6. First name | |

For example, an input record might appear as

| Marital status | Sex | Age | Contentment | |
|:---:|:---:|:---:|:---:|:---:|
| 2 | 2 | 1 | 2 | Oaks Zan |

Write a program using only *one* PRINT/WRITE statement to transcribe this data into sentences with the following structure:

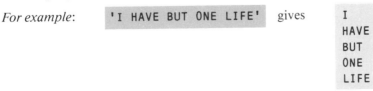

$$\textit{first name  family name}\ \text{IS} \left\{ \begin{matrix} \text{OVER 30} \\ \text{UNDER 30} \end{matrix} \right\}. \left\{ \begin{matrix} \text{SHE} \\ \text{HE} \end{matrix} \right\} \text{IS} \left\{ \begin{matrix} \text{SINGLE} \\ \text{MARRIED} \\ \text{DIVORCED} \\ \text{WIDOWED} \end{matrix} \right\} \text{AND} \left\{ \begin{matrix} \text{HAPPY} \\ \text{UNHAPPY} \end{matrix} \right\}$$

For example, given the above input record the program should produce the following sentence:

```
ZAN OAKS IS OVER 30. HE IS MARRIED AND UNHAPPY.
```

6. a. Write a program to read a sentence and list each word on a separate line.

*For example*:     `'I HAVE BUT ONE LIFE'`   gives
```
I
HAVE
BUT
ONE
LIFE
```

b. Write the code to extract all blank spaces from a sentence to form one string. Given the above example, we get   `IHAVEBUTONELIFE`.

7. The following string contains a sentence without spaces between words, where the first word is 1 character long, the second word is 2 characters long, the third word is 3 characters long, ..., up to the ninth word which is 9 characters long.

    ```
    SENT = 'IAMTOOMUCHTIREDEATINGSAUSAGEAMERICANJALAPINOS'
    ```

    a. Print each word on a separate line.
    b. Separate each word by a blank space and print the entire sentence on one line.

8. You may have received personalized form letters like the one shown below. Write a program to read sets of names dates and addresses and produce individualized letters similar to the following: (within the letter, words should be separated from one another by only one blank space).

    ```
    THE COCOZZAS
    6501 S 19 AVE
    PENSACOLA
    FLORIDA              AUGUST 12 1984

    DEAR MR AND MRS COCOZZA

    ONLY YOU HAVE BEEN SELECTED IN THE PENSACOLA AREA TO APPLY FOR OUR
    ONCE IN A LIFETIME SPECIAL ALUMINUM SIDING BARGAIN OF THE YEAR.
    THE COCOZZA FAMILY SHOULD INDEED REJOICE IN HAVING THEIR CHARMING
    HOME AT 6501 S 19 AVE RESTYLED WITH THE FINEST MATERIAL FROM FLORIDA.

                            SINCERELY


    THE DELLA TROCES
    11 N 123 ST.
    AMARILLO             JULY 12 1984
    TEXAS

    DEAR MR AND MRS DELLA TROCE

    ONLY YOU HAVE BEEN SELECTED IN THE AMARILLO AREA TO APPLY FOR OUR
    ONCE IN A LIFETIME SPECIAL ALUMINUM SIDING BARGAIN OF THE YEAR.
    THE DELLA TROCE FAMILY SHOULD INDEED REJOICE IN HAVING THEIR CHARMING
    HOME AT 11 N 123 ST. RESTYLED WITH THE FINEST MATERIAL FROM TEXAS.
                            SINCERELY
    ```

9. Read a paragraph of five lines and determine the number of occurrences of the word "is". Be sure to ignore occurrences of the string "is" imbedded in other words such as "th*is*."

10. Each record of a class roster consist of a name entry typed as follows:

    *first-name    middle-initial    last-name*

    where one or more blank spaces separate each item. Write the code to read a class roster to produce a new class roster, edited as follows:

    *last-name,    first-name    middle-initial.*

    For example:    SUEbbLbbbDOE    gives    DOE,bSUEbL.

11. To facilitate transmission, words in telegrams are usually separated by slashes (/). Regenerate the original line of a telegraph message by substituting blanks wherever slashes appear.

12. Do the same problem as in exercise 11, but now compute the cost of the telegram. Each word up to and including the twentieth word costs 15 cents; thereafter, each word costs 12 cents.

13. Addresses in telegrams are transmitted serially. A double slash indicates a new line. Read five such addresses and recreate them as envelope addresses.

    *Example:* 1301/NORTH12TH/AVE//ATLANTA//GEORGIA/ 75603//

14. Write a program to convert military time to civilian time.

    *Example:* 1818 should produce THE TIME IS 18 PAST 6 PM
    1545 should produce THE TIME IS 15 BEFORE 4 PM

15. Write a program to convert civilian time to 24-hour time. Civilian time should contain only the key words P.M. and A.M. The format for the input is

$$\text{hours, minutes, } \begin{Bmatrix} \text{``PM''} \\ \text{``AM''} \end{Bmatrix}$$

    *Example:* 2 15 PM should produce 1415.

16. Translate dates expressed numerically into the usual month, day, and year representation.

    *Example:* 11/07/84 should produce NOVEMBER 7 1984

17. Determine the number of syllables in a word; in a sentence.

18. Determine the number of sentences and words in a paragraph (The end of sentence identifiers are: . ? ! .).

19. A palindrome is a sequence of characters that is the same read from left to right as from right to left. For example 22, 303, 111 and 4224 are examples of palindromes. Write a program to generate all 2-digit, 3-digit, and 4-digit palindromes.

20. Write a program to determine if a number accepted as input is a palindrome.

21. Write a program to determine if a character string accepted as input is a palindrome.

22. Write a program to determine whether the following logical equations are always satisfied regardless of the values of A, B, and C.

    a. .NOT. (A .AND. B) = .NOT. A .OR. (.NOT. B)
    b. A .OR. (B .AND. C) = (A .OR. B) .OR. (A .OR. C)
    c. .NOT.(A .AND. B) .OR. A = .TRUE.
    d. A .AND. B .OR.(.NOT. A .AND. C) =
       .NOT. A .AND. (.NOT. B) .AND. C .OR. A .AND. B .AND. (.NOT. C) .OR. B .AND. C

    Exercise a can be partially verified by observing that if A = .TRUE. and B = .FALSE. then:

    .NOT.(.TRUE..AND..FALSE.) = .NOT..TRUE..OR.(.NOT..FALSE.)
    .NOT.(.FALSE.)            = .FALSE..OR..TRUE.
         .TRUE.               = .TRUE.

The results for other combinations of A and B remain to be shown. A table of all the possible values that A, B, and C can assume is constructed as follows:

| A | B | C |
|---|---|---|
| .FALSE. | .FALSE | .FALSE. |
| .FALSE. | .FALSE. | .TRUE. |
| .FALSE. | .TRUE. | .FALSE. |
| .FALSE. | .TRUE. | .TRUE. |
| .TRUE. | .FALSE. | .FALSE. |
| .TRUE. | .FALSE. | .TRUE. |
| .TRUE. | .TRUE. | .FALSE. |
| .TRUE. | .TRUE. | .TRUE. |

Prepare eight data records with three items on each (the first record contains F,F,F; the second record contains F,F,T, and so forth) and write the code to determine whether parts a,b,c, and d are true. If any equation does not hold true, write the values of A, B, and C for which the equation does not hold true.

23. A resistor network using standard EIA resistors consists of 3 meshes as shown in the schematic diagram below. 1000 volts D.C. is impressed across the input. The values of the various resistors are shown on the schematic diagram. Assume the wattage rating of the resistors is adequate. Write a program to calculate the total current, in amperes, supplied by the 1000 volt supply to the network.

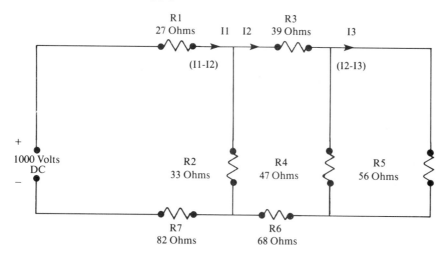

Use Cramers rule to solve for I1, I2, and I3 using

$$aI1 + dI2 + gI3 = j$$
$$bI1 + eI2 + hI3 = k$$
$$cI1 + fI2 + iI3 = l$$

$$I1 = \frac{\begin{vmatrix} j & d & g \\ k & e & h \\ l & f & i \end{vmatrix}}{\begin{vmatrix} a & d & g \\ b & e & h \\ c & f & i \end{vmatrix}} \quad I2 = \frac{\begin{vmatrix} a & j & g \\ b & k & h \\ e & l & i \end{vmatrix}}{\begin{vmatrix} a & d & g \\ b & e & h \\ c & f & i \end{vmatrix}} \quad I3 = \frac{\begin{vmatrix} a & d & g \\ b & e & h \\ c & f & i \end{vmatrix}}{\begin{vmatrix} a & d & g \\ b & e & h \\ c & f & i \end{vmatrix}}$$

where the determinant $\begin{vmatrix} a & d & g \\ b & e & h \\ c & f & i \end{vmatrix} = a(e \cdot i - f \cdot h) - d(b \cdot i - c \cdot h) + g(b \cdot f - c \cdot e)$

**24.** The effect of round-off using floating-point arithmetic can be demonstrated as follows: Suppose we are working with a decimal machine capable of storing four significant digits. Suppose further that we wish to perform the following computation:

$$2000 + .1 = .2000 + 10^4 + .1000 \times 10^0.$$

When an addition is to be performed and the exponents are not equal, the fractional part of the variable having the smaller exponent is shifted to the right and the exponent is increased until it is equal to the larger exponent. Thus:

$$.1000 \times 10^0 = .00001 \times 10^4$$

and $\quad .2000 \times 10^4 + .00001 \times 10^4 = (.2000 + .00001) \times 10^4 = .200001 \times 10^4.$

However, the machine can store only four digits; hence the digits calculated must either be rounded or truncated (some machines do it one way, some another) to four digits. In either case, the value stored for this example will be $.2000 \times 10^4$. Devise an experiment to show this effect using your computer. Can you determine whether your machine rounds or truncates when storing a floating-point value?

**25.** Floating-point arithmetic does not obey all of the usual rules of real numbers. In particular, the associative property does not hold. For example, consider the four-digit based, floating-point machine described in Exercise 28, and suppose that truncation is performed. Let us evaluate $(2000. + .4) + .6$ and $2000. + (.4 + .6)$.

$$
\begin{aligned}
(2000. + .4) + .6 &= (.2000 \times 10^4 + .4000 \times 10^0) + .6000 \times 10^0 \\
&= (.2000 \times 10^4 + .00004 \times 10^4) + .6000 \times 10^0 \\
&= (.20004 \times 10^4) + .6000 \times 10^0 \\
&= (.2000 \times 10^4) + .6000 \times 10^0 \qquad \text{Truncation occurs.} \\
&= (.2000 + .00006) \times 10^4 \\
&= .20006 \times 10^4 \\
&= .2000 \times 10^4 \qquad \text{Truncation occurs.}
\end{aligned}
$$

$$
\begin{aligned}
2000. + (.4 + .6) &= .2000 \times 10^4 + (.4000 \times 10^0 + .6000 \times 10^0) \\
&= .2000 \times 10^4 + (.1000 \times 10^1) \\
&= .2000 \times 10^4 + .0001 \times 10^4 \\
&= (.2000 + .0001) \times 10^4 \\
&= .2001 \times 10^4
\end{aligned}
$$

Devise an experiment to show that the associative property does not hold for floating-point arithmetic on your machine.

## 6-8-3 Answers to Test Yourself

**1.** a. F    b. T    c. T    d. F    e. Depends on code    f. F    g. T

**2.** 

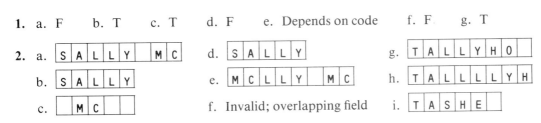

3. a. | A | B |   |   |   |     b. | 5 | 5 | 4 | 2 |   |

4. a. | E | H | C | I | M |     b. | 1 | 2 | 3 | 4 | 5 |

5. Trailing blanks of sentence now become leading blanks. For example:

| H | E |   | I | S |   |   |   | becomes |   |   |   | H | E |   | I | S |

6. Double precision mode allows more significant digits to be computed but takes more time to compute and more space to store each value.

7. Specification statements must precede executable statements. IMPLICIT statements come first.

8. a. 0.00032
   b. 34000000
   c. − 132400000
   d. − .0001324
   e. 43240
   f. − .000000016394872
   g. 0.0163254311
   h. 32400000000

9. a. $0.6320000 \times 10^5$
   b. $-0.6230000 \times 10^{14}$
   c. $0.1234000 \times 10^2$
   d. $-0.1234000 \times 10^{-3}$
   e. $0.6952000 \times 10^6$
   f. $0.3241000 \times 10^1$
   g. $-0.2561000 \times 10^4$
   h. $0.3334470 \times 10^{-47}$

10. a. Ø.32E-Ø2
    b. _____-Ø.1E_Ø3
    c. _Ø.3246E-Ø2
    d. _____Ø.31E-26
    e. ___-Ø.1234E_Ø8
    f. ___-Ø.1234ØØØD_Ø8
    g. -Ø.7E-Ø6
    h. Ø.2E_29
    i. .2E_29
    j. _Ø.1234567891E_Ø3
    k. __Ø.12345679D_Ø3

11. a. F.   b. F.   c. T.   d. T.   e. F.   f. T.
    g. F.   h. T.   i. F.   j. F.   k. T.   l. F.
    m. T.   n. T.   o. T.   p. T.   q. F.   r. T.

12. a. F.   b. T.   c. F.   d. T.   e. T.   f. T.

13. a. F.   b. F.   c. T.   d. F.   e. T.   f. F.
    g. T.   h. T.

14. a. T.   b. T.   c. F.   d. T.   e. F.   f. T.

15. a. IF(J.GT.Ø AND.J.LT.1Ø)STOP
    b. IF(X.GT.1Ø.OR.X.LT.Ø.)STOP

16. (A.AND.(.NOT.B)).OR.((.NOT.A).AND.B)

17. a. A.AND.(B.OR.C).OR.D.AND.(E.OR.F)
    b. A.AND.(B.OR.C.OR.(D.AND.(E.OR.F))).AND.G
    c. ((A.OR.B.OR.C).AND.((D.AND.E).OR.F).AND.G).OR.H
    d. (A.OR.B.OR.C).AND.(D.OR.E).AND.F.AND.G
    e. (A.AND.B.AND.C).OR.((D.OR.E).AND.F).OR.G

18. a. Invalid.   b. Invalid.   c. Valid.   d. Invalid.

19. a. (2.8, − 7.4).   b. (− 1.0, 0.0).   c. (2.0, − 3.0).   d. (− 1.0, − 5.0).

20. Print CHAR(I) as I varies from 1 to 255.

# one-dimensional arrays and the dimension statement

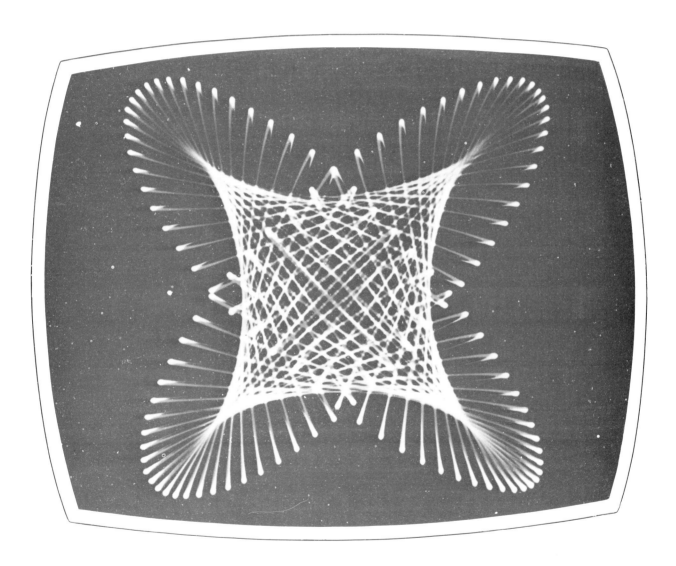

CHAPTER SEVEN

# one dimensional arrays and the dimension statement

## 7-1  Arrays

### 7-1-1  Background and Justification

Some problems can only be solved with the use of arrays; consider the following examples.

*Example 1*

> Suppose an input file consists of five records, where each record contains a grade. We want to print the difference between each grade and the average. Computing the average of the grades poses no problem: each time a grade G is read, it can be accumulated into a variable S through the statement S = S + G. But a problem arises when the average has been computed and it is time to determine the difference between each grade and the average. The grades that have been read are no longer in memory, since only one variable G was used to successively store the grades.
>
> Determining the difference between each grade and the average requires the computer to remember (store) the grades as they are read, so that after the average is computed, the computer can remember (retrieve) each grade one at a time and compute the difference between it and the average. The computer can remember these grades only it if stores them in different memory locations, i.e., if each grade is provided with a separate name, as shown in Figure 7–1. The code in Figure 7–1 is laborious and impractical because each grade is individually processed; what would happen if the input file consisted of 100 grades or, even worse, an unknown number of grades?

A more convenient approach would be to design a system or a notation that would create a table of five scores, store that table in the memory of the computer, and then be able to refer to any grade in the table by its position in the table (i.e., the first one, the second one, and so forth). For example, we could designate G(3) to mean the third grade in the table G, or G(I) to be the fourth grade if I were set to 4. With this capability, we could then index the table, allowing us to access successive entries of the table simply by manipulating the index I (for example, adding 1 to I to "get to" the next table element). With such an indexing mechanism, a word problem such as "Given a table of 100 grades, determine how many of those grades exceed 90" could be restated as "Determine the number of times G(I) is greater than 90 as I varies from 1 to 100".

*Example 2*

> Another problem that would be difficult to solve without tables is this: Given the tax table shown in Figure 7–2, write a program to compute the amount of tax owed on an adjusted gross income read from an input record.

The problem is, how can the computer compute the tax if it doesn't have the tax tables in its memory? This type of problem obviously requires a data structure different from any we have encountered so far. One approach might be to create an amount table (A), a tax table (T), and a percent over table (V), as shown in Figure 7–3, and store these in memory.

**FIGURE 7-1**    AVERAGE AND DEVIATION WITHOUT AN ARRAY

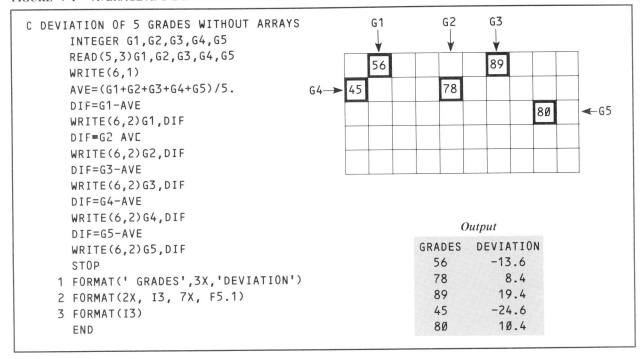

```
C DEVIATION OF 5 GRADES WITHOUT ARRAYS
      INTEGER G1,G2,G3,G4,G5
      READ(5,3)G1,G2,G3,G4,G5
      WRITE(6,1)
      AVE=(G1+G2+G3+G4+G5)/5.
      DIF=G1-AVE
      WRITE(6,2)G1,DIF
      DIF=G2 AVE
      WRITE(6,2)G2,DIF
      DIF=G3-AVE
      WRITE(6,2)G3,DIF
      DIF=G4-AVE
      WRITE(6,2)G4,DIF
      DIF=G5-AVE
      WRITE(6,2)G5,DIF
      STOP
    1 FORMAT(' GRADES',3X,'DEVIATION')
    2 FORMAT(2X, I3, 7X, F5.1)
    3 FORMAT(I3)
      END
```

*Output*

| GRADES | DEVIATION |
|--------|-----------|
| 56 | -13.6 |
| 78 | 8.4 |
| 89 | 19.4 |
| 45 | -24.6 |
| 80 | 10.4 |

**FIGURE 7-2**    A TAX TABLE

| Adjusted Income | But Not Over— | Tax | Of the Amount Over— |
|-----------------|---------------|-----|---------------------|
| $1,000 | $2,000 | $140 + 15% | $1,000 |
| $2,000 | $3,000 | $290 + 16% | $2,000 |
| $3,000 | $4,000 | $450 + 17% | $3,000 |
| $4,000 | $8,000 | $620 + 19% | $4,000 |
| $8,000 | $12,000 | $1,380 + 22% | $8,000 |
| $12,000 | $16,000 | $2,260 + 25% | $12,000 |
| $16,000 | $20,000 | $3,260 + 28% | $16,000 |
| $20,000 | $24,000 | $4,380 + 32% | $20,000 |
| $24,000 | $28,000 | $5,660 + 36% | $24,000 |
| $28,000 | $32,000 | $7,100 + 39% | $28,000 |
| $32,000 | $36,000 | $8,660 + 42% | $32,000 |
| $36,000 | $40,000 | $10,340 + 45% | $36,000 |
| $40,000 | $44,000 | $12,140 + 48% | $40,000 |
| $44,000 | $52,000 | $14,060 + 50% | $44,000 |
| $52,000 | $64,000 | $18,060 + 53% | $52,000 |
| $64,000 | $76,000 | $24,420 + 55% | $64,000 |
| $76,000 | $88,000 | $31,020 + 58% | $76,000 |
| $88,000 | $100,000 | $37,980 + 60% | $88,000 |
| $100,000 | $120,000 | $45,180 + 62% | $100,000 |
| $120,000 | $140,000 | $57,580 + 64% | $120,000 |
| $140,000 | $160,000 | $70,380 + 66% | $140,000 |
| $160,000 | $180,000 | $83,580 + 68% | $160,000 |
| $180,000 | $200,000 | $97,180 + 69% | $180,000 |
| $200,000 | ..... | $110,980 + 70% | $200,000 |

**FIGURE 7-3**    TABLES A, T, AND V

| Adjusted Income | But Not Over— | Tax | Of the Amount Over— |
|-----------------|---------------|-----|---------------------|
| $1,000 | $2,000 | $140 + 15% | $1,000 |
| $2,000 | $3,000 | $290 + 16% | $2,000 |
| $3,000 | $4,000 | $450 + 17% | $3,000 |
| $4,000 | $8,000 | $620 + 19% | $4,000 |
| $8,000 | $12,000 | $1,380 + 22% | $8,000 |
| $12,000 | $16,000 | $2,260 + 25% | $12,000 |
| $16,000 | $20,000 | $3,260 + 28% | $16,000 |
| $20,000 | $24,000 | $4,380 + 32% | $20,000 |
| $24,000 | $28,000 | $5,660 + 36% | $24,000 |
| $28,000 | $32,000 | $7,100 + 39% | $28,000 |
| $32,000 | $36,000 | $8,660 + 42% | $32,000 |

| Amount (A) | Tax (T) | Over (V) |
|-----------|---------|----------|
| $1,000 | $140 | .15 |
| $2,000 | $290 | .16 |
| $3,000 | $450 | .17 |
| $4,000 | $620 | .19 |
| $8,000 | $1,380 | .22 |
| $12,000 | $2,260 | .25 |
| $16,000 | $3,260 | .28 |
| $20,000 | $4,380 | .32 |
| $24,000 | $5,660 | .36 |
| $28,000 | $7,100 | .39 |

A(5)

$9,800 gross → $8,000    $1,380 ← T(5)    .22 ← V(5)

Then, for example, we could compute the tax due on an adjusted income of $9,800 by successively comparing $9,800 with the first, second, third, … entries of Table A until an entry is found that is larger than 9800—in this case, the sixth entry of table A or A(6). The tax due on $9,800 would then be:

Due = $1,380 + 22% over $8,000

Due = 5th entry of Tax + 5th entry of Percent over * (9800 − 5th entry of amount)

D =        T(5)         +            V(5)         * (9800 −        A(5))

The last statement is actually the correct FORTRAN expression to compute the tax due.

The examples just described require the use of tables. In FORTRAN and in most non-business programming languages, such tables are called *arrays*.

### 7-1-2  Definition

An array is a sequence of consecutive memory locations in which entries (numbers or character data) can be stored. In essence, it is a chunk of memory that can be sliced into a certain number of memory locations as specified by type statements such as the REAL, INTEGER, CHARACTER, DOUBLE PRECISION, and LOGICAL statements. The type statement specifies the name of the array and its size (the number of entries in the array). For example, INTEGER GRADE(5) means reserve five memory locations called GRADE(1), GRADE(2), GRADE(3), GRADE(4), and GRADE(5). Each element of the array can be referred to by specifying the name of the array and the element's position (subscript).

Internally these five locations are equal in length. In fact, there is no internal difference between GRADE(2), which is called a subscripted variable, and a variable such as X, which is just called a variable. They are the same size, and they can hold the same number, i.e., we can write GRADE(2) = −1.4 and X = −1.4. The only difference in terms of memory arrangement is that we know what item precedes GRADE(2) (GRADE(1)) and what item follows it (GRADE(3)). We do not know what follows or precedes X. This indexing structure gives rise to the notion of a list (something very important in life!). So far we have been able to process only one item of information at a time (a variable). Now, with arrays, we can process a list of items.

The problem of Figure 7–1 can be solved with or without arrays. Each method uses the same number of memory locations (see Figure 7–4). If we call the array GRADE, a block of five sequential memory locations GRADE(1), GRADE(2), …, GRADE(5) is reserved for the five grades; five memory locations are also used for the individual labeling of the grades G1, G2, G3, … What makes the array concept different and powerful is that elements within the array can be indexed with a subscript, thereby greatly simplifying the task of manipulating array elements for processing and for input/output operations.

The grade problem in our example could be broken into the following three tasks:

1. reading the grades from the input file into the array GRADE,

2. accumulating the grades in the array and computing the average, and

3. printing the grades and the deviations (grade − average).

Some of these tasks could be consolidated, but let us illustrate these three tasks independently.

**FIGURE 7–4**    INDIVIDUAL LABELING OF GRADES VERSUS AN ARRAY OF GRADES

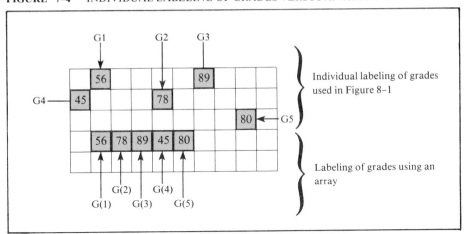

**Task 1**    Reading the 5 grades into the array GRADE

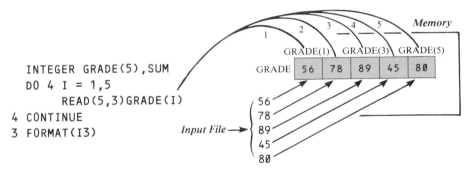

```
INTEGER GRADE(5),SUM
DO 4 I = 1,5
      READ(5,3)GRADE(I)
4 CONTINUE
3 FORMAT(I3)
```

Note that the statement READ GRADE(I) is processed five times as I takes on values 1 to 5. I is both the array subscript and the index of the DO loop. Initially I is 1, so the first time the READ statement is executed, GRADE(I) will refer to GRADE(1) and the value read from the input file will be stored in GRADE(1); the second time, I is 2, GRADE(I) will identify GRADE(2), and a new grade will be stored in GRADE(2). Eventually, I will be 5, GRADE(I) will refer to GRADE(5), and the last grade will be read into GRADE(5), completing the task of reading the grades into the array.

**Task 2**    Accumulating the grades in the array and computing the average

The variable SUM is used to accumulate the sum of the grades

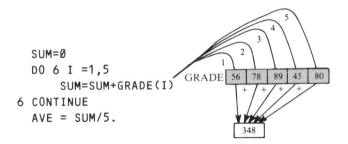

```
SUM=0
DO 6 I =1,5
      SUM=SUM+GRADE(I)
6 CONTINUE
AVE = SUM/5.
```

The 1st time (I = 1) through the loop, SUM = 0 + GRADE(I) = 0 + GRADE(1) = 56
The 2nd time (I = 2) through the loop, SUM = 56 + GRADE(I) = 56 + GRADE(2) = 56 + 78 = 134
The 3rd time (I = 3) through the loop, SUM = 134 + GRADE(I) = 134 + GRADE(3) = 134 + 89 = 223
The 4th time (I = 4) through the loop, SUM = 223 + GRADE(I) = 223 + GRADE(4) = 223 + 45 = 268
The 5th time (I = 5) through the loop, SUM = 268 + GRADE(I) = 268 + GRADE(5) = 268 + 80 = 348

Note that the grades are *not* read from the array by means of the READ statement, but are simply retrieved or accessed from memory by their own names, such as GRADE(1). (READ can be used only to read data from an input file.)

**Task 3**   Printing the elements of array GRADE and the deviations from the average

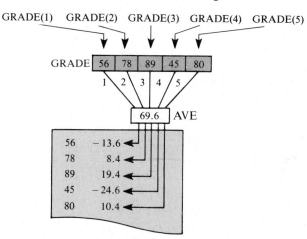

```
DO 7 I = 1,5
    DIF = GRADE(I) - AVE
    WRITE(6,2)GRADE(I),DIF
7 CONTINUE
2 FORMAT(2X,I3,7X,F5.1)
```

The first time through the loop, I = 1, and GRADE(1) and DIF = GRADE(1) – AVE are printed. By varying the subscript from 1 to 5, all the elements of the array and their differences from the average are printed.

The entire program is illustrated in Figure 7–5.

### 7-1-3   Do It Now

**1.** Could the grades be read into the array and accumulated at the same time?

**2.** How would the program of Figure 7–5 handle 97 grades?

**3.** Think of a problem that you could not handle without arrays.

### *Answers*

**1.** Yes. Use the following code:

```
SUM = Ø
DO 5 I = 1,5
    READ(5,3) GRADE(I)
    SUM = SUM + GRADE(I)
5 CONTINUE
```

**2.** Change the three DO statements to DO  xx  I = 1,97

**3.** Sorting a list of names.

**FIGURE 7-5**    COMPUTING A DEVIATION OF GRADES

```
C GRADE DEVIATION PROBLEM USING ARRAYS
C    GRADE:   ARRAY TO HOLD GRADES
C    SUM:     ACCUMULATES SUM OF GRADES
C    I:       SUBSCRIPT FOR ARRAY GRADE
C    AVE:     GRADE AVERAGE
C    DIF:     DIFFERENCE BETWEEN GRADE AND AVERAGE
C
         INTEGER GRADE(5),I,SUM          Reserve 5 memory locations for array GRADE.
         REAL AVE, DIF
         WRITE(6,1)
         DO 5 I = 1, 5                    Read all grades into array.
            READ(5,3)GRADE(I)             When I = 1, G(I) is G(1) and 56 is read into G(1).
    5    CONTINUE                         Do the same thing for I = 2, 3, 4 and 5.
         SUM = 0.                         Initialize sum of grades to 0.
         DO 6 I = 1,5
            SUM = SUM + GRADE(I)          Add all grades one at a time to SUM.
    6    CONTINUE
         AVE = SUM / 5.                   Compute the average of the grades.
         DO 7 I = 1, 5
            DIF = GRADE(I) - AVE          Compute the difference between each grade and average.
            WRITE(6,2) GRADE(I), DIF      Print the grade and corresponding difference.
    7    CONTINUE
         STOP
    1    FORMAT(' GRADES',3X,'DEVIATION')
    2    FORMAT(2X, I3, 7X, F5.1)
    3    FORMAT(I3)
         END
```

| GRADES | DEVIATION |  | *Input File* |
|--------|-----------|--|--------------|
| 56 | -13.6 |  | ↓ |
| 78 | 8.4 |  | 056 |
| 89 | 19.4 |  | 078 |
| 45 | -24.6 |  | 089 |
| 80 | 10.4 |  | 045 |
|  |  |  | 080 |

## 7-2    **FORTRAN Statements**

### 7-2-1  **Array Declarator Statements**

The following specification statements can be used to declare arrays:

> DIMENSION
> REAL
> INTEGER
> LOGICAL                *array name₁* (*limit₁*) [,*array name₂* (*limit₂*) ... ]
> DOUBLE PRECISION
> CHARACTER
> COMPLEX

where *array name₁*, *array name₂*, ... are names of the various arrays (any valid variable names) and

*limit₁*, *limit₂*, ... are unsigned integer constants representing the maximum number of memory locations reserved for each array.

It is not necessary to use all the reserved locations when processing the array. Array subscripts can vary from 1 to the limit declared in the type or DIMENSION statement but cannot exceed that limit. Any array used in a program must first be declared in a type or DIMENSION statement; any number of arrays can be declared in one type or DIMENSION statement, for example, the statements

```
DIMENSION X(6), K(3)
INTEGER Z1(20),J(107),TAB
```

declares X as a real array and MAT as an integer array, while arrays Z1 and J are integer arrays. If the DIMENSION statement is used to declare arrays, then the name of the array determines the array type (integer if the array name starts with I through N, real otherwise).

The elements of these various arrays can be visualized as shown in Figure 7–6.

Recall that type specification statements should precede executable statements and DATA statements. A typical FORTRAN program might start as follows:

| | |
|---|---|
| `INTEGER GRADE(30),JSUM(30)` | All 30 elements of GRADE are integer values. |
| `REAL A(336),K(32),T,L` | Two arrays and two variables. |
| `DOUBLE PRECISION B(5),LT(6)` | Both B and LT are double precision (real) arrays. |
| `LOGICAL M` | M becomes a logical variable. |
| `CHARACTER*10 N(50),PIT(7)` | Each element of these two arrays contains 10 characters. |
| `CHARACTER N(6)*8,TAB(15)*3` | Elements of N and TAB are 8 and 3 characters long respectively |
| `DATA M/.TRUE./, T,L/2*0./` | |
| `READ(5,6)...` | |

**FIGURE 7–6** REPRESENTATION OF LINEAR ARRAYS

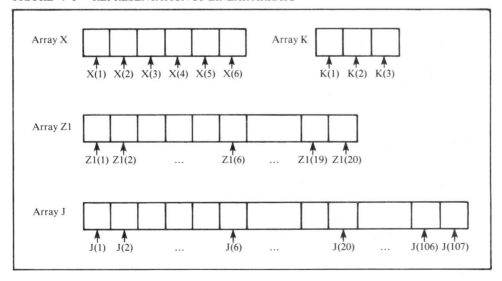

The following array declaration statements are invalid:

| | |
|---|---|
| DIMENSION A(3.) | Invalid limit; the limit must be an integer constant. |
| DIMENSION A(N) | N is not an integer constant. |

These examples stress one more time that the size of an array must be declared with an *integer* value in a type or DIMENSION statement. The size of an array may *not* be declared as a variable. The maximum value that can be specified as a limit to an array size depends on the size of the particular computer's memory.

Character arrays are conceptually similar to numeric arrays. For example, if TEXT is an array declared as CHARACTER∗5 TEXT(6) then TEXT(1), TEXT(2), ..., TEXT(6) are the 6 elements that make up array TEXT. Each array element consists of 5 characters, for example, array TEXT might have the following configuration:

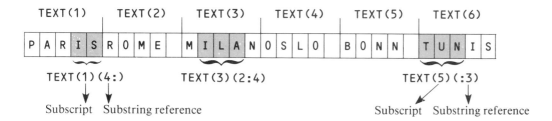

Note that declaring an array does *not* initialize the array elements to any particular values; it simply reserves memory locations.

## 7-2-2  Subscripts

Subscripts must be used with array names to refer to specific elements within an array. The subscript is enclosed in parentheses following the array name and can be an integer constant, an integer variable, or an integer expression. Some systems allow real expressions, in which case the subscript value is truncated.

Suppose arrays A and L and variables I and R have the following values:

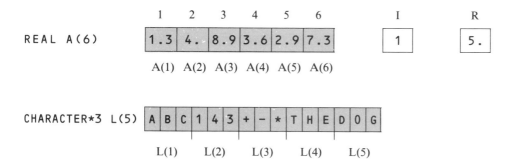

The following examples illustrate the use and meaning of the subscripts (assuming the subscript expression can be real).

| | | A | L | I | R |
|---|---|---|---|---|---|
| *Subscript Form* | *Example* | 1.3 4. 8.9 3.6 2.9 7.3 | A B C \| 1 4 3 \| + − * \| T H E D O G | 1 | 5. |

| | | |
|---|---|---|
| constant | A(4) | The value in the fourth location of A is 3.6. |
| constant | A(3.7) | When the subscript is real, it is truncated to just the whole number portion. This refers to the third element of array A, or 8.9. |
| variable | A(I) | The subscript is evaluated first. Since I = 1, this refers to the first element of A, which is 1.3. |
| variable | A(R) | Since R is 5., the value of A(R) would be 2.9, since A(R) is equivalent to A(5). |
| expression | A(24./R-2.3) | The arithmetic expression is evaluated first to $4.8 - 2.3 = 2.5$, which is then truncated to 2. A(2) is the second element in array A, or 4. |
| library function | A(SQRT(4.)) | Since the square root of 4. is 2., this also refers to the second element in array A. |
| subscripted variable | A(A(4)) | Since the fourth element in array A is 3.6, this example becomes A (3.6) which is A(3) or 8.9. |
| constant | L(3) | Third element of array (+ − *). |
| constant/substring | L(3)(1:1) | First character of the array third element (+). |
| expression | L(2*I) | $2*I = 2$, so this refers to the second element, i.e., characters 143. |
| expression/substring | L(2*I)(2:3) | This refers to characters 2 and 3 of the second element which are 4 and 3. |
| expression/substring | L(2*I)(I:5*I-3) | This evaluates to L(2)(1:2), so it refers to characters 1 thru 2 of the second element (1 and 4). |
| | L(4)(2:)//' '//L(5) | This refers to the characters HE DOG |

It is important to differentiate between the subscript value and the corresponding array element value. The value of A(3) generally has nothing to do with the number 3; for instance, A(3) = 8.9. Also, the same subscript can be used to refer to two different array elements for example, A(I) and L(I).

**Caution:**

1. Since subscripts identify the position of an element in an array, it is important that no subscripts evaluate to zero or a negative number.

2. When you have dimensioned an array to a particular size, say REAL X(33), you must make sure that any subscripts used with array X do not exceed 33. This is easier said than done! If, in your program, you use X(I) anywhere in a replacement statement or in an input or output statement, the value of I *must* be less than or equal to 33. If I is greater than 33, some systems will give an execution time error message such as "invalid index"; other systems may process A(I) with unpredictable results (see question 9 section 7-9). After all what would you do if you had a list of 10 names and someone asked you, "What is the name of the 15th person on your list?"!

Consider the following example:

```
       DIMENSION A(100),B(10)
       I = 101
       Y = A(I)
       B(11) = 3.
       DO 10 I = 1,11
  10    B(I) = Ø.
```

Invalid use of A(I), since I = 101, which exceeds 100.
Invalid; maximum subscript for B is 10.
On the last pass of the DO loop, I will be eleven,
causing an invalid reference to B(11).

**3.** In a replacement statement, you *must* use subscripts to refer to an array element. Using the name of an array without subscripts is illegal in a replacement statement, for example, if WEEK is an integer array, then

```
       DAY = WEEK/7 }
       WEEK = 7      }  are invalid.
```
```
       DAY = WEEK(3) /7. }
       WEEK(2) = 7.       }  are valid.
```

**4.** When declaring an array in a type specification statement, make sure you specify the size of the array with an integer constant. If a program written for some particular application requires that array X be large enough to contain 10 elements one day and 100 elements another day, *don't* write the following:

```
       REAL X(N)
       READ*, N        (Decide on the size depending on the application)
```

This will *not* work. Simply use the statement REAL X(100) and don't fret about the fact that you may not be using array X efficiently.


## 7-2-3  Do It Now

**1.** Write type statement(s) to create an array Q containing 10 real elements and an array R containing 25 character elements, each 3 characters long.

**2.** Suppose arrays X and T are as follows

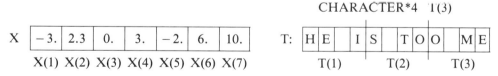

and suppose I = 3 and J = 2. Evaluate each of the following expressions:

a.  X(3)
b.  X(1 + 4)
c.  X(1) + X(4)
d.  X(I)
e.  X(I − J)
f.  X(I) − X(J)
g.  X(X(4))
h.  (X(7) − 3) / X(4)

i.  X(X(I/J)**.5 + 1) / 2.
j.  X(2*I + 1) − X(J/I)
k.  T(2)
l.  T(3)(3:)
m.  T(1)//T(3)(2:)
n.  T(2)(3:)//T(3)(1:1)
o.  T(3)//T(2)//T(1)

## Answers

1. ```
   REAL Q(10)
   CHARACTER*3 R(25)
   ```

2. a. 0.
   b. $-2.$
   c. $-3. + 3. = 0.$
   d. 0.
   e. $-3.$
   f. $0 - 2.3 = -2.3$
   g. $X(3) = 0.$
   h. 2.333333

   i. Invalid; square root
   of negative number.
   j. X(0) is undefined.
   k. SbTO
   l. ME
   m. HEbIbME
   n. TOO
   o. ObMESbTOHEbI

# 7-3 Array Manipulation

When working with arrays, it is often necessary to initialize arrays to certain values, create duplicate arrays, interchange elements within arrays, merge two or more arrays into one, search or accumulate array entries, or sort arrays. This section illustrates some of the commonly used array manipulation techniques so that the reader can become more familiar with the array index mechanism. In the following examples, it is assumed that values have already been stored in the various arrays.

## 7-3-1 Array Initialization and Duplication

The following code sets all elements of array A to zeroes, sets each element of array B to the variable X, sets $C(1) = 1$, $C(2) = 2$, ..., $C(N) = 10$, and creates a copy of array D in array S.

```
REAL A(10),B(10),C(10)
REAL S(10),D(10)
READ*,X
DO 5 I = 1,10            As I varies from 1 to 10,
      A(I) = 0.         A(1), A(2), ..., A(10) are set to 0., one at a time,
      B(I) = X          B(1), B(2), ... are set to the value X,
      C(I) = I          C(1) = 1., C(2) = 2., ..., C(10) = 10.,
      S(I) = D(I)       S(1) = D(1), S(2) = D(2), ..., S(10) = D(10)
5 CONTINUE
```

Sometimes it may be necessary to set an array C equal to the sum of two other arrays A and B in such a way that $C(1) = A(1) + B(1)$, $C(2) = A(2) + B(2)$, ..., $C(100) = A(100) + B(100)$. The following code could be used:

```
REAL A(100), B(100), C(100)
DO 5 I = 1,100
      C(I) = A(I) + B(I)
5 CONTINUE
```
```

Suppose we want to initialize two arrays A and B, as follows:

A(1) = B(10) = 1.      The code on the right          ```
A(2) = B(9)  = 2.      could be used:                 REAL A(10),B(10)
A(3) = B(8)  = 3.                                     DO 5 I = 1,10
         .                                                A(I) = I
         .                                                B(11-I) = I
A(10) = B(1) = 10.                               5 CONTINUE
                                                      ```

Note that $11 - I$ generates the numbers 10, 9, 8..., 1 as I ranges from 1 to 10. If I ranged from 1 to N, the subscript $N + 1 - I$ would generate the numbers $N, N - 1, N - 2, ..., 3, 2, 1$.

## 7-3-2  Reversing Arrays

Suppose A is an array of size N, where N has been defined previously, and we want to reverse the array, i.e., interchange A(1) with A(N), A(2) with A(N − 1), A(3) with A(N − 2), and so forth. The following code could be used (assuming A has already been loaded):

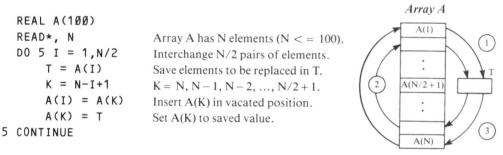

```
REAL A(100)
READ*, N          Array A has N elements (N <= 100).
DO 5 I = 1,N/2    Interchange N/2 pairs of elements.
   T = A(I)       Save elements to be replaced in T.
   K = N-I+1      K = N, N - 1, N - 2, ..., N/2 + 1.
   A(I) = A(K)    Insert A(K) in vacated position.
   A(K) = T       Set A(K) to saved value.
5 CONTINUE
```

*Array A*

Since each interchange step involves a pair of elements $(A_1, A_N)$, $(A_2, A_{N-1})$, ... The interchange process needs to be repeated only N/2 times. If N is odd, the middle element remains the same. T is a temporary location needed to save A(1) before we move A(N) into A(1). If we simply wrote A(1) = A(N), the value of A(1) would be lost.

## 7-3-3  Accumulation of Array Elements

To compute the product of the elements of the array A = | 10 | 20 | 30 | 40 | 50 | , the following code could be used:

```
INTEGER P,A(5)
P = 1             P is initially set to 1 before the loop is entered.
DO 5 K = 1,5      The first time through the loop, P = P*A(1) = 1*10 = 10
   P = P*A(K)     The second time through the loop, P = P*A(2) = 10*20 = 200
5 CONTINUE
```

To compute the sum of two arrays A and B such that $S = A(1) + B(1) + A(2) + B(2) + ... + A(50) + B(50)$ we could use:

```
REAL A(50),B(50)
S = 0.
DO 5 K = 1,50
   S = S + A(K) + B(K)
5 CONTINUE
```
```

*Example*

Assume a store keeps track of its inventory as follows: array C identifies the cost of each of 100 different items that the store retails, and array Q identifies the corresponding item quantities:

| **Array C Contains Item Costs** | **Array Q Contains Item Quantities** |
|---|---|
| $C(1) = 4.5$   Item 1 costs $4.50. | $Q(1) = 40.$   There are 40 of item 1. |
| $C(2) = 3.74$   Item 2 costs $3.74. | $Q(2) = 60.$   There are 60 of item 2. |
| . | . |
| . | . |
| . | . |
| $C(100) = 1.76$  Item 100 costs $1.76. | $Q(100) = 48.$ There are 48 of item 100. |

The store wishes to determine its market value inventory, which is simply:

$$\text{inventory value} = C(1) * Q(1) + C(2) * Q(2) + \ldots + C(100) * Q(100)$$

The code to compute the inventory value is:

```
REAL INV,C(100),Q(100)
INV = 0.                  Set inventory to 0.
DO 5 J = 1,100
    INV = INV + C(J) * Q(J)
5 CONTINUE
PRINT*,INV
```

## 7-3-4 Array Merge

Suppose A and B are two arrays of size 10 and we want the array C to contain the data

$$A_1, B_1, A_2, B_2, \ldots, A_{10}, B_{10}$$

arranged in that order. Any of the following codes could be used:

1.
```
   K = 1
   DO 10 I=1,10
       C(K) = A(I)
       K    = K + 1
       C(K) = B(I)
       K    = K + 1
10 CONTINUE
```

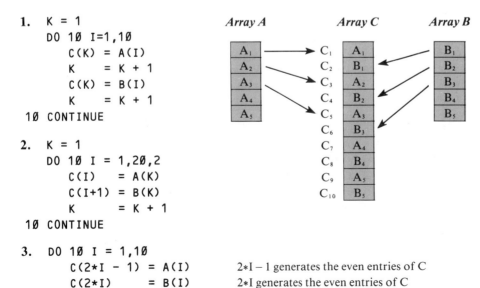

2.
```
   K = 1
   DO 10 I = 1,20,2
       C(I)   = A(K)
       C(I+1) = B(K)
       K      = K + 1
10 CONTINUE
```

3.
```
   DO 10 I = 1,10
       C(2*I - 1) = A(I)      2*I – 1 generates the even entries of C
       C(2*I)     = B(I)      2*I generates the even entries of C
10 CONTINUE
```

### 7-3-5 Array Searches

*Example 1*

Assume array A contains 100 grades and we want to determine the number of grades over 53. The following code can be used:

```
    K = 0
    DO 10 I = 1,100                  If A(I) > 53 increment counter K by 1.
        IF(A(I).GT.53.)K=K+1         Otherwise compare next grade with 53.
10 CONTINUE
```

*Example 2*

Assume array A contains N scores that are supposed to be in ascending order. Write the code to perform a sequence check and write an error message if the scores are out of sequence. If the scores are in sequence, write an appropriate message. Stop as soon as the first out-of-sequence score is detected.

```
    DO 5 L = 2,N
        IF(A(L) .LT. A(L-1)) GO TO 35
5  CONTINUE
    PRINT*,'NOS. IN SEQUENCE'
    STOP
35 PRINT*,A(L),'IS OUT OF SEQUENCE'
    STOP
```

*Example 3*

Assume an array G contains 10 scores and we want to determine the highest score. One way to do this is to use a variable L to contain the current highest score and keep comparing L with the next score. If the next score is larger than L, then L is set to that score; otherwise L is compared to the score that follows. Initially, L is set to the first score.

```
    INTEGER G(10),L
    L = G(1)                         Set L initially to the first score.
    DO 50 I = 2,10                   Start comparing L with the second entry.
        IF(L .GE. G(I)) GO TO 50     If the largest score (L) so far is less than the
            L = G(I)                 new score G(I), replace L by new score G(I).
50 CONTINUE                          Otherwise, look at the next score.
    PRINT*,'LARGEST VALUE', L
```

This code does not, however, indicate the position of the largest element of the array G, i.e., it does not show whether the largest number was found at the 5th or 7th position, for example. That could be done with the following code:

```
    L = G(1)
    IPOS = 1                         Assume largest element is in position 1
    DO 50 I = 2,10                   (subject to later change).
        IF(L.GE.G(I))GO TO 50
            L = G(I)                 Every time a new larger number is found, store it in
            IPOS = I                 L and keep track of its array position in IPOS.
50 CONTINUE
    PRINT*, 'MAX=',L, 'POSITION=', IPOS
```

### 7-3-6 Do It Now

1. What will be the content of each element of the array Y after the following code is executed:

```
INTEGER Y(10)
Y(1) = 1
Y(2) = 1
DO 5 I = 3,10
    Y(I) = Y(I-1) + Y(I-2)
5 CONTINUE
```

2. Write the code to fill successive elements of an array with the values 5, 7, 9, 11, ..., 225. Do not use a READ statement.

3. Assume array X has 50 elements. Write the code to compute the sum of the squares of the elements of X.

4. Array C with N elements is supposed to be in ascending order. Write the code to perform a sequence check and print all numbers that are out of sequence.

5. Array C contains 17 elements. Print the element in C closest to 5.37 and identify its position, i.e., was that element the first? second? fourteenth?

6. Given an array G containing 5 scores, would the following code print the position of the highest score and the highest score itself?

```
K = 1
DO 5 I = 2,5
    IF(G(K) .LT. G(I)) K = I
5 CONTINUE
PRINT*,'POSITION HIGHEST SCORE IS',K,'HIGHEST SCORE IS',G(K)
```

### *Answers*

1.

| 1 | 1 | 2 | 3 | 5 | 8 | 13 | 21 | 34 | 55 |
|---|---|---|---|---|---|----|----|----|----|

$Y_1$  $Y_2$  $Y_3$  $Y_4$  $Y_5$  $Y_6$  $Y_7$  $Y_8$  $Y_9$  $Y_{10}$

2.
```
    INTEGER A(150)
    K = 1
    DO 5 I = 5,225,2
        A(K) = I
        K = K + 1
5 CONTINUE
```

3.
```
    S = 0.
    DO 5 I = 1,50
        S = S + X(I)**2
5 CONTINUE
```

4.
```
    T = C(1)
    DO 5 I = 2,N
        IF(T .LT. C(I)) THEN
            T = C(I)
        ELSE
            PRINT*,C(I)
        ENDIF
5 CONTINUE
```

**5.**
```
      K = 1
      X = C(1) - 5.37
      IF(X .LT. 0.) X = -X
      DO 5 I = 2,17
          D = C(I) - 5.37
          IF(D .LT. 0.) D = -D
          IF(D .GT. X) GO TO 5
          X = D
          K = I
    5 CONTINUE
      PRINT*,'POSITION IS',K,'NUMBER IS',C(K)
```

**6.** K will identify the position of the highest score, while G(K) will be the highest score.

# 7-4 Input and Output of Arrays

There are essentially two methods for loading (reading) and writing out arrays. The first method uses the *explicit* form of the DO loop, and the second method uses an implied form of the DO loop that is equivalent to listing all array entries individually in the READ/WRITE list. The second method is called the *implied DO list*; it can do everything that the explicit form of the DO loop does and much more, as will be seen in the following sections, where the two methods are discussed in more detail.

## 7-4-1 Explicit Use of the DO Loop

A straightforward approach for reading five grades from five data records (one grade per record) into an array GRADE is to use five READ statements, each specifying the five memory locations into which the grades are to be stored:

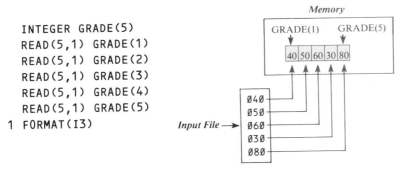

This method is clearly tedious. A preferable approach is to read GRADE(I) as I varies from 1 to 5, i.e., the READ statement is part of a DO loop where the array subscript is also used as the idex of the DO loop. For example, to read five data items from records (one data item per record), the following code can be used:

*Example 1*

```
      INTEGER GRADE(5)
      DO 10 I = 1,5
          READ(5,1) GRADE(I)
   10 CONTINUE
    1 FORMAT(I3)
```

The first time through the loop I is 1, and GRADE(1) is read from the data record. The second time through the loop I is 2, and the data item on the second record is stored into GRADE(2). Finally, I is 5, and the fifth data item (from fifth record) is read into GRADE(5). Because there is only one variable in the READ list, the corresponding format should only specify one data format code.

To read two numbers per record into two different arrays HR and RATE, the following code can be used:

*Example 2*

| | | | *Array Storage* | | | |
|---|---|---|---|---|---|---|
| | *Input Data* | | **HR** | | **Rate** | |

```
     REAL RATE(10)
     INTEGER HR(10)
     DO 10 I = 1,10
        READ(5,5)HR(I),RATE(I)
10 CONTINUE
 5 FORMAT(I3,3X,F4.0)
```

Input Data:
```
040bbbb05·1
020bbbb03·0
050bbbb02·5
   :
060bbbb10·0
```

HR:
| 40 | HR(1) |
| 20 | HR(2) |
| 50 | HR(3) |
| : | |
| : | |
| 60 | HR(10) |

Rate:
| 5.1 | RATE(1) |
| 3. | RATE(2) |
| 2.5 | RATE(3) |
| : | |
| : | |
| 10. | RATE(10) |

*Example 3*

Assume that each element of array SALES contains a daily sales amount and that you want to print the daily sales with each corresponding day. The following code could be used:

```
     REAL SALES(7)
     WRITE(6,12)
     DO 10 I = 1,7
        WRITE(6,11)I,SALES(I)
10 CONTINUE
11 FORMAT(1X,I2,5X,F6.2)
12 FORMAT(' DAYS',3X,'SALES')
```

*Output*

| DAYS | SALES |
|------|-------|
| 1 | 101.00 |
| 2 | 200.00 |
| 3 | 50.50 |
| 4 | 35.50 |
| 5 | 100.00 |
| 6 | 300.00 |
| 7 | 50.00 |

Note that I represents the day and SALES(I) represents the corresponding day's sales, i.e., SALES(I) is the sales for the Ith day.

*Example 4*

If more than one number per record (two, for instance) is to be read into array A, the following code can be used:

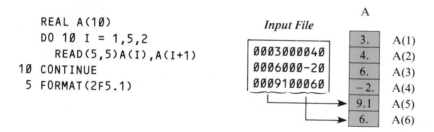

```
     REAL A(10)
     DO 10 I = 1,5,2
        READ(5,5)A(I),A(I+1)
10 CONTINUE
 5 FORMAT(2F5.1)
```

Input File:
```
0003000040
0006000-20
0009100060
```

A:
| 3. | A(1) |
| 4. | A(2) |
| 6. | A(3) |
| -2. | A(4) |
| 9.1 | A(5) |
| 6. | A(6) |

Note that only six elements of the array are read. If six numbers were to be read per record, the READ list in the DO loop would have to specify A(I),A(I+1),A(I+2),A(I+3), A(I+4),A(I+5), which is somewhat inconvenient. In this case the DO list is advantageous.

## 7-4-2 Implied DO List

The implied DO list is essentially a shorthand notation for listing subscripted variables in a READ/WRITE list. Instead of writing

$$READ(5,5)A(1),A(2),A(3),A(4),A(5),A(6)$$

we can use a more compact and convenient notation:

$$READ(5,5)(A(I),I=1,6,1)$$

This statement can be interpreted as follows: Read the numbers A(I) as I ranges from 1 to 6 in steps of 1. The incremental step 1 can be omitted, resulting in an automatic increment of 1. Six values will then be read from one or more records, as determined by the number of data format codes in the format. Once again, the implied DO list specifies the total number of values to be read into memory or written out, and the format specifies how many of these values will be read per record (or written per line). As with the DO loop, the index of the DO list is undefined at the conclusion of the READ operation if the DO list goes through its complete cycle. If transfer is made out of the DO list through the END option, the value of the index is preserved. Consider the following examples:

*Example 1*

```
    READ(5,10)(A(I),I=1,5)              WRITE(6,10)(B(I),I=1,5)
10  FORMAT(F5.0)                    10  FORMAT(2X,2F6.0)
```

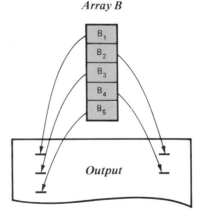

In both cases five elements are to be read or written. The format specifies the number of entries per record. For the READ operation there is one item per record, hence five records will be read. For the WRITE operation there are two items (2F6.0) per line; hence three lines will be printed, with only one item printed on the last line.

*Example 2*

```
    READ(5,10)(A(I),I=1,13)                WRITE(6,20)(A(I),I=1,13)
 10 FORMAT(3F5.0)                       20 FORMAT(1X,12F6.0)
```

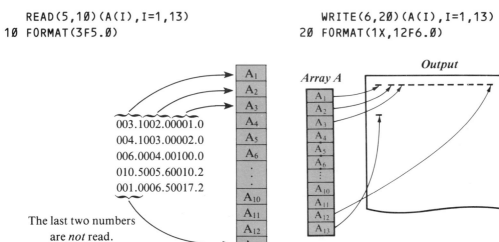

The last two numbers
are *not* read.

In both cases 13 elements are processed. For the READ operation there are three items per record (3F5.0), hence five records will be read, reading only the first entry on the fifth record. For the WRITE operation 12 items are printed per line (12F6.0), hence two lines will be printed, with only one field printed on the second line.

*Example 3*      Printing the index of the DO list

```
    WRITE(6,12)
    READ (5,5)(SALES(I),I=1,7)
                                          ── 14 entries in all are written
    WRITE(6,11)(I,SALES(I),I=1,7)
  5 FORMAT(F5.2)
 11 FORMAT(1X,I2,6X,F6.2)◄────── 2 entries per line
 12 FORMAT(' DAYS',4X,'SALES')
```

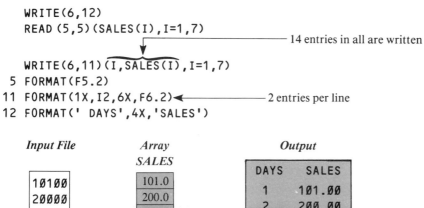

Seven sales are read into array SALES. The list of variables in the WRITE statement specifies 14 items to be printed: 1,SALES(1); 2,SALES(2); …; 7,SALES(7). The output format indicates that only two entries are to be printed per line. If FORMAT 6 had been (6(I3,2X,F6.2)) then the 14 values would have been printed on the same line.

*Example 4*

```
    READ(5,10)(A(I),B(I),I=1,5)              WRITE(6,10)(A(I),B(I),I=1,5)
10 FORMAT(2F5.0)                         10 FORMAT(3F6.0)
```

| Array A | Input File | Array B | Output |
|---------|-----------|---------|--------|

Array A: $A_1$, $A_2$, $A_3$, $A_4$, $A_5$

Input File:
```
012.4001.5
001.3003.0
003.0010.4
034.5010.6
010.6100.8
```

Array B: $B_1$, $B_2$, $B_3$, $B_4$, $B_5$

Output:
$A_1$   $B_1$   $A_2$
$B_2$   $A_3$   $B_3$
$A_4$   $B_4$   $A_5$
$B_5$

Both examples process the elements A(I) and B(I) as I varies from 1 to 5. This is equivalent to the list of variables A(1),B(1),A(2),B(2),A(3),...,A(5),B(5). The READ statement reads pairs of A and B elements, hence five data records are needed. In the WRITE operation, three numbers are written per line (3F6.0).

*Example 5*

```
    WRITE(6,4)(A(I),I=1,5),(B(I),I=1,4)       WRITE(6,6)(A(I),I=1,5),(B(I),I=1,4)
 4 FORMAT(1X,3F4.0)                        6 FORMAT(1X,6F4.0/1X,3F4.0)
```

$A_1$   $A_2$   $A_3$
$A_4$   $A_5$   $B_1$
$B_2$   $B_3$   $B_4$

$A_1$   $A_2$   $A_3$   $A_4$   $A_5$   $B_1$
$B_2$   $B_3$   $B_4$

In both examples, nine values are to be printed. Format 4 specifies three entries per line, hence three lines with three entries will be printed. Format 6 specifies six values on the first line and three values on the second line.

*Example 6*

```
    CHARACTER*3 TEXT(15)                     WRITE(6,4)(TEXT(K),K=1,15)
    READ(5,6)(TEXT(I),I=1,15)             4 FORMAT(1X,3A4,A1)
 6 FORMAT(2A3,A1,1X,A4)
```

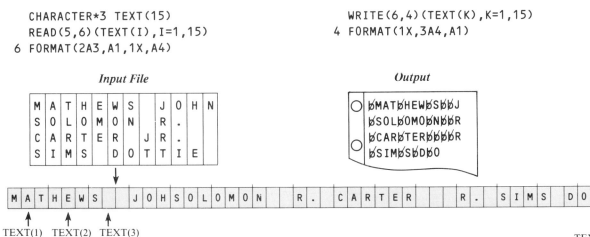

Recall that on input if *w* of *Aw* is greater than the length *l* of the variable to be read (*l* is defined in the CHARACTER statement, then the rightmost *l* characters of the input data field are read into the variable; likewise on output, if *w* is greater then *l*, then the *l* characters are right justified in the output field with *w* − *l* leading blanks.

*Example 7*

Suppose the correct answers to a multiple choice test (maximum of 25 questions) are recorded on an input record with the first entry on the record indicating the number of test questions that follow, for example

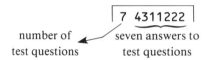

number of        seven answers to
test questions      test questions

The following code first reads the number of test questions (7) into N and then reads the N answers to the test questions into array TEST. The TEST array is then printed out on one line.

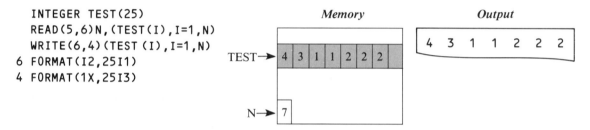

```
      INTEGER TEST(25)
      READ(5,6)N,(TEST(I),I=1,N)
      WRITE(6,4)(TEST (I),I=1,N)
    6 FORMAT(I2,25I1)
    4 FORMAT(1X,25I3)
```

Note that formats 6 and 4 specify 25I1 and 25I3. Since N will always be less than or equal to 25, only N entries will be printed per line.

*Example 8*

Suppose that for a particular report the following heading is required at the top of a new page:

```
   PARTNO.   MACHINE 1   MACHINE 2   MACHINE 3 ... MACHINE 9
```

The literal "MACHINE" is repeated nine times, and the numbers 1,2,3,...,8,9 can be generated by the implied DO list, as follows:

```
      WRITE(6,1)(I,I=1,9)        Write I as I varies from 1 to 9.
    1 FORMAT('1',9X,'PARTNO.',4X,9('MACHINE',I1,2X))
```

### 7-4-3 Do It Now

**1.** Consider the data file shown below:

| 0 | 2 | 0 | 3 | 0 | 0 | 0 | 0 | 1 | 2 |
|---|---|---|---|---|---|---|---|---|---|
| 0 | 4 | − | 6 | 0 | 0 | 0 | 0 | 2 | 2 |
| 0 | 5 | 0 | 7 | 0 | 0 | 0 | 0 | 0 | 0 |
| − | 2 | − | 1 | 0 | 0 | 0 | 0 | 1 | 4 |
| 0 | 0 | 0 | 0 | 0 | 0 | 0 | 0 | 0 | 0 |

What values will be stored in arrays X and Y as a result of executing the following instructions? (Repeat each part of the problem with all the FORMATS shown for that part.) Assume REAL X(5),Y(5).

a.
```
   READ(5,6)(X(I),I=1,5)
 1 FORMAT(F2.0)
 2 FORMAT(5F2.0)
```

*Data File*

| 0 | 2 | 0 | 3 | 0 | 0 | 0 | 0 | 1 | 2 |
|---|---|---|---|---|---|---|---|---|---|
| 0 | 4 | – | 6 | 0 | 0 | 0 | 0 | 2 | 2 |
| 0 | 5 | 0 | 7 | 0 | 0 | 0 | 0 | 0 | 0 |
| – | 2 | – | 1 | 0 | 0 | 0 | 0 | 1 | 4 |
| 0 | 0 | 0 | 0 | 0 | 0 | 0 | 0 | 0 | 0 |

b.
```
   READ(5,6)(X(I),Y(I),I=1,5)
 1 FORMAT(2F2.0)
 2 FORMAT(3F2.0)
 3 FORMAT(10F1.0)
```

c.
```
   READ(5,6)(X(I),I=1,5,2),(Y(I),I=2,5,2),X(2)
 1 FORMAT(2F2.0)
 2 FORMAT(3F2.0)
```

d.
```
   READ(5,6)N,(X(I),Y(I),I=1,N)
 1 FORMAT(I2,6F2.0)
 2 FORMAT(/I2,4F2.0/6F1.0)
 3 FORMAT(I2,3F2.0)
```

e.
```
    I = 0
10 READ(5,14)A,B
    IF(A .EQ. 0.) GO TO 30
    I = I+1
    X(I) = A
    Y(I) = B
    GO TO 10
30 ...
14 FORMAT(2F2.0)
```

*Data File*

| 0 | 2 | 0 | 3 | 0 | 0 | 0 | 0 | 1 | 2 |
|---|---|---|---|---|---|---|---|---|---|
| 0 | 4 | – | 6 | 0 | 0 | 0 | 0 | 2 | 2 |
| 0 | 5 | 0 | 7 | 0 | 0 | 0 | 0 | 0 | 0 |
| – | 2 | – | 1 | 0 | 0 | 0 | 0 | 1 | 4 |
| 0 | 0 | 0 | 0 | 0 | 0 | 0 | 0 | 0 | 0 |

**2.** Determine the number of lines printed by
```
       WRITE(6,4)(X(I),I=1,3),Z,(Y(I),I=1,4)
```
using the following FORMATS

a.  `FORMAT(1X,F5.0)`
b.  `FORMAT(1X,9F5.0)`
c.  `FORMAT(1X,3F5.0)`
d.  `FORMAT(1X,/1X,F4.0)`
e.  `FORMAT(1X,6F4.0/1X,F4.0)`

**3.** What will be printed by the following WRITE statements? Give the value of the variable, if known, or the corresponding variable name, if the value is unknown.

a.  `WRITE(6,4)(A(I),I,I=1,2)`
b.  `WRITE(6,5)(B(I),I,C(I),I=1,3)`
c.  `WRITE(6,6)(K,A(I),B(I),I=1,5,2)`

**4.** Assume CHARACTER*3 A(4) and the data file shown below.

| S | O | M | E |   | P | E | O | P | L | E |
|---|---|---|---|---|---|---|---|---|---|---|
| S | E | E |   | T | H | I | N | G | S |   | A |
| S |   | T | H | E | Y |   | A | R | E |   | A |
| N | D |   | S | A | Y |   | W | H | Y |

Display the contents of array A resulting from the following input statements:

```
READ(5,6)(A(I),I=1,4)
```

a. FORMAT(3A3)
b. FORMAT(A1)
c. FORMAT(1X,A3)
d. FORMAT(2A2)
e. FORMAT(A6)
f. FORMAT(2A5)

*Data File*

| S | O | M | E |   | P | E | O | P | L | E |   |
| S | E | E |   | T | H | I | N | G | S |   | A |
| S |   | T | H | E | Y |   | A | R | E |   | A |
| N | D |   | S | A | Y |   | W | H | Y |   |   |

**5.** An input file consists of 100 records, where each record contains a student name, a 3-digit ID, a final score in management, and a final score in algebra.

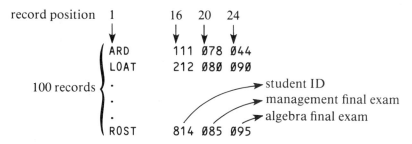

record position  1       16  20  24

```
            ⎧ ARD     111 078 044
            ⎪ LOAT    212 080 090
100 records ⎨  ·                         ───► student ID
            ⎪  ·                         ───► management final exam
            ⎪  ·                         ───► algebra final exam
            ⎩ ROST    814 085 095
```

Write the code to load all the algebra scores into Array A and all the names into array NAME.

## Answers

**1.** a. 1
     2

| 2. | 4. | 5. | − 2. | 0. |
| 2. | 3. | 0. | 0. | 12. |

b. 1
   2
   3

| 2. | 4. | 5. | − 2. | 0. |
| 2. | 0. | − 6. | 5. | 0. |
| 0. | 0. | 0. | 0. | 1. |

| 3. | − 6. | 7. | − 1. | 0. |
| 3. | 4. | 0. | 7. | − 2. | ──► Y
| 2. | 3. | 0. | 0. | 2. |

c. 1
   2

| 2. | 7. | 3. | ? | 4. |
| 2. | 0. | 3. | ? | 0. |

| ? | − 6. | ? | 5. | ? |
| ? | 4. | ? | − 6. | ? |

d. 1
   2
   3

| 3. | 0. | ? | ? | ? |
| − 6. | 0. | 0. | 0. | ? |

Invalid format I2 for Y(2)

| 0. | 12. | ? | ? | ? |
| 0. | 22. | 5. | 7. | ? |

| 2 |
| 4 | ──► N

e.

| 2. | 4. | 5. | − 2. | ? |

| 3. | − 6. | 7. | − 1. | ? |

**2.** a. 8   b. 1   c. 3   d. 16   e. 3

**3.** a. A(1), 1, A(2), 2
     b. B(1), 1, C(1), B(2), 2, C(2), B(3), 3, C(3)
     c. K, A(1), B(1), K, A(3), B(3), K, A(5), B(5)

**4.**

| | $A_1$ | | | $A_2$ | | | $A_3$ | | | $A_4$ | | |
|---|---|---|---|---|---|---|---|---|---|---|---|---|
| a. | S | O | M | E | | P | E | O | P | S | E | E |
| b. | S | | | S | | | S | | | N | | |
| c. | O | M | E | E | E | | | T | H | D | | S |
| d. | S | O | | M | E | | S | E | | E | | |
| e. | E | | P | | T | H | H | E | Y | S | A | Y |
| f. | M | E | | O | P | L | E | | T | N | G | S |

**5.**
```
      CHARACTER*15 NAME(100)
      INTEGER A(100)
      DO 5 I = 1,100
         READ(5,6) NAME(I),A(I)
    5 CONTINUE
    6 FORMAT(A15,8X,I3)
```

## 7-4-4 Nested DO Lists

Implied DO lists can be nested, and in such a case each DO list must have a different index.
Consider the following example:

*Nested DO List*

```
 WRITE(6,5)(A(I),B(I),(M(J),J=1,4),I=1,3)
 5 FORMAT(1X,2F5.0,4I5)
```

$$\downarrow$$

| $A_1$ | $B_1$ | $M_1$ | $M_2$ | $M_3$ | $M_4$ |
|---|---|---|---|---|---|
| $A_2$ | $B_2$ | $M_1$ | $M_2$ | $M_3$ | $M_4$ |
| $A_3$ | $B_3$ | $M_1$ | $M_2$ | $M_3$ | $M_4$ |

*Equivalent*

```
 DO 6 I = 1,3
    WRITE(6,5)A(I),B(I),(M(J),J=1,4)
 6 CONTINUE
 5 FORMAT (1X,2F5.0,4I5)
```

The cycles of the inner and outer loop subscripts are as follows:

Inner loop

```
WRITE(6,5)(A(I),B(I),(M(J),J=1,4),I=1,3)
```

Outer loop

The outer loop subscript changes slowly; the inner loop subscript runs through its complete
range of values for each value of the outer subscript. For the preceding statement

I is 1 and J runs through 1,2,3,4
I is 2 and J runs through 1,2,3,4
I is 3 and J runs through 1,2,3,4

## 7-4-5 Do It Now

**1.** Specify the list (or values) of the variables generated by the following nested DO lists:

a. `WRITE(6,4)(I,I=1,10),(I,I=10,-1,-1)`

```
  b. WRITE(6,5)(A(I),B(I),I,I=1,K)
  c. WRITE(6,5)(A(I),(B(J),I,J=1,2),A(I+1),I=1,2)
  d. WRITE(6,5)(A(I),(B(J),C(J),J=1,2),I=1,2)
```

**2.** Write the code to produce the following outputs:

```
  a. 10 10 10 10 10 10 10 10 10 10          b.   1
      9  9  9  9  9  9  9  9  9                   2  2
      8  8  8  8  8  8  8  8                       3  3  3
      .                                            4  4  4  4
      .                                            .
      .                                            .
      2  2                                         10 10 10 10 10 10 10 10 10 10
      1
```

## Answers

**1.**   a.  1,2,3,4,5,6,7,8,9,10,10,9,8,7,6,5,4,3,2,1,0, − 1
       b.  $A_1 B_1 1 A_2 B_2 2 \ldots A_K B_K K$
       c.  $A_1 B_1 1 B_2 1 A_2 A_2 B_1 2 B_2 2 A_3$
       d.  $A_1 B_1 C_1 B_2 C_2 A_2 B_1 C_1 B_2 C_2$

**2.**   a.   `DO 5 I = 10,1,-1`              b.   `DO 5 I = 1,10`
            `WRITE(6,6)(I,K=1,I)`                 `WRITE(6,6)(I,K=1,I)`
        `5 CONTINUE`                         `5 CONTINUE`
        `6 FORMAT(1X,10I3)`                  `6 FORMAT(1X,10I3)`

### 7-4-6  Common Misunderstandings

One of the most confusing aspects of input/output of arrays is the relationship between the list of variables specified by the READ/WRITE statement and the corresponding FORMAT. Consider the following example (which is frequently misinterpreted)—how many data records will be read by the following code?

```
    DO 5 I = 1,9            The reader might think that this code will read A(I) as I goes
       READ(5,6)A(I)        from 1 to 9, and since three numbers are specified in the
    5 CONTINUE              FORMAT, three records will be read altogether. That is not
    6 FORMAT(3F5.3)         the case.
```

Initially I is 1, and the first time through the loop the READ statement becomes READ(5,6)A(1). This statement says "just read one element, A(1)"; the format says "the maximum number of entries that can be read from a record is three," but that's just a maximum—in this case the program will only read one element. Hence each cycle through the DO loop results in one record being read, so altogether nine records will be read.

Contrast the preceding code with the following one:

```
    READ(5,6)(A(I),I=1,9)
    6 FORMAT(3F5.3)
```

In this case the READ statement says "read nine elements altogether." The FORMAT says "no more than three elements per record." Hence to satisfy the READ list, three records will have to be read altogether.

## 7-4-7 Do It Now

**1.** How many records will be read by the following?

a.
```
DO 5 I = 1,9
    READ(5,6)A(I),B(I)
5 CONTINUE
6 FORMAT(F5.1)
```

b.
```
DO 5 I = 1,3
    READ(5,6)(A(I),I=1,4)
5 CONTINUE
6 FORMAT(3F4.0)
```

**2.** How many lines will be printed as a result of the different formats?

```
WRITE(6,4)(I,A(I),I=1,5)
```
a. `FORMAT(1X,F4.1)`

b. `FORMAT(1X,I1,F4.1)`

c. `FORMAT(1X,2(I1,F4.1))`

d. `FORMAT(1X,I1,F4.1,I1)`

## *Answers*

**1.** a. 18    b. 6    (2 records per READ statement)

**2.** a. Invalid; the variable I needs an I type format.
   b. 5
   c. 3; the last line will print 5 and A(5).
   d. Invalid starting with line 2; A(2) needs an F type format.

## 7-4-8 Input/Output of an Entire Array

If an array name is used by itself without subscripts in a READ or WRITE operation, *all* the elements of the array (as many as are declared in the type or DIMENSION statement) are either read or written.

*Example*

```
REAL X(10) ⎫                    ⎧REAL X(10)
           ⎬ equivalent to      ⎨
READ(5,6)X ⎭                    ⎩READ(5,6)(X(I),I=1,10)
```

Care must be exercised when just using names of arrays without subscripts in an input/output operation. Consider the following code:

```
REAL HRS(3),RATE(3)      40. bb05.50
READ(5,3)HRS,RATE        20.bb03.00  ◄── Input File
3 FORMAT(F3.0,2X,F5.2)   50.bb02.50
```

This code would load arrays HRS and RATE as follows:

| HRS | RATE | *not* | HRS | RATE |
|-----|------|-------|-----|------|
| 40. | 3.   |       | 40. | 5.5  |
| 5.5 | 50.  |       | 20. | 3.   |
| 20. | 2.5  |       | 50. | 2.5  |

The statement READ(5,3)HRS,RATE reads the list of variables:

HRS(1),HRS(2),HRS(3),RATE(1),RATE(2),RATE(3)

### 7-4-9 The DATA Statement

The DATA statement was used earlier to establish initial values for nonsubscripted variables. It can also be used to initialize arrays. Recall that the DATA statement should be placed after the various type statements. Through the DATA statement an array is initialized either by explicitly listing the named array elements and their corresponding values, or by defining the array elements through the DO list, or by specifying the name of the array by itself, as in section 7-4-8.

*Example 1*

```
      REAL A(5)
      DATA A(1),A(2),A(3),A(4),A(5) /1.,2.1,-3.,4.,5.6/     Explicit form.
   or DATA (A(I),I=1,5)/1.,2.1,-3.,4.,5.6/     DO list.
   or DATA A/1.,2.1,-3.,4.,5.6/     Just the array name.
```

In the third case the number of array elements initialized is equal to the size of the array declared in the DIMENSION or type statement (5 elements for A in this case).

The duplication factor "*" can be used to simplify the constant list.

*Example 2*

To initialize 100 elements of arrays A, B and C to zeroes, blanks, and .TRUE. values, we write:

```
      INTEGER A(200)
      CHARACTER*3 B(100)
      LOGICAL C(100)
      DATA (A(I),I = 1,100)/100*0 /, B, C/100 * ' ', 100 * .TRUE./
```

A(101),A(102),...,A(200) remain undefined. Note that the * in the constant list means repetition of a constant, not multiplication.


# 7-5 End-of-File Conditions

More often than not, an input file consists of an unknown number of records. How do we know how many entries to reserve for our arrays if the input data is to be read into arrays? The type or DIMENSION statements require an integer constant for the size of the array—we cannot specify a variable size for the array (such as REAL X(N) where N varies from one application to the next). One way to take care of the problem is to estimate a maximum size. Frequently, the particular problem will specify the maximum number of records to be processed, so use that maximum! Remember, not all reserved array entries have to be used.

In the next sections we will illustrate two ways to deal with an unknown number of input records. Let us consider the following problem: An input file consists of an unknown number of records. Each record contains a student's name and two test scores. Read into array NAME the name of each student and store in array SCORE the average of each student's scores. Print the number of records processed. Assume a maximum of 100 student records.

## 7-5-1  Last-Record-Code or Sentinel Method

An additional record containing a trip code (sentinel) is appended to the input file, for example, the trip code could be a negative test score.

*Example*

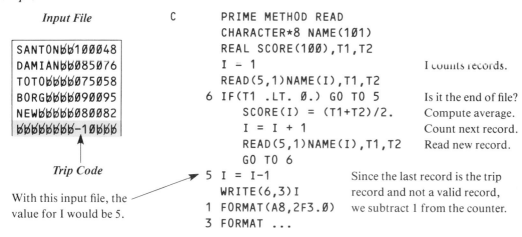

| Input File | | |
| --- | --- | --- |

```
                         C     PRIME METHOD READ
                               CHARACTER*8 NAME(101)
SANTONbb100048                 REAL SCORE(100),T1,T2
DAMIANbb085076                 I = 1                    I counts records.
TOTObbbb075058                 READ(5,1)NAME(I),T1,T2
BORGbbbb090095            6 IF(T1 .LT. 0.) GO TO 5      Is it the end of file?
NEWbbbbb080082                    SCORE(I) = (T1+T2)/2.  Compute average.
bbbbbbb-10bbb                     I = I + 1              Count next record.
                                  READ(5,1)NAME(I),T1,T2 Read new record.
                                  GO TO 6
                          5 I = I-1                     Since the last record is the trip
                            WRITE(6,3)I                 record and not a valid record,
                          1 FORMAT(A8,2F3.0)            we subtract 1 from the counter.
                          3 FORMAT ...
```

*Trip Code*

With this input file, the value for I would be 5.

Note that the WHILE DO statement could be used in this example by replacing line 6 by WHILE (T1 .GE. 0.) DO and GO TO 6 by ENDWHILE.

## 7-5-2  Automatic End-of-File Method

Since the automatic end-of-file method is probably the most widely used technique to terminate reading an input file, we present two methods that can be used interchangeably.

**Method 1**

```
        Option 1                           Option 2
  CHARACTER*8 NAME(101)              CHARACTER*8 NAME(100),TEMP
  REAL SCORE(100)                    REAL SCORE(100)
  I = 1                              I = 0
7 READ(5,9,END=8) NAME(I),T1,T2    7 READ(5,9,END=8)TEMP,T1,T2
     SCORE(I) = (T1+T2)/2.              I = I + 1
     I = I + 1                          NAME(I) = TEMP
     GO TO 7                            SCORE(I) = (T1+T2)/2.
8 I = I - 1                            GO TO 7
  WRITE(6,5)I                     8 WRITE(6,5)I
```

In option 1 the names are directly read into array NAME; however, the terminal value of the index I is one more than the number of grades read, since I counts the end-of-file record. Hence 1 must be subtracted from I. In option 2 the index I reflects the exact number of grades read; however, the name is read into TEMP first, before the name is stored into the array.

**Method 2**

The DO loop can be used to read an input file, however, an upper limit for the number of records to be read must be known in advance since the DO statement must indicate the number of times the loop is to be carried out. Suppose we expect no more than 100 records; we must tell the DO loop to read at least one more record than the maximum number of records expected—in our case 101, or 200, or even 10,000. This forces the loop to read the end-of-file record and therefore take an exit from the loop through the END = 8 option of the READ statement. With this approach the value of the DO index upon the end-of-file exit will always reflect the number of records read plus one (for the end-of-file record). The index I is *not* undefined outside the loop, since the loop never runs through its complete cycle, i.e., it is forced to exit prematurely through the END = 8 option.

***Option 1***

```
      REAL SCORE(100)
      CHARACTER*8 NAME(101)
      DO 5 I = 1,101
         READ(5,9,END=8) NAME(I),T1,T2
         SCORE(I)=(T1+T2)/2.
    5 CONTINUE
    8 I = I - 1
      WRITE(6,7)I
         .
         .
         .
```

If there are exactly 100 records, I will be 101 when the READ statement encounters the end of the file. Transfer is then made out of the loop to statement 8. The loop never gets a chance to go through its complete cycle, therefore the value of the index is preserved.

***Option 2***

```
      DO 5 I = 1, 100
         READ(5,9,END=8) NAME(I),T1,T2
         SCORE(I) = (T1+T2)/2.
    5 N = I
    8 WRITE(6,7)N
         .
         .
         .
```

If there are exactly 100 records the value for N will be 100; the end of file is not encountered in this case.

The value of N reflects the number of elements read whether the end of file is encountered or not.

When the DO loop is terminated, the value of N represents the number of elements read into the array whether normal exit is taken (100 times exactly) or whether an end of file condition exists.

*Example 1*

An input file consists of an unknown number of scores ranging from 1 to 10. Write the code to determine the number of scores below the average. Assume at least one score.

```
      INTEGER SCORE(100),BELOW
      REAL SUM,AVE
      SUM = 0.
      I = 1
      BELOW = 0
    4 READ(5,6,END=88)SCORE(I)
         SUM = SUM+SCORE(I)
         I = I+1
         GO TO 4
   88 AVE = SUM/(I-1)
      DO 5 K = 1,I-1
         IF(SCORE(K).LT.AVE)BELOW = BELOW+1
    5 CONTINUE
      WRITE(6,3)BELOW
         .
         .
         .
```

Accumulates the scores.
Index for the array SCORE.
Counts the number of scores below the average.
Read a score.
Add it to the sum.
Count it.
Go back and read more records.
I − 1 because of the end-of-file record.
Process I − 1 scores.

The DO list option can also be used to read input files with an unknown number of records. Naturally it is not possible to analyze the data as it is read into the array with this form of input.

*Example 2*

Temperature readings have been recorded 50 per record. Write the code to read an input file consisting of no more than 10 such records and compute and print the average temperature. *Then* print the temperature readings, one per line.

```
      REAL TEMP(501),AVE,SUM          Force the automatic end-of-file exit
      READ(5,6,END=88) (TEMP(I),I=1,501)  in case there are exactly 10 records.
   88 N = I-1                         Count of temperature readings.
      SUM = 0.
      DO 5 I = 1,N                    There are N temperature readings.
         SUM = SUM+TEMP(I)
    5 CONTINUE
      AVE = SUM/N
      WRITE(6,4) (TEMP(I),I=1,N)      Write the temperature readings
      WRITE(6,8) AVE                  one per line.
    4 FORMAT(1X,F5.1)
    6 FORMAT(50F4.1)
    8 FORMAT(1X,F5.1)
```

In conclusion, the implied DO list is a convenient method for loading or writing out arrays. The implied DO list cannot be used if the data items are to be analyzed as they are read into memory or written out. For example, if one wishes to read an array and stop the reading process when a particular item is encountered in the input file, an explicit DO loop must be used, since the implied DO list does not allow testing while reading; likewise for output.

# 7-6  Programming Examples

## 7-6-1  Table Look-Up

Table look-up is a fast and efficient method to directly access data in a table without searching the table elements, something like looking up your taxes in the tax table (fast and painful!).

*Problem/Specification*:   United Package Service operates under a cost delivery system based on article weight and destination zone. The rate table per pound is as follows:

| Zone Code | Cost Per Pound | Meaning |
|-----------|----------------|---------|
| 1 | $ .55 | The cost to ship 1 pound to zone 1 is $ .55 |
| 2 | $ .80 | . |
| 3 | $1.03 | The cost to ship 1 pound to zone 3 is $1.03. |
| 4 | $1.30 | . |
| 5 | $1.75 | . |
| 6 | $2.01 | . |

Let us write a program that will read an input file where each record contains two entries: a destination zone and a shipment weight. The program will print the destination zone, the weight, and the corresponding shipping cost.

To understand the problem, let us look at the following example. Suppose we wanted to send a two-pound parcel to zone 6. We would look up the zone 6, and identify the corresponding cost per pound entry, which is $2.01. Since the parcel weighs two pounds, the total cost would be $2 * 2.01 = 4.02$. An attractive output design might be:

| ZONE | WEIGHT | COST |
|------|--------|------|
| 6 | 2.0 | 4.02 |
| 2 | 3.5 | 2.80 |

A convenient way to look up the cost associated with a particular zone is to create an array RATE such that RATE(1) = $.55, RATE(2) = $.80, ..., RATE(6) = $2.01. In this way, if the zone is 6, for example, we can immediately look up the sixth entry of RATE ($2.01). In general, the cost associated with zone ZONE is simply RATE(ZONE). Hence if we read a zone ZONE and a weight WGHT, the corresponding shipment cost is simply WGHT * RATE (ZONE).

The program in Figure 7-7 reads a zone ZONE and a weight WGHT, and prints the zone ZONE, the weight WGHT, and the resulting cost RATE(ZONE)*WGHT.

**FIGURE 7-7**    A TABLE LOOKUP PROBLEM

```
C TABLE LOOKUP PROBLEM
C   RATE: RATE TABLE
C   COST: COST TO CUSTOMER
C   ZONE: TARGET ZONE FOR SHIPMENT
C   WGHT: WEIGHT OF PACKAGE
C
      REAL WGHT, COST, RATE(6)
      INTEGER ZONE
      DATA RATE/.55,.8,1.03,1.30,1.75,2.01/      Define the rate table.
      WRITE(6,3)
    1 READ(5,6,END=60) ZONE,WGHT                 Read a zone and a weight.
      IF(ZONE .LT. 7) THEN                        Check for valid zone.
         COST = WGHT * RATE(ZONE)                 Compute corresponding shipment cost.
         WRITE(6,11) ZONE,WGHT,COST
      ELSE
         WRITE(6,12)ZONE                          Print invalid zone number.
      ENDIF
      GO TO 1                                     Go back and read more records.
   60 STOP
    6 FORMAT(I2,1X,F4.1)
    3 FORMAT(' ZONE    WEIGHT   COST')
   11 FORMAT(1X,I2,6X,F4.1,3X,F5.2)
   12 FORMAT(1X,'CHECK ZONE',I2)
      END
```

*Input File*

| ZONE | WEIGHT | COST |
|------|--------|------|
| 6 | 2.0 | 4.02 |
| 3 | 23.5 | 24.21 |
| 1 | 8.0 | 4.40 |
| 5 | 10.0 | 17.50 |
| 2 | 5.0 | 4.00 |

ZONE⟶    ⟵WGHT

```
06 02.0
03 23.5
01 08.0
05 10.0
02 05.0
```

## 7-6-2 Inventory Update Program

*Problem/Specification:* An input file consists of two sets of records:

1. The first set of records is the master file which reflects an item inventory at the start of the business day. Each master file record contains a part number and a corresponding item stock quantity. The end of the master file is identified by a record containing negative entries. Let us assume that the master file contains no more than 100 records.

2. The second set of records, which follows the master file, reflects the transactions for each of the various items during that day. Transaction records have the same format as the master file records: they contain the item number and the corresponding total number of items sold that day.

Write a program to update the master file against the transaction file to produce the new master file at the end of the day. A reorder notice should accompany any item number for which fewer than 10 items remain in stock. A list of invalid item numbers, if any, should be printed before the final master file is printed. Invalid items are incorrectly recorded items in the transaction file for which there are no corresponding items in the master file. The input and output should be similar to:

```
                Input File

   Item Number      Item Quantity                Output File

                  444  40              CURRENT  INVENTORY
                  111  30           ITEM NO        QUANTITY
Master file       222  15              444            40
                  134  20              111            30
                  353  05              222            15
                                       134            20
End of master file → -3  -4            353             5
                  134  03            UPDATED  INVENTORY
                  111  29           ITEM NO        QUANTITY
                  112  09                               INVALID ITEM 112
Transaction file  353  02                               INVALID ITEM 352
                  352  12              444            40
                  222  10              111             1 REORDER
                                       222             5 REORDER
                                       134            17
                                       353             3 REORDER
```

In the input file shown above, the master file consists of 5 items that represent the inventory at the beginning of the business day. Sales are reflected in the master file by subtracting the number of units sold for each item from the corresponding master item quantity. For example, originally there are 20 of item 134; three of these are sold during the day, hence the updated master file quantity for item 134 should be 17 (20 − 3).

The master file should be read into two arrays: one contains the master item numbers (in this case there are five), and the other contains the corresponding item quantities.

We then read the transaction file one record at a time; every time an item is read (sold), the master file is updated to reflect the current number of items on the shelf. This requires a search of the master table to identify which master file item number is to be updated. In the transaction for item 134, we look for an entry equal to 134 in the master item table; in this case it is the 4th entry of the table. We then subtract the item quantity (3) from the 4th element of the master file quantity table.

If there is an incorrect item number in the transaction file, there will be no matching item in the master item table. If this should happen, we print the invalid item and read the next record. When all transaction records have been read, the master file will be updated. Then the master file is printed, two entries at a time. If the quantity entry is less than 10, a reorder message is printed.

The program to solve this problem is shown in Figure 7-8.

**FIGURE 7-8**    AN INVENTORY UPDATE PROGRAM

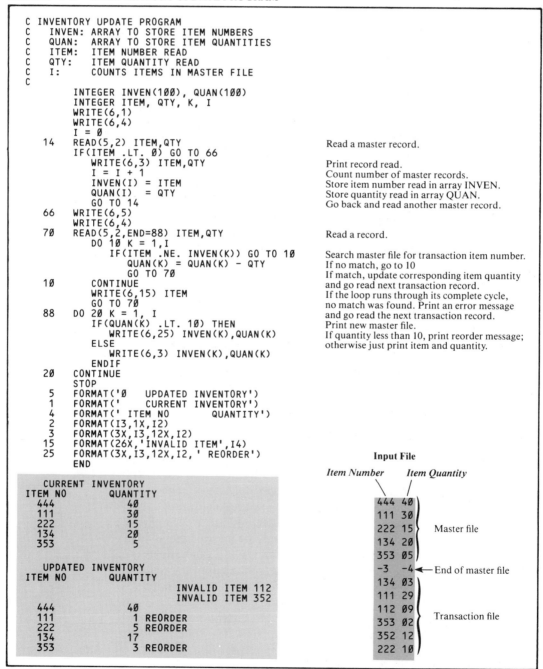

```
C INVENTORY UPDATE PROGRAM
C    INVEN: ARRAY TO STORE ITEM NUMBERS
C    QUAN:  ARRAY TO STORE ITEM QUANTITIES
C    ITEM:  ITEM NUMBER READ
C    QTY:   ITEM QUANTITY READ
C    I:     COUNTS ITEMS IN MASTER FILE
C
        INTEGER INVEN(100), QUAN(100)
        INTEGER ITEM, QTY, K, I
        WRITE(6,1)
        WRITE(6,4)
        I = 0
   14   READ(5,2) ITEM,QTY                   Read a master record.
        IF(ITEM .LT. 0) GO TO 66
           WRITE(6,3) ITEM,QTY               Print record read.
           I = I + 1                         Count number of master records.
           INVEN(I) = ITEM                   Store item number read in array INVEN.
           QUAN(I)  = QTY                    Store quantity read in array QUAN.
           GO TO 14                          Go back and read another master record.
   66   WRITE(6,5)
        WRITE(6,4)
   70   READ(5,2,END=88) ITEM,QTY            Read a record.
           DO 10 K = 1,I                     Search master file for transaction item number.
              IF(ITEM .NE. INVEN(K)) GO TO 10    If no match, go to 10
                 QUAN(K) = QUAN(K) - QTY     If match, update corresponding item quantity
                 GO TO 70                    and go read next transaction record.
   10      CONTINUE                          If the loop runs through its complete cycle,
           WRITE(6,15) ITEM                  no match was found. Print an error message
           GO TO 70                          and go read the next transaction record.
   88   DO 20 K = 1, I                       Print new master file.
           IF(QUAN(K) .LT. 10) THEN          If quantity less than 10, print reorder message;
              WRITE(6,25) INVEN(K),QUAN(K)   otherwise just print item and quantity.
           ELSE
              WRITE(6,3) INVEN(K),QUAN(K)
           ENDIF
   20   CONTINUE
        STOP
    5   FORMAT('0   UPDATED INVENTORY')
    1   FORMAT('     CURRENT INVENTORY')
    4   FORMAT(' ITEM NO      QUANTITY')
    2   FORMAT(I3,1X,I2)
    3   FORMAT(3X,I3,12X,I2)
   15   FORMAT(26X,'INVALID ITEM',I4)
   25   FORMAT(3X,I3,12X,I2,' REORDER')
        END
```

```
    CURRENT INVENTORY
ITEM NO      QUANTITY
    444            40
    111            30
    222            15
    134            20
    353             5

    UPDATED INVENTORY
ITEM NO      QUANTITY
                          INVALID ITEM 112
                          INVALID ITEM 352
    444            40
    111             1 REORDER
    222             5 REORDER
    134            17
    353             3 REORDER
```

**Input File**

*Item Number*    *Item Quantity*

```
444 40  ┐
111 30  │
222 15  ├ Master file
134 20  │
353 05  ┘
-3  -4  ◄─ End of master file
134 03  ┐
111 29  │
112 09  │
353 02  ├ Transaction file
352 12  │
222 10  ┘
```

### 7-6-3 A Frequency Distribution

*Problem/Specification*: Each record of an input file contains a score (1–100). Write a program to determine the number of times each score occurs. The input and output will have the following form:

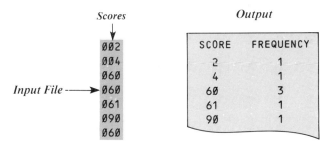

Given a list of scores in the range 1 to 100, we must determine how many times score 1 appears, how many times score 2 appears, and so forth. It is possible that many of these scores will not appear at all in the input list.

Since we do not know what scores will occur, we need 100 different counters to count all possible score occurrences. Also, since it would be quite impractical to have 100 differently labeled variable names to count the occurrence of each score, we will use 100 array elements as counters to count all possible score occurrences. We need to choose which of the array elements will count which score. We decide on the following:

KOUNT(1) will count the occurrence of score 1
KOUNT(2) will count the occurrence of score 2
 .
 .
 .
KOUNT(36) will count the occurrence of score 36, and
KOUNT(SCORE) will count how many times the score SCORE appears in the input list.

Thus every time we read a SCORE, we will use that SCORE as the subscript of KOUNT to designate which counter to increment, i.e., we add 1 to KOUNT(SCORE):

$$\text{KOUNT(SCORE)} = \text{KOUNT(SCORE)} + 1$$

After all scores have been read the set of counters will appear as follows:

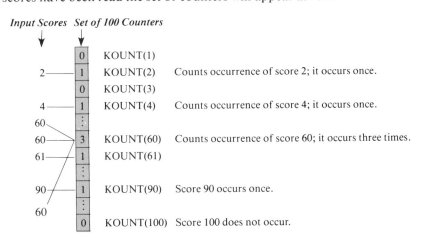

Every time we read a score SCORE we add 1 to the appropriate counter through the statement KOUNT(SCORE) = KOUNT(SCORE) + 1, i.e., if SCORE = 80 then KOUNT(80) = KOUNT(80) + 1, meaning that the count of score 80 is equal to the old count of score 80 plus 1. Obviously KOUNT(80) and all other counters should also be initialized to 0's.

When all the scores have been read, we must print all those scores whose frequency counts are nonzero. This means going through the array of counters, starting with KOUNT(1), and asking the question: Is KOUNT(1) = 0? If KOUNT(1) = 0, there were no scores equal to 1 so we do not print the score 1. If KOUNT(1) = 3, this means that the score 1 occurred three times in the list, so we write the score 1 and its corresponding frequency 3. In general, if the answer to the question "Is KOUNT(I) = 0?" is yes, then the score I is *not* printed, otherwise the score I and the frequency count KOUNT(I) are printed.

The FORTRAN code for this problem is shown in Figure 7–9.

**FIGURE 7-9** A FREQUENCY DISTRIBUTION

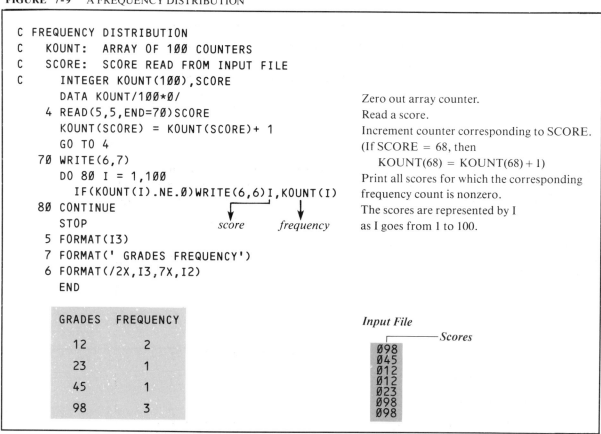

### 7-6-4 Do It Now

Modify the program of Figure 7–9 to produce a sorted list of scores, i.e., if score 64 occurs 3 times, print 64,64,64. Scores should be written one per line.

## Answer

Change the DO 80 loop to the following:

```
   DO 80 I = 1,100
      IF (KOUNT .EQ. 0) GO TO 80
      DO 60 J = 1,KOUNT(I)
         WRITE(6,5)I
60    CONTINUE
80 CONTINUE
```

### 7-6-5 Bar Graphs

It is often desirable to produce graphic output from a computer program. A scientific problem might require the graph of a function; a business problem might require a bar graph. Consider, for example, the following problem. Data regarding company sales for a week have been tabulated as shown:

| Day | Sales | | DAY | SALES |
|-----|-------|---|-----|-------|
| 1 | 3 | To visualize the sales trend, we can represent | 1 | *** |
| 2 | 7 | each day's sales with an equivalent number of * | 2 | ******* |
| 3 | 10 | symbols. The output on the right might be suit- | 3 | ********** |
| 4 | 6 | able. | 4 | ****** |
| 5 | 8 | | 5 | ******** |
| 6 | 2 | | 6 | ** |
| 7 | 0 | | 7 | |

The solution to this problem is shown in Figure 7–10 (we assume SALES does not exceed 20). Note that the variable STAR is initialized to the character *; every time a sale is read (SALES) a number of stars (*) equal to SALES is printed by the implied DO list in statement 15.

**FIGURE 7-10    EXAMPLE OF A BAR GRAPH**

```
C BAR GRAPH EXAMPLE
C   SALES:  DAILY SALES VOLUME
C   DAY:    TO COUNT THE DAYS
C   STAR:   GRAPHIC SYMBOL FOR PLOTTING
      INTEGER SALES,DAY
      CHARACTER STAR
      DATA STAR/'*'/
      WRITE(6,1)                          Skip to next page to print titles.
      DO 20 DAY = 1,7
        READ(5,2) SALES                   Read sales for the day.
        IF(SALES.EQ.0) THEN               If sales are 0, print only the day.
          WRITE(6,3)DAY
        ELSE
15        WRITE(6,3)DAY,(STAR,J=1,SALES)   Print the day and number of stars
        ENDIF                              corresponding to the sales for that day.
20    CONTINUE
 1 FORMAT('1DAY',T8,'SALES')
 3 FORMAT(T3,I1,T8,20A1)                   Assume sales do not exceed 20(20A1).
 2 FORMAT(I2)
      STOP
      END
```

### 7-6-6 Array Input/Output

To be admitted to the Mensa club, candidates must score a minimum of 74 points on an intelligence test. Each candidate's name and test score are recorded on records as shown below. Write a program to read an input file (no more than 50 records) to produce the following information in the form illustrated by the same input and output shown below:

1. Two separate paragraph listings of names of successful and unsuccessful candidates. Each line should contain four names.

2. Two consecutive vertical lists of names and scores of successful and unsuccessful candidates (one name and corresponding score per line).

3. If there are no successful candidates, the caption "SUCCESSFUL CANDIDATES" should not be printed; the same holds true if there are no unsuccessful candidates.

```
                    Output                              Input File

                                                 Name          Score
        SUCCESSFUL CANDIDATES
        ADAMS       PENSKE      MICHAEL   SALAAM     ADAMS      074
        JONES       CLARK       WILLS     MOUTON     PENSKE     081
        HENGSIU                                      LOUD       056
        UNSUCCESSFUL CANDIDATES                      MICHAEL    090
        LOUD        LAZY        MILLS     ANTONE      LAZY       048
        MONISH      GAMBINO     BOILLOT   DERNIER     MILLS      044
                    NAMES       SCORES                ANTONE     046
        PASSING     ADAMS        74                   MONISH     046
                    PENSKE       81                   SALAAM     100
                    MICHAEL      90                   GAMBINO    035
                    SALAAM      100                   BOILLOT    048
                    JONES        76                   JONES      076
                    CLARK        79                   CLARK      079
                    WILLS        94                   WILLS      094
                    MOUTON       86                   DERNIER    010
                    HENGSIU      96                   MOUTON     086
        FAIL        LOUD         56                   HENGSIU    096
                    LAZY         48
                    MILLS        44
                    ANTONE       46
                    MONISH       46
                    GAMBINO      35
                    BOILLOT      48
                    DERNIER      10
```

A program to solve this problem is shown in Figure 7–11. Since the names of the candidates must be printed by group (success/failure), two arrays are needed to store the names of successful candidates and unsuccessful candidates.

A name and a score are read from a record. If the score is not greater than 74, the name is stored in the array FNAME and its corresponding score in array FAIL. The index F is used to place each name and score in successive array locations. Arrays PNAME, PASS, and index P are used similarly to record the passing candidates' data. When the end-of-file is reached, P contains the number of passing candidates while F contains the number of failing candidates.

The implied DO list WRITE(6,2)(PNAME(I),I = 1,P) specifies the list of all passing candidates, while FORMAT 2 tells the computer to print first a heading, then four names per line under the heading. Similarly, the names of passing candidates and their scores are specified by the statement WRITE(6,4)(PNAME(I),PASS(I),I = 1,P). FORMAT 4 specifies that one name and one score are to be printed per line. Note the position of the literals PASSING and FAILING in FORMAT 4 and note the use of the parentheses in

**FIGURE 7-11**    INPUT OUTPUT OF ARRAYS

```
C INPUT OUTPUT OF ARRAYS
C    PNAME: TABLE OF NAMES OF PASSING CANDIDATES
C    FNAME: TABLE OF NAMES OF FAILING CANDIDATES
C    PASS:  ARRAY CONTAINING PASSING SCORES
C    FAIL:  ARRAY CONTAINING FAILING SCORES
C    P:     VARIABLE USED TO INDEX "PASSING" ARRAYS
C           ALSO COUNTS NUMBER OF PASSING CANDIDATES
C    F:     VARIABLE USED TO INDEX "FAILING" ARRAYS
C    NAME:  CANDIDATE'S NAME READ FROM INPUT RECORD
C    SCORE: CANDIDATE'S SCORE READ FROM INPUT RECORD
C    MESSG: CHARACTER VARIABLE TO HOLD CAPTIONS FOR OUTPUT PURPOSES
C
      CHARACTER*8 PNAME(50),FNAME(50),NAME
      CHARACTER*23 MESSG
      INTEGER PASS(50),FAIL(50),SCORE,P,F
      DATA P,F/0,0/,MESSG/'SUCCESSFUL CANDIDATES'/
   10 READ(5,1,END=88)NAME,SCORE
        IF(SCORE .LT. 74) THEN
C         CANDIDATE FAILS; RECORD NAME & SCORE IN "FAIL" ARRAYS
          F = F + 1
          FNAME(F) = NAME
          FAIL(F)  = SCORE
        ELSE
C         CANDIDATE PASSES; RECORD NAME & SCORE IN "PASS" ARRAYS
          P = P + 1
          PNAME(P) = NAME
          PASS(P)  = SCORE
        ENDIF
        GO TO 10
   88 WRITE(6,2) MESSG, (PNAME(I),I=1,P)      This statement is bypassed if P = 0.
      MESSG = 'UNSUCCESSFUL CANDIDATES'
      WRITE(6,2) MESSG, (FNAME(I),I=1,F)      This statement is bypassed if F = 0.
      WRITE(6,3)
      MESSG = 'PASSING'
      WRITE(6,4) MESSG, (PNAME(I),PASS(I),I=1,P)   bypassed if P = 0.
      MESSG = 'FAIL'
      WRITE(6,4) MESSG, (FNAME(I),FAIL(I),I=1,F)   bypassed if F = 0.
      STOP
    1 FORMAT(A8,I3)
    2 FORMAT('0',A23//(1X,4A9))
    3 FORMAT('0',11X,'NAMES    SCORES')
    4 FORMAT('0  ',A9,A8,1X,I3/(12X,A8,1X,I3))
      END
```

SUCCESSFUL CANDIDATES

| ADAMS | PENSKE | MICHAEL | SALAAM |
|-------|--------|---------|--------|
| JONES | CLARK | WILLS | MOUTON |
| HENGSIU | | | |

UNSUCCESSFUL CANDIDATES

| LOUD | LAZY | MILLS | ANTONE |
|------|------|-------|--------|
| MONISH | GAMBINO | BOILLOT | DERNIER |

|  | NAMES | SCORES |
|--|-------|--------|
| PASSING | ADAMS | 74 |
| | PENSKE | 81 |
| | MICHAEL | 90 |
| | SALAAM | 100 |
| | JONES | 76 |
| | CLARK | 79 |
| | WILLS | 94 |
| | MOUTON | 86 |
| | HENGSIU | 96 |
| FAIL | LOUD | 56 |
| | LAZY | 48 |
| | MILLS | 44 |
| | ANTONE | 46 |
| | MONISH | 46 |
| | GAMBINO | 35 |
| | BOILLOT | 48 |
| | DERNIER | 10 |

*Input File*

| Name | Score |
|------|-------|
| ADAMS | 074 |
| PENSKE | 081 |
| LOUD | 056 |
| MICHAEL | 090 |
| LAZY | 048 |
| MILLS | 044 |
| ANTONE | 046 |
| MONISH | 046 |
| SALAAM | 100 |
| GAMBINO | 035 |
| BOILLOT | 048 |
| JONES | 076 |
| CLARK | 079 |
| WILLS | 094 |
| DERNIER | 010 |
| MOUTON | 086 |
| HENGSIU | 096 |

(12X,A8,1X,F6.1)) to force format control to restart at the rightmost open parenthesis in the format to print all remaining names and scores. (See section 7–8–1 for a complete discussion of this feature.) Note that if P = 0 (no passing candidates) or F = 0 (no failing candidates) the corresponding names/scores will not be printed.

# 7-7 **Sorting and Plotting**

Given a list of any type of unprocessed or raw information, such as a lists of names or employee numbers, one's first impulse is, generally, to sort out these items into some particular order (descending or ascending) so that looking them up will be a great deal easier. Hence it should come as no surprise that sorting is one of the most practiced forms of data processing (for directories, tax tables, book retrieval, identifications, and so forth). Arrays obviously lend themselves to this type of manipulation.

There are many clever and sophisticated ways to sort arrays (see exercise 40 in section 7–10–2). Two traditional methods are presented in this section: the *bubble sort* and the *mini/ max* methods. Although these methods may not be used often in a real-life environment, they will give you some insight into the sorting process, as well as an appreciation of array indexing.

### 7-7-1 **The Bubble Sort**

Assume the following list of numbers is to be sorted into ascending sequence:

> 4   5   3   2

One systematic approach begins by comparing the first pair of numbers and interchanging the first number with the second number if the first number is greater than the second number. Then we move on to the next pair, 5 and 3, and do the same thing—this time we interchange 5 and 3. Then move on to the next pair, 5 and 2, and perform an interchange if necessary (in this case we interchange 2 and 5). In this way we ensure that the largest number is continuously moved to the right. At the end of this first pass through the list, the numbers are

> 4   3   2   5

We now repeat the procedure:

Compare the first pair 4, 3 and obtain 3, 4.

Compare the second pair 4, 2 and obtain 2, 4.

Compare the third pair 4, 5 and obtain 4, 5.

Actually we do not need to process the third pair since we already know that the largest number is in the last position. At the end of this second pass, the second largest

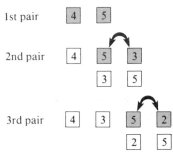

The largest number is now in the right-most position

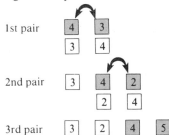

number is in the second-to-last position and the numbers are now:

$$3 \quad 2 \quad 4 \quad 5$$

We now carry out the same procedure for the third time.

Compare the first pair 3, 2 and obtain 2, 3.

1st pair  3  2  ☐  ☐
          2  3

Compare the second pair 3, 4 and obtain 3, 4.

2nd pair  2  3  4

Compare the third pair 4, 5 and obtain 4, 5.

3rd pair  2  3  4  5

Actually, we only needed to compare the first pair of numbers, since we know the last two numbers are already in order.

Before we write the complete code to sort an array of five elements into ascending order, let us just write the code to take care of just the first pass (moving the largest number in the right-most position):

```
INTEGER G(4)
DO 4 I = 1,3
    IF(G(I).LT.G(I+1)) GO TO 4
    T     = G(I)
    G(I)  = G(I+1)
    G(I+1) = T
4 CONTINUE
```

The upper limit for I is 3. When I is 3, we will be comparing G(3) with G(4), which is G(I+1). G(I) and G(I + 1) are interchanged if the next number G(I + 1) is less than the previous number G(I).

This code will move the largest number in the array G into the right-most position. To sort the entire array, we need to make three passes through the list as explained previously. Hence we will carry out the above procedure three times by using the following code:

```
INTEGER G(4)
DO 5 J = 1,3
    DO 4 I = 1,3
        IF(G(I).LT.G(I+1)) GO TO 4
            T     = G(I)
            G(I)  = G(I+1)
            G(I+1) = T
4       CONTINUE
5 CONTINUE
```

Repeat the 1st pass three times.

This code will sort all elements of the array. You might find this code easy to remember at the expense of efficiency—on the second pass, the code compares G(3) with G(4), when we already know that G(4) is the largest. This also happens on the third pass: G(2) is compared with G(3) when we already know that G(3) is larger than G(2). It would be better to stop the second pass at G(3) and stop the third pass at G(2), i.e., we would like the index I to be 3 for the first pass, 2 for the second pass, and 1 for the third and last pass. To do this, we replace the statement DO 4 I = 1,3 with the statement DO 4 I = 1,4-J since 4 − J will generate the numbers 3, 2, and 1.

The sort program in Figure 7–12 reads an input file containing an unknown number of scores (maximum of 30 scores) and sorts these scores into ascending order.

FIGURE 7-12 A BUBBLE SORT

```
C BUBBLE SORT PROGRAM: ASCENDING ORDER SORT
C   SCORES: ARRAY OF SCORES TO BE SORTED
C   N:       NUMBER OF SCORES
C   PASSES: NUMBER OF PASSES (N - 1)
C   TEMP:    TEMPORARY LOCATION FOR INTERCHANGE PROCEDURE
C
      INTEGER SCORES(31),N,PASSES,TEMP
      READ(5,3,END=88)(SCORES(I),I=1,31)        Force transfer out of DO list
88    N = I - 1                                 I − 1 because of the end-of-file record.
      WRITE(6,1) (SCORES(I),I=1,N)
      PASSES = N - 1
      DO 5 L = 1, PASSES                         The outer loop controls the number of passes.
         DO 6 J = 1, N-L                         The first pass shifts highest score into the
            IF(SCORES(J).LT.SCORES(J+1))GOTO6   right-most position, ie., SCORES(N). The second
7              TEMP      = SCORES(J+1)           pass shifts the second-highest score into next-to-last
8              SCORES(J+1) = SCORES(J)           position (SCORES(N − 1)), etc.
9              SCORES(J)   = TEMP                N − L represents the size of the ever shrinking
6         CONTINUE                               array as it gets smaller with each pass.
5     CONTINUE                                   J is used to index the interchange procedure that
4     WRITE(6,2) (SCORES(I),I=1,N)               moves the largest numbers to the right.
      STOP
1     FORMAT(' UNSORTED SCORES:',30I4)
2     FORMAT(' SORTED SCORES  :',30I4)
3     FORMAT(I3)
      END
```

UNSORTED SCORES   42  65  36  48  92  78  50
SORTED SCORES     36  42  48  50  65  78  92

## 7-7-2 Interchange Minimum/Maximum (Mini/Max) Sort

Another method that can be used to sort an array of numbers into ascending order is to determine the location (position) of the smallest element in the array and interchange that element with the first element of the array (see Figure 7–13). At the end of this first search pass, the smallest element is in the first position. The array is then searched for the next smallest element, with the search starting at position 2 of the array; the smallest element is then swapped with the number in position 2 of the array. At the end of the second search pass, the first two elements of the array are in ascending sequence order. The search for the next smallest number starts in position 3, and the same search and interchange process is repeated until the last two (rightmost) array elements are processed. Using this sorting procedure, an array of **N** elements requires N − 1 passes for the search and interchange procedure. The search for the smallest number involves comparing N numbers during the first pass, N − 1 numbers during the second pass, ..., and two numbers during the last pass. Figure 7–13 illustrates the sorting process with an integer array SCORES containing 4 scores.

To understand the process better, let us consider the problem of sorting an array of four scores into ascending order and write the code just for the first pass. This pass determines the position of the smallest score of the array and interchanges the smallest score with the score in the first position of the array.

| | |
|---|---|
| `S = SCORES(1)` | Assume the smallest score is SCORES(1) before the search starts. |
| `K = 1` | Assume the position K of smallest score is 1, subject to later change. |
| `DO 6 J = 2,4` | Start comparing S with the remaining scores. |
| `IF(S.LE.SCORES(J))GO TO 6` | If S ≤ SCORES(J), then S is still the smallest |
| `S = SCORES(J)` | and its position K does not change. |
| `K = J` | If S > SCORES(J), then the new smallest score is |
| `6 CONTINUE` | at location J, so we set K equal to J and we |
| `TEMP = SCORES(K)` | reset S to SCORES(J) to keep track of current smallest score. |
| `SCORES(K) = SCORES(1)` | After the loop is completed, we switch the smallest score with |
| `SCORES(1) = TEMP` | the score in the first position. |

This code takes care of the first pass. At the end of the first pass, the smallest score is in position 1, so we start looking for the next smallest score at position 2 of the array. Hence, prior to the second pass, we set S to SCORES(2) and K to 2. At the conclusion of the second pass, we interchange the smallest score (at position K) with the score in the second position and the process continues. The complete FORTRAN code, which is shown in Figure 7–14, reads N scores into an array SCORES (assume there are no more than 25 scores).

**FIGURE 7-13** MINI/MAX SORTING PROCESS

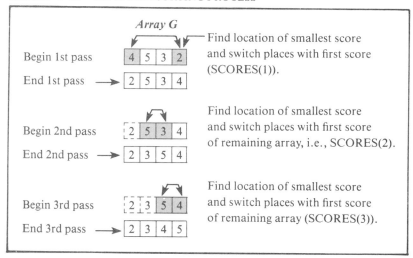

**FIGURE 7-14** THE MINI/MAX SORT

```
C MINI/MAX ASCENDING ORDER SORT PROGRAM
C   S:      TEMPORARY LOCATION TO HOLD SMALLEST SCORE
C   K:      TEMPORARY LOCATION TO IDENTIFY POSITION OF SMALLEST SCORE IN ARRAY
C   SCORES: ARRAY OF SCORES TO BE SORTED
C   N:      NUMBER OF SCORES
C   PASSES: NUMBER OF PASSES (N - 1)
C   TEMP:   TEMPORARY LOCATION FOR INTERCHANGE PROCEDURE
C
         INTEGER SCORES(26),N,PASSES,TEMP,S,K
         READ(5,3,END=88)(SCORES(I),I=1,26)
88       N = I - 1
         WRITE(6,1) (SCORES(I),I=1,N)
         PASSES = N - 1
         DO 5 L = 1, PASSES
            S = SCORES(L)
            K = L
            DO 6 J = L+1, N
               IF(S .LE. SCORES(J))GO TO 6
                  S = SCORES(J)
                  K = J
6           CONTINUE
            TEMP      = SCORES(K)
            SCORES(K) = SCORES(L)
            SCORES(L) = TEMP
5        CONTINUE
         WRITE(6,2) (SCORES(I),I=1,N)
         STOP
1        FORMAT(' UNSORTED SCORES:',25I4)
2        FORMAT(' SORTED SCORES   :',25I4)
3        FORMAT(I3)
         END
```

N keeps track of the number of scores.

Number of passes
L controls the number of passes. Before starting a pass, assume S = SCORES(L) is the smallest score and that its location in the array is K = L.
Find the real smallest score S and its location K in the array.
S is smallest number so far.
Current position of smallest number is K.
At end of loop smallest number is SCORES(K).
Interchange the smallest score found
during the first pass with the first element, then the smallest score found during the second pass with the second element, and so forth.

```
UNSORTED SCORES:   12  45 100    3  98  67  76
SORTED SCORES  :    3  12  45  67  76  98 100
```

## 7-7-3 Do It Now

**1.** Tabulate the bubble sort program in Figure 7–12 for the following score input file:

input file ⟶ 5 1 2 3  (4 scores)

**2.** In the bubble sort program of Figure 7–12, can you stop the sort process if all numbers are sorted before all passes are completed?

**3.** Tabulate the mini/max sort program of Figure 7–14 for the following score file:

input file ⟶ 5 3 2  (3 scores)

## *Answers*

**1.**

| I | Scores(1) | Scores(2) | Scores(3) | Scores(4) | N | Passes | L | J | Temp |
|---|-----------|-----------|-----------|-----------|---|--------|---|---|------|
| 1 | 5 | 1 | 2 | 3 | 4 | 3 | 1 | 1 | 1 |
| 2 | 1 | 5 | 5 | 5 | | | | 2 | 2 |
| 3 | | 2 | 3 | | | | | 3 | 3 |
| 4 | | | | | | | 2 | 1 | |
| 5 | | | | | | | | 2 | |
| | | | | | | | 3 | 1 | |

**2.** The sort process can be terminated as soon as it is discovered that no elements are interchanged during any one pass. If the numbers are all in sequence, lines 7, 8 and 9 in Figure 7–12 are not executed. Hence before any given pass, we will set a variable to 0 and reset that variable to 1 if lines 7, 8 and 9 are executed. If the variable is still 0 at the end of a pass, the sort process is stopped. To carry this out, make the following changes in the DO loops:

```
      DO 5 L = 1,PASSES
         M=0
         DO 6 J = 1,N-L
            IF(SCORES(J) .LT. SCORES(J+1))GO TO 6
               TEMP       = SCORES(J+1)
               SCORES(J+1) = SCORES(J)
               SCORES(J)   = TEMP
               M = 1
6         CONTINUE
          IF(M .EQ. 0) GO TO 4
5     CONTINUE
```

**3.**

| I | Scores(1) | Scores(2) | Scores(3) | N | Passes | L | S | K | J | Temp |
|---|-----------|-----------|-----------|---|--------|---|---|---|---|------|
| 1 | 5 | 3 | 2 | 3 | 2 | 1 | 5 | 1 | 2 | |
| 2 | | | | | | | 3 | 2 | | |
| 3 | 2 | | 5 | | | | 2 | 3 | 3 | 2 |
| 4 | | 3 | | | | 2 | 3 | 2 | 3 | |
| | | 3 | | | | | | | | 3 |

### 7-7-4  Graph Plotting: General Considerations

Let us write a program to graph the function $y = x^2/5 + 1$ in the first quadrant, for values of $x$ ranging from 1 to 7 in steps of 1. Before we write the program, let us get a general idea about how to proceed by looking at the function $y = x^2/5 + 1$. Graphing the function means plotting various points that belong to the curve and then joining these points together. We pick various values of $x$ such as 1, 2, 3, ..., 7, then we determine the corresponding values for $y$ and plot the corresponding points, as follows:

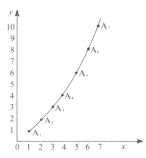

| x | y |
|---|---|
| 1 | 1.2 |
| 2 | 1.8 |
| 3 | 2.8 |
| 4 | 4.2 |
| 5 | 6 |
| 6 | 8.2 |
| 7 | 10.8 |

It is a little more difficult to print the graph of this function using the computer, because the printer paper moves up in increments of one line. Thus it is difficult to print $A_1$ first and then print $A_2$, since the computer first prints $A_1$ and then prints $A_2$ on the next line, i.e., $A_2$ would lie below $A_1$ on the printer form. You might ask, "Why not print $A_7$, then $A_6$, and down to $A_1$ to keep the points coming down the page? Use incremental values of $y$ equal to 10, 9, 8, ..., 1 and compute the corresponding values of $x$ using the formula $x = \sqrt{5y - 5}$ instead of $y = x^2/5 + 1$." This, of course, would work in this particular case, but what if you had to graph the function $y = x^4 - 16x^3 + 2x^2 - 1$ ? How would you compute $x$ in terms of $y$?

We will solve this problem by using the vertical axis as the $x$ axis so that each new printer line corresponds to a unit increment of $x$; the horizontal axis will be the y axis. For each value of $x$, we will print a graphic symbol $y$ units away from the $x$ axis. With this switching of axes, the graph of the function will appear as:

| $x$ | $y$ | $y$ rounded |
|-----|-----|-------------|
| 1 | 1.2 | 1 |
| 2 | 1.8 | 2 |
| 3 | 2.8 | 3 |
| 4 | 4.2 | 4 |
| 5 | 6 | 6 |
| 6 | 8.2 | 8 |
| 7 | 10.8 | 11 |

**Physical Positioning of y**

*y axis*

*x axis*

line array containing graphic symbol * at position $y$ of line while all remaining positions are blanks.

From this diagram, the graphing process becomes more evident. We use an array to print one horizontal line at a time. The line array is initially set to blanks. For a given value of $x$, the corresponding value of the function $y$ is computed, and a graphic symbol such as * is inserted at position $y$ in the line array. The array (line) is then printed, and the process is repeated for the different values of $x$. Thus any graph can be visualized as follows on your printer:

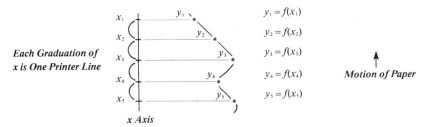

Care must be exercised if $y$ is negative. In this case, an appropriate constant should be added to all values of $y$ to shift the graph to the right on the output line (translation).

If the changes in the magnitude of $y$ are fractional, $y$ should be scaled (multiplied by a constant) appropriately; for example, if for $x = 2$ the value of $y$ is 1.3, and if for $x = 3$ the value for $y$ is 1.4, you might wish to multiply $y$ by 10 to obtain 13 and 14; then the graphic symbol on the first line will be one position to the left of the graphic symbol on the second line. Otherwise the graph might be represented by a vertical straight line, since LINE(1.3) is equal to LINE(1.4).

The code to graph the function $y = \dfrac{x^2}{5} + 1$ is shown in Figure 7–15 for values of $x$ ranging from 1 to 10 in increments of 1 (line).

**FIGURE 7-15**   PLOTTING THE FUNCTION Y = X²/5 + 1

```
C PLOTTING Y = X**2/5 + 1
C   LINE: ARRAY CONTAINING BLANKS EXCEPT FOR GRAPHIC SYMBOL *
C         THE LINE ARRAY SIMULATES THE LINE TO BE PRINTED
C   X:    RANGES IN VALUE FROM 1 TO 10 IN INCREMENTS OF 1 LINE
C   Y:    DISTANCE BETWEEN A POINT ON THE CURVE AND THE X AXIS
C
      CHARACTER LINE(21)
      INTEGER X
      REAL Y
      DATA LINE/21*' '/          Initialize array line to blanks.
      WRITE(6,2)
      DO 5 X = 1, 10
        Y = X**2/5. + 1.         Compute the value of the function.
        LINE(Y + .5) = '*'        Insert the asterisk in its proper place in the line.
        WRITE(6,1)X, Y, LINE      and write out the line array.
        LINE(Y + .5) = ' '        Blank out the asterisk to prepare for the next line.
    5 CONTINUE
      STOP
    1 FORMAT(1X,I2,3X,F4.1/
     *         '+',13X,21A1)
    2 FORMAT(' X       Y')
      END
```

*Output*

| X | Y |
|---|---|
| 1 | 1.2 |
| 2 | 1.8 |
| 3 | 2.8 |
| 4 | 4.2 |
| 5 | 6.0 |
| 6 | 8.2 |
| 7 | 10.8 |
| 8 | 13.8 |
| 9 | 17.2 |
| 10 | 21.0 |

$y = \dfrac{x^2}{5} + 1$

*x axis*

## 7-7-5  A Polynomial and Sine Curves

Let us plot the functions $y = x^2 + x - 6$ in the interval $(-4, 3.6)$ and $y = \sin x$ in the interval 0 to 7.2. Our approach is as follows:

**1.** Fill an array PLINE with blanks.

**2.** Compute a value YPOLY $= x^2 + x - 6$ for $x = -4$, insert the symbol * in position YPOLY of the array (PLINE(YPOLY) = '*') and print the array PLINE.

**3.** Repeat steps 1 and 2 for values of $x = -3.6, -3.2, ..., 3.6$ (the incremental value is arbitrary).

There is one minor problem: For some values of $x$, YPOLY is negative (see Figure 7-16); YPOLY cannot be negative, since it is used as a subscript of PLINE to indicate the position of the symbol * on the output line. This problem can be taken care of by adding to $x^2 + x - 6$ a constant C that will neutralize the largest negative value of $x^2 + x - 6$ in the given interval and ensure that YPOLY $\geq 1$. Adding such a constant does not change the shape of the graph but results in the translation of the $x$ axis by C. In this example, a constant C = 7.25 could be used, since the largest negative value for YPOLY is $-6.25$ ($x = -.5$). With YPOLY $= x^2 + x - 6 + 7.25$, the smallest and largest value for YPOLY in the interval are YPOLY $= 1$ ($x = -.5$) and YPOLY $= 18$ ($x = 3.6$). Hence the array PLINE must be dimensioned to a size of at least 18.

In the case of the sine function, a constant of 2 is added to YSINE $= \text{SIN}(X)$ to ensure that YSINE $\geq 1$, since $\text{SIN}(X) = -1$ for some values of $x$. Plotting YPOLY $= \text{SIN}(X) + 2$ is somewhat difficult, since most of the values taken by YSINE will be in the interval 1 to 2. To magnify or stretch the graph over a wider area of print columns, we can multiply $\text{SIN}(X) + 2$ by a factor (let us use 8 in this case) that will spread out YSINE from a minimum of 1*8 when SIN(X) = −1 to a maximum of 3*8 = 24 when SIN(X) = 1. An array of a size of at least 24 must be reserved for the array to print the sine function. Multiplying the function by 8 does not plot the original function exactly, but it gives a fairly good idea of the shape of the curve while preserving the roots (see Figure 7–16).

**FIGURE 7-16** PLOTTING TWO FUNCTIONS

```
C PLOTTING A POLYNOMIAL AND A SINE FUNCTION
C   XPOLY: X VALUE FOR THE POLYNOMIAL
C   XSINE: X VALUE FOR THE SINE
C   YPOLY: VALUE OF THE POLYNOMIAL FUNCTION
C   YSINE: VALUE OF THE SINE FUNCTION
C   PLINE: IMAGE OF THE LINE TO BE PRINTED FOR POLYNOMIAL
C   SLINE: IMAGE OF THE LINE TO BE PRINTED FOR THE SINE
C
      CHARACTER PLINE(28), SLINE(28)
      REAL XPOLY, XSINE, YPOLY, YSINE
      DATA PLINE,SLINE/56*' '/            Initialize both line arrays to blanks.
      WRITE(6,9)
      XPOLY = -4.0
      XSINE = 0.0
   18 IF(XPOLY .GT. 4.0) GO TO 20
      YPOLY = XPOLY**2 + XPOLY - 6.
      YSINE = SIN(XSINE)
      PLINE(YPOLY +7.25)  = '*'
      SLINE(8*(YSINE + 2)) = '*'
      WRITE(6,11)XPOLY,YPOLY,PLINE,XSINE,YSINE,SLINE
      XPOLY = XPOLY + .4
      XSINE = XSINE + .4
      PLINE(YPOLY + 7.25)  = ' '           erase the graphic symbol
      SLINE(8*(YSINE + 2)) = ' '           erase the graphic symbol
      GO TO 18
   20 STOP
    9 FORMAT(3X,'X',4X,'Y'/'+',34X,'X',4X,'Y')    Print captions.
   11 FORMAT(2F5.1,2X,28A1/'+',31X,2F5.1,28A1)    Print both graphs on same line.
      END
```

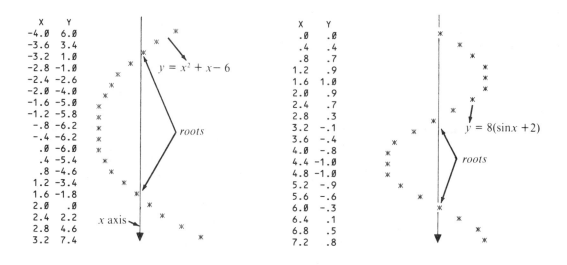

## 7-8 Probing Deeper

### 7-8-1 Format Reuse and the Slash

In general, if *n* variables are specified in a READ/WRITE list, the system scans the format for *n* corresponding data format codes (I,F,A,L,E,D) in the FORMAT statement. If there are *m* data format codes in the FORMAT and *m* is less than *n* (fewer format codes than variables), reading or writing will start at the beginning of a new record and scanning for data format codes will resume at the right-most *open* (left) parenthesis in the format in order to complete processing the *n* − *m* variables left in the READ/WRITE list.

*Example 1*

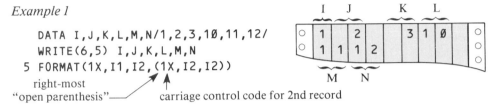

```
    DATA I,J,K,L,M,N/1,2,3,10,11,12/
    WRITE(6,5) I,J,K,L,M,N
  5 FORMAT(1X,I1,I2,(1X,I2,I2))
```
right-most "open parenthesis" ──── carriage control code for 2nd record

Variables I,J,K, and L will be printed on the first line; at this point format control encounters the very last parenthesis in the format—this signals the "end of record" (line, in this case); format control then resumes scanning at the right-most "open parenthesis" and prints M and N on the second line since the carriage control for the new record is blank (1X).

*Example 2*

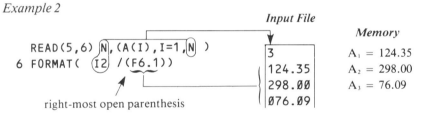

```
    READ(5,6) N,(A(I),I=1,N )
  6 FORMAT( I2 /(F6.1))
```
right-most open parenthesis

**Input File**

```
3
124.35
298.00
076.09
```

**Memory**

$A_1 = 124.35$
$A_2 = 298.00$
$A_3 = 76.09$

In this example, N is first read, and then N is used as the terminal value in the implied DO list to control the number of variables to be read. All values for the array A will be read under the format F6.1, since after encountering the right-most parenthesis, format scanning resumes at the right-most *open* parenthesis, forcing a new record. If we had used (I2/F6.1) instead, then A(2) would be read with format code I2, which would be invalid.

*Example 3*

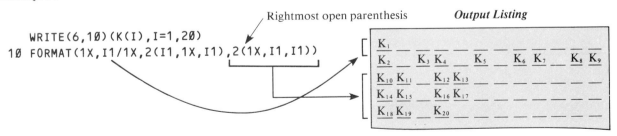

Rightmost open parenthesis

**Output Listing**

```
    WRITE(6,10)(K(I),I=1,20)
 10 FORMAT(1X,I1/1X,2(I1,1X,I1),2(1X,I1,I1))
```

After the right-most parenthesis has been encountered the first time, FORMAT control will resume scanning at 2(1X,I1,I1), which is equivalent to 1X,I1,I1,1X,I1,I1. From then on, all the variables in the WRITE list will be processed according to this format, beginning a new line each time. Note that scanning does *not* resume at (1X,I1,I1) but at 2(1X,I1,I1) i.e., the duplication factor 2 is included. Also note the importance of 1X in 2(1X,I1,I1)—it serves as carriage control. If the 1X had been omitted then part of $K_{10}$, $K_{14}$, and $K_{18}$ would *not* be printed.

*Example 4*

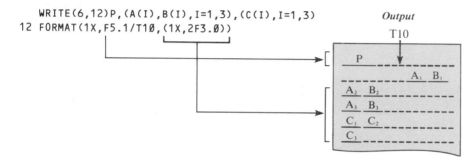

```
    WRITE(6,12)P,(A(I),B(I),I=1,3),(C(I),I=1,3)
12 FORMAT(1X,F5.1/T10,(1X,2F3.0))
```

Note that after P, $A_1$, and $B_1$ are written, all remaining variables are written under the same format (1X,2F3.0). If we had used (1X,F5.1/(T10,2F3.0)), then $A_2$, $B_2$, $A_3$, $B_3$, $C_1$, $C_2$ and $C_3$ would be aligned under $A_1$ and $B_1$.

*Example 5*

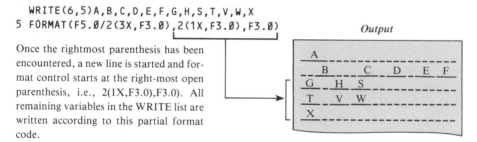

```
    WRITE(6,5)A,B,C,D,E,F,G,H,S,T,V,W,X
5 FORMAT(F5.0/2(3X,F3.0),2(1X,F3.0),F3.0)
```

Once the rightmost parenthesis has been encountered, a new line is started and format control starts at the right-most open parenthesis, i.e., 2(1X,F3.0),F3.0). All remaining variables in the WRITE list are written according to this partial format code.

## 7-8-2 Programming Example

Consider, for example, the following problem, which requires the reuse of the format: Each pair of records of an input file contains a student's class schedule for the week. The first record contains the student's Monday schedule (identical to Wednesday's and Friday's) and the second record contains the student's Tuesday schedule (same as Thursday's). Write a program to produce weekly class schedules comparable to the following:

| TIME | M | T | W | TH | F |
|------|------|------|------|------|------|
| 8 | DP101 | | DP101 | | DP101 |
| 9 | | FH100 | | FH100 | |
| 10 | MS312 | | MS312 | | MS312 |
| 11 | | BY101 | | BY101 | |
| 12 | EH202 | | EH202 | | EH202 |
| 13 | | | | | |
| 14 | | | | | |
| | TOTAL CLASS MEETINGS 13 | | | | |

Each data record is divided into seven fields reflecting the times when classes may meet:

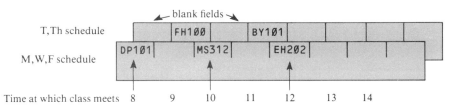

A program to solve this problem is shown in Figure 7-17.

**FIGURE 7-17** CLASS SCHEDULE

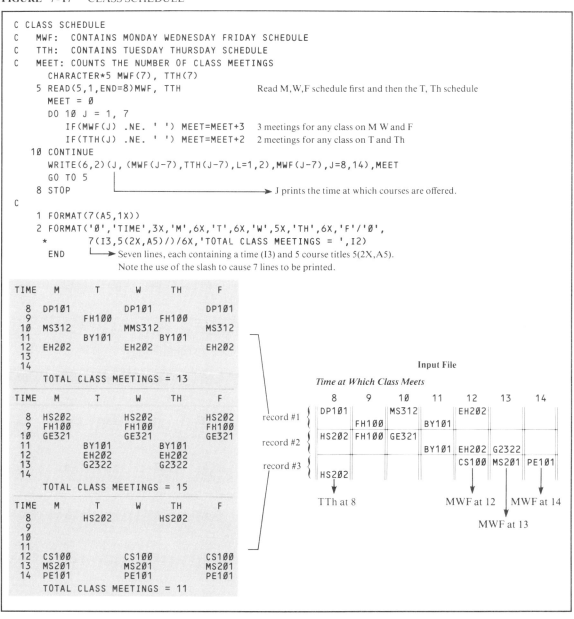

If the final caption "TOTAL CLASS MEETINGS = " were to be omitted from the report a much simpler format could be used:

FORMAT('OTIME',3X,'M',6X,'T',6X,'W',5X,'TH', 6X,'F'//(1X,I3,5(2X,A5)))

Each line following the header line is printed according to this format, starting at the right most open parenthesis.

## 7-9  You Might Want to Know

**1.** What happens if I have dimensioned PRICE as an array and I use PRICE in a statement such as Y = PRICE*QUAN(J)?

*Answer:* On a few systems, PRICE will be interpreted as PRICE(1). On most systems, however, this is an error. PRICE should be subscripted, i.e., provided with an index.

**2.** Is there any limit to the size of an array?

*Answer:* Yes, the maximum size for an array is a function of the memory size of the system in use.

**3.** Does a DIMENSION statement initialize array elements to any specific values?

*Answer:* No, it is the programmer's responsibility to initialize arrays.

**4.** What differentiates a FORTRAN function from a subscripted variable? For instance, when I write Y = SIN(X), is SIN(X) a subscripted variable?

*Answer:* Unless you dimension an array called SIN in your program, SIN(X) is not a subscripted variable name but a function name.

**5.** Can I use an implied DO list in an arithmetic statement to process an array? For example, can I write:

$$SUM = (TAB1(I) + TAB2(I),I = 1,10) \text{ or}$$
$$(A(I),I = 1,10) = 0.$$

*Answer:* No, implied DO lists are valid only in input/output and DATA statements.

**6.** What if I use a subscripted variable name in my program and I forget to dimension it?

*Answer:* No compilation error will occur, since the compiler will think that it is a function. An error will occur later on, since no such function is defined anywhere.

**7.** Can the same index be used more than once in implied DO lists as follows:

$$READ(5,5)((A(I),I = 1,5),SAM,I = 1,9)$$

*Answer:* No, the inner implied DO list A(I),I = 1,5 will change the value of I used to control the outer implied DO list, i.e., I = 1,9. Note, however, that the following is permissible.

$$READ(5,6)(A(I),I = 1,4),(B(I),I = 1,6),I$$

In this case I is used to control three independent entities.

**8.** My friend was running a FORTRAN program with a statement X = A(J), in which J exceeded the limit expressed in the REAL statement that declared A as an array. Although the program gave erroneous results, no error message was printed. Why?

*Answer:* The programmer uses the REAL statement to inform the compiler of the maximum number of memory locations for the array. If the user inadvertently at execution time refers to an array element A(J) in which J exceeds the size declared in the REAL statement, some systems may fail to inform the user that the array dimension has been exceeded and may actually process A(J) as that element J positions away from the first element of A. This can result in destruction of data or machine instructions representing FORTRAN instructions, depending on the value of J and depending on whether A(J) is on the left or the right of the equals sign in a replacement statement. With many versions of FORTRAN, however, if the index goes outside its specified range during execution, an error message is printed and execution of the program terminates at that point.

# 7-10  Exercises

## 7-10-1  Test Yourself

**1.** Which of the following are legal array declarations for arrays A and B?

| | |
|---|---|
| a. INTEGER B(3) | d. INTEGER(2*100) |
| b. CHARACTER A(100),B(N) | e. CHARACTER A(3)*2,B(4)*5 |
| c. REALA | f. CHARACTER*2 A(3),B(2)*3 |

**2.** In terms of memory arrangement, what is the difference between a three-element array and any three variable names?

**3.** State whether the following statements are true or false:

a. The REAL statement is an executable statement.
b. An implied DO list is an executable statement.
c. A FORMAT is an executable statement.
d. END is a nonexecutable statement.
e. The DATA statement is an executable statement.
f. If A is an array, then READ(5,1)A will cause reading of just A(1).
g. Subscripted variables can be used in any FORTRAN statement in the same way that nonsubscripted variables are used.
h. The INTEGER and REAL statements can be placed anywhere in the program.
i. If K = 3 and L = 3, then G(K) = G(L).
j. If X(I) = X(J), then I = J.
k. If X(2 + 1) = 4 then it is always true that X(2) + X(1) = 4.
l. If K is the location (position) of the largest value in array X, then X(K) is the largest value.
m. Given CHARACTER A(20), the instruction READ(5,1) A(1) will store in A(1) a maximum of 20 characters.
n. X(A(31)) is a valid subscripted variable.
o. T(7) = 'BOY' is a valid replacement statement.

4. Assume G is an array consisting of 5 entries, REAL G(5) ⟶ | 1.4 | 3. | − 4. | 1. | 3. |
   Are the following statements valid or invalid? If valid, specify the resulting values; if invalid, explain why.

   a. `L = G(1)`

   b. `L = 2`
      `L = G(G(L))`

   c. `K = 1`
      `G(K) = G(K) + 1`

   d. `K = -2`
      `K = G(K**2-1) + K ** 2`

   e. `L = 2`
      `G(2*L) = 'HELLO'`

   f. `G(3) = (G(2)-3.)/G(G(4)-1.)`

5. A and B are integer arrays of size 5; both are initially set to zeros. Use the code in parts a, b, c, and d to read the indicated data files and identify the contents of A and B. Case 1 refers to 10 input records, while case 2 refers to just 1 record.

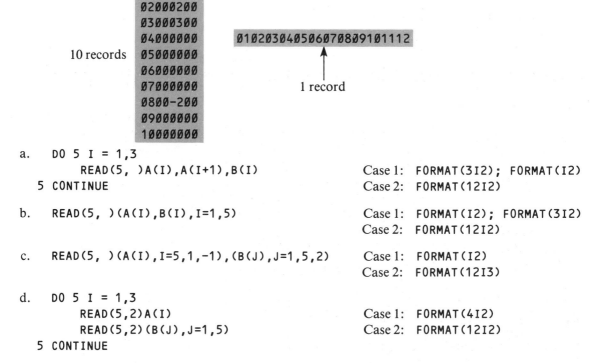

Case 1. Input file       Case 2.  Input file

```
              01000100
              02000200
              03000300
              04000000
10 records    05000000       01020304050607080901 01112
              06000000
              07000000
              0800-200              ↑
              09000000
              10000000            1 record
```

   a. ```
         DO 5 I = 1,3
            READ(5, )A(I),A(I+1),B(I)
       5 CONTINUE
      ```
      Case 1: FORMAT(3I2); FORMAT(I2)
      Case 2: FORMAT(12I2)

   b. ```
         READ(5, )(A(I),B(I),I=1,5)
      ```
      Case 1: FORMAT(I2); FORMAT(3I2)
      Case 2: FORMAT(12I2)

   c. ```
         READ(5, )(A(I),I=5,1,-1),(B(J),J=1,5,2)
      ```
      Case 1: FORMAT(I2)
      Case 2: FORMAT(12I3)

   d. ```
         DO 5 I = 1,3
            READ(5,2)A(I)
            READ(5,2)(B(J),J=1,5)
       5 CONTINUE
      ```
      Case 1: FORMAT(4I2)
      Case 2: FORMAT(12I2)

6. Determine the number of records processed by the following codes:

   a. ```
         DO 10 I = 1,5
            READ(5,6)A(I)
       6    FORMAT(3F5.0)
      10 CONTINUE
      ```

   b. ```
         DO 10 J = 1,9
            READ(5,6)A(J),B(J)
       6    FORMAT(F5.3)
      10 CONTINUE
      ```

   c. ```
         DO 10 K = 1,6,2
            READ(5,7)(A(I),I = 1,K)
       7    FORMAT(3F5.0)
      10 CONTINUE
      ```

   d. ```
         REAL A(4),J
         DO 5 I = 1,4
       5    WRITE(6,6)J,A
       6 FORMAT(1X,2F4.1)
      ```

**7.** Convert the following implied DO lists to the explicit DO loop form:

a. 
```
READ(5,5)(A(I),I = 1,6)
  5 FORMAT(2F5.0)
```
b. 
```
READ(5,6)(A(I),K(I),I = 2,9,2)
  6 FORMAT(2(F5.1,I2))
```

**8.** Specify the exact output (print positions, etc.) for the following WRITE operations, given the arrays A and B, and K:

array A | 1.5 | − 3.2 | 3. | 4.8 | .34 |   constant K = 3

array B | − 1. | 2. | 3. |

a. 
```
WRITE(6,11)(I,I = 1,5)
```
```
FORMAT(I1)
FORMAT(I2,I2)
FORMAT(1X,20I1)
FORMAT(4X,2I2,('+',2I1))
```

b. 
```
WRITE(6,11)(K,I,I = 1,4)
```
```
FORMAT(I2,5F5.0)
FORMAT(I3,1X,I1)
FORMAT(5I2)
```

c. 
```
WRITE(6,11)(J,(A(I),I = 1,5),J = 1,2)
```
```
FORMAT(I2,5F4.0)
FORMAT(I1/5F4.0,I2/5F4.0)
FORMAT(I2/(5F4.0))
```

d. 
```
WRITE(6,11)((A(I),I = 1,2),(B(I),I = 1,2),L = 1,2)
```
```
FORMAT(2F4.0,3F3.1)
FORMAT(1X,F4.1)
FORMAT(12F3.0)
```

**9.** Write possible formats for the following input/output statements.

a. READ(5,5)(A(I),I = 1,5),(K(I),I = 1,1000)
b. WRITE(6,5)(A(I),B(I), I,I = 1,500)
c. WRITE(6,5)(A(I),I = 1,3),(JPAY(I),I = 1,1000),COST, K

**10.** Given the input data file shown below, specify the contents of arrays X and or Y.

*Data File*

```
bbb1.3bbb4.2bbb6.8bbb1.9bbb3.3  ←——— First record
   4.1   -2.3   6.0   8.5   4.1
   7.8    2.1   0.6   4.9  -2.0
  18.3    7.1   4.2   8.1   7.3
   0.0   10.0  20.0  30.0  40.0  ←——— Last record
```

a.
```
     INTEGER C
     REAL X(5)
     C = 1
   3 READ(5,1)X(C)
     IF(C.EQ.5)GO TO ...
     C = C + 1
     GO TO 3
   1 FORMAT(F6.1)
```

b.
```
     INTEGER C
     REAL X(3),Y(2)
     READ(5,1)X,Y
   1 FORMAT(5F6.1)
```

c.
```
    INTEGER C
    REAL X(5)
    C = 1
  3 READ(5,1)X(C)
    IF(C.EQ.5) GO TO...
    C = C + 2
    GO TO 3
  1 FORMAT(F6.1)
```

```
ЬЬЬ1.3ЬЬЬ4.2ЬЬЬ6.8ЬЬЬ1.9ЬЬЬ3.3 ◀—— First record
   4.1   -2.3   6.0   8.5   4.1
   7.8    2.1   0.6   4.9  -2.0
  18.3    7.1   4.2   8.1   7.3
   0.0   10.0  20.0  30.0  40.0 ◀—— Last record
```

d.
```
    REAL X(4),Y(3)
    READ(5,1)X
    READ(5,1)Y
  1 FORMAT(4F6.1)
```

e.
```
    REAL X(3),Y(3)
    READ(5,1)(X(I),Y(I),I = 1,3)
  1 FORMAT(5F6.1)
```

f.
```
    REAL X(3),Y(3)
    READ(5,1)(X(I),I = 1,3),(Y(I),I = 1,3)
  1 FORMAT(4F6.1)
```

g.
```
    INTEGER C
    REAL X(5)
    READ(5,1)X(5)
    READ(5,1)X(1),X(4)
    X(3) = X(1)*5
    X(2) = X(1) + X(5)
  1 FORMAT(F6.1)
```

h.
```
    REAL X(16)
    READ(5,1)(X(I),A,I = 1,4)
  1 FORMAT(3F6.1)
```

11. Which of the following DO lists are invalid? If the implied DO list is valid, specify the number of records read or lines written. If the implied DO list is invalid, state the reason, and state whether an error will occur at compilation or execution time.

a.
```
    READ(5,5)(A(I),I = 1,5),(B(J),J = 1,3)
  5 FORMAT(3F5.2)
```

b.
```
    WRITE(6,6)(K,A(I),B(I),I,I = 1,5)
  6 FORMAT(I2,2F3.0,I3)
```

c.
```
    READ(5,5)(A(J),B(J),J = 1,9)
  5 FORMAT(F5.1)
```

d.
```
    WRITE(6,8)(A(J),J = 1,N,K-J)
  8 FORMAT(F10.1)
```

e.
```
    READ(5,7)A,(A(J),J = 1,7),B,KK
  7 FORMAT(4F3.0)
```

f.
```
    READ(5,8)(A(I),(B(J),J = 1,5),I = 1,5)
  8 FORMAT(F5.1)
```

g.
```
    WRITE(6,11)(PAY(J),J = 1,3)
 11 FORMAT(2F6.1)
```

h.
```
    WRITE(6,4)(I,(A(I),I = 1,3),B,K = 1,5)
  4 FORMAT(1X,I1,3F5.0,F3.0)
```

12. Given an array, A, of size 100, write the code to generate the following output; use both the implied DO list and explicit DO loop for the WRITE statement.

a.
$$\begin{array}{ll} A_1 & A_2 \\ A_3 & A_4 \\ A_5 & A_6 \\ \vdots & \vdots \\ A_{99} & A_{100} \end{array}$$

b.
$$\begin{array}{ll} A_1 & A_{51} \\ A_2 & A_{52} \\ A_3 & A_{53} \\ \vdots & \vdots \\ A_{50} & A_{100} \end{array}$$

c.
$$\begin{array}{ll} 1 & A_{100} \\ 2 & A_{99} \\ 3 & A_{98} \\ \vdots & \vdots \\ 100 & A_1 \end{array}$$

d.
$$\begin{array}{l} A_2 \\ A_4 \\ A_6 \\ \vdots \\ A_{100} \\ A_1\ A_2\ A_3\ \ldots\ A_9\ A_{10} \\ A_{11}A_{12}A_{13}\ \ldots\ A_{19}A_{20} \\ \vdots \\ A_{91}A_{92}A_{93}\ \ldots\ A_{99}A_{100} \end{array}$$

13.  Array POS contains 12 numbers. Using only one WRITE statement, write the code to produce exactly the following output:

```
POS LISTING: 1  2  3  4
             5  6  7  8
             9 10 11 12
```

14.  Given the following complete programs, infer potential execution-time/logical errors:

a.
```
DIMENSION A(100)
I = 1
X = 4.
A(J) = X**2+2.*X+I
STOP
END
```

c.
```
DIMENSION A(100)
WRITE(6,5)A
READ(5,5)(A(I),I = 1,110)
5 FORMAT(10F5.0)
STOP
END
```

b.
```
DIMENSION A(100)
I = 1
X = 4
A(I) = X**A(J)
STOP
END
```

d.
```
DIMENSION A(6)
DO 10 I = 1,5
    READ(5,7)A(I),A(I + 1)
7   FORMAT(2F5.0)
10 CONTINUE
STOP
END
```

15.  Specify the list of variables that are read or written by the following instructions; for example the list might be: N, L, $M_1$, $M_2$,... . Indicate the position of each of the variables on the input or output medium. (Repeat part b for each of the FORMATs given.)

a.
```
INTEGER M(20)
WRITE(6,5)(N,L,(M(J),J = 1,4),K,K=1,2)
5 FORMAT(1X,3I3/(1X,4I2))
```

b.
```
REAL T(10)
READ(5,6)A,B,(T(I),I = 1,5)
6 FORMAT(3F5.1)
6 FORMAT(3F5.1/F5.1)
6 FORMAT(F5.1/(2F5.1))
```

c.
```
WRITE(6,4)(A(I),I = 1,7)
4 FORMAT(1X,2F4.0/1X,2(F3.1,1X)/2(1X,F3.0))
```

**16.** Find at least five syntax errors in the following code:

```
        REALA(10),B(20),IBIG
        DIMENSION A(10),C(3)
        DATA C/4,5,6/
     20 READ(5,1)(A(I),I = 1,10)
        DO 3 I = 1,10
           IF(A(I).GE.IBIG) THEN IBIG = A(I)
           IF(A(I).LT ISMALL) ISMALL = A(I)
      3 CONTINUE
        IF(IBIG = 0)GO TO 20
        STOP
        END
```

**17.** Array SOCSEC contains 100 different social security numbers. Write the code to determine whether the number in T matches any number in array SOCSEC. The code should print either MATCH or NO MATCH.

**18.** An input record contains an unknown number of numbers (at least 51 but no more than 100). Write the code to read the first 20 numbers into array A, the next 30 into array B, and the remainder into array C.

**19.** Arrays A and B contain integers between 1 and 100. Array A has 10 elements, and array B has 16. Write the code to print the numbers that are common to both arrays and the number of equal elements.

*Example*

A: | 3 | 5 | 3 | 7 | 9 |

B: | 5 | 3 | 7 | 3 | 8 |

*Output*

```
                3
                5
                7
NUMBER OF EQUAL ITEMS = 3
```

**20.** First load an array A with 20 integers between 1 and 20. **Then** write the code to perform a frequency distribution on the numbers in array A. The output should list the numbers in ascending order and their corresponding frequency, as follows:

| NUMBERS | 1 | 3 | 4 | 5 | 10 | 12 | 13 | 14 | 15 | 17 | 18 | 19 |
|---------|---|---|---|---|----|----|----|----|----|----|----|----|
| FREQUENCY | 1 | 4 | 2 | 1 | 1 | 1 | 2 | 2 | 1 | 2 | 2 | 1 |

**21.** Determine whether an array that has 10 numbers (not necessarily integers) has any two equal entries.

**22.** Array A consists of 11 entries; the first 10 entries contain numbers arranged in ascending sequence. Read a number X and insert it in its proper position in array A. For example, if X = 23 and array A is

| 10 | 20 | 30 | 40 | 50 | 60 | 70 | 80 | 90 | 95 | |

The edited array is:

| 10 | 20 | 23 | 30 | 40 | 50 | 60 | 70 | 80 | 90 | 95 |

**23.** Write the code to produce the following multiplication tables

```
1 X  1 =  1    2 X  1 =  2    3 X  1 =  3   . . .   10 X  1 =  10
1 X  2 =  2    2 X  2 =  4    3 X  2 =  6            10 X  2 =  20
1 X  3 =  3    2 X  3 =  6    3 X  3 =  9            10 X  3 =  30
      .              .              .                      .
      .              .              .                      .
      .              .              .                      .
1 X 12 = 12    2 X 12 = 24    3 X 12 = 36            10 X 12 = 120
```

## 7-10-2 Programming Problems: General/Business

**1.** Assume array A with 50 elements has already been loaded. Write the code to compute the sum of the squares of the elements of array A.

**2.** A and B are tables of size 100 and 50, respectively. Write the code to store the numbers 1, 2, 3, ..., 100 in table A, and the first 50 positive odd integers starting at 101 in table B. Do not read data from input records.

**3.** A data file is composed of packets of scores. The first packet contains final scores obtained by an algebra class, while the second packet contains scores obtained by an accounting class. The packets are separated by a negative number. Read the class scores into two arrays and print the number of scores in each packet. The input file (one entry per record) can be visualized as follows:

$$10, 80, 64, 86, 44, 28, -3, 43, 74, 86, 94, 21, -7$$

| Algebra scores | Accounting scores |
| --- | --- |
| At most 100 scores | At most 50 scores |

**4.** An input file consists of many packets of scores, each terminated by a negative number. Write a program to compute the average of each packet and compute the overall average of all scores. (No more than 30 scores in each packet.) Print the number of scores below the overall average; for example:

| *Input* | *Output* | |
| --- | --- | --- |
| | SET 1:      10   20   30 | AVG = 20.0 |
| 10 20 30 -4 | SET 2:      30   40   50   60   70 | AVG = 50.0 |
| 30 40 50 60 70 -2 | SET 3:      50   60   70 | AVG = 60.0 |
| 50 60 70 -4 | TOTAL SET: 10  20  30  30  40  50  60  70  50  60  70 | AVG = 44.5 |
| | NUMBER OF SCORES BELOW 44.5 = 5 | |

**5.** Each record of an input file (maximum 15 records) consists of an account number and an amount deposited. Write the code to:

  **a.** Print the account numbers of all the accounts in which $50,000 or more has been deposited.
  **b.** *Then* print the numbers of all the accounts in which amounts between $10,000 and $50,000 have been deposited.

**6.** For each student in a class, there is one record with his/her name and 10 test scores. The student's average is based on his/her nine best scores. Write a program to produce an output similar to the following:

```
                      GRADE REPORT
   NAME: WOODRUFF    AVERAGE = 60.0
   TESTS:   10    20   30   40   50   60   70   80   90   100


   NAME: ZIEGLER     AVERAGE = 58.9
   TESTS:  100   50   60   40   35   65   80   20   30    70
```

7. Write the code to produce the following tables:

   a. ```
      1 2 3 4 5 6 7 8 9 10
      1 2 3 4 5 6 7 8 9
      1 2 3 4 5 6 7 8
      1 2 3 4 5 6 7
      1 2 3 4 5 6
      1 2 3 4 5
      1 2 3 4
      1 2 3
      1 2
      1
      ```

   b. ```
      1 2 3 4 5 6 7 8 9 10
        2 3 4 5 6 7 8 9 10
          3 4 5 6 7 8 9 10
            4 5 6 7 8 9 10
              5 6 7 8 9 10
                6 7 8 9 10
                  7 8 9 10
                    8 9 10
                      9 10
                        10
      ```

   c. ```
      10
      10 9
      10 9 8
      10 9 8 7
      10 9 8 7 6
      10 9 8 7 6 5
      10 9 8 7 6 5 4
      10 9 8 7 6 5 4 3
      10 9 8 7 6 5 4 3 2
      10 9 8 7 6 5 4 3 2 1
      ```

   d. ```
                        1
                      2 1
                    3 2 1
                  4 3 2 1
                5 4 3 2 1
              6 5 4 3 2 1
            7 6 5 4 3 2 1
          8 7 6 5 4 3 2 1
        9 8 7 6 5 4 3 2 1
      10 9 8 7 6 5 4 3 2 1
      ```

8. The following diagram shows Pascal's triangle for N = 6:

   ```
   1                    1
   2                  1   1
   3                1   2   1
   4              1   3   3   1
   5            1   4   6   4   1
   6          1   5  10  10   5   1
   ```

   Find the rule for generating successive rows of Pascal's triangle and use it in a program that will accept a value of N and print the appropriate triangle.

9. Write a program to calculate the exact Julian date equivalent to the date specified in the form: month, day, year. The Julian date is the day of the year. January 1 has Julian date 1, February 2 has Julian date 33, December 31 has Julian date 365 and so forth. Use a table showing the number of days that have occurred since the beginning of the year for each month, i.e.

   | Month | Days |
   |-------|------|
   | 1 | 0 |
   | 2 | 31 |
   | 3 | 59 |
   | 4 | 90 |
   | . | . |
   | . | . |

   How would you change your program to account for leap years, in which February has one more day. [Hint: See exercise 22 chapter 3 section 3–10–1.]

10. Write a program to convert dates in the form month-number, day, year to the form month-name, day, 19year. For example, the input 11 18 84 should produce the output NOVEMBER 18, 1984.

11. Write a program that will input a value for N and draw the following axis graduated in units of 5:

```
If N = 31    ----5----0----5----0----5----0-
If N =  7    ----5--
If N =  3    ---
```

12. Use Exercise 11 to draw a graduated axis for the bar graph problem of section 7-6-5. The last graduation symbol should reflect the maximum sales for the week, as shown in the following example:

```
DAY   SALES

1      15      ***************
2      19      *******************
3      23      ***********************
4      16      ****************
5      21      *********************
6      12      ************
7      15      ***************
               ----5----0----5----0--  ➤ graduated axis
```

13. The correct answers (1,2,3, or 4) to a multiple choice test of 10 questions are recorded on the first record of an input file. Succeeding records contain the name of a student and the student's 10 answers. Write the code to compute each student's final score (each question is worth 10 points). The input and output have the following form:

*Correct Answer to Test*

```
1 1 2 3 1 4 2 4 3 3
JONES   1 1 2 3 1 4 2 4 3 3
HILL    1 1 2 3 1 1 1 3 2 4
CLAM    4 1 2 3 1 4 2 4 3 2
```

| NAME | SCORES | GRADE |
|------|--------|-------|
| JONES | 1 1 2 3 1 4 2 4 3 3 | 100 |
| HILL | 1 1 2 3 1 1 1 3 2 4 | 50 |
| CLAM | 4 1 2 3 1 4 2 4 3 2 | 80 |

14. At the beginning and at the end of each month, members of the U-WATCH-UR-WEIGHT club are weighed in. Each member's name and initial and terminal weights are typed on a record. Write a program to read such records and print out each member's name, initial and final weight, and weight loss. Also print the average weight loss for the group and the number of members whose weight loss was greater than the average weight loss. For example:

```
GREEN    200    180    20    *
FARAH    130    120    10
TODINI   161    154     7

AVERAGE WEIGHT LOSS IS 12.3 POUNDS
1 MEMBER WITH WEIGHT LOSS OVER 12.3 POUNDS
```

Note that a * is printed beside the name each member's name whose weight loss is above the average.

**15.** Using the schedule shown below, write a program to read an adjusted gross income and compute and print the amount of tax owed.

| | |
|---|---|
| Not over $3,400 . . . . . . . . . . . . . . | No tax. |
| Over $3,400 but not over $5,500 . . . . . | 14% of excess over $3,400 |
| Over $5,500 but not over $7,600 . . . . . | $294, plus 16% of excess over $5,500 |
| Over $7,600 but not over $11,900 . . . . | $630, plus 18% of excess over $7,600 |
| Over $11,900 but not over $16,000. . . . | $1,404, plus 21% of excess over $11,900 |
| Over $16,000 but not over $20,200. . . . | $2,265, plus 24% of excess over $16,000 |
| Over $20,200 but not over $24,600. . . . | $3,273, plus 28% of excess over $20,200 |
| Over $24,600 but not over $29,900. . . . | $4,505, plus 32% of excess over $24,600 |
| Over $29,900 but not over $35,200. . . . | $6,201, plus 37% of excess over $29,900 |
| Over $35,200 but not over $45,800. . . . | $8,162, plus 43% of excess over $35,200 |
| Over $45,800 but not over $60,000. . . . | $12,720, plus 49% of excess over $45,800 |
| Over $60,000 but not over $85,600. . . . | $19,678, plus 54% of excess over $60,000 |
| Over $85,600 but not over $109,400. . . | $33,502, plus 59% of excess over $85,600 |
| Over $109,400 but not over $162,400 . . | $47,544, plus 64% of excess over $109,400 |
| Over $162,400 but not over $215,400 . . | $81,464, plus 68% of excess over $162,400 |
| Over $215,400 . . . . . . . . . . . . . . . | $117,504, plus 70% of excess over $215,400 |

**16.** Klinkon Headquarters has received personnel secrets for the spaceship Renderprize from two of its spies.

| **The First Spy Reports** | | **The Second Spy Reports** | |
|---|---|---|---|
| *Number* | *Name* | *Number* | *Title* |
| 455-30-1980 | Kiik | 465-29-9136 | Engineer |
| 465-29-9136 | Skolly | 432-98-2316 | Navigator |
| 408-32-6166 | Spark | 446-66-2366 | Navigator |
| 432-98-2316 | Thekov | 433-27-8107 | Doctor |
| 492-38-7213 | Uhula | 455-30-1980 | Captain |
| 433-27-8107 | Mc Joy | 408-32-6166 | First Officer |
| 446-66-2366 | Lusu | 492-38-7213 | Communications |

As a Klinkon programmer, your job is to program the computer to match up crew member names with their titles. (Star Fleet Command has evidence that when Klinkon programmers make syntax errors, they mysteriously disappear!) Write the code to produce a list of numbers and the corresponding names and titles, i.e.

```
455-30-1980    KIIK     CAPTAIN
465-29-9136    SKOLLY   ENGINEER
     :           :         :
     :           :         :
     :           :         :
```

**17.** A table contains 27 numbers that can be either positive or negative. Write a program to print the positive numbers and the negative numbers 4 per line as follows:

```
-14   -12   -34   -56
 -2    -6   -45   -67
            :
-34   -23

 12    56    90    21
 56    89     6     4
            :
 78
```

Don't print the positive numbers if none exist; do the same for the negative numbers.

**18.** Write the code to produce the following multiplication tables:

```
1 x 1 =  1   2 x 1 =  2   3 x 1 =  3   4 x 1 =  4   5 x 1 =  5   6 x 1 =  6   7 x 1 =  7   8 x 1 =  8
1 x 2 =  2   2 x 2 =  4   3 x 2 =  6   4 x 2 =  8   5 x 2 = 10   6 x 2 = 12   7 x 2 = 14   8 x 2 = 16
1 x 3 =  3   2 x 3 =  6   3 x 3 =  9   4 x 3 = 12   5 x 3 = 15   6 x 3 = 18   7 x 3 = 21   8 x 3 = 24
1 x 4 =  4   2 x 4 =  8   3 x 4 = 12   4 x 4 = 16   5 x 4 = 20   6 x 4 = 24   7 x 4 = 28   8 x 4 = 32
1 x 5 =  5   2 x 5 = 10   3 x 5 = 15   4 x 5 = 20   5 x 5 = 25   6 x 5 = 30   7 x 5 = 35   8 x 5 = 40
1 x 6 =  6   2 x 6 = 12   3 x 6 = 18   4 x 6 = 24   5 x 6 = 30   6 x 6 = 36   7 x 6 = 42   8 x 6 = 48
```

**19.** The following integers have been recorded on a record.

$$36, 27, 43, 18, 5, 6, 9, 33, 45, 34, 22, 42$$

Read these numbers into an array and write a program to accomplish the following:

a. Compute the average (mean) of these 12 numbers, rounded to the nearest whole number.
b. Compute the difference between each of these 12 numbers and the mean (subtract the mean from each number) and store each of these deviations in an array.
c. Determine which of the 12 numbers in the array deviates the most from the mean (this corresponds to the deviation having the largest absolute value) and print that number (not its deviation).

The output should be as follows:

```
ARRAY     DEVIATION
 36          6
 27         -3
 43         13
 .           .
 .           .
 38          8
NUMBER DEVIATING MOST FROM MEAN IS 43
```

**20.** Professor X records her final grades as follows: The first data item N (N < 20) in the record identifies the number of grades for her entire class. N is followed by N grades entered on the same record. Write a program to produce a grade frequency report. A sample input and output are shown below:

```
9  80  80  20  25  20  80  79  64  64
↑
N              N = 9 grades
```

```
GRADES    COUNT
  20        2
  25        1
  64        2
  79        1
  80        3
```

**21.** a. Without reading any data records (initialize the three following arrays to the constants specified below), create and print the following inventory file for an auto parts dealer:

```
PART NUMBER   QUANTITY   COST/PART
    115          50          90
    120          60          91
    125          70          92
    130          80          93
     .            .           .
     .            .           .
    160         140          99
```

For example, there are 50 of item 115 at a cost of 90 cents each. During the day, sales transactions are recorded on records as follows:

Part number   Quantity sold

b. Write a program to read the day's transaction, produce a parts inventory, print a "reorder" message whenever fewer than 20 items are in stock, and discount the price of any part for which there were no sales, by 10% of the original cost (rounded to the nearest penny).

The inventory report, for example, might be drawn as follows:

| PART NUMBER | STOCK | NUMBER SOLD | COST/PART | |
|---|---|---|---|---|
| 115 | 40 | 10 | 90 | |
| 120 | 0 | 60 | 91 | **REORDER** |
| 125 | 70 | 0 | 83 | DISCOUNT |
| 130 | 5 | 75 | 93 | **REORDER** |
| . | . | . | . | |
| . | . | . | . | |
| . | . | . | . | |
| 160 | 70 | 70 | 99 | |

c. If a parts number is incorrectly recorded in the transaction data file, generate the same report as in part b with a list of the incorrect part numbers following the inventory report. For example:

| PART NUMBER | STOCK | NUMBER SOLD | COST/PART |
|---|---|---|---|
| 115 | 40 | 10 | 90 |
| . | . | . | . |
| . | . | . | . |
| . | . | . | . |
| 160 | 70 | 70 | 99 |

117***NO SUCH EXISTING PART. CHECK RECORD***
126***NO SUCH EXISTING PART. CHECK RECORD***

d. To prepare for the following day, recreate a new inventory file by deleting all part numbers with exhausted stock and print the new inventory table as follows:

| PART NUMBER | QUANTITY | COST/PART | |
|---|---|---|---|
| 115 | 40 | 90 | ← Note absence of part number 120. |
| 125 | 70 | 83 | |
| 130 | 5 | 93 | |
| . | . | . | |
| . | . | . | |
| . | . | . | |
| 160 | 70 | 99 | |

e. During the day, a parts salesperson persuades the manager to add three new parts to the current line. These parts have numbers between 100 and 170, different from those already in stock. The manager decides to purchase 300 of each of the new parts. Read three records with new part numbers and corresponding costs, and produce a new inventory table by inserting the new records in their appropriate ascending position in the file:

| PART NUMBER | QUANTITY | COST/PART | |
|---|---|---|---|
| 100 | 300 | 60 | ← |
| 115 | 40 | 90 | |
| 125 | 70 | 83 | > Note new inserts. |
| 130 | 5 | 93 | |
| 132 | 300 | 95 | ← |
| ⋮ | ⋮ | ⋮ | |

22. On NBC's *Today* show weather report, temperatures from various cities in the United States are listed by geographical area. Temperature readings are collected from various weather-measuring stations and typed on records in no special sequence order. Each record contains the following data (rp = record position):

| City | Temperature | Section code | $\left(\begin{array}{ll}1 = \text{East Coast} & 2 = \text{Midwest}\\ 3 = \text{South} & 4 = \text{Pacific}\end{array}\right)$ |
|---|---|---|---|
| rp 1–8 | rp 10–12 | rp 16 | |

a. Write a program segment to produce a list of cities and corresponding temperatures by geographical area in the order the cities are encountered in the input file. The output should identify each of the geographical areas by name, as shown below:

```
        Input                        Output

    BOSTON    45   1     EAST COAST
    FRESNO    66   4                   BOSTON    45
    NEW YORK  51   1                   NEW YORK  51
    MOBILE    73   3     MIDWEST
    MADISON   -5   2                   MADISON   -5
    CHICAGO   57   2                   CHICAGO   57
    MIAMI     88   3     SOUTH
                                       MOBILE    73
                                       MIAMI     88
                        PACIFIC
                          ⋮            FRESNO    66

                        HIGHEST TEMP:  MIAMI     88
```

b. Write another program segment to list cities in ascending temperature order (four cities per printed line) as follows:

```
MADISON -5  BOSTON    45  NEW YORK   51  CHICAGO   57
FRESNO  66  MOBILE    73  MIAMI      88
```

23. Write a program to determine the day of the week for any date in the twentieth century. Use the following algorithm:

Let J be the Julian date (see problem 9 in this section) and Y be the year (last two digits only).

a.  Compute $X = 365.25*Y + J$
b.  If the decimal part of X is zero, subtract one from X.
c.  Compute the remainder after dividing the integer part of X by seven.

The remainder corresponds to the days of the week as follows:
$$0 = \text{Sunday}, 1 = \text{Monday}, 2 = \text{Tuesday}, ...$$

24.  An encyclopedia company has hired part-time salespeople. The name of each salesperson and the number of encyclopedia sets he/she has sold are recorded on separate data records (one record per salesperson). Each salesperson is paid $90.00 for each set sold, as well as $15.00 extra for each set (or fraction) sold over the average number of sets sold by all the salespeople. Write a program to print the name, the number of sets sold, and the amount earned by each employee. For example, if the average number of sets sold is 5.8 and a salesperson has sold 8 sets, the difference is 2.2, which counts as 3 sets over the average (the fractional part counts as an entire set). Do not forget to print the average number of sets sold.

25.  The Meals on Wheels Company operates a fleet of vans used for the delivery of cold foods at various local plants and construction sites. The management is thinking of purchasing a specially built $18,000 van equipped to deliver hot foods. This new addition to the fleet is expected to generate after-tax earnings $E_1, E_2, ..., E_6$ (as displayed below) over the next six years, at which time the van's resale value will be zero. Projected repair and maintenance costs $C_0, C_1, C_2, ..., C_6$ over the six years are shown below.

| *Projected Earnings* | | *Projected Costs* | | |
|---|---|---|---|---|
| $E_1$ | $2,500 | $C_0$ | $18,000 | (purchase cost of the van) |
| $E_2$ | 2,500 | $C_1$ | 1,000 | |
| $E_3$ | 3,000 | $C_2$ | 1,500 | |
| $E_4$ | 4,500 | $C_3$ | 2,000 | |
| $E_5$ | 6,000 | $C_4$ | 2,000 | |
| $E_6$ | 6,000 | $C_5$ | 2,100 | |
| | | $C_6$ | 2,400 | |

The decision to purchase the van depends on the benefit/cost ratio (BCR) (grossly speaking, earnings/expenditures) given by the formula

$$BCR = \frac{E_1 (1 + i)^6 + E_2 (1 + i)^5 + ... + E_6 (1 + i)^1}{C_0 + C_1 (1 + i)^6 + C_2 (1 + i)^5 + ... + C_6 (1 + i)^1}$$

where $i$ is the rate of investment of earnings by the company. If $BCR > 1$, then the company should acquire the van. Write a program to determine how high the investment rate ($i$) would have to be raised to permit the purchase of the vehicle. Write a program to compute the BCR for investment rates starting at 6% and increasing by amounts of 0.1%. The output should be as follows:

```
BENEFIT/COST RATIO        INVESTMENT RATE
        .                        6.0
        .                        6.1
        .                         .
        .                         .
        .                         .
```

Stop when the BCR is greater than 1 and print the following message:

PURCHASE OF VAN REQUIRES INVESTMENT RATE OF XX.XX.

26. The department of psychology offers a maximum of ten sections of introduction to psychology. Each section contains no more than 25 students. At the end of the semester final grades for each section are recorded as follows:

a. Write a program to produce the above output.
b. Write a program to produce the following output showing the class averages:

```
CLASS1   CLASS2   CLASS3   ...  CLASS?
  70       45       65             ?
```

Note that there might be fewer than ten classes.

27. An input file consists of an unknown number of grades in random order. Compute and print the median. The median is the score that divides a distribution of scores into two equal parts. For example,

10, 30, 87, 12        The median is (12 + 30)/2 = 21
                      (Half are above 21, half are below 21.)

53, 16, 99            The median is 53 (Half are above 53, half below 53.)

28. Write a program to record in an array P the relative ascending order position of each element of array A. For example, if

array A = | 51 | 20 | 90 | 80 | 100 |      then      array P = | 2 | 1 | 4 | 3 | 5 |

The interpretation for array P is given on the next page.

array A = | 51 | 20 | 90 | 80 | 100 |     then     array P = | 2 | 1 | 4 | 3 | 5 |

1 is stored in P(2), to indicate that the second element of A is the smallest (20).

2 is stored in P(1), to indicate that the first element of A is the next-to-smallest (51).

$\vdots$

5 is stored in P(5), to indicate that the fifth element of A is the largest (100).

The following code would then print the elements of A in ascending numerical sequence

```
WRITE(6,6)(A(P(I)),I=1,5)
```

In what programming situation would this sort algorithm be preferable to the bubble or mini/max sorts?

**29.** Dr. X is an information-science teacher. A file consisting of his students' names and their respective grades is stored in memory as follows:

| Student | Grade 1 | Grade 2 | Total |
|---------|---------|---------|-------|
| MARGULIES | 91 | 56 | 147 |
| GLEASON | 40 | 50 | 90 |
| HORN | 50 | 65 | 115 |
| MONISH | 70 | 70 | 140 |
| $\vdots$ | $\vdots$ | $\vdots$ | $\vdots$ |

a. Write a program to read input records and create such a file (table) for about ten students.

b. Add the necessary code to allow Dr. X to correct his file in the event grades are recorded incorrectly. Grade changes are read according to the following format:

STUDENT NAME          GRADE 1          GRADE 2

For grades that need not be changed, enter a negative number. For example, HORN –1    98 means change HORN's second grade to 98 and compute new total.

**30.** You work for the National Weather Service. They are going to measure changes in wind direction by sending up 3 balloons on each of 5 different days. Each of the 15 balloons is assigned a unique identification number (ID) between 100 and 999 (in no particular order). One balloon is released in the morning, one is released at noon, and one is released in the evening on each of the five days. When the balloons are returned, the ID number (integer), the day each balloon was sent up (1, 2, 3, 4, or 5), and the distance traveled (real number) will be recorded, with one record for each balloon (see test data on next page). Write a program to:

a. Read the records shown on next page (one at a time) into three tables.

b. Sort the tables into ascending order by ID number.

c. Print the sorted table with three entries per line (ID, day, and distance).

d. Find the maximum distance traveled for each day (5 maximums). Print the ID, day, and maximum distance for each of the 5 days (print the results for the first day, then the second, third, etc.).

e. Find the average distance traveled by balloons released on the first and fifth days combined and print this average distance (one result).

*Input:*   15 records with 3 data items/record: ID, day and distance.
*Output:*  15 printed lines of sorted ID's and corresponding days and distances (ID, day, distance).

5 printed lines of maximum distances for each day (1 through 5) (ID, day, distance).

1 printed line of the average distance traveled on the first and fifth days (average).

Use the following test data.

| Identification | Day | Distance |
|---|---|---|
| 123 | 2 | 143.7 |
| 269 | 3 | 976.4 |
| 120 | 1 | 370.2 |
| 460 | 5 | 980.8 |
| 111 | 1 | 111.3 |
| 986 | 4 | 1320.6 |
| 629 | 3 | 787.0 |
| 531 | 2 | 429.2 |
| 729 | 2 | 726.1 |
| 833 | 4 | 433.1 |
| 621 | 3 | 962.4 |
| 143 | 4 | 714.3 |
| 972 | 5 | 320.1 |
| 410 | 5 | 820.4 |
| 511 | 1 | 1240.0 |

**31.** Repeat the inventory problem of section 7–6–2 and print a reorder notice whenever the stock falls below ten percent of the original stock. Identify any item that has not been sold that day with two asterisks on the output. All invalid items should be listed after the updated inventory has been printed. The output should be similar to:

```
              NEW INVENTORY

ITEM NO.        QUANTITY
    444            40              **
    111             1           REORDER
    222             5
    134            17
    353             3

INVALID ITEM NUMBER 112
INVALID ITEM NUMBER 352
```

**32.** At the Kilpatrick Community College, General Mathematics MS101 has always been offered in the traditional teacher/lecture format. This year, for the first time, students may take MS101 using a self-paced approach to instruction through a computer-assisted instructional method (CAI). Because of the novelty of the CAI approach, the mathematics faculty has formulated the following policies concerning grades and tests for those taking MS101 in the CAI mode:

1.  Students may take one or two or three tests during the semester.

2.  The final score is based on the student's average score, scaled as follows: If the CAI class average AV is less than 80 (the standardized average for the traditional tea-

cher/lecture form), then the difference 80 − AV should be added to each student's average score; otherwise, the difference, AV − 80, is subtracted from each student's average. The input data is formatted as follows:

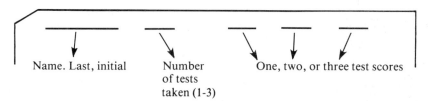

Name. Last, initial        Number              One, two, or three test scores
                           of tests
                           taken (1-3)

Write a program to produce the following score information. For example, the following input data would produce the output shown:

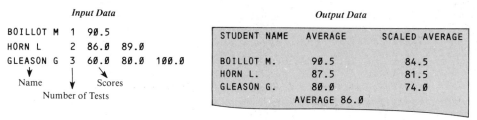

*Input Data*

```
BOILLOT M  1  90.5
HORN L     2  86.0  89.0
GLEASON G  3  60.0  80.0  100.0
```
Name / Scores
Number of Tests

*Output Data*

```
STUDENT NAME    AVERAGE      SCALED AVERAGE

BOILLOT M.       90.5            84.5
HORN L.          87.5            81.5
GLEASON G.       80.0            74.0
              AVERAGE 86.0
```

Can you rewrite the code for this exercise in such a way that each student's scores are printed after the student name but before the average? After the scaled average?

33. The Triple Star Corporation maintains a file in which each record contains a date (year) and the yearly sales in millions of dollars. These figures lie between 0 and 70 million. Write a program to produce a graph of this data, similar to the following one:

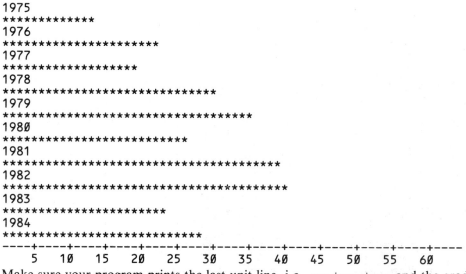

```
1975
*************
1976
*********************
1977
*******************
1978
******************************
1979
***********************************
1980
*************************
1981
*******************************************
1982
**********************************************
1983
**********************
1984
***************************
----+----+----+----+----+----+----+----+----+----+----+----+----
    5   10   15   20   25   30   35   40   45   50   55   60
```

Make sure your program prints the last unit line, i.e., ---- + ---- + ---- and the graduations 0,5,10,15,...

34. You are the organizer for the National Swimming Finals. You want to have a program that will seed the swimmers in the correct preliminary heat (race). You have 36 swimmers, each with an identification number and a submitted time. The swimming pool has only six lanes, so only six swimmers can swim at a time. The procedure for seeding

is to (1) sort the swimmers according to submitted times, and (2) assign to the first heat the swimmers with the first, seventh, thirteenth, ..., and thirty-first fastest times. (Note that a person whose time is 52.1 is *faster* than someone whose time is 55.8.) The swimmers in the second heat should be those with the second, eighth, fourteenth, ..., and thirty-second fastest times. Swimmers should be assigned to the other four heats in a similar manner.

Write a program to:

a. Read a file in which each record contains an integer ID and a submitted time, and store these data into an integer array and a real array.

b. Sort both arrays in ascending order *by time*.

c. Starting with the first heat, print the heat number (integer), then print the ID number and time of each swimmer in that heat in ascending order by time. Repeat for each heat.

d. Print on a separate line (1) the number of swimmers who swam faster (less time) than the average submitted time and (2) the average submitted time.

35. The BOISUPP company employs a variable number of salespersons. The input file consists of records of sales by each salesperson; that the records are already sorted in ascending order by salesperson number but not by date. For example, a typical data file might be:

```
JOHN DOE        111     011784      50.00
JOHN DOE        111     011584     150.00
MARY SMITH      212     011584     100.00
JAMES BROWN     314     011984     400.00
        |                 |            |
   Salesperson name    Date of sales
            Salesperson number      Amount of sales
```

The management wants to print out a monthly sales report to summarize the total sales for each salesperson and the total amount of all sales. Also, a salesperson-of-the-month award will go to the salesperson with highest sales for the month. Entries are to be listed in ascending order by salesperson number and date of sales. Arrange the output in the following form:

```
SALESPERSON              DATE OF   AMOUNT OF   TOTAL SALES/
NAME           NUMBER    SALES      SALES      SALESPERSON
JOHN DOE        111     01 15 84   150.00
                        01 17 84    50.00       200.00

MARY SMITH      212     01 15 84   100.00       100.00

JAMES BROWN     314     01 19 84   400.00       400.00
                              TOTAL SALES       700.00

**AWARD GOES TO JAMES BROWN**
```

Write a program to read a transaction file and produce a summary report like the one shown. Be sure you include more than one transaction for some of the salespersons and note that in such a case you print the number of the salesperson only once.

36. A radio station has hired you to write a program to help them plan their air time. You are given twenty input records at most, with the following entries on each record:

1st entry: Record identification
2nd entry: Record type (1 = Punk rock, 2 = Acid rock, 3 = Classical)
3rd entry: Playing time (3.6 means 3 minutes and 6/10 of a minute)

Write a program to

a. Read the input file and store the record identification, the record type, and the playing time into three separate tables.
b. Sort the three tables in ascending order by playing time.
c. Print the sorted tables with each record identification, record type, and corresponding playing time on one output line (3 data items/line).
d. Determine total playing time for each type of record and print the result as:

```
PUNK ROCK    14.6
ACID ROCK    21.0
CLASSICAL     9.2
```

e. Determine the classical record with the playing time closest to 2.4 minutes and print the located record's identification and playing time.

37. The Language Department at Johns College offers five courses and is now registering students. Each student completes a form with his/her name and one course number. More than one course can be taken by the same student, in which case the student fills out different forms. The list of courses, the maximum enrollment per class, and the room number in which each class meets are described as follows:

| Course | Size | Room No | Input |
|--------|------|---------|-------|
| FRE 110 | 5 | 204 | ADAMS FRE 110 |
| FRE 120 | 10 | 200 | BEVIS GER 100 |
| GER 100 | 6 | 100 | ADAMS FRE 120 |
| SPN 100 | 10 | 212 | ADAMS SPN 100 |
| SPN 105 | 15 | 220 | KERR  SPN 105 |

a. Each record of the input file consists of a student name and a course number. Write a program to read this file and provide the following enrollment information:

```
COURSE    ROOM NO    ENROLLMENT    MAX ENROLLMENT
FRE 110    204          5                5
FRE 120    200          6               10
  :
  :
SPN 105    220          4               15
```

If a course is filled up, either identify that course by placing a * next to the maximum enrollment figure or list the students who could not enroll.

b. At the conclusion of the enrollment procedure, the department head would like to inquire directly in this data base to obtain one of the following:

| | Query-code | Item |
|---|---|---|
| • A list of student names in any particular course: | 1 and | Course number |
| • A list of courses taken by a particular student: | 2 and | Student name |
| • An actual class size for a particular room: | 3 and | Room number |
| • To stop the inquiry process | 4 | |

For example, the following set of queries would produce the following output (perform input validation on all fields):

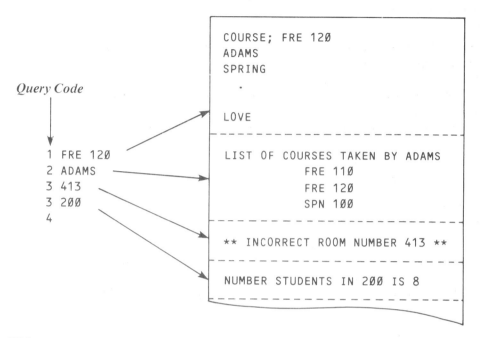

*Query Code*

1 FRE 120
2 ADAMS
3 413
3 200
4

```
COURSE; FRE 120
ADAMS
SPRING
     ·

LOVE
- - - - - - - - - - - - - - - - - - - - -
LIST OF COURSES TAKEN BY ADAMS
            FRE 110
            FRE 120
            SPN 100
- - - - - - - - - - - - - - - - - - - - -
** INCORRECT ROOM NUMBER 413 **
- - - - - - - - - - - - - - - - - - - - -
NUMBER STUDENTS IN 200 IS 8
- - - - - - - - - - - - - - - - - - - - -
```

Write a program to accept the query information and produce the requested information. Another option for inquiries, instead of numerical codes is for the computer to display a menu of inquiries.

38. Wrap-around sales averaging. The management at Food Stores, Inc., likes to compare their monthly sales with a running average of their sales for the preceding 11 months. Write a program to read sales data for the preceding 11 months (Jan. to Nov. '83) and read "dummy" sales projections for the next 12 months (Dec. '82 through Nov. '83). Then compute the preceding 11-month's running average for Dec. '83 through Nov. '84. The process can be visualized as follows:

| Jan.–Nov. 1983 | | | | | | | | | | | Dec. '83–Nov. '84 | | | | | | | 11 months running average |
|---|---|---|---|---|---|---|---|---|---|---|---|---|---|---|---|---|---|---|
| J | F | M | A | M | J | J | A | S | O | N | D | J | F | M | A | M ... N | |
| 10 | 11 | 12 | 10 | 11 | 14 | 10 | 11 | 12 | 11 | 12 | 13 | | | | | | 11.27 |
| | 11 | 12 | 10 | 11 | 14 | 10 | 11 | 12 | 11 | 12 | 13 | 16 | | | | | 11.54 |
| | | 12 | 10 | 11 | 14 | 10 | 11 | 12 | 11 | 12 | 13 | 16 | 11 | | | | 12.00 |
| | | | 10 | 11 | 14 | 10 | 11 | 12 | 11 | 12 | 13 | 16 | 11 | 13 | | | 11.90 |
| | | | | ⋮ | | | | | | | | ⋮ | | | | | ⋮ |

For the month of December, for example, management will compare the December volume (13) with the running average of the 11 previous months 11.27
$[(10 + 11 + 12 + 10 + 11 + 14 + 10 + 11 + 12 + 11 + 12)/11]$
See desired output on next page.

The output should be similar to:

```
MONTHS      11-MONTH RUNNING AVERAGE   MONTH SALES
DECEMBER             11.27                  13
JANUARY              11.54                  16
FEBRUARY             12.00                  11
MARCH                11.90                  13
  .                    .                     .
  .                    .                     .
  .                    .                     .
```

**39.** Systems planning involves estimating development time and projection of costs associated with the completion of a particular task. An example might be planning the construction of a house. A list of tasks and a time schedule might be:

| Sequence of Events | Task Description | Time in Days |
|:---:|:---|:---:|
| 1 | Laying of foundation | 15 |
| 2 | Plumbing installment | 12 |
| 3 | Frame and roof | 20 |
| 4 | Electrical work | 7 |
| 5 | Plastering | 4 |
| 6 | Carpentry | 7 |
| 7 | Landscaping | 3 |

Write a program to produce a bar graph like the following one to represent the duration of each task.

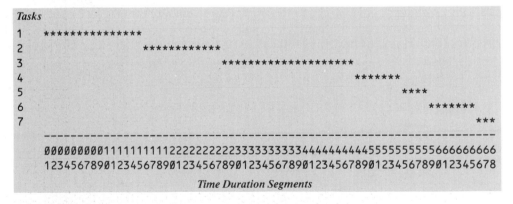

**40.** Two sort methods have been presented in this chapter, the bubble and the mini/max sort. These two sorting techniques are not the most efficient methods, however. An extremely efficient sorting method is the Shell-Metzner sort displayed here in flowchart form. In an article entitled "A Comparison of Sorts" in *Creative Computing*, Volume 2, John Grillo compared the three methods and determined that to sort 100,000 numbers would take 7.1 days, 3.8 days, and 15 minutes for the bubble, mini/max, and Shell-Metzner sort, respectively. To sort 10,000,000 numbers would take 93 years, 50 years, and 2.5 days respectively! Write a program to sort N numbers using the following flowchart.

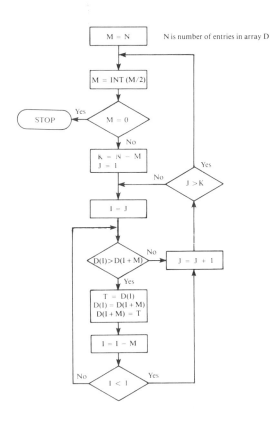

**41.** Write a program to convert decimal numbers to Roman numerals, employing the usual rules required in Roman numerals. Recall that the basic correspondence between roman and decimal numerals is as follows:

| Roman | Decimal (Hindu-Arabic) |
|-------|------------------------|
| M     | 1000                   |
| D     | 500                    |
| C     | 100                    |
| L     | 50                     |
| X     | 10                     |
| V     | 5                      |
| I     | 1                      |

Test your program with the following:

| Decimal | Expected Roman | Decimal | Expected Roman |
|---------|----------------|---------|----------------|
| 3       | III            | 49      | XLIX           |
| 4       | IV             | 50      | L              |
| 5       | V              | 58      | LVIII          |
| 7       | VII            | 75      | LXXV           |
| 9       | IX             | 90      | XC             |
| 10      | X              | 200     | CC             |
| 12      | XII            | 350     | CCCL           |
| 24      | XXIV           | 400     | CD             |
| 29      | XXIX           | 500     | D              |
| 38      | XXXVIII        | 900     | CM             |
| 40      | XL             | 2900    | MMCM           |
| 44      | XLIV           |         |                |

**42.** Read a word and write it in reverse order, then read and reverse a sentence one word at a time.

**43.** A very simple method to encode a message is to substitute each letter of the message with another according to some scheme such as

$$\text{letter A B C D E...Y Z}$$
$$\text{substitute Z Y X W V...B A}$$

Write a program to encode a message using this method.

**44.** Write a program to read a five-letter word and generate all possible combinations of two-letter words using those five letters. Can you avoid duplication of two-letter words?

### 7-10-3 Programming Problems: Scientific/Mathematical/ Use of Random Numbers

**1.** This exercise requires interactive communications with a terminal. Guess a number between 1 and 10 and let the computer guess it randomly, using random numbers between 1 and 10. The computer should not guess the same number twice.

**2.** A weighted average is computed as

$$f_1 x_2 + f_2 x_2 + f_3 x_3 + \ldots + f_n x_n \text{ where } f_1 + f_2 + f_3 + \ldots + f_n = 1.$$

Write a program to read $n$ values of $f$ and $x$ and compute the weighted average. Write an error message if the sum of the $f$s is not equal to 1. Test your program with the following:

| $n$ | $f_1$ | $x_1$ | $f_2$ | $x_2$ | $f_3$ | $x_3$ | *Expected Output* |
|---|---|---|---|---|---|---|---|
| 3 | .4 | 3 | .5 | 2 | .1 | 5 | 2.7 |
| 2 | .6 | 4 | .6 | 8 | | | Error message |

**3.** Write a program to read an unknown number of grades and calculate the standard deviation of those grades using the following formula:

$$sd = \sqrt{\frac{(x_1 - \bar{x})^2 + (x_2 - \bar{x})^2 + (x_3 - \bar{x})^2 + \ldots + (x_n - \bar{x})^2}{n(n - 1)}}$$

where $n$ = number of grades;
$\bar{x}$ = average of grades;
$x_1, x_2, x_3, \ldots, x_n$ are the grades.

**4.** Read the coordinates of two vectors A and B and compute the dot product

$$A_1 \cdot B_1 + A_2 \cdot B_2 + \ldots + A_N \cdot B_N$$

The coordinates are recorded on one data record as follows

$$\boxed{\text{N } A_1 \text{ } B_1 \text{ } A_2 \text{ } B_2 \ldots A_N \text{ } B_N} \text{ assume N} \le 10.$$

**5.** Write a program to generate 1,000 random integer numbers between 1 and 100 and print their frequency. Compare the observed frequency with the expected frequency for randomly selected numbers.

**6.** a. In the maze game of chapter 5 section 5–5–3 you placed a mole 500 times at row 3, column 4 of the island and counted the number of times the mole escaped. Now, if the mole were clever, it could remember the route it took the first time it found the way out, so that from then on it would never drown! Write a program to do just that; i.e., keep track in an array of the sequence of steps leading to a safe exit and reject any sequence of steps leading to drowning. Sooner or later the mole will find a way out, then that path will be recorded in an array and from that point on the mole will always escape.

   b. Of course, the mole's first path to freedom may not be the shortest way out. Write a program to force the mole to select the shortest escape path out of some 20 escape routes. From then on the mole should remember that particular path. Print the mole's final exit path using a coordinate system, for example,

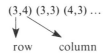

**7.** Using the bar graph method discussed in section 7–6–5, produce abstract computer art as follows: Fill an array S of size 60 with random numbers between 1 and 100 and graph the corresponding bar graph for each element of S.

**8.** Using the bar graph method discussed in section 7–7–4, write the code to graph the function $y = x^2$ and $y = 10 |\sin x|$ to obtain a graph similar to:

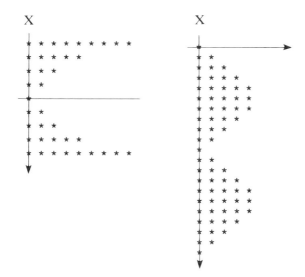

Recall that the vertical axis represents the independent variable ($x$) and the horizontal axis represents the dependent variable ($y$). Rotation of the graphs 90° counterclockwise will yield the usual positions of the $x$ and $y$ axes.

9. Load an array of size 8 with any digits from 1 to 9, then write the code to store these eight digits as a single number in memory location KNUMB.

For example, if A = $\boxed{3\ 5\ 2}$ then KNUMB = 352.

A(1)   A(2)   A(3)

[*Hint:* KNUMB = ((0 + A(1) * 10) + A(2)) * 10 + A(3) = (3 * 10 + 5) * 10 + 2 = 352]

10. Read a three-digit number, N, and store each individual digit of N in three consecutive array locations. For example, if N = 193, then J(3) = 1, J(2) = 9, J(1) = 3.

[*Hint:* Divide N by 100 to get J(3) = 1, then divide N − J(3)*100 (93) by 10 to obtain J(2) = 9, and so on.]

11. Write a program to compute $n! = n(n − 1)*(n − 2)* \ldots *2*1$ for values of $n$ that are so large that the result cannot fit in a single integer memory location. For example, 25! = 15,511,210,043,330,985,984,000,000. One way to solve the problem is to use an array to store the answer (and partial results), using one array memory location per digit. Thus 12! = 479,001,600 would be stored as follows (see exercise 10):

J(8)  J(6)  J(4)  J(2)

J(9)↓ J(7)↓ J(5)↓ J(3)↓ J(1)

$\boxed{4\ 7\ 9\ 0\ 0\ 1\ 6\ 0\ 0}$

To compute 13!, multiply each memory location by 13 (taking care to move the carries) to obtain:

J(9)  J(7)  J(5)  J(3)  J(1)

J(10)↓ J(8)↓ J(6)↓ J(4)↓ J(2)↓

$\boxed{6\ 2\ 2\ 7\ 0\ 2\ 0\ 8\ 0\ 0}$

12. Two integer numbers containing a maximum of 80 digits are contained on two data records. Write a program to compute the sum of these numbers.

13. A data record contains the degree $n$ and the coefficients $a_n, a_{n-1}, \ldots a_1, a_0$ of a polynomial function: $f(x) = a_n x^n + a_{n-1} x^{n-1} + \ldots a_1 x + a_0$. Write a program to produce a table of values of $f(x)$ for $x$ varying from 0 to 5 in units of .5. Assume the maximum value of $n$ is 10.

14. *Binary Search.* In this chapter we discussed a sequential method of searching for a particular entry in a table. Sequential searches are time-consuming in the sense that searching starts with the first entry and proceeds with successive entries. A shorter search is the binary search, which is essentially a guessing game. The binary search, however, requires that the table already be arranged in a particular order (ascending or descending). The array is split into two sections at the midpoint; then the desired entry is in either the right section or the left section. If it is in the right section that section is again split up into two subsections, and the desired number is in one section or the other; this splitting-in-half procedure is carried out until the entry has been found.

   The end points of a section are identified by two pointers, L (left) and R (right). Initially L = 0 and R = number of entries + 1. The method can be visualized by studying the following example. We want to determine whether 51 is in array A, which has 11 elements.

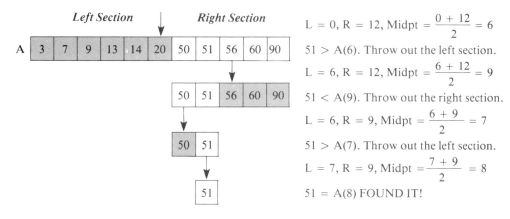

$L = 0$, $R = 12$, Midpt $= \dfrac{0 + 12}{2} = 6$

$51 > A(6)$. Throw out the left section.

$L = 6$, $R = 12$, Midpt $= \dfrac{6 + 12}{2} = 9$

$51 < A(9)$. Throw out the right section.

$L = 6$, $R = 9$, Midpt $= \dfrac{6 + 9}{2} = 7$

$51 > A(7)$. Throw out the left section.

$L = 7$, $R = 9$, Midpt $= \dfrac{7 + 9}{2} = 8$

$51 = A(8)$ FOUND IT!

Note that the number 51 is found in four moves as opposed to eight moves that would have been required if a sequential search had been performed.

Write a program to perform a binary search on an array containing no more than 50 elements.

## 7-10-4 Answers to Test Yourself

1.  a. valid      b. invalid      c. valid      d. invalid      e. valid      f. valid

2.  All can hold the same amount of information. The notion of "order" does not exist for locations X1, X2, and X3, i.e., no one can predict what the next variable after X2 is. In contrast, we know that the item physically next to X(2) in memory is X(3).

3.  a. F.      b. T except in DATA statement      c. F.      d. T.      e. F.
    f. F.      g. T      h. F.      i. T.      j. F.      k. F.
    l. T.      m. F.      n. T.      o. T if T is character type.

4.  a. 1                    d. 0
    b. $-4$                 e. Invalid; G is not a character array.
    c. 2.4                  f. Invalid; G(0) is invalid.

5.  a. case 1:   FORMAT(3I2)      A = | 1 | 2 | 3 | 0 | 0 | B = | 1 | 2 | 3 | 0 | 0 |

            FORMAT (I2)       A = | 1 | 4 | 7 | 8 | 0 | B = | 3 | 6 | 9 | 0 | 0 |

    case 2:   FORMAT(12I2)     A = | 1 | 2 | 0 | 0 | 0 | B = | 3 | 0 | 0 | 0 | 0 |

            end of file encountered when trying to read A(2) the 2nd time around

    b. case 1:   FORMAT(I2)      A = | 1 | 3 | 5 | 7 | 9 | B = | 2 | 4 | 6 | 8 | 10 |

            FORMAT(3I2)      A = | 1 | 1 | 0 | 3 | 3 | B = | 0 | 2 | 2 | 0 | 4 |

    case 2:   FORMAT(12I2)     A = | 1 | 3 | 5 | 7 | 9 | B = | 2 | 4 | 6 | 8 | 10 |

    c. case 1:   FORMAT(I2)      A = | 5 | 4 | 3 | 2 | 1 | B = | 6 | 0 | 7 | 0 | 8 |

    case 2:   Read error format on some systems: too few digits on input record.

    d.  case 1:        FORMAT(4I2)        A = | 1 | 4 | 7 | 0 | 0 |  B = | 8 | 0 |-2 | 0 | 9 |

          case 2:        FORMAT(12I2)      A = | 1 | 0 | 0 | 0 | 0 |  B = | 0 | 0 | 0 | 0 | 0 |

              end of file encountered when trying to read B(1) for first time.

**6.** a. 5.   b. 18.   c. 4.   d. 12

**7.** a.   `DO 1 I = 1,6,2`       b.   `DO 2 I = 2,9,4`
      `1 READ(5,5) A(I),A(I + 1)`    `2 READ(5,6)A(I),K(I),A(I + 2),K(I + 2)`

**8.** a.  (1.) Skip to the top of a new page, space down four lines (no printed output).

      (2.) <u>1</u>  <u>2</u>           (3.) <u>1</u> <u>2</u> <u>3</u> <u>4</u> <u>5</u>
          <u>3</u>  <u>4</u>         (4.) <u>5</u>     <u>1</u>  <u>2 + 3</u> <u>4</u>
          <u>5</u>              ↑—because of carriage control code +

   b.  (1.) Invalid; mixed modes.    (3.) <u>3</u>  <u>1</u>  <u>3</u>  <u>2</u>  <u>3</u>
                                   <u>3</u>  <u>3</u>  <u>4</u>
      (2.)   <u>3</u>  <u>1</u>
            <u>3</u>  <u>2</u>
            <u>3</u>  <u>3</u>
            <u>3</u>  <u>4</u>

   c.  (1.) <u>1</u>   <u>2</u> .  <u>− 3</u> .   <u>3</u> .   <u>5</u> .   <u>0</u> .
          <u>2</u>   <u>2</u> .  <u>− 3</u> .   <u>3</u> .   <u>5</u> .   <u>0</u> .

      (2.) Starting on a new page, 2nd line
       <u>2</u> .  <u>− 3</u> .   <u>3</u> .   <u>5</u> .   <u>0</u> .   <u>2</u>
       <u>2</u> .  <u>− 3</u> .   <u>3</u> .   <u>5</u> .   <u>0</u> .

      (3.) <u>1</u>
       <u>2</u> .  <u>− 3</u> .   <u>3</u> .   <u>5</u> .   <u>0</u> .
      J cannot be described by an F format the second time around.

   d.  (1.)   <u>2</u> .  <u>− 3</u> . * * * <u>2</u> . <u>0</u> <u>1</u> . <u>5</u>
        <u>− 3</u> .  <u>− 1</u> . <u>2</u> . <u>0</u>

      (2.)  <u>1</u> . <u>5</u>     (3.) <u>2</u> . <u>− 3</u> . <u>− 1</u> .  <u>2</u> .  <u>2</u> . <u>− 3</u> . <u>− 1</u> .  <u>2</u> .
        <u>− 3</u> . <u>2</u>
        <u>− 1</u> . <u>0</u>
        <u>2</u> . <u>0</u>
        <u>1</u> . <u>5</u>
        <u>− 3</u> . <u>2</u>
        <u>− 1</u> . <u>0</u>
        <u>2</u> . <u>0</u>

**9.** a. 5 FORMAT(5F10.0/(10I8))
   b. 5 FORMAT(1X,2F10.0,I5)
   c. 5 FORMAT(1X,3F10.0/100 (1X,10I6/),2X,F5.0,I3)

**10.**

|   | 1 | 2 | 3 | 4 | 5 |
|---|---|---|---|---|---|

a. X  | 1.3 | 4.1 | 7.8 | 18.3 | 0. |

b. X  | 1.3 | 4.2 | 6.8 |   |   Y | 1.9 | 3.3 |

c. X  | 1.3 |   | 4.1 |   | 7.8 |

d. X  | 1.3 | 4.2 | 6.8 | 1.9 |   Y | 4.1 | −2.3 | 6. |

e. X  | 1.3 | 6.8 | 3.3 |   Y | 4.2 | 1.9 | 4.1 |

f. X  | 1.3 | 4.2 | 6.8 |   Y | 1.9 | 4.1 | −2.3 |

g. X  | 4.1 | 5.4 | 20.5 | 7.8 | 1.3 |

h. X  | 1.3 | 6.8 | −2.3 | 7.8 | A = 2.1 |

**11.**

a. Valid; 3 records.
b. Valid; 5 records.
c. Valid; 18 records.
d. Invalid; problems with $K - J$ (execution time).
e. Invalid; integer variable read with real format code (execution-time error).
f. Valid; 30 records.
g. Valid; 2 records.
h. Valid; 5 records.

**12.** a.
```
   WRITE(6,5)(A(I),I = 1,100)
 5 FORMAT(T10,F5.0,1X,F5.0)
```
```
   DO 10 I=1,100,2
10 WRITE(6,5)A(I),A(I+1)
```

b.
```
   WRITE(6,5)(A(I),A(I+50),I=1,50)
 5 FORMAT(T10,F5.0,IX,F5.0)
```
```
   DO 10 I=1,50
10 WRITE(6,5)A(I),A(I+50)
```

c.
```
   WRITE(6,5)(I,A(101-I),I = 1,100)
 5 FORMAT(T10,I1,1X,F5.0)
```
```
   DO 10 I=1,100
10 WRITE(6,5)I,A(101-I)
```

d.
```
   WRITE(6,5)(A(I),I = 2,100,2),(A(I),I = 1,100)
 5 FORMAT(50(T10,F5.0/)/(2X,10F5.0))
```

**13.**
```
   WRITE(6,5)(I,I = 1,12)
 5 FORMAT(T5,'POS LISTING:',(T20,4I3))
```

**14.**
a. Value of J is undefined; this could destroy a memory location and blow the program.
b. Value of J is undefined, but this cannot blow the program; results may be meaningless.
c. Program may blow since values will be read into A(101), A(102), ..., A(110), which have not been reserved for the array A.
d. The values initially read for A(2), A(3), A(4), and A(5) will be destroyed by successive values.

**15.** a.

| N | L | $M_1$ |   |
|---|---|-------|---|
| $M_2$ | $M_3$ | $M_4$ | 1 |
| N | L | $M_1$ | $M_2$ |
| $M_3$ | $M_4$ | 2 |   |

b.

| Format 1 | | | Format 2 | | | Format 3 | |
|---|---|---|---|---|---|---|---|
| A | B | $T_1$ | A | B | $T_1$ | A |   |
| $T_2$ | $T_3$ | $T_4$ | $T_2$ |   |   | B | $T_1$ |
| $T_5$ |   |   | $T_3$ | $T_4$ | $T_5$ | $T_2$ | $T_3$ |
|   |   |   |   |   |   | $T_4$ | $T_5$ |

c.

| $A_1$ | $A_2$ |
|-------|-------|
| $A_3$ | $A_4$ |
| $A_5$ | $A_6$ |
| $A_7$ |   |

**16.** The size of array A should not be declared in both the REAL and the DIMENSION statement.

The list of constants in the DATA statement should be real constants.

FORMAT 1 is omitted.

THEN I BIG may be truncated to six characters to form variable THENIB

.LT should be written as .LT.

IBIG = 0 is incorrect in the last IF statement.

**17.**
```
      CHARACTER*9 SOCSEC,T
      READ*,T
      DO 5 I = 1,100
          IF(SOCSEC(I).EQ.T)GO TO 6
    5 CONTINUE
      PRINT*,'NO MATCH'
      STOP
    6 PRINT*,'MATCH'
```

**18.**
```
      REAL A(20),B(30),C(51)
      READ(5,6,END=88)A,B,C
   88 ----
```

**19.**
```
      INTEGER A(10),B(16),K(100)
      DATA K/100*0/
      READ(5,1)(A(I),I=1,10),B
      DO 5 I = 1,10
         DO 6 J = 1,16
             IF(A(I).EQ.B(J))K(A(I))=1
    6    CONTINUE
    5 CONTINUE
      L = 0
      DO 7 I = 1,100
         IF(K(I) .EQ. 0) GO TO 7
             PRINT*,I
             L = L+1
    7 CONTINUE
      PRINT*,'NUMBER EQUAL ITEMS=',L
```

**20.**
```
      INTEGER A(20),K(20),NUMB(20),FREQ(20)
      DATA K/20*0/
      READ(5,1)A
      DO 5 I = 1,20
         K(A(I)) = K(A(I))+1
    5 CONTINUE
      L = 0
      DO 6 I = 1,20
         IF(K(I) .EQ. 0) GO TO 6
         L = L+1
         NUMB(L) = I
         FREQ(L) = K(I)
    6 CONTINUE
      WRITE(6,8)(NUMB(I),I=1,L)
      WRITE(6,9)(FREQ(I),I=1,L)
    8 FORMAT(' NUMBERS  ',20I4)
    9 FORMAT(' FREQUENCY',20I4)
      STOP
```

**21.**
```
      REAL A(10)
      READ(5,1)A
      DO 5 I = 1,9
         DO 6 J = I+1,10
             IF(A(I).EQ.A(J))GOTO9
    6    CONTINUE
    5 CONTINUE
      PRINT*,'NO EQUAL ENTRIES'
      STOP
    9 PRINT*,'MATCH EXISTS'
      STOP
```

**22.**
```
      REAL A(11)
      READ(5,9)(A(I),I=1,10)
      READ(5,9)R
      DO 5 I = 1,10
          IF(A(I).GT.R)GO TO 8
    5 CONTINUE
      A(11) = R
      STOP
    8 DO 6 J = 11,I+1,-1
          A(J) = A(J-1)
    6 CONTINUE
      A(I) = R
      STOP
```

**23.**
```
      INTEGER K(10)
      DO 5 J = 1,12
         DO 6 I = 1,10
            K(I) = I*J
    6    CONTINUE
         WRITE(6,4)(I,J,K(I),I=1,10)
    5 CONTINUE
    4 FORMAT(10(I3,'X',I3,'=',I3,3X))
```

# two-and three-dimensional arrays

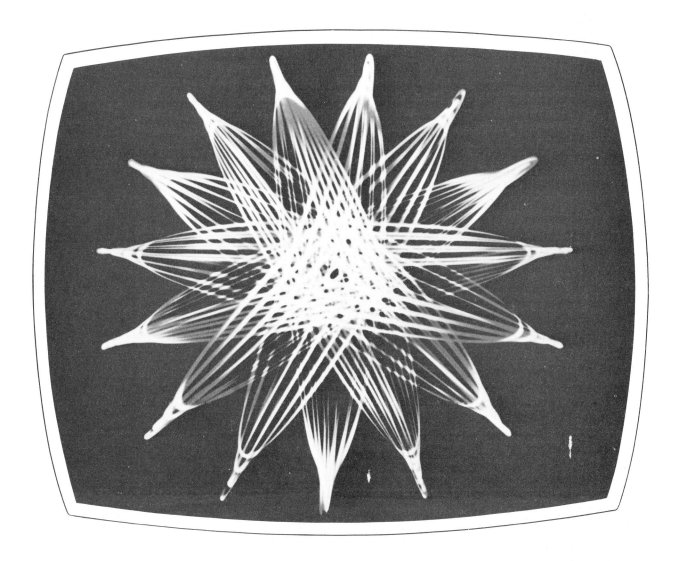

## CHAPTER EIGHT

# two- and three-dimensional arrays

## 8-1   Two-Dimensional Tables

### 8-1-1   Background and Justification

Much of the information that we deal with in our everyday lives is arranged in rows and columns. In a movie house, in an airplane, or in a typical classroom, seats are identified by their row and column positions (aisles). For some of us, looking up our taxes means reading a number at the intersection of an income level row and a number of dependents column. Chess boards and teachers' grade notebooks are also examples of two-dimensional tables or two-dimensional arrays.

The power of a two-dimensional array lies in its "lookup" procedure, which allows us to access any entry in the table directly, without searching through array entries. We access the array entries by specifying the row and column. For example, in the sales tax deduction table shown below, the deduction allowed a family with four children and an income of $8,000 to $8,999 is $117.

|  |  | *Number of Children* | | | | | |
|---|---|---|---|---|---|---|---|
| *Income Array* |  | 1 | 2 | 3 | 4 | 5 | 6 |
|  | $0,000. | 35. | 48. | 49. | 59. | 59. | 60. |
|  | $3,000. | 44. | 58. | 61. | 71. | 73. | 75. |
|  | $4,000. | 51. | 68. | 72. | 82. | 85. | 88. |
|  | $5,000. | 58. | 76. | 82. | 91. | 97. | 100. |
|  | $6,000. | 64. | 84. | 91. | 100. | 107. | 112. |
|  | $7,000. | 70. | 92. | 100. | 109. | 117. | 123. |
| 7th entry | $8,000. | 76. | 99. | 108. | 117. | 127. | 133. |
|  | $9,000. | 81. | 106. | 116. | 124. | 136. | 143. |
|  | $10,000. | 86. | 112. | 124. | 131. | 145. | 153. |
|  | $11,000. | 91. | 118. | 132. | 138. | 154. | 163. |
|  | $12,000. | 96. | 124. | 139. | 145. | 162. | 172. |
|  | $13,000. | 101. | 130. | 146. | 151. | 170. | 181. |
|  | $14,000. | 106. | 136. | 153. | 157. | 178. | 190. |
|  | $15,000. | 110. | 141. | 160. | 163. | 186. | 198. |
|  | $16,000. | 114. | 146. | 167. | 169. | 194. | 206. |
|  | $17,000. | 118. | 151. | 173. | 175. | 201. | 214. |
|  | $18,000. | 122. | 156. | 179. | 181. | 208. | 222. |
|  | $19,000. | 126. | 161. | 185. | 186. | 215. | 230. |

Once the correct income entry has been located in the INCOME array (position 7 for $8,000), we simply look up the figure at the 7th row and 4th column of the table, i.e., we use the number of children to identify the proper column directly (no IF statements). This table is an example of a two-dimensional array consisting of 18 rows and 6 columns; any entry in the table can be successively accessed by varying the row and/or column subscript.

## 8-1-2  Programming Example

Mr. Spandex does his daily grocery shopping at 4 stores (he store-hops for bargains) and he records his daily purchases at the various stores as follows:

| | | Stores | | | Explanation |
|---|---|---|---|---|---|
| | 1 | 2 | 3 | 4 | |
| 1 | 10.00 | 20.00 | 10.50 | 40.45 | On day 1 he spent $10 at store 1, $20 at store 2, ... |
| 2 | 0.00 | 15.00 | 20.00 | 35.55 | On day 2 he spent $0 at store 1, $15 at store 2, ... |
| Days 3 | 10.90 | 31.65 | 30.78 | 12.64 | |
| 4 | 0.00 | 0.00 | 9.87 | 5.50 | |
| 5 | 21.35 | 32.56 | 3.75 | 1.98 | On day 5 he spent $21.35 at store 1, $32.56 at store 2, ... |

Over the weekend, Mr. Spandex likes to analyze his grocery expenses by asking such questions as:

1. How much did I spend on Monday, on Tuesday, ..., on Friday?
2. How much did I spend for the whole week at store 1, store 2, ..., store 4?
3. On which day did I spend the least? the most?
4. At which store(s) did I spend the least? the most?
5. Which store(s) did I not go to on a particular day?
6. What are my total weekly expenses?
7. What were my expenses for a given day?
8. What was the average amount spent that week at each of the stores?
...and his questions go on and on!

Mr. Spandex has a microcomputer at home. He quickly realizes that he needs to store the above table in the memory of the computer and then write the code (manipulate the array) to get the answers to his questions easily. For example, if the array is called A, Mr. Spandex could type PRINT*, A(3,4) and the computer would print 12.64 (day 3, store 4).

In this introductory example, we will help Mr. Spandex do the following:

1. Load his expense table into a 5 by 4 array called A (5 rows and 4 columns).
2. Print his total expenses for each day.
3. Allow him to print the amount he spent on any given day at any given store.

**Task 1**  Loading the array A

To load the various entries into the array A, we first record the entries in row sequence on five input records, simulating the original data arrangement.

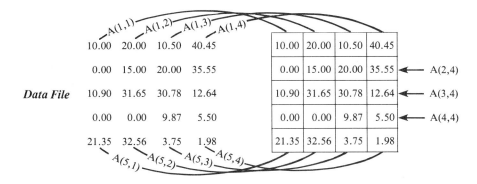

Since the input records give the entries in row fashion, we must also load the array in row fashion, i.e., when we load the first row,

the 1st item (10.00) must go into ⟶ | A(1,1) | A(1,2) | A(1,3) | A(1,4) |
the 2nd item (20.00) must go into ⟶
the 3rd item (10.50) must go into ⟶
the 4th item (40.45) must go into ⟶

and the same process must be repeated for rows 2, 3, 4, and 5. One code for reading these five rows in the order shown is:

```
      REAL A(5,4)      Reserve a 5 row by 4 column array.
      READ(5,1)A(1,1),A(1,2),A(1,3),A(1,4)
      READ(5,1)A(2,1),A(2,2),A(2,3),A(2,4)
      READ(5,1)A(3,1),A(3,2),A(3,3),A(3,4)
      READ(5,1)A(4,1),A(4,2),A(4,3),A(4,4)
      READ(5,1)A(5,1),A(5,2),A(5,3),A(5,4)
    1 FORMAT(4F5.2)
```

If we use a DO loop, this code could be reduced to:

```
      REAL A(5,4)
      DO 5 I = 1,5
         READ(5,1)A(I,1),A(I,2),A(I,3),A(I,4)
    5 CONTINUE
    1 FORMAT(4F5.2)
```

If we use a DO list, the list of variables could be shortened to:

```
      REAL A(5,4)
      DO 5 I = 1,5
         READ(5,1)(A(I,J),J=1,4)
    5 CONTINUE
    1 FORMAT(4F5.2)
```

Finally, we could also use two implied DO lists as follows:

```
    1 FORMAT(4F5.2)
      READ(5,1)((A(I,J),J=1,4),I=1,5)
```

The inner loop cycles rapidly:
when I = 1 J runs through 1, 2, 3, 4 (generates 1st row elements)
when I = 2 J runs through 1, 2, 3, 4 (generates 2nd row elements)

the outer loop moves slowly: for each value of I,
the inner index J runs from 1 to 4.

Once again, the implied DO list is nothing more than a compact technique to generate a list of variables. The DO list actually generates the following code:

```
READ(5,3)A(1,1),A(1,2),A(1,3),A(1,4),A(2,1),A(2,2),A(2,3),A(2,4),A(3,1), ..., A(5,4)
```

Hence 20 values are to be read in memory. The number of values read per record is specified by the format. FORMAT(4F5.2) specifies that four values are to be read per record. Since 20 variables are to be read, five records will be required. Had the format specified 7F5.2, three records would have been read, reading only six entries on the last record.

Specifying the proper sequence of the array elements in the READ/WRITE list is the basic task to be accomplished when an input or output operation is to be performed on a two-dimensional array. There are always alternative ways to accomplish this task, and some are more compact and efficient than others, but there may be several acceptable solutions, as displayed in this example.

**Task 2** Printing the Total Daily Expenses

Computing total daily expenses means adding the elements of a particular row. Since each row can be thought of as a one-dimensional array, we are back to the problem of accumulating the elements of a one-dimensional array. For example, to compute the sum of the first row, we could write

```
SUM = A(1,1) + A(1,2) + A(1,3) + A(1,4)     or     SUM = 0.
                                                   DO 5 STORE = 1,4
              varying column index                    STORE
                                                      SUM = SUM+A(1,STORE)
                                                 5 CONTINUE
```

Since the same process needs to be repeated for each of the remaining rows 2 through 5, we let the row index DAY vary from 1 to 5:

```
    INTEGER DAY,STORE
    DO 6 DAY = 1,5
        SUM = 0.
        DO 7 STORE = 1,4
            SUM = SUM + A(DAY,STORE)
7       CONTINUE
        WRITE(6,2)SUM
6   CONTINUE
2   FORMAT (F6.2)
```

Process 5 days (rows).
Initialize the accumulator for total expenses to 0.
Each row consists of 4 column entries (stores).
Add the 4 column entries of a given row to compute the total expenses for the particular day.
Print each day's total expenses.

**Task 3** Interactive Communication between Mr. Spandex and His Computer

To enable Mr. Spandex to determine how much he spent at a particular store on a particular day, we add the following code. (This form of communication is valid if you are using a screen and a printer. The asterisk used in the READ and WRITE statements refers to the user's screen, i.e., the screen is used both as an input and output device. In some installations 0 is used instead of *. Check your system for other conventions.)

```
    INTEGER DAY,STORE
11  WRITE(*,3)
    READ(*,4)DAY,STORE
    IF(DAY .EQ. 0) GO TO 9
      WRITE(*,8)A(DAY,STORE),DAY,STORE
      GO TO 11
9   STOP
8   FORMAT(' YOU SPENT',F6.2,' DOLLARS ON DAY',I2,' AT STORE',I2)
3   FORMAT(' ENTER DAY AND STORE. TO STOP ENTER 0,0')
4   FORMAT(2I1)
```

Write message on screen instead of printer.
Read from the screen. Mr. Spandex enters day and store.

Print expense for a given day and store.

The complete program to solve this three-part problem is shown in Figure 8–1.

## 8-1-3 Do It Now

1. Could the printing of the day's total purchases have been taken care of while loading the array into memory?

**FIGURE 8-1** A GROCERY SHOPPING ANALYSIS

```
C GROCERY SHOPPING ANALYSIS
C   A(5,4): ARRAY CONTAINING WEEKLY EXPENSES BY DAY & STORE
C   SUM:    USED TO ACCUMULATE TOTAL DAILY EXPENSES
C   DAY:    IDENTIFIES THE DAY
C   STORE:  IDENTIFIES A PARTICULAR STORE
C
      REAL A(5,4), SUM
      INTEGER DAY, STORE
      DO 5 DAY = 1, 5
         READ(5,1)(A(DAY,STORE),STORE=1,4)
    5 CONTINUE
      DO 6 DAY = 1, 5                Process 5 days.
         SUM = 0.                    Set the sum of expenses for each day to 0.
         DO 7 STORE = 1, 4           Add the expenses at the 4 stores for a given day.
            SUM = SUM + A(DAY,STORE)
    7    CONTINUE
         WRITE(6,2)DAY, SUM
    6 CONTINUE
   11 WRITE(*,3)                     Write the cue on the screen (terminal).
      READ(*,4)DAY, STORE            Enter the day and store on the screen (terminal).
      IF(DAY .EQ. 0) GO TO 9
         WRITE(*,8)A(DAY,STORE),DAY,STORE      Print answers on terminal.
         GO TO 11
    9 STOP
    8 FORMAT(' YOU SPENT',F6.2,' DOLLARS ON DAY',I2,' AT STORE',I2)
    3 FORMAT(' ENTER DAY AND STORE. TO STOP ENTER 00')
    4 FORMAT(2I1)
    1 FORMAT(4F5.2)
    2 FORMAT(' TOTAL DAILY EXPENSES FOR DAY',I2,' IS',F6.2)
      END
```

*Input File*

```
TOTAL DAILY EXPENSES FOR DAY 1 IS 80.95
TOTAL DAILY EXPENSES FOR DAY 2 IS 70.55
TOTAL DAILY EXPENSES FOR DAY 3 IS 85.97
TOTAL DAILY EXPENSES FOR DAY 4 IS 15.37
TOTAL DAILY EXPENSES FOR DAY 5 IS 59.64
ENTER DAY AND STORE. TO STOP ENTER 00
32

YOU SPENT 31.65 DOLLARS ON DAY 3 AT STORE 2
ENTER DAY AND STORE. TO STOP ENTER 00
11 ←──── day 1, store 1 entered on the screen by Mr. Spandex.

YOU SPENT 10.00 DOLLARS ON DAY 1 AT STORE 1
ENTER DAY AND STORE. TO STOP ENTER 00
34

YOU SPENT 12.64 DOLLARS ON DAY 3 AT STORE 4
ENTER DAY AND STORE. TO STOP ENTER 00
00
```

| | A(1,1) | A(1,2) | A(1,3) | A(1,4) |
|---|---|---|---|---|
| day 1 | 10.00 | 20.00 | 10.50 | 40.45 |
| day 2 | 00.00 | 15.00 | 20.00 | 35.55 |
| day 3 | 10.90 | 31.65 | 30.78 | 12.64 |
| day 4 | 00.00 | 00.00 | 09.87 | 05.50 |
| day 5 | 21.35 | 32.56 | 03.75 | 01.98 |

Printed on the screen.

**2.** Write the code to enable Mr. Spandex to print the total daily expenses (interactive communication) for any given day.

**3.** Write the code to enable Mr. Spandex to print the list of purchases at the four stores for any given day (interactive communication).

## Answers

1. No; at least not in any efficient manner.

2.
```
      REAL A(5,4)
      INTEGER DAY,STORE
      WRITE(*,4)
      READ(*,7)DAY
      SUM = 0.
      DO 5 STORE = 1,4
        SUM = SUM + A(DAY,STORE)
    5 CONTINUE
      WRITE(*,6) DAY,SUM
    6 FORMAT(' TOTAL EXPENSES FOR DAY',I2,'IS',F6.2)
    4 FORMAT(' ENTER DAY')
    7 FORMAT(I1)
```

3.
```
      REAL A(5,4)
      INTEGER DAY,STORE
      WRITE(*,4)
      READ(*,7)DAY
      WRITE(*,8)(A(DAY,STORE),STORE = 1,4)
    4 FORMAT(' ENTER DAY')
    7 FORMAT(I1)
    8 FORMAT(1X,4F6.2)
```

# 8-2  FORTRAN Statements

## 8-2-1  Two-Dimensional Arrays

In chapter 7 we discussed one-dimensional or linear arrays, where only one subscript is needed to address elements of the array. With two-dimensional tables or arrays, we address a particular array element by specifying the row and the column. Thus, the element in the second row and third column of array A is addressed as A(2,3). In general, A(I,J) refers to the element found in the Ith row and Jth column of array A. Note the comma separating the two subscripts. Figure 8–2 displays a 3 by 3 array. Analyze the subscripts carefully.

**FIGURE 8-2**    A TWO-DIMENSIONAL ARRAY

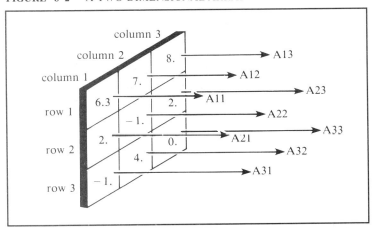

## 8-2-2  Array Declaration Statements and Subscripts

The general form of the declaration statement for a two-dimensional array is:

$$\begin{bmatrix} \text{DIMENSION} \\ \textit{type statement} \end{bmatrix} \textit{variable (row limit,column limit)} [,\ldots]$$

where *variable* is the name of the array

> *type statement* can be REAL, INTEGER, CHARACTER, DOUBLE PRECISION, COMPLEX, or LOGICAL
> *row limit* is a positive integer constant specifying the maximum number of rows
> *column limit* is a positive integer constant specifying the maximum number of columns

Any number of two- or one-dimensional arrays can be specified in a declarative statement. For example, the statement REAL B(6,8),C(10),J(10,25) reserves 48 memory locations for the array B, 10 memory locations for array C, and 250 locations for array J. Any reference to the variable name B or J must include two subscripts. For example, the statement B(I) = 0 is invalid, since only one subscript is included.

The row subscript value in a reference to a two-dimensional array must be between 1 and the row limit specified in the type statement. A similar restriction applies to the column subscript. For example, given an array A defined by REAL A(3,5), the references A(1,1), A(2,4), and A(3,5) are valid, whereas A(4,1) and A(3,6) are invalid, since they contain subscripts outside the allowable subscript range (there is no 4th row and no 6th column!).

Subscript expressions for two-dimensional arrays follow the same rules as subscripts for one-dimensional arrays. The following references to a two-dimensional array are valid:

| | |
|---|---|
| T(3*X,I + 2) | If X = 1.4 and I = −1, then we have T(4,1). |
| B(10/L,J*2) | If L = 3 and J = 1, then we have B(3,2). |
| C(SQRT(X),X**2) | If X = 9, then we have C(3,81). |

In these examples, the subscript expressions are first evaluated and then truncated to their integer values. Note that functions *can* be part of subscript expressions. As in the case of one-dimensional arrays, some FORTRAN versions may restrict subscript expressions to integer expressions.

### 8-2-3  Do It Now

Consider the following arrays A and B:

A

| | | | |
|---|---|---|---|
| 1. | −2. | .5 | 3. |
| 3. | 0. | 0. | −1. |
| 2. | 1. | 5. | 6. |
| 3. | 1. | 0. | 1. |

B

| | |
|---|---|
| 10. | 5. |
| 0. | 6. |
| −1. | .5 |

1. Compute the following values:
   a. A(3,4) = ?
   b. A(2,3) + B(1,2) = ?
   c. A(3,2) * A(4,3) = ?
   d. B(2,1) + B(2,2) = ?
   e. 1/(A(4,4)*2) + B(3,1) = ?

2. List the variable names (not the values) for the following:
   a. the diagonal elements of A
   b. the 2nd row of B
   c. the 3rd column of A

**3.** If I = 2, J = 4, what values will be printed by the following codes?

a. `PRINT*,A(J,I)`

b. `PRINT*,B(I + 1,2)`

c.
```
      S = 0.
      DO 5 K = 1,3
         S = S + A(I,K)
    5 CONTINUE
      PRINT*,S
```

d.
```
      DO 5 L = 1,4
         M = 5 - L
         PRINT*,A(M,J)
    5 CONTINUE
```

e.
```
      DO 5 L = 1,2
         PRINT*, B(L,L)
    5 CONTINUE
```

## Answers

**1.**  a. 6.     b. 5.     c. 0.     d. 6.     e. −0.50

**2.**  a. A(1,1), A(2,2), A(3,3), A(4,4)
   b. B(2,1), B(2,2)
   c. A(1,3), A(2,3), A(3,3), A(4,3)

**3.**  a. 1.     b. 0.5     c. 3.     d. 1., 6., −1., 3.     e. 10., 6.

### 8-2-4 Processing Two-Dimensional Arrays

Two-dimensional arrays can be processed in essentially the same way as one-dimensional arrays, except that an additional subscript must be used. In general, this means that we will need two loops: one to control the rows, and one to control the columns. The order of these loops, i.e., which one is the inner one, is generally immaterial since a table can be processed in row fashion or in column fashion. The following examples illustrate some common procedures.

*Example 1*    Initializing all elements of an array to 0

```
      REAL A(10,6), B(10,6)          REAL A(10,6), B(10,6)
      DO 6 J = 1,6                   DO 6 J = 1,6
         DO 5 I = 1,10                  DO 5 I = 1,10
            A(I,J)=0.0                     A(I,J)=0.0
            B(I,J)=0.0                     B(I,J)=0.0
    5    CONTINUE                  5    CONTINUE
    6 CONTINUE                     6 CONTINUE
              ⇓                              ⇓
```
The elements are zeroed out        The elements are zeroed out
in row fashion.                    in column fashion.

The DATA statement can also be used to initialize two-dimensional arrays (see question 3, section 8–5).

*Example 2*    Array Addition

Given the arrays

$$A = \begin{array}{|c|c|c|} \hline 1 & 2 & 3 \\ \hline 2 & 1 & 4 \\ \hline \end{array} \qquad B = \begin{array}{|c|c|c|} \hline -1 & 2 & 0 \\ \hline 1 & 3 & 4 \\ \hline \end{array}$$

We would like to add these two arrays to obtain another array C such that each element of C is equal to the sum of the corresponding entries of A and B, i.e.

$$C = \begin{array}{|c|c|c|} \hline 1+(-1) & 2+2 & 3+0 \\ \hline 2+1 & 1+3 & 4+4 \\ \hline \end{array} \quad \text{or} \quad C = \begin{array}{|c|c|c|} \hline 0 & 4 & 3 \\ \hline 3 & 4 & 8 \\ \hline \end{array}$$

This means that, in general, we want C(I,J) = A(I,J) + B(I,J) as I goes from 1 to 2 and as J goes from 1 to 3:

```
      INTEGER A(2,3),B(2,3),C(2,3)          DO 6 J = 1, 3
      DO 5 I = 1, 2                          DO 5 I = 1, 2
         DO 6 J = 1, 3              or           C(I,J)=A(I,J)+B(I,J)
            C(I,J)=A(I,J)+B(I,J)          5    CONTINUE
    6    CONTINUE                         6 CONTINUE
    5 CONTINUE
```

*Example 3*  Array Search

Suppose we are to identify the row and column position of the largest number in array A. To start the search process, we assume the largest number is at row R = 1 and column C = 1. We then compare A(R,C) with the entries of the array, moving successively along rows from one to the next (columns could also be used). Whenever we find an entry larger than A(R,C), we reset R and C to the row and column position of the larger number just found. The procedure can be visualized as follows:

```
      INTEGER R,C
      REAL A(10,15)
      R = 1                          Assume the largest number is at row R = 1 and at
      C = 1                          column C = 1 (subject to later change, of course).
      DO 5 I = 1,10
         DO 6 J = 1,15
            IF(A(R,C).GE.A(I,J)GOTO6     Determine if A(R,C) is still largest.
               R = I                     Since A(R,C) is no longer the largest, but A(I,J)
               C = J                     is, reset R and C to the location of the current
    6    CONTINUE                        largest number.
    5 CONTINUE
```

*Example 4*  Row Summation and Column Interchange

Given an array A of size 10 by 17, write the code to:

1. Add all the entries of the Nth row of array A, where N is accepted from input.
2. Interchange column 3 with column 17.

The row sum is SUM = A(N,1) + A(N,2) + A(N,3) + ... + A(N,16) + A(N,17). Hence the row index is fixed to N, while the column index varies from 1 to 17.

The interchange procedure can be accomplished by successively moving each element of column 3 into a temporary location, TEMP, then moving the corresponding element of column 17 into the vacated column 3 position, and finally moving the saved value in TEMP into the corresponding location of column 17, as shown below. If no temporary location were used, the elements of column 3 would be destroyed by the statement A(I,3) = A(I,17), as I ranges from 1 to 10. The code to perform the sum and the interchange procedure is:

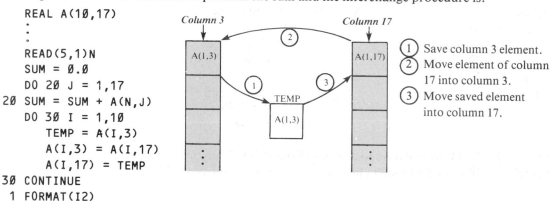

```
      REAL A(10,17)
      .
      .
      .
      READ(5,1)N
      SUM = 0.0
      DO 20 J = 1,17
   20 SUM = SUM + A(N,J)
      DO 30 I = 1,10
         TEMP = A(I,3)
         A(I,3) = A(I,17)
         A(I,17) = TEMP
   30 CONTINUE
    1 FORMAT(I2)
```

*Example 5*    Row Summation for an Entire Array

Given the array A, shown below, we would like to compute the sum of the elements of the 1st row and store that sum in S(1), compute the sum of the elements of the 2nd row and store it in S(2), and so forth.

| A | | | | S | | Compute sum of each row |
|---|---|---|---|---|---|---|

$$S(1) = 1 + 4 + 7$$
$$S(2) = 2 + 5 + 8$$
$$S(3) = 3 + 6 + 9$$

(A: row1 = 1, 4, 7; row2 = 2, 5, 8; row3 = 3, 6, 9) (S: 12, 15, 18)

Two methods are shown:

**Row Method**

The sum of each row can be computed by fixing the row index I of A to 1 and varying the column index from 1 to 3, and repeating the same process for I equal to 2 and 3.

```
      INTEGER S(3),A(3,3)
      DATA S/3*0/
      DO 5 I = 1,3
         DO 6 J = 1,3
            S(I)=S(I)+A(I,J)
6        CONTINUE
5     CONTINUE
```

$$I = 1 \quad S(1) = S(1) + A(1,1) + A(1,2) + A(1,3) = 1 + 4 + 7 = 12$$
$$I = 2 \quad S(2) = S(2) + A(2,1) + A(2,2) + A(2,3) = 2 + 5 + 8 = 15$$
$$I = 3 \quad S(3) = (S3) + A(3,1) + A(3,2) + A(3,3) = 3 + 6 + 9 = 18$$

**Column Method**

The same results can be obtained, in a less apparent way, if we interchange the two DO loops as follows:

```
      DATA S/3*0/
      DO 6 J = 1,3
         DO 5 I = 1,3
            S(I)=S(I)+A(I,J)
5        CONTINUE
6     CONTINUE
```

| $J = 1$ | $J = 2$ | $J = 3$ |
|---|---|---|
| $S_1 = A_{11}$ | $S_1 = A_{11} + A_{12}$ | $S_1 = A_{11} + A_{12} + A_{13}$ |
| $S_2 = A_{21}$ | $S_2 = A_{21} + A_{22}$ | $S_2 = A_{21} + A_{22} + A_{23}$ |
| $S_3 = A_{31}$ | $S_3 = A_{31} + A_{32}$ | $S_3 = A_{31} + A_{32} + A_{33}$ |

## 8-2-5  Do It Now

1. What values will be stored in array X after each of the following codes is executed?

a.
```
      INTEGER X(3,4)
      DO 5 I = 1,3
         DO 6 J = 1,4
            X(I,J) = I*J
6        CONTINUE
5     CONTINUE
```

b.
```
      INTEGER X(3,4)
      L = 1
      DO 5 I = 1,4
         DO 6 J = 1,3
            X(J,I) = L
            L = L+1
6        CONTINUE
5     CONTINUE
```

2. If A is a table of size 10 by 6, write the code to initialize the first column of A with 1's, the second column with 2's, the third column with 3's, ..., and column 6 with 6's.

3. Write the code to load a 10 by 10 array with 100 random numbers between 0 and 1, *then* compute the average of all the entries of the array. What would you expect the answer to be?

4. Write the code to input a value for C and print the largest value in column C of the array A(3,7).

5. Given an array A of size 6 by 6, write the code to compute the sum of the elements of its first diagonal and the sum of the elements of its second diagonal. These diagonals are defined as follows:

1st diagonal          2nd diagonal

## Answers

**1.** a.

| 1 | 2 | 3 | 4 |
|---|---|---|---|
| 2 | 4 | 6 | 8 |
| 3 | 6 | 9 | 12 |

X:

b.

| 1 | 4 | 7 | 10 |
|---|---|---|---|
| 2 | 5 | 8 | 11 |
| 3 | 6 | 9 | 12 |

X:

**2.**
```
    REAL A(10,6)
    DO 5 J = 1,6
        DO 6 I = 1,10
            A(I,J) = J
6       CONTINUE
5   CONTINUE
```

**3.**
```
    REAL A(10,10)
    DO 5 I = 1,10
        DO 5 J = 1,10
            A(I,J) = RAND(1)
5   CONTINUE
    SUM = 0.
    DO 6 I = 1,10
        DO 6 J = 1,10
            SUM = SUM + A(I,J)
6   CONTINUE
    PRINT*,SUM/100.
```
The answer should be close to .5.

**4.**
```
    INTEGER A(3,7)
    READ*,C
    L = A(1,C)
    DO 5 I = 2,3
        IF(L.LT.A(I,C))L=A(I,C)
5   CONTINUE
    PRINT*,L
```

**5.**
```
    REAL A(6,6)
    D1 = 0.
    D2 = 0.
    DO 5 I = 1,6
        D1 = D1 + A(I,I)
        D2 = D2 + A(I,7-I)
5   CONTINUE
    PRINT*,D1, D2
```

## 8-2-6 Input and Output of Two-Dimensional Arrays

In section 8–1–2 we discussed various methods of loading a two-dimensional array with data arranged in row fashion.

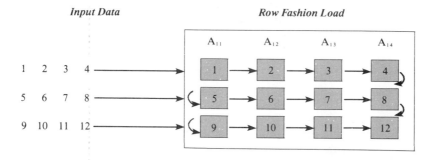

| Input Data | Row Fashion Load |

It is, of course, also possible to load a two-dimensional array in column fashion *if* the data file specifies a sequence of entries that reflect a column arrangement. For example, to load the above array with the same numbers, but in column fashion, we must have the following input file:

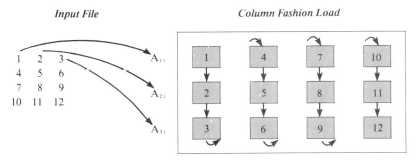

Various methods of loading an array in row or column fashion are illustrated in Figure 8–3. Study this figure carefully; options 3 and 4 are probably the methods used most frequently. Note that options 4 and 5 do not nescessarily require that the input data be arranged as

**FIGURE 8-3**   VARIOUS METHODS OF LOADING A TWO-DIMENSIONAL ARRAY

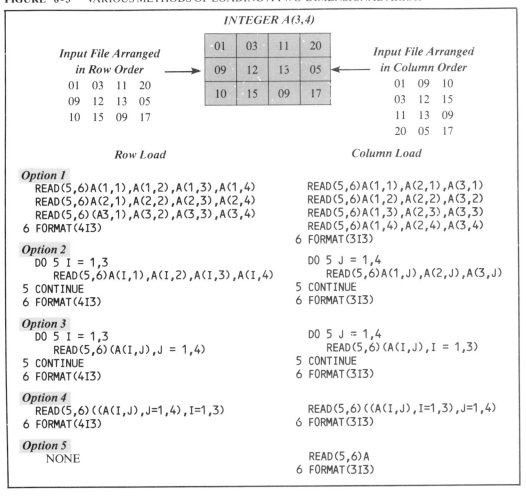

shown. The input data could also be recorded on just one record in row or column sequence and be read into array A as follows:

**Input Record**

Row order

```
01 03 11 20 09 12 13 05 10 15 09 17     READ(5,6)((A(I,J),J=1,4),I=1,3)
                                        6 FORMAT(12I3)
```

Column order

```
01 09 10 03 12 15 11 13 09 20 05 17    {READ(5,6)((A(I,J),I=1,3),J=1,4)
                                       {READ(5,6)A
                                        6 FORMAT(12I3)
```

Note the simple method in option 5 for loading an array when the data file is organized in column sequence. READ(5,6)A is equivalent to READ(5,6)((A(I,J),I=1,3),J=1,4) if the array A is declared as INTEGER A(3,4).

Consider the following examples of array input/output.

*Example 1*

Assume three arrays A, B, and C are to be read row-wise, according to the data layout shown below:

| | |
|---|---|
| record #1 | A(1,1) A(1,2) A(1,3)   B(1,1) B(1,2) B(1,3) B(1,4)   C(1) |
| record #2 | A(2,1) A(2,2) A(2,3)   B(2,1) B(2,2) B(2,3) B(2,4)   C(2) |
| record #3 | A(3,1) A(3,2) A(3,3)   B(3,1) B(3,2) B(3,3) B(3,4)   C(3) |
| record #4 | A(4,1) A(4,2) A(4,3)   B(4,1) B(4,2) B(4,3) B(4,4)   C(4) |

The implied DO list to load these arrays might be

```
1 FORMAT(8F5.0)
  READ(5,1)((A(I,J),J=1,3),(B(I,K),K=1,4),C(I),I=1,4)
```

This can be interpreted as

When I = 1, read A(1,J) as J = 1 to 3, then B(1,K) as K = 1,4 and C(1)

or

read A(1,1), A(1,2), A(1,3), B(1,1),...,B(1,4), C(1)

then repeat the process for I = 2, 3, and 4.

Altogether, three elements of A, four elements of B, and one element of C will be read from each record as I ranges from 1 to 4. Hence $(3 + 4 + 1)\cdot 4 = 32$ elements will be read. The list of variables contains 32 elements, and the format specifies eight values per record, hence four records will be read.

*Example 2*

In this example, the array B is to be read column-wise and the elements of C are reversed

| | |
|---|---|
| record #1 | A(1,1) A(1,2) A(1,3)   B(1,1) B(2,1) B(3,1) B(4,1)   C(4) |
| record #2 | A(2,1) A(2,2) A(2,3)   B(1,2) B(2,2) B(3,2) B(4,2)   C(3) |
| record #3 | A(3,1) A(3,2) A(3,3)   B(1,3) B(2,3) B(3,3) B(4,3)   C(2) |
| record #4 | A(4,1) A(4,2) A(4,3)   B(1,4) B(2,4) B(3,4) B(4,4)   C(1) |

The following code might be used to read this data:

```
    READ(5,1)((A(I,J),J=1,3),(B(K,I),K=1,4),C(5-I),I=1,4)
  1 FORMAT(8F5.0)
```

If the user finds the preceding method too confusing, he/she can use a combination of a DO loop and an implied DO list as follows:

```
    DO 10 I = 1,4
    READ(5,1) (A(I,J),J=1,3), (B(K,I),K=1,4), C(5-I)
 10 CONTINUE
```

*Example 3*

Two-dimensional arrays are very useful when printing tables of numbers that require some form of column/row identification and headings. Consider, for example, the problem in Figure 8–1 where A is an "expense" array; we would like to print the input data in the following form:

| DAY 1 | XX.XX | XX.XX | XX.XX | XX.XX |
| DAY 2 | XX.XX | XX.XX | XX.XX | XX.XX |
| DAY 3 | XX.XX | XX.XX | XX.XX | XX.XX |
| DAY 4 | XX.XX | XX.XX | XX.XX | XX.XX |
| DAY 5 | XX.XX | XX.XX | XX.XX | XX.XX |

The following code can be used to generate this output:

```
           Day    Expense
            ↓        ↓
    WRITE(6,1)(I,(A(I,J),J=1,4),I=1,5)
  1 FORMAT(8X,'DAY',I2,5X,4F11.2)
```

The DO list generates $1, A_{11}, A_{12}, A_{13}, A_{14}, 2, A_{21}, A_{22}, A_{23}, A_{24}, 3, \ldots, 5, A_{51}, A_{52}, A_{53}, A_{54}$ on 5 lines.

We could also generate the more sophisticated output

**Shopping Analysis**

|  | *Store 1* | *Store 2* | *Store 3* | *Store 4* |
|---|---|---|---|---|
| DAY 1 | XX.XX | XX.XX | XX.XX | XX.XX |
| DAY 2 | XX.XX | XX.XX | XX.XX | XX.XX |
| DAY 3 | XX.XX | XX.XX | XX.XX | XX.XX |
| DAY 4 | XX.XX | XX.XX | XX.XX | XX.XX |
| DAY 5 | XX.XX | XX.XX | XX.XX | XX.XX |

with just one WRITE statement:

```
       Store numbers    Day number     Expense entries
             ↘              ↓              ↙
    WRITE(6,1)(K,K=1,4),(I,(A(I,J),J=1,4),I=1,5)
  1 FORMAT('1',T35,'SHOPPING ANALYSIS'//T24,4('STORE',I2,2X)//
  *  (8X,'DAY',I3,5X,4F11.2))
             ↓         ⌣                        ↓
       Day number     Data                Store number
         (I)         (A(I,J))                   K
```

The beginning programmer may prefer to use two or three separate WRITE statements instead of the one shown.

428

*Example 4*

Professor X's grade (100 records maximum) roster contains the following information:

| Name | Number test scores (N ≤ 4) | Test scores (max of 4) | | | |
|------|------|------|------|------|------|
| ANTON | 3 | 80 | 74 | 68 | |
| BEVIS | 1 | 70 | | | |
| HUGHES | 4 | 20 | 30 | 60 | 80 |
| TERN | 2 | 74 | 86 | | |
| WATS | 3 | 80 | 60 | 20 | |

*Input File* appears to the left of the Name column.

Write the code to read the name and number of tests into one-dimensional arrays NAME and NO, and the grades into a two-dimensional array GRADES while producing the following report as the input file is read.

**Input Records**

| *Name* | *No* | *Grades* | | | |
|--------|------|------|------|------|------|
| ANTON | 3 | 80 | 74 | 68 | |
| BEVIS | 1 | 70 | | | |
| HUGHES | 4 | 20 | 30 | 60 | 80 |
| TERN | 2 | 74 | 86 | | |
| WATS | 3 | 80 | 60 | 20 | |
| ⋮ | ⋮ | ⋮ | ⋮ | ⋮ | ⋮ |

*Output*

| NAME | TESTS | TEST 1 | TEST 2 | TEST 3 | TEST 4 |
|------|-------|--------|--------|--------|--------|
| ANTON | 3 | 80 | 74 | 68 | |
| BEVIS | 1 | 70 | | | |
| HUGHES | 4 | 20 | 30 | 60 | 80 |
| TERN | 2 | 74 | | | |
| WATS | 3 | 80 | 60 | 20 | |

The following code could be used:

```
      CHARACTER*8  NAME(101)
      INTEGER GRADES(101,4),NO(100),N
      WRITE(6,1)(I,I=1,4)
      DO 5 I = 1,101
         READ(5,8,END=88)NAME(I),N,(GRADES(I,J),J=1,N)
         WRITE(6,2)NAME(I),N,(GRADES(I,J),J=1,N)
         NO(I) = N
    5 CONTINUE
   88 STOP
    1 FORMAT(' NAME',5X,'TESTS',2X,4('TEST',1X,I1,2X))
    2 FORMAT(1X,A8,3X,I1,5X,4(I3,5X))
    8 FORMAT(A8,I1,4I3)
      END
```

## 8-2-7  Do It Now

Given the data file shown below, specify the contents of the array INTEGER A(3,4) after carrying out the following input instructions. Assume that array A initially is set to 0's.

*Input File*
```
01020304 ←— 1st Record
05060708
09101112
```

**1.** a.
```
   DO 5 I = 1,3
 5    READ(5,6)(A(I,J),J = 1,3)
 6 FORMAT(4I2)
```

b.
```
   DO 5 I = 1,3
 5    READ(5,6)(A(J,I),J = 1,3)
 6 FORMAT(4I2)
```

c.
```
   READ(5,6)A
 6 FORMAT(4I2)
```

d.
```
   READ(5,6)((A(I,I),J=1,4),I=1,3)
 6 FORMAT(4I2)
```

**2.** Given the arrays REAL A(3,4) and INTEGER B(3,4), write the necessary WRITE instruction and FORMAT statement to produce the following output arrangements. (Use only one WRITE statement for each part.)

   a. First row of A on one line, first row of B on next line, ... (alternating in that way).
   b. All entries of A in row fashion followed by all entries of B in row fashion, all on one line.
   c. All entries of A in row fashion on one line, followed by all entries of B in row fashion on the next line.
   d. $A_{11} B_{11} A_{12} B_{12} A_{13} B_{13} ... A_{34} B_{34}$ all on just one line.
   e. First column of A on first line, second column of A on second line, ..., fourth column of A on fourth line, followed by first column of B on line 5, second column of B on line 6, ...
   f. First row of A on line 1, second row of A on line 2, third row of A on line 3, first row of B on line 4, second row of B on line 5, ...
   g. All entries of A in column fashion, one entry per line, followed by all entries of B in column fashion, one entry per line.

**3.** Modify the program of Figure 8–1 to allow Mr. Spandex to obtain the following report:

|         | STORE 1 | STORE 2 | STORE 3 | STORE 4 |
|---------|---------|---------|---------|---------|
| DAY 1   | 10.00   | 20.00   | 10.50   | 40.45   |
| DAY 2   | .00     | 15.00   | 20.00   | 35.55   |
| DAY 3   | 10.90   | 31.65   | 30.78   | 12.64   |
| DAY 4   | .00     | .00     | 9.87    | 5.50    |
| DAY 5   | 21.35   | 32.56   | 3.75    | 1.98    |
| AVERAGE | 8.45    | 19.84   | 14.98   | 19.22   |

**4.** Write the code to produce the following report for Professor X (see example 4 in section 8-2-6). Read the names and grades in the same arrays as in example 4.

| NAME   | TESTS | TEST 1 | TEST 2 | TEST 3 | TEST 4 | AVERAGE |
|--------|-------|--------|--------|--------|--------|---------|
| ANTON  | 3     | 80     | 74     | 68     |        | 74.0    |
| BEVIS  | 1     | 70     |        |        |        | 70.0    |
| HUGHES | 4     | 20     | 30     | 60     | 80     | 47.5    |
| TERN   | 2     | 74     | 86     |        |        | 80.0    |
| WATS   | 3     | 80     | 60     | 20     |        | 53.3    |
| AVERAGE|       | 64.8   | 62.5   | 49.3   | 80.0   |         |

*Input File*

```
ANTON    3080074068
BEVIS    1070
HUGHES   4020030060080
TERN     2074086
WATS     3080060020
```

## Answers

**1.** a. 
```
1    2    3    0
5    6    7    0
9   10   11    0
```
b.
```
1    5    9    0
2    6   10    0
3    7   11    0
```
c.
```
1    4    7   10
2    5    8   11
3    6    9   12
```
d.
```
4    0    0    0
0    8    0    0
0    0   12    0
```

**2.** a.
```
   WRITE(6,6)((A(I,J),J = 1,4),(B(I,J),J = 1,4),I = 1,3)
 6 FORMAT(1X,4F6.0/1X, 4I6)
```

b.  
```
    WRITE(6,6)((A(I,J),J=1,4),I=1,3),((B(I,J),J=1,4),I=1,3)
  6 FORMAT(1X,12F6.1,2X,12I3)
```

c. Same WRITE statement as part b, with  
```
  6 FORMAT(1X,12F6.0/1X,12I3)
```

d.  
```
    WRITE(6,6)((A(I,J),B(I,J),J = 1,4),I = 1,3)
  6 FORMAT(1X,12(F6.0,1X,I3))
```

e.  
```
  WRITE(6,6)A,B
  6 FORMAT(4(1X,3F6.0/),(1X,3I3))
```

f. Same WRITE statement as part b with  
```
  6 FORMAT(3(1X,4F6.0/),(1X,4I3))
```

g.  
```
  WRITE(6,6)A,B
  6 FORMAT(12(1X,F6.0/),(1X,I3))
```

3.
```
    C GROCERY SHOPPING ANALYSIS
    C    A(5,4): ARRAY CONTAINING WEEKLY EXPENSES BY DAY & STORE
    C    SUM:    USED TO ACCUMULATE TOTAL DAILY EXPENSES
    C    DAY:    IDENTIFIES THE DAY
    C    STORE:  IDENTIFIES A PARTICULAR STORE
    C
          REAL A(5,4), SUM, COLUMN(4)
          INTEGER DAY, STORE
          DO 5 I = 1, 5
             READ(5,1)(A(I,J),J=1,4)
    5     CONTINUE
          DO 4 J = 1,4
             SUM = 0.
             DO 6 I = 1,5
                SUM = SUM + A(I,J)
    6        CONTINUE
             COLUMN(J) = SUM/5.
    4     CONTINUE
          WRITE(6,7)(I,I=1,4),(I,(A(I,J),J=1,4),I=1,5),COLUMN
          STOP
    7     FORMAT(8X,4('STORE ',I1,3X)//5(' DAY ',I1,3X,4(F5.2, 5X)/),
          A        ' AVERAGE ',4(F5.2,5X))
    1     FORMAT(4F5.2)
          END
```

4.
```
    C COLNO(4):   RECORDS NUMBER OF ENTRIES IN EACH COLUMN
    C               I.E., COLNO(1) = 5 AND COLNO(4) = 1 IN THIS EXAMPLE
    C COLSUM(4): RECORDS THE SUM OF ENTRIES OF EACH COLUMN
    C               I.E., COLSUM(1) = 324  AND COLSUM(4) = 80 IN THIS EXAMPLE
    C TESTAV(4): COMPUTES THE AVERAGES OF EACH COLUMN
    C               I.E., TESTAV(1) = 324/5 =64.8 AND TESTAV(4) = 80/1 = 80
    C
          REAL TESTAV(4),AVER,SUM
          CHARACTER*8  NAME(101)
          INTEGER GRADES(101,4),N,COLNO(4),COLSUM(4)
          DATA COLNO,COLSUM/8*0/
          WRITE(6,1)(I,I=1,4)
          DO 5 I = 1,101
             READ(5,8,END=88)NAME(I),N,(GRADES(I,J),J=1,N)
             WRITE(6,2)NAME(I),N,(GRADES(I,J),J=1,N)
             SUM = 0.0
             DO 6 J = 1, N
                SUM = SUM + GRADES(I,J)
                COLSUM(J) = COLSUM(J) + GRADES(I,J)
                COLNO(J) = COLNO(J) + 1
             CONTINUE
    6     AVER = SUM/N
          WRITE(6,3)AVER
```

**Input File**

| *Name* | *N* | *Grades* |
|--------|-----|----------|
| ANTON  | 3080074068 | |
| BEVIS  | 1070 | |
| HUGHES | 4020030060080 | |
| TERN   | 2074086 | |
| WATS   | 3080060020 | |

Compute sum of each row.
Accumulate four separate column sums.
Count number of entries in each of the
  four columns.
Compute average of scores for each row.

```
5         CONTINUE
88        L = 0
          DO 7 I = 1, 4
             IF(COLNO(I) .EQ. 0)GO TO 12          If a column contains no entries, exit from loop.
                L = L + 1                         Count number of averages to be printed.
                TESTAV(I) = COLSUM(I)/(1.*COLNO(I))   Compute average of each column.
7         CONTINUE                                Note 1. for real division.
12        WRITE(6,4)(TESTAV(I),I=1,L)             Write out the column averages.
          STOP
1         FORMAT(' NAME',5X,'TESTS',2X,4('TEST',1X,I1,2X),2X,'AVERAGE'/)
2         FORMAT(1X,A8,3X,I1,5X,4(I3,5X))
3         FORMAT('+',50X,F5.1)
4         FORMAT('0AVERAGE',10X,4(F5.1,3X))
8         FORMAT(A8,I1,4I3)
          END
```

# 8-3 Programming Examples

### 8-3-1 A Frequency Distribution

*Problem/Specification:* Data on the smoking habits of students at a university have been gathered. Each student's class (1 = freshman, 2 = sophomore, 3 = junior, 4 = senior, 5 = graduate) and a code representing the student's smoking habits (1 = don't smoke, 2 = one pack or less a day, 3 = more than one pack a day) have been recorded, with each record containing data for one student. Let us write a program to generate a frequency table showing students' smoking habits by class.

This problem essentially deals with counting, i.e., we need to count how many freshmen do not smoke, how many freshmen smoke one pack or less a day, how many freshmen smoke in excess of one pack, and so forth. Altogether we need 15 counters (5 student classifications and 3 habits). One simple way to solve the problem manually is to draw a table with 5 rows and 3 columns, and proceeds as follows:

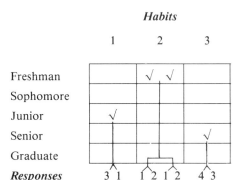

If the first record is 3,1 (3 = junior, 1 = no smoke), we place a check mark in the box at row 3 and column 1. We read the next record (1,2) and check the corresponding box. We repeat the process until we run out of records, then we add up the checks in each box.

This table shows the counts (frequencies) obtained by processing the four data records shown.

To simulate this process in our program, we create a two-dimensional array COUNT with 5 rows and 3 columns, where each entry serves as a counter. Initially, these counters are set to 0; then every time we read a class and a habit code, we add 1 to the corresponding array entry, e.g., if class = 1 and habit = 2, we add 1 to COUNT(class,habit), which is COUNT(1,2). When all data have been read, COUNT(I,J) will contain the count of class I students with smoking habit J. The input and output will have the following form:

**Input**                                                    **Output**

*Class*   *Habit Code*

```
   11
   12
   13
   11
   13
   21
   23
   51
   23
   32
   33
   41
   41
   43
   51
   23
   52
   53
```

|  | FREQUENCY DISTRIBUTION | | |
|---|---|---|---|
| CLASS | DON'T SMOKE | 1 PACK OR LESS | MORE THAN 1 |
| FRESHMAN | 2 | 1 | 2 |
| SOPHOMORE | 1 | 0 | 3 |
| JUNIOR | 0 | 1 | 1 |
| SENIOR | 2 | 0 | 1 |
| GRADUATE | 2 | 1 | 1 |

The program to solve this problem is shown in Figure 8–4.

### 8-3-2  An On-line Airline Reservation Problem

You have been asked to write an on-line reservation system for a small commuter airline company. Each plane has 5 rows of seats, with 4 seats per row, and can carry up to 20 passengers. The ticket agent is to ask each passenger's name and his or her row and seat preference; the name and seat request are then entered on a computer terminal. If the seat requested is available, the system should reserve that seat. If that seat is already taken, the system is to assign the first available seat, starting with row 1, row 2, ..., up to row 5. A message should appear on the screen as soon as the seating capacity has been reached. When all passenger requests have been taken care of, the program should then print the seating arrangement, by passenger name, as follows:

```
ENTER ROW THEN SEAT AND NAME
11BOILLOT
ENTER ROW THEN SEAT AND NAME
11ADKINS
ENTER ROW THEN SEAT AND NAME
44FORD
ENTER ROW THEN SEAT AND NAME
44CABERAS
ENTER ROW THEN SEAT AND NAME
0000000000
```

System displays the cue on the terminal.
The agent enters the passenger's request and name.

11 means row 1 and seat 1.

When the agent enters the special code 00, the system prints the seating arrangement.

```
              FINAL SEATING ARRANGEMENT
ROW 1    BOILLOT_  ADKINS__  CABERAS_  _____
ROW 2    _____  _____  _____  _____
ROW 3    _____  _____  _____  _____
ROW 4    _____  _____  _____  FORD____
ROW 5    _____  _____  _____  _____
```

Note that ADKINS is assigned 1,2 and that CABERAS is assigned 1,3!

(Note that the program instructs the printer to underline each seat.)

The idea behind this problem is to represent the plane's seating configuration with a 5 by 4 array SEAT, which will eventually contain all the passenger's names. Initially we set

**FIGURE 8-4** A FREQUENCY DISTRIBUTION PROGRAM

```
C FREQUENCY DISTRIBUTION USING A TWO-DIMENSIONAL ARRAY
C    COUNT(5,3): COUNTS STUDENT'S SMOKING HABITS BY CLASS & NO. PACKS
C    KLASS(4):   CONTAINS THE 5 CLASSIFICATIONS: FRESHMAN,...,GRADUATE
C    CLASS:      STUDENT CLASSIFICATION READ FROM A RECORD
C    HABIT:      NUMERIC CODE: 1=DON'T SMOKE 2=1 PACK OR LESS 3=OVER 1
C
      CHARACTER*9 KLASS(5)
      INTEGER COUNT(5,3), CLASS, HABIT
      DATA COUNT/15*0/
      DATA KLASS/'FRESHMAN ','SOPHOMORE','JUNIOR','SENIOR','GRADUATE'/
      WRITE(6,1)
5     READ(5,2,END=88)CLASS,HABIT
      IF(CLASS.EQ.0 .OR. CLASS.GT.5 .OR. HABIT.EQ.0 .OR. HABIT.GT.3)THEN
         WRITE(6,4)CLASS,HABIT
      ELSE
         COUNT(CLASS,HABIT) = COUNT(CLASS,HABIT) + 1
      ENDIF
      GO TO 5
88    WRITE(6,3)(KLASS(I),(COUNT(I,J),J=1,3),I=1,5)
      STOP
C
1     FORMAT(15X,'FREQUENCY DISTRIBUTION'/' CLASS',6X,
     A 'DON''T SMOKE',2X,'1 PACK OR LESS',2X,'MORE THAN 1'/)
2     FORMAT(2I1)
3     FORMAT(1X,A9,6X,I2,13X,I2,12X,I2)
4     FORMAT(1X,'CHECK INPUT PARAMETERS',2I3)
      END
```

| Input File | |
|------------|------|
| *Class* | *Habit* |
| 1 | 1 |
| 1 | 2 |
| 1 | 3 |
| 1 | 1 |
| 1 | 3 |
| 2 | 1 |
| 2 | 3 |
| 5 | 1 |
| 2 | 3 |
| 3 | 2 |
| 3 | 3 |
| 4 | 1 |
| 4 | 1 |
| 4 | 3 |
| 5 | 1 |
| 2 | 3 |
| 5 | 2 |
| 5 | 3 |

```
                FREQUENCY DISTRIBUTION
CLASS        DON'T SMOKE   1 PACK OR LESS   MORE THAN 1

FRESHMAN          2              1               2
SOPHOMORE         1              0               3
JUNIOR            0              1               1
SENIOR            2              0               1
GRADUATE          2              1               1
```

these 20 seats to blanks to indicate nonreserved seats. Thus SEAT(3,4) = ' ' means that seat number 4 in the 3rd row is empty. If a passenger wishes to reserve SEAT(3,4), we store the passenger's name in that array location.

If there are fewer than 20 passengers at departure time, the agent enters a special code (R = 0) to terminate the reservation process; the system then prints the seating arrangement of the airplane. If all seats are taken, the system alerts the agent and prints the final seating map.

The program to solve this problem is shown in Figure 8–5.

**FIGURE 8-5** AN ON-LINE RESERVATION SYSTEM

```
C AIRPLANE SEATING RESERVATION SYSTEM
C    SEAT(5,4): ARRAY DISPLAYING PLANE SEATING ARRANGEMENT
C    R:        PASSENGER'S ROW REQUEST
C    C:        PASSENGER'S SEAT PREFERENCE (COLUMN)
C
      CHARACTER*8 SEAT(5,4), NAME
      INTEGER R, C
      DATA SEAT/20*' '/              Initialize all seats to blanks.
   35 WRITE(*,1)                      System writes cue on terminal
      READ(*,2)R,C,NAME               Accept a passenger seating request.
      IF(R .EQ. 0)GO TO 77            If no more passengers, print the seating arrangement.
         IF(SEAT(R,C) .EQ. ' ') THEN  If seat is not taken,
            SEAT(R,C) = NAME          reserve it.
            GO TO 35
         ELSE                         Otherwise check for 1st available seat starting at (1,1).
            DO 5 I = 1,5
               DO 7 J = 1, 4
                  IF(SEAT(I,J) .EQ. ' ') THEN }  Assign passenger a seat other than
                     SEAT(I,J) = NAME           the one requested.
                  GO TO 35
                  ENDIF
    7          CONTINUE
    5       CONTINUE
            WRITE(*,3)                 If we have gone through both DO loops,
         ENDIF                         all the seats must be taken, i.e., plane is full.
   77 WRITE(*,4)
      DO 8 I = 1, 5
         WRITE(*,6)I, (SEAT(I,J),J=1,4) }  Print the plane's seating arrangement.
    8 CONTINUE
      STOP
    1 FORMAT(' ENTER ROW THEN SEAT AND NAME')
    2 FORMAT(2I1,A8)
    3 FORMAT(' PLANE IS FILLED TO CAPACITY'/)
    4 FORMAT(15X,'FINAL SEATING ARRANGEMENT'/)
    6 FORMAT(' ROW ',I1,4X,4(A8,2X)/'+',9X,4(8('_'),2X))      Underline seats.
      END
```

```
ENTER ROW THEN SEAT AND NAME
11BOILLOT
ENTER ROW THEN SEAT AND NAME
11ADKINS
ENTER ROW THEN  SEAT AND NAME
44FORD
ENTER ROW THEN SEAT AND NAME
44CABERAS
ENTER ROW THEN SEAT AND NAME
0000000000
```

```
              FINAL SEATING ARRANGEMENT

ROW 1    BOILLOT_  ADKINS_  CABERAS_  _____
ROW 2    _____  _____  _____  _____
ROW 3    _____  _____  _____  _____
ROW 4    _____  _____  _____  FORD____
ROW 5    _____  _____  _____  _____
```

## 8-3-3  A Bar Graph

The daily volume of a major stock exchange is given in millions of shares for the three weeks starting July 8:

| JULY 8 | | JULY 15 | | JULY 22 | |
|---|---|---|---|---|---|
| VOLUME | WORKDAY | VOLUME | WORKDAY | VOLUME | WORKDAY |
| 5 | 1 | 5 | 1 | 3 | 1 |
| 7 | 2 | 3 | 2 | 2 | 2 |
| 8 | 3 | 5 | 3 | 1 | 3 |
| 9 | 4 | 4 | 4 | 2 | 4 |
| 7 | 5 | 2 | 5 | 4 | 5 |

Write a program to produce the bar graph shown below for the 15 work days starting July 8. The transactions have been recorded on 1 record as follows: 5 7 8 9 7 5 3 5 4 2 3 2 1 2 4

```
Volume
  9                 *
  8           *     *
  7      *    *     *    *
  6      *    *     *    *
  5 *    *    *     *    *    *          *
  4 *    *    *     *    *    *     *                        *
  3 *    *    *     *    *    *     *         *              *
  2 *    *    *     *    *    *     *    *    *    *    *    *    *
  1 *    *    *     *    *    *     *    *    *    *    *    *    *
      1 _ 2 _ 3 _ 4 _ 5 _ 1 _ 2 _ 3 _ 4 _ 5 _ 1 _ 2 _ 3 _ 4 _ 5  ➔Days
```

## Understanding the Problem

In this problem we will use an array G consisting of at least 9 rows (for the maximum volume during the entire 15-day period) and 15 columns (for the 15 days). Initially, we set the array G to blanks. We then read the transaction for the first day of the first week (5) and insert five asterisks in the first column of G. We then proceed with the next transaction volume (7) and insert 7 asterisks in the second column to represent the second day's volume. The same steps are carried out up to the 15th day, where we insert asterisks in G(1,15), G(2,15), G(3,15), and G(4,15). The process can be visualized as follows:

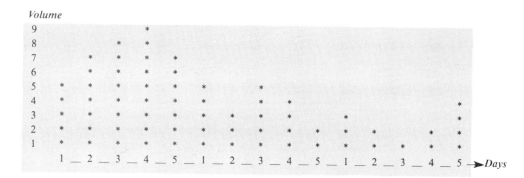

During Day 1 of the 2nd week, 5 million shares were transacted. Store 5 asterisks in the first 5 positions of column 6.

July 15 week

On day 5 of the 2nd week, 2 million shares were transacted. Store 2 asterisks in the first two positions of column 10.

Week of July 8   Week of July 15   Week of July 22

In this diagram, the bar graph peaks down rather than up. We want to turn it upside down, i.e., rotate it 180°, as follows:

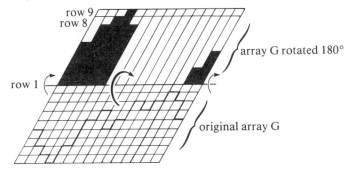

This rotation can be achieved by printing the "bottom" of the array first, i.e., by printing row 9 on the first line, row 8 on the second line, and so forth.

The problem is essentially broken down into the following activities:

1.  Initialize array G(9,15) with blank characters.

2.  Read the number of transactions for the first day and call it V.
    Store V asterisks in the 1st column of G.
    Then read the number of transactions for the second day, call it V.
    Store V asterisks in the 2nd column of G.
    Repeat these steps for days 3, 4, ..., 15.

3.  Print the array G, starting with row 9, then row 8, ..., to row 1.

4.  Print the gradations for the day axis, i.e., 1 2 3 4 5 1 2 3 ...

The FORTRAN code to solve this problem is shown in Figure 8–6. Notice how the horizontal gradations are printed.

### 8-3-4  Do It Now

In the bar graph of Figure 8–6, replace the graphic symbol * by the darker rectangular symbol ■ to print a more forceful bar graph. Your output should be similar to the following one:

[*Hint*: Use a combination of multistrike characters to obtain the symbol ■.]

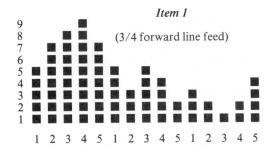

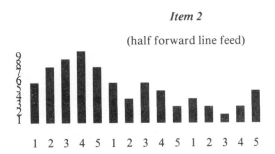

## Answer

The program is shown in Figure 8–8.

**FIGURE 8-6**   A TWO-DIMENSIONAL BAR GRAPH

```
C  TWO-DIMENSIONAL BAR GRAPH
C     G(9,15): EACH COLUMN DEPICTS A DAY'S TRANSACTION VOLUME
C     V(15):   THE 15 DAILY TRANSACTION VOLUMES ARE STORED IN V
      I:        IS USED TO PRINT THE VERTICAL GRADUATIONS OF THE GRAPH
C     J:        IS USED TO PRINT THE HORIZONTAL GRADUATIONS OF THE GRAPH
C
         CHARACTER G(9,15)
         INTEGER V(15)                 Stores the 15 daily transaction volumes.
         DATA G / 135*' '/             Initialize all entries to blanks.
         READ(5,1)V                    Read all transactions
         DO 5 J = 1,15
            DO 4 I = 1, V(J)           V(J) represents the transaction volume for day J.
               G(I,J) = '*'            Store V(J) asterisks in column J.
4           CONTINUE
5        CONTINUE
         WRITE(6,7)(I,(G(I,J),J=1,15),I=9,1,-1)    Print the array starting with bottom row.
         WRITE(6,8)((I,I=1,5),J=1,3)               Print the horizontal graduations.
         STOP
1        FORMAT(15I1)
8        FORMAT(4X,15I2)
7        FORMAT(' VOLUME'/(3X,I1,15A2))
         END
```

VOLUME

```
 9                    *
 8              *  *
 7        *  *  *  *
 6        *  *  *  *
 5     *  *  *  *  *  *        *
 4     *  *  *  *  *  *     *  *                 *
 3     *  *  *  *  *  *  *  *     *              *
 2     *  *  *  *  *  *  *  *  *  *  *     *  *
 1     *  *  *  *  *  *  *  *  *  *  *  *  *  *  *
       1  2  3  4  5  1  2  3  4  5  1  2  3  4  5
```

**Input File**

*Transaction Volumes*

$V_1$  $V_2$  $V_{15}$

578975354232124

## 8-3-5  A Warehouse Problem

You own six warehouses across the country; each warehouse stocks five particular items (see table on next page). The stock quantities for each of the five items are recorded in a data file, with one record for each warehouse. Write a program to read the data into a two-dimensional array and produce the output shown below.

Identify on the output any item that has zero stock in three or more warehouses. Also print those warehouses and item numbers where the stock is below 10. When listing those item numbers with stock levels less than 10, note that commas separate each item, i.e., the list should terminate with an item number, not a comma.

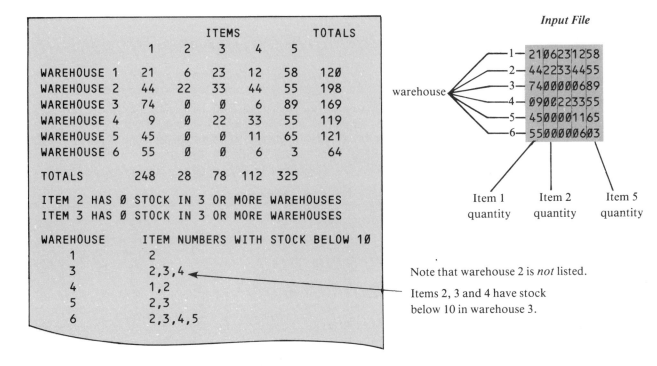

```
                         ITEMS            TOTALS
                1    2    3    4    5
WAREHOUSE 1     21   6    23   12   58    120
WAREHOUSE 2     44   22   33   44   55    198
WAREHOUSE 3     74   0    0    6    89    169
WAREHOUSE 4     9    0    22   33   55    119
WAREHOUSE 5     45   0    0    11   65    121
WAREHOUSE 6     55   0    0    6    3     64

TOTALS          248  28   78   112  325

ITEM 2 HAS 0 STOCK IN 3 OR MORE WAREHOUSES
ITEM 3 HAS 0 STOCK IN 3 OR MORE WAREHOUSES

WAREHOUSE          ITEM NUMBERS WITH STOCK BELOW 10
    1              2
    3              2,3,4
    4              1,2
    5              2,3
    6              2,3,4,5
```

*Input File*

warehouse
1— 2106231258
2— 4422334455
3— 7400000689
4— 0900223355
5— 4500001165
6— 5500000603

Item 1        Item 2        Item 5
quantity      quantity      quantity

Note that warehouse 2 is *not* listed.

Items 2, 3 and 4 have stock below 10 in warehouse 3.

The problem consists of four parts:

1. Computing the sum of each row of the array.

2. Computing the sum of each column of the array.

3. Searching each column to determine whether 3 or more entries are 0.

4. Searching each row to find entries that are less than 10.

The last part is probably the most interesting part of the problem. It requires us to look at a row and identify in that row the column number whose corresponding array element is less than 10. It is that column number (item number) that we need to print, not the entry (stock). The program to solve this problem is shown in Figure 8–7.

Initially the array COLSUM is set to 0's. The array COLSUM is used to compute the five sums of the five columns of array W. As each record is read, we accumulate the sums of each row (line 15) while accumulating partial column totals (line 16). Line 17 prints each row as well as the sum of its entries. When the entire array has been printed, we print the column totals (line 18).

In the third part of the problem, we check each column (line 22) for entries that have value 0. If there are three or more zero entries in a particular column, we print the column number (item number) and the message. K is used as a counter to count each occurrence of a zero entry. If K is less than 3, no message is printed.

In the fourth part of the problem, we analyze each row and record in the array BELOW the item numbers whose stock level is below 10. The variable M counts these items (line 19); when each row has been analyzed we print the M elements of array BELOW. A comma is inserted between each item (line 21). To avoid printing a comma to the right of the last entry, we print BELOW(M) all by itself.

**FIGURE 8-7**    A WAREHOUSE PROBLEM

```
C WAREHOUSE PROBLEM
C    W(6,5):     6 WAREHOUSES EACH CONTAINING 5 DIFFERENT ITEMS
C    ROWSUM:     ACCUMULATES SUM OF EACH ROW OF W
C    COLSUM(5): ACCUMULATES SUM OF EACH COLUMN OF W
C    K:          COUNTS NO. WAREHOUSES WITH 0 STOCK LEVEL FOR A GIVEN ITEM
C    BELOW(5):   IDENTIFIES ITEMS WITH STOCK < 10 FOR A GIVEN WAREHOUSE
C    COMMA:      REPRESENTS A COMMA TO SEPARATE ITEM NUMBERS
C    M:          COUNTS NUMBER OF ITEMS WHOSE STOCK LEVEL IS < 10 IN EACH ROW
      INTEGER W(6,5), COLSUM(5), ROWSUM, BELOW(5)
      CHARACTER COMMA
      DATA COMMA / ','/,COLSUM / 5*0/
      READ(5,1)((W(I,J),J=1,5),I=1,6)
      WRITE(6,2)(I,I=1,5)
C
      DO 5 I = 1, 6
15       ROWSUM = 0
         DO 6 J = 1, 5
            ROWSUM = ROWSUM + W(I,J)
16          COLSUM(J) = COLSUM(J) + W(I,J)
6        CONTINUE
17       WRITE(6,3)I,(W(I,J),J=1,5), ROWSUM
5     CONTINUE
18    WRITE(6,4) COLSUM
C
      DO 7 J = 1, 5
         K = 0
         DO 8 I = 1, 6
22          IF(W(I,J) .EQ. 0) K = K + 1
8        CONTINUE
         IF(K .LT. 3)GO TO 7
            WRITE(6,9)J
7     CONTINUE
C
      WRITE(6,11)
      DO 20 I = 1, 6
         M = 0
         DO 30 J = 1, 5
            IF(W(I,J) .GE. 10) GO TO 30
19             M = M + 1
               BELOW(M) = J
30       CONTINUE
         IF(M .EQ. 0) GO TO 20
21          WRITE(6,12)I, (BELOW(L),COMMA,L=1,M-1), BELOW(M)
20    CONTINUE
      STOP
C
1     FORMAT(5I2)
2     FORMAT(24X,'ITEMS',10X,'TOTALS'/16X,5(I1,4X)/)
3     FORMAT(' WAREHOUSE ',I1,3X,5(I2,3X),I3)
4     FORMAT('0TOTALS',7X,5(I3,2X)/)
9     FORMAT(' ITEM ',I1,' HAS 0 STOCK IN 3 OR MORE WAREHOUSES')
11    FORMAT('0WAREHOUSE',5X,'ITEM NUMBERS WITH STOCK BELOW 10')
12    FORMAT(5X,I1,10X,5(I1,A1))
      END
```

**FIGURE 8-8** A BAR GRAPH PROBLEM

```
C TWO-DIMENSIONAL BAR GRAPH
C   G(9,5): EACH COLUMN REPRESENTS A DAY'S TRANSACTION VOLUME
C   V(15):  THE 15 DAILY TRANSACTION VOLUMES ARE STORED IN V
C   I:      IS USED TO PRINT THE VERTICAL GRADATIONS OF THE GRAPH
C   J:      IS USED TO PRINT THE HORIZONTAL GRADATIONS OF THE GRAPH
C   SYMBOL(4) IS USED FOR MULTISTRIKING GRAPHIC SYMBOLS
        CHARACTER G(9,15), SYMBOL(6)
        INTEGER V(15)
        DATA G /135*' '/
        DATA SYMBOL /'M','W','A','*','L','E'/        Multistrike these 6 characters to obtain ■.
        READ(5,1)V
        DO 5 J = 1,15
           DO 4 I = 1, V(J)                    ⎫ Same as in Figure 8-6.
              G(I,J) = '*'                     ⎭
4          CONTINUE
5       CONTINUE
        DO 40 I = 9,1,-1
           DO 60 K = 1,6 ─────────────────→Print each line 6 times on "top" of itself.
              DO 50 J = 1, 15
                 IF(G(I,J) .NE. ' ') G(I,J)=SYMBOL(K)
50            CONTINUE
              WRITE(6,10)I,(G(I,J),J=1,15)
60         CONTINUE
           WRITE(6,9)
40      CONTINUE
        WRITE(6,8)((I,I=1,5),J=1,3)        Print the graduations 1 2 3 4 5 1 2 3 4 5....
        STOP
1       FORMAT(15I1)
8       FORMAT(4X,15I2)
10      FORMAT('+',2X,I1,15A2)
9       FORMAT(1X)
        END
```

## 8-4 Three-Dimensional Arrays

### 8-4-1 Definition and Background Information

A three-dimensional array is a data structure whose elements can be accessed using three subscripts. A three-dimensional table can be visualized as a cube sliced into several two-dimensional tables.

Three-dimensional arrays are declared through the DIMENSION or the type statement, just as one- and two-dimensional arrays are declared, except that three size limits must be declared.

Consider the following two arrays: REAL Q(3,2,4), TABL(3,4,2)

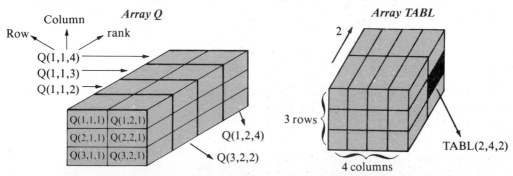

Any element of the cube Q can be referred to by Q(IR,IC,ID),
where IR indicates the row.

IC indicates the column.

ID indicates the rank, i.e., which of the two-dimensional arrays the element is in.
The rules for subscripts are similar to those for one- and 2-dimensional arrays.

Input/output and processing techniques for three-dimensional arrays are similar to
the techniques for two-dimensional arrays. Suppose, for example, that a company has two
factories, each containing 3 shops, each having 5 machines. A study of the repair records of
machines (machine down-time expressed in hours) is to be made. The log of repairs is recorded in table A. The technical manager may want to compute the number of hours lost
for each machine in shop 1, factory 2, or find out which shops in both factories exceeded
100 hours in down-time for machine 4, and so forth. Using a three-dimensional table to
identify the various factories, shops, and machines can greatly facilitate the logic of the
program.

An array to store the data on the repair records could be specified by:

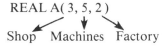

REAL A( 3, 5, 2 )

Shop   Machines   Factory

Suppose the repair data for each shop has been entered in a file with factory 1 data,
followed by factory 2 data. The data can be visualized as:

| Hours lost on machine 1<br>Shop 1, Factory 1<br>↓ | | Hours lost on machine 4<br>Shop 1, Factory 1<br>↓ | | | |
|---|---|---|---|---|---|
| A(1,1,1) | A(1,2,1) | A(1,3,1) | A(1,4,1) | A(1,5,1) | Shop 1 |
| A(2,1,1) | A(2,2,1) | A(2,3,1) | A(2,4,1) | A(2,5,1) | Shop 2   Factory 1 |
| A(3,1,1) | A(3,2,1) | A(3,3,1) | A(3,4,1) | A(3,5,1) | Shop 3 |
| A(1,1,2) | A(1,2,2) | A(1,3,2) | A(1,4,2) | A(1,5,2) | Shop 1 |
| A(2,1,2) | A(2,2,2) | A(2,3,2) | A(2,4,2) | A(2,5,2) | Shop 2   Factory 2 |
| A(3,1,2) | A(3,2,2) | A(3,3,2) | A(3,4,2) | A(3,5,2) | Shop 3 |

The FORTRAN code to read the input data, compute the average time lost on each machine, and write out the results is shown in Figure 8–9.

## 8-4-2 Internal Representation of Multidimensional Arrays

Internally, two-dimensional arrays are stored as a linear sequence of elements in column order. For example, an array A with three rows and three columns is stored as follows:

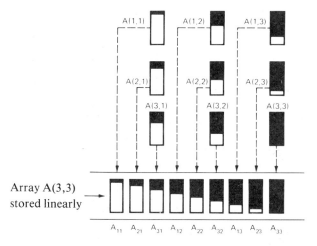

Although the array A is stored column-wise in memory, this does not mean that A has to be read into memory by columns. It can be read row-wise as in:

$$\text{READ}(5,3)(A(I,J),J, = 1,3),I = 1,3)$$

Three-dimensional arrays are stored linearly in memory. The internal order of storage for the array A(3,5,3) is column-wise across each depth plane.

*Order*

A(1,1,1)
A(2,1,1)
A(3,1,1)
A(1,2,1)
A(2,2,1)
A(3,2,1)
A(1,3,1)
A(2,3,1)
A(3,3,1)
A(1,4,1)
A(2,4,1)
A(3,4,1)
A(1,5,1)
A(2,5,1)
A(3,5,1)
A(1,1,2)
A(2,1,2)
A(3,1,2)
A(1,2,2)
    :
    :

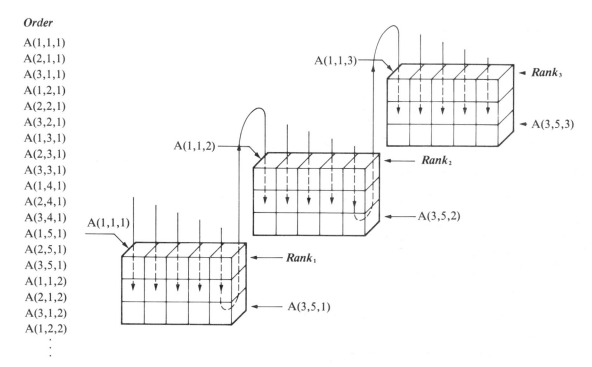

An array name can be used in a READ or WRITE list without subscripts. In that case the elements are processed in column order.

*Example*

```
    REAL X(3,4)←      Note
    READ(5,3)X←
 3 FORMAT(3F4.0)
```

This code will read all 12 elements of X, with three data items per record. The data will be read into the array as follows:

$$\left. \begin{array}{ccc} X(1,1) & X(2,1) & X(3,1) \\ X(1,2) & X(2,2) & X(3,2) \\ X(1,3) & X(2,3) & X(3,3) \\ X(1,4) & X(2,4) & X(3,4) \end{array} \right\}$$ order in which data items will be read from input file.

These array considerations apply to output as well. For example, suppose the array IX contains the following data:

$$IX = \begin{array}{|c|c|c|c|} \hline 17 & 9 & 8 & 73 \\ \hline 4 & 6 & 18 & 14 \\ \hline 5 & 10 & 21 & 5 \\ \hline \end{array}$$

The following WRITE statements are equivalent:

```
      INTEGER IX(3,4)              INTEGER IX(3,4)
          ⋮                            ⋮
      WRITE(6,1Ø)IX                WRITE(6,1Ø)((IX(I,J),I=1,3),J=1,4)
   1Ø FORMAT(2X,3I3)           1Ø FORMAT(2X,3I3)
```

This would produce the following printout:

```
   17    4    5
    9    6   10
    8   18   21
   73   14    5
```

**FIGURE 8-9**   SAMPLE PROGRAM TO PROCESS A THREE-DIMENSIONAL ARRAY

```
C PROCESSING A THREE-DIMENSIONAL ARRAY
C   A(3,5,2):  HOURS LOST FOR 3 SHOPS, 5 MACHINES & 2 FACTORIES
C   LOSTIM(5): CONTAINS HOURS LOST FOR EACH OF THE 5 MACHINES
C
      REAL A(3,5,2), LOSTIM(5)
      INTEGER SHOP, MACHIN, FACTRY
      READ(5,1)(((A(I,J,K),J = 1,5), I = 1,3),K = 1,2)
      DO 3Ø MACHIN = 1, 5
         LOSTIM (MACHIN) = Ø.Ø
         DO 2Ø FACTRY = 1, 2
            DO 15 SHOP = 1, 3
               LOSTIM(MACHIN) = LOSTIM(MACHIN) + A(SHOP,MACHIN,FACTRY)
   15       CONTINUE
   2Ø    CONTINUE
         LOSTIM(MACHIN) = LOSTIM(MACHIN)/6.
   3Ø CONTINUE
      DO 4Ø FACTRY = 1, 2
         WRITE(6,2)FACTRY,(SHOP,(A(SHOP,MACHIN,FACTRY),MACHIN=1, 5),SHOP=1,3)
   4Ø CONTINUE
      WRITE(6,3)(LOSTIM(MACHIN,MACHIN = 1,5)
      STOP
C
    1 FORMAT(5F4.1)
    2 FORMAT('Ø',16X,'FACTORY',I3/ (' SHOP',I2,4X,5F6.1))
    3 FORMAT('Ø','AVERAGES',1X,5F6.1)
      END
```

*Input File*

| | FACTORY | 1 | | | |
|---|---|---|---|---|---|
| SHOP 1 | 1.1 | 2.2 | 3.3 | 4.4 | 5.5 |
| SHOP 2 | 1.1 | 1.2 | 1.3 | 1.4 | 1.5 |
| SHOP 3 | .1 | .2 | .3 | .4 | .5 |
| | FACTORY | 2 | | | |
| SHOP 1 | 3.0 | 4.0 | 5.0 | 6.0 | 7.0 |
| SHOP 2 | 4.0 | 5.0 | 6.0 | 7.0 | 8.0 |
| SHOP 3 | 1.0 | 2.0 | 3.0 | 4.0 | 5.0 |
| AVERAGES | 1.7 | 2.4 | 3.1 | 3.9 | 4.6 |

```
           A(1,2,1)   A(1,4,1)
  A(1,1,1)    A(1,3,1)   A(1,5,1)
  Ø1.1Ø2.2Ø3.3Ø4.4Ø5.5
  Ø1.1Ø1.2Ø1.3Ø1.4Ø1.5
  ØØ.1ØØ.2ØØ.3ØØ.4ØØ.5
  Ø3.ØØ4.ØØ5.ØØ6.ØØ7.Ø
  Ø4.ØØ5.ØØ6.ØØ7.ØØ8.Ø
  Ø1.ØØ2.ØØ3.ØØ4.ØØ5.Ø
        A(3,2,2)  A(3,4,2)
  A(3,1,2)   A(3,3,2)   A(3,5,2)
```

### 8-4-3 Do It Now

1. Given array R(4,6,5) write the code to compute the sums of each row of R and store these in a 2-dimensional array S(4,5) in such a way that:
   S(1,1) = sum of row 1   rank 1;   S(1,2) = sum of row 2   rank 2; ... S(2,3) = sum of row 2   rank 3.

2. List the internal sequence of arrays X(3,2) and Y(2,3,2).

### *Answers*

1.
```
    REAL R(4,6,5),S(4,5)
    DATA S/20 * 0./
    DO 5 I = 1,4
        DO 5 J = 1,6
            DO 5 K = 1,5
  5 S(I,K) = S(I,K) + R(I,J,K)
```

2. X(1,1), X(2,1), X(3,1), X(1,2), X(2,2), X(3,2)
   Y(1,1,1), Y(2,1,1), Y(1,2,1), Y(2,2,1), Y(1,3,1), Y(2,3,1)
   Y(1,1,2), Y(2,1,2), Y(1,2,2), Y(2,2,2), Y(1,3,2), Y(2,3,2)

### 8-4-4 A Three-Dimensional Table Problem

Each record of an input file (maximum of 50 records) consists of a student name followed by 8 scores. The first four scores were obtained on mathematics tests, and the last four scores were obtained on computer science tests. Write a program to compute the class average (all tests in both disciplines) and "pass" those students whose averages on both mathematics and computer tests are above the overall class average (place two asterisks by their grades). Sample input and output files are shown as follows:

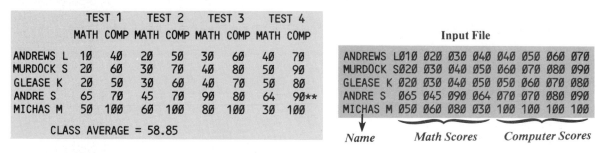

|  | TEST 1 | | TEST 2 | | TEST 3 | | TEST 4 | | | **Input File** |
|---|---|---|---|---|---|---|---|---|---|---|
|  | MATH | COMP | MATH | COMP | MATH | COMP | MATH | COMP | | |
| ANDREWS L | 10 | 40 | 20 | 50 | 30 | 60 | 40 | 70 | | ANDREWS L010 020 030 040 040 050 060 070 |
| MURDOCK S | 20 | 60 | 30 | 70 | 40 | 80 | 50 | 90 | | MURDOCK S020 030 040 050 060 070 080 090 |
| GLEASE K | 20 | 50 | 30 | 60 | 40 | 70 | 50 | 80 | | GLEASE K 020 030 040 050 050 060 070 080 |
| ANDRE S | 65 | 70 | 45 | 70 | 90 | 80 | 64 | 90** | | ANDRE S 065 045 090 064 070 070 080 090 |
| MICHAS M | 50 | 100 | 60 | 100 | 80 | 100 | 30 | 100 | | MICHAS M 050 060 080 030 100 100 100 100 |

CLASS AVERAGE = 58.85

*Name*     *Math Scores*     *Computer Scores*

The FORTRAN code to solve this problem is shown in Figure 8–10. (Note how the input data is read into the three-dimensional array SCORES at line 10). The SCORES array can be visualized as a three-dimensional table as follows:

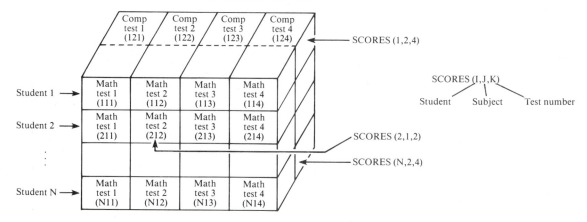

**FIGURE 8-10** A THREE-DIMENSIONAL ARRAY PROBLEM

```
C A 3-DIMENSIONAL ARRAY PROBLEM
C    SCORES(50,2,4): MAXIMUM OF 50 STUDENTS; 2 SUBJECTS, 4 TESTS
C    NAME(50): ARRAY OF STUDENTS' NAMES
C    N:        NUMBER OF STUDENTS
C    AWARD:    CONTAINS '**' IF BOTH AVERAGES > CLASS AVERAGE, ELSE BLANK
C    COMPAV:   COMPUTES STUDENT'S AVERAGE SCORE ON COMPUTER TESTS
C    MATHAV:   COMPUTES STUDENT'S AVERAGE SCORE ON MATH TESTS
C
      CHARACTER NAME(10)*9, AWARD*2
      REAL MATHAV, COMPAV, CLASAV
      INTEGER SCORES(51,2,4), N
C
      WRITE(6,1) (I,I=1,4)
10    READ(5,2,END=88) (NAME(I), ((SCORES(I,J,K),K=1,4),J=1,2),I=1,51)
88    N = I - 1
      CLASAV = 0.0
      DO 5 I = 1, N
         DO 6 J = 1, 2
            DO 7 K = 1, 4
               CLASAV = CLASAV + SCORES(I,J,K)       ⎫
7           CONTINUE                                 ⎬ Compute class average.
6        CONTINUE                                    ⎭
5     CONTINUE
      CLASAV = CLASAV/(8*N)
C
      DO 11 I = 1, N
         AWARD = '  '
         MATHAV = 0.0
         DO 8 K = 1,4                                ⎫
            MATHAV = MATHAV + SCORES(I,1,K)          ⎬ Compute math average.
8        CONTINUE                                    ⎭
         MATHAV = MATHAV/4.
         IF(MATHAV .GT. CLASAV) THEN                 No award if math average < class average.
            COMPAV = 0.0
            DO 9 K = 1, 4                            ⎫
               COMPAV =COMPAV + SCORES(I,2,K)        ⎬ Compute computer test average.
9           CONTINUE                                 ⎭
            COMPAV = COMPAV/4.                       If both test averages > class average,
            IF(COMPAV .GT. CLASAV) AWARD='**'        the student is awarded stars (**)
         ENDIF
         WRITE(6,3)NAME(I), ((SCORES(I,J,K),J=1,2),K=1,4), AWARD
11    CONTINUE
      WRITE(6,4)CLASAV
      STOP
C
1     FORMAT(16X,4('TEST ',I1,6X)/14X,4('MATH COMP   ')/)
2     FORMAT(A9,8(I3,1X))
3     FORMAT(1X,A9,4(4X,I3,2X,I3),A3)
4     FORMAT('0',14X,'CLASS AVERAGE = ',F6.2)
      END
```

| | TEST 1 | | TEST 2 | | TEST 3 | | TEST 4 | |
|---|---|---|---|---|---|---|---|---|
| | MATH | COMP | MATH | COMP | MATH | COMP | MATH | COMP |
| ANDREWS L | 10 | 40 | 20 | 50 | 30 | 60 | 40 | 70 |
| MURDOCK S | 20 | 60 | 30 | 70 | 40 | 80 | 50 | 90 |
| GLEASE K | 20 | 50 | 30 | 60 | 40 | 70 | 50 | 80 |
| ANDRE S | 65 | 70 | 45 | 70 | 90 | 80 | 64 | 90** |
| MICHAS M | 50 | 100 | 60 | 100 | 80 | 100 | 30 | 100 |

CLASS AVERAGE = 58.85

**Input File**

*Scores(1,1,1)*   *Scores(1,1,2)*   *Scores (1,2,4)*

| | | | | | | | | |
|---|---|---|---|---|---|---|---|---|
| ANDREWS L | 010 | 020 | 030 | 040 | 040 | 050 | 060 | 070 |
| MURDOCK S | 020 | 030 | 040 | 050 | 060 | 070 | 080 | 090 |
| GLEASE K | 020 | 030 | 040 | 050 | 050 | 060 | 070 | 080 |
| ANDRE S | 065 | 045 | 090 | 064 | 070 | 070 | 080 | 090 |
| MICHAS M | 050 | 060 | 080 | 030 | 100 | 100 | 100 | 100 |

## 8-5 You Might Want to Know

**1.** Does FORTRAN allow most arrays of more than three dimensions?

*Answer:* Some versions of FORTRAN allow 31 dimensions for an array (Burroughs 6700/7700), while most others offer 7 dimensions.

**2.** What will happen to my program if I use a subscript reference that is illegal? For example, suppose my array is declared by DIMENSION X(3,5) and I reference X(5,7).

*Answer:* The handling of this problem may differ among FORTRAN systems. Many FORTRAN compilers translate an array reference into an address without checking whether the subscripts are in the range allowed by the declarator statement. If the address is invalid (outside the user's program) an execution-time diagnostic will be produced. If the address is valid, the data or instruction contained in that location will be fetched or changed, depending on whether X(5,7) is to the left or to the right of the equal sign in a replacement statement. The effects of such a mistake may be apparent when the desired output is not produced by the program. The cause of the error may be difficult to determine, since the erroneous output will usually provide no clue that can be traced to an invalid array reference.

**3.** Can I initialize two- or three-dimensional arrays in a DATA statement?

*Answer:* Yes. For example:

```
    REAL X(3,2,4)
    DATA(((X(I,J,K),I=1,3),J=1,2),K=1,4)/12*2.,6*1.,6*2.1/
or
    DATA X/12*2., 6*1., 6*2.1/
```

meaning: $X(1,1,1)$ through $X(3,2,2) = 2$.
$X(1,1,3)$ through $X(3,2,3) = 1$.
$X(1,1,4)$ through $X(3,2,4) = 2.1$

**4.** Is there any limit to the size of a multidimensional array?

*Answer:* Theoretically, no. Practically, yes. Restrictions on array sizes are dictated by the size of the memory of the particular system. For example, on a system with memory size of 32,000 bytes the statement INTEGER A(100,10,10) exceeds the memory size. On larger systems the operating system may take up a large portion of memory; the programmer requiring large arrays should check on memory available at his or her particular installation.

## 8-6 Exercises

### 8-6-1 Test Yourself

**1.** Which of the following are valid array declarations? Specify errors, if any.

a. INTEGER A(100,3),IB(3,5)
b. DIMENSION A3(3),A4(4,4)
c. CHARACTER ST(50,40),J(3,1,7)*3
d. DIMENSION Z100
e. DIMENSION UT(3.,2)

f. REAL N,X(3,2,N)
g. LOGICAL Z(7,2,3,4,5,6)
h. DIMENSION (MIKE)10
i. DIMENSION BIG(3*10,2)
j. DOUBLE PRECISION I(2,2)

**2.** List the internal order of storage for arrays A and B specified by:

INTEGER A(2,4),B(3,1,4),K(2,2,2)

**3.** Explain in words what arrays TC and TR will contain as a result of the following code.

```
REAL A(5,4),TC(4),TR(5)
DATA TC,TR/9*0./
READ array A from input file
DO 3 J = 1,4
   DO 2 I = 1,5
      TC(J) = TC(J) + A(I,J)
      TR(I) = TR(I) + A(I,J)
 2    CONTINUE
 3 CONTINUE
```

**4.** Using implied DO lists, write I/O statements corresponding to the following lists of variables:

a. `WRITE(6,10)A(4),A(5),A(6),A(7),...,A(90)`
b. `WRITE(6,4)B(1),B(3),B(5),B(7),B(9),...,B(99)`
c. `READ(5,2)C(2,1),C(2,2),C(2,3),C(2,4),C(2,5)`
d. `READ(5,1)A(1,1),B(1),A(2,1),B(2),A(3,1),B(3)`
e. `WRITE(6,5)K,A(1,1),B(1),B(2),B(3),K,A(2,1),B(1),B(2),B(3)`
f. `READ(5,3)A(1,1),A(1,2),A(1,3),B(2,1),B(2,2),B(2,3),C(1),`
   `*C(2),C(3)`
g. `WRITE(6,1)A(1,1),B(1,1),C(1,1),I,A(1,2),B(1,2),C(1,2),I,`
   `*A(1,3),B(1,3),C(1,3),I`
h. `WRITE` *the values* 1 2 3 4 1 2 3 4 1 2 3 4 (12 values)

**5.** Generate the corresponding READ/WRITE list of variables for the following implied DO lists, and specify the number of records that would be processed by the accompanying FORMATs.

a. `((A(I,J),I = 1,3),J = 1,2)`          `FORMAT(8F3.1)`
b. `((A(I,J),I,I = 1,3),J = 1,2)`          `FORMAT(2(F3.1,I2)/F3.1,I2)`
c. `((A(I,J),I = 1,3),J,J = 1,3)`          `FORMAT(3F3.1,I1/(3F3.1,I1))`
d. `((A(I,J),B(I,J),J=1,2),I=1,3)`          `FORMAT(F3.1)`
e. `(C(I),(A(I,J),J = 1,3),`          `FORMAT(6F4.1)`
   `*(P(K,I),K = 1,2),I = 1,2)`
f. `(((A(I,J,K),I=1,2),K=1,3),J=1,2)` `FORMAT(11F3.0)`

**6.** Assume arrays A, JSUM, and VAR contain the following data:

A(3,4)

| 1. | 2. | 3. | 4. |
|----|----|----|----|
| 5. | 6. | 7. | 8. |
| 9. | 10. | 11. | 12 |

JSUM(3,4)

| 10 | 20 | 30 | 40 |
|----|----|----|----|
| 50 | 60 | 70 | 80 |
| 90 | 100 | 110 | 120 |

VAR

| 500. |
|------|

Write the necessary implied DO lists to generate the following output using only these three arrays (no computations are to be performed). Show formats.

```
a. 1.  2.  3.  4. ... 12.  10  20  30  40  ...  120  500.

b. 1.  2.  3.  4.     10  20  30  40     500.
   5.  6.  7.  8.     50  60  70  80     500.
   9. 10. 11. 12.     90 100 110 120     500.

c. 1.  5.  9.     500.     10  50  90
   2.  6. 10.     500.     20  60 100
   3.  7. 11.     500.     30  70 110
```

d. 1. 10   2.   20   3.   30   4.   40
   5. 50   6.   60   7.   70   8.   80
   9. 90  10.  100  11.  110  12.  120

e. 1. 10   5.   50   9.   90   2.   20   6.   60  10.  100
   3. 30   7.   70  11.  110   4.   40   8.   80  12.  120

For part e, you may want to use a combination of a DO loop and an implied DO list.

7. Write one READ statement with a DO list and an appropriate FORMAT statement to read each of the following input files:

a. $A_{11}$  $A_{21}$  $A_{31}$  $A_{41}$
   $A_{12}$  $A_{22}$  $A_{32}$  $A_{42}$
   $A_{13}$  $B_{23}$  $A_{33}$  $A_{43}$

b. $A_{11}$  $A_{12}$  $A_{13}$
   $A_{14}$  $A_{15}$  $A_{16}$
   $B_1$  $B_2$  $B_3$
   $B_4$  $B_5$  $B_6$

c. $A_{11}$  $B_{11}$  $A_{21}$  $B_{21}$
   $A_{31}$  $B_{31}$  $A_{41}$  $B_{41}$
   $A_{51}$  $B_{51}$  $A_{61}$  $B_{61}$

d. $A_{11}$  $B_{11}$  $A_{21}$  $B_{12}$
   $A_{31}$  $B_{13}$  $A_{41}$  $B_{14}$
   $A_{51}$  $B_{15}$  $A_{61}$  $B_{16}$

e. $A_{11}$  $A_{12}$  $A_{13}$  $B_{11}$  $B_{12}$
   $A_{21}$  $A_{22}$  $A_{23}$  $B_{21}$  $B_{22}$
   .         .
   .         .
   $A_{91}$  $A_{92}$  $A_{93}$  $B_{91}$  $B_{92}$

f. $A_{11}$  $A_{12}$  ... $A_{19}$
   $A_{21}$  ...        $A_{29}$
   .
   .
   $A_{81}$  ...        $A_{89}$
   $B_{11}$  $B_{21}$  $B_{31}$
   $B_{41}$  $B_{12}$  $B_{22}$
   $B_{32}$  $B_{42}$

8. If A is an array of size $16 \times 6$, write the code to initialize the first column of A with 1's, the second column with 2's, the third column with 3's, ..., and the sixth column with 6's.

9. An array A of size $5 \times 5$ is to be read from five records (five entries per record, one record for each row). Write the codes to

   a. Read in the array and write it out in row form (one row per line), then print each column on one line, i.e., $A_{11}$, $A_{21}$, ..., $A_{51}$ on one line then $A_{12}$, $A_{22}$, ..., $A_{52}$ on the second line, etc.
   b. Calculate the sum of the elements in the third row.
   c. Find the largest value in the first column.
   d. Create an array B consisting of five elements initialized to zero. Calculate the sum of each column of A, storing the result in the corresponding column position of B.
   e. Add the corresponding elements of rows 2 and 3 of the array A, storing the results in row 3; i.e., A(3,1) = A(3,1) + A(2,1), and so forth.
   f. Interchange column 3 and column 4.
   g. Compute the sum of the entries of the main diagonal, i.e., $A_{11}$, $A_{22}$, $A_{33}$, ..., $A_{55}$.
   h. Compute the sum of the entries of the secondary diagonal and determine the largest entry of that diagonal. (The secondary diagonal consists of elements $A_{15}$, $A_{24}$, $A_{33}$, $A_{42}$, $A_{51}$)
   i. Print the smallest element of the array A and its position in the array (row, column).

10. Write the READ statement to read in two arrays C and D of size $5 \times 5$ given the following input description: (5 entries per record)

| 1,2,3,4,5 | 1,2,3,6,8 | 4,5,6,7,8 | 4,5,6,7,6 ... |
|-----------|-----------|-----------|---------------|
| Row 1 of C | Row 1 of D | Row 2 of C | Row 2 of D |

11. Assume an array F of size 40 by 17 that already contains data. Write the code to store the rows of the array F sequentially into a one-dimensional array G of size 680 (40 × 17), as follows:

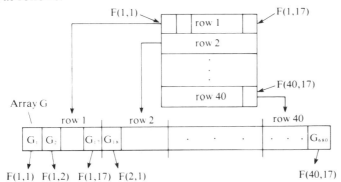

12. Assume the array A(10,3) has been read in; write a program segment to compute the sum of the elements of the array A, and print the following with *one* WRITE statement.

```
                        FINAL

COLUMN 1      COLUMN 2      COLUMN 3    ...    COLUMN 10
   A₁ ₁          A₂ ₁          A₃ ₁     ...       A₁₀ ₁
   A₁ ₂          A₂ ₂          A₃ ₂     ...       A₁₀ ₂
   A₁ ₃          A₂ ₃          A₃ ₃     ...       A₁₀ ₃
       SUM IS XXX.X
```

13. The result of multiplying two arrays A(5,4) and B(4,3) is another array C of size 5 by 3, defined as follows (matrix multiplication):

$$
\begin{array}{l}
A \\
A_{11}\,A_{12}\,A_{13}\,A_{14} \\
A_{21}\,A_{22}\,A_{23}\,A_{24} \\
A_{31}\,A_{32}\,A_{33}\,A_{34} \\
A_{41}\,A_{42}\,A_{43}\,A_{44} \\
A_{51}\,A_{52}\,A_{53}\,A_{54}
\end{array}
\;\times\;
\begin{array}{l}
B \\
B_{11}\,B_{12}\,B_{13} \\
B_{21}\,B_{22}\,B_{23} \\
B_{31}\,B_{32}\,B_{33} \\
B_{41}\,B_{42}\,B_{43}
\end{array}
\;=\;
\begin{array}{l}
C \\
C_{11}\,C_{12}\,C_{13} \\
C_{21}\,C_{22}\,C_{23} \\
C_{31}\,C_{32}\,C_{33} \\
C_{41}\,C_{42}\,C_{43} \\
C_{51}\,C_{52}\,C_{53}
\end{array}
$$

where

$$C_{11} = A_{11} * B_{11} + A_{12} * B_{21} + A_{13} * B_{31} + A_{14} * B_{41}$$
$$C_{21} = A_{21} * B_{11} + A_{22} * B_{21} + A_{22} * B_{31} + A_{24} * B_{41}$$
$$C_{31} = A_{31} * B_{11} + A_{32} * B_{21} + A_{33} * B_{31} + A_{34} * B_{41}$$
$$C_{41} = A_{41} * B_{11} + A_{42} * B_{21} + A_{43} * B_{31} + A_{44} * B_{41}$$
$$C_{51} = A_{51} * B_{11} + A_{52} * B_{21} + A_{53} * B_{31} + A_{54} * B_{41}$$

$$C_{12} = A_{11} * B_{12} + A_{12} * B_{22} + A_{13} * B_{32} + A_{14} * B_{42}$$
$$C_{22} = A_{21} * B_{12} + A_{22} * B_{22} + A_{23} * B_{32} + A_{24} * B_{42}$$
$$C_{32} = A_{31} * B_{12} + A_{32} * B_{22} + A_{33} * B_{32} + A_{34} * B_{42}$$
$$C_{42} = A_{41} * B_{12} + A_{42} * B_{22} + A_{43} * B_{32} + A_{44} * B_{42}$$
$$C_{52} = A_{51} * B_{12} + A_{52} * B_{22} + A_{53} * B_{32} + A_{54} * B_{42}$$

$$C_{13} = A_{11} * B_{13} + A_{12} * B_{23} + A_{13} * B_{33} + A_{14} * B_{43}$$
$$C_{23} = A_{21} * B_{13} + A_{22} * B_{23} + A_{23} * B_{33} + A_{24} * B_{43}$$
$$C_{33} = A_{31} * B_{13} + A_{32} * B_{23} + A_{33} * B_{33} + A_{34} * B_{43}$$
$$C_{43} = A_{41} * B_{13} + A_{42} * B_{23} + A_{43} * B_{33} + A_{44} * B_{43}$$
$$C_{53} = A_{51} * B_{13} + A_{52} * B_{23} + A_{53} * B_{33} + A_{54} * B_{43}$$

Write a program to read an array A of size 5 by 4 and an array B of size 4 by 3 and compute the product array C of size 5 by 3. For example:

$$
\begin{array}{l}
A \\
1\;\;2\;\;3\;\;4 \\
6\;\;7\;\;8\;\;9 \\
5\;\;4\;\;3\;\;2 \\
2\;\;3\;\;4\;\;5 \\
1\;\;2\;\;3\;\;4
\end{array}
\;\times\;
\begin{array}{l}
B \\
\\
1\;\;2\;\;3 \\
4\;\;5\;\;6 \\
7\;\;8\;\;7 \\
3\;\;4\;\;5
\end{array}
\;=\;
\begin{array}{l}
C \\
42\;\;\;52\;\;\;56 \\
117\;\;147\;\;161 \\
48\;\;\;62\;\;\;70 \\
57\;\;\;71\;\;\;77 \\
42\;\;\;52\;\;\;56
\end{array}
$$

[*Hint*: Note that any element of C is such that: C(I,J) = A(I,1)*B(1,J) + A(I,2)*B(2*J) + A(I,3)*B(3,J) + A(I,4)*B(4,J) where I varies from 1 to 5 and J varies from 1 to 3, i.e., C(I,J) is equal to the product of the Ith row of A and the Jth column of B as illustrated above.]

## 8-6-2 Programming Problems: Business/General

1. An array A has size 4 by 9. Write the code to interchange the first column with the ninth column, the second column with the eighth column, and so forth.

2. Each record in a file consists of six data items, a student name followed by five test scores, for example:

| DOE | 10 | 20 | 30 | 40 | 50 |
|-----|----|----|----|----|----|

| SLY | 10 | 10 | 70 | 60 | 40 |
|-----|----|----|----|----|----|

*Five Test Scores*

There are at most 100 records. Read the data into a two-dimensional table. For example, A(3,I), with I ranging from 1 to 5, represents the third student's test scores. Compute the average score for each student and the average score on each test. The output should have the following format:

```
NAME          TEST1    TEST2    TEST3    TEST4    TEST5    AVERAGE
DOE            10       20       30       40       50       30.0
SLY            11       10       71       60       40       38.0
AVERAGE/TEST   10.5     15.0     50.5     50.0     45.0
```

3. The personnel department of a small insurance company maintains a payroll file for its insurance representatives, who work in different states. Each employee's record contains (among other information) the following data:

| Employee Name | Hours Worked | Rate of Pay | State Tax |
|---------------|--------------|-------------|-----------|
| Anton D. | 45 | 10.00 | .05 |

Read an unknown number of input records (maximum 100). Load array NAME with the employee names and load a two dimensional array A with the corresponding set of 3 entries per record. *Then*

   a. Compute and print each employee's pay before and after tax.
   b. Compute the total payroll for the firm (not including state tax withdrawals).
   c. Give a $1,000 bonus to the employee with lowest hourly rate who has worked more hours than any other employee. Such a condition may or may not be satisfied.

Overtime is paid at 1.5 times the regular rate. The output should be similar to

```
EMPLOYEE   HOURS    RATE OF   GROSS    STATE    NET
NAME       WORKED   PAY       PAY      TAX      PAY
ANTON D    45       10.00     475.00   .05      451.25
  .          .        .         .        .        .
  .          .        .         .        .        .
  .          .        .         .        .        .
COMPANY PAYROLL = XXXX.XX
$1,000 BONUS GOES TO ANTON D. WITH 45 HOURS AT $ 10 PER HOUR
```

**4.** Write a program to compute itemized sales tax deductions using the following instructions and table:

Your itemized deduction for general sales tax paid can be estimated from these tables. To use the tables:

**Step 1**—Figure your total available income.

**Step 2**—Count the number of exemptions for you and your family. Do not count exemptions claimed for being 65 or over or blind as part of your family size.

**Step 3 A**—If your total available income is not over $40,000, find the income line on the table and read across to find the amount of sales tax for your family size.

**Step 3 B**—If your income is over $40,000, but not over $100,000, find the deduction listed on the income line "$38,001–$40,000" for your family size. For each $5,000 (or part of $5,000) of income over $40,000, increase the deduction by the amount listed on the line "$40,000–$100,000."

| Alabama |  |  |  |  |  |  |
|---|---|---|---|---|---|---|
| *Income* | *Family Size* |  |  |  |  | *Over* |
|  | 1 | 2 | 3 | 4 | 5 | 5 |
| $1–$8,000 . . . . . . . . . . | 93 | 115 | 122 | 131 | 142 | 160 |
| $8,001–$10,000. . . . . . | 109 | 132 | 142 | 153 | 165 | 185 |
| $10,001–$12,000. . . . . | 124 | 147 | 161 | 173 | 187 | 208 |
| $12,001–$14,000. . . . . | 138 | 161 | 178 | 191 | 206 | 228 |
| $14,001–$16,000. . . . . | 152 | 174 | 194 | 209 | 225 | 248 |
| $16,001–$18,000. . . . . | 164 | 186 | 210 | 226 | 242 | 266 |
| $18,001–$20,000. . . . . | 176 | 197 | 225 | 242 | 259 | 284 |
| $20,001–$22,000. . . . . | 188 | 208 | 239 | 257 | 275 | 301 |
| $22,001–$24,000. . . . . | 199 | 218 | 253 | 271 | 290 | 317 |
| $24,001–$26,000. . . . . | 210 | 228 | 266 | 285 | 305 | 332 |
| $26,001–$28,000. . . . . | 221 | 238 | 279 | 299 | 320 | 347 |
| $28,001–$30,000. . . . . | 231 | 247 | 291 | 313 | 334 | 362 |
| $30,001–$32,000. . . . . | 241 | 256 | 303 | 326 | 347 | 376 |
| $32,001–$34,000. . . . . | 251 | 265 | 315 | 338 | 360 | 390 |
| $34,001–$36,000. . . . . | 261 | 274 | 327 | 350 | 373 | 403 |
| $36,001–$38,000. . . . . | 271 | 282 | 338 | 362 | 386 | 416 |
| $38,001–$40,000. . . . . | 280 | 290 | 349 | 374 | 399 | 429 |
| $40,001–$100,000 . . . . (See Step 3B) | 14 | 15 | 17 | 19 | 20 | 21 |

**Step 3 C**—If your income is over $100,000, your sales tax deduction is limited to the deduction for income of $100,000. To figure your sales tax deduction, use Step 3 B but don't go over $100,000

**5.** A data file contains the following information: (maximum of 100 records)

```
DOE    3  20  30  40
HARON  2  10  60
LUCAS  4  20  30  40  50
```

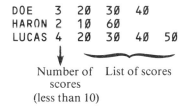

Number of    List of scores
scores
(less than 10)

If the average of all the scores in the input file is less than 80, five points are added to the average of each student; otherwise 5 points are subtracted from the average of each student. Write a program to produce the following output:

| NAME | TEST1 | TEST2 | TEST3 | TEST4 | ... | TEST10 | AVERAGE | UPDATED AVERAGE |
|---|---|---|---|---|---|---|---|---|
| DOE | 20 | 30 | 40 |  |  |  | 30.00 | 35.00 |
| HARON | 10 | 60 |  |  |  |  | 35.00 | 40.00 |
| LUCAS | 20 | 30 | 40 | 50 |  |  | 35.00 | 40.00 |

**6.** At the end of every semester, Dr. Landrum, head of the business data systems department, likes to check grade reports of the department's freshman class (100 students at most). Each student's final grades in three subject areas are entered on records, one record per student, for example:

| SMITH | 58 | 78 | 44 |
|---|---|---|---|
| Student Name | Accounting I | Business Law | Principles of Management |

Enter in an array NAME all student names and enter each student's grades into a corresponding two-dimensional array G. For example, G(3,2) represents the third student's score in Business Law.

Write a program for Dr. Landrum, using the array G to

a. Compute the average score of each student across all disciplines.

b. Compute the freshman average score for all Accounting I, the average score for Business Law, and average score for Principles of Management.

c. Provide a list of all students whose three final scores are all above the freshman average scores for each of the three subject areas.

d. Award a prize to student(s) with highest scores in Principles of Management. Print the name(s) of the recipient(s).

e. Award a scholarship to any student who obtains the three highest scores in the three subject areas (if there is such a student).

The output should be similar to the following report:

```
                    SEMESTER END REPORT
                         BUSINESS
                 ACCT. I     LAW      MANAGEMENT    AVERAGE
HORNET             40         50          60         50.0
BOIL               50         90          40         60.0
SMITHEN            20         60          10         30.0

CLASS AVERAGE      36.7       66.7        36.7

STUDENT NAMES WHOSE 3 TESTS EXCEED THE 3 CLASS AVERAGES
                         BOIL
AWARD GOES TO HORNET
SCHOLARSHIP IS AWARDED TO NO ONE
```

**7.** Read into an array named WORD eight of each of the following: nouns, pronouns, verbs, adverbs, adjectives, and articles (repeated if necessary) and store their corresponding numerical word codes into an integer array called KODE. The word codes are: 1 = pronoun, 2 = verb, 3 = adverb, 4 = adjective, 5 = noun, 6 = article. A typical input file might appear as:

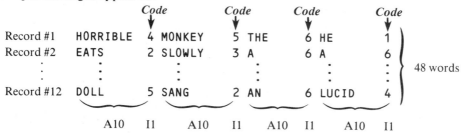

|  |  | *Code* |  | *Code* |  | *Code* |  | *Code* |  |
|---|---|---|---|---|---|---|---|---|---|
| Record #1 | HORRIBLE | 4 | MONKEY | 5 | THE | 6 | HE | 1 | |
| Record #2 | EATS | 2 | SLOWLY | 3 | A | 6 | A | 6 | } 48 words |
| : | : | | : | | : | | : | : | |
| Record #12 | DOLL | 5 | SANG | 2 | AN | 6 | LUCID | 4 | |
|  | A10 | I1 | A10 | I1 | A10 | I1 | A10 | I1 | |

After reading this input file, the two arrays WORD and KODE would appear as follows:

| WORD | HORRIBLE | MONKEY | THE | HE | EATS | SLOWLY | ... | DOLL | SANG | AN | LUCID |
|------|----------|--------|-----|-----|------|--------|-----|------|------|-----|-------|

| KODE | 4 | 5 | 6 | 1 | 2 | 3 | ... | 5 | 2 | 6 | 4 |
|------|---|---|---|---|---|---|-----|---|---|---|---|

KODE(1)      KODE(2)                                          KODE(48)

a. Write a program to load an array TABLE(8,6) in such a way that column 1 of TA-
   BLE contains all pronouns, column 2 contains all verbs, and so forth; then write
   out TABLE to produce the following arrangement:

```
PRONOUNS    VERBS   ADVERBS   ADJECTIVES   NOUNS    ARTICLES
   HE        EATS    SLOWLY     HORRIBLE    MONKEY     THE
   .           .        .          .           .        .
   .           .        .          .           .        .
   .           .        .          .           .        .
             SANG                 LUCID      DOLL        AN
```

b. Using the random-number generator routine to extract entries from the 48-word
   array (not from the six sorted word arrays), construct two English sentences to fit
   the following grammatical structure:

   *Article, noun, verb, adjective. Pronoun, verb, article, adverb, adjective, noun.*

   For example, the following sentences might be generated:

   ```
   THE ANIMAL IS TALL. HE IS A VERY BEAUTIFUL MONKEY.
   ```

   Analyze the selected numerical codes to keep rejecting words until they satisfy the
   desired grammatical structure. [*Hint*: You might want to store the numerical word
   codes for the sentence in an array where NUM(1) = 6, NUM(2) = 5, NUM(3) = 2,
   ..., NUM(10) = 5 and compare NUM(I) with KODE(J), where I varies from 1 to
   10 and J is a random number between 1 and 48.]

8. Grid analysis is a marketing strategy technique used to examine product-related needs
   of customers. The following market grid for apartments was developed in Dallas to
   help builders better understand the needs (grey squares) of customers:

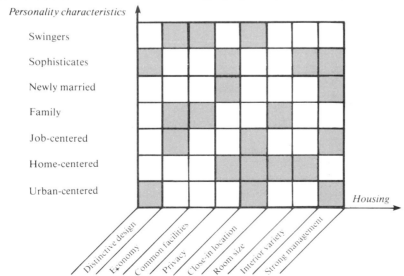

Write a program to read the data shown (using any code you wish) into an array to perform the following functions:

a. Accept one personality characteristic from input and list corresponding housing needs. For instance given the following response and cue

ENTER PERSONALITY CHARACTERISTICS? FAMILY

The computer should print

FOR FAMILY CHARACTERISTIC THE NEEDS ARE:
  1 ECONOMY
  2 COMMON FACILITIES
  3 ROOM SIZE

b. Accept one housing need from input and list personality characteristics sharing that need. Use the same input/output format as in part a.

c. Accept one housing need from input and list the personality characteristics that do *not* require that need.

d. Accept a pair of personality characteristics and list all the corresponding needs. For example, newly wed, urban-centered: distinctive design, privacy, close-in location, strong management.

9. The table on the left shows life expectancy, and the table on the right shows how long a savings amount will last if this amount is invested at a fixed interest rate and a fixed percentage of the amount is withdrawn consistently every year. For example, if one's savings earns 10% interest and one withdraws 10% of the amount every year, the withdrawal process can go on indefinitely; however, if 11% of the amount is withdrawn every year, then the withdrawal process will last only 25 years.

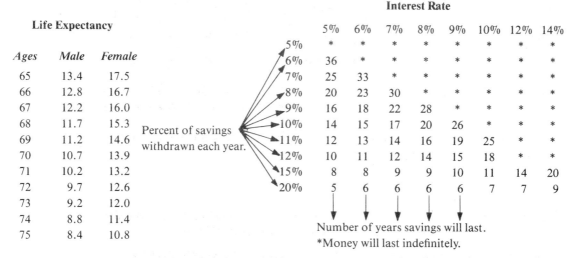

| Interest Rate | | | | | | | | |
| --- | --- | --- | --- | --- | --- | --- | --- | --- |
| | 5% | 6% | 7% | 8% | 9% | 10% | 12% | 14% |
| 5% | * | * | * | * | * | * | * | * |
| 6% | 36 | * | * | * | * | * | * | * |
| 7% | 25 | 33 | * | * | * | * | * | * |
| 8% | 20 | 23 | 30 | * | * | * | * | * |
| 9% | 16 | 18 | 22 | 28 | * | * | * | * |
| 10% | 14 | 15 | 17 | 20 | 26 | * | * | * |
| 11% | 12 | 13 | 14 | 16 | 19 | 25 | * | * |
| 12% | 10 | 11 | 12 | 14 | 15 | 18 | * | * |
| 15% | 8 | 8 | 9 | 9 | 10 | 11 | 14 | 20 |
| 20% | 5 | 6 | 6 | 6 | 6 | 7 | 7 | 9 |

Life Expectancy

| Ages | Male | Female |
| --- | --- | --- |
| 65 | 13.4 | 17.5 |
| 66 | 12.8 | 16.7 |
| 67 | 12.2 | 16.0 |
| 68 | 11.7 | 15.3 |
| 69 | 11.2 | 14.6 |
| 70 | 10.7 | 13.9 |
| 71 | 10.2 | 13.2 |
| 72 | 9.7 | 12.6 |
| 73 | 9.2 | 12.0 |
| 74 | 8.8 | 11.4 |
| 75 | 8.4 | 10.8 |

Percent of savings withdrawn each year.

Number of years savings will last.
*Money will last indefinitely.

a. Write a program to store both tables in memory, and write the code to read an interest rate and a withdrawal percentage and determine the number of years the withdrawal process can continue. For example, a savings amount earning 8% interest with an 11% withdrawal rate will last for 16 years.

b. Given an individual's age (65 or over), a sex code, a savings amount, and an interest rate, determine the largest possible yearly savings withdrawal that will leave the individual as close to broke as possible (as allowed by the table) at the time of death!

For example, a male, age 75, with $10,000 in savings at 10% interest rate, has a life expectancy of 8.4 years. His maximum percentage of withdrawal is then 15%. Twenty percent would be too high (the withdrawal process could last only 7 years). Hence his maximum yearly withdrawal would be $1500. (This would still leave a little extra for funeral expenses!)

Another example: A male, age 65, with $10,000 savings invested at 7% interest rate, has a life expectancy of 13.4 years. His maximum withdrawal would be 11%, for a yearly withdrawal of $1,100.

10. You are calculating returns from a primary election in which five candidates were running for office: Aiken, Andover, Hilary, Martin, and Watson. Each vote is recorded on one record with two entries per record. The first entry is a number identifying the party of the voter (1 = Democrat, 2 = Republican, 3 = Independent). The second entry identifies the name of the candidate.

a. Write a program to determine the total number of votes obtained by each candidate. If a candidate obtains 6 or more votes from any party, print the number of votes from that party and the party. For example:

```
CANDIDATE    TOTAL VOTES      PARTY        NUMBER OF VOTES

AIKEN            4

WATSON                        DEMOCRAT            6
WATSON           21           INDEPENDENT        10

ANDOVER          8

HILARY          14           INDEPENDENT        10

MARTIN                        DEMOCRAT            6
MARTIN                        REPUBLICAN          6
MARTIN           20           INDEPENDENT         8
```

Note for example that Mr. Watson must have gotten 5 votes from the Republican party; the name of the party is not printed, however, since he did not obtain at least 6 votes in that party.

b. List the candidates who obtained votes from each of the three parties. For the example given above, the output might be:

```
WATSON
MARTIN
```

c. Identify candidates who were elected by one or more democrats, by one or more republicans, etc. Given the above input the output could be as follows:

```
BY AT LEAST 1 DEMOCRAT:     AIKEN    ANDOVER MARTIN WATSON
BY AT LEAST 1 REPUBLICAN:   MARTIN   HILARY  WATSON
BY AT LEAST 1 INDEPENDENT:  ANDOVER  HILARY  MARTIN WATSON
```

11. A large computer company decided some years ago to study whether there was any relationship between the major of a college student and his or her success in the computer field. Four hundred graduates were selected as follows: 70 in mathematics, 156 in engineering, and 174 in liberal arts. At the end of the company training period, overall scores revealed the following:

**Performance**

|  | Excellent | Fair | Unsatisfactory |
|---|---|---|---|
| Mathematics | 37 | 23 | 10 |
| Liberal arts | 56 | 76 | 42 |
| Engineering | 25 | 64 | 67 |

The formula used to determine whether "major" is a significant factor in success is:

$$x = \frac{1}{4} \sum_{j=1}^{3} \sum_{i=1}^{3} (f_{ij} - e_{ij})^2 = \frac{1}{4} [(f_{11} - e_{11})^2 + (f_{12} - e_{12})^2 + (f_{13} - e_{13})^2 + (f_{21} - e_{21})^2 + \dots (f_{33} - e_{33})^2]$$

where $f_{ij}$ is $\dfrac{(\text{sum of row } i)\cdot(\text{sum of column } j)}{\text{sum of all entries of performance array}}$

(row and column refer to the above performance array)

For example, $f_{23} = \dfrac{(56 + 76 + 42)\cdot(10 + 42 + 67)}{400}$

$e_{ij}$ is number of students in cell at row $i$ and column $j$. For example, $e_{23} = 42$.

Write a program to read the given numbers in an array and determine whether there is a relationship between major and future success in the computer field. If $x > 9.488$, the relationship exists; otherwise, it does not.

**12.** The region shown below is a two-dimensional model of a section of a nuclear reactor. The point marked S is the source of particles that are free to travel one mesh step in any direction with equal probability. Points marked A are centers of absorption; any particle reaching such a point is considered to have been absorbed. Points marked R are reflectors and return a particle to the point from which it came, taking a total of two steps for the process. Points marked E indicate that a particle escapes through the absorbing medium. Blank points are scattering centers from which the particle moves one mesh step in any direction with equal probability. Motion can be in the horizontal or vertical direction only. The source is to be considered a normal mesh point.

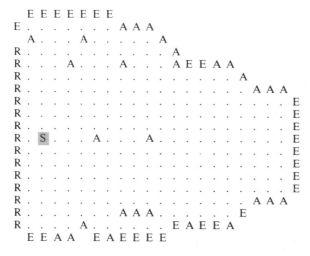

Write a program to start individual particles one at a time from point S and follows them one at a time to their escape or absorption.

a. Run 500 particles; keep track of each particle in an array that records the number of steps taken and whether the particle was absorbed or escaped. Terminate any particles remaining in the reactor after 500 moves and count them (such particles are neither absorbed nor escaped).

b. Print out the percentage of particles that escaped and the percentage that were absorbed.

c. Print out the number of particles that escaped versus the number of steps taken (so many escaped on the fifth step, so many escaped on the sixth step, and so forth). Do the same for the particles that were absorbed.

d. Print how many particles escaped through the right-most points.

The output should be similar to:

```
PERCENTAGE ESCAPED                    XXX.X
PERCENTAGE ABSORBED                   XXX.X
ESCAPES THROUGH RIGHT-MOST POINTS      XX
PARTICLES OVER 500 MOVES               XX

   ABSORBED    ESCAPED    NO. STEPS
      2           0           4
      4           3          10
      0          22          96
      .           .           .
      .           .           .
      .           .           .
     24           0         126
      .           .           .
      .           .           .
      .           .           .
      0           1         500
```

Interpretation: Two particles were absorbed in 4 steps.
Four particles were absorbed in 10 steps; 3 particles also escaped in 10 steps (output line 2), and so forth.

The number-of-steps column should be in ascending order. Use a random number generator to generate the numbers 1, 2, 3 and 4 and associate four directions to these four random numbers.

13. An input file contains at most 100 records. Each record contains a student name, the number of tests the student took that semester, and the test scores themselves (see sample input below). Students may take only the final if they want to, or both the 12 weeks test and the final, or the 6 and 12 weeks tests and the final. The tests are recorded on the input record in the following order: final, 12 weeks test (test 2), 6 weeks test (test 1).

Write the code to first read the input data into arrays NAME, GRADES, and N (number of tests), but do *not* accumulate or compute anything during this initial reading phase. After the scores have been read into the two-dimensional table GRADES, process the data. List the names, the scores, and the test averages of all students who took three tests. Provide similar lists of the students who took two tests and those who took one test. Finally, print the class average for the three tests.

No grades other than the scores read from the input record should be stored in the GRADES table; i.e., unused elements of GRADES should not be initialized to 0's or to any other values.

The input and output have the following form:

**Sample Input**

```
GAYMAL     N  2  59   67
SYMMES     L  3  91   65  87
GAELID     W  1  67
ANTONINA   T  1  95
JONES      A  1  78
CHAMID     S  2  99   87
ANDROS     K  3  29   38  64
TELEAIKEN  G  3  65  100  50
GLZSINSKI  Y  1  76
```

*Number of Tests    Final    Test2    Test1*

**Sample Output**

| NAME | | TEST 1 | TEST 2 | FINAL | AVERAGE |
|------|---|--------|--------|-------|---------|
| SYMMES | L | 87 | 65 | 91 | 81.0 |
| ANDROS | K | 64 | 38 | 29 | 43.7 |
| TELEAIKEN | G | 50 | 100 | 65 | 71.7 |
| | | | | | |
| GAYMAL | N | | 67 | 59 | 63.0 |
| CHAMID | S | | 87 | 99 | 93.0 |
| | | | | | |
| GAELID | W | | | 67 | 67.0 |
| ANTONINA | T | | | 95 | 95.0 |
| JONES | A | | | 78 | 78.0 |
| GLZSINSKI | Y | | | 76 | 76.0 |
| | | | | | |
| AVERAGE | | 67.0 | 71.4 | 73.2 | |

*Array*
*GRADES*

*Array*
*N*

| | | | |
|---|---|---|---|
| 59 | 67 | | 2 |
| 91 | 65 | 87 | 3 |
| 67 | | | 1 |
| 95 | | | 1 |
| 78 | | | 1 |
| 99 | 87 | | 2 |
| 29 | 38 | 64 | 3 |
| 65 | 100 | 50 | 3 |
| 76 | | | 1 |

**14.** *A Digital Data Noise-Elimination Problem.* A common problem in the collection of digital data via telecommunications is the phenomenon of noise—momentary fluctuations in the signal. When the transmitted data represents an image, as in pictures transmitted by satellites and space vehicles, noise results in obviously invalid random black, white, and gray spots when the image is reconverted to visual form. In order to eliminate at least some noise from a picture, it is possible to examine the image in digital form prior to converting it to visual form and replace noise elements by an estimate of the correct signal. Noise elements can be found by examining the difference between each element and the elements surrounding it. Noise elements generally differ drastically from the surrounding elements, for example, a white element surrounded by black elements or a black element surrounding by white. An estimate of the correct signal can be made by replacing the noise element by the average of the surrounding elements.

Write a program to eliminate noise from a digitized image stored in a 30 × 30 array. Each element of the array represents one "spot" in the image and stores a value from 0 to 9. Zero represents white; 9 represents black; the values between 0 and 9 represent shades of gray. An element is assumed to be a noise element if it differs in absolute value by 4 or more from five of its surrounding elements. For example, consider the element A(3,3) in the array below:

There are eight elements surrounding A(3,3); the relevant differences are:

$$|7 - 3| = 4$$
$$|6 - 3| = 3$$
$$|9 - 3| = 6$$
$$|9 - 3| = 6$$
$$|2 - 3| = 1$$
$$|8 - 3| = 5$$
$$|8 - 3| = 5$$
$$|1 - 3| = 2$$

*Array A* →

| 7 | 2 | 1 | 2 | 5 |
|---|---|---|---|---|
| 6 | 7 | 6 | 9 | 7 |
| 8 | 9 | 3 | 2 | 2 |
| 7 | 8 | 8 | 1 | 2 |
| 5 | 6 | 7 | 1 | 7 |

Five of the differences are greater than or equal to 4, hence the element can be classified as a noise element. Noise elements should be replaced by the average of the surrounding elements; in this case

$$A(3,3) = \frac{7 + 6 + 9 + 9 + 2 + 8 + 8 + 1}{8} = 6$$

Assume boundary elements (rows 1 and 30 and columns 1 and 30) are not distorted. How would you change your program to account for possible distorted boundary elements?

15. *A Digital Image Enhancement.* Another problem in the analysis of images in digitized form is that objects are sometimes difficult to recognize because of insufficient contrast between the object and its background. One method that can be used to enhance digital images is to reduce the number of distinct shades of gray from the number represented in the initial signal (ten in the previous problem) to a lesser number such as five (black, white, and three shades of gray), three (black, white, and gray), or even two (black and white). This process is somewhat like increasing the contrast on a black-and-white television set. With increased contrast some detail is lost but remaining images are more prominent.

Write a program to enhance contrast in the 30 × 30 digitized images described below. Perform three enhancements: translate the image from the original ten different values to five (low contrast), three (medium contrast), and two (high contrast) different values using the following table of transformations:

| Original Value | Low Contrast | Medium Contrast | High Contrast |
|---|---|---|---|
| 0 | 0 | 0 | 0 |
| 1 | 0 | 0 | 0 |
| 2 | 2 | 0 | 0 |
| 3 | 2 | 4 | 0 |
| 4 | 4 | 4 | 0 |
| 5 | 4 | 4 | 9 |
| 6 | 6 | 4 | 9 |
| 7 | 6 | 9 | 9 |
| 8 | 8 | 9 | 9 |
| 9 | 8 | 9 | 9 |

For example, given the following $3 \times 3$ digitized image, we generate 3 "contrast" images:

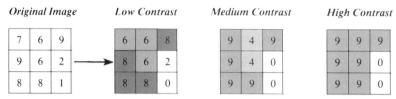

*Original Image*    *Low Contrast*    *Medium Contrast*    *High Contrast*

The following examples are two images that have been digitized and processed for high and low contrast images. To give the images more tone/contrast, many characters have been multi-struck with different characters to give the picture varying tones of grey. Each printer line was made to advance half its usual vertical spacing. For a hint on how to proceed, look at the program at the end of this chapter following the answers to the "Test Yourself."

*Original Digital Image*      *Low Contrast Image*      *High Contrast Image*

*Digitized Image*      *Low Contrast Image*      *High Contrast Image*

**16.** The world is at war, and the only hope to conquer the enemy is to destroy its command post. Army intelligence agents have intercepted a chart (see diagram that follows) of an area in the Mohave desert, showing exactly where the enemy command post is located.

This chart divides a certain region of the desert into areas of square yards. Each square yard on the chart is identified by two numbers. The first number represents its north-south position on the chart and the second number represents its east-west position on the chart. The chart has a total of ten yards running north to south and a total of ten yards running east to west. The top of the chart is north and the bottom is south (rows), while the left side of the chart is west and the right side is east (columns). (For example, area (1,1) on the chart is the area in the upper left corner and (10,10) is the area on the lower right corner; area (3,4) means the third area down and the fourth area to the right.) To fully protect the enemy's command post, explosive land mines are planted in every square yard around the post except for a *single* path so that men and supplies can move in and out. On the chart, zeros are placed where a clear path exists, and ones are placed in every area where a land mine is set (any person who steps on any portion of the square yard with a mine will be blown up). Using the provided chart you are to follow the path free from mines and destroy the enemy command post, being careful not to step on any areas with mines.

Initialize a two-dimensional array with ones for the squares in the gray area and zeroes for the path free of mines (light area).

*Output:*

a. Print out the map of zeroes and ones using an attractive format.

b. Once all the data is read you are to follow the path that must be taken to safely reach the command post and print out the two integer identification numbers for each area you travel through (including the area where you start and end). The following assumptions must be made:

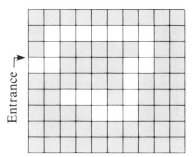

(1) The path starts at (4,1).

(2) You cannot go back and retrace your steps.

(3) When the path ends and you can go no further (mines are all around you), you have reached the command post and are not to try to travel any further!

(4) You can travel only north, south, east, or west (you cannot travel diagonally).

(5) Once you have found the correct path, you radio the path coordinates to your second in command who is to follow your footsteps directly to the command post, without ever testing for mines. To ensure that he obeys, you order him to replace all 0's of the clear path by 3's and to print the region once safe at the command post.

17. A matrix is a rectangular array of numbers. Addition and multiplication of matrices is illustrated in the following examples: (see exercise 13 section 8–6–1)

*Addition*

$$\begin{pmatrix} a_{11} & a_{12} & a_{13} \\ a_{21} & a_{22} & a_{23} \end{pmatrix} + \begin{pmatrix} b_{11} & b_{12} & b_{13} \\ b_{21} & b_{22} & b_{23} \end{pmatrix} = \begin{pmatrix} a_{11} + b_{11} & a_{12} + b_{12} & a_{13} + b_{13} \\ a_{21} + b_{21} & a_{22} + b_{22} & a_{23} + b_{23} \end{pmatrix}$$

*Multiplication*

$$\begin{pmatrix} a_{11} & a_{12} & a_{13} \\ a_{21} & a_{22} & a_{23} \end{pmatrix} \cdot \begin{pmatrix} b_{11} & b_{12} \\ b_{21} & b_{22} \\ b_{31} & b_{32} \end{pmatrix} = \begin{pmatrix} a_{11} \cdot b_{11} + a_{12} \cdot b_{21} + a_{13} \cdot b_{31} & a_{11} \cdot b_{12} + a_{12} \cdot b_{22} + a_{13} \cdot b_{32} \\ a_{21} \cdot b_{11} + a_{22} \cdot b_{21} + a_{23} \cdot b_{31} & a_{21} \cdot b_{12} + a_{22} \cdot b_{22} + a_{23} \cdot b_{32} \end{pmatrix}$$

In general, if A is *m* by *n* (*m* rows and *n* columns) and B is *n* by *q*, then the product matrix C = A·B is of size *m* by *q*. The number of columns in A must equal the number of rows in B. Such matrices are said to be *conformable*.

a. Write a program to read two 4 by 3 matrices and compute their sum and difference (to subtract, the corresponding entries are subtracted).
b. Write a program to read a 3 by 3 matrix A and a 3 by 3 matrix B. Compute A·B and (A + B)·(A − B).
c. Write a program to read a value for N and compute $A^N$ where A is a 3 by 3 matrix that has been read in.

$$A^N = \underbrace{A \cdot A \cdot \ldots \cdot A}_{\text{N matrices}}$$

d. Read in a square matrix A and print out its tranpose $A^T$ (the rows of $A^T$ are equal to the columns of A; row $i$ of $A^T$ = column $i$ of A).

18. The XYZ Company manufactures four products: P1, P2, P3, P4. Each of these products must undergo some type of operation on five different machines: A, B, C, D, E. The time (in units of hours) required for each of these products on each of the five machines is shown below:

|      | A    | B   | C    | D   | E   |
|------|------|-----|------|-----|-----|
| P1   | .2   | .2  | .1   | .58 | .15 |
| P2   | .26  | .1  | .13  | .61 | .3  |
| P3   | .5   | .21 | .56  | .45 | .27 |
| P4   | .6   | .17 | 1.3  | .25 | .31 |

For example, product P1 requires .2 hour on machine A, .2 hour on machine B, .1 hour on machine C, and so on.

a. The XYZ Company has been requested to fill an order of 356 products P1, 257 products P2, 1,058 products P3, and 756 products P4. Write a program to determine the total number of hours that *each* machine will be used. [*Hint*: Express the table as a 4 by 5 matrix; express the order as a 1 by 4 matrix, and multiply the two matrices. You do not·need to know about matrices to solve this problem, however!]
b. The XYZ Company is renting the five machines A, B, C, D, E from a tooling company. The hourly rental cost for each machine is as follows:

| Machines         | A       | B      | C      | D       | E      |
|------------------|---------|--------|--------|---------|--------|
| Rental cost/hour | $10.00  | $5.75  | $3.50  | $10.00  | $5.76  |

Write a program to compute the total rental expense for all the machines. [*Hint*: Express rental costs as a 1 by 6 matrix and multiply by matrix result of part a. This problem can be solved without matrices.]

19. Write a program to verify that for any conformable matrices X, Y, Z of your choice the following are true:

a. $(X + Y) \cdot Z = X \cdot Z + Y \cdot Z$
b. $(X \cdot Y) \cdot Z = X \cdot (Y \cdot Z)$
c. $X \cdot X^{-1} = X^{-1} \cdot X = I$

The inverse of a matrix is only defined for square matrices. Not all square matrices have inverses however. A matrix X multiplied by its inverse yields the identity matrix I which consists of 1's down the main diagonal and 0's elsewhere. For part c above use the following matrices

$$X = \begin{pmatrix} 1 & 2 & -3 \\ 4 & -1 & 2 \\ 14 & -1 & 3 \end{pmatrix} \text{ and } X^{-1} = \begin{pmatrix} -1 & -3 & 1 \\ 16 & 45 & -14 \\ 10 & 29 & -9 \end{pmatrix}$$

20. Let us refer to A' (A prime) as the transpose of matrix A (see problem 17.d.). Write a program to demonstrate that
$$(A')^{-1} = (A^{-1})'$$
Use the X matrices shown in exercise 19.

21. An $n$ by $n$ matrix A is said to be *symmetric* if and only if A = A'. Write a program to demonstrate that
   a. A·A' is symmetric and
   b. A + A' is symmetric.

22. A strictly triangular matrix is a square matrix with all entries on and below the main diagonal equal to zero. Write a program to demonstrate that if A is a 4 by 4 strictly triangular matrix, then $A^4 = A·A·A·A$ is the zero matrix (in general $A^n$ is the zero matrix if A is an $n$ by $n$ strictly triangular matrix).

23. Write a program to verify that DET(A·B) = DET(A)·DET(B) where A and B are square matrices and DET refers to the determinant of the matrix.

24. Write a program to verify that the determinant of a triangular matrix is equal to the product of its diagonal elements; use a square matrix of size 4.

25. An iterative method[1] for computing the inverse of a matrix A is given by
$$A^{-1} = I + B + B^2 + B^3 + B^4 + ...,$$
where B = I − A (I is the identity matrix). Compute the inverse of
$$A = \begin{pmatrix} 1/2 & 1 & 0 \\ 0 & 2/3 & 0 \\ -1/2 & -1 & 2/3 \end{pmatrix}$$
Stop at $B^{10}$ in the expansion for $A^{-1}$. Check result by computing $A^{-1}*A$.

26. The trace of a matrix is defined as the sum of its diagonal elements. Let A be a 5 by 5 matrix and B be a 5 by 5 matrix. Write a program to determine that tr(A·B) = tr(B·A) and tr(A + B) = tr(A) + tr(B).

27. A method for computing the inverse of any matrix on a computer is as follows:
$$A^{-1} = -\frac{1}{c_n}(A^{n-1} + c_1 A^{n-2} + c_2 A^{n-3} + ... + c_{n-1}I)$$
where the $c$'s are all constants defined as
$$c_1 = -tr(A) \text{ (See exercise 26 for the definition of the trace.)}$$
$$c_2 = -1/2(c_1 tr(A) + tr(A^2))$$
$$c_3 = -1/3(c_2 tr(A) + c_1 tr(A^2) + tr(A^3))$$
$$\vdots$$
$$c_n = -1/n(c_{n-1}tr(A) + c_{n-2}tr(A^2) + ... + c_1 tr(A^{n-1}) + tr(A^n))$$

Write a program to compute the inverse of a 5 by 5 matrix A and check that it is indeed the inverse by verifying that $A·A^{-1} = I$ where I is the identity matrix.

For example, the inverse of a 2 by 2 matrix X is $X^{-1} = -\frac{1}{c_2}(X + c_1 I)$ where $c_2 = -1/2(c_1 tr(X) + tr(X^2))$ and $c_1 = -tr(X)$.

[1]This method will work only when the Eigenvalues of A are less than 1 in absolute value.

**28.** The following is the daily schedule of a small Pennsylvania airline.

| Flight Number | Origin | Stops | Plane Capacity | Departure Time |
|---|---|---|---|---|
| 700 | State College | Harrisburg<br>Baltimore<br>Washington | 5 | 7:05 A.M. |
| 701 | Washington | Harrisburg<br>State College | 5 | 9:00 A.M. |
| 430 | State College | Harrisburg<br>Baltimore<br>Washington | 5 | 4:15 P.M. |
| 431 | Washington | Baltimore<br>Harrisburg<br>State College | 5 | 6:15 P.M. |

If a plane is full, assume the passenger will accept the next available flight.

After all transactions have been processed, print a listing by flight and stops of the passengers scheduled. The planes are very small; there is a maximum of five passengers per flight. Use a three-dimensional array to store reservations.

The output should have the following form:

```
DATE    FLIGHT                     PASSENGER
2/25    700     STATE COLLEGE TO   B. BALDRIGE
                HARRISBURG         H. DAVIS
                                   .

                HARRISBURG TO      B. BALDRIGE
                BALTIMORE          H. DAVIS
                                   .

                BALTIMORE TO       H. DAVIS   (Baldrige gets off at Baltimore)
                WASHINGTON
        701     WASHINGTON TO      A. CHARLES
                HARRISBURG         .
                                   .
                                   .

                HARRISBURG TO      (Charles gets off in Harrisburg)
                STATE COLLEGE
                                   .
                                   .

        430     STATE COLLEGE TO   .
                HARRISBURG         .
                        .          .

        431             .          .
                        .          .
                        .          .

2/26    700             .          .
         .       .      .          .
         .       .      .          .
```

Write a program for maintaining passenger reservations for three days, using the following list of reservation requests:

**Transactions (Requests for Seats)**

| *Name* | *Date Desires* | *From* | *To* | *Flight Number* |
|---|---|---|---|---|
| B. Baldrige | 2/25 | State College | Baltimore | 700 |
| W. Bartlett | 2/26 | Harrisburg | State College | 431 |
| W. Broderick | 2/25 | Harrisburg | Washington | 430 |
| R. Cheek | 2/26 | Baltimore | State College | 431 |
| E. Cooley | 2/27 | State College | Washington | 700 |
| H. Davis | 2/25 | State College | Washington | 700 |
| S. Dalles | 2/26 | Harrisburg | State College | 431 |
| L. Donald | 2/25 | Baltimore | Washington | 700 |
| F. John | 2/26 | Baltimore | Harrisburg | 431 |
| L. Line | 2/26 | Washington | State College | 431 |
| M. Dohert | 2/25 | State College | Baltimore | 700 |
| W. Howard | 2/26 | Washington | Harrisburg | 431 |
| J. Jacks | 2/25 | Washington | State College | 431 |
| J. Jacks | 2/26 | State College | Washington | 430 |
| G. Holland | 2/26 | Harrisburg | Washington | 700 |
| G. Holland | 2/27 | Washington | Harrisburg | 431 |
| C. Italia | 2/26 | State College | Washington | 700 |
| C. Italia | 2/26 | Washington | Harrisburg | 431 |
| H. Kent | 2/25 | Baltimore | Harrisburg | 431 |
| H. Kent | 2/27 | Harrisburg | Baltimore | 430 |
| C. Murray | 2/25 | State College | Washington | 700 |
| C. Murray | 2/26 | Washington | State College | 431 |
| R. Steel | 2/25 | State College | Washington | 700 |
| R. Steel | 2/25 | Washington | State College | 431 |
| A. Charles | 2/25 | Washington | Harrisburg | 701 |
| A. Charles | 2/26 | Harrisburg | Washington | 430 |
| A. Jabbari | 2/25 | State College | Washington | 700 |
| B. Jolly | 2/27 | Baltimore | Harrisburg | 431 |
| J. Hay | 2/26 | State College | Harrisburg | 430 |
| D. Day | 2/27 | Washington | State College | 431 |
| C. Mead | 2/25 | State College | Baltimore | 700 |
| Z. Mattern | 2/26 | Washington | Harrisburg | 431 |
| D. Davidson | 2/25 | Harrisburg | State College | 431 |
| M. West | 2/26 | State College | Washington | 700 |
| L. Mudd | 2/27 | Baltimore | Harrisburg | 431 |
| R. Frat | 2/25 | Washington | Harrisburg | 701 |

## 8-6-3 Answers to Test Yourself

**1.** a. Valid.
   b. Valid.
   c. Valid.
   d. Missing parentheses.
   e. Real number is invalid for size specification.
   f. Variable may not be used to specify array size.
   g. Valid.
   h. Misplaced parenthesis
   i. 3*10 not allowed.
   j. Valid.

**2.** A(1,1),A(2,1),A(1,2),A(2,2),A(1,3),A(2,3)A(1,4),A(2,4)
B(1,1,1),B(2,1,1),B(3,1,1),B(1,1,2),B(2,1,2),B(3,1,2),B(1,1,3),B(2,1,3),
B(3,1,3),B(1,1,4),B(2,1,4),B(3,1,4),
K(1,1,1),K(2,1,1),K(1,2,1),K(2,2,1), K(1,1,2),K(2,1,2),K(1,2,2),K(2,2,2)

**3.** TC will contain the sum of each column of A.
TR will contain the sum of each row of A.

**4.** a. `WRITE( )(A(I),I = 4,9Ø)`
b. `WRITE( )(B(J),J = 1,99,2)`
c. `READ( )(C(2,K),K = 1,5)`
d. `READ( )(A(J,1),B(J),J = 1,3)`
e. `WRITE( )(K,(A(I,1),(B(J),J = 1,3),I = 1,2))`
f. `READ( )(A(1,J),J = 1,3),(B(2,J),J = 1,3),(C(J),J = 1,3)`
g. `WRITE( )(A(1,J),B(1,J),C(1,J),I,J = 1,3)`
h. `WRITE( )((I,I = 1,4), J = 1,3)`

**5.** a. $A(1,1),A(2,1),A(3,1),A(1,2), A(2,2),A(3,2)$.  1 record.
b. $A(1,1),I,A(2,1),I,A(3,1),I,A(1,2),I,A(2,2), I,A(3,2),I$.  4 records.
c. $A(1,1),A(2,1),A(3,1),J,A(1,2),A(2,2),A(3,2),J,A(1,3),A(2,3),A(3,3),J$.  3 records.
d. $A(1,1),B(1,1),A(1,2),B(1,2),A(2,1),B(2,1),A(2,2),B(2,2),A(3,1),B(3,1),A(3,2),B(3,2)$.  12 records.
e. $C(1),A(1,1),A(1,2),A(1,3),P(1,1),P(2,1),C(2),A(2,1),A(2,2),A(2,3),P(1,2),P(2,2)$.  2 records.
f. $A(1,1,1),A(2,1,1),A(1,1,2),A(2,1,2),A(1,1,3),A(2,1,3), A(1,2,1),A(2,2,1),A(1,2,2),A(2,2,2),$
$A(1,2,3),A(2,2,3)$.  2 records.

**6.** a. `WRITE( )((A(I,J),J = 1,4),I = 1,3),(JSUM(I,J),J=1,4),I=1,3),VAR`
`FORMAT (2X,12F4.Ø,12I4,F5.Ø)`
b. `WRITE( )((A(I,J),J = 1,4),(JSUM(I,J),J = 1,4),VAR,I = 1,3)`
`FORMAT(2X,4F4.Ø,4I4,F5.Ø)`
c. `WRITE( )((A(I,J),I = 1,3),VAR,(JSUM(I,J),I = 1,3),J = 1,3)`
`FORMAT(2X,3F4.Ø,F5.Ø,3I4)`
d. `WRITE( )((A(I,J),JSUM(I,J),J = 1,4),I = 1,3)`
`FORMAT(4(F5.Ø,I5))`
e. `WRITE( )((A(I,J),JSUM(I,J),I = 1,3),J = 1,4)`
`FORMAT(6(F5.Ø,I5))`

**7.** a. `READ( )((A(I,J),I = 1,4),J = 1,3)`
`FORMAT(4F5.Ø)`
b. `READ( )(A(1,J),J = 1,6),(B(I),I = 1,6)`
`FORMAT(2(3F5.Ø/),(3F3.Ø))`
c. `READ( )(A(I,1),B(I,1),I = 1,6)`
`FORMAT(2(F4.Ø,1X,F5.Ø))`
d. `READ( )(A(I,1),B(1,I),I = 1,6)`
`FORMAT(2(F5.Ø,F6.Ø))`
e. `READ( )((A(I,J),J = 1,3),(B(I,J),J = 1,2),I = 1,9)`
`FORMAT(3F5.Ø,2F3.Ø)`
f. `READ( )((A(I,J),J = 1,9),I = 1,8),((B(I,J),I = 1,4),J = 1,2)`
`FORMAT(8(9F3.Ø/),(3F4.Ø))`

**8.** 
```
   DO 2 I = 1,16
   DO 2 J = 1,6
 2    A(I,J) = J
```

**9.** a.
```
   DIMENSION A(5,5),B(5)
   READ(5,1)((A(I,J),J=1,5),I=1,5)
 1 FORMAT(5F1Ø.Ø)
   WRITE(6,2)((A(I,J),I=1,5),J=1,5)
 2 FORMAT(2X,5F1Ø.Ø)
```

b.
```
   SUM = Ø.
   DO 3 I = 1,5
 3    SUM = SUM + A(3,I)
```

c.
```
   ALARG = A(1,1)
   DO 4 I = 2,5
      IF(ALARG.LT.A(I,1))ALARG=A(I,1)
 4 CONTINUE
```

d.
```
   DO 5 I = 1,5
 5    B(I) = Ø.
   DO 6 I = 1,5
   DO 6 J = 1,5
 6    B(J) = B(J) + A(I,J)
```

```
e.    DO 7 I = 1,5                              SSUM = SSUM + A(I,J)
     7     A(3,I) = A(3,I)+A(2,I)                IF(SLARG.LT.A(I,J))SLARG = A(I,J)
                                          16 CONTINUE
f.    DO 8 I = 1,5
            HOLD = A(I,3)             i.    KROW = 1
            A(I,3) = A(I,4)                 KOLUMN = 1
     8     A(I,4) = HOLD                    ASMAL = A(1,1)
                                            DO 5 I = 1,10
g.    SUM2 = Ø.                             DO 5 J = 1,10
      DO 9 I = 1,5                             IF(ASMAL.LE.A(I,J))GO TO 5
     9     SUM2 = SUM2 + A(I,I)                 ASMAL = A(I,J)
                                               KROW = I
h.    SSUM = Ø.                                KOLUMN = J
      SLARG = A(1,5)                    5 CONTINUE
      DO 16 I = 1,5                      PRINT*, ASMAL, KROW, KOLUMN
            J = 6 - I  (continued in next column)
```

```
10.       READ(5,3)((C(I,J),J=1,5),(D(I,J),J=1,5),I=1,5)
```

```
11.       REAL F(4Ø,17),G(68Ø)
                  .
                  .
          K = 1
          DO 1Ø I = 1,4Ø
          DO 1Ø J = 1,17
                G(K) = F(I,J)
      1Ø     K = K + 1
```

```
12.       REAL A(1Ø,3)
          SUM = Ø.
          DO 1Ø I = 1,1Ø
          DO 1Ø J = 1,3
      1Ø     SUM = SUM + A(I,J)
          WRITE(6,5)(J,J = 1,1Ø),((A(I,J),I = 1,1Ø),J = 1,3),SUM
       5 FORMAT(T3Ø,'FINAL'/T5,1Ø('COLUMN',I3,2X)/3(T5,1ØF6.1/)/ T5,
        *'SUM IS',F5.1)
```

```
13.       INTEGER A(5,4), B(4,3), C(5,3),SUM
          READ(5,1)((A(I,J),J=1,4),I=1,5)
          READ(5,2)((B(I,J),J=1,3),I=1,4)
          DO 4 I = 1, 5
              DO 5 J = 1, 3
                 SUM = Ø
                 DO 6 K - 1, 4
                    SUM = SUM + A(I,K) * B(K,J)
      6          CONTINUE
                 C(I,J) = SUM
      5       CONTINUE
      4    CONTINUE
          WRITE(6,3)((A(I,J),J=1,4),I=1,5)
          WRITE (6,7)((B(I,J),J=1,3),I=1,4)
          WRITE(6,8)((C(I,J),J=1,3),I=1,5)
          STOP
      1    FORMAT(4I1)
      2    FORMAT(3I1)
      3    FORMAT(1X,4I3)
      7    FORMAT(1X,3I3)
      8    FORMAT(1X,3I6)
          END
```

*Hint for problem 15 (digitized images)*

```
      CHARACTER ICON(5),MOD(30,30)
      INTEGER IMAGE(30,30)
      DATA ICON/' ','0','1','X','*'/
      READ(5,15)LIM1,LIM2          LIM1 = number rows; LIM2 = number columns.
      READ(5,25)((IMAGE(K,L),L=1,LIM2),K=1,LIM1)
      WRITE(6,90)
      WRITE(6,30)((IMAGE(K,L),L=1,LIM2),K=1,LIM1)
      N=1
77    IF(N.EQ.2) THEN          digitized image       contrast character
         WRITE(6,60)                code                   ICON
         KODKEY = 5                  ↓                      ↓
         KODADD = 4                 0,1                  blank
      ELSE                          2,3                  0
         WRITE(6,40)                4,5                  multistrike 0 and 1
         KODKEY = 2                 6,7                  multistrike 0, 1, and X
         KODADD = 1                 8,9                  multistrike 0, 1, X and *
      ENDIF
      KODMIN = 0                Any contrast characters can be chosen.
      DO 200 K = 1, LIM1
         DO 250 I = 1 ,5
            DO 300 L = 1, LIM2
               NUMCOM = (IMAGE(K,L)/KODKEY) + KODADD - KODMIN
               IF (NUMCOM .LT. 1) NUMCOM = 1
               IF(N.EQ.3 .AND. IMAGE(K,L).LT.5)NUMCOM = 1
300            MOD(K,L) = ICON(NUMCOM)
            WRITE(6,10)(MOD(K,M),M=1,LIM2)
250      KODMIN = KODMIN + 1
         KODMIN = 0
200   WRITE(6,20)
      N = N + 1
      IF(N.LT.3) GO TO 77
      STOP
15    FORMAT(2I2)
25    FORMAT(30I1)        number of elements per line (LIM2)
40    FORMAT(/1X,'LOW CONTRAST IMAGE' /1X)
60    FORMAT(/1X,'HIGH CONTRAST IMAGE'/1X)
10    FORMAT('+',30A1)
20    FORMAT(1X)
90    FORMAT(1X,'ORIGINAL DIGITAL IMAGE'/1X)
30    FORMAT(1X,30I1)
      END
```

# functions

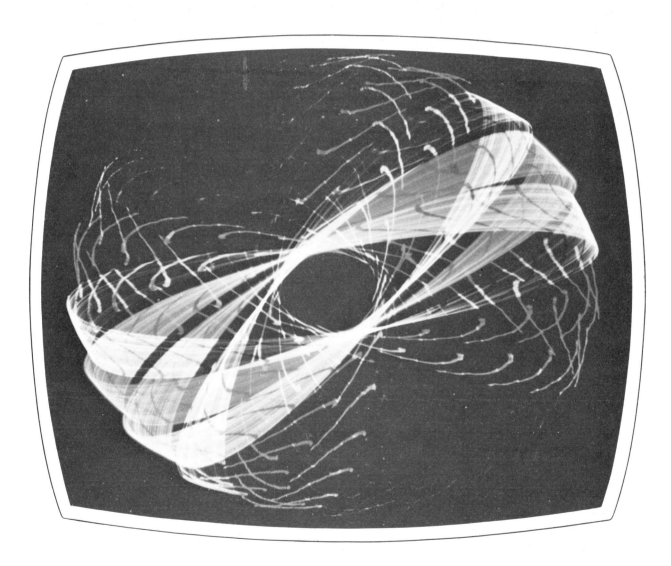

## CHAPTER NINE

# functions

## 9-1   Introduction

You are probably familiar with many mathematical functions such as the square root and the exponential and trigonometric functions. These functions and others are available to the FORTRAN programmer through libraries that are provided by the computer system. FORTRAN also allows you to define and write your own functions, which you may want to incorporate in the library (user or system library). In either case functions allow you to transfer to a prewritten block of code to perform a specific task. This is very convenient when the same task is to be repeated numerous times or at different places in a program. Functions relieve you of writing the code for routine tasks, and certain user-written functions can be shared by different users, resulting in a significant economy of effort.

In this chapter we shall examine functions that are included with FORTRAN and also describe procedures for defining your own functions. Consider, for example, the following problem: An observer on shore sights a ship one mile away, moving along a line perpendicular to the line of sight. One hour later the observer sights the ship and finds an angle of 25° between the two sightings (see Figure 9–1). How far has the ship traveled?

Using trigonometric methods, it can be shown that the distance traveled in one hour is $x = \tan 25°$. A FORTRAN program to perform this calculation is shown in Figure 9–1.

**FIGURE  9-1**     DISTANCE CALCULATION USING TAN FUNCTION

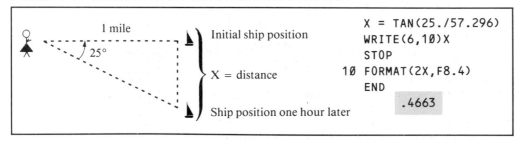

The program uses the function TAN; the programmer does not have to write a routine to evaluate the tangent function. Note that the argument of the function TAN must be expressed in radians. One radian is equivalent to 57.296° ($180° = \pi$ radians), hence $25° = 25/57.296$ radians.

## 9-2   FORTRAN-Supplied Functions

### 9-2-1   Definition

A function is a correspondence between one set of numbers, called *arguments*, and another set of numbers, called *values* of the function. The purpose of a function is to take one or more arguments and come up with a single result. For example, the square root function can be used in a FORTRAN statement as follows:

Function value     Argument
```
Y=SQRT(16.)
```

Figure 9-2 illustrates the use of the square root function to produce the square root of the numbers 1 through 7.

The type of the argument depends on the function used; for example, the TAN function requires its argument to be real, while for some other functions such as the absolute value function ABS, the argument can be either real or integer (see Figures 9-3 and 9-4). Functions can be part of any arithmetic expression. The general form of a function reference is:

> *function name* (*argument expression*[,...])

where *function name* is the name of the function.

The *argument expression* (there must be at least one) can be a constant, a variable, another function reference, or an expression containing constants, variables, arithmetic operations, and function references. The argument expression is evaluated to a single value, which is then passed to the function as an argument.

Logically, we can think of the function as being evaluated at the point it is used (where it appears in the statement). Internally, a transfer is made to a set of instructions that calculates the value of the function based on the value of the argument(s). Control is then returned to the point where the function was called. Some functions can have more than one argument, as in the case of the function MIN, which selects the smallest value of its integer arguments:

```
AK = MIN(I,J,K,L,3,N,NT)
```

Function value is stored in AK as a real number.     The function returns an integer value.     More than one argument.

The type of the argument generally determines the type of the result (functional value); thus ABS(X) returns a real value while ABS(N) returns an integer value.

**FIGURE 9-2**     PROGRAM USING FUNCTION SQRT

```
      WRITE(6,10)
      DO 20 I = 1,7
         X = I              The argument of the SQRT function must be real.
13       Y = SQRT(X)
         WRITE(6,11)X,Y
20    CONTINUE
      STOP
10    FORMAT(' ARGUMENT',4X,'VALUE')
11    FORMAT(4X,F3.1,4X,F6.3)
      END
```

| ARGUMENT | VALUE |
| --- | --- |
| 1.0 | 1.000 |
| 2.0 | 1.414 |
| 3.0 | 1.732 |
| 4.0 | 2.000 |
| 5.0 | 2.236 |
| 6.0 | 2.449 |
| 7.0 | 2.646 |

The argument of the function must always be enclosed in parentheses. The argument itself may contain parentheses, as in:

Outer parentheses identify the argument.

$$Y = SQRT((3.*(X1 + X2 + X3) - (X1 + X2 + X3)**2)/(X*(X-1.)))$$

Expression is to be evaluated as the argument.

FORTRAN-supplied functions are furnished with the FORTRAN compiler by the computer manufacturer. These functions are stored in system libraries on magnetic disks or other types of storage devices. The FORTRAN library of functions consists of mathematical functions and other special functions described in the next two sections.

### 9-2-2 Mathematical Functions

Standard built-in mathematical functions known as *intrinsic* functions are part of the FORTRAN compiler. These functions are shown in Figure 9–3. Note that there are restrictions on the range of values acceptable as arguments; for example, the square root and logarithmic functions cannot have negative arguments. If an invalid argument is detected by a function, an error message will be printed. Certain functions also require a particular type argument (real, integer, and so forth); a real argument can be either single or double precision.

*Examples*

```
Y = SQRT(A**2 + B**2)
IF(ABS(Y).LT.0.01)GO TO 5

I = COS(X)**2 + C*EXP(-SIN(X))

Q = LOG(R)
```

Evaluate the expression $\sqrt{a^2 + b^2}$.
If the value of $y$ is in the range $-0.01 < y < 0.01$, go to statement 5.

Evaluates to $\cos^2 x + ce^{-\sin x}$. The result is truncated since it is stored in I.

The natural logarithm (base $e$) is computed. If $r$ is negative, an error message will be printed, since logarithms of negative numbers are not defined.

### 9-2-3 Do It Now

**1.** Write FORTRAN statements for each of the following:

a. $\sin x + \cos x$   
b. $\sin^2 x + \cos^2 x$   
c. $\tan x^{-1}$   
d. $\ln (x+y)$   
e. $|a+b|$   
f. $\sqrt{a+b}$   

g. $(\tan x)^{-1}$   
h. $\dfrac{1}{\sin x^2 + \cos x^2}$   
i. $e^x + e^{-x}$   
j. $\sqrt{\sin^2 x + \cos^2 x}$   
k. $|a-b|\,|x-y|$   

**2.** What is the value of each of the following if A = $-3$. and B = 4.?

a. SQRT(A+B)   
b. ABS(A+B)   
c. LOG(EXP(B))   

d. LOG10(A+B)   
e. LOG(A)

**FIGURE 9-3** FORTRAN-SUPPLIED MATHEMATICAL FUNCTIONS

| *Function* | *Form* | *Argument* | *Value* | *Example* |
|---|---|---|---|---|
| Absolute value<br>$\lvert x \rvert = x$ if $x \geq 0$<br>$\quad = -x$ if $x < 0$ | ABS(X) | 1 real<br>1 integer<br>1 complex | real<br>integer<br>real | ABS(1.7)=1.7<br>ABS(-2)=2<br>ABS(3.,2.)=$\sqrt{13}$ |
| Square root<br>$\sqrt{r}$ | SQRT(X)<br>X $\geq$ 0 | 1 real<br>1 complex | real<br>complex | SQRT(3.)=1.732...<br>SQRT(2) is invalid. |
| Exponential<br>$e^x$ | EXP(X) | 1 real<br>1 complex | real<br>complex | EXP(1.)=2.718...<br>EXP(-1.)=0.367... |
| Natural log<br>$\text{Log}_e(x)$ | LOG(X)<br>X > 0 | 1 real<br>1 complex | real<br>complex | LOG(2.718...)=1.<br>LOG(2) is invalid. |
| Common log<br>$\text{Log}_{10}(x)$ | LOG10(X)<br>X > 0 | 1 real<br>1 complex | real<br>complex | LOG10(100.)=2.<br>LOG10(20.)=1.301... |

Trigonometric functions: Given the angles, find the corresponding arcs. Sine, cosine, and tangent require arguments in radians; to use degrees, divide by 57.3 ($180/\pi = 57.3$), e.g., $\text{SIN}(\pi) = \text{SIN}(180°/57.3)$

| | | | | |
|---|---|---|---|---|
| Sine | SIN(X) | 1 real<br>1 complex | [$-1$. to 1.] | SIN(90./57.3)=1.<br>SIN(1.)=.8414 |
| Cosine | COS(X) | 1 real<br>1 complex | [$-1$. to 1.] | COS(3.1)=-.999... |
| Tangent | TAN(X) | 1 real | $-\infty$. to $+\infty$. | TAN(1.571)=-4900... |

The arc functions: Given the arc values, find the corresponding angles. The values returned by these functions are expressed in radians: divide by 57.3 to get degrees.

| | | | | |
|---|---|---|---|---|
| Arcsine | ASIN(X)<br>$-1 \leq X \leq 1$ | 1 real | [$-\pi/2, \pi/2$] | ASIN(.5)=0.523... |
| Arcosine | ACOS(x)<br>$-1 \leq X \leq 1$ | 1 real | [$0, \pi$] | ACOS(.5)=1.047... |
| Arctangent | ATAN(X)<br>$-\infty < X < +\infty$ | 1 real | [$-\pi/2, \pi/2$] | ATAN(1.)=0.785... |
| Real arc tangent $x/y$ | ATAN2(X,Y)<br>$-\infty < X,Y < \infty$ | 2 real | ($-\pi, \pi$] | ATAN2(5.8,-4.7)=2.251 |

For the hyperbolic functions, the arguments must be in radians.

| | | | | |
|---|---|---|---|---|
| Hyperbolic sine | SINH(X) | 1 real | real | SINH(.2)=0.201... |
| Hyperbolic cosine | COSH(X) | 1 real | real | COSH(.2)=1.02... |
| Hyperbolic tangent | TANH(X) | 1 real | real | TANH(2.99)=.994... |

## Answers

1. a. SIN(X) + COS(X)
   b. SIN(X)**2 + COS(X)**2
   c. TAN(X**(−1)) or TAN(1./X)
   d. LOG(X+Y)
   e. ABS (A+B)
   f. SQRT(A+B)
   g. 1./(TAN(X)) or TAN(X)**(−1)
   h. 1./(SIN(X**2) + COS(X**2)) or (SIN(X**2) + COS(X**2))**(−1)
   i. EXP(X) + EXP(−X)
   j. SQRT(SIN(X)**2 + COS(X)**2)
   k. ABS(A−B)*ABS(X−Y)

2. a. 1.     b. 1.     c. 4.     d. 0.     e. Error. Argument must be $\geq$ 0.

### 9-2-4  Special Functions

Certain other functions shown in Figure 9–4 are also included in the FORTRAN libraries. The type conversion functions INT, NINT and REAL are used to change the type of an argument. This type conversion, of course, can also be accomplished with a replacement statement in which the type of the expression on the right is different from that of the variable on the left. The type conversion functions allow this operation to be performed within an arithmetic expression.

*Example 1*

The INTeger function converts to integer type, truncating any fractional part.
If A = 3. and B = 2. then INT(A/B) + INT(A/4.) = 1 + 0 = 1

Some functions such as the transfer of sign (SIGN) and positive difference (DIM) functions require two arguments. SIGN (x,y) is equal to the absolute value of x times the sign of y while the value of DIM (x,y) is x − y if that difference is positive, zero otherwise.

*Example 2*

| Function Reference | Value | Function Reference | Value |
|---|---|---|---|
| SIGN(3, −2) | −3 | DIM(3, −2) | 5 |
| SIGN(3,2) | 3 | DIM(3.,2.5) | 0.5 |
| SIGN(−3., −2.) | −3. | DIM(−3, −2) | 0 |
| SIGN(−3,2) | 3 | DIM(−3.,2.) | 0. |

Some other functions may have any number of arguments; the functions that return the largest and smallest of a sequence of arguments require at least two arguments, all of the same type.

*Example 3*   Suppose J = 3 and K = −2

| Function Reference | Value |
|---|---|
| MIN (3,9,7, −1,4) | −1 |
| MAX (3.,9.,7., −1.,4.) | 9. |
| MIN (J, K, J*K,J+K) | −6 |
| MAX (J,K,J*K,J +K,14) | 14 |

**FIGURE 9-4**    OTHER FORTRAN-SUPPLIED FUNCTIONS

| *Function* | *Purpose* | *Form* | *Argument* | *Value* | *Example* |
|---|---|---|---|---|---|
| Mode conversion | Conversion to integer (truncation of fractional part) | INT(X) | 1 real<br>1 integer<br>1 complex | integer | INT(3.6)=3<br>INT(-2.5)=-2<br>INT(-3.79)=-3 |
| | Rounding to nearest integer | NINT(X) | 1 real | integer | NINT(7.3)=7<br>NINT(-7.5)=-8 |
| | Conversion to real | REAL(X) | 1 real<br>1 integer<br>1 complex | real | REAL(2)=2.<br>REAL(3.2)=3.2 |
| | Character conversion to integer value | ICHAR | 1 character*1 | integer | ICHAR('A')=65<br>(ASCII CODE) |
| | Integer conversion to character value | CHAR | 1 integer | character*1 | CHAR(65)='A'<br>(ASCII CODE) |
| Truncation to real | | AINT(X) | 1 real | real | AINT(7.4)=7.<br>AINT(-2.5)=-2. |
| Rounding to nearest real integer | | ANINT(X) | 1 real | real | ANINT(.1)=0.<br>ANINT(-1.5)=-2. |
| Positive difference | Whichever of the following two values is larger:<br>$x_1 - x_2$ or 0 | DIM(X1,X2) | 2 real<br>2 integer | real<br>integer | DIM(3.2,1.0)=2.2<br>DIM(1,3)=0 |
| Remainder | Remainder $= x_1 - \text{INT}(\frac{x_1}{x_2}) * x_2$<br><br>(remainder of $\frac{17}{5} = 2$) | MOD(X1,X2) | 2 real<br>2 integer | real<br>integer | MOD(6,4)=2<br>MOD(6.,5.)=1.<br>MOD(-5,3)=-2<br>MOD(-7.5,2.)=-1.5<br>MOD(4.123,1.)=.123 |
| Transfer of sign | $\|x_1\|$ if $x_2 \geq 0$<br>$-\|x_1\|$ if $x_2 < 0$ | SIGN(X1,X2) | 2 real<br>2 integer | real<br>integer | SIGN(2,-3)=-2<br>SIGN(-2,-3)=-2<br>SIGN(-4.,2.)=4.0 |
| Choose largest value | Largest of $(x_1, x_2, ..., x_n)$ | MAX(X1,X2,...) | $\geq$ 2 real<br>$\geq$ 2 integer | real<br>integer | MAX(-1.,-2.,-3.)=-1.<br>MAX(-2,7,3)=7 |
| Choose smallest value | Least of $(x_1, x_2, ..., x_n)$ | MIN(X1,X2,...) | $\geq$ 2 real<br>$\geq$ 2 integer | real<br>integer | MIN(0,-1,3)= 1<br>MIN(10.,3.1,1.)=1. |

The following functions determine the order relationship between characters according to the collating sequence in use by the computing system (ASCII or EBCDIC codes)

| | | | | | |
|---|---|---|---|---|---|
| Lexically $\geq$ | True if $x_1 \geq x_2$ | LGE(X1,X2) | 2 character*n | logical | LGE('B','A')=.TRUE. |
| Lexically $>$ | True if $x_1 > x_2$ | LGT(X1,X2) | 2 character*n | logical | LGT(WORD,'HI')=? |
| Lexically $\leq$ | True if $x_1 \leq x_2$ | LLE(X1,X2) | 2 character*n | logical | LLE('a','A')=.FALSE.<br>(ASCII CODE) |
| Lexically $<$ | True if $x_1 < x_2$ | LLT(X1,X2) | 2 character*n | logical | LLT('5','R')=.TRUE.<br>(ASCII CODE) |

### 9-2-5 Do It Now

**1.** Write a single FORTRAN statement for each of the following:

    a. Place the largest value of a one-dimensional array A of length 5 into variable X.
    b. Compute the remainder after dividing X by Y.
    c. Compute the square root of integer variable I.

**2.** What will be the value of each of the following expressions if $A = -3.$ and $B = 4.$?

    a. INT (A)
    b. SIGN (A,B)
    c. DIM (A,B)

    d. MAX (A, 2.*A, B)
    e. MIN (A, 2.*A, B)
    f. MOD (B,A)

**3.** What will be the values of the following expressions?

    a. INT(0.5)
    b. INT(1.9)
    c. INT(−1.5)
    d. INT(1−2.9)
    e. REAL(−5)
    f. NINT(−1.1)
    g. NINT(−0.75)
    h. AINT(0.7)
    i. AINT(−1.5)

    j. ANINT(0.6)
    k. ANINT(−2.5)
    l. CHAR(ICHAR'A')
    m. ICHAR(CHAR(65))
    n. MOD(17,13)
    o. MOD(2.14,1.)
    p. MAX(ABS(−1.3),2.,ABS(2.1))
    q. MIN(−1,−3,NINT(−2.5))
    r. LLT('Z','A')
    s. LGT('NEWARK','NEW YORK')

**4.** The date for any Easter Sunday in any year can be computed as follows (let Y be the year):

    Let A be the remainder of the division of Y by 19.
    Let B be the remainder of the division of Y by 4.
    Let C be the remainder of the division of Y by 7.
    Let D be the remainder of the division of (19A + 24) by 30.
    Let E be the remainder of the division of (2B + 4C + 6D + 5) by 7.

The date for Easter Sunday is March (22 + D + E), which may give a date in April. Write the code to read a year and determine its Easter date.

### *Answers*

**1.**  a. `X = MAX(A(1),A(2),A(3),A(4),A(5))`
    b. `R = MOD(X,Y)`
    c. `X = SQRT(REAL(I))`

**2.**  a. −3
    b. 3.
    c. 0.

    d. 4.
    e. −6.
    f. 1.

**3.**

| | | | |
|---|---|---|---|
| a. 0 | f. −1 | k. −3.0 | p. 2.1 |
| b. 1 | g. −1 | l. 'A' | q. −3 |
| c. −1 | h. 0.0 | m. 65 | r. .FALSE. |
| d. −1 | i. −1.0 | n. 4 | s. .FALSE. |
| e. −5. | j. 1.0 | o. 0.14 | |

```
4.   IMPLICIT INTEGER(A-Z)
     READ(*,1)YEAR
     A = MOD(YEAR,19)
     B = MOD(YEAR,4)
     C = MOD(YEAR,7)
     D = MOD(19*A+24,30)
     E = MOD(2*B+4*C+6*D+5,7)
     R = 22 + D + E
     IF(R.GT.31)THEN
        R = R-31
        PRINT*,'EASTER SUNDAY IS APRIL',R
     ELSE
        PRINT*,'EASTER SUNDAY IS MARCH',R
     ENDIF
     STOP
```

## 9-3 Programming Examples

### 9-3-1 Prime Numbers

The program in Figure 9–5 provides a list of all the prime numbers between 5 and 10,000. A prime number is a number that is evenly divisible only by 1 and by itself. To determine whether a number N is prime, it suffices to check whether N is divisible by any integer up to the integer value of $\sqrt{N}$. For example, to determine whether 43 is prime one needs only to check if 43 is divisible by 2, 3, 4, 5, or 6.

Notice the use of the REAL function to make the argument of the square root function a real argument. Also note the use of the MOD function to determine whether I (possible prime candidate) is divisible by J. If I is divisible by J, then I is not prime.

**FIGURE 9-5**   LIST OF PRIME NUMBERS

```
     DO 5 I = 5,10000,2          Skip all even numbers.
        K = SQRT(REAL(I))        Determine √I. Argument of SQRT must be real.
        DO 4 J = 3,K,2
           IF(MOD(I,J).EQ.0)GO TO 5   Check if I is divisible by any integer
   4    CONTINUE                      up to and possibly including √I.
        WRITE(6,31)I               Number is prime; print it.
  5 CONTINUE
     STOP
 31 FORMAT(1X,I6)
     END
```

### 9-3-2 Break-Even Analysis

Systems analysts at the XYZ Company computed the revenue function associated with the manufacture and marketing of a new company product. A cost function was also projected for that product. The functions are as follows:

Revenue function:   $y = 15xe^{-x/3} + 0.5$

Cost function:   $y = \dfrac{x^3}{16} - \dfrac{x^2}{2} + \dfrac{7x}{4} + 4$

Determine the breakeven point(s) graphically.

A solution to the problem is shown in Figure 9–6. Note that

$$y = \frac{x^3}{16} - \frac{x^2}{2} + \frac{7x}{4} + 4 = \frac{x^3 - 8x^2 + 28x + 64}{16}$$

The numerator of this expression is then factored to yield $((x - 8)x + 28)x + 64$. This form of the cost function expression is more efficient in terms of computations, since it contains only two multiplications and one division as opposed to four and three, respectively, in the original cost function. The cost and revenue functions are graphed for values of $x$ ranging from 0 to 12.

In Figure 9–6, the array LINE is used to print each line of the graph. This array is initially filled with 70 blanks. The integer value J of the revenue function and the integer value L of the cost function are then computed for X = 0,1,2,..., 12. Each time, the graphic symbols R and C are inserted in positions J and L of the array LINE, then the array is printed.

### 9-3-3   A Graph of the TAN Function

Figure 9–7 shows a program that produces a rough graph of the function $y = \tan x$ in the interval $0, 5\pi/2$ for values of $x$ in steps of 0.2 radian. Special precautions must be taken, however, since in that interval $\tan x$ is $\mp \infty$ at $\pi/2$, $3\pi/2$ and $5\pi/2$ as shown:

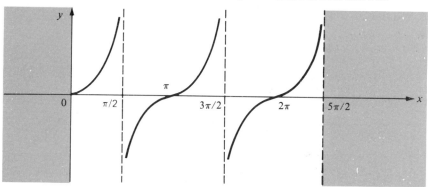

We must decide what portion of the graph we want to retain, since we cannot graph all those points close to the asymptotes. We might decide, as in the program of Figure 9–7, to graph only those points that fall in the area where $y$ lies between $-9$ and $9$. Then, when writing the program, we must test the values for $y$ and graph only those points falling in the restricted area.

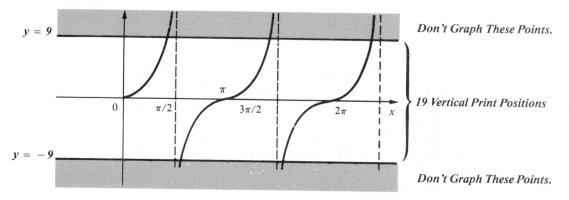

**FIGURE 9-6** A BREAKEVEN ANALYSIS

```
C GRAPHICAL BREAK-EVEN ANALYSIS
C    LINE(70): ARRAY WHICH PRINTS EACH LINE WITH GRAPHIC SYMBOLS
C    R:   VALUE OF THE EXPONENTIAL FUNCTION
C    C:   VALUE OF THE POLYNOMIAL FUNCTION
C    J:   ROUNDED INTEGER VALUE OF THE EXPONENTIAL FUNCTION
C    L:   ROUNDED VALUE OF THE POLYNOMIAL VALUE FUNCTION
C    X:   GRADUATION UNITS FOR THE X AXIS
C
      CHARACTER LINE(70)*1
      REAL R, C
      INTEGER J, L, X
      DATA LINE/70*' '/                   Initialize line to be printed to blanks.
      WRITE(6,10)
      DO 6 X = 0, 12
         C = (((X - 8.)*X + 28.)*X + 64.)/16.
         R = 15.*X*EXP(-X/3.) + .5
         J = R + .5
         L = C + .5
         LINE(J) = 'R'                    Insert graphic symbols in line to be printed
         LINE(L) = 'C'
         WRITE(6,11)X, R, C, LINE
         LINE(J) = ' '                    Replace graphic symbols by blank characters
         LINE(L) = ' '                    to blank out the LINE array.
6     CONTINUE
      STOP
10    FORMAT(' X    REVENUE    COST'/)
11    FORMAT(I3,4X,F4.1,4X,F4.1,12X,70A1)
      END
```

| X | REVENUE | COST |
|---|---------|------|
| 0 | .5 | 4.0 |
| 1 | 11.2 | 5.0 |
| 2 | 15.9 | 6.0 |
| 3 | 17.1 | 6.0 |
| 4 | 16.3 | 7.0 |
| 5 | 14.7 | 8.0 |
| 6 | 12.7 | 10.0 |
| 7 | 10.7 | 13.0 |
| 8 | 8.8 | 18.0 |
| 9 | 7.2 | 24.0 |
| 10 | 5.9 | 34.0 |
| 11 | 4.7 | 45.0 |
| 12 | 3.8 | 61.0 |

$y = 15xe^{-x/3}$

$y = \dfrac{x^3}{16} - \dfrac{x^2}{2} + \dfrac{7x}{4} + 4$

First break-even point

Second break-even point

$x$ axis

Since graphs are printed on the printer output form with the $y$ axis horizontal and the $x$ axis vertical, only 19 print positions ($-9$ to 9) could be used to print $y = \tan(x)$. To avoid negative values, we add 9 to $\tan x$ to neutralize the $y$ range $-9$ to 0; this means that the range of $\tan x + 9$ is now 0 to 18. To spread out the graph over more than 19 positions on the line we multiply the range 0–18 by 4 with the expression $4(\tan x + 9)$. This gives us a range of 73 print positions in which to insert the graphic symbol '*' ($4 \times 18 = 72 + 1$). The graph is then drawn one horizontal line at a time using the array LINE to print a line that is blank except for the graphic character * inserted at position $4(\tan x + 9)$. For example

*Example:*

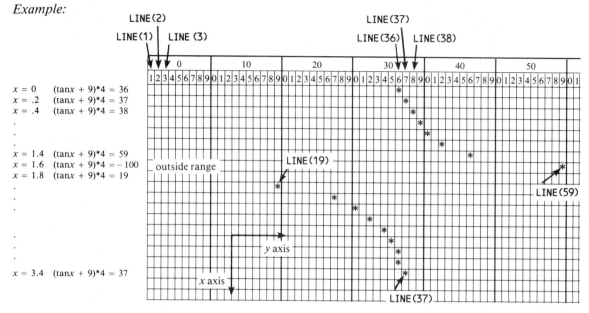

$x = 0$  $(\tan x + 9)*4 = 36$
$x = .2$  $(\tan x + 9)*4 = 37$
$x = .4$  $(\tan x + 9)*4 = 38$
.
.
$x = 1.4$  $(\tan x + 9)*4 = 59$
$x = 1.6$  $(\tan x + 9)*4 = -100$
$x = 1.8$  $(\tan x + 9)*4 = 19$
.
.
.
.
$x = 3.4$  $(\tan x + 9)*4 = 37$

In Figure 9–7, the variable J is used to place the asterisk at the Jth position in the array LINE (the asterisk will be in LINE(J)). If J is zero or negative or J ≥ 72, the asterisk cannot be graphed, since it is outside the designated interval 1–72 for the array LINE.

## 9-4  Subprograms

Subprograms are powerful, convenient, and at times necessary programming tools to help you better structure, document, code, test, and debug your programs. This section will discuss function subprograms, while chapter 10 will discuss subroutine subprograms.

### 9-4-1  Program Structure: Modularity

One way to improve the structure of a program is to decompose the original problem or task to be solved into independent subtasks and then execute these subtasks in a predefined sequence. In the process, you must clearly identify each subtask, document each subtask, and show the order in which these subtasks are to be executed. Such a well-organized plan results in code that is easier to write, follow, test, and debug and is easier for others to read. You will also find that you will use the GOTO statement less frequently. This in itself is very important, since the undisciplined use of the GOTO statement often gives rise to the "spaghetti code syndrome," which makes it very difficult for the program reader to remember where in the program he/she is coming from and where he/she is going! Mr. E. W. Dijkstra, who played a critical role in the formulation and early development of structured program design, was an outspoken critic of the GOTO statement and felt that the GOTO statement should be abolished from all higher level programming languages. Breaking a program into subtasks or subprograms, however, minimizes the need for the GOTO statement and improves the clarity and readability of the resulting code.

Decomposing a problem into smaller pieces, modules, or subprograms allows you to focus more easily on a particular part of the problem without worrying about the overall problem. The tasks become easier to solve and are much more manageable when each per-

**FIGURE 9-7**    GRAPH OF THE SCALED TANGENT FUNCTION

```
C GRAPH OF THE TANGENT FUNCTION
C   LINE: LINE CONTAINING THE GRAPHIC SYMBOLS
C
        CHARACTER LINE(72)
        DATA LINE/72*'.'/                    Initialize LINE array to dots.
        WRITE(6,3)
        X = 0.0
10      IF(X .GT. 8.) STOP
          Y = TAN(X)
          J = (Y + 9.)*4. + .5
          IF(J.LT 1  OR. J.GT.72) THEN       Check for points that cannot be graphed
            WRITE(6,15) X, Y, J               because they are outside the range 0-72.
          ELSE
            LINE(J) = '*'
            WRITE(6,15) X, Y, J, LINE
          ENDIF
          LINE(J) = '.'                       Reset line aray to all dots.
          X = X + .2
          GO TO 10
3       FORMAT(3X,'X',7X,'Y',5X,'J')
15      FORMAT(1X,F4.1,2X,F6.2,2X,I4,3X,72A1)
        END
```

|   |  X   |   Y    |   J  |
|---|------|--------|------|
|         | .0   |  .00   |  36  |
|         | .2   |  .20   |  37  |
|         | .4   |  .42   |  38  |
|         | .6   |  .68   |  39  |
|         | .8   | 1.03   |  40  |
|         | 1.0  | 1.56   |  42  |
|         | 1.2  | 2.57   |  46  |
| $\pi/2$ | 1.4  | 5.80   |  59  |
|         | 1.6  | -34.23 | -100 |
|         | 1.8  | 4.29   |  19  |
|         | 2.0  | -2.19  |  27  |
|         | 2.2  | -1.37  |  31  |
|         | 2.4  | -.92   |  32  |
|         | 2.6  | -.60   |  34  |
|         | 2.8  | -.36   |  35  |
| $\pi$   | 3.0  | -.14   |  35  |
|         | 3.2  | .06    |  36  |
|         | 3.4  | .26    |  37  |
|         | 3.6  | .49    |  38  |
|         | 3.8  | .77    |  39  |
|         | 4.0  | 1.16   |  41  |
|         | 4.2  | 1.78   |  43  |
|         | 4.4  | 3.10   |  48  |
| $\frac{3\pi}{2}$ | 4.6 | 8.86 | 71 |
|         | 4.8  | -11.38 |  -9  |
|         | 5.0  | -3.38  |  22  |
|         | 5.2  | 1.89   |  28  |
|         | 5.4  | -1.22  |  31  |
|         | 5.6  | -.81   |  33  |
|         | 5.8  | -.52   |  34  |
|         | 6.0  | -.29   |  35  |
| $2\pi$  | 6.2  | -.08   |  36  |
|         | 6.4  | .12    |  36  |
|         | 6.6  | .33    |  37  |
|         | 6.8  | .57    |  38  |
|         | 7.0  | .87    |  39  |
|         | 7.2  | 1.30   |  41  |
|         | 7.4  | 2.05   |  44  |
|         | 7.6  | 3.85   |  51  |
| $\frac{5\pi}{2}$ | 7.8 | 18.51 | 110 |
|         | 8.0  | -6.80  |  9   |

forms a very specific function. Typically, you can code each module independently of the others and even test and debug each module separately. Once all modules are working properly, you can link them together by writing the coordinating code (generally called the root segment or the main code), which specifies the order in which the modules are to be executed. In essence, the coordinating code activates the various modules in a predetermined sequence. These principles are illustrated in Figure 9–8. Note that the resulting problem consists of 5 modules: the coordinating module and the four subtask modules A, B, C, and D. It is, of course, possible that a particular module itself might be broken down into other modules.

By breaking down a problem into independent modules, a programmer in charge of a very complex problem can easily assign various members of his/her team the responsibility for developing one or more modules. Such modules can then be run and tested independently. (Making one change in one module is a very local intervention that does not require an understanding of all other modules. On the other hand, making one change in a non-modular program, held together by myriads of GOTO statements, not only requires an understanding of the whole program but can well result in dramatic repercussions throughout the program; these in turn can produce masses of error messages as well as unwanted output!) When all modules are completed, they can be joined together to form the complete program, which can then be tested. In FORTRAN such modules are referred to as subprograms.

In a modular environment, each module can be respecified as a sequence of smaller modules describing what is to be done at increasing levels of detail. This technique of expanding a program plan into levels of detailed subplans is sometimes referred to as *top-down* design, where the structure of the program is presented as a hierarchy of tasks. A hierarchy chart, sometimes called a structure diagram, is a useful tool to illustrate module relationships and hierarchies. Figure 9–9 shows a hierarchy chart for the problem of Figure 9–8.

**FIGURE 9-8**   PROGRAM DECOMPOSITION

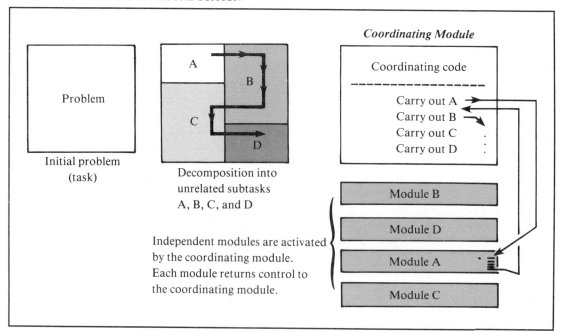

**FIGURE 9-9** A STRUCTURED DIAGRAM

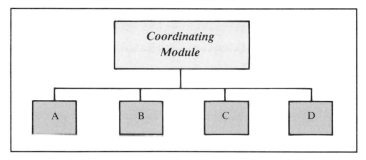

## 9-4-2 Do It Now

In the problem of Figure 9–8, assume module B requires module X, which requires module P, and assume that module C requires 2 different modules Y and Z. Draw the corresponding structured diagram.

*Answer*

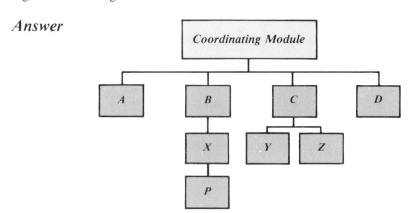

## 9-4-3 Programming Example

Professor X agrees with her students at the beginning of the semester on the way in which their final grades will be determined. If the average of their three test scores (6 weeks test, 12 weeks test, and final) is higher than their final, that average becomes their semester grade; otherwise their score on the final is their final grade. (They pass if their semester grade is more than 70 and fail otherwise.)

Let us write a program to read an input file consisting of student records (each record contains three test scores) to determine each student's best score combination and final grade. We will also determine the letter grade for the class as a whole, i.e., the letter grade based on the average of the students' semester grades. The output will have the following form:

| STUDENT NAME | TEST1 | TEST2 | FINAL | SEMESTER GRADE | LETTER GRADE |
|---|---|---|---|---|---|
| DENTON | 30 | 90 | 80 | 80.0 | PASS |
| AMAURY | 90 | 80 | 70 | 80.0 | PASS |
| MALLORY | 100 | 20 | 60 | 60.0 | FAIL |
| MANARIN | 80 | 80 | 70 | 76.7 | PASS |

CLASS LETTER GRADE = PASS

We will organize our program by dividing it into three parts:

1. The main program, which will coordinate the use of the other two parts (subprograms).

2. A function subprogram called BEST that will determine the student's best score combination.

3. A function subprogram called LETTER that will determine whether grades will be pass or fail.

The structured diagram for the program of Figure 9–10 is

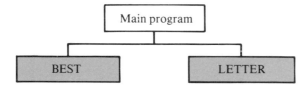

The complete program is shown in Figures 9–10 and 9–11. Both solve the problem, but Figure 9–11 is fully documented with a data dictionary, while Figure 9–10 explains how the functions work. Notice how the functions BEST and LETTER are used in the main program and how their arguments are used in the function subprograms to carry out the desired computations.

In the main program, the statement AV = BEST(T1,T2,FINAL) sets up the internal linkage to communicate (send values to and from the calling and called program) between two distinct areas of memory—one containing the main program and the other containing the BEST subprogram.

The reader should understand that the arguments S1, S2, and S3 specified in FUNCTION BEST (S1, S2, S3) refer to the same memory locations as T1, T2, and FINAL defined in the main program. Different names can be used, since the person writing the subprogram may not be the one writing the main program. For example, in the case of the square root function the user might refer to the argument X for SQRT(X) or to the argument TEMP for SQRT(TEMP), and so forth, but the internal name of the argument used by the SQRT function is known only to its author!

The correspondence between arguments can be visualized as follows:

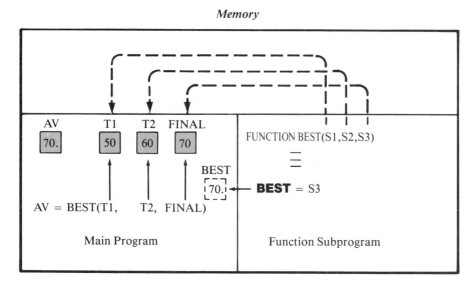

**FIGURE 9-10**    FUNCTION SUBPROGRAM PROBLEM

```
      CHARACTER GRADE*4, CLASS*4, NAME*8
      INTEGER T1, T2, FINAL, N
      REAL AV, SUM
C FUNCTIONS USED
      CHARACTER*4 LETTER
      REAL BEST
      DATA SUM, N/0., 0/
C
      WRITE(6,1)
    5 READ(5,2,END=88)NAME,T1,T2,FINAL
        N = N + 1
        AV = BEST(T1, T2, FINAL)
        SUM = SUM + AV
        GRADE = LETTER(AV)
        WRITE(6,3)NAME,T1,T2,FINAL,AV,GRADE
        GO TO 5
   88 CLASS = LETTER(SUM/N)
      WRITE(6,4)CLASS
      STOP
C
    1 FORMAT(' STUDENT   TEST1  TEST2  FINAL  SEMESTER  LETTER'/
     A       '  NAME                          GRADE   GRADE'/)
    2 FORMAT(A8,3I3)
    3 FORMAT(1X,A8,2X,I3,4X,I3,4X,I3,5X,F5.1,5X,A4)
    4 FORMAT('0CLASS LETTER GRADE = ',A4)
      END
```

N counts the number of students.

T1, T2, FINAL are the arguments passed to the function to compute the student's semester average.

LETTER is a function that will return either a PASS or a FAIL depending on whether the student's average is greater than 70.

Find the letter grade for the entire class. Note that SUM/N is a valid argument.

Write the letter grade for the class as a whole.

```
      REAL FUNCTION BEST(S1,S2,S3)
      INTEGER S1, S2, S3
      BEST = (S1 + S2 + S3)/3.
      IF(BEST .LE. S3) BEST = S3
      RETURN
      END
```

BEST determines a student's best score combination, either the final score or the average of the three scores. S1, S2, and S3 are the same as T1, T2, and FINAL. They are just different variable names referring to the same memory locations.

If the average of the scores is less than the final, the final score is passed on to the main program, otherwise the average is passed on. Note how the name of the function BEST is used to communicate the result to the main program.

The key word RETURN is used to pass control back to the main program.

```
      CHARACTER*4 FUNCTION LETTER(A)
      LETTER = 'PASS'
      IF(A .LE. 70.) LETTER = 'FAIL'
      RETURN
      END
```

LETTER returns either 'PASS' or 'FAIL' to the main program.

This function is called from two different locations in the main program, the first time to compute the letter grade for each student and the second time to compute the overall class average.

```
STUDENT    TEST1   TEST2   FINAL   SEMESTER   LETTER
NAME                               GRADE      GRADE

DENTON      30      90      80      80.0       PASS
AMAURY      90      80      70      80.0       PASS
MALLORY    100      20      60      60.0       FAIL
MANARIN     80      80      70      76.7       PASS

CLASS LETTER GRADE = PASS
```

**Input File**

| *Name* | *T1* | *T2* | *Final* |
|--------|------|------|---------|
| DENTON | 030090080 | | |
| AMAURY | 090080070 | | |
| MALLORY | 100020060 | | |
| MANARIN | 080080070 | | |

**FIGURE 9-11**  FUNCTION SUBPROGRAM EXAMPLE

```
C FUNCTION SUBPROGRAM EXAMPLE
C   T1, T2, FINAL: 1ST, 2ND AND FINAL TEST SCORES
C   GRADE: LETTER GRADE FOR SEMESTER (PASS OR FAIL)
C   AV:    STUDENT'S SEMESTER GRADE (FINAL OR (T1+T2+FINAL)/3)
C   CLASS: LETTER GRADE FOR ENTIRE CLASS (AVERAGE OF ALL AV'S)
C   N:     TOTAL NUMBER OF STUDENTS
C   NAME:  STUDENT NAME
C   LETTER: RETURNS LETTER GRADE FOR EACH STUDENT AND FOR CLASS
C
      CHARACTER GRADE*4, CLASS*4, NAME*8
      INTEGER T1, T2, FINAL, N
      REAL AV, SUM
C FUNCTIONS USED
      CHARACTER*4 LETTER
      REAL BEST
      DATA SUM, N/0., 0/
C
      WRITE(6,1)
5     READ(5,2,END=88)NAME,T1,T2,FINAL
         N = N + 1
         AV =  BEST(T1, T2, FINAL)
         SUM = SUM + AV
         GRADE = LETTER(AV)
         WRITE(6,3)NAME,T1,T2,FINAL,AV,GRADE
         GO TO 5
88    CLASS = LETTER(SUM/N)
      WRITE(6,4)CLASS
      STOP
C
1     FORMAT(' STUDENT   TEST1   TEST2   FINAL   SEMESTER   LETTER'/
     A        '  NAME                              GRADE     GRADE'/)
2     FORMAT(A8,3I3)
3     FORMAT(1X,A8,2X,I3,4X,I3,4X,I3,5X,F5.1,5X,A4)
4     FORMAT('0CLASS LETTER GRADE = ',A4)
      END
C
C FUNCTION BEST TO COMPUTE STUDENT'S SEMESTER GRADE
C   S1, S2, S3: REPRESENT T1, T2 AND FINAL
C   AV:         STUDENT'S AVERAGE SCORE (T1+T2+T3)/3
C   BEST        EITHER EQUALS TO FINAL OR (T1+T2+T3)/3
      REAL FUNCTION BEST (S1, S2, S3)
      INTEGER S1, S2, S3)
      BEST = (S1 + S2 + S3)/3.
      IF(BEST .LE. S3) BEST = S3
      RETURN
      END
C
C FUNCTION LETTER TO DETERMINE STUDENT'S LETTER GRADE
C   A:     STUDENT'S SEMESTER GRADE
C   LETTER: GETS PASS IF BEST > 70 , FAIL OTHERWISE
      CHARACTER*4 FUNCTION LETTER(A)
      LETTER = 'PASS'
      IF(A .LE. 70) LETTER = 'FAIL'
      RETURN
      END
```

| STUDENT NAME | TEST1 | TEST2 | FINAL | SEMESTER GRADE | LETTER GRADE |
|---|---|---|---|---|---|
| DENTON | 30 | 90 | 80 | 80.0 | PASS |
| AMAURY | 90 | 80 | 70 | 80.0 | PASS |
| MALLORY | 100 | 20 | 60 | 60.0 | FAIL |
| MANARIN | 80 | 80 | 70 | 76.7 | PASS |

CLASS LETTER GRADE = PASS

**Input File**

| Name | T1 | T2 | Final |
|---|---|---|---|
| ↓ | | | |
| DENTON | 030090080 | | |
| AMAURY | 090080070 | | |
| MALLORY | 100020060 | | |
| MANARIN | 080080070 | | |

Note that if for some reason any of the arguments S1, S2, or S3 are changed in the subprogram, the corresponding argument T1, T2, or FINAL would also change in the main program, since S1 refers to the same memory location as T1, and so forth. To understand the return mechanism from the subprogram to the main program, the user should think of BEST as a memory location defined in the main program. The subprogram causes the value of the function (either S3 or (S1 + S2 + S3)/3) to be stored in that memory location (BEST). Note that any reference to BEST in the main program must include arguments, since BEST is a function name.

Since a function returns a particular value to the calling program, the value returned can be integer, real, double precision, logical, complex, or character type. For that reason the function itself should be typed. In Figure 9–10 we have typed LETTER as CHARACTER*4 since that function returns a 4-character value; likewise the function BEST has been typed REAL since BEST returns an average. If the function is *not* typed, then the value returned is either integer or real as defined implicitly by the name of the function. It is good practice to always type functions just as we have always typed variables and array names. The function names should be typed in the function program and in the program that uses them.

Through the function call statement, data is passed from one program to another by means of the arguments specified in the function call statement and in the FUNCTION definition statement. The flowpath between the three blocks of code or programs is illustrated in Figure 9–12.

**FIGURE 9-12**    FLOWPATH BETWEEN A MAIN PROGRAM AND FUNCTION SUBPROGRAMS

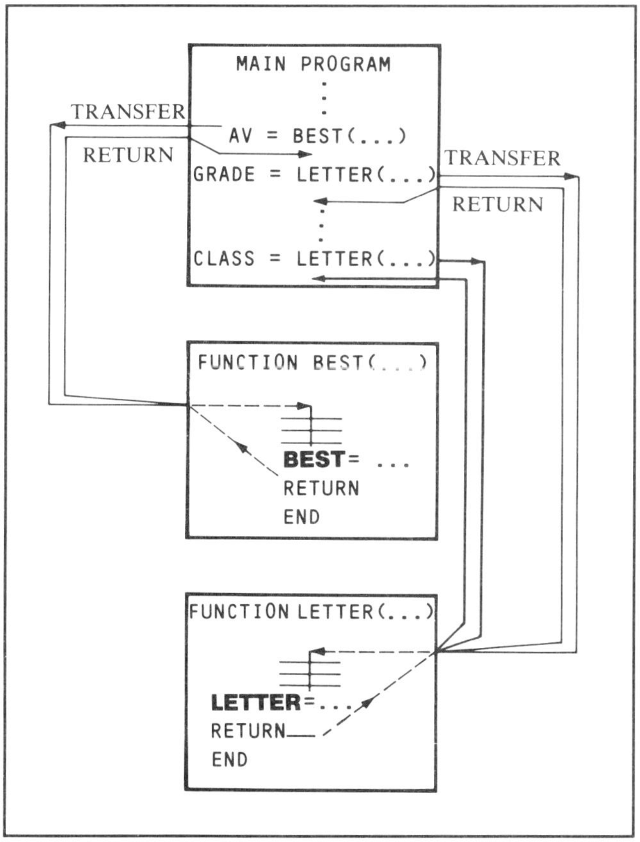

Notice how it is possible to avoid duplication of code through the use of functions. Whenever a task is to be performed, a transfer is made to that task; when the task is completed, it returns control to the program that called it. In the program in Figure 9–10, the task to determine the letter grade needs to be done at two different places in the program, once to compute the letter grade for each student and again to compute the overall class letter grade when all records have been read. Instead of writing the code to determine the letter grade every time it is needed, one block of code is written to perform this task, then it can be called any number of times by the main program (or even by other subprograms).

### 9-4-4 Function Subprograms

One form of a programmer-defined function is the function subprogram. Another form is the arithmetic statement function, which will be discussed in section 9–5. The function subprogram can be a separately compiled program that can be executed by another program. The prefix *sub-* in subprogram implies that the function subprogram is not really a complete program; if it were executed by itself it would not produce meaningful results. Function subprograms are usually written to carry out generalized procedures that are data-independent, for example, determining the largest element of any array, computing the average or the standard deviation of any set of grades, and so forth. Arguments (sometimes called *dummy* arguments because they are used as place holders) are used to illustrate the way in which the task (function) is to be carried out. These arguments in turn must be specified by the program that uses the function, for example, the program must name the array (argument would be a score array) whose largest score is to be found, or specify the number of scores (argument would be the number) for which an average is to be calculated.

A function subprogram should be viewed as one logical component (module) of a total program that might consist of numerous other logical components (subprograms).

Function subprograms can be catalogued in the system or user libraries if these functions are to be shared by other users or used repeatedly by the programmer (in the same way as the mathematical functions are stored in libraries). They can also be part of the job-stream, i.e., part of the job that is submitted each time the program is to be run. Functions can be accessed or executed from another program (main program or other subprograms) by using the name of the function and specifying a list of arguments.

### 9-4-5 The Function Invocation Statement

The general form of a function invocation statement is:

$$\textit{function name } (a_1, a_2, a_3, \ldots, a_n)$$

where *function name* is the name of the function (any valid variable name) and $a_1, a_2, a_3, \ldots, a_n$ are arguments to be passed to the function subprogram. These arguments can be variables, subscripted variable names, array names, constants, expressions, or function names. The value of the function is returned through the name of the function (acting as a variable). If not typed, the value returned by the function is implicitly typed by the function name. If the name begins with I,J,K,L,M, or N, the function value is integer; otherwise it is real.

Consider the following examples:

```
X = 3.*SUB(Y)/SAM + 3.6          One argument is passed to the function.
AX = A(T,J,3) + B(X**2,1.5)      The function A has three arguments, while
                                 the function B has two arguments.
IF(TRAP(X,K) - 8.3)THEN ...      The function TRAP is part of an IF state-
                                 ment. It is first evaluated and its value is
                                 compared to 8.3.
Z = S1(A,R(1),3*I + K,J)         S1 has four arguments.
T = SUB2(SIN(X),Y) - SUB2(3.1,0.0)  Arguments can be functions, too.
```

The reader may wonder how the compiler differentiates between a function and a reference to an array. For example, B(3) could be a reference to a function or to an element of the array B. If the variable B is typed as an array, then B is an array; if B is not typed as an array, the compiler will treat any reference to B as a reference to a function subprogram even though the user may never have defined a function B (after the compilation process an error will occur when the system tries to locate the function B in its libraries and cannot find such a function!).

### 9-4-6 The FUNCTION Definition Statement and the RETURN Statement

The first statement in every function subprogram must be the FUNCTION statement. The general form of this statement is:

> [*type*] FUNCTION *function name* $(p_1, p_2, p_3, \ldots, p_n)$

where *function name* is the name of the function, and

$p_1, p, p_3, \ldots, p_n$ are dummy arguments used to pass the data to and from the calling program. These arguments can either be variable names, expressions, array names, or function names. Subscripted variables and constants are not permitted as arguments in the function definition (they are permitted in the function invocation statement, however).

*type* is an optimal parameter that specifies the mode of the value returned by the function. Functions can be typed as REAL, INTEGER, CHARACTER, DOUBLE PRECISION, COMPLEX, and LOGICAL. It is a good practice to always type the function both in the subprogram and in the program using the function. If type is omitted, the function value is implicitly defined by the function name. If the name starts with I,J,K,L,M, or N, the value is integer; otherwise, it is real.

The dummy arguments used in the subprogram are dummy names for the actual arguments listed in the invocation statement. When the function is executed, the dummy arguments take on the values of the "real" arguments specified in the calling program. More precisely, the function directly processes the real arguments through the dummy arguments.

**The arguments in the invocation statement should correspond in number, order, and type with the dummy arguments of the FUNCTION statement.** The argument names used may be the same or different. The order of the arguments in the invocation statement and in the FUNCTION statement must be the same; that is, there must be a one-to-one correspondence between the two sets of arguments.

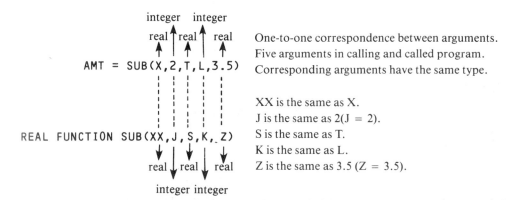

One-to-one correspondence between arguments.
Five arguments in calling and called program.
Corresponding arguments have the same type.

XX is the same as X.
J is the same as 2(J = 2).
S is the same as T.
K is the same as L.
Z is the same as 3.5 (Z = 3.5).

If an argument in a function subprogram is an array name, the array name must be declared in a DIMENSION or type statement in the function subprogram.

The value of the function that is computed in the function subprogram is passed or transmitted back to the calling program by setting the function name all by itself (no arguments) equal to that value (*name of function* = *value*) and then returning to the calling program by means of the RETURN statement. The RETURN statement returns control to the statement in the calling program where the invocation was made. Many RETURN statements can be included in a function subprogram. A distinguishing feature of the function subprogram is that at its conclusion the statement to which the return is made is variable (unlike the GO TO statement). The return point depends on which statement called (invoked) the function.

The last statement in every function subprogram must be the END statement. Some examples of function subprograms follow.

*Example 1*    Function ALARG returns the larger value of any two arguments.

| **Calling Program** | **Function Subprogram** |
|---|---|
| . | REAL FUNCTION **ALARG**(A,B) |
| . | REAL A,B |
| Z = ALARG(X,Y) | IF(A .GT. B) THEN |
| WRITE(6,3)Z | **ALARG** = A |
| . | ELSE |
| . | **ALARG** = B |
| IF(ALARG(Z,T).LT.3.1)THEN... | ENDIF |
| | RETURN |
| | END |

*Example 2*

| | |
|---|---|
| REAL QUIZZ | REAL FUNCTION **QUIZZ**(J,K,L) |
| : | INTEGER J,K,L |
| : | **QUIZZ** = (J + K + L)/3. |
| IF(QUIZZ(30,40,50).GT.T)THEN | RETURN |
| : | END |
| : | |
| Y = QUIZZ(J,30,L) | |

Note the REAL specification
in both programs.
QUIZZ returns a real value.

*Example 3*

```
REAL BAKER,A              REAL FUNCTION BAKER (X,Y,J)
I = 2                     REAL X,Y
A = 7.0                   INTEGER J
Y = BAKER(3.2,9.8*A,I)       .
   .                         .
   .
```

The arguments of BAKER must be two real
values followed by an integer value.

When control is passed to BAKER,
X = 3.2, Y − 9.8*7 − 68.6 and J = 2

*Example 4*

In this example, the function name participates as a variable in the subprogram. The function SUM computes the sum of the entries of a 10-element real array.

```
INTEGER A(10),B(10)       REAL FUNCTION SUM(Z)
REAL SUM                  INTEGER Z(10)
   .                      SUM = 0.
   .                      DO 10 I = 1,10
X = SUM(A)                    SUM = SUM + Z(I)
   .                  10 CONTINUE        Note the array declaration statement required in
   .                     RETURN          the subprogram. SUM (the name of the function)
Y = SUM(B)               END             is used as an accumulator.
   .
   .
```

*Example 5*   Function LARG returns the largest element in a real array of size 10.

```
REAL A(10),B(10),LARG     REAL FUNCTION LARG(X)
   .                      REAL X(10)
   .                      LARG = X(1)
X = LARG(A) + LARG(B)     DO 10 I = 2,10
                            IF(LARG.LT.X(I)) LARG = X(I)
```
When the RETURN statement is executed,   `10 CONTINUE`
control is passed to the point at which the   `RETURN`
function was invoked. First LARG(A)          `END`
is executed, then LARG(B), then the
sum of the two largest numbers is stored in X.

*Example 6*   This example illustrates character arguments.

The function RATE(USAGE) returns

the value 'LOW'      if      USAGE ≤ 300.
the value 'MEDIUM' if 300 < USAGE ≤ 500.
the value 'HIGH'     if      USAGE > 500.

```
CHARACTER*6 RATE,POWER    CHARACTER*6 FUNCTION RATE(USAGE)
READ( ) USAGE             REAL USAGE
POWER = RATE(USAGE)       IF(USAGE.LE.300.) THEN
   .                      RATE = 'LOW'
   .                      ELSE IF (USAGE .LE.500.) THEN
POWER = RATE(X)                     RATE = 'MEDIUM'
   .                           ELSE
   .                               RATE = 'HIGH'
                          ENDIF
                          RETURN
                          END
```

*Example 7*   The character function HINAME returns the name that is alphabetically last
in a list of names.

```
CHARACTER*15 NAME(50)              CHARACTER*15 FUNCTION HINAME(NOM)
CHARACTER*15 HINAME                CHARACTER*15 NOM(50)
        .                          HINAME = NOM(1)
        .                          DO 6 I = 2,50
IF(HINAME(NAME).GT.'ZEUS') THEN        IF(HINAME.LT.NOM(I))HINAME = NOM(I)
        .                        6 CONTINUE
        .                          RETURN
                                   END
```

It is often necessary to write function subprograms that will process arrays of varying sizes. In this case it is possible to use an integer variable to specify the size of the array in the declarator statement in the function subprogram (not in the main program). A more detailed and complete discussion of variable dimension for multidimensional arrays is presented in section 10-5-2. In the following example, the subprogram will process arrays of varying sizes. The number rows and columns are passed as the second and third arguments.

*Example 8*

The function AVER computes the average of the grades stored in arrays class 1, class 2 and class 3. Being able to use the variable dimension in the function subprogram allows the user to write one subprogram to find the grade average of any size grade arrays.

| *Calling Program* | *Function Subprogram* |
|---|---|

```
REAL CLASS1(10,10)          REAL FUNCTION AVER(ARAY,NR,NC)
REAL CLASS2(5,5)            REAL ARAY(NR,NC)
REAL CLASS3(7,17)          INTEGER NR,NC
REAL AVER, A,B,C,TOT        AVER = 0.              variable dimension
A = AVER(CLASS1,10,10)      DO 6 I = 1,NR
B = AVER(CLASS2,5,5)            DO 5 J = 1,NC
C = AVER(CLASS3,7, 17)              AVER = AVER + ARAY(I,J)
TOT = (A+B+C)/3.        5       CONTINUE
                                AVER = AVER/(NR*NC)
                        6   CONTINUE
                            RETURN
                            END
```

Since subprograms are separate programs that are treated independently by the compiler, identical variable names that are totally unrelated, can appear in the calling and called programs with no risk of confusion; likewise, duplicate statement numbers in the calling and called programs are permissible, since the programs are compiled separately. For the same reason, if the programmer wishes to refer in a function subprogram to a variable that is defined in the calling program, he/she cannot use the same name and hope that it will refer to the variable with the identical name in the calling program. The only way to "communicate" variables between programs is either through the COMMON statement (see section 10-2-4) or by passing the variable name as an argument in the function-calling sequence. Consider the following example:

| *Calling Program* | *Subprogram* |
|---|---|
| `REAL A(10),B(6),SUM` | `FUNCTION ADD(X,Y,Z)` |
| `READ( )P,Q,A` | `SUM = X+Y+Z` |
| `SUM = 0.` | `PROD = X*Y*Z` |
| `DO 8 I = 1,6` | `IF(SUM.GT.PROD)GO TO 8` |
| `    SUM = SUM + A(I)` | `    .` |
| `8  CONTINUE` | `    .` |
| `R = SUM + P` | `8    ADD =` |
| `T - ADD(P,Q,R)` | `    .` |
| `    .` | `    .` |
| `    .` | |

The only variables common to the two programs are P and X, Q and Y, and R and Z. The variable SUM in the main program has *no* relationship to the variable SUM in the subprogram; similarly, statement 8 in the main program will not be confused with statement 8 in the subprogram.

The following are *invalid* function references or function definition statements:

| Calling Program | Function Subprogram | |
|---|---|---|
| X = AMAX(2.1,3,4.) | FUNCTION AMAX(X,Y,Z) | "3" is integer and "Y" is real. |
| INTEGER SMALL<br><br>.<br>.<br>.<br><br>J = SMALL(3.1,X) | FUNCTION SMALL(T,X) | SMALL should be declared as INTEGER in the subprogram. |
| S = COT(A,B,T(3)) | FUNCTION COT(X,Y,Z)<br>X = COT(T,Z,P) | Function cannot invoke itself. |
| REAL Q(100)<br>C = DAM(Q(1),Q(2), – 4) | FUNCTION DAM(T(1),T(2),J)<br>REAL T(100) | Function arguments may not be subscripted variable names. |
| MIM = SUB(X,2*J,9.8) | FUNCTION SUB(X,J) | Arguments disagree in number. |
| INTEGER CART(10)<br>.<br>.<br>X = TIP(3.9,X,CART) | FUNCTION TIP(X,Y,Z)<br>TIP = (X + Y)/2.<br>.<br>. | Z must be declared as an array in the function subprogram. |
| READ*, INCOME<br>G = TAX(INCOME) | FUNCTION TAX(INCOME)<br>REAL TAX | The type statement must precede the word FUNCTION. |
| A = PAY(EARN,DEP,3)<br>PRINT*,A<br>C = PAY(10.,A*2 + K) | FUNCTION PAY (A,B,N)<br>PAY = A*B + N<br>RETURN<br>END | PAY must be invoked with three arguments. |

### 9-4-7 Do It Now

1. Write a function subprogram to compute the determinant of a 2 by 2 matrix.

   [*NOTE*: Determinant of A $= |A| = \begin{vmatrix} a_{11} & a_{12} \\ a_{21} & a_{22} \end{vmatrix} = a_{11} \cdot a_{22} - a_{21} \cdot a_{12}$]

2. Write a function to calculate the approximate number of days that have elapsed between two dates: M1, D1, Y1 and M2, D2, Y2, where M, D, and Y refer to month, day, and year.

   [*Hint*: There are an average of 365.25 days in each year and an average of 30.4 days in each month; express both quantities in days.]

3. Write a function subprogram to compute the cost of postage for a first class letter weighing P ounces. The postage is 20 cents for the first ounce and 17 cents for each additional ounce or part thereof.

### *Answers*

1.
```
REAL FUNCTION DET(A)
REAL A(2,2)
DET = A(1,1) * A(2,2) - A(2,1) * A(1,2)
RETURN
END
```

2.
```
REAL FUNCTION MDIF(M1,D1,Y1,M2,D2,Y2)
REAL M1,D1,M2,D2,Y1,Y2,JD1,JD2,MDIF
JD1 = 365.25 * Y1 + (M1-1) * 30.4 + D1
JD2 = 365.25 * Y2 + (M2-1) * 30.4 + D2
MDIF = ABS(JD1 - JD2)
RETURN
END
```

3.
```
REAL FUNCTION POSTGE(P)
REAL P
POSTGE = .20
IF(P .GT. 1.) POSTGE = .20 + .17*(P-1.)
RETURN
END
```

### 9-4-8 Position of the Function Subprogram in the Job

All user-defined subprograms are separate physical and logical entities and as such are compiled independently of one another. The compiler treats each function subprogram as a new program in the job. When a FORTRAN program requires user-written subprograms, the various subprograms should be placed immediately after the END statement of the main program. The order of the various subprograms is immaterial. Each subprogram should start with the FUNCTION statement and terminate with the END statement.

In a batch environment, some systems may require job control statements between each subprogram; in such systems, the input data should be placed after the last subprogram in the file. In other systems, the input data is stored as a separate data file on disk.

You should check the proper control statements for your system, since control statements vary greatly from one installation/system to another.

### 9-4-9  Why Use Function Subprograms?

Subprograms can help the programmer write shorter and more compact programs. The programmer can break his/her program into smaller logical components that are easier to work with, resulting in a more readable program. A subprogram can also result in an economy of code for procedures or tasks that are to be performed repeatedly at different places in a program. The code for the procedure is written just once and is not recoded wherever it is needed in the program.

Function subprograms that are to be used frequently should be compiled, debugged, and thereafter stored in a library. This saves computer time, since the subprogram need not be recompiled each time it is to be used. User-written subprograms can be shared through "share" libraries. A brief subprogram description and its use (calling sequence) should be included in the listing of the subprogram through comment statements.

In long, complex problems, it is sometimes possible to segment the tasks that make up a complete program; the programmer can write these tasks as subprograms and verify that each subprogram executes properly. The complete program can then be constructed from the debugged subprograms.

### 9-4-10  Program Example

Write a program to compute the binomial expression

$$C(n,m) = \frac{n!}{m!(n-m)!}$$

$C(n,m)$ represents the number of ways to choose $m$ objects from $n$ different objects. For example, if six people are on a ship and the lifeboat can hold only two, then

$$C(6,2) = \frac{6!}{2!4!} = \frac{6\cdot5\cdot4\cdot3\cdot2\cdot1}{(2\cdot1)\cdot(4\cdot3\cdot2\cdot1)} = 15$$

$C(6,2) = 15$ represents the number of different combinations of people who could be saved.

Two approaches to this problem are shown in Figure 9–13. Both assume N > M. The factorial calculation must be repeated three times to compute the result. The program is greatly simplified by using a function subprogram to calculate the factorials.

### 9-4-11  Message Encryption

*Problem/Specification*:   Write a program to read a message and code it in such a way that each letter of the alphabet in the message is replaced by the "next" letter, for example, A will be replaced by B, ..., Y by Z, and Z by A, while all other special characters remain unchanged. Use a function that accepts a character as an argument—if the argument is a letter of the alphabet, the function returns the "next" letter, otherwise the function leaves the argument unchanged. For example, the message I AM 30 YRS. OLD! becomes J BN 30 ZST. PME!

**FIGURE 9-13** COMBINATION WITH AND WITHOUT FUNCTION SUBPROGRAM

*Program without Function Subprogram*

```
      INTEGER COMB
      READ(5,1)N,M
      NFACT = 1
      DO 10 I = 1,N        } Factorial
         NFACT = NFACT*I
   10 CONTINUE
      MFACT = 1
      DO 20 I = 1,M        } Factorial
         MFACT = MFACT*I
   20 CONTINUE
      NM = N - M
      NMFACT = 1
      DO 30 I = 1,NM       } Factorial
         NMFACT = NMFACT*I
   30 CONTINUE
      COMB = NFACT/(MFACT*NMFACT)
      WRITE(6,2)N,M,COMB
      STOP
    2 FORMAT(' COMBINATIONS OF',I3,'ITEMS'
     */'TAKEN',I3,' AT A TIME IS',I4)
    1 FORMAT(2I2)
      END
```

```
COMBINATIONS OF 6 ITEMS
TAKEN  2 AT A TIME IS  15
```

*Program with Function Subprogram*

```
      INTEGER COMB,FACT
      READ(5,1)N,M
      COMB=FACT(N)/(FACT(M)*FACT(N-M))
      WRITE(6,2)N,M,COMB
      STOP
    2 FORMAT(' COMBINATIONS OF',I3,'ITEMS'
     */'TAKEN',I3,' AT A TIME IS',I4)
    1 FORMAT(2I2)
      END
```

```
      INTEGER FUNCTION FACT(N)
      FACT = 1
      DO 10 I = 1,N
         FACT = FACT*I
   10 CONTINUE
      RETURN
      END
```

```
COMBINATIONS OF 6 ITEMS
TAKEN  2 AT A TIME IS  15
```

*Problem/Solution:* Many versions of FORTRAN use the ASCII code to represent letters of the alphabet; for example the letter A is coded internally as 65, the letter B as 66, C as 67, .., Y as 89 and, Z as 90. This means that for any letter L of the alphabet, the "next" letter has an internal code value equal to the (internal code of L) + 1. Hence if L is any letter of the alphabet other than Z, the letter following L is

$$LETTER = CHAR(ICHAR(L) + 1)$$

For example, if the ASCII code for Y is 89 then the "next" letter after Y is

$$LETTER = CHAR(ICHAR(Y) + 1) = CHAR(89 + 1) = CHAR(90) = Z$$

The function NCRYPT can then be written as follows:

```
CHARACTER FUNCTION NCRYPT(L)           L is the character to be encrypted.
CHARACTER L*1
IF(L .GE. 'A' .AND. L .LE. 'Y')THEN    Check whether character L
   NCRYPT = CHAR(ICHAR(L) + 1)         is a letter of the alphabet.
ELSE IF (L .EQ. 'Z')THEN
      NCRYPT = 'A'                      If L is 'Z' change L to 'A'.
ELSE
      NCRYPT = L                        Don't change character if it is
ENDIF                                   not a letter of the alphabet.
RETURN
END
```

The program using this function might be:

```
      CHARACTER LINE*80,C,L
  10  READ(5,6,END=88)LINE          Read a line of text.
      DO 5 I = 1,80
         L = NCRYPT(LINE(I:I))       Convert each character and
         LINE(I:I) = L               replace it in the text.
   5  CONTINUE
      GO TO 10                       Read more lines.
  88  STOP
   6  FORMAT(A80)
      END
```

### 9-4-12  Do It Now

1. Could the program of Figure 9–13 have been simply coded as

```
      DO 10 I = N-M+1,N
  10     NMFACT = NMFACT*I
```

2. Could function NCRYPT in section 9–4–11 have been written as follows?

```
      CHARACTER FUNCTION NCRYPT(L)
      CHARACTER L*1
      LOGICAL LETTER
      NCRYPT = L
      IF(LETTER(L))THEN
        IF(L.EQ.'Z')THEN
          NCRYPT = 'A'
        ELSE
          NCRYPT = CHAR(ICHAR(L)+ 1)
        ENDIF
      ENDIF
      RETURN
      END
      LOGICAL FUNCTION LETTER(L)
      CHARACTER L*1
      LETTER = L.GE.'A' .AND. L.LE.'Z'
      RETURN
      END
```

### *Answer*

Yes to both questions.

### 9-4-13  A Lottery Example

As a promotional gimmick, every patron of the Circle K gas station gets a lucky card with three numbers on it ranging from 1 to 1,000. The station manager then draws at random a number from 1 to 1,000. If any of the customers' numbers matches the one drawn by the manager, the customer gets an amount in cents equal to one-tenth of his lucky number. Write a program to read ten customer lucky cards and determine the dollar amount of any lucky winner. For example, if the lucky card contains the numbers 50, 100 and 200 and the manager draws the number 50, the customer wins five cents.

To solve this problem we will write:

**1.** A function called IRAND to generate random numbers between two specified integers named IBEG and ITER. This function can be copied to generate random numbers if your installation does not have a random number generator.

**2.** A function called WIN to determine whether the customer has a lucky number and if so, to compute the amount won.

The complete program shown in Figure 9–14 consists of three independent blocks of code (or subprograms), which perform very specific tasks: the main program, which acts as a coordinator between the other two subprograms; the IRAND program, which generates random numbers; and the WIN program, which computes an amount won or lost.

## 9-5 Statement Functions

### 9-5-1 Introduction

As we have seen, FORTRAN allows you to define your own functions through the use of function subprograms. The function subprogram, in general, can require several lines of code and can produce several answers, even though only one value can be returned to the calling program. In cases where the function is so simple that it can be expressed in one line of code and can produce only one possible answer, the statement function can be used to great advantage. Statement functions are generally used when a particular arithmetic expression needs to be evaluated for different values of the variable at different places in the program. Unlike function subprograms, which are compiled independently, statement functions are defined in the program that uses the statement function. For example, if a second-degree polynomial is to be evaluated several times in a program for different values of the variable, the statement function POLY could be used as follows:

| *Program without Statement Function* | *Program with Statement Function* |
|---|---|
| `X = -5.6` | **`POLY`**`(X) = 2.1*X**2 - 3.*X + 1.` |
| `Y = 2.1*X**2 - 3.*X + 1.` | `X = -5.6` |
| `X = 2.12347` | `Y = `**`POLY`**`(X)` |
| `.` | `.` |
| `.` | `.` |
| `IF(2.1*X**2 - 3.*X + 1. .GT. 3.)THEN` | `IF(`**`POLY`**`(2.12347).GT. 3.) THEN` |
| `.` | `.` |
| `.` | `.` |
| `T = 10.6` | `T = 10.6` |
| `SUM = SUM + SQRT(2.1*T**2 - 3.*T + 1.)` | `SUM = SUM + SQRT(`**`POLY`**`(T))` |

The general form of the statement function definition is:

*function name* $(a_1, a_2, a_3, ..., a_n) =$ *expression*

where *function name* is the name of the function (any variable name).

**FIGURE 9-14**    RANDOM NUMBER LUCKY WIN

```
C LOTTERY PROBLEM
C    CARD(3): CONTAINS 3 LUCKY NUMBERS
C    IRAND:   RANDOM NUMBER GENERATOR FUNCTION
C    WIN:     DETERMINES A WINNING AMOUNT
C    AMT:     AMOUNT OF LUCKY WIN
C    NAME:    NAME OF CUSTOMER
      INTEGER K,CARD(3)
      REAL AMT
      CHARACTER*5 NAME
C FUNCTION NAMES USED IN PROGRAM ARE:
      INTEGER IRAND
      REAL WIN
C
5     READ(5,1,END=8)NAME, CARD
         K = IRAND(1,1000)
         AMT = WIN(CARD, K)
         WRITE(6,2)NAME, AMT
         GO TO 5
8     STOP
1     FORMAT(A5,3F5.0)
2     FORMAT(1X,A5,' GETS',F10.0,'CENTS')
      END
C
C FUNCTION WIN RETURNS WINNING AMOUNT
      REAL FUNCTION WIN(SLIP, N)
      INTEGER SLIP(3)
      WIN = 0.
      DO 15 I = 1, 3
         IF(SLIP(I).EQ.N)WIN=SLIP(I)/10.
15    CONTINUE
      RETURN
      END
C
C FUNCTION IRAND GENERATES A RANDOM NUMBER
C BETWEEN THE INTEGER VALUES IBEG & ITER
      INTEGER FUNCTION IRAND(IBEG,ITER)
      INTEGER M, B, A
      REAL X
      DATA M, B, A/25211, 32767, 19727/
      A = MOD(M*A, B)
      X = REAL(A)/REAL(B)
      IRAND = X*(ITER - IBEG + 1) + IBEG
      RETURN
      END
```

Read the records one at a time.
Call the function IRAND to choose a random number from 1 to 1,000. The arguments of the random routine are 1 and 1,000. The function WIN computes the amount won. If the customer loses, AMT = 0. The array CARD is transmitted to the function WIN along with the lucky number K, which is the random number returned by the function IRAND.

The array SLIP in the function WIN really refers to the array CARD in the calling program. Similarly, N is just a dummy name for the variable K, defined in the calling program.

If no match exists between the numbers on the card and the number drawn by the manager, the value of the function is WIN = 0. If there is a match, WIN is one-tenth of the lucky number.

Note how the name of the function WIN returns the value of the function to the calling program.

Function IRAND returns any integer value between IBEG and ITER (IBEG < ITER). In this program, IBEG and ITER take on those values passed by the calling program, i.e., IBEG = 1 and ITER = 1,000. The value X, as a result of the computations, is always a real number from 0 to 1. The value IRAND becomes any number from 1 to 1,000. Note how IRAND transmits the function value to the calling program.

$a_1$, $a_2$, $a_3$, ..., $a_n$ are dummy arguments that must be nonsubscripted variable names, and

*expression* is any arithmetic expression that contains $a_1$, $a_2$, $a_3$, ..., $a_n$ and possibly other constants, variables, array elements, or references to function subprograms or previously defined statement functions.

The statement function definition should precede the first executable statement of the program but follow all DIMENSION and specification statements. The following code illustrates the use of a statement function.

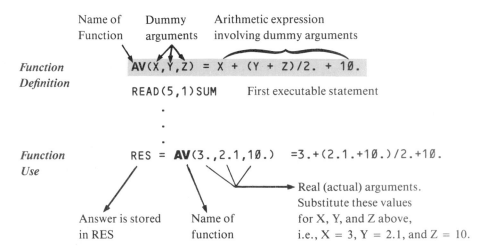

Name of Function — Dummy arguments — Arithmetic expression involving dummy arguments

*Function*
*Definition*

$$AV(X,Y,Z) = X + (Y + Z)/2. + 10.$$

READ(5,1)SUM      First executable statement

.
.
.

*Function*
*Use*

RES = **AV**(3.,2.1,10.)   =3.+(2.1.+10.)/2.+10.

Answer is stored in RES   Name of function   Real (actual) arguments. Substitute these values for X, Y, and Z above, i.e., X = 3, Y = 2.1, and Z = 10.

When a statement function is executed, the values of the real (actual) arguments replace the dummy arguments in the expression in the function definition. If variables other than the dummy arguments are used in the expression, then their current values will be used when the function is evaluated. The use of a variable as a dummy argument does not preclude its use as a variable in the program. The only purpose of the dummy argument is to illustrate the way in which the real arguments are manipulated to produce the function value.

In the expression in the function definition, the dummy arguments must be nonsubscripted variable names. In the calling statement for the function, the real arguments *can* be subscripted variables or arithmetic expressions. **As with function subprograms, the real arguments must agree in number, order, and type with the dummy arguments in the function definition.** The type of the value returned is determined implicitly by the name of the function but can be changed by appropriate type statements.

### 9-5-2  Examples

*Example 1*

F(X) = (X+2.)/(X-2.) + X**2       $F(X) = \dfrac{X + 2}{X - 2} + X^2$
.
.
.

Y = **F**(4.0)      The value of Y will be 19.
Y = **F**(T)       The value of Y is computed, substituting T for X in the function definition.

*Example 2*

BETA(Y) = A*Y**2 + B*Y + C        The expression involves variables other than the formal argument Y.
.
.
.

READ(5,1)A,B,C        The values of A, B, and C are established. The function will be
DO 10 IX = 1,10       evaluated for values of IX varying from 1 to 10. Note that the
   Q = **BETA**(REAL(IX))   mode of the actual argument and the formal argument must be
10 WRITE(6,2)IX,Q      the same. The REAL function converts the integer IX to real
                       mode.

*Example 3*

```
RAD(DEGREE) = DEGREE/57.296
    .
    .
    .
Y = SIN(RAD(30.))
```

RAD converts degrees into radians.

Statement functions can be used as arguments of any other functions.

*Example 4*

```
B1(Y) = ABS(Y - 1.)
B2(Y) = LOG(B1)/10.
    .
    .
    .
Z = B2(-5.)
```

Statement functions can reference other previously defined statement functions. B1 and B2 are functions.

$Z = LOG(|-5-1|)/10 = LOG(6)/10$

*Example 5*

```
COMB(N,M) =
*FACT(N)/(FACT(M)*FACT(N-M))
    .
    .
K = COMB(8,2)
```

The COMB function could be used in the program of Figure 9–13. Note the use of the user-defined function subprogram FACT.

*Example 6*

```
PAY(HRS,RATE) = HRS*RATE+BONUS
    .
    .
BONUS = 50.
X = PAY(40.,5.)
BONUS = BONUS + 10.
Y = PAY(50.,4.)
```

$X = 5*40 + 50 = 250$

$Y = 4*50 + 60 = 260$

*Example 7*

```
FAHR(C) = 9./5.*C + 32.
    .
    .
    .
C = 0.
TEMP = FAHR(100.)
C = C + 1.
```

The variable C is used as an ordinary variable in the program, even though it is also used as a dummy argument in the function definition.

The value of C is 1.

*Example 8*

```
REAL INT
INT(R,N) = PRIN*(1.+R)**N
    .
    .
    .
DUE = INT(A(3),K*360 + J)
```

The FORTRAN-supplied function INT is redefined as a user function.

Note the use of the subscripted variable A(3). In this case, R = A(3) and N = K*360 + J.

*Example 9*

```
T(X) = SQRT(X**2 + 9.) + A
A = 11.
S = T(4) + SQRT(T(5))
```

$S = \sqrt{25} + 11 + \sqrt{\sqrt{34} + 11}$

*Example 10*

```
LOGICAL LETTER
CHARACTER C,L
LETTER(C) = C.GE.'A'.AND.C.LE.'Z'          LETTER(C) is .TRUE. if C is a letter of the alphabet.
  :
  :
READ*,L
IF(LETTER(L))K = 1                          If L is a letter of the alphabet, set K to 1.
```

The following examples show *invalid* statement function definitions or invalid references to statement functions:

a.
```
PAY = HRS*RATE
RES = PAY(40,5)
```
Arguments needed for PAY.

b.
```
CONS(X,3) = 3*X + 1
```
3 is an invalid dummy argument.

c.
```
DUE(X,A(1),Z) = A(1) + X + Z
```
Subscripted variables cannot be used as dummy arguments.

e.
```
DOG(X,Y,Z) = X + Y*DOG(C,D,F)
```
Recursive definition of DOG—a function cannot refer to itself.

f.
```
TRUE(NCY) = NCY*3/256
DIMENSION A(100)
```
Statement functions should follow specification statements.

g.
```
SIGN(X) = -X
Y = SIGN(3)
```
Real and dummy arguments differ in type.

h.
```
BRA(VO,S) = (VO + S)**3
Z = BRA(3.12*X)
```
Arguments differ in number.
Only one argument in BRA.

### 9-5-3  Do It Now

Write statement functions for the Do It Now exercises 1 and 2 in section 9–4–7.

### Answers

1.
```
DET(A1,A2,A3,A4) = A1*A4-A3*A2
```

2.
```
JD(M,ID,IY) = 365.25*IY + (M-1.)*30.4 + ID
MDIF(M1,ID1,IY1,M2,ID2,IY2) = ABS(JD(M1,ID1,IY1) - JD(M2,ID2,IY2))
```

### 9-5-4  Programming Example

The program in Figure 9–15 illustrates the use of a statement function to solve a set of linear equations of the following form:

$$a_1x + b_1y = c_1$$
$$a_2x + b_2y = c_2$$

The program uses the Gauss-Seidel iteration procedure, which involves starting with an approximation $x_0$, $y_0$ of the solution and computing successive approximations for $x$ and $y$ using the following formulas:

$$x_{n+1} = \frac{1}{a_1}(c_1 - b_1 y_n)$$

$$y_{n+1} = \frac{1}{b_2}(c_2 - a_2 x_{n+1})$$

It can be shown that this sequence of approximations $x_i$, $y_i$ converges towards the solution of the system of linear equations if:

$$|a_1| \cdot |b_2| > |b_1| \cdot |a_2|.$$

The program in Figure 9–15 accepts as input the values $a_1$, $b_1$, $c_1$, $a_2$, $b_2$, $c_2$ and tests to see if the Gauss-Seidel iteration procedure will converge. If it will not converge, an appropriate message is produced; if it will converge, the first eight terms of the sequence are computed.

**FIGURE 9-15**    GAUSS-SEIDEL METHOD

```
C GAUSS SEIDEL ITERATIVE METHOD
C   XNEW: FUNCTION TO COMPUTE X VALUES
C   YNEW: FUNCTION TO COMPUTE Y VALUES
C
C     IMPLICIT REAL(A-M,O-Z), INTEGER(N)
C
      XNEW(Q) = (1./A1)*(C1 - B1*Q)
      YNEW(Q) = (1./B2)*(C2 - A2*Q)
C
   10 READ(5,6,END=88)A1,B1,C1,A2,B2,C2
      WRITE(6,2) A1,B1,C1,A2,B2,C2
      IF(ABS(A1)*ABS(B2) .GT. ABS(B1)*ABS(A2)) THEN
         WRITE(6,3)
         Y = 0.
         DO 20 N = 1, 8
            X = XNEW(Y)
            Y = YNEW(X)
            WRITE(6,4)N, X, Y
   20    CONTINUE
      ELSE
         WRITE(6,5)
      ENDIF
      GO TO 10
   88 STOP
    2 FORMAT(1X/(1X,F4.1,'*X+',F4.1,'*Y=',F4.1))
    3 FORMAT('0',2X,'N',5X,'X',6X,'Y')
    4 FORMAT(2X,I2,2X,F5.2,2X,F5.2)
    5 FORMAT('0',2X,'SYSTEM WILL NOT CONVERGE')
    6 FORMAT(6F4.0)
      END
```

**Input File**

| $A_1$ | $B_1$ | $C_1$ | $A_2$ | $B_2$ | $C_2$ |
|-------|-------|-------|-------|-------|-------|
| 8.00 | 2.00 | 18.0 | 1.00 | 1.00 | 3.00 |
| 3.00 | -4.0 | -1.0 | 2.00 | 6.00 | 8.00 |
| 1.00 | 3.00 | 4.00 | 4.00 | 2.00 | 6.00 |

```
8.0*X+ 2.0*Y=18.0
1.0*X+ 1.0*Y= 3.0

N      X       Y
1    2.25     .75
2    2.06     .94
3    2.02     .98
4    2.00    1.00
5    2.00    1.00
6    2.00    1.00
7    2.00    1.00
8    2.00    1.00

3.0*X+-4.0*Y=-1.0
2.0*X+ 6.0*Y= 8.0

N      X       Y
1    -.33    1.44
2    1.59     .80
3     .74    1.09
4    1.12     .96
5     .95    1.02
6    1.02     .99
7     .99    1.00
8    1.00    1.00

1.0*X+ 3.0*Y= 4.0
4.0*X+ 2.0*Y= 6.0

SYSTEM WILL NOT CONVERGE
```

## 9-6    **You Might Want to Know**

1. I was looking at another FORTRAN book and I saw many functions such as IABS, AMAX1, and MIN0 that are not listed in Figures 9–3 and 9–4. What are these functions and can I use them?

   *Answer*: FORTRAN 77 has many built-in intrinsic functions. Most of these functions have a generic name; this means that the argument is not restricted to any specific type and that the function returns a value of the same type as that of its argument(s). In earlier FORTRAN versions, a function might have as many as four or five specific names depending on the argument, for example, the absolute value function might be IABS for integer arguments, ABS for real arguments, DABS for double precision arguments, and CABS for complex arguments. A list of such nongeneric functions is shown in Figure 9–16. These functions can still be used in FORTRAN 77.

2. Can an argument expression contain a reference to another function?

   *Answer*: Yes. For example:

   ```
   SQRT(ABS(X))
   SQRT(SQRT(Y))
   ```

3. Is it better to use SQRT or **.5 to calculate the square root?

   *Answer*: In general, SQRT is more efficient if not more accurate than exponentiation. In either case the result will be a close approximation to the actual square root. Logarithms are used to perform exponentiation in most systems; iterative methods may be used in evaluation of SQRT.

4. What other functions are available?

   *Answer*: The lists of functions in Figures 9–3 and 9–4 are by no means exhaustive. Refer to the manufacturer's reference manual for your FORTRAN system for a complete listing. Also, most installations have packages of statistical and other mathematical functions with a wide variety of capabilities. When available, these functions may considerably reduce the amount of effort involved in program development.

5. Can an array element be used as a function argument?

   *Answer*: Yes. For example, if A and XYZ are arrays, the following are valid function references:

   ```
   SQRT(A(4))
   ABS(XYZ(L,J))
   ```

6. Can the MAX/MIN functions return the value of the largest/smallest value contained in an array?

   *Answer*: Yes, but each element of the array must be listed as a separate argument. For example:

   ```
   SMALL = MIN(X(1),X(2),X(3),X(4),X(5),X(6),X(7))
   ```

   It would, of course, be better to write a function subprogram that would accept the array as an argument and return the smallest element.

7. Are all FORTRAN-supplied functions stored in the system library?

   *Answer*: No. Some functions, such as ABS, INT, are said to be *in-line* functions, while others are said to be *out-of-line* functions. In-line functions are inserted in the FOR-

**FIGURE 9-16    NONGENERIC FUNCTIONS**

| Function | Definition (Argument = a) | Number of Arguments | Name | Mode of Argument | Value of Function |
|---|---|---|---|---|---|
| Absolute value | $\lvert a \rvert = a$ if $a \geq 0$ <br> $\quad -a$ if $a < 0$ | 1 | IABS <br> ABS <br> DABS <br> CABS | Integer <br> Real <br> Double precision <br> Complex | Integer <br> Real <br> Double precision <br> Real |
| Square root | $\sqrt{a},\; a \geq 0$ | 1 | SQRT <br> DSQRT <br> CSQRT | Real <br> Double precision <br> Complex | Real <br> Double precision <br> Complex |
| Exponential | $e^a$ <br> note $e = 2.718\ldots$ | 1 | EXP <br> DEXP <br> CEXP | Real <br> Double precision <br> Complex | Real <br> Double precision <br> Complex |
| Natural logarithms | $ln(a),\; a > 0$ | 1 | ALOG <br> DLOG <br> CLOG | Real <br> Double precision <br> Complex | Real <br> Double precision <br> Complex |
| Common Logarithms | $\log_{10}(a),\; a > 0$ | 1 | ALOG10 <br> DLOG10 | Real <br> Double precision | Real <br> Double precision |
| Sine | $\sin(a)$ <br> $a$ is expressed in radians | 1 | SIN <br> DSIN <br> CSIN | Real <br> Double precision <br> Complex | Real <br> Double precision <br> Complex |
| Cosine | $\cos(a)$ <br> $a$ is expressed in radians | 1 | COS <br> DCOS <br> CCOS | Real <br> Double precision <br> Complex | Real <br> Double precision <br> Complex |
| Tangent | $\tan(a)$ <br> $a$ is expressed in radians | 1 | TAN <br> DTAN | Real <br> Double precision | Real <br> Double precision |
|  | Conversion to real | 1 | FLOAT <br> SNGL <br> REAL | Integer <br> Double precision <br> Complex | Real <br> Real <br> Real |
|  | Conversion to double precision | 1 | DFLOAT <br> DBLE | Integer <br> Real | Double precision <br> Double precision |
| Transfer of sign | $\lvert a_1 \rvert$ if $a_2 \geq 0$ <br> $-\lvert a_1 \rvert$ if $a_2 < 0$ | 2 | ISIGN <br> SIGN <br> DSIGN | Integer <br> Real <br> Double precision | Integer <br> Real <br> Double precision |
| Positive difference | $a_1 - a_2$ if $a_1 > a_2$ <br> 0 if $a_1 \leq a_2$ | 2 | IDIM <br> DIM <br> DDIM | Integer <br> Real <br> Double precision | Integer <br> Real <br> Double precision |
| Choose the largest value | The largest of $(a_1, a_2, \ldots)$ | $\geq 2$ | MAX0 <br> AMAX1 <br> DMAX1 <br> AMAX0 <br> MAX1 | Integer <br> Real <br> Double precision <br> Integer <br> Real | Integer <br> Real <br> Double precision <br> Real <br> Integer |
| Choose the smallest value | The smallest of $(a_1, a_2, \ldots)$ | $\geq 2$ | MIN0 <br> AMIN1 <br> DMIN1 <br> AMIN0 <br> MIN1 | Integer <br> Real <br> Double precision <br> Integer <br> Real | Integer <br> Real <br> Double precision <br> Real <br> Integer |
| Remainder function | Remainder of the division of $a_1$ by $a_2$. <br> $r = a_1 - \mathrm{INT}\,(a_1/a_2)\,^{*}a_2$ | 2 | MOD <br> AMOD <br> DMOD | Integer <br> Real <br> Double precision | Integer <br> Real <br> Double precision |

TRAN program by the FORTRAN compiler whenever a reference to that function is made, i.e., the compiler generates the code for the function during the compilation process. An out-of-line function, on the other hand, is stored in the system library, and the FORTRAN compiler generates external references to it; i.e., the compiler generates the necessary instructions to link the FORTRAN program to the library function program so that transfer can be established between the two programs.

8. What if I dimension an array SIN(10), and in my program I refer to Y = SIN(X) will the sine function of X be computed?

   *Answer*: No. The compiler will treat any reference to SIN as an array reference. There are no "reserved words" in the FORTRAN language.

## 9-7 Exercises

### 9-7-1 Test Yourself

1. Write FORTRAN statements for each of the following:

   a. $a = \sin^2 x - \cos^2 x$      d. Find the largest of A, B, C, D, and E.
   b. $z = e^x - e^{-x}$      e. Find the smallest of I, J, K, and 3.
   c. $x = \sqrt{|p - q|}$

2. How could INT be used to round to the nearest hundred? To the nearest thousandth?

3. What will be the value of each of the following if A = 100., B = −2.4, C = 81., D = 0.?

   a. SQRT(C)          e. SIGN(B,A)          i. MAX(A,B,4.*B,C,D)
   b. SQRT(SQRT(C))    f. DIM(A,B)           j. ABS(B) + ABS(C)
   c. INT(B)           g. DIM(B,A)           k. LOG10(A)
   d. SIGN(A,B)        h. MIN(A,B,C,D)       l. SIN(D) + COS(D)

4. In the graph of Figure 9–7, what would be the difference if instead of using J = (TAN(X) + 9.)*4. to determine the position of the graphic character on the line we used J = TAN(X) + 35. Why do you think it is necessary to have a magnifying factor such as 4 in this case?

5. What statement in the program of Figure 9–7 would you change in order to display the graph of the tangent function in 126 print positions instead of 72?

6. Determine which of the following calling program/function subprograms pairs are invalid. Give reasons.

   | Calling Program | Function Subprogram |
   |---|---|
   | a. X = MAX(2.1,3.1,4) | FUNCTION MAX(X,Y,Z) |
   | b. IF(LOW(I,J,K))1,2,3 | FUNCTION LOW(K,I,J) |
   | c. REAL MALL | FUNCTION MALL(X,T) |
   |    X = MALL(X,T) | |
   | d. REAL A(5) | FUNCTION A(I,J,T) |
   |    INTEGER X,S | |
   |    Z = A(X,K,3*S) | |
   | e. T = BAD(1,2.+S,3*I) | FUNCTION BAD(I,J,K) |
   | f. M = TUT(SQRT(R),S) | FUNCTION TUT(RT,T) |
   | g. S = MAD(3.,2*S,−1) | FUNCTION MAD(X,Y,K) |
   | h. P = MAT(ABS(K),2,SIN(T)) | FUNCTION (X,I,T) |

| Calling Program | Function Subprogram |
|---|---|
| i. `S = COT(A,B,COT(1.,1.,1.))` | `FUNCTION COT(X,Y,Z)` |
| j. `REAL Q(100)` | `FUNCTION DAM(T(1),T,J)` |
| `  T = DAM(Q(1),Q,-4)` | `REAL T(100)` |
| k. `WRITE(6,11)FUNC(1.,2.)` | `FUNCTION FUNC(X,Y)` |
| l. `MIM = SUB(X,2*J,9.8)` | `INTEGER FUNCTION SUB(X,K,S)` |
| m. `SON = OF(A,OF(A,GUN))` | `FUNCTION OF(A,NON)` |
| n. `IF(MAT(2.,X).GT.3.) THEN` | `INTEGER FUNCTION MAT(X+Y,Z)` |
| o. `REAL B(5)` | `FUNCTION TIP(A,B,C)` |
| `  X = TIP(B(1),X,B(5))` | `REAL A(5)` |
| p. `REAL A(5)` | `FUNCTION CAN(T,J,3)` |
| `  Z = CAN(T,3,6/L)` | |
| q. `A = PAT(L,M,N)` | `FUNCTION PAT(N,M,L)` |
| | `DATA N,M,L/1,1,3/` |
| | `RETURN` |
| | `END` |
| r. `S = LARG(2,LARG(3,4))` | `FUNCTION LARG(I,J)` |
| s. `X = COT(X)` | `FUNCTION COT(X)` |

7. Which of the following function subprogram declarative statements are incorrect? State the reason in each case.

a. `FUNCTION AD(A,B,C+D)`      e. `FUNCTION A(A,B,C)`
b. `FUNCTION SORT(X,Y,Z)`      f. `FUNCTION B(A,C(1))`
c. `FUNCTION FUNCTION(X)`      g. `FUNCTION (A,AA,B)`
d. `FUNCTION SQRT(I)`      h. `FUNCTION C(3,B,B)`

8. Which of the following statement function definition statements are invalid? State reasons.

a. `SOME(A(I),B) = A(I)*2`      g. `HI(2,B,C) = (B-C)/2`
b. `SQRT(A,B) = SQRT(A) + SQRT(B)`      h. `A(L) = REAL(L) + AL + SIM`
c. `T(Y) = Y**2 + 2.`                `Y = A(K) - AL - SIM`
    `A(X) = T(X) + 1.`      i. `ADD(X,Y,Z) = X + Y + Z`
d. `SQRT(X) = X**0.5`          `T = ADD(X*Y,T)`
e. `ROOT = -B + SQRT(B*B - 4.*A*C)`    j. `C(X + 1.,A) = (X + 1.)*3. + A`
    `C(B) = B**2 + FUN`      k. `MIX(K) = LOG(K + 1.)`
f. `LONE(I,J,K) = I*J*K`          `S = MIX(3.1) + 3.`
    `L = LONE(1,2,3) + I*J*K`

9. Are the following statements true or false?

a. In most cases the type of a FORTRAN-supplied mathematical function is determined by its arguments.
b. The argument of the ABS function must be real.
c. In-line functions are part of the function libraries.
d. Y = SQRT(3) could mean to store the third element of array SQRT into Y if SQRT is dimensioned.
e. The trigonometric supplied functions are actually function subprograms.
f. The END statement in some cases is not needed in function subprograms.
g. Function subprograms can return only one value to the calling program.

h. The function reference I = STAN(X,Y) is invalid, since I and STAN are not of the same type.
i. In some cases, function subprograms can be compiled concurrently with the calling program.
j. Since only one value can be returned by a function subprogram, only one RETURN statement is allowed in the subprogram.
k. In the definition of a function subprogram, a dummy argument cannot be a subscripted variable name.
l. Array names are permitted as arguments in a function subprogram.
m. Statement functions are compiled independently of the program in which they are used.
n. A statement function can be coded in only one statement.
o. Real arguments used in a reference to a statement function can be subscripted variables.

10. Write one statement function that could be used for all statements 5,6,7,8 and show how the function would be used in each case.

```
5 Y = 3.*X**2 + 2.*X -1.
  WRITE(6,1)Y
6 T = I*X**2 + 7.*X - TOT
7 S = 3.*X**2 - K(2)*X + SIN(T)
  SUM = S + T
8 IF(17.*X**2 + MIN (A,B)*X - SQRT(A) .GT. 0.3) THEN
```

11. Same exercise as 10, except that 5 is coded as $Y = 3.*T**2 + 2.*T - 1$.

12. Write a statement function to perform the following:

a. $C = A^2 + B^2 - 2AB \cos(C)$ — Length of one side of a triangle.
b. $A = P(1 + I/J)^{J \cdot T}$ — Compound interest: P is fixed.
c. $A = P(1 + R)^N$ — Simple interest: P is fixed.
d. $1/R = 1/R1 + 1/R2 + 1/R3$ — Compute R: Total resistance.
e. $Q = .92A(T_1 - T_0)/H$ — Heat flow: H is fixed.
f. $E = 1 + X + X^2/2! + X^3/3!$ — Approximation to $e^x$.
g. $Y = Be^{-ax} \cos(\sqrt{B^2 - A^2 X - T})$ — A is fixed.

13. What output will be printed by the following two programs?

a.
```
    IMPLICIT INTEGER(A-Z)
    READ(5,7)A,B,C
    DO 10 I = 1,2
        Y = (10 - I)*POL(A,B,C,-I)
10  WRITE(6,14)Y
    STOP
14  FORMAT(1X,I7)
 7  FORMAT(3I2)
    END
    INTEGER FUNCTION POL(A,B,C,X)
    INTEGER A,B,C,X
    POL = A*X**2 + B*X + C
    RETURN
    END
```

*Data for Part a*

+2+3-1

↑
1st position

b.
```
      IMPLICIT INTEGER(A-Z)
      INTEGER ITEM(3)
      REAL PRICE(3)
      DO 10 I = 1,3
10       READ(5,11)ITEM(I),PRICE(I)
      READ(5,12)J
      L = FIND(ITEM,J)
      IF(L.LT.0)GO TO 8
      WRITE(6,15)ITEM(L),PRICE(L)
      STOP
    8 WRITE(6,13)J
      STOP
   13 FORMAT(1X,I4,1X,'COULD NOT BE FOUND')
   15 FORMAT(1X,I4,2X,F5.2)
   12 FORMAT(I4)
   11 FORMAT(I4,F4.2)
      END
      INTEGER FUNCTION FIND(A,B)
      INTEGER A(3),B
      FIND = -1
      DO 10 I = 1,3
         IF(A(I).EQ.B)FIND = I
   10 CONTINUE
      RETURN
      END
```

*Data for Part b*

11461733   record 1
11720845
11661042
1172

14. Write a statement function that computes the approximate difference between two dates M1, D1, Y1 and M2, D2, Y2. (M = month, D = day, Y = year; assume 365.25 days per year and 30.4 days per month. Then compute the number of hours that you have slept since you have been born. Assume you sleep eight hours per day.

15. Write a statement function that rounds a value $Q$ to the nearest hundredth.

16. Write a statement function that computes the remainder after dividing argument X by argument Y, i.e., 15/7 has remainder 2.

17. Write a statement function that computes the length of the hypotenuse of a right triangle, given sides A and B. Note $H^2 = A^2 + B^2$.

18. The length of a vector is defined as $\sqrt{A_1^2 + A_2^2 + ... + A_N^2}$. A data record contains the N components of the vector as follows:

$$\boxed{N \quad A_1 \, A_2 \, ... \, A_N} \quad N = \text{number of coordinates}$$

Write a main program to read records of this form (for $N \le 10$) and a function subprogram to compute the length of the vector associated with the components read.

19. Write a main program to read the coefficients $a_1, a_2, ..., a_n$, of the polynomial $P(x) = a_1 x^n + a_2 x^{n-1} + ... + a_{n-1} x^1 + a_n$ ($n \le 10$) into an array A. Print a table of the values of $P(x)$ for $x = -5., -4.5, -4., ..., 4.5, 5.$ using a function to compute the polynomial values. The input data layout is

$$\boxed{N \quad a_1 \, a_2 \, ... \, a_n}$$

### 9-7-2 Programming Problems: Business/General

1. The coordinates of three ships are accepted as input. Write a program to print the distances between each ship. If $x_1$ and $y_1$, and $x_2$ and $y_2$ are the coordinates of any two ships, the formula to compute the distance separating them is

$$d = \sqrt{|x_1 - x_2|^2 + |y_1 - y_2|^2}$$

where the symbol $|x_1 - x_2|$ means the absolute value of $x_1 - x_2$

2. You are dealt 13 cards. These are entered on one data record in the following manner: the numbers 01–13 represent the spades from the 2 to the ace; 14–26 represents the hearts from the 2 to the ace; 27–39, diamonds from the 2 to the ace; 40–52, clubs from the 2 to the ace. The 13 numbers are not in order. Write a program to count the number of kings. Use the MOD library function.

3. A salesperson is assigned a commission on the following basis:

| Sales | Commission |
|-------|------------|
| $0.00–$ 500.00 | 1% |
| $500.01–$5000.00 | 5% |
| over $5000.00 | 8% |

   a. Write a main program to read a name and a sale (one set per record) and a subprogram to compute the commission. Print the name and commission.
   b. Same as part a with eight sales set recorded on one record.

4. a. Array A contains N elements (N < 100). Write a function subprogram to perform a sequence check on the elements of A. If the array is in sequence (ascending), return a value of 1.
   b. Same as part a, except that it is not know whether the elements of A are in ascending or descending order. The first entry sets the ordering sequence.

5. Each student record of an input file consists of a name and ten test scores. The student is allowed to drop his or her lowest score before an average is figured. Use a subprogram to find the sum of the scores for each student and another subprogram to find the minimum score. Print the student's name and average. (The subprograms should be general, allowing an array of up to 100 in size.)

6. Write a function subprogram to calculate the difference in absolute value between the largest and smallest elements of an array of variable length.

7. a. Write a function to accept a number between 1 and 10 and return the corresponding word. For example, 3 would yield THREE.
   b. Write another function to accept a number between 20 and 99 and return the corresponding words. For example, 25 would yield TWENTY FIVE.

8. Write a function subprogram to return a three-character abbreviation for the name of a month given the month number as an argument. Test your program with appropriate data.

9. On the first record of an input file we have entered the answers (1, 2, 3, 4) to a multiple choice test of 10 questions. On the second record, we have entered the number of students taking the test. Each following record consists of a student's name and 10 answers to the 10 questions. Write a subprogram to determine the percentage of correct answers for each student and another subprogram to determine the student's grade

(90–100 = A, 80–89 = B, 60–79 = C, below 60 = D). The output should be performed by a function that prints the student's name, the letter grade, and percentage of correct answers. Given the following input, the output should be as follows:

Correct answers to the 10 questions

```
1123142433
3 ← number of students
JONES 1123142433
SATO  1123111324
LAKY  4123142432
```

```
NAME    GRADE   PERCENTAGE
JONES     A         100
SATA      D          50
LAKY      B          80
```

10. A store maintains an inventory data file in the following form: The first record in an input file contains the current date in the form YYDDD where YY refers to the year and DDD the number of days elapsed since the year started. Each succeeding record contains the date (same format as above) of the last time an item was sold, the number of items on hand, the cost per item, and the regular selling price. The store plans a sale to try to sell slow-moving items. A program is needed to produce a report showing the recommended sale price using the following guidelines:

> If the item has not been sold in last 30 days, the discount is 10%.
> If the item has not been sold in last 60 days, the discount is 20%.
> If the item has not been sold in last 90 days, the discount is 40%.

However, any item that has been sold in the last 30 days is not to be put on sale, and if there is only one of an item left in stock, it is not to be placed on sale no matter when the last date of sale was. In addition, the sale price may not be lower than the cost. Write a subprogram to return the sale price of a particular item, and use a main program to read the data and produce a report for all the items read. Note that some of the sales may have occurred in a prior year.

11. a. Each record of an input file contains an employee name, a number of hours worked, and a rate of pay. Write a main program to read the records and call a function subprogram to compute each employee's pay. Hours in excess of 40 are paid at a rate of time and a half. The printout should list the employee name, number of hours worked, rate of pay, and pay.

    b. Same as part a, except that the input file is recorded on one record as follows:

number of employee records

    c. Same as part a, except that the input file consists of at most 100 records where each record contains 10 employee records. For example, the input file might be as follows:

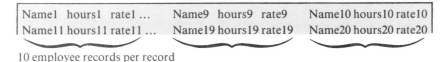

10 employee records per record

12. Write a program to read sets of data records with the following form: The first entry on a record is N, which tells how many numbers are to be read from that record. N may not exceed 25. All numbers read must be stored in just one array, i.e., use only one ar-

ray for this exercise. Write a program to compute the average of each of the sets of numbers and then the average of all the numbers, using a function subprogram to compute the average of each set of numbers. The input and output can be visualized as follows:

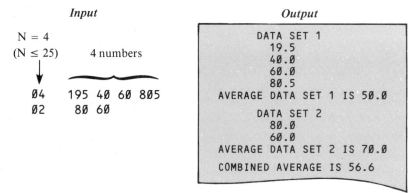

13. You are the personnel director of a large company, and for every person you place in a job you enter the following two entries on a record:

Sex code (2 = male, 1 = female) and first year's starting salary

Read all the input data into a two dimensional array and *then* write the code using different subprograms to determine each of the following:
   a. Total number of persons placed in jobs.          d. Maximum salary paid to males.
   b. Total amount of salaries paid the first year.     e. Average salary paid to females.
   c. Average salary per person.

14. The president of the XSTAR Company realizes that the company's present accounting procedures are too slow, too inefficient, and not sufficiently accurate to deal with the company's increasing annual processing volume. Plans have been made to replace manual accounting operations with a wholly computerized system. The current total manual operating costs in millions of dollars in terms of annual processing volume is given by $y = x + .5$ (where $y$ is the dollar cost and $x$ is the annual processing volume). Projected total computerized cost is given by the formula $y = .75x + 2$. The anticipated annual processing volume will be close to four units. Write a program to:
   a. Determine graphically whether the president's decision to switch to a computerized system is economically sound (graph both lines).
   b. Determine graphically the breakeven point (the annual volume of processing that would justify the president's plan for changing methods of operation).
   Realizing that an annual volume of processing of four units is not sufficient to warrant such a change in operations, a compromise is effected. The new operational procedures will involve both manual and computer operations. The cost attached to such a new system is given by $y = .445x + 1.5$. Write a program to:
   c. Determine graphically whether such a system would be economically beneficial to the company.
   d. Determine graphically the breakeven point for the total computerized system versus the computer manual plan.

15. The Toystar Corporation is marketing a new toy. Expected revenues are approximated by the function $y = 3\sqrt{x}$. Costs associated with the production and the sales of the toy are defined by the function $y = 2 + x^2/4$. Write a program to determine graphically the breakeven point for the production of the new toy.

**16.** Write a program to graph the total profit function of the example in Exercise 15. The total profit function is defined as the difference between the cost and revenue function, that is, $T(x) = |R(x) - C(x)|$, where $R$, $C$, and $T$ are, respectively, the revenue, the cost, and the total profit functions. Identify on the total profit graph the point at which profit is maximum.

## 9-7-3 Programming Problems: Mathematical/Scientific

**1.** Find the square roots of ten positive real numbers read from one record. Remember there are two roots, a positive and a negative root.

**2.** Modify the program in Figure 9–1 to produce a table showing the distance traveled by the ship for angles varying from $1°$ to $45°$. How is the program changed if the ship is two miles offshore?

**3.** Use a statement function to compute the square root of 43, using the formula

$$x = \frac{1}{2}(x + \frac{43}{x})$$

Start with $x = 1$ to get a new value for $x$, then use that new value in the formula to get a newer value. Proceed in this fashion until the refined value is such that

$$|x^2 - 43| < .01$$

**4.** Given $ax^2 + bx + c = 0$, the roots (values for $x$ that make the statement true) are given by $\frac{-b \pm \sqrt{b^2 - 4ac}}{2a}$. Write a main program to read values for $a$, $b$, and $c$. If $a$ is zero, then there is only one real value for $x$ ($x = -c/b$). If $b^2 - 4ac$ is negative, then there are two complex roots for $x$. If $b^2 - ac$ is positive or zero, then there are two real roots for $x$, which are given by the formula. Write a subprogram that returns a 1 if $a = 0$, returns a 2 if $b^2 - 4ac$ is negative, and returns a 3 if $b^2 - 4ac$ is positive or zero. Then, depending on the value returned, write an appropriate message or answer.

**5.** Write a function to calculate the standard deviation of a set of measurements contained in an array of variable length (see section 7–10–3, exercise 3).

**6.** Write statement functions for each of the following:
   a. $V = \pi r^3$
   b. $y = ax^3 + bx^2 + cx + d$
   c. $q = x\sin(x) + x^2 \cos(x)$ where $x$ is to be expressed in degrees
   d. the difference between the largest and smallest values in a list of six real values

**7.** Iterative methods for solving systems of linear equations (illustrated in Figure 9–15) can be terminated under either of the following conditions:

   a. When $|x_{n+1} - x_n| < \epsilon$ and $|y_{n+1} - y_n| < \epsilon$, where $\epsilon$ is a prescribed degree of accuracy.
   b. When $x_n$ and $y_n$ are substituted back into the equations and the numerical results are within $\epsilon$ of the constants on the righthand side of the original system of equations.

Write a program using the Gauss-Seidel method to solve a system of equations and use programmer-defined functions to terminate the iterative process using both of the above termination criteria. Set $\epsilon = .01$. Which criterion terminates the process first for the given set of equations.

**8.** It can be shown that:

$$\sin(x) = x - \frac{x^3}{3!} + \frac{x^5}{5!} - \frac{x^7}{7!} + \ldots$$

where $x$ is expressed in radians. Write a program to calculate values of $\sin(x)$ using the first five terms of the formula for values of $x$ ranging from $0°$ to $90°$ in increments of $10°$. Compare your results with the values returned by the FORTRAN function SIN.

**9.** The number $e$ can be defined as the limit of $\left(\frac{n+1}{n}\right)^n$ as $n$ tends to infinity:

$$e = \lim_{n \to \infty} \left(\frac{n+1}{n}\right)^n$$

Using this definition of $e$, write a program to determine $n$ so that:

$$\left| e - \left(\frac{n+1}{n}\right)^n \right| < .001 \qquad \text{Use the function EXP for } e.$$

**10.** Write a program to show that as $n$ gets larger and larger, each of the following expressions converges to a limit. Can you guess the limits from your printouts?

a. $\left(\frac{n^2+1}{n+1}\right)$  
b. $\frac{\log(n)}{n}$  
c. $n \cdot \log\left(1 + \frac{1}{n}\right)$

**11.** Write a program to determine the limits of the following expressions as $x$ approaches 0. (Let $x$ range from $1°$ to $.1°$ in steps of $.1°$.)

a. $\frac{\sin(x)}{x}$  
c. $\frac{\tan(2x)}{\sin(7x)}$  
e. $\frac{15t}{\tan(6t)}$

b. $\frac{\tan(x)}{x}$  
d. $\frac{x \cdot \sin(x)}{1 - \cos(x)}$

Recall that $x$ must be expressed in radians.

**12.** Using the exponential function EXP(X), compute EXP(1). The value of $e$ to eight places is 2.71828182. Can you obtain a better approximation than EXP(1) by using the following series definition?

$$e^x = 1 + \frac{x}{1!} + \frac{x^2}{2!} + \frac{x^3}{3!} + \ldots + \frac{x^n}{n!} + \ldots$$

How many terms of the series do you need to improve on EXP(1)? Use double precision for the computations.

**13.** Write a function subprogram to evaluate the determinant of a 3 by 3 matrix. Recall that

$$\begin{vmatrix} a_{11} & a_{12} & a_{13} \\ a_{21} & a_{22} & a_{23} \\ a_{31} & a_{32} & a_{33} \end{vmatrix} = a_{11} \begin{vmatrix} a_{22} & a_{23} \\ a_{32} & a_{33} \end{vmatrix} - a_{21} \begin{vmatrix} a_{12} & a_{13} \\ a_{32} & a_{33} \end{vmatrix} + a_{31} \begin{vmatrix} a_{12} & a_{13} \\ a_{22} & a_{23} \end{vmatrix}$$

**14.** Write a function subprogram to evaluate C(N,M) (see section 9-4-10).

**15.** Sometimes it is helpful to expand or contract a graph. Scale factors are used for this purpose. Rewrite the breakeven analysis program of Figure 9-6 to change both graphs by using the functions:

$$y = n(15xe^{-x/3}) \quad \text{and} \quad y = n\left(\frac{x^3}{16} - \frac{x^2}{2} + \frac{7x}{4} + 4\right)$$

where $n$ is a scale factor accepted from input. If $n = 1$, the graph should be identical to the one depicted in Figure 9–6. If $n = 10$, the graph should be steeper, and if $n = .5$ the graph should be wider (more elongated). Try various scale factors.

16. Determine graphically the roots of $y = x \sin(x)$ as $x$ varies from 0 to $3\pi$. You may have to use a scale factor. Remember that this does not affect the roots.

17. What scale factors could you use on $y = 1/x$ to get a feel for the shape of the graph of that function? Experiment by graphing that function.

18. Write a program to plot a circle.

   [*Hint*: The equation of a circle of radius $r$ centered on the $y$ axis passing through the origin is given by:

   $$(y - r)^2 + x^2 = r^2 \text{ or } y = \pm \sqrt{r^2 - x^2} + r$$

   Plot both branches by adding .5 to the $y$ positive branch and $-.5$ to the $y$ negative branch. Use $r = 4.5$ initially.]

19. Generalize exercise 19 to accept the radius from input.

20. A company has 10 delivery trucks. It uses a 2-dimensional coordinate scheme to keep track of the location of each truck:

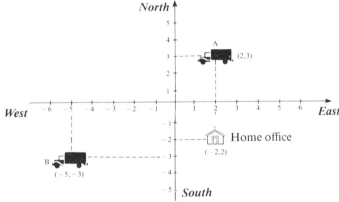

   a. Write a program to read 10 truck coordinates and vehicle numbers to determine which truck is closest to the home office. Write a subprogram to compute the distances between each truck and the home office and another subprogram to determine the least distance. The main program should print the location of the closest truck and its vehicle number.

   b. In an interactive environment, how would you structure your program to keep accepting new truck coordinates (as some of these move about) and determine which is closest at any given time?

## 9-7-4 Answers to Test Yourself

1.  a. A = SIN(X)**2 - COS(X)**2
    b. Z = EXP(X) - EXP(-X)
    c. X = SQRT(ABS(P - Q))
    d. ALARG = MAX(A,B,C,D,E)
    e. KSMAL = MIN(I,J,K,3)

2. To round the value in A to the nearest hundred:

       A = 100. * INT((A + 50.)/100.)

   To round the value in A to the nearest thousandth:

       A = INT(A + .0005)*1000.)/1000.

**3.** a. 9.     b. 3.     c. $-2$     d. $-100$.     e. 2.4.     f. 102.4.
    g. 0.     h. $-2.4$    i. 100.    j. 83.4.     k. 2.     l. 1.

**4.** The values for $\tan x$ for values of $x$ close to 0, $2\pi$, etc., would appear to fall on a straight line, because the differences among successive values of the function are small in these intervals. The factor 4 is needed to "magnify" the differences so that they are visible on the graph.

**5.**
```
CHARACTER LINE(126)
    .
    .
    .
J = (Y + 9)*7 + 0.5
IF(J.LT.0 .OR. J.GT.126) THEN
```

**6.** a. Invalid; 4 and Z different types.
    b. Valid.
    c. Invalid; type of function must be the same in the calling program and in the function definition.
    d. Invalid reference to a singly dimensioned array A.
    e. Invalid; 2 + S and J different types.
    f. Valid.
    g. Valid.
    h. Invalid; function has no name.
    i. Invalid; COT(3) should have three arguments.
    j. Invalid; subscripted variable T(1).
    k. Invalid; function reference cannot occur in I/O statement list.
    l. Invalid; function name type conflict.
    m. Invalid; GUN, NON different types.
    n. Invalid dummy argument X + Y.
    o. Valid.
    p. Dummy argument cannot be a constant.
    q. Invalid; function is not assigned a value.
    r. Valid.
    s. Valid.

**7.** a. Invalid; dummy argument cannot be an expression.
    b. Valid.
    c. Invalid; function name too long.
    d. Valid (user defines own SQRT).
    e. Invalid; function name and argument cannot be the same.
    f. Invalid; argument cannot be subscripted variable.
    g. Invalid; function name is missing.
    h. Invalid, dummy argument cannot be a constant.

**8.** a. Invalid; dimensioned variable cannot be in dummy argument list.
    b. Invalid; function cannot refer to itself.
    c. Valid.
    d. Valid.
    e. Invalid; function definition must precede executable statements.
    f. Valid; dummy variables may be used as actual variables in a program.
    g. Invalid; dummy arguments may not be constants.

h. Valid.
i. Invalid; number of arguments in function reference and in function definition do not match.
j. Invalid; expression (X + 1) cannot be used as a dummy argument.
k. Invalid; type of actual arguments must match type of dummy arguments.

9. a. T.   b. F.   c. F.   d. T.   e. T.   f. F.   g. F.   h. F.
   i. T.   j. F.   k. T.   l. T.   m. F.   n. T.   o. T.

10. 
```
REAL L,J,I
FN(L,J,A) = L*X*X + J*X - A
Y = FN(3.,2.,1.)
T = FN(I,7.,TOT)
S = FN(3.,-K(2),-SIN(T))
IF(FN(17.,MIN(A,B),SQRT(A)).GT.0.3) THEN
```

11. 
```
REAL L,J,I
FN(L,J,A,Y) = L*Y*Y + J*Y - A
Y = FN(3.,2.,1.,T)
T = FN(I,7.,TOT,X)
S = FN(3.,-K(2),-SIN(T),X)
IF(FN(17.,MIN(A,B),SQRT(A),X).GT.0.3) THEN
```

12. 
```
a. SIDE(A,B,C) = A*A + B*B + 2.*A*B*COS(C)
b. A(T,AI,J) = P*(1. + AI/J)**(J*T)
c. SINT(R,N) = P*(1. + R)**N
d. R(R1,R2,R3) = (1./R1 + 1./R2 + 1./R3)**(-1)
e. HF(A,TI,T0) = .92*A*(TI - T0)/H
f. E(X) = 1. + X*X + X*X/2. + X**3/6.
g. F(B,ASM,X,T) = B*EXP(-A*X)*COS(SQRT(B*B-A**2*X - T))
```

13. a. −18,8    b. 1172,8.45.

14. 
```
APPROX(M,D,Y) = 365.25*Y + (M-1)*30.4 + D
PROX(M1,D1,Y1,M2,D2,Y2)=ABS(APPROX(M1,D1,Y1)-APPROX(M2,D2,Y2))
```

15. 
```
ROUND(Q) = INT((Q + 0.005)*100.)/100.
```

16. 
```
REM(X,Y) = X - INT(X/Y)*Y
```

17. 
```
HYP(A,B) = SQRT(A**2 + B**2)
```

18. 
```
      REAL A(10),VECLEN
    3 READ(5,1,END=88) N,(A(I),I = 1,N)
      ALEN = VECLEN(A,N)
      PRINT*, ALEN
      GO TO 3
   88 STOP
    1 FORMAT(I2,10F4.1)
      END
      REAL FUNCTION VECLEN(A,N)
      REAL A(N)
      VECLEN = 0.
      DO 9 I = 1,N
         VECLEN = VECLEN + A(I)**2
    9 CONTINUE
      VECLEN = VECLEN**.5
      RETURN
      END
```

19. 
```
      REAL A(10),FUNC,PX,X
      READ*,N,(A(I),I = 1,N)
      X = -5.
    6 IF(X.GT.5.) STOP
      PX = FUNC(N,A,X)
      PRINT*,X,PX
      X = X + .5
      GO TO 6
      END
      REAL FUNCTION FUNC(N,A,X)
      REAL A(10)
      FUNC = 0.
      DO 5 I = 1,N+1
         FUNC = FUNC + A(I)*X**(N+1-I)
    5 CONTINUE
      RETURN
      END
```

# subroutines

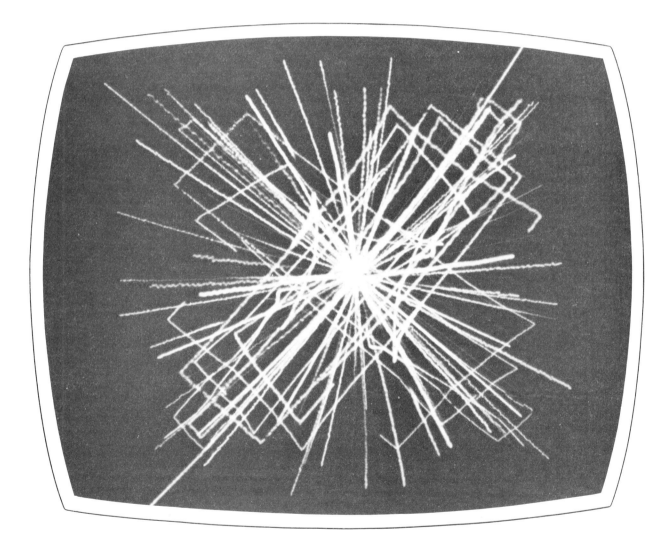

CHAPTER TEN

# subroutines

## 10-1 Programming Example

Dr. D teaches two FORTRAN classes. Array CLASS1 contains the 10 final scores of class 1, while array CLASS2 contains the 8 final scores of class 2. To ensure fairness, Dr. D assigns final scores as follows:

■ If the average of class 1 is less than the average of class 2, all class 1 students get 5% of their class's average added to their scores.

■ If the average of class 2 is less than the average of class 1, all class 2 students get 5% of their class's average added to their scores.

■ If the difference between the two class averages is less than 5 points, the scores are left unchanged.

Write a program to do the following (in the sequence shown):

1. Read the scores in arrays CLASS1 and CLASS2 and print both sets of scores.

2. Compute the average scores for CLASS1 and CLASS2 and print the averages (use a subroutine).

3. Compute the 5% bonus, add the bonus to each score, and print the bonus and the adjusted scores (use a subroutine).

Given the following input file, the output should be as follows:

```
Ø6Ø.ØØ7Ø.ØØ8Ø.ØØ9Ø.ØØ5Ø.ØØ6Ø.ØØ7Ø.ØØ8Ø.ØØ8Ø.ØØ65.Ø ──────► class 1 input scores
Ø1Ø.ØØ2Ø.ØØ3Ø.ØØ4Ø.ØØ5Ø.ØØ6Ø.ØØ7Ø.ØØ9Ø.Ø ─────────────► class 2 input scores
```

```
CLASS 1 SCORES:          60.0 70.0 80.0 90.0 50.0 60.0 70.0 80.0 80.0 65.0
CLASS 2 SCORES:          10.0 20.0 30.0 40.0 50.0 60.0 70.0 90.0
CLASS 1 AVERAGE = 70.50
CLASS 2 AVERAGE = 46.25
BONUS= 2.3
ADJUSTED SCORES CLASS 2  12.3 22.3 32.3 42.3 52.3 62.3 72.3 92.3
```

A program to solve this problem is shown in Figure 10–1. The program in the left column of Figure 10–1 is written without subroutines and the program in the right column is written with subroutines. In the program with subroutines, note the use of:

1. The CALL statement, which calls for the execution of a subroutine and passes arguments to the subprogram.

2. The SUBROUTINE statement, which declares that a subprogram is a subroutine and lists the set of expected arguments.

**FIGURE 10-1**   PROGRAMMING EXAMPLE WITH SUBROUTINES

```
C PROGRAM WITHOUT SUBROUTINES
C   AV1, AV2: CLASS 1 & CLASS 2 AVERAGES
C   SUM: ACCUMULATES SCORES OF BOTH CLASSES SUCCESSIVELY
C   CLASS1(10): CLASS1 SCORES
C   CLASS2(08): CLASS2 SCORES
C   BONUS: 5% OF EITHER AVERAGE CLASS1 OR AVERAGE CLASS2
C   N: NUMBER OF STUDENTS IN CLASS1 OR IN CLASS2
C   K: CLASS NUMBER (1 OR 2)
      REAL AV1, AV2, SUM, BONUS
      REAL CLASS1(10), CLASS2(8)
      READ(5,3) CLASS1, CLASS2
      WRITE(6,1)CLASS1, CLASS2

      SUM = 0.
      DO 5 I = 1, 10
         SUM = SUM + CLASS1(I)
5     CONTINUE
      AV1 = SUM / 10.

      SUM = 0.
      DO 6 I = 1, 8
         SUM = SUM + CLASS2(I)
6     CONTINUE
      AV2 = SUM / 8.

      WRITE(6,4) AV1,AV2
      IF(ABS(AV1 - AV2) .LT. 5.) STOP
      IF(AV1 .GT. AV2) THEN

         BONUS = AV2 * .05
         DO 7 I = 1, 8
            CLASS2(I)=CLASS2(I)+BONUS
7        CONTINUE
         K = 2
         WRITE(6,2) BONUS, K,CLASS2

      ELSE

         BONUS = AV1 * .05
         DO 8 I = 1, 10
            CLASS1(I)=CLASS1(I)+BONUS
8        CONTINUE
         K = 1
         WRITE(6,2) BONUS, K, CLASS1

      ENDIF
      STOP
1     FORMAT(' CLASS 1 SCORES:',9X,10F5.1/
     *        ' CLASS 2 SCORES:',9X,10F5.1)
2     FORMAT(' BONUS=',F5.1/1X,
     *'ADJUSTED SCORES CLASS',I2,1X,10F5.1)
3     FORMAT(10F5.1)
4     FORMAT(' CLASS 1 AVERAGE = ',F6.2/
     *        ' CLASS 2 AVERAGE = ',F6.2)
      END
```

*Program with Subroutines*

```
      REAL AV1, AV2
      REAL CLASS1(10), CLASS2(8)
      READ(5,3) CLASS1, CLASS2
      WRITE(6,1)CLASS1, CLASS2
      CALL AVRGE(CLASS1,AV1,10)
      CALL AVRGE(CLASS2,AV2, 8)
      WRITE(6,4) AV1,AV2
      IF(ABS(AV1 - AV2).LT.5.)STOP
      IF (AV1 .GT. AV2) THEN
         CALL ADJUST(CLASS2, AV2, 8, 2)
      ELSE
         CALL ADJUST(CLASS1, AV1, 10, 1)
      ENDIF
      STOP
1     FORMAT(' CLASS 1 SCORES:',9X,10F5.1/
     *        ' CLASS 2 SCORES:',9X,10F5.1)
3     FORMAT(10F5.1)
4     FORMAT(' CLASS 1 AVERAGE = ',F6.2/
     *        ' CLASS 2 AVERAGE = ',F6.2)
      END

      SUBROUTINE AVRGE(CLASS, AVG, N)
      REAL CLASS(10), AVG, SUM
      INTEGER N
      SUM = 0.
      DO 5 I = 1, N
         SUM = SUM + CLASS(I)
5     CONTINUE
      AVG = SUM / N
      RETURN
      END

      SUBROUTINE ADJUST(CLASS, AVG, N, K)
      REAL CLASS(10), AVG, BONUS
      INTEGER K, N
      BONUS = AVG * .05
      DO 9 I = 1, N
         CLASS(I) = CLASS(I) + BONUS
9     CONTINUE
      WRITE(6,2) BONUS,K,(CLASS(I),I=1,N)
      RETURN
2     FORMAT(' BONUS=',F5.1/1X,
     *'ADJUSTED SCORES CLASS',I2,1X,10F5.1)
      END
```

```
CLASS 1 SCORES:          60.0 70.0 80.0 90.0 50.0 60.0 70.0 80.0 80.0 65.0
CLASS 2 SCORES:          10.0 20.0 30.0 40.0 50.0 60.0 70.0 90.0
CLASS 1 AVERAGE = 70.50
CLASS 2 AVERAGE = 46.25
BONUS=  2.3
ADJUSTED SCORES CLASS 2  12.3 22.3 32.3 42.3 52.3 62.3 72.3 92.3
```

The program in Figure 10–2 explains the essential features of the program with subroutines; each of three independent program segments performs specific tasks. These program segments are:

1. The main program, which coordinates the use of the two subroutines AVRGE and ADJUST.

2. The AVRGE program, which computes and returns to the main program the average of N scores stored in array CLASS.

3. The ADJUST program, which adds a constant (BONUS) to each of the N grades in the array CLASS and prints the adjusted scores.

**FIGURE 10-2**   SAMPLE PROGRAM WITH EXPLANATIONS

```
      REAL CLASS1(10),CLASS2(8)
```
CLASS1 contains the ten scores of class 1, CLASS2 contains the eight scores of class 2.

```
      READ(5,3)CLASS1,CLASS2
    3 FORMAT(10F5.1)
      WRITE(6,1)CLASS1,CLASS2
```
Read scores from both classes into CLASS1 and CLASS2 and write them out.

```
      CALL AVRGE(CLASS1,AV1,10)
```
Call the AVRGE program to compute the average (AV1) of ten scores stored in array CLASS1. In subroutine AVRGE the array CLASS1 is referred to as CLASS, AV1 is referred to as AVG, and N is equal to ten. The subroutine stores the result (average) into AVG, which is the same memory location as AV1.

```
      CALL AVRGE(CLASS2,AV2,8)
      .
      .
      IF(AV1.GT.AV2) THEN
         CALL ADJUST(CLASS2,AV2,8,2)
      ELSE
         CALL ADJUST(CLASS1,AV1,10,1)
      ENDIF
      .
      .
      END
```
The AVRGE program is called again, this time to compute the average of eight scores stored in CLASS2. The resulting average is stored in memory location AV2 (called AVG in subprogram).

Determine which class has lowest average. If AV2 is lowest, the 8 scores in CLASS2 and the average of class 2 (AV2) are transmitted to program ADJUST. The argument 2 identifies the class number (K in subroutine ADJUST).

Program ADJUST adds five percent of AV1 or AV2 (BONUS) to each class 1 or class 2 score and stores the resulting adjusted scores in CLASS.

Upon return from ADJUST, the adjusted scores will either be in CLASS1 and CLASS2, and BONUS will be equal to five percent of AV1 or AV2.

```
      SUBROUTINE AVRGE(CLASS,AVG,N)
      REAL CLASS(10),AVG,SUM
      SUM = 0.
      DO 5 I = 1,N
        SUM = SUM + CLASS(I)
    5 CONTINUE
      AVG = SUM/N
      RETURN
      END
```
This is a general program to compute the average of N scores stored in array CLASS, and store the average in AVG. The array argument must be declared as an array in the subroutine. If AV1 < AV2, CLASS is just another name for array CLASS1. If AV2 < AV1, then array CLASS refers to array CLASS2. Likewise AVG refers to either AV1 or AV2 in the calling program.

```
      SUBROUTINE ADJUST(CLASS,AVG,N,K)
      REAL CLASS(10),AVG,BONUS
      BONUS = AVG*0.05
      DO 9 I = 1,N
        CLASS(I) = CLASS(I) + BONUS
    9 CONTINUE
      WRITE(6,6)BONUS, K,(CLASS(I),I=1,N)
      RETURN
    6 FORMAT(1X,'BONUS = ',F5.1/1X,
     *'ADJUSTED SCORES CLASS',I2,1X,10F5.1)
      END
```
This program performs the following general procedure: Add 5% of AVG to each of the N scores in array CLASS, and print out these scores and the class number (K).

BONUS equals 5% of the average AVG.

K is either 1 or 2 and is used to print the class.

CLASS corresponds to either CLASS1 or CLASS2.

N is either 10 or 8.

AVG corresponds to either AV1 or AV2.

The three programs are compiled independently of one another.

Information (the score arrays, the number of scores, and so forth) is passed from the *calling* program to the *called* program through the arguments specified in the CALL statement and in the SUBROUTINE definition statement. Arguments can be used as two-way or one-way communication links between the calling and the called program. In the AVRGE program, array CLASS is a two-way argument: it sends the values to the subroutine, where they are modified and then sent back to the calling program (through the same array)! The AVG argument in subroutine AVRGE is used to transmit a result from the subroutine back to the main program. The correspondence between the arguments in the CALL and SUBROUTINE statements is illustrated in Figure 10–3. Information and results are thus passed between the called and calling program by means of arguments.

The sequence of execution for the three blocks of code is shown in Figure 10–4. Note how the use of subroutines eliminate duplication of code as shown on the righthand side of

**FIGURE 10-3** CORRESPONDENCE BETWEEN THE ARGUMENTS IN THE CALL AND SUBROUTINE STATEMENTS

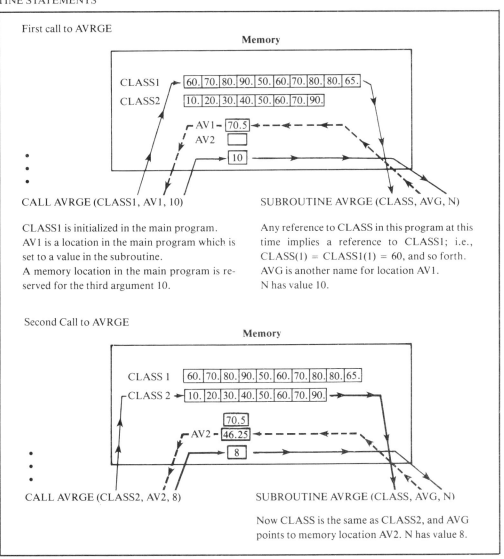

Figure 10–4. Whenever a procedure (task) is to be performed, a transfer is made to that procedure through the CALL statement; when the task is completed, the procedure returns (RETURN) to the program that called the procedure. In the program in Figure 10–1, instead of writing the codes to determine the average and adjust the scores twice, one block of code is written for each of these tasks, and each block is called twice by the main program.

The reader may think that there is not much difference between a function and a subroutine subprogram. The difference is barely noticeable—in fact, the AVRGE program could have been written as a function subprogram since only *one* result is passed from the subprogram to the main program. In the ADJUST program, however, *eight* or *ten* results are passed back to the main program; i.e., the entire array CLASS1 or CLASS2 is changed by the subprogram and sent back to the main program. (An ADJUST function subprogram could have been written to modify the scores in array CLASS and pass them back to the calling program, but functions are supposed to return only one value to the calling program. Hence it would be very bad practice to use a function to pass values back to the main program through its arguments.)

**FIGURE 10-4** FLOWPATH BETWEEN MAIN PROGRAM AND SUBPROGRAMS

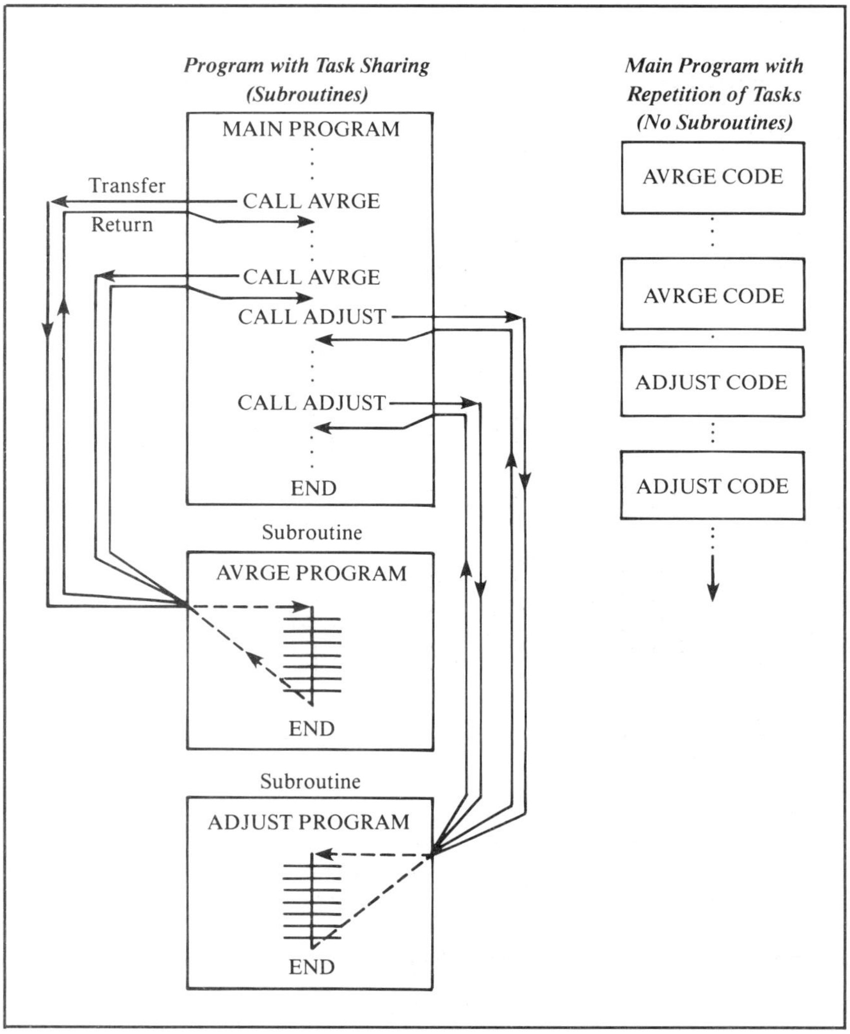

## 10-2 FORTRAN Statements

### 10-2-1 Subroutines

A subroutine is an independently compiled block of code sometimes called a *subprogram*. The prefix *sub-* implies that a subroutine is not really a complete program, in the sense that if it were executed by itself it would not produce meaningful results. Subroutines are usually written to carry out generalized procedures that are data-independent, for example, sorting or merging arrays of any size and so forth. Arguments (sometimes called *dummy arguments*) provide the data for the subroutine to use in its procedures. These arguments must be specifically identified by the program wishing to use the subroutine. The name of the particular array to be sorted and the exact number of grades for which an average is to be computed are examples of arguments that might be passed to a subroutine.

A subroutine should be viewed as one logical component of a total program that might consist of numerous other logical components (subprograms). A subroutine can be accessed (executed) from another program (main program or other subprogram) through the CALL statement.

### 10-2-2 The CALL Statement

The general form of the CALL statement is:

> CALL *subroutine name* $[(a_1, a_2, a_3, ..., a_n)]$

where CALL is a required key word,

> *subroutine name* is the name of the subroutine (any valid variable name), and
> $a_1, a_2, ..., a_n$ are arguments to be passed to the subroutine. These arguments can be variables, subscripted variables, array names, constants, expressions, or function names. Arguments are used either to transmit data from the calling program or to receive data (values, results) from the called program. Arguments are optional.

*Examples*

| | |
|---|---|
| CALL SUB(X) | One argument is passed to the subroutine called SUB. |
| CALL XRAY | No arguments (print headings only, for example). |
| CALL S1(A,B(1),3*I + K,J) | Four arguments are passed to the subroutine; $3*I + K$ is evaluated and passed to the third argument of S1. |
| CALL SUB2(SIN(X),Y) | The sine of X will be evaluated and the value passed to the first argument of SUB2. |

### 10-2-3 The SUBROUTINE Statement

The SUBROUTINE statement must be the first statement in every subroutine subprogram. The general form of the SUBROUTINE statement is:

> SUBROUTINE *subroutine name* $[(p_1, p_2, p_3, ..., p_n)]$

where SUBROUTINE is a required key word,

subroutine name is the name of the subroutine (any valid variable name), and $p_1$, $p_2$, $p_3$, ..., $p_n$ are dummy arguments used to communicate data to and from the calling program. These arguments can either be variables, array names, or function names (no subscripted variable names or constants).

If an argument is an array name, the array name must be declared in a type or DIMENSION statement within the subroutine. The size of that array should be the same as the size of the corresponding argument (array) in the calling program (see section 10–4–2 for exceptions). The dummy arguments used in the subroutine refer to the actual names or arguments listed in the invocation statement of the calling program. When the subroutine is executed, the dummy arguments take on the values of the "real" arguments specified in the CALL statement of the calling program. More precisely, the subroutine directly processes the real arguments through the dummy arguments.

**The arguments in the CALL statement should correspond in number, order, and type with the dummy arguments of the SUBROUTINE statement. The names used may be the same or different.** The order of the arguments in the CALL statement and in the SUBROUTINE statement must be the same; that is, there must be a one-to-one correspondence between the two sets of arguments.

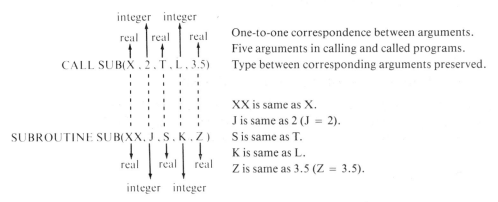

One-to-one correspondence between arguments.
Five arguments in calling and called programs.
Type between corresponding arguments preserved.

XX is same as X.
J is same as 2 (J = 2).
S is same as T.
K is same as L.
Z is same as 3.5 (Z = 3.5).

The RETURN statement returns control to the statement immediately following the CALL statement in the calling program. Many RETURN statements can be included in a subroutine. A distinguishing feature of the subroutine is that at its conclusion the statement to which transfer (return) is made in the calling program is variable (unlike the GO TO statement)

*Example 1*

| Main Program | Subprogram | Comments |
|---|---|---|
| DATA X,Y/3.,4./ | SUBROUTINE ADD(A,B,C) | |
| CALL ADD(X,Y,R) | C = A + B | C is same as R. |
| WRITE(6,1)R | RETURN | The value of R is 7. |
| CALL ADD(X,R,Z) | END | C is same as Z. |
| WRITE(6,1)Z | | The value of Z is 10. |

In the first call to ADD, arguments A, B, and C correspond to X, Y, and R, respectively. In the second call to ADD, arguments A, B, and C correspond to X, R, and Z, respectively.

It should be emphasized again that the subroutine can change the value of a variable in the main program. Consider the following example:

*Example 2*

| Main Program | Subprogram | Comments |
|---|---|---|
| | `SUBROUTINE TRI(X,C)` | |
| : | : | |
| : | : | |
| : | : | |
| `A = 4.0` | `X = 7.0` | The subroutine changes |
| `CALL TRI (A,B)` | `C = 3.1` | the value of A to 7.0 |
| `WRITE(6,1)A` | `RETURN` | since X really refers to A. |
| : | `END` | |
| : | | |

A is 4. when the call is made to the subroutine; on return to the main program, the value for A will be 7.; the value for B will be 3.1.

The value of any expression in the CALL statement is calculated before passing values of parameters to the subroutine.

*Example 3*

| Main Program | Subprogram |
|---|---|
| : | `SUBROUTINE SUB4(A,B,C)` |
| : | : |
| `X = 3.0` | : |
| `Y = 2.0` | |
| `CALL SUB4(X,X+Y,3.*Y)` | |

The value of A will be 3.0; the value of B will be 5.0; the value of C will be 6.0.

If an array is to be passed to a subroutine, the name of the array is specified in the CALL statement. The array name used in the subroutine must be specified in a type or DI-MENSION statement and its size must equal the size of the corresponding array in the calling program.

*Example 4*          Note

| Main Program | Subprogram |
|---|---|
| `REAL A(10),B(10)` | `SUBROUTINE SUMIT(X,S)` |
| : | `REAL X(10),S` |
| : | `S = 0.0` |
| `CALL SUMIT(A,SUM1)` | `DO 10 I = 1,10` |
| : | `10 S = S + X(I)` |
| : | `RETURN` |
| `CALL SUMIT(B,SUM2)` | `END` |

Two calls to subroutine SUMIT are made. As a result, SUM1 and SUM2 will contain the sums of the elements of arrays A and B, respectively.

The following are incorrect SUBROUTINE statements:

| Main Program | Subprogram | Comments |
|---|---|---|
| `CALL SUM(A,B,C)` | `SUBROUTINE SUM(A,B)` | Invalid. Two subroutine arguments. |
| `CALL PROD(A,3,N)` | `SUBROUTINE PROD(X,Y,I)` | Type mismatch in second argument. |
| `CALL TOT(X,3.1,2)` | `SUBROUTINE TOT(X,B(1),J)` | B(1) not allowed as argument. |
| `CALL SIS(T(3),M)` | `SUBROUTINE SIS(S,4)` | 4 is not a variable name. |
| `CALL TW(A + B,C)` | `SUBROUTINE TW(X + Y,D)` | X + Y is an invalid argument. |

Since subprograms are really separate programs that are treated independently by the compiler, identical variable names can appear in both the calling and called programs with no risk of confusion; the same holds true for statement numbers.

### 10-2-4 The COMMON Statement

One method that can be used to pass data from one subprogram to another is to specify each data item (variable) in the argument list of the CALL and SUBROUTINE statements or in the FUNCTION invocation statement and FUNCTION subprogram. It should be noted that the dummy (arguments) of the subroutine function do not really have a fixed memory address. When a dummy variable is encountered in the subprogram, the system must look up the address of the corresponding argument in the calling program and process the contents (value) of that memory location or use it for storage. The address of the dummy variable changes depending on what argument it represents in the main program. For example,

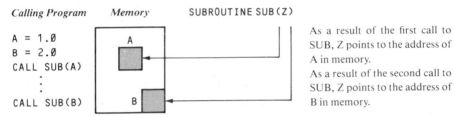

As a result of the first call to SUB, Z points to the address of A in memory.
As a result of the second call to SUB, Z points to the address of B in memory.

Another method to pass data from one subprogram to another is to use the COMMON statement. Variables to be shared among subprograms are declared in a COMMON statement. COMMON can be thought of as a block of memory locations that can be accessed (shared) by any programs containing a COMMON statement. The names of variables used to refer to the data in the COMMON block may be different in the various subprograms—the ordering and length of the variables in COMMON determines which names in one program will be associated with which names in another program. The use of COMMON in a subprogram offers immediate access to data in memory; there is no "look-up address" procedure as in the case of dummy variables (subroutine arguments), since each variable in COMMON has a predetermined (fixed) memory address:

*Example 1*

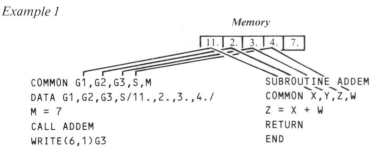

G1 and X identify the first element of the COMMON block, G2 and Y refer to the second element of the COMMON block, and so forth. M refers to the fifth element of the block. It is not used by subroutine ADDEM; it could be used by another subprogram. This subroutine adds the first and fourth elements of the COMMON block and stores the result in the third location. Hence Z = 11. + 4. = 15. In the main program the name of the third element of the COMMON block is G3. Hence G3 = 15. Note that M is not shared by the subroutine ADDEM.

*Example 2*

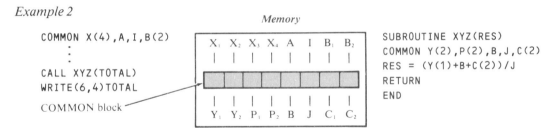

```
COMMON X(4),A,I,B(2)
      .
      .
      .
CALL XYZ(TOTAL)
WRITE(6,4)TOTAL
```
COMMON block

```
SUBROUTINE XYZ(RES)
COMMON Y(2),P(2),B,J,C(2)
RES = (Y(1)+B+C(2))/J
RETURN
END
```

As a result of the CALL statement in the main program, TOTAL = $(X(1) + A + B(2))/I$.

*Example 3*

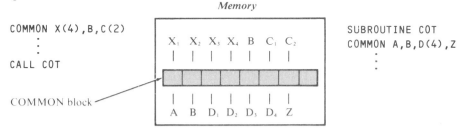

```
COMMON X(4),B,C(2)
      .
      .
      .
CALL COT
```
COMMON block

```
SUBROUTINE COT
COMMON A,B,D(4),Z
      .
      .
      .
```

Note the correspondence between the data items in COMMON.

The general form of the COMMON statement is:

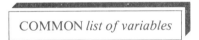

COMMON *list of variables*

where the *list of variables* can contain either variables or array names.

Dummy arguments specified in a subroutine or function argument list may not be declared in a COMMON statement. COMMON statements are specification statements that must be placed after IMPLICIT but before executable and DATA statements. Variables listed in COMMON may not be initialized through the DATA statement. The COMMON statement can be used instead of a type or DIMENSION statement to declare arrays. The following three coding sequences have same effect:

```
REAL X           or    REAL X(100)  or   COMMON X(100)
COMMON X(100)          COMMON X
```

However, `REAL X(100)`      is illegal:
         `COMMON X(100)`

Note that
```
COMMON A,B
COMMON D(5)
COMMON K
```
is equivalent to COMMON A,B,D(5),K. These give rise to the following COMMON block arrangement.

These give rise to the following COMMON block arrangement.

| A | B | $D_1$ | $D_2$ | $D_3$ | $D_4$ | $D_5$ | K | ◄—— COMMON block arrangement.

COMMON can be used to great advantage when there is a data base that is needed by several subprograms. It is often more convenient to transmit a lengthy sequence of variables with a COMMON statement than to transmit them as arguments in the calling sequence of a subprogram. A list of COMMON statements can be copied and included in the various subprograms requiring it.

The only way to communicate variables between programs is to either use the COMMON statement or to pass the variable name as an argument in the calling sequence.

### 10-2-5 Position of Subprograms in the Complete Program (JOB)

All user-defined function or subroutine subprograms are separate logical entities and as such are generally compiled independently of one another. Special system control statements (job control, workflow, and so forth) may be required to separate each program from one another as depicted in Figure 10–5. The student should determine the proper control statements required by his or her computer system. In many systems the input data is not part of the job stream but is stored as a separate file on disk.

**FIGURE 10-5** SUBPROGRAM JOB MAKE-UP

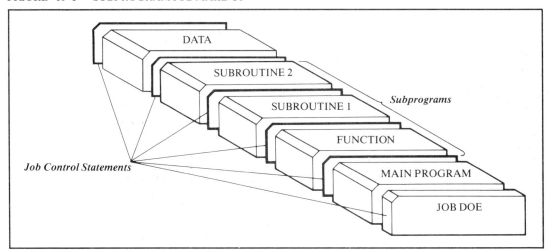

## 10-3 Programming Examples

### 10-3-1 An Investment Decision

Ms. X. must decide whether to buy a condominium now at a relatively high interest rate or wait one year and buy at what is anticipated to be a lower interest rate. She is looking at a $55,000 condo that she can purchase with 20% down and a 30-year mortgage at 14%. The current rate of inflation for housing is 8–10% per year; thus in one year the condominium is expected to be worth $60,000. However, the interest rate may decline to 11.5% in the next year. Should Mrs. X. buy the condominium now or wait? The program in Figure 10–6 can be used to help make the decision. Note the use of a subroutine to calculate the total cost for each option. The formula to compute the monthly payment is:

$$\text{monthly payment} = \frac{\text{principal} * \dfrac{\text{interest}}{12}}{1 - \left(\dfrac{1}{1 + \dfrac{\text{interest}}{12}}\right)^{12*\text{years}}}$$

**FIGURE 10-6**   INVESTMENT DECISION PROGRAM

```
C INVESTMENT DECISION PROGRAM
C   I1,I2:   INTEREST RATES (.14 and .115)
C   P1,P2:   PRINCIPALS     ($55,000 AND $60,000)
C   PAYMT:   MONTHLY PAYMENT
C   TOT1,TOT2:  TOTAL PAYMENTS OVER THE YEARS
C   DIF:  DIFFERENCE IN COST(TOT1-TOT2)
      IMPLICIT REAL(A-Z)
      READ(5,6)I1,I2,P1,P2
      WRITE(6,5)
      CALL CALC(I1,P1,PAYMT,TOT1)
      WRITE(6,1)I1,P1,PAYMT,TOT1
      CALL CALC(I2,P2,PAYMT,TOT2)
      WRITE(6,1)I2,P2,PAYMT,TOT2
      DIF = TOT1 - TOT2
      WRITE(6,2)DIF
      STOP
    2 FORMAT('0THE DIFFERENCE IN TOTAL COST IS',F9.2)
    1 FORMAT(T5,F5.3,T19,F6.0,T37,F6.2,T49,F10.2)
    5 FORMAT(T4,'INTEREST',4X,'PRINCIPAL',4X,'MONTHLY PAYMENT',4X,'TOTAL')
    6 FORMAT(2F5.0,2F6.0)
      END
C SUBROUTINE CALC COMPUTES MONTHLY AND TOTAL PAYMENT
C   I:        INTEREST RATE
C   DOWN:     20% DOWN PAYMENT
C   P:        PRINCIPAL
C   PAYMT:    MONTHLY PAYMENT
C   TOT:      TOTAL PAYMENT OVER 30 YEARS
      SUBROUTINE CALC(I,P,PAYMT,TOT)
      IMPLICIT REAL(A-Z)
      DOWN = .2*P
      PAYMT = (P - DOWN)*(I/12.)/(1.-(1.+I/12.)**(-360.))
      TOT = PAYMT*360. + DOWN
      RETURN
      END
```

```
      INTEREST    PRINCIPAL    MONTHLY PAYMENT      TOTAL
      0.140        55000.          521.34        198683.66
      0.115        60000.          475.34        183122.31

      THE DIFFERENCE IN TOTAL COST IS 15561.35
```

## 10-3-2  Solution to a Quadratic Equation

The two solutions to quadratic equations of the form $ax^2 + bx + c = 0$ are given by the following formulas:

$$x_1 = \frac{-b + \sqrt{b^2 - 4ac}}{2a} \qquad x_2 = \frac{-b - \sqrt{b^2 - 4ac}}{2a}$$

If $b^2 - 4ac < 0$, then the solutions are complex. The program shown in Figure 10-7 uses a subroutine to solve quadratic equations. If the solution cannot be found because the roots are complex or because the equation is not a quadratic ($a = 0$), the subroutine sets a flag that is tested by the main program. Otherwise, the two solutions are calculated.

**FIGURE 10-7** SOLUTION OF QUADRATIC EQUATIONS

```
C SOLUTION OF A QUADRATIC EQUATION
      INTEGER FLAG
100 READ(5,8,END=10)A,B,C
      CALL QUAD(A,B,C,X1,X2,FLAG)
      WRITE(6,11)A,B,C
      IF(FLAG.EQ.0)THEN              If FLAG = 0 the roots are real
          WRITE(6,13)X1,X2
      ELSE
          WRITE(6,12)                otherwise they are imaginary.
      ENDIF
      GO TO 100
 10 STOP
 12 FORMAT('+',T50,'NO SOLUTION')
 13 FORMAT('+',T50,'X1=',F11.3, 2X,'X2=',F11.3)
 11 FORMAT('0A=',F11.3,2X,'B=',F11.3,2X,'C=',F11.3)
  8 FORMAT(3F10.0)
      END
C FLAG: FLAG IS SET TO 1 IF NO REAL ROOTS
      SUBROUTINE QUAD(A,B,C,X1,X2,FLAG)
      INTEGER FLAG
      FLAG = 0
      IF(A.NE.0.) THEN
        DISC = B**2 - 4.*A*C
        IF(DISC .GE. 0.) THEN
          X1 = (-B+SQRT(DISC))/(2.*A)
          X2 = (-B-SQRT(DISC))/(2.*A)
        ELSE
          FLAG = 1
        ENDIF
      ELSE IF(B.NE.0.)THEN
        X1 = -C/B
        X2 = X1
      ELSE
        PRINT*,'INVALID COEFFICIENTS'
      ENDIF
      RETURN
      END
```

### 10-3-3 Sort Example

An input file consists of an unknown number of records, where each record contains the scores obtained by a particular FORTRAN class. The first two digits in each record identify the number of scores for a particular class (record). The department head wants to sort the scores of each FORTRAN class into ascending order, then sort all the combined scores into ascending order. The sorted scores are to be printed 12 per line. Assume there will be no more than 45 students in each class and no more than 500 students in all. A sample input and output are shown in Figure 10–8.

Since the code for sorting is fairly long and since the program requires that the sorting procedure be performed several times, a subroutine is to be used to carry out the sort. The program is shown in Figure 10–8.

### 10-3-4 A Class Report

An input file consists of grade rosters, each containing grades for different classes. Each roster is identified by a header record specifying the course name and number and the num-

**FIGURE 10-8    SORT PROGRAM WITH SUBROUTINES**

```
C SORT SUBROUTINE
C   CLASS:   COUNTS NO. OF CLASSES
C   J:       COUNTS TOTAL NO. OF SCORES READ
C   TEMP:    ARRAY CONTAINING SCORES OF A CLASS
C   GRADE:   ARRAY CONTAINING ALL SCORES READ
C   N:       NUMBER OF SCORES IN ONE CLASS
C
      INTEGER TEMP(45),GRADE(500),CLASS
      DATA CLASS,J/2*0/
   10 READ(5,6,END=88)N,(TEMP(I),I=1,N)         Read number of scores N and then load N scores in TEMP.
      CALL SORT(TEMP,N)                          Call subroutine SORT to sort the N scores
      CLASS = CLASS + 1
      WRITE(6,5)CLASS,(TEMP(I),I=1,N)            Print out the class number and the sorted scores
C MERGE ALL SCORES INTO ARRAY GRADE
      DO 15 I = 1, N
         J = J + 1                               Count all scores
         GRADE(J) = TEMP(I)                      and store them in array GRADE.
   15 CONTINUE
      GO TO 10                                   Go read another record.
   88 CALL SORT(GRADE,J)                         When all class records have been read, go sort all scores.
      WRITE(6,7) (GRADE(I),I=1,J)
      STOP
    5 FORMAT(1X,'CLASS',I2,':',4X,12I4/(13X,12I4))
    6 FORMAT(I2,25I3)
    7 FORMAT('0','ALL  CLASSES:',12I4/(13X,12I4))
      END
C
      SUBROUTINE SORT(G,N)                        Bubble sort.
      INTEGER G(500)
      M = N - 1                                   Number of passes = M.
      DO 15 I = 1, M
         DO 10 J = 1, N - I
            IF(G(J) .LE. G(J+1))GO TO 10
            Q     = G(J)
            G(J)     = G(J+1)
            G(J+1) = Q
   10    CONTINUE
   15 CONTINUE
      RETURN
      END
```

| CLASS 1:      | 50 | 50 | 60 | 70 | 70 | 80 | 80 | 90 | 90 | 100 |    |
|---------------|----|----|----|----|----|----|----|----|----|-----|----|
| CLASS 2:      | 10 | 11 | 20 | 22 | 30 | 33 | 40 | 44 | 50 | 51  | 52 | 53 |
|               | 55 | 55 | 56 | 60 | 66 | 70 | 77 | 78 | 80 | 88  | 90 | 95 |
|               | 99 |    |    |    |    |    |    |    |    |     |    |
| CLASS 3:      | 49 | 57 | 66 | 69 | 79 | 87 |    |    |    |     |    |
| ALL CLASSES:  | 10 | 11 | 20 | 22 | 30 | 33 | 40 | 44 | 49 | 50  | 50 | 50 |
|               | 51 | 52 | 53 | 55 | 55 | 56 | 57 | 60 | 60 | 66  | 66 | 69 |
|               | 70 | 70 | 70 | 77 | 78 | 79 | 80 | 80 | 80 | 87  | 88 | 90 |
|               | 90 | 90 | 95 | 99 | 100 |   |    |    |    |     |    |

**Input File**

*Number of Scores Per Record        Scores*

```
10 050100070080090050060070080090
25 010020030040050060070080090007801102203304405500660770880990950510520530550 56
06 057087069079049066
```

ber of students for that class. The following records contain one student grade per record. No class is expected to contain more than 100 students. Write a complete program to determine each class's grade average and the number of grades below the average. Print the course name and number, the grades, the average, and the count of grades below the average. The input file must be read in the main program. One subroutine should take care of all output functions, while another subroutine should calculate the class average and the number of grades less than the average. The input and output will have the following form:

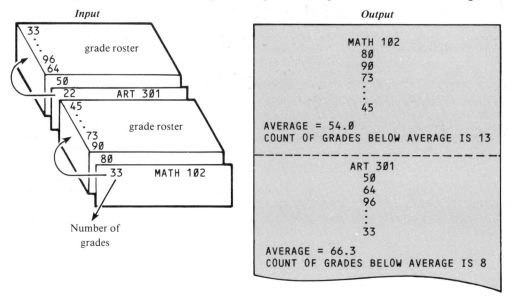

A program to solve this problem is shown in Figure 10–9.

## 10-4 **Probing Deeper**

### 10-4-1 **Flowchart Symbols for Subroutines**

The predefined process block ⊏▢⊐ is used to show a branch to a subroutine in a program flowchart. For example, ⊏▢ sort array X ▢⊐ could be translated into a FORTRAN program as CALL SUB(X,N).

The terminal block ◯ is used in a program flowchart to show the entry point and exit point(s) in a subroutine. The entry point corresponds to the first instruction in the subroutine and could be indicated by placing the name of the subroutine and a list of the dummy arguments in a begin/end block, for example, (SUB(X,Y)) . The RETURN instruction is the exit point and would be shown on the program flowchart as (RETURN) . A complete program flowchart for the program of Figure 10–6 is shown in Figure 10–10.

### 10-4-2 **Variable Dimension**

Arrays that are passed as arguments from one program to another through the CALL sequence (or COMMON statements) must be declared as arrays in the subprogram through appropriate type statements. If the size of the array to be processed in the subprogram is to be the same size as the corresponding array in the main program (or calling program), the size of the subprogram array can be set to the particular size of the array defined in the call-

**FIGURE 10-9** A SUBPROGRAM CALLING TWO SUBROUTINES

```
      CHARACTER*11 HEADER
      REAL AVG
      INTEGER GRADE(100),N,BELOW
    5 READ(5,6,END=8)N,HEADER,(GRADE(I),I=1,N)
      CALL AVRGE(GRADE,N,AVG,BELOW)



      CALL PRINT(GRADE,N,AVG,BELOW,HEADER)
      GO TO 5
    8 STOP
    6 FORMAT(I3,2X,A11/(I3))
      END

      SUBROUTINE AVRGE(SCORE,L,AV,BLOW)
      INTEGER SCORE(100),L,BLOW
      REAL AV
      AV = 0.
      BLOW = 0
      DO 1 I = 1, L
         AV = AV + SCORE(I)
    1 CONTINUE
      AV = AV/L
      DO 2 I = 1, L
         IF(SCORE(I).LT.AV)BLOW=BLOW+1
    2 CONTINUE
      RETURN
      END

      SUBROUTINE PRINT(GRADE,N,AV,BLOW,HDNGS)
      CHARACTER*11 HDNGS
      INTEGER GRADE(100),N,BLOW
      REAL AV
      WRITE(6,5)HDNGS,(GRADE(I),I=1,N)
      WRITE(6,6)AV,BLOW
      RETURN
    5 FORMAT('1',15X,A11/(18X,I3))
    6 FORMAT(1X,'AVFRAGE IS',F5.1/1X,
     *'COUNT OF GRADES BELOW AVERAGE IS',I2)
      END
```

HEADER gives the course name and number.
No more than 100 students per class.
Read the number of grades N, the header, and the grades in a given class.
Transfer control to subroutine AVRGE.
GRADE transfers the grades to the subprogram.
N transfers the number of grades.
AVG returns the average from the subprogram.
BELOW returns the number of scores below the average.
Transfer control to subroutine for printout.
HEADER communicates the course name and number to the subroutine.
The subroutine prints the heading, the N grades, the average, and the number of grades below average.

Subroutine AVRGE will compute the average of L grades stored in an array SCORE and store the result in AV. The count of grades below the average is stored in BLOW. Initially, BLOW is set to 0.
The array SCORE is really the array GRADE, which has been read in the main program, and L (or N) is the number of grades to be processed. Note that the subroutine does not change the array SCORE and the variable L, and hence these are not changed in the main program. The average and the count of grades below average are returned to AVG and BELOW in the main program via AV and BLOW.

Subroutine PRINT will print a heading found in HDNGS on a new page, with N grades listed vertically. The average grade AV and the count below average BLOW will also be printed.
Note that none of the arguments are changed in the subroutine (set to any value).
HDNGS is another name for HEADER defined in the main program.

ing program. Suppose, for example, we wished to add two arrays, A and B, of the same size (adding corresponding elements), and store the resulting entries in a third array, C. The following code could be used.

*Main Program*

```
INTEGER A(3,3),B(3,3),C(3,3)
K = 3
CALL ADD(A,B,C,K)
```

Note equal sizes.

*Subprogram*

```
      SUBROUTINE ADD(X,Y,Z,K)
      INTEGER X(3,3),Y(3,3),Z(3,3)
      DO 15 I = 1,K
         DO 10 J = 1,K
            Z(I,J) = X(I,J) + Y(I,J)
   10    CONTINUE
   15 CONTINUE
      RETURN
      END
```

536

CHAPTER TEN / SUBROUTINES

**FIGURE 10-10** FLOWCHART FOR INVESTMENT DECISION PROGRAM

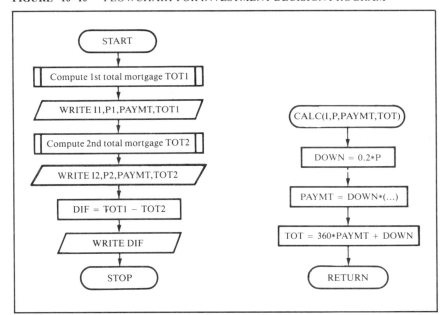

The only drawback to subroutine ADD is that it is coded to add only arrays of size 3 by 3. This restricts the generality of the subroutine, since it cannot be used to add arrays that are of size 2 by 2, 5 by 5, and so forth. One way to remedy this problem is to use the variable type declaration feature, which allows the user to adjust the size of the array in the subroutine to the size of the corresponding array in the main program (calling program). In this way a subroutine can process arrays of different sizes. For example, the problem of adding corresponding elements of two arrays could be coded as follows:

| *Main Program* | *Subprogram* |
|---|---|

```
INTEGER A(3,3),B(3,3),C(3,3)      SUBROUTINE ADD(X,Y,Z,M,N)
INTEGER T(2,3),Q(2,3),R(2,3)      INTEGER X(M,N),Y(M,N),Z(M,N)
M = 3                             DO 10 I = 1,M
N = 3                             DO 10 J = 1,N
CALL ADD(A,B,C,M,N)                   Z(I,J) = X(I,J) + Y(I,J)
      :                        10 CONTINUE
      :                           RETURN
CALL ADD(T,Q,R,2,3)               END
```

In the first call to ADD, X, Y, and Z are 3 by 3 arrays, while in the second call arrays X, Y, and Z are 2 by 3.

## 10-4-3 Named COMMON Blocks

Recall that variables located in COMMON are available to any program containing the COMMON statement. In many instances the number of variables contained in COMMON is large and all subprograms do not require access to all variables. In such cases it is possible to construct named blocks of COMMON. These named or labeled COMMON blocks allow subprograms to access only those COMMON blocks that are needed.

*Example*

| *Main Program* | *Subprograms* |
|---|---|

```
COMMON/BLK1/X,Y/BLK2/Q,R,T          SUBROUTINE SUB1
       .                            COMMON/BLK1/A,B
       .                                   .
       .                                   .
CALL SUB1                                  .
       .                            END
       .                            SUBROUTINE SUB2
CALL SUB2                           COMMON/BLK2/X,Y,Z
                                           .
                                           .
```

In this example, two blocks of COMMON are defined in the main program. Note that the two subroutines do not share any COMMON area with one another; however, each shares a separate COMMON area with the main program. In BLK1, A refers to X while B refers to Y. In BLK2, X refers to Q, Y refers to R, and Z refers to T.

The general form of the COMMON specification statement is:

COMMON [/*block name*/] *list of variables* [/*block name*/] *list of variables...*

where COMMON is a required key word,
  *block name* is the name of the block COMMON, and
  slashes (/) are a required part of the statement.

If the block name is omitted, the variables are placed in unnamed (sometimes called *blank*) COMMON (see section 10-2-4). The COMMON statement must follow any IMPLICIT statement and precede any DATA, statement functions or executable statements. A standard practice is to place the COMMON statement after DIMENSION or type statements which refer to items within the COMMON block. Standard FORTRAN requires that all COMMON blocks of the same name must have the same length in all subprograms in which they appear. Also if a COMMON block contains any character variables or character arrays, then it cannot contain any variables or arrays of any other type.

*Examples*

```
COMMON/XYZ/X(10),Y(100)/ABC/RR(100)
COMMON A,B,C(10)/BLOCK3/Q,R,S
```

Three blocks of COMMON are named XYZ, ABC, and BLOCK3, while blank COMMON contains the variables A, B, and ten elements of C.

## 10-4-4  BLOCK DATA

One way to initialize variables or arrays that appear in named COMMON is through the BLOCK DATA subprogram.

Suppose that each element of array R in block BLK2 is to be initialized to 0 and the variable BE in block BLK1 is to be initialized to "GOOD". The following code can be used:

| *Main Program* | *Subprogram* |
|---|---|
| ```
CHARACTER*4 BE,M*1,Y(4)*3
REAL R(10),ITEM
COMMON /BLK1/M,Y,BE/BLK2/R,ITEM
        ·
        ·
        ·
``` | ```
BLOCK DATA
REAL R(10),ITEM
CHARACTER*4 NE,L,Z(4)*3
COMMON /BLK2/R,ITEM
COMMON /BLK1/L,Z,NE
DATA R/10*0./
DATA NE/'GOOD'/
END
``` |

Note that the first statement of the subprogram is:

```
BLOCK DATA
```

and the last statement is:

```
END
```

**There are no executable statements and no RETURN statement.** The only statements allowed besides the COMMON statements are specification statements. If a variable or array is to be initialized, the entire named COMMON block in which it is stored must be specified. All dimensions and type specifications must agree with those in the main program. Standard FORTRAN disallows blank COMMON in BLOCK data.

NE, which corresponds to BE, is declared a CHARACTER*4 variable and is initialized to "GOOD" in the DATA statement. Since BLK1 contains character data, no other type of data except character data can be specified in BLK1.

Note how the array R is initialized to zeroes in the BLOCK DATA subprogram, while ITEM is not initialized at all.

### 10-4-5 Multiple Entries in Subprograms

A method that allows one to enter subroutines or functions at different points in the subprogram is the ENTRY statement. The general form of this statement, which appears in the subprogram, is:

ENTRY *name* $(p_1, p_2, p_3, \ldots)$

where *name* is any valid variable name (in a function subprogram, this name returns a value to the calling program);

$p_1$, $p_2$, ... are dummy arguments used to communicate data to and from the calling program (following the rules discussed previously).

Notice that the words SUBROUTINE or FUNCTION do not procede the word ENTRY.

Consider the following example where subroutine RMAT calculates the sum of the rows of an array and then the sum of the columns of the same array. If it is desired to just calculate the sums of the columns of an array, that corresponding portion of the code in RMAT can be used by simply entering RMAT at the proper place (ENTRY CMAT):

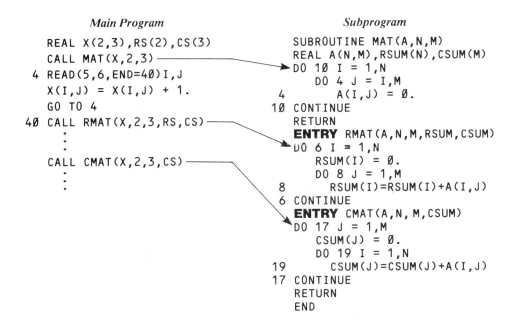

```
      Main Program                        Subprogram
    REAL X(2,3),RS(2),CS(3)        SUBROUTINE MAT(A,N,M)
    CALL MAT(X,2,3) ───────────┐   REAL A(N,M),RSUM(N),CSUM(M)
                               └─► DO 10 I = 1,N
  4 READ(5,6,END=40)I,J              DO 4 J = I,M
    X(I,J) = X(I,J) + 1.      4        A(I,J) = 0.
    GO TO 4                  10 CONTINUE
 40 CALL RMAT(X,2,3,RS,CS) ──┐   RETURN
       .                     │   ENTRY RMAT(A,N,M,RSUM,CSUM)
       .                     └─► DO 6 I = 1,N
       .                           RSUM(I) = 0.
    CALL CMAT(X,2,3,CS) ──┐        DO 8 J = 1,M
       .                  │   8      RSUM(I)=RSUM(I)+A(I,J)
       .                  │   6 CONTINUE
       .                  └─► ENTRY CMAT(A,N, M,CSUM)
                              DO 17 J = 1,M
                                CSUM(J) = 0.
                                DO 19 I = 1,N
                          19      CSUM(J)=CSUM(J)+A(I,J)
                          17 CONTINUE
                              RETURN
                              END
```

The first CALL in the main program is to SUBROUTINE MAT. This causes each element of the two-dimensional array X to be set to zero, then control is returned to the main program. (If there had been no RETURN statement after 10 CONTINUE, then the statements after ENTRY RMAT(A,N,M,RSUM,CSUM) and ENTRY CMAT(A,N,M, CSUM) would have been executed also. ENTRY statements are nonexecutable statements and are ignored at execution time.) The second CALL is to RMAT. This causes execution to start at the first executable statement after ENTRY MAT. First the row sums are calculated and then the column sums. Finally, the last CALL is to CMAT, and entry occurs at that point in the subroutine. The column sums are calculated and returned to the main program. Notice that all DIMENSION and specification statements are positioned after the SUBROUTINE statement, and *not* after the ENTRY statements.

## 10-4-6 Multiple Returns from Subroutines

When a RETURN is executed in a subroutine, execution in the main program resumes at the statement immediately following the CALL statement. If you want to return to different points in the main program depending on outcomes in the subroutine, the multiple return can be used.

The general form of the multiple return is:

$$\text{CALL } name\ (p_1, p_2, * s_1, p_3, * s_2, \ldots)$$

where *name* is a valid subroutine name;

$p_1, p_2, \ldots$ are arguments used to communicate data to and from the subroutine;

$s_1, s_2, \ldots$ are statement numbers of statements in the main program where control is to be returned (these *must* be preceded by the asterisk or the ampersand (&) symbol in the argument list to differentiate them from constants). These can be specified in any order in the CALL argument list.

In the subprogram the following format is used:

```
SUBROUTINE  name (p₁, p₂, * , p₃, * ,...)
  .
  .
  .
RETURN 1
  .
  .
  .
RETURN 2
  .
  .
  .
RETURN
END
```

where *name* is a valid subroutine name:

$p_1$, $p_2$, ... are dummy arguments used to communicate data to and from the calling program;

Asterisks(*) are used to correspond with the * $s_1$, * $s_2$, ... in the main program's CALL argument list;

RETURN 1 means execution returns to the main program to the statement corresponding to the first * encountered in the CALL argument list;

RETURN 2 means execution returns to the statement corresponding to the second * encountered in the CALL argument list, and so on.

It is also valid to specify RETURN N where N is an integer variable.

*Example*

The following main program and subroutine determine the roots of the equation $ax^2 + bx + c = 0$.

|  |  |
|---|---|
| **Main Program** | **Subroutine** |

```
60 READ(5,3,END = 80)A,B,C          SUBROUTINE ROOTS(A,*,B,C,*,*)
   CALL ROOTS(A,&5,B,C,&8,&10)       IF (A.EQ.0.0 .AND. B.NE.0.0)RETURN 1
   DI = SQRT(B**2 - 4.*A*C)          DISC = B**2 - 4.*A*C
   R1 = (-B - DI)/(2.*A)             IF (DISC .EQ. 0.0) RETURN 3
   R2 = (-B + DI)/(2.*A)             IF (DISC .LT. 0.0) RETURN 2
   WRITE(6,7)R1,R2                   RETURN
   GO TO 60                          END
 5 R = -C/B
   WRITE(6,7)R
   GO TO 60
 8 WRITE(6,81)
   GO TO 60
10 RD = -B/(2.*A)
   WRITE(6,7)RD,RD
   GO TO 60
 3 FORMAT(3F5.1)
 7 FORMAT(1X,2(F10.2,2X))
81 FORMAT(1X,'COMPLEX ROOTS')
80 STOP
   END
```

In the subroutine, if A = 0 and B ≠ 0, execution is returned to statement 5 in the main program. If $B^2 - 4AC = 0$, execution returns to statement 10 (the statement that corresponds to the third asterisk). If $B^2 - 4AC < 0$, return is to statement 8. If none of these conditions is true; that is if $B^2 - 4AC > 0$, control is returned to the statement following the CALL. In each case appropriate messages are printed about the roots.

## 10-4-7 The EXTERNAL and INTRINSIC Statements

Suppose you wanted to determine the maximum value taken on by each of the following functions in the specified intervals:

**1.** $y = 3x^3 - 2x^2 - 14$       $x$ ranges from 2 to 10 in increments of 3.

**2.** $y = \sqrt{(x - 4)(x + 6)}$       $x$ ranges from $-4$ to 5 in increments of 1.

**3.** $y = sin(x)$       $x$ ranges from .1 to 1.1 in increments of .1.

We can write two function subprograms, POLY for the first function and SQPOLY for the second function as shown in Figure 10–11. The third function, sin $x$, does not need to be written since it is a library function. Explanations are given on next page.

**FIGURE 10-11**    USE OF THE EXTERNAL STATEMENT

```
      EXTERNAL POLY,SQPOLY          In the main program POLY, SQPOLY, and SIN are to be con-
      INTRINSIC SIN                 strued as function names.
      CALL MAXI(2.,10.,3.,POLY)     The interval for POLY is [2, 10], and the increment value is 3.
                                    Find the maximum value of POLY in that interval.
      CALL MAXI(-4.,5.,1.,SQPOLY)   Go find the maximum value taken on by function SQPOLY in
                                    the interval [-4, 5]. Increment is 1.
      CALL MAXI(.1,1.1.,.1,SIN)     Find maximum sine value in interval .1 and 1.1.
      STOP
      END

      SUBROUTINE MAXI(INIT,TER,INC,FUNC)   The range of the function FUNC is [INIT, TER].
      REAL INIT,TER,INC,MAX
      MAX = FUNC(INIT)
    7 INIT = INIT + INC             Assume maximum function value is FUNC(INIT).
      IF(INIT.GT.TER) GO TO 8
      IF(FUNC(INIT).GT.MAX)MAX=FUNC(INIT)  The first time FUNC is actually POLY, and hence POLY(2),
      GO TO 7                       POLY(5), ... will be computed.
    8 WRITE(6,3)MAX
    3 FORMAT(1X,F10.2)              Later on, FUNC will be the sine function, and the maximum
      RETURN                        value for the sine function in the interval .1 and 1.1 will be
      END                           printed.

      FUNCTION POLY(X)
      POLY = 3.*X**3 - 2.*X**2 - 14.0
      RETURN
      END

      FUNCTION SQPOLY(X)
      SQPOLY = SQRT((X - 4.)*(X + 6.))
      RETURN
      END
```

A subroutine MAXI (See Figure 10–11) can be written to calculate the maximum value for any function within a given range. In order for MAXI to know which of the above three functions are to be processed, the name of the function must be one of the arguments transmitted to MAXI. To ensure against the function name arguments POLY, SQPOLY, and SIN being interpreted by MAXI as ordinary variable names in the calling program, the calling program must declare the names of the user written functions in the EXTERNAL statement, and the names of any other compiler available functions (SIN,SQRT, etc.) in the INTRINSIC statement. In Figure 10–11 the name of the dummy argument representing the particular function to be processed in MAXI, is FUNC.

The general forms of the INTRINSIC and EXTERNAL specification statements are:

> EXTERNAL *name1*, *name2*, ...
> INTRINSIC *name*a, *name*b, ...

where *name1*, *name2*,... are names for user written subprograms that are to be passed as arguments to a function or subroutine subprogram.

name*a*, name*b*,... are names of intrinsic functions (functions available to the FORTRAN compiler) that are to be passed as arguments to a function or subroutine subprogram.

These statements must be placed after BLOCK DATA and IMPLICIT statements and before DATA and statement function statements.

## 10-4-8 Sharing Storage: The EQUIVALENCE Statement

The EQUIVALENCE statement can be used to share storage; it assigns two or more names to the same storage unit. For example, EQUIVALENCE(A,B) causes the variables A and B to have the same address; i.e., any reference to A is equivalent to a reference to B and vice versa. A and B should be thought of as different names for the same memory location. Consider the following example:

```
EQUIVALENCE(A,B)
A = 1.
B = 3.
WRITE(6,11)A          The value written for A will be 3.
```

The general form of the EQUIVALENCE statement is:

> EQUIVALENCE (*list of variables*)...

Each variable in the *list of variables* is thus declared to be equivalent to the others. The variables can be subscripted variable names. The EQUIVALENCE statement must follow any IMPLICIT statements and precede any DATA, statement functions or executable statements. Any equivalenced variables should be of the same type.

*Example*

```
CHARACTER*5 FIRST,LAST
INTEGER ZZZ,R,STU
REAL X,Y
EQUIVALENCE (X,Y),(ZZZ,R,STU),(FIRST,LAST)
```

The variables X and Y share the same memory locations. ZZZ, R, and STU all refer to the same storage location. FIRST and LAST occupy the same storage units.

Arrays or parts of arrays can be equivalenced by specifying the starting location at which sequential matching between array elements is desired. Assume arrays A and B are to be equivalenced:

*Examples*

```
   INTEGER A(5),B(5)
   EQUIVALENCE (A(1),B(1))
or EQUIVALENCE (A(5),B(5))         yields the pairing
```
$$A_1\ A_2\ A_3\ A_4\ A_5$$
$$B_1\ B_2\ B_3\ B_4\ B_5$$

```
   INTEGER A(5),B(5)
   EQUIVALENCE (A(1),X),(B(5),Y)   yields the pairing
```
$$A_1\ B_5$$
$$X\ \ Y$$

```
   REAL A(5),B(4),C(2)
   EQUIVALENCE (A(3),B(2),C(1))    yields the pairing
```
$$A_1\ A_2\ A_3\ A_4\ A_5$$
$$B_1\ B_2\ B_3\ B_4$$
$$C_1\ C_2$$

Character strings may be equivalenced causing an overlap situation as shown in the following example.

```
   CHARACTER A*7, B*7, C(2)*5      yields
   EQUIVALENCE (A(6:7),B),(B(4:),C(2))
```

For two-dimensional arrays, the matching sequence is performed according to the linear memory sequence in which multidimensional arrays are represented.

The EQUIVALENCE statement is sometimes used when two or more programmers working independently on program segments have used different names for the same variable. Rather than rewrite the entire program with the same variable names, the EQUIVALENCE statement can be used. The EQUIVALENCE statement also allows the programmer to reuse arrays that might otherwise be used only once in a program. To reuse the same array for a different purpose and to avoid name confusion, the same array can be given a different name.

*Example*

```
   REAL A(10,10),AINVER(10,10),TEMP(10,10)
   EQUIVALENCE (AINVER(1,1),TEMP(1,1))
      .
      .
      .
   WRITE(6,1)AINVER
      .
      .
   READ(5,11)TEMP
```

The inverse matrix has now been computed. Write it out. At this point in the program AINVER is no longer needed.

Let us use the storage of AINVER for some temperatures. Calling the array AINVER could be misleading so we call it TEMP.

## 10-5 You Might Want to Know

**1.** Why use subroutines?

*Answer:* A subroutine can be an aid in writing shorter and more compact programs. The programmer can break a program into smaller logical components that are easier to work with, resulting in a more readable program. A subroutine can result in an economy of code for procedures or tasks that are to be performed repeatedly at different places in a program(s). The code for the procedure is written just once and is not recoded wherever it is needed in the program.

Subroutines that are to be used frequently should be compiled and tested until thoroughly debugged. They can then be stored in object form in a user's library or on the user's diskette where they can be retrieved by other FORTRAN programs. This saves computer time, since the subroutine need not be recompiled each time it is to be used. For this purpose, subroutines can be written and shared by users through "share" libraries. A brief subroutine description and its use (calling sequence) should be included in the listing of the subprogram by means of comment statements.

**2.** There are no repetitive tasks in most of the programs I write. Are subroutines of any value to me?

*Answer:* Perhaps, particularly in long or complex problems. It may be possible to segment the tasks that make up the complete program, write subprograms to perform these tasks, and verify that each subprogram executes properly. The complete program can then be constructed using the already written and debugged subprograms.

**3.** What statements can be used in a subroutine?

*Answer:* Any FORTRAN statements except other SUBROUTINE or FUNCTION declarative statements.

**4.** Is a STOP statement necessary after the RETURN statement?

*Answer:* No. The STOP instruction cannot be executed, since RETURN will pass control back to the calling program.

**5.** If an argument in a CALL statement is just used by the subroutine to pass a particular result to the calling program, need that argument be initialized to a specific value in the calling program?

*Answer:* No. For example:

```
CALL ADD(X,Y,RES)    SUBROUTINE ADD(A,B,RES)
                     RES = A + B
```

There is no need to initialize RES to any value in the calling program.

**6.** If I use a DATA statement to initialize a variable in a subroutine, will that variable be reinitialized every time the subroutine is called?

*Answer:* No. For example:

```
CALL TX (Y,3)        SUBROUTINE TX(X,K)
     :               DATA SUM/0./
     :               SUM =SUM + X
CALL TX(Y,4)         RETURN
```

As a result of the first call to TX, the value of SUM is 3. The second time through TX, SUM will equal 7, not 4. If you need to reset SUM to 0, use the statement SUM = 0.0.

7. Can a subroutine use a STOP statement?

*Answer:* Yes. Consider the following example:

```
    SUBROUTINE QUAD(A,B,C,X,ROOT1,ROOT2)
         .
         .
    DISC = B**2 - 4.*A*C
    IF(DISC.NE.0)GO TO 1
  2 WRITE(6,11)
 11 FORMAT(T20,'ROOTS ARE IMAGINARY')
    STOP
  1 ROOT1 = · · ·          Note the STOP statement.
         .
         .
```

The practice of using the STOP statement in a subroutine is *not* recommended, as many programmers feel it should be the privilege of the main program to stop execution of the complete program. A flag can be used in the subroutine and tested in the main program if there is cause for immediate termination of the job.

8. Can a subroutine call another subroutine or a function subprogram?

*Answer:* Yes, as long as the subroutine does not call itself. Nor can a subroutine call a subroutine that calls the original subroutine. You must avoid calling sequences that result in a closed loop, such as:

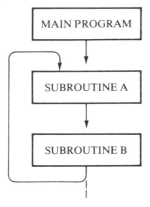

9. Is a subroutine permitted to change the value of any argument?

*Answer:* Yes. However, care must be exercised to avoid problems such as those shown in the following example:

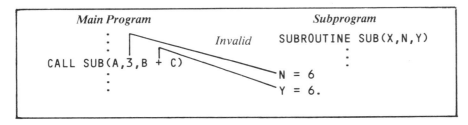

The value of the second argument is changed to 6 by the subroutine; however, the actual argument is a constant 3. This can have an unpredictable effect in the program. Similarly, the value of the third argument is changed by the subroutine, but the actual argument is an expression, not a storage location.

**10.** Functions and subroutines seem to have a lot in common. Can I change the value of an argument in a function subprogram as I can in a subroutine subprogram?

*Answer:* Yes, you can write a function to perform the exact same tasks as a subroutine; however, this is contrary to the purpose of a function subprogram. A function is generally used to return a single value to the calling program via the function name. A subroutine should be written when the value of more than one variable is to be changed.

**11.** Why would I ever want to write a subroutine without arguments such as CALL SUB?

*Answer:* Perhaps you might want to write a subroutine just to set up headings for each page of a lengthy computer-generated report or to control the printer for special editing effects, or you might want to use SUB in conjunction with a data set defined in a COMMON statement in order to operate directly on that common data.

**12.** Can a subroutine use arrays that are not declared as arguments or in a COMMON statement?

*Answer:* Yes. For example:

```
SUBROUTINE SUB(A,B,K)
REAL A(100),C(50,10)
DATA C/500*0./
```

The array C is to be used in the subroutine even though it is not part of the argument list of the subroutine.

## 10-6  Exercises

### 10-6-1  Test Yourself

1. What would happen if you tried to execute a subroutine all by itself?
2. List two distinct differences between function and subroutine subprograms.
3. What advantages are there in using subroutines?
4. What are two ways to pass data to a subroutine?
5. Why can't you write the code equivalent to a subroutine in the main program and branch to it whenever you want to execute that code?
6. Would the statement REAL X(N) be valid in a main program? In a subroutine? In a function subprogram? What restrictions would be placed on X and N?
7. Is it a good idea to use the DATA statement in a subroutine to initialize accumulators and counters that are used in the subroutine?
8. Find the error in each of the following:

| Main Program | Subprogram |
|---|---|
| a. `DIMENSION A(10),B(10)`<br><br>`    .`<br>`CALL SUB(A,B)`<br>`    .`<br>`    .` | `SUBROUTINE SUB(I,J)`<br>`DIMENSION I(10),J(10)`<br>`DO 10 K = 1,10`<br>`    I(K) = J(K)`<br>`10 CONTINUE`<br>`RETURN`<br>`END` |
| b. `REAL X(100)`<br>`    .`<br>`    .`<br>`CALL SUB(X,14.)`<br>`    .`<br>`    .` | `SUBROUTINE SUB(A,X)`<br>`REAL A(100)`<br>`X = 0.0`<br>`DO 3 I = 1,100`<br>`3    X = X + A(I)`<br>`RETURN`<br>`END` |
| c. `REAL X(10,10),Y(3,4)`<br>`    .`<br>`    .`<br>`CALL SUBC(X)`<br>`    .`<br>`    .`<br>`CALL SUBC(Y)` | `SUBROUTINE SUBC(A)`<br>`REAL A(10,10)`<br>`    .`<br>`    .`<br>`RETURN`<br>`END` |
| d. `REAL A(15)`<br>`    .`<br>`    .`<br>`CALL SUBD(A,B)`<br>`    .`<br>`    .` | `SUBROUTINE SUBD(P,Q)`<br>`REAL Q(15)`<br>`DO 10 I = 1,15`<br>`10    Q(I) = P`<br>`RETURN`<br>`END` |
| e. `REAL X(3,4)`<br>`    .`<br>`    .`<br>`CALL SUBE(X)`<br>`    .`<br>`    .` | `SUBROUTINE SUBE(X,N,M)`<br>`REAL X(N,M)`<br>`    .`<br>`    .` |
| f. `REAL X(3,4)`<br>`    .`<br>`    .`<br>`CALL SUBF(X,3,4)`<br>`    .`<br>`    .` | `SUBROUTINE SUBF(X,A,B)`<br>`REAL X(A,B)`<br>`INTEGER AB`<br>`    .`<br>`    .` |
| g. `REAL JSUM(10)`<br>`    .`<br>`    .`<br>`CALL SUB(JSUM,N,3.1)`<br>`    .`<br>`    .` | `SUBROUTINE (JSUM,K,R)`<br>`REAL JSUM(1)`<br>`    .`<br>`    .` |
| h. `REAL A(5),B(5),C(5),E(5,5)`<br>`COMMON D(3)`<br>`    .`<br>`    .`<br>`CALL SUB(B,E,3,D)`<br>`    .`<br>`    .` | `SUBROUTINE SUB(B,E,K,DD)`<br>`COMMON DD(3)`<br>`REAL E(5,5),B(5)`<br>`    .`<br>`    .` |
| i. `INTEGER C(50)`<br>`CHARACTER B*2`<br>`    .`<br>`    .`<br>`CALL L(C,3.,B)` | `SUBROUTINE L(K,S,C)`<br>`INTEGER K(50)`<br>`CHARACTER*2 B` |

**9.** Which of the following statements are invalid or false? State the reason.

a. SUBROUTINE(A,X,Z,3.126)

b. CALL A(X,Y,Z(JNE))

c. COMMON A/I,J,K,L

d. EQUIVALENCE TABLE(100),B(100)

e. ENTRY D(C)

f. INTRINSIC COS,TAN,SINE

g. REAL A(10),B(10)
   EQUIVALENCE/A(5),B(5)/

h. SUBROUTINE BC(K,L(10),M)

i. COMMON W/T/

j. REAL A(10),B(10)
   EQUIVALENCE(A(5),B(5)),(MSUM,B(5))

k. The statement A(10),B(5,5),C(P) is valid in some cases.

l. Only one RETURN is allowed in a subroutine.

m. Two-dimensional arrays are stored in memory in column sequence.

n. The COMMON statement can be placed anywhere in the program before the first executable statement.

o. It is possible for subroutines to have no arguments.

p. Arguments in a subroutine arguments list can be declared in a COMMON statement.

q. EQUIVALENCE and COMMON statements really mean the same thing.

r. Arguments in a calling sequence and in a subroutine must always agree in number and type.

s. Subroutine names cannot have more than six characters.

t. The EXTERNAL statement can be used to pass statement function names to subprograms.

u. More than one COMMON statement is allowed per subroutine.

v. If a statement number is the same in a main program and in a subprogram, there will be a syntax error.

w. In a subroutine the statement END is not necessary because of the RETURN statement.

x. Subscripted variable names cannot be used in a CALL argument list.

y. At least one RETURN statement should immediately precede the END statement in a subroutine.

z. The French revolution took place in 1791.

**10.** Determine what the following program does.

```
      CHARACTER*10 NAME(4)
      CHARACTER*3 BLOOD(4),TYPE
      COMMON /A/ NAME,BLOOD
      DO 10 I = 1,4
   10 READ(5,11) NAME(I),BLOOD(I)
      READ(5,12)TYPE
      WRITE(6,13)TYPE
      CALL SEARCH(TYPE)
      STOP
   11 FORMAT(A10,A3)
   12 FORMAT(A3)
   13 FORMAT(1X, 'THESE PEOPLE HAVE BLOOD',2X,A3)
      END
      SUBROUTINE SEARCH(L)
      CHARACTER*10 NOM(4)
      CHARACTER*3, BLOOD(4),L
      COMMON /A/ NOM ,BLOOD
      DO 10 I = 1,4
         IF(BLOOD(I).EQ.L)WRITE(6,19)NOM(I)
   10 CONTINUE
   19 FORMAT(T11,A10)
      RETURN
      END
```

*Data*

```
MICHELLEbb+Ab
MICHAELbbb+Ob
MARCbbbbbb+AB
ROBERTbbbb+Ab
+Ab
```

10-6-2 **Programming Problems**

1. A toy store sells 20 different toys.

    a. Write a main program to read the prices of the toys into a one-dimensional array.
    b. Write a subroutine to print all items over $5.00.
    c. The store decides to run a sale on all its merchandise; everything is reduced to 60% of its original price. Write a subroutine to output the new prices.

2. Write a subroutine that accepts a one-dimensional array and returns the largest and the smallest elements of that array.

3. Write a subroutine that accepts a one-dimensional array and returns the positions of the largest and the smallest elements.

4. Repeat exercise 2 with a two-dimensional array. Specify the rows and columns.

5. Repeat exercise 3 with a three-dimensional array.

6. Rewrite the program of Figure 10–6 without subroutines. Compare the length and the complexity of the two programs. Is there any advantage to using subroutines for this program?

7. Rewrite the program of Figure 10–1 without using arguments for either subroutine.

8. Modify the program of Figure 10–6 to find the break-even point for the future interest rate. How low does the interest rate have to go before it does not matter whether Ms. X buys now or waits? Also generalize the program to enter a variable interest rate, house purchase cost, and percentage of house purchase price for down payment.

9. Write and test subroutines to perform the following tasks on two-dimensional arrays.

    a. Set all elements of an array to a constant.
    b. Add corresponding elements of two arrays, storing results in a third array.
    c. Multiply each element of an array by a constant.

10. Write a subroutine that accepts a one-dimensional array and reverses the order of the elements of the array.

11. Write a subroutine that accepts any integer and sets a flag to one if the integer is a prime number and sets the flag to zero otherwise.

12. Each record of an input file (no more than 50) contains a name and an address. Read the names and corresponding addresses into a 50 by 2 array with names in column 1 and addresses in column 2, for example:

| K(1,1) | MARTIN | 1 NORTH ST. | K(1,2) |
|--------|--------|-------------|--------|
| K(2,1) | JONATH | 3 ELM ST. | K(2,2) |
| | : | : | |

Write a subroutine to sort this data on demand either by name or by address in ascending order and let the main program produce a table of names and corresponding addresses.

**13.** Student X has been asked by two of her teachers to write a program to compute two class's average grades and the numbers of A's (grades > 90) in each class. Teacher 1's grades are recorded on just one record, 25 grades in all, while teacher 2's grades are recorded one grade per record (number of records unknown).

     Write a main program to read the data. The main program should call a subroutine to be used to compute the average and the number of A's and another subroutine to perform the output functions. The input and output can be visualized as follows:

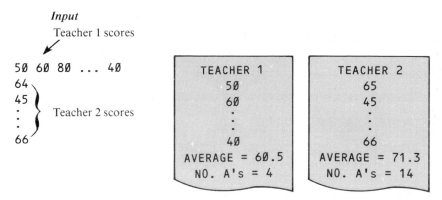

**14.** Write a subroutine to accept a number from 1 to 10 and return a variable (argument) spelling out the number; for example, 3 yields THREE. Should a function subprogram be used in this case? What would be the difference between a function subprogram and a subroutine?

**15.** Each record of a file consists of the names of cities and the average daily temperatures for those cities. For example,

```
MOBILE,17,   MADISON,-3,   PARIS,0,     NEW YORK,33
TAMPA,65,    TUCSON,48,    WAUSAU,-5,   SEATTLE,0
```

Write a program to produce an output similar to

```
ABOVE ZERO:     MOBILE      NEW YORK      TAMPA
                TUCSON
AT ZERO:        PARIS       SEATTLE
BELOW ZERO:     MADISON     WAUSAU
```

Use a subroutine for the output functions. Note that only three city names are printed per line.

**16.** Each record of an input file consists of an employee name, a number of hours worked, and a rate of pay. Write a main program to read the input file and a subroutine to compute each employee's pay. Hours over 40 are paid at time-and-a-half the regular rate. The printout should list the employee name, number of hours, rate of pay, and pay.

     Use a subroutine to perform the input data validation. The rate of pay should not exceed $50.00 per hour, and the hours worked should not exceed 80 hours. The main program should write the error messages, if any; note that there could be two error messages if both the rate and the hours exceed their maximums.

**17.** On the first record of an input file we have entered the answers (1, 2, 3, 4) to a multiple choice test of ten questions. On each of the next records is a student's name followed by the student's ten answers to the ten questions. Write a main program to read the input file. Use one subroutine to determine the percentage of correct answers for each student and another subroutine to determine the grade (90–100 = A, 80–89 = B, 60–79 = C, and below 60, D). The output should be performed by a third subroutine that prints the student name, the letter grade, and percentage. The input and output have the following form:

*Input*

correct answers to the 10 questions

```
 1123142433
 JONES    1123142433
 SATO     1123111324
 LAUGHLIN 4123142432
```

student's responses

*Output*

```
NAME        GRADE    PERCENTAGE

JONES         A         100
SATO          D          50
LAUGHLIN      B          80
```

**18.** The Stayfirm Company accounting system keeps sales records for each salesperson on a day-to-day basis. This data is transcribed on records as follows:

| Salesperson | Date of Sale | Amount of Sale |
|---|---|---|
| MONISH | 011584 | 100.00 |
| MONISH | 011384 | 50.00 |
| GLEASON | 012784 | 10.00 |
| MONISH | 012784 | 150.00 |
| GLEASON | 012684 | 190.00 |
| HORN | 011384 | 100.00 |

Note that the transactions are not arranged alphabetically by salesperson name. Also note that the dates are not sorted in ascending order.

Write a program using a sort subroutine to produce a monthly sales report for January 84 summarizing the company's total sales and the total sales for each salesperson. Entries in the report must be listed by salesperson's name in alphabetical order, and these in turn must sorted by sales date. For example, given the above data, the output should be as follows:

| SALESPERSON | DATE OF SALES | SALES AMOUNT | TOTAL AMOUNT |
|---|---|---|---|
| GLEASON | 012684 | 190.00 | |
| | 012784 | 10.00 | |
| | | | 200.00 |
| HORN | 011384 | 100.00 | |
| | | | 100.00 |
| MONISH | 011384 | 50.00 | |
| | 011584 | 100.00 | |
| | 012784 | 150.00 | |
| | | | 300.00 |
| | TOTAL SALES | | 600.00 |

**19.** The Department of Management Science has received the final scores obtained by their students in the various sections of Introduction to Management. The input file consists of the various class records, where each record contains the section number and the section's corresponding scores. A negative value terminates the list of scores (maximum of 20 scores per class). An example of an input file is as follows:

```
MNGM 102    30 20 60 -4
MNGM 103    10 40 -4
MNGM 104    10 90 20 80 -4
```

Write a program for the department to sort the scores in ascending order for each class and then produce one list of sorted scores containing all the scores from all the sections.

Use a subroutine for the sorting procedure and write another subroutine for the output functions. The output should be similar to the following:

```
MNGM 102         20  30  60
MNGM 103         10  40
MNGM 104         10  20  80  90
COMBINED SCORES  10  10  20  20  30  40  60  80  90
```

20. There are five sections of a financial management course FI 550. For each of these sections, we have entered on separate records the section number and the number of students who enrolled in that section during preregistration (two entries per record). Following these five records, we have other records for students wishing to add FI 550. These student records contain two entries: a name and the section number the student wants to add. The maximum number of students permitted in sections 1 through 5 is 13, 15, 17, 9, and 8, respectively. Write a program using subroutines to register these "add" student. If a request for a section cannot be filled, print out the student name and the section requested. At the conclusion of the program, print out each section number and the updated enrollment. For example, the following input would produce the output shown:

| Input | | | Output |
|---|---|---|---|
| **Section Number** | **Pre Enrollment** | **Max** | SECTIONS CLOSED |

Pre-registration File:

| Section Number | Pre Enrollment | Max |
|---|---|---|
| 100 | 13 | 13 |
| 110 | 14 | 15 |
| 105 | 10 | 17 |
| 121 | 9 | 9 |
| 107 | 3 | 8 |

Late Registration File:

| Name | Section |
|---|---|
| JOE | 100 |
| SUE | 110 |
| CLO | 107 |
| FLO | 100 |
| MIK | 110 |

Output:

```
SECTIONS CLOSED

   SECTION 100

      JOE
      FLO

   SECTION 110

      MIK


   UPDATED FILE
SECTION    ENROLLMENT

  100          13
  110          15
  105          10
  121           9
  107           4
```

21. Dr. X has unusual grading practices. He assigns random grades (1–100) to his class of N students (where N < 99 is accepted from input). Each student gets three random test

scores for three tests. Write a program to assign the grades (use a random number routine, if available) and compute the average grade of each student and the average of the entire class. First read the entire input file into a two dimensional array and *then* work from the array. The results should be tabulated in page form as follows:

```
                                                        PAGE 1

        STUDENT
        NUMBER    SCORE 1    SCORE 2    SCORE 3    AVERAGE

           1        20         30         40         30
           2        20         80         20         40
           .         .          .          .          .
           .         .          .          .          .
          15         1          0         98         33
```

2 blank lines
1 dotted line  → ------------------------------------------------------------

2 blank lines
```
                                                        PAGE 2

        STUDENT
        NUMBER    SCORE 1    SCORE 2    SCORE 3    AVERAGE
```
1 blank line
```
          16        50         60         70         60
          17         .          .          .          .
           .         .          .          .          .
          30
```

2 blank lines
1 dotted line  → ------------------------------------------------------------

2 blank lines
```
                                                        PAGE 3

        STUDENT
        NUMBER    SCORE 1    SCORE 2    SCORE 3    AVERAGE

           .         .          .          .          .
           .         .          .          .          .
```

A subroutine should be used to simulate automatic ejection to the top of a new page and provide a page number, headings, and a demarcation line to be used by Dr. X. to cut each page and bind them in booklet form. The average class grade should be printed by itself on a new numbered page. Would you expect the class average grade to be close to 50?

22. LUXURMART is an exclusive clothing store where Luxurmart members are required to maintain $1,000 in their accounts at all times. Members charge all purchases on Luxur credit cards. Write a main program to create a master member file (array) consisting of member names with an initial $1,500 credit for all members.

There are several types of transactions that require members' accounts to be updated. Some members return merchandise that must be credited to their accounts. Other members purchase items; if a purchase causes a member's credit to fall below $1,000, a message should be printed requesting the member to write a check for an amount to bring his/her credit back to $1,000. In some cases, the name listed on a transaction might not be on the master file, and an appropriate message should be printed.

Write a subroutine to update each customer's account. Transaction records contain member names and dollar amounts for credit or debit. The subroutine tells the main program whether a message is to be printed. The main program performs all output functions and should produce an updated member file after all transaction records have been processed. Sample input and output data are shown below.

| *Input* | *Output* |
|---|---|
| MASTER FILE<br><br>HOWARD   1500<br>NIARCO   1500<br>PELLON   1500<br>ROCKER   1500<br><br>TRANSACTION FILE<br><br>PELLON   106.00<br>MOCKER   500.00<br>NIARCO    -10.00<br>HOWARD   -600.00<br>NIARCO     -5.00 | \*\*NO MATCHING NAME FOR MOCKER\*\*<br>--HOWARD MUST PAY 100.00 NOW--<br><br>   UPDATED MASTER FILE<br>   HOWARD    900.00<br>   NIARCO   1485.00<br>   PELLON   1606.00<br>   ROCKER   1500.00 |

23. Repeat the preceding exercise with the following variation:

    To simplify and minimize transcription errors, the transaction records contain tag numbers, instead of dollar amounts, for items purchased or returned. D or C signifies debit or credit, respectively. For example:

    HOWARD    9 D        means debit Howard's account by whatever item 9 costs.
    NIARCO   10 C        means credit Niarco's account by the value of item 10.

    Create a table of costs for the different items. For example:

    | Item Tag | Cost |
    |---|---|
    | 1 | 44.50 |
    | 2 | 100.75 |
    | 3 | 94.50 |
    | . | . |
    | . | . |
    | 10 | 46.00 |

24. Write a subroutine that will accept an integer number and return via an array all permutations of the digits that make up the number. The subroutine should also compute the number of digits and return this value.

    Example

| *Input* | *Output* |
|---|---|
| 321 | NUMBER OF DIGITS   3<br>PERMUTATIONS       1 2 3<br>                   1 3 2<br>                   2 1 3<br>                   2 3 1<br>                   3 1 2<br>                   3 2 1 |

25. An interesting method of encoding data is to load a message to be encoded into a two-dimensional array and then interchange rows and interchange columns a number of

times. The resulting sequence of characters is the encoded message. In order to decode the message, the sequence of steps used in the encoding process is followed in reverse order. For example, consider the message I HAVE BUT ONE LIFE TO GIVE FOR MY COUNTRY. Let us load the message into a 6 × 7 array:

| I |   | H | A | V | E |   |
|---|---|---|---|---|---|---|
| B | U | T |   | O | N | E |
|   | L | I | F | E |   | T |
| O |   | G | I | V | E |   |
| F | O | R |   | M | Y |   |
| C | O | U | N | T | R | Y |

Now consider the following encoding process:

(1.) Interchange rows 1 and 3

| L | I | F | E |   |   | T |
|---|---|---|---|---|---|---|
| B | U | T |   | O | N | E |
| I |   | H | A | V | E |   |
| O |   | G | I | V | E |   |
| F | O | R |   | M | Y |   |
| C | O | U | N | T | R | Y |

(2.) Interchange columns 2 and 5

| E | I | F | L |   |   | T |
|---|---|---|---|---|---|---|
| B | O | T |   | U | N | E |
| I | V | H | A |   | E |   |
| O | V | G | I |   | E |   |
| F | M | R |   | O | Y |   |
| C | T | U | N | O | R | Y |

(3.) Interchange rows 4 and 6

| E | I | F | L |   |   | T |
|---|---|---|---|---|---|---|
| B | O | T |   | U | N | E |
| I | V | H | A |   | E |   |
| C | T | U | N | O | R | Y |
| F | M | R |   | O | Y |   |
| O | V | G | I |   | E |   |

(4.) Interchange columns 1 and 5

| L | E | I | F |   |   | T |
|---|---|---|---|---|---|---|
| U | O | T |   | B | N | E |
|   | V | H | A | I | E |   |
| O | T | U | N | C | R | Y |
| O | M | R |   | F | Y |   |
|   | V | G | I | O | E |   |

The resulting string is LEIF   TUOT BNE  VHAIE OTUNCRYOMR FY  VGIOE. In order to decode the message, the encoding process is reversed; i.e., the encoded message would be loaded into a 6 by 7 array and then the following interchanges would be performed:

> columns 1 and 5
> rows 4 and 6
> columns 2 and 5
> rows 1 and 3

Write a main program to encode and decode messages, using subroutines to perform the column interchange and row interchange operations.

26. A variation on the encoding technique just described is to include in the encoded message the transformations required to decode the message. These instructions may be embedded into the body of the message using any scheme you desire. Repeat exercise 25 with embedded instructions.

27. Write a subroutine to accept the coordinates of up to 20 ships and determine which two ships are the closest. If $(X_1, Y_1)$ are the coordinates of ship 1 and $(X_2, Y_2)$ are the coordinates of ship 2, then the distance $d$ separating the two ships is given by:

$$d = \sqrt{(X_1 - X_2)^2 + (Y_1 - Y_2)^2}$$

**28.** Grades for a particular class are based on homework, quizzes, and tests. For each student there is record with his or her name, eight homework scores, four quiz scores, and three test scores. Print out each student's name, homework average, quiz average, and test average. To do this, write a *general* subprogram to find the average of an array of real numbers. There are at most 100 students.

**29.** Given a record containing three values A, B, and C, write a subprogram to determine whether they make up the sides of a triangle (the sum of any two is more than the third). If they do, let K = 1 and find the area of the triangle where area = S*(S − A)*(S − B)*(S − C) and S = .5 (A + B + C). If the three values do not make up the sides of a triangle, let K = 0 and let the area = 0. Then, if they do make up the sides of a triangle, write another subprogram to determine whether it is a right triangle. Let RIGHT = 1 if it is; let RIGHT = 0 if it is not. The main program should print out appropriate messages and answers.

**30.** Each record in a data file contains two, forty digit integer numbers. Write a program to print the two numbers and their sum.

**31.** Write a subroutine to compute the trace of a matrix (defined in exercise 26, section 8–6–2,) and then use it to compute the inverse of the matrix (see exercise 27 of section 8–6–2).

**32.** The Furniture Company has stock in three different warehouses. The controller-dispatcher needs to know at any given time the number of a particular furniture item at each of the three warehouses; he may also need to know the number of each particular item at one warehouse. Initially the stock of items in all warehouses is as follows:

|        | *Warehouse 1* | *Warehouse 2* | *Warehouse 3* |
|--------|---------------|---------------|---------------|
| Desks  | 123           | 44            | 76            |
| Chairs | 789           | 234           | 12            |
| Beds   | 67            | 456           | 90            |

He has at his fingertips a terminal where he can inquire about a particular item. For example, when he types BEDS the system furnishes him with the number of beds at the three warehouses. He can also type a warehouse number to list all items at that warehouse. Write a program to allow the following communications between the dispatcher and the data base.

```
ENTER REQUEST
BEDS

              WAREHOUSE1  WAREHOUSE2  WAREHOUSE3
     BEDS           67         456          90       TOTAL   613

ENTER REQUEST
WAREHOUSE3

                  DESKS       CHAIRS        BEDS
  WAREHOUSE3         76           12          90       TOTAL   178

ENTER REQUEST
CHAIRS

              WAREHOUSE1  WAREHOUSE2  WAREHOUSE3
   CHAIRS          789         234          12       TOTAL  1035

ENTER REQUEST
```

Note that the message "ENTER REQUEST" is printed after each request has been satisfied. If the dispatcher enters an invalid request, the system should print an appropriate error message to force him to renew his request.

**33.** If you have access to a conversational computing system, write a program to play tic-tac-toe. The program should allow the user to make the first move, then calculate its next move, and so forth. Can you make the program always win? If not, can you design the program so that it can never lose?

**34.** If you have access to a conversational computing system, write a program to play blackjack. The program should deal cards from the deck in a randomized fashion. You may choose to start with a new deck for each hand or keep track of all cards dealt until the entire deck has been used. The program should act as the dealer and include routines to evaluate its own hand to determine whether to deal itself more cards or stand pat. It must also evaluate the player's hand to determine the winner of each hand.

**35.** 1. Write separate subroutines to print each of the following geometric symbols:

2. Write a main program to generate primitive art artificially (through random generator routine) by printing the above geometric symbols vertically in random fashion. For example:

**36.** You work for the BCD Polling Company. They want you to write a program that will evaluate data from questionnaires of the following form:

1. There are three groups of questions on each questionnaire. The first group has four questions, the second group has eight questions, and the third group has seven questions.
2. Each question will be answered with a number between one and five inclusively: 1 = strongly disagree; 2 = disagree; 3 = don't care; 4 = agree; 5 = strongly agree.

You are asked to write a program to do the following for each questionnaire, in this order:
   a. Use a subprogram AVE to find the average response for each group of questions (this subprogram must be invoked three times for each questionnaire).
   b. Use a subprogram HIST to draw a histogram (bar graph) showing the average response to each of the three groups of questions.
   c. Use a subprogram OP to write the respondent's (person's) average opinion (in words) for each of the three groups of questions.

You will process an unknown number of questionnaires.

*Input:* When a person answers the questionnaire, the answers are recorded on a record in the following manner:

*Column positions*:

| | |
|---|---|
| 1–3 | ID number for the person responding (integer). |
| 5–8 | The four responses to the questions in group 1, one column each (each is an integer between 1 and 5, inclusive). |
| 10–17 | The eight responses to the questions in group 2, one column each (each is an integer between 1 and 5, inclusive). |
| 19–25 | The seven responses to the questions in group 3, one column each (each is an integer between 1 and 5, inclusive). |

A sample record might look like:

$$218 \quad 4213 \quad 43145244 \quad 4944535$$

Your main program should read in a record and use the subprograms described for each record.

Write a *general* real function AVE with two arguments, an integer array (the answers to a particular group of questions) and the length (integer) of the array (the number of questions). AVE should compute the average of the numbers in the array. Use this same subprogram three times for each questionnaire to find the average response for each of the three groups of questions. An example of a call to AVE is:

$$Y = AVE \text{ (}array \ name, \ length \ of \ array\text{)}.$$

Store the three averages in an array (in the main program).

Write another subroutine HIST with one real argument, the array of average responses to the three groups of questions. An example of a call to this subroutine is:

CALL HIST (*array name*)

The subroutine HIST should make a histogram of the three averages using the following description that follow:

Start the histogram at the top of a new page.

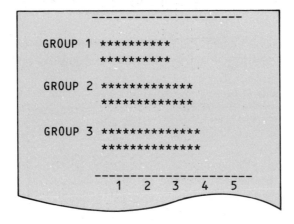

For each .25 points an asterisk is printed. For example, if the average response for group 3 is 3.71, then 14 asterisks are used, since there are 14 full .25 points in 3.71. Do not round off. Any fraction less than .25 is ignored. Note that a double line of asterisks is drawn for each average. The preceding histogram shows what the output would be if the averages were 2.5, 3.3333, and 3.71 for the three groups, respectively. (This is only an example.) Be sure to have your histogram print the dashed lines (minus signs), the words GROUP 1, GROUP 2, and GROUP 3 in the left-hand columns, and the numbers one through five on the bottom, as shown.

Write a subroutine OP with two arguments. The first is the respondent's ID number (INTEGER); the second argument is a REAL array containing the averages of the responses to the three groups of questions. This subroutine should print the following:

```
PERSON xxxS VIEW ABOUT GROUP 1 QUESTIONS IS ____
PERSON xxxS VIEW ABOUT GROUP 2 QUESTIONS IS ____
PERSON xxxS VIEW ABOUT GROUP 3 QUESTIONS IS ____
```

The xxx is to be replaced by the person's ID number, and the blank spaces are to be filled with the appropriate capitalized words shown below:

If the average is 1, the person STRONGLY DISAGREES.
If the average is greater than 1 but less than or equal to 2, the person DISAGREES.
If the average is greater than 2 but less than or equal to 3, the person DOES NOT CARE.
If the average is greater than 3 but less than or equal to 4, the person AGREES.
If the average is greater than 4 but less than or equal to 5, the person STRONGLY AGREES.

**37. a.** Store into a three-dimensional array, K(9, 7, 6), the geometric sets representing the digits 1–9 as follows:

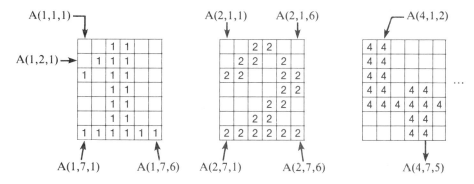

Read a record containing three digits and write a subroutine to display the three digits as a continuous geometric ensemble. For example, if the digits 2, 1, 4 are read, the subroutine should produce the following output:

```
      2 2                 1 1           4 4
    2 2       2         1 1 1           4 4
  2 2         2 2   1     1 1           4 4
              2 2         1 1           4 4       4 4
            2 2           1 1           4 4 4 4 4 4
          2 2             1 1                 4 4
  2 2 2 2 2 2       1 1 1 1 1 1               4 4
```

**b.** (This exercise is for patient artists only.) Represent each letter of the alphabet as a geometric ensemble (as in the preceding exercise) and write a subroutine to accept a name and print its corresponding geometric symbols as shown.

**38.** Write a program that will read in a bridge hand for each of four players (West, North, East, and South, in that order). Each hand has 13 cards. There are four data records, each containing one hand. For example, one data record might be

02 14 41 12 42 01 49 48 22 21 13 40 24

Each two-digit number represents one playing card. The numbers 1–13 represent the spades, 2–ace (1 represents the 2 of spades, 11 represents the queen of spades, and 13 represents the ace). The numbers 14–26 represent the hearts, 2–ace; the numbers 27–39, the diamonds; and 40–52, the clubs. (25 represents the king of hearts.) The 13 numbers of a hand should be stored in an integer array. Call a subroutine SORT to sort the numbers into ascending order. (Notice that by representing the cards this way, SORT arranges the cards into their separate suits and puts them in ascending order *within* the suits.) Call an integer function ITOTAL to calculate the number of points in the hand (a definition of points follows). Write the name of the hand (West, North, East, or South) in the main program and then call a subroutine SHOW to write out the contents of the hand and the number of points in the hand. Repeat these steps for each hand.

Write a general subroutine SORT that will take any integer array and return an array containing the same elements sorted into ascending order. An example of a call to SORT is:

CALL SORT (*array*, *length of array*)

where both *array* and *length of array* are integers.

Write a general integer function ITOTAL that calculates the number of points in a given hand. This subprogram has two arguments. An example of the use of ITOTAL is:

IX = ITOTAL (*array*, *length of array*)

where both *array* and *length of array* are integers.

The points are calculated as follows:

4 points for each ace
3 points for each king
2 points for each queen
1 point for each jack

[*Hint*: the MOD function might help in this routine.]

Write a subroutine SHOW with two arguments. The first argument is an integer array of length 13 containing the sorted cards, and the second argument is an integer variable containing the number of points in the hand. An example of a call to SHOW is:

CALL SHOW (*array*, *number of points*).

Subroutine SHOW prints the contents of the hand passed to it as an argument and prints the number of points in the hand. It prints out the cards by suit, in ascending order within a suit. The printed order of the suits is spades, hearts, diamonds, and then clubs. Print the information according to the sample shown below. Note: The array will have already been sorted into ascending order of spades, hearts, and so forth, by the subroutine SORT; subroutine SHOW is merely a "print" routine.

Print an A for an ace, a K for a king, a Q for queen, and a J for jack. Output for sample data card given is shown below:

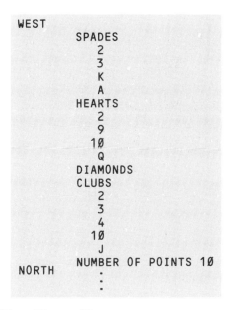

```
WEST
        SPADES
        2
        3
        K
        A
        HEARTS
        2
        9
        10
        Q
        DIAMONDS
        CLUBS
        2
        3
        4
        10
        J
        NUMBER OF POINTS 10
NORTH   .
        .
        .
```

## 10-6-3 Answers to Test Yourself

1. The dummy variables are not initialized properly and might destroy memory; also the return address is unknown.

2. (1) a function generally returns one value; a subroutine returns many values, (2) a subroutine is invoked by the CALL statement, whereas a function is invoked implicitly by using its name in an expression.

3. Program segmentation, utilization of coding segments from program libraries.

4. (1) COMMON statement, (2) argument lists.

5. Return to a variable point (location) is not possible using the simple GO TO statement.

6. A variable as a size declarator is valid only in a subprogram. X and N must be dummy variables.

7. No; they will be initialized *only* on the first call to the subroutine.

8. a. Type of real and dummy arguments must match.
   b. Value of the constant 14. cannot be changed in the subprogram.
   c. Dimension of an array in a subprogram must match dimensions in the calling program (except for one-dimensional arrays). Use variable dimension.
   d. P should be declared as an array instead of Q.
   e. Number of arguments does not match.
   f. The dimensions of X in the REAL statement must be integers.
   g. Subroutine name is missing.
   h. A dummy argument cannot also be in COMMON (D).
   i. Dummy argument C should be typed CHARACTER.

9. a. Subroutine name is missing; a constant appears in list of dummy arguments.
   b. Valid.
   c. Missing / at beginning of name of common block, or / should be a comma!

    d.  Missing parentheses.

    e.  Valid.

    f.  Function SINE undefined.

    g.  Use parentheses instead of slashes.

    h.  Subscripted variables not allowed as dummy arguments.

    i.  Invalid syntax.

    j.  Valid.

    k.  True.

    l.  As many RETURN statements as desired can be used.

   m.  True.

    n.  False.

    o.  True.

    p.  False.

    q.  False.

    r.  True.

    s.  True.

    t.  False; can only pass names of user written subprograms.

    u.  True.

    v.  False: Statement labels are independent among main programs and subprograms.

   w.  False: The END statement is required at the end of every main program or subprogram.

    x.  False.

    y.  False.

    z.  False (1789).

**10.** It will produce the following printout:

THESE PEOPLE HAVE BLOOD + A

MICHELLE

ROBERT

# file
# processing

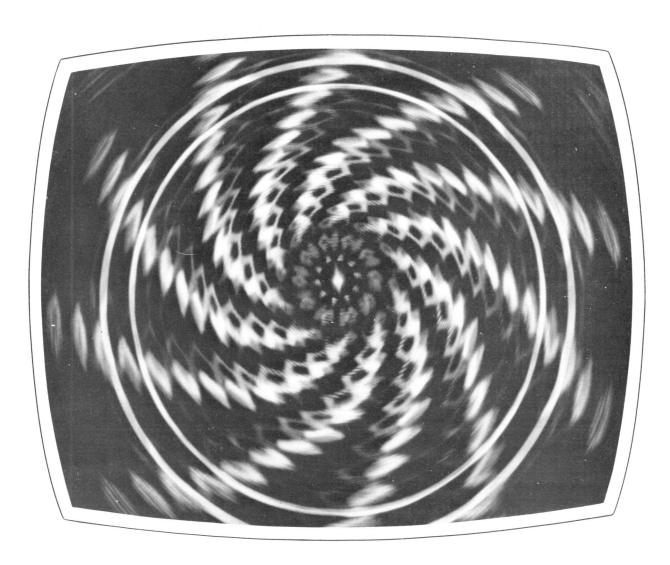

## CHAPTER ELEVEN

# **file processing**

## 11-1 **Introduction**

### 11-1-1 **File Concepts**

Many applications of computers, particularly in business environments, require the storage and processing of large amounts of data. Typically there is too much data to store in memory at one time, so the data is stored externally. The earliest computers used punched cards and magnetic tapes for storage of data. Later computers used magnetic disks and drums as external storage devices.

Data is organized into *records* containing related data items. Groups of related records compose a *file*. For example, a personnel file might contain one record for each employee in a company. Each record would be composed of such data items as the employee's name, social security number, age, date hired, and so on. For convenience in processing, the data items in each record are stored in the same order.

Records within a file are organized for easy access to process the data they contain. A data item that has a unique value for each record is designated as the *record key* and is used as the basis for the file organization. In the example just given, the employee social security number might be the record key as shown in the following illustration:

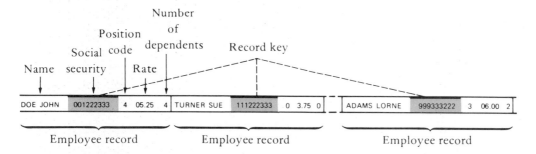

The file might be organized sequentially, randomly, or in any one of a number of other schemes. Using sequential organization, records are placed in the file in order by record keys; each record has a record key value larger than that of its predecessor. A file that is organized sequentially is usually processed sequentially; a program processes each record in turn, starting with the first record in the file. Using random organization, records are placed in the external storage device in a location that is calculated from the value of the record key. This organization allows a program to have random access to any specified record in a file without processing other records in the file. This type of file organization is not commonly supported in FORTRAN systems. Direct-access file organization (discussed in section 11–4) offers a compromise between the limitations of sequential and the advantages of random organization.

### 11-1-2 Programming Example

Mr. X wishes to use a computer to maintain data on the number of parts on hand at his store. He has just taken inventory and now knows the number of parts on hand. The part numbers and corresponding quantities are entered into the computer system and retained on a disk file. Later, as parts are sold or as parts are added to the inventory, the parts file is updated. Then, on either a daily or a weekly basis, reports are produced to list the contents of the inventory file to identify those parts that need to be ordered.

Such an information-processing system inevitably leads to the following file-processing considerations: Once the initial file is created, certain procedures must be defined to maintain the file, i.e., to keep the file current. In the case of personnel or payroll files, new employees are hired, others retire, and some may be fired, the marital status and the number of exemptions may change, certain employees may be promoted thereby causing a change in their pay/salary formula, and so forth. Clearly the files must be updated to reflect such changes before paychecks can be written. In any type of information-processing system, one or more of the following tasks will generally need to be performed:

1. Creating files.
2. Merging files, i.e., combining the records of two or more files into one new file.
3. Adding records.
4. Deleting records.
5. Changing individual items within file records.
6. Generating detailed or summary reports.

Such processes are illustrated in Figure 11–1 where a master file is created and then run against a transaction file to produce a newly updated master file. In real-life applications, of course, the updated master file becomes the current master file, which continually evolves into new updated master files as a result of continual transactions.

A short FORTRAN program shown in Figure 11–2 is used to create Mr. X's inventory file on external storage. The physical device used for storage will vary from one system to another. The device number used on the WRITE statement will be associated by the operating system with an appropriate file-storage device. In Figure 11–2, notice the END FILE statement and the unformatted WRITE.

Later, as parts are used from or added to the inventory, it will be necessary to update the data recorded in this file. A second program shown in Figure 11–3 could be used for this purpose. Notice the unformatted READ statement and the REWIND statement.

Finally, a program will be required to list the contents of the file to see how many parts are available, how many should be ordered, and so forth. Such a program is shown in Figure 11–4. A system flowchart showing the relationship among these programs is shown in Figure 11–5.

## 11-2 File Processing Statements

### 11-2-1 Formatted vs Unformatted I/O

If the format statement number is omitted from the READ or WRITE statement, data is read or written without undergoing translation by FORMAT specifications. FORMATs are required to translate data in character form to internal form for input and from internal form to character form for output. Numerical data on input records is in character form and hence must be translated into internal number representation before it can be pro-

**FIGURE 11-1** FILE PROCESSING TASKS

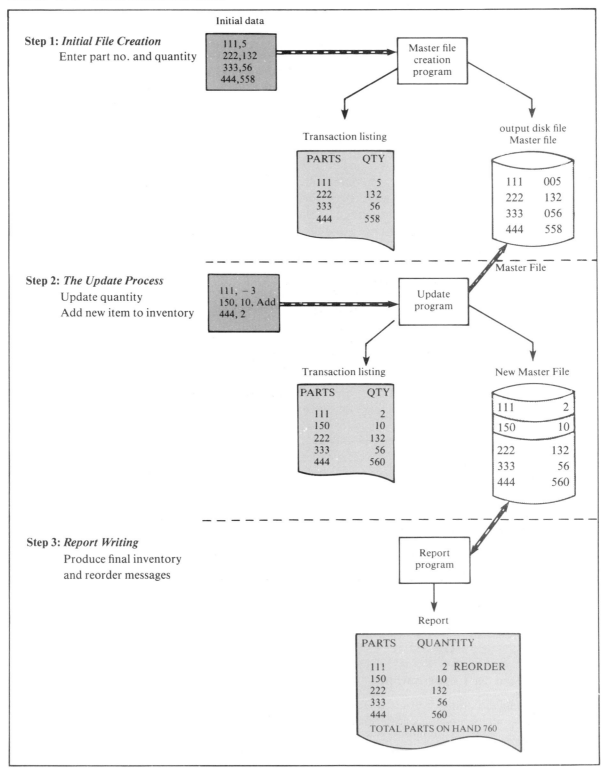

**FIGURE 11-2** FILE CREATION PROGRAM

```
C CREATING A MASTER PARTS FILE
      INTEGER PARTN,QTY
      WRITE(6,3)
100   READ(5,1,END=44)PARTN,QTY        Read a record from the input file.
         WRITE(7)PARTN,QTY             Write record on file 7.
         WRITE(6,2)PARTN,QTY           Write same record on printer.
      GO TO 100
 44   END FILE 7
      REWIND 7
      STOP
   1  FORMAT(I6,I3)
   2  FORMAT(1X,I6,3X,I3)
   3  FORMAT('1PART #',2X,'QUANTITY')
      END

PART #    QUANTITY
111111       20
222222        3
333333       25
444444      123
```

**FIGURE 11-3** FILE UPDATE PROGRAM

```
C UPDATING A MASTER FILE
      INTEGER P(100),Q(100),PART,QUANTY    Read into appropriate arrays all part
C     READ FILE 7 INTO ARRAYS P AND Q      numbers and associated quantities.
      DO 10 N = 1,101                      Assume 100 records at most.
         READ(7,END = 11)P(N),Q(N)         Read the file, one record at a time.
 10   CONTINUE
 11   N = N - 1                            N represents the number of records.
 12   READ(5,1,END = 21)PART,QUANTY        Read a change record.
 14   DO 13 I = 1,N                        Find a part number in the file which is
         IF(P(I).EQ.PART)GO TO 15          equal to the part number on the change
 13   CONTINUE                             record.
      WRITE(6,2)PART                       If the part number is not on file, write the
      GO TO 12                             appropriate error message.
 15   Q(I) = Q(I) + QUANTY                 Update appropriate quantity.
      GO TO 12
 21   REWIND 7                             Reposition file 7.
      DO 30 I = 1,N                        Rewrite file 7 with updated data.
         WRITE(7)P(I),Q(I)
 30   CONTINUE
      END FILE 7
      REWIND 7
      STOP
   1  FORMAT(I6,I3)
   2  FORMAT('0INVALID PART NUMBER',I7)
      END
```

**FIGURE 11-4** LISTING PROGRAM

```
C LISTING THE MASTER FILE
      INTEGER PARTN,QTY
      WRITE(6,1)
 10      READ(7,END = 99)PARTN,QTY
         WRITE(6,2)PARTN,QTY
         GO TO 10
 99   REWIND 7
      STOP
   1  FORMAT('1PART #',4X,'QUANTITY')
   2  FORMAT(1X,I6,6X,I3)

PART #    QUANTITY
111111       26◄——Note change in quantities which
222222        3      resulted from the file update.
333333       25
444444      223
```

**FIGURE 11-5**    SYSTEM FLOWCHART FOR INVENTORY SYSTEM

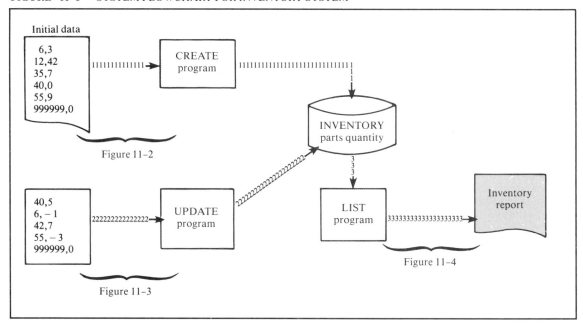

cessed by the arithmetic unit. The printer or terminal requires its data in character form; FORMATs are thus used to translate an internal number representation into character form before that number can be printed. Data may, however, be stored on devices such as tapes and disks in either internal (binary form) or character form (see Figure 11–6). The unformatted WRITE statement will write the internal form of the numbers on a storage medium. Data that has been written out in the internal form on a storage medium does not need to be retranslated when it is read, and hence the unformatted READ statement is used. Using unformatted (binary) data whenever possible may save space on the external storage device being used and speed up the processing of data by the program.

*Example*

```
READ(7)A,B,K
```

Three values will be read from a record on device 7. No conversion will take place; the data will be assumed to be in internal form.

```
WRITE(10)X,Y,LL,KK
```

Four values in internal form will be written on device 10. Carriage control codes do not apply in this context, since we are not trying to control "paper movement" on disk or tape.

## 11-2-2  The END FILE Statement

Every file must have a system end-of-file record following the last data record of the file. The END FILE statement is used to write this record when a disk or tape file is being created by a FORTRAN program. The general form of this statement is:

END FILE *device number*

where *device number* is the number associated with the disk or tape file.

**FIGURE 11-6**   FORMATTED VS. UNFORMATTED READ/WRITE

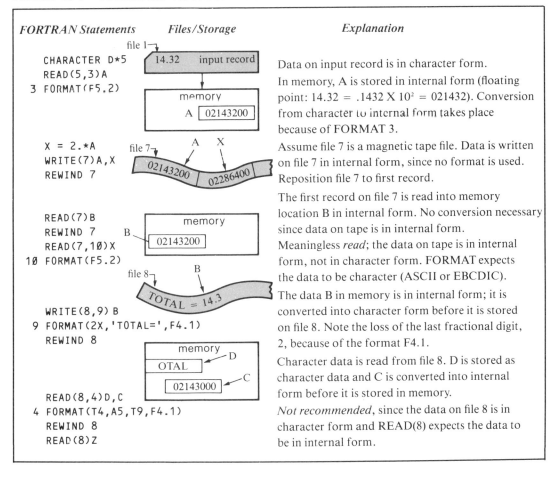

| *FORTRAN Statements* | *Files/Storage* | *Explanation* |
|---|---|---|

CHARACTER D*5
READ(5,3)A
3 FORMAT(F5.2)

Data on input record is in character form.
In memory, A is stored in internal form (floating point: 14.32 = .1432 X 10² = 021432). Conversion from character to internal form takes place because of FORMAT 3.

X = 2.*A
WRITE(7)A,X
REWIND 7

Assume file 7 is a magnetic tape file. Data is written on file 7 in internal form, since no format is used. Reposition file 7 to first record.

READ(7)B
REWIND 7
READ(7,10)X
10 FORMAT(F5.2)

The first record on file 7 is read into memory location B in internal form. No conversion necessary since data on tape is in internal form.
Meaningless *read*; the data on tape is in internal form, not in character form. FORMAT expects the data to be character (ASCII or EBCDIC).

WRITE(8,9)B
9 FORMAT(2X,'TOTAL=',F4.1)
REWIND 8

The data B in memory is in internal form; it is converted into character form before it is stored on file 8. Note the loss of the last fractional digit, 2, because of the format F4.1.

READ(8,4)D,C
4 FORMAT(T4,A5,T9,F4.1)
REWIND 8
READ(8)Z

Character data is read from file 8. D is stored as character data and C is converted into internal form before it is stored in memory.
*Not recommended*, since the data on file 8 is in character form and READ(8) expects the data to be in internal form.

*Example*

```
  1 READ(5,10,END = 100)A,B,C
      SUM = A + B + C
      WRITE(7)A,B,C,SUM
      GO TO 1
100 END FILE 7
 10 FORMAT(3F5.0)
      .
      .
      .
```

Statement 100 will cause the system end-of-file record to be written on device number 7.

## 11-2-3  The REWIND Statement

A major advantage of a disk or tape file is that it can be processed repeatedly by a program. The REWIND statement causes the next input operation addressed to a file to return to the program the first record of the file. When the file is on tape, the tape is physically rewound and repositioned so that the first record of the file is available at the next operation. When the file is on disk, the rewinding is logical rather than physical. The result, however, is the same; the first record of the file is the next one available for processing. The general form of the REWIND statement is:

REWIND *device number*

where *device number* is the number associated with the file to be rewound.

*Example*

```
      .
      .
      .
    END FILE 7
    REWIND 7
  2 READ(7,END = 1000)A,B,C,SUM
      WRITE(6,110)A,B,C,SUM
      GO TO 2
1000 STOP
```

After processing of the file on device 7 is terminated, the file is rewound and processed again (statement 2).

## 11-3  Programming Examples

### 11-3-1  File Creation

In the following program examples, we shall assume that a file MASTER (device number 7) has been established, containing payroll data records with identification numbers, names, and hourly wages. The program used to create the file is shown in Figure 11–7; the program used to list the file is shown in Figure 11–8. In both examples the END = option is used to control the program when end-of-file is reached.

### 11-3-2  Merging

As new employees are hired, records must be added to the file MASTER. If there is no ordering in the file MASTER, adding records at the end of the file presents no special difficulties. However, it is usually advantageous to store a file in ascending order by record key. Note that the sample file listed in Figure 11–8 is sorted into ascending sequence by identification number. We will write a program that will accept new items to be added to the file and then merge the new items with the old items in a way that preserves the order of the records in the new file.

Throughout this discussion, we will assume that there are too many items in the file MASTER to be stored into arrays. If such storage were available, techniques like those used in the program of section 11–1 would be appropriate. We will assume that there is sufficient space available in memory for the new items to be added to the file. The program in Figure 11–9 will accept new items to be added, store them in arrays, and print a listing of each new item. When all new items have been entered, the program will merge the new items with the old and create a file NEW MASTER (device number 8) containing the new file.

If tapes are used for file storage, a common procedure would be to store the file MASTER as a backup in case errors are discovered and use the file NEW MASTER in subse-

**FIGURE 11-7** FILE CREATION PROGRAM

```
C THIS PROGRAM CREATES THE FILE MASTER FROM INPUT FILE
        CHARACTER NAME*20
    1   READ(5,100,END = 60)ID,NAME,H
            WRITE(7)ID,NAME,H                    Create file 7 in unformatted form.
            GO TO 1
   60   END FILE 7
        REWIND 7
        STOP
  100   FORMAT(I9,A20,F5.2)
        END
```

**FIGURE 11-8** FILE-LISTING PROGRAM

```
C THIS PROGRAM PRODUCES A LISTING OF THE FILE MASTER
        CHARACTER NAME*20
        WRITE(6,10)
        WRITE(6,11)
    1   READ(7,END = 100)ID,NAME,H               Access to file 7 is made through an
    2       WRITE(6,12)ID,NAME,H                  unformatted READ, since this was the way the
            GO TO 1                               file was initially created (binary file).
  100   WRITE (6,13)
        STOP
   10   FORMAT('1',60('*'))
   11   FORMAT(1X,'ID NUMBER',8X,'NAME',16X,'HOURLY WAGE')
   12   FORMAT(1X,I9,8X,A20,2X,F7.2)
   13   FORMAT(1X,60('*'))
        END
```

```
**********************************************************
ID NUMBER          NAME                HOURLY WAGE
123456789          DOE JOHN               5.00
222222222          BROWN JIM              2.50
333333333          GREEN MARY             7.25
456789000          SMITH SAM              4.21
**********************************************************
```

quent processing. If disk storage is used, there may not be room to store both MASTER and NEW MASTER permanently. In this case a typical procedure would be to copy the contents of the file MASTER onto tape for backup storage and copy the file NEW MASTER onto MASTER. The file MASTER is used in subsequent processing; the area used by the file NEW MASTER is released for other uses. The program in Figure 11-9 assumes that disk storage is used and that a backup copy of the file MASTER has been produced prior to execution of this program; hence the program copies the contents of NEW MASTER into MASTER.

In the program of Figure 11-9 it is assumed that the new items are in ascending sequence. If this is not the case, a sort algorithm could be used prior to merging the new items. In all file processing, it is important to institute error checks with appropriate messages to ensure that erroneous data does not enter the system. Note, for example, the check in the program of Figure 11-9 that ensures that records with duplicate identification numbers are not allowed to enter the file. If a duplicate identification number appears, a message is written on the report. The new contents of the file MASTER are shown in Figure 11-10.

**FIGURE 11-9** FILE-MERGING PROGRAM

```
      DIMENSION NID(100), WAGNEW(100)
      CHARACTER*20 NAME,NEWNAM(100)
      DO 10 I = 1,101                        Read new records into arrays.
      READ(5,100,END=20)NID(I),NEWNAM(I),WAGNEW(I)
 10   WRITE(6,102)NID(I),NEWNAM(I),WAGNEW(I)
 20   N = I - 1                              N is the number of itesm to be added.
      I = 1
 21   READ(7,END = 50)ID,NAME,H              Read a record from master file.
 23   IF(ID.EQ.NID(I))GO TO 33               Check for duplicate identification numbers.
      IF(ID.GT.NID(I))GO TO 30
      WRITE(8)ID,NAME,H                      If ID on master file is less than new record ID,
      GO TO 21                               then output master file record onto new file.
 30   WRITE(8)NID(I),NEWNAM(I),WAGNEW(I)
 22   I = I + 1
      IF(I.GT.N)GO TO 40                     If all new records have been used, go to
      GO TO 23                               40; otherwise continue the loop.
 33   WRITE(6,101)ID                         Write error message.
      GO TO 22
 50   IF(I.GT.N)GO TO 60
 51   WRITE(8)NID(I),NEWNAM(I),WAGNEW(I)
      I = I + 1                              Output remainder of new records when
      GO TO 50                               master has been exhausted.
 40   WRITE(8)ID,NAME,H                      Output remainder of master file when all
      READ(7,END = 60)ID,NAME,H              new records have been exhausted.
      GO TO 40
 60   END FILE 8                             New file has been completed.
      REWIND 8
      REWIND 7
 61   READ(8,END = 70)ID,NAME,H              Copy new file onto master file.
      WRITE(7)ID,NAME,H
      GO TO 61
 70   END FILE 7
      REWIND 7
      REWIND 8
      STOP
100   FORMAT(I9,A20,F5.2)
101   FORMAT(2X,'DUPLICATE ID',I10)
102   FORMAT(2X,I9,2X,A20,F7.2)
      END

100000000    ABLE BAKER    3.00
222222222    BROWN JIM     2.50
555555555    JONES MARK    7.50
DUPLICATE ID 222222222
```

**FIGURE 11-10** NEW CONTENTS OF FILE MASTER

```
***************************************************
ID NUMBER          NAME              HOURLY WAGE
100000000          ABLE BAKER            3.00
123456789          DOE JOHN              5.00
222222222          BROWN JIM             2.50
333333333          GREEN MARY            7.25
456789000          SMITH SAM             4.21
555555555          JONES MARK            7.50
***************************************************
```

## 11-3-3  Report Generation

A second file (HOURS) is to be created containing records in the form:

Identification number, hours-worked

The program used to create and list the file HOURS is shown in Figure 11–11. Note the use of the REWIND statements to enable processing the file after its creation.

**FIGURE  11-11**    CREATION OF THE FILE HOURS

```
C THIS PROGRAM CREATES AND LISTS THE FILE HOURS
   1    READ(5,100,END = 20)ID,HOURS
        WRITE(8)ID,HOURS                    Create the file HOURS on device number 8.
        GO TO 1
  20    END FILE 8
        REWIND 8
        WRITE(6,101)
  21    READ(8,END = 30)ID,HOURS            List the file HOURS.
        WRITE(6,102)ID,HOURS
        GO TO 21
  30    WRITE(6,103)
        REWIND 8
        STOP
 100    FORMAT(I9,F6.2)
 101    FORMAT('1',40('*')/'0','ID NUMBER',9X,'HOURS WORKED')
 102    FORMAT(1X,I9,10X,F7.2)
 103    FORMAT('0',40('*'))
        END
```

```
******************************
ID NUMBER        HOURS WORKED
123456789           40.00
222222222           53.00
444444444           30.00
456789000           24.00
555555555           50.00
******************************
```

A report is needed to show the employee's name, identification number, hourly wage, hours worked, and gross pay. The program in Figure 11–12 could be used to generate this report. We assume that there are more data in both files than can be contained in memory; hence data on one employee at a time is read from each of the files. When identification numbers match, a line of the report is written. In this case, there are two end-of-file problems to consider. When end-of-file is detected in the file HOURS, this signifies the end of the report. When end-of-file is detected on the file MASTER, however, there may be items left on HOURS that have not been processed. This case is treated as an error condition.

## 11-3-4  Do It Now

Modify the program of Figure 11–11 to reject any record which does not have a matching ID number in the MASTER file.

**FIGURE 11-12** GROSS PAY REPORT

```
C THIS PROGRAM READS THE FILE HOURS AND MASTER AND PRODUCES GROSS PAY REPORT
        CHARACTER NAME*20
        WRITE(6,100)
  1     READ(7,END = 700)MASTID,NAME,WAGE          Read a record on MASTER file.
  2     READ(8,END = 600)ID,HOURS                  Read a record on HOURS file.
  3     IF(MASTID.EQ.ID) GO TO 200                 If ID's are equal, to to 200.
        IF(MASTID.LT.ID) GO TO 190                 If MASTER ID is greater than HOURS ID,
        WRITE(6,101)ID                             write error message.
        GO TO 2
 190    READ(7,END = 500)MASTID,NAME,WAGE          Read new record on MASTER file if
        GO TO 3                                    MASTER ID is less than HOURS ID.
 200    PAY = HOURS*WAGE                           Compute pay and write report line when
        WRITE(6,102)ID,NAME,WAGE,HOURS,PAY         MASTER ID is equal to hours ID.
        GO TO 1
 500    WRITE(6,101)ID
        READ(8,END = 600)ID,HOURS                  If end is reached on MASTER, current hours
        GO TO 500                                  record and remaining HOURS are in error.
 700    READ(8,END = 600)ID,HOURS                  If end is reached on MASTER, remaining
        WRITE(6,101)ID                             HOURS records are in error.
        GO TO 700
 600    WRITE(6,103)
        REWIND 7
        REWIND 8
        STOP
 100    FORMAT('1',70('*')/2X,'ID NUMBER',3X,'NAME',17X,'HOURLY WAGE',
       #5X,'HOURS',5X,'PAY')
 101    FORMAT(2X,'NO MATCHING RECORD ID NUMBER',I10)
 102    FORMAT(2X,I9,3X,A20,2X,F7.2,6X,F7.2,2X,F8.2)
 103    FORMAT(1X,70('*'))
        END
```

```
*****************************************************************
ID NUMBER     NAME                   HOURLY WAGE     HOURS      PAY
123456789     DOE JOHN                     5.00      40.00    200.00
222222222     BROWN JIM                    2.50      53.00    132.50
NO MATCHING RECORD ID NUMBER 444444444
456789000     SMITH SAM                    4.21      24.00    101.04
555555555     JONES MARK                   7.50      50.00    375.00
*****************************************************************
```

## Answer

```
  DIMENSION NAME(5)                    20 WRITE(8)ID,HOURS
  READ(7) MASTID, NAME, WAGE              GO TO 1
1 READ(5,100,END = 200)ID,HOURS        30 READ (7)MASTID,NAME,WAGE
2 IF (MASTID .EQ. ID) GO TO 20            GO TO 2
  IF (MASTID. LT. ID) GO TO 30        200 STOP
  WRITE (6, 101)ID, HOURS             100 FORMAT(I9,F6.2)
  GO TO 1                             101 FORMAT(3X,'INVALID ID NUMBER',2X,I9,3X,F7.2)
                                          END
```

## 11-4 You Might Want to Know

**1.** Is there any way to get the system to backspace a record in processing a file?

*Answer:* Yes. On some FORTRAN versions the BACKSPACE statement causes the system to back up one record at a time from the current position of the file. For example, to backspace four records in a file the following code could be used:

```
   DO 10 I = 1,4
      BACKSPACE 7
10 CONTINUE
```

In some cases where FORTRAN stores more than one logical record per unit area of disk or tape (automatic blocking), BACKSPACE may result in skipping over more than one logical record. Look in your reference manual under *blocking*.

**2.** Can a file be used as both an input file and an output file in the same program?

*Answer:* Yes. For example, combine the program segments in sections 11–2–2 and 11–2–3. This program would create a file, rewind it, and read it back.

**3.** Can I skip files if there are more than one on a tape?

*Answer:* Yes. For example, the following code would skip over one file.

```
10 READ(7,END = 88)DATA
      GO TO 10
88 _____
```

**4.** How can I read data from more than one logical unit using one READ statement?

*Answer:* Some FORTRAN versions allow you to refer to the input/output logical device as a variable name as in:

```
 7 READ(N,8)A,B,C
```

**5.** What is the advantage of using unformatted READ/WRITE statements as opposed to formatted READ/WRITE statements?

*Answer:* Time is saved by unformatted READ, since no translation of the data read is necessary. Unformatted WRITE may save space, since less space may be used by the internal form of a data item than by the character form.

**6.** Can I write formatted and unformatted records on the same file? For example:

```
   WRITE(7)A
   WRITE(7,4)B
 4 FORMAT(2X,'SUM IS',F4.2)
```

*Answer*: Yes. See the discussion in section 11–4–2.

## 11-5  Exercises

### 11-5-1  Test Yourself

**1.** What purpose is served by each of the following FORTRAN features?
   a. The END = option.
   b. The END FILE statement.
   c. The REWIND statement.
   d. The BACKSPACE statement.

**2.** What is the difference between formatted and unformatted processing of data?

**3.** What is a record key? Why is it important?

**4.** Differentiate among the following: data item, data record, data file.

**5.** What are the disadvantages of sequential access to data? Are there advantages?

## 11-5-2 Programming Problems: Business/General

**1.** Write a program to add records, delete records, and change existing records for the inventory file discussed in section 11–1. Use a code on the input record to indicate the action to be performed. For example, you might use 1 for addition, 2 for deletion, and 3 for change.

**2.** In the program in Figure 11–9, suppose the new items are not in sorted sequence. Add the code to perform the sort.

**3.** Write a program to delete items from the file MASTER discussed in section 11–3.

**4.** Write a program to process changes in names and hourly wages for the file MASTER discussed in section 11–3.

**5.** Rewrite the program in Figure 7–9 using a file to store the students' names and grades.

**6.** Write programs for the Widget Manufacturing Company's sales information system. A sales file is to be created with records in the following format:

salesperson number, amount of sales

A master file must also be created with records in the format:

salesperson number, name, amount of sales to data

Programs are needed to:
a. Create the files.
b. Update the master file from data in the sales file.
c. Produce a report showing each salesperson's totals to date.

**7.** Dr. X teaches an introduction to computers course to 15 students. Three equally weighted tests are given in the course. A file is created for the class; each record consists of a student name followed by the student's grade. Records are sorted by name in alphabetical order. Each time a test is given, the file is updated to reflect the total score (sum of grades) obtained by each student so far. At the end of the semester Dr. X computes the average of the three scores and assigns letter grades as follows:

| | |
|---|---|
| 90 and above | A |
| 80–89 | B |
| 70–79 | C |
| 60–69 | D |
| Below 60 | F |

a. Write a program to create a class file for Dr. X. Initially, the students' scores are all zero.
b. Simulate three sets of test scores for the 15 students; update the class file three times.
c. Write the code to produce a listing of names with their corresponding averages and letter grades.

   d. Write a program to input a student's name and print out that student's total test score so far.

**8.** In exercise 7 make necessary changes to the student's record and to the program to allow for the following message to be printed out when assigning the letter grade for each student: "Cannot determine student's final grade. Student did not take all three tests."

**9.** A bank maintains its accounts' master file with items in the following format:

account number, name, present balance

Checks must be processed against the master file. Write a program that accepts information about checks to be processed as input and updates the master file. Note that checks will be presented in any order, so some sorting will be required before updating the file. Also note that more than one check may be processed against an account. What type of error conditions might be encountered? If your system supports random access binary files, this problem should be greatly simplified.

**10.** Rewrite the airline reservation problem of exercise 28, section 8–6–2b to maintain passenger reservation information in files.

**11.** The PAYROLL file at Tricity College consists of records containing the following information:

(1) Employee social security number.
(2) A federal tax coefficient that is applied to gross pay to determine federal taxes for each pay period.

(3) A year-to-date gross pay.
(4) A year-to-date federal tax.
(5) A year-to-date social security tax.
(6) A year-to-date net pay.

Create a disk payroll file for the Tricity College personnel department and a transaction file consisting of records containing an employee's social security number and an employee's gross pay for a pay period.

   a. Write a program to update the PAYROLL file with the TRANSACTION file and print each employee's check and check stub, as follows:

```
TRICITY COLLEGE
DATE  4/16/84
PAY TO   DOE  JON              $    668.84
------------------------------------------
CHECK DATE  4/16/84
SOCIAL SECURITY    NAME
109-84-8224        JON  DOE

GROSS PAY      FED. TAX      FICA      NET PAY
1 008.77        272.85      67.08      668.84

Y-T-D         Y-T-D        Y-T-D     Y-T-D
GROSS PAY     FED. TAX     FICA      NET PAY
8 070.16      2246.90      536.64    3057.90
------------------------------------------
TRICITY COLLEGE
DATE  4/16/84
PAY TO   CHARMS  LINDA         $   1664.48
------------------------------------------
CHECK DATE  4/16/84
SOCIAL SECURITY    NAME
304-12-3334        LINDA  CHARMS
        :            :        :        :
        :            :        :        :
        :            :        :        :
------------------------------------------
```

b. Using tables, try writing the code to complete the above paychecks by writing out the pay amount in words, as in:

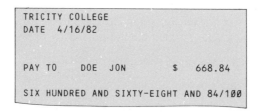

```
TRICITY COLLEGE
DATE  4/16/82



PAY TO    DOE  JON        $    668.84

SIX HUNDRED AND SIXTY-EIGHT AND 84/100
```

12. At the end of the semester, students' final grades are recorded in a file called GRADE-ROSTER-FILE. The file is organized sequentially using each student's social security number as a key. Identical social security numbers occur in groups, i.e., each group identifies a particular student's grades in each course taken by the student. An example of GRADE-ROSTER-FILE is as follows:

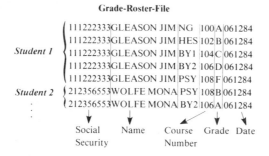

**Grade-Roster-File**

Student 1
```
111222333GLEASON JIM NG  100 A 061284
111222333GLEASON JIM HES 102 B 061284
111222333GLEASON JIM BY1 104 C 061284
111222333GLEASON JIM BY2 106 D 061284
111222333GLEASON JIM PSY 108 F 061284
```
Student 2
```
212356553WOLFE MONA PSY 108 B 061284
212356553WOLFE MONA BY2 106 A 061284
```

Social    Name    Course   Grade Date
Security          Number

The Registrar's office also has a list of student names organized sequentially by social security key on a disk file called STUDENT-ADMISSION-FILE. Each disk record contains the student's name and social security number, the student's current cumulative hours (credits) and cumulative grade point, and the student's major field of study and classification. An example of STUDENT-ADMISSION-FILE is:

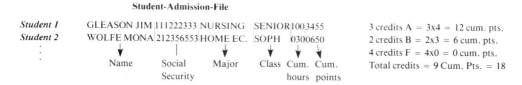

**Student-Admission-File**

Student 1   GLEASON JIM 111222333 NURSING   SENIOR 100 3455     3 credits A = 3x4 = 12 cum. pts.
Student 2   WOLFE MONA 212356553 HOME EC.   SOPH   030 0650     2 credits B = 2x3 = 6 cum. pts.
                                                                4 credits F = 4x0 = 0 cum. pts.
            Name     Social    Major   Class  Cum.  Cum.        Total credits = 9 Cum. Pts. = 18
                     Security                 hours points

Since each record of the GRADE-ROSTER-FILE indicates neither the number of credits associated with the particular course nor the verbal description of the course, a file called COURSE-CATALOG-FILE is used as a course identification directory to look up the number of credits for a particular course (using the three-digit course number) and the corresponding verbal description. An example of such a file is shown below:

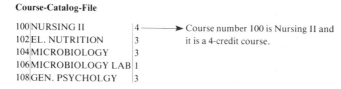

**Course-Catalog-File**

```
100 NURSING II         4  ────►  Course number 100 is Nursing II and
102 EL. NUTRITION      3            it is a 4-credit course.
104 MICROBIOLOGY       3
106 MICROBIOLOGY LAB   1
108 GEN. PSYCHOLGY     3
```

Write a program that will:

a. Read the GRADE-ROSTER-FILE and print each student's end-of-semester grade report.
b. Compute each student's grade point average for the semester, as well as his or her cumulative grade point average.
c. Print the semester total hours, as well as the cumulative hours.
d. Update the student admission file to reflect updated entries for both the cumulative points and cumulative hours.

An example of a student's end-of-semester grade report is shown as follows:

```
FIELD STUDY   CLASS   STUDENT NAME          DATE       SS. NUMBER
NURSING       SENIOR  GLEASON JIM           06 12 81   111222333
*****************************************************************
COURSE        NUMBER  DESCRIPTION     HOURS  GRADE  POINTS   GPA
*************CUMULATIVE TOTALS        100           345.5
NG            100     NURSING II      4      A      16.0
HES           102     EL. NUTRITION   3      B      9.0
BY1           104     MICROBIOLOGY    3      C      6.0
BY2           106     MICROBIOLOGY LA 1      D      1.0
PSY           108     GEN. PSYCHOLOGY 3      F      0.0
*****************************************************************
                      SEMESTER TOTALS 14            32.0    2.285
                      CUM.    TOTALS  114           377.5   3.311
```

The interaction (and relationship) between the various transaction files and the master file is shown below, illustrating the way in which data is captured from the various files to produce a complete end-of-semester grade report.

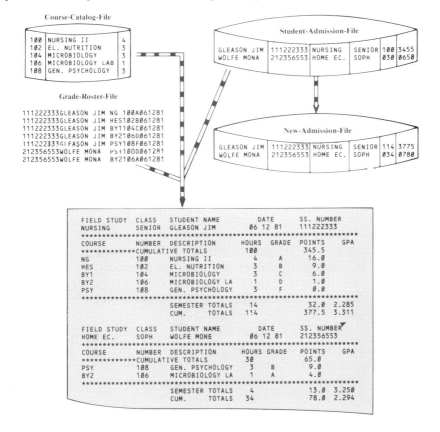

**13.** Problem 12 did not include error checking. Rewrite the program to take care of the following situations:

  a. A social security number in GRADE-ROSTER-FILE has no corresponding match in STUDENT-ADMISSION-FILE. In such a case, print an appropriate error message identifying the name of the student not listed in the STUDENT-ADMISSION-FILE.

  b. A course number in the GRADE-ROSTER-FILE has been incorrectly typed and is not found in the course directory. Type an appropriate message and abort the report for the particular student. Note that in such a case successive social security numbers may still belong to that student. Such records should be flushed out before continuing with the next record(s) for a different student.

  c. The grade specified in the GRADE-ROSTER-FILE is incorrectly recorded; i.e., the grade is neither F, D, C, B or A. Abort the current report and continue with the next report.

**14.** Dr. Teach keeps her students' grades on diskettes on her own microcomputer system. She has already entered the following information on each student into her master file: name, two test scores, and two blank entries for the final average and the corresponding letter grade. Dr. Teach's input file might be similar to:

| Name | Test 1 | Test 2 | Average | Grade |
|------|--------|--------|---------|-------|
| DOE J | 80 | 90 | ? | ? |
| HILL K | 60 | 62 | ? | ? |
| : | | | | |

| | |
|---|---|
| A | = 90 or above |
| B+ | = 85–89 |
| B | = 80–84 |
| C+ | = 75–79 |
| C | = 60–74 |
| D | = 50–59 |
| F | = below 50 |

Dr. Teach is now ready to write a program to compute each student's final score and corresponding letter grade. She realizes that in some cases, either or both test scores may have to be changed. Some students have withdrawn from the class and need their names deleted from the master file. Write a program to:

  a. Create a class file arranged alphabetically by student name. Each record should contain a name, two test scores, and two initial blank fields for the final average and the letter grade.

  b. Create a transaction file consisting of change records. Such records can cause deletion of certain records or changes in either one or both test scores. Use change codes of your choice.

  c. Print an updated grade roster file listing the names of the students as well as their scores and letter grade. Identify transaction names that do not have corresponding matches in the master file.

The master file, transaction file, and output have the following form:

*Master file*

| | | |
|---|---|---|
| DOE JOE | 50 | 70 |
| LIKE SALLY | 80 | 90 |
| TASS MIKE | 65 | 70 |
| TURAN LEO | 80 | 70 |

*Transaction file*

| | | | |
|---|---|---|---|
| DOE JOE | DELETE | | |
| LIKE SALLY | CHANGE | 1 | 70 |
| TASS MIKE | CHANGE | 1 | 80 |
| TURAN LEO | CHANGE | 2 | 80 |
| TURAN LEO | CHANGE | 1 | 60 |
| AMIGO LUIS | CHANGE | 1 | 60 |

*Output*

```
NAME          T1  T2  AVG   GRADE
LIKE SALLY    70  90  80    B
TASS MIKE     80  70  75    C+
TURAN LEO     60  80  70    C
NO MATCH FOR AMIGO
```

**15.** WKNE station's meteorologist has access to a master file containing weather data on most of the cities that lie within a 50-mile radius of the WKNE broadcasting station. Each record contains the name of the city and its record high and low temperatures for each of the past 20 years. The master file records have the following layout:

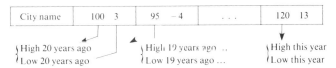

| City name | 100  3 | 95  −4 | . . . | 120  13 |

{ High 20 years ago / Low 20 years ago    { High 19 years ago ... / Low 19 years ago ...    { High this year / Low this year

a.  Write a program to read a data file where each record contains the name of a city and the corresponding high and low temperatures for the day. Such records are as follows:

| City | 90 | 70 |

High and    Low for the day

The program should list the temperature (high and low) of the day for each city and indicate whether any temperature records were broken during the day. A typical listing might be:

```
CITY        HIGH    LOW
ATMORE       98     70
BEULAH       95     68    PREVIOUS RECORD HI WAS 94 IN 1971
CHUMUCKLA    92     65    PREVIOUS RECORD LO WAS 66 IN 1979
MILTON       98     62
MARYESTHER  100     58    PREVIOUS RECORD HI WAS 98 IN 1965
                          PREVIOUS RECORD LO WAS 60 IN 1974
  :           :      :
  :           :      :
  :           :      :
PACE         94     71
```

Be sure to update the master file if any record temperatures are broken; i.e., change the records in the master file to identify new highs or lows.

b.  Design an on-line inquiry system that allows the meteorologist to perform the following functions:

(1) Key in a city name and a year and list the high and low for that city and year.

(2) Key in a city name and identify the year of its record high and low for the last 20 years. Print the city, year, and record high and low.

(3) Key in a year and identify the city (cities) with record high and low for that year.

(4) Produce a listing arranged in year sequence order, identifying the record high and low for each city during the year. Over the 20-year period the output might be as follows:

```
YEAR    CITIES       HI    LO
1964    ATMORE       94    15
        BEULAH       91    21
        CHUMUCKLA    96    16
        MILTON       89    23
        MARYESTHER   90    20
        PACE         94     9

1965    ATMORE       98    10
        BEULAH       94    16
        CHUMUCKLA    89    14
                      :     :
                      :     :
1984    ATMORE       91    10
        BEULAH       90    12
                      :     :
                      :     :
        PACE         99    20
```

**16.** The Chique Boutique is an exclusive ladies' fashion store where the Chique Boutique members are required to maintain at least $1,000 in their accounts at all times. Members charge purchases on Chique Boutique credits cards.

a. Write a program to create a master file consisting of customer numbers, customer names, and an initial balance of over $1,500 for each member.

b. Members may return merchandise, in which case their account is credited appropriately. In some cases, purchases cause the member's credit to fall below $1,000, in which case a notice is sent to the member requesting that a check be written to bring back the member's credit to at least $1,000.

A transaction file for the month consists of various purchase records sorted by ascending customer numbers. Such records include a customer number, an item number and description, and a date of purchase. Individual customer transactions, if there are more than one, occur in groups.

Write a program to update the master file and produce a monthly customer invoice similar to the following:

```
CHIQUE BOUTIQUE
ACCT NO: 1215
DATE 02/05/84

                        DATE        BALANCE       PURCHASES
                                    10000.00
***JOVANT BOOTS         01/20/82     360.00
   ENSEMBLE LINGERIE    01/25/82                    550.75
   FLEURETTE FOUNDATION 01/25/82                    145.25
   PENDANT 20 KT.       01/27/82                   2600.00
                                    7064.00        3296.00
```

Note that *** is a credit entry (return).

```
CHIQUE BOUTIQUE
ACCT NO: 1315
DATE 02/05/84

                           DATE        BALANCE       PURCHASES
                                       2000.00
   NEGLIGEE EXQUIS         01/15/82                    600.00
   PEIGNOIR BROCADE        01/20/82                    400.00
   ILUNA ESSENCE 6 OZ. FL. 01/23/82                    300.00
                                        700.00        1300.00

PLEASE REMIT MINIMUM OF $300.00
```

c. The Chique Boutique sales department would like to produce the following monthly sales activity report by ascending customer account number:

Write the code to generate such a report.

```
MONTHLY SALES REPORT: APRIL 1984

ACCOUNT NO.    TOTAL SALES    CUSTOMER BALANCE
   1215          3296.00          7064.00
   1315          1300.00           700.00
   1446         10432.00          5600.00
                15028.00         13364.00
```

d. Write the code to produce a sales summary report for the internal auditor; this report shows the sales for each day of the month as follows:

```
      SUMMARY DAILY SALES

    DATE              SALES

  01/01/82           23452.00
  01/02/82           13452.00
  01/03/82           33400.70
     :                  :
     :                  :
```

e. Write another code for the auditor to produce a summary of daily sales by items, as follows:

```
               DETAILED DAILY SALES

     DATE      ITEMS      SALES       TOTALS
   01/01/82
                112       344.00
                209       246.00
                321       410.00
                400     22452.00
                                     23,452.00

   01/02/82
                112       344.00
                216     10000.00
                312      3108.00
                                     13,452.00
      :           :          :           :
      :           :          :           :
```

17. The Tricity College library staff is thinking about using computers to assist them in dealing with the high volume of book transactions. Four types of transactions must be considered:

(1) Books checked in.   (3) New books put into circulation.
(2) Books checked out.   (4) Old books withdrawn from circulation.

Books have an 8-digit numeric code identification, the last two digits of which indicate a multicopy identification number:

```
              11112001
              11112003
```

Book number ⟵      ⟶ Copy identification number
        Number of copies in library      (1–20)

The library clerks deal manually with four types of files:

(1) The CHECK-IN-OUT-FILE.

This file consists of a daily list of books that have been checked in or checked out. The record layout for each file is as follows:

| Item | Nature |
|---|---|
| 1 | Book number identification |
| 2 | Disposition code (1 = check in, 2 = check out) |
| 3 | Julian date (025 means Jan. 25, 365 is Dec. 31) |
| 4 | Patron's identity (1 = faculty, 2 = student) |
| 5 | Patron's telephone number |

Book id. | Patron

1111 20 02   1 034 1 4345410
1111 20 17   2 034 1 4762500
2222 02 01   2 034 2 4785660

Book no.  # copies    Date    Telephone
        Copy number  Disposition code

(2) The NEW-BOOK-FILE.

This file consists of books that have been either purchased or donated and do not exist in the master file. The record layout for such file records is:

| Item | Nature |
|------|--------|
| 1 | Book number identification |
| 2 | Year of edition |
| 3 | Disposition status (1 = available, 2 = reserve) |
| 4 | Author |
| 5 | Acquisition code (1 = purchased, 2 = donation) |

(3) The DELETE-FILE.

Transaction records in this file allow the librarian to delete books from the master file or to change the status field of a particular book. The record layout for such file records is:

Item   Nature

1  Book number identification

2  Change code { 1 = delete / 2 = make status available / 3 = make status reserve

All 1130 books are deleted from the inventory.

1 1 3 0|1
1 4 0 0|2

All 1400 books are now changed to available status (however many there were).

(4) The MASTER-FILE.

All records in the master file have the following layout:

| Item | Nature |
|------|--------|
| 1 | Book identification number |
| 2 | Author |
| 3 | Edition Year |
| 4 | Status disposition (1 = on loan, 2 = on shelf) |
| 5 | Date loaned       (0 if book is not loaned) |
| 6 | Patron's identity  (1 = faculty, 2 = student, 3 = on the shelf) |
| 7 | Acquisition code  (1 = purchased, 2 = donation) |
| 8 | Reserve status    (1 = available, 2 = reserve) |
| 9 | Patron's telephone number |

Write a program to perform the following tasks:

a. Create the above four files and store them on disk. Assume the records are arranged sequentially according to the 8-digit book identification number.

b. Print the four disk files.

c. (1) Assume that all disk file records are in sequence and that all transaction records are valid; i.e, transaction keys all have corresponding keys in the master file. Update MASTER-FILE with CHECK-IN-OUT-FILE.

(2) Print a listing of the updated file.

(3) Print a list of telephone numbers of patrons who possess overdue books. A book is overdue if it has been kept 30 days or more. A fine of 10 cents a day is charged for each day over 30 days. This report should indicate the telephone number, the number of days overdue, the original checkout day, and the corresponding fine in dollars and cents. No fines are listed for faculty members.

Books that have not been returned after a 100-day overdue period are considered stolen. Flag such books on the output to allow the librarian to charge the patron for the cost of the book plus the 100-day fine. (These books will be deleted in part f. of this exercise by their inclusion in the DELETE-FILE.)

(4) List each book identification number of MASTER-FILE and summarize for each volume the number of copies in (on the shelf) or out (on loan). The report should be similar to:

```
BOOK IDENTIFICATION    IN    OUT

    1111 20 03
    1111 20 08
    1111 20 17
                        3     17

    2000 18 02
    2000 18 12
                        2     16
            .
            .
```

(5) Determine the percentage of books currently held by faculty and the percentage of books currently held by the students.

d. (1) Update the current MASTER-FILE with NEW-BOOK-FILE; i.e., merge the two files. It is understood that no book in NEW-BOOK-FILE exists in the current MASTER-FILE. (See part g. for additions of books that currently exist in the master file.) Print an updated inventory listing.

(2) During the update pass (i.e., do not reprocess the master file), keep track of all the book identification numbers that have been donated, and print a list of such titles at the conclusion of the update process.

e. (1) Identify any author who has written two or more different books. Specify the author and corresponding list of books.

(2) Produce a list of books arranged by ascending author order.

f. (1) Update MASTER-FILE with DELETE-FILE.

(2) Print the list of books that have been deleted (all such books are assumed to be currently on the shelf). Remember, there may be more than one of the same title.

(3) Any book that has not been returned 100 days after the checkout date is considered stolen and hence should be deleted and brought to the attention of the librarian by means of an appropriate message.

(4) Print the updated file.

g. On many occasions, the library purchases additional copies of existing books. Design a system to allow the librarian to add these books to the master file. Such purchases of new books can give rise to the following situations; Either the new books purchased need to be added to similar copies already on the shelf, in which case the quantity of existing books on hand needs to be changed; or the books to be added are newer editions, in which case all books with edition years less than that of the new edition must be taken out of circulation, i.e., deleted. If this is the case, the librarian would like to obtain a list of all books that are to be deleted, so that these entries can be added to the DELETE file of part f. of this problem. Write the code to take care of the above possibilities.

## 11-5-3 Answers to Test Yourself

1.  a. The END = option allows automatic branching when the end-of-file record is read.
    b. The END FILE statement causes an end-of-file record to be written.
    c. The REWIND statement causes a file to be repositioned so that the first record in the file is available for processing.
    d. The BACKSPACE statement causes the repositioning of a file one record backwards.

2. Unformatted processing of data works with data in its internal form; formatted processing of data cuases translation of data between internal and external forms.

3. A record key is a field in a record. It is important because it is used to identify the record in order to retrieve data from a file.

4. A data file is a collection of data records. A data record is composed of data items.

5. Sequential access to data requires that each record in a file be processed (read) to obtain any record from the file. It is the only file-access method available on certain devices (e.g., tape). There is less overhead involved in accessing a sequential file than in using other methods.

# index